THE END OF THE WORLD

THE END OF THE WORLD

A Theological Interpretation

Ulrich H. J. Körtner

Translated by
Douglas W. Stott

WESTMINSTER JOHN KNOX PRESS
Louisville, Kentucky

Originally published as *Weltangst und Weltende*, copyright 1988 Vandenhoeck & Ruprecht, Göttingen, Germany.

Book design by Publishers' WorkGroup
Cover design by Vickie Arrowood

First edition

Published by Westminster John Knox Press
Louisville, Kentucky

This book is printed on acid-free paper that meets the American National Standards Institute Z39.48 standard. ♾

PRINTED IN THE UNITED STATES OF AMERICA

95 96 97 98 99 00 01 02 03 04 — 10 9 8 7 6 5 4 3 2 1

Library of Congress Cataloging-in-Publication Data

Körtner, Ulrich H. J.
[Weltangst und Weltende. English]
The end of the world : a theological interpretation / Ulrich H. J. Körtner ; translated by Douglas Stott. — 1st ed.
p. cm.
Includes bibliographical references.
ISBN 0-664-25631-7 (alk. paper)
1. Apocalyptic literature—History and criticism. 2. End of the world. 3. Anxiety—Religious aspects—Christianity. I. Title.
BT876.K6713 1995
236—dc20 95-5531

We would rather be ruined than changed,
We would rather die in our dread
Than climb the cross of the moment
And let our illusions die.

—*Wystan Hugh Auden*

Only a god can still save us.

—*Martin Heidegger*

CONTENTS

PREFACE TO THE ENGLISH EDITION

We live in an age of anxiety. With technological civilization caught in a serious crisis, one that may well end in catastrophe for humankind, it is no wonder that prophets of doom are enjoying considerable currency. Apocalyptic is an important part of the present age, and the idea of a possible end of the world at once both terrifies and fascinates us. And here at the threshold of the third millennium, apocalyptic anxiety and hope are gaining additional momentum.

The topic of apocalyptic is much too important for enlightened theology to leave to the plethora of sects and to fundamentalism. Even if the present study came about within a European context, touching only tangentially on the American discussion, it can perhaps nonetheless contribute indirectly to the debate with fundamentalism by attempting to specify more precisely, in a systematic-theological fashion, the fundamental relationship between Christianity and apocalyptic. Such an undertaking is in any case of fundamental significance for any understanding of Christianity and by no means represents merely some fashionable topic of the day, for Christianity itself, from its very beginnings, carries an apocalyptic heritage within.

The geopolitical situation has changed considerably since the appearance of the German edition. The dissolution of the Soviet Union and the end of the East-West conflict have ameliorated the danger of nuclear war; yet at the same time, fear of Islam has grown significantly in the West. The basic problems with which my book concerns itself, however, have remained the same, and for this reason I have not altered the text of this English version from the original. Otherwise I would have had to write a completely new book.

The German edition is dedicated to my wife, and may the present edition also be so dedicated.

ULRICH H. J. KÖRTNER

Vienna
November 1994

PREFACE

Apocalyptic thinking is currently attracting a great deal of interest, interest drawn neither to a merely historical phenomenon nor to a marginal affair rooted in sectarian thinking. Rather, apocalyptic is a contemporary phenomenon manifesting itself in the public sphere in the form of new patterns and configurations, and this renewed interest is less historical than existential. In view of the various developments threatening all humankind, apocalyptic thinking seems increasingly plausible.

The time seems right for a theological reevaluation of apocalyptic. Situational theology cannot avoid entering into new dialogue with apocalyptic thinking, dialogue involving at the same time a reevaluation of the apocalyptic legacy of theology and Christianity. Now that the theology of hope is dogged more and more by crisis, we must reevaluate our view of apocalyptic. Apocalyptic can be understood as a form of pastoral care for those in anxiety, and theology at large must ask itself to what extent it in its own turn is yet capable of providing such pastoral care in an age characterized by world anxiety. The present investigation attempts to provide a systematic-theological answer to this question.

The objection might be raised that this interpretation of apocalyptic, given its point of departure in an analysis of existence, reduces the pressing problems of an unprecedented historical situation completely to the subjective, yet without investigating the causes of this situation of unprecedented danger in which humankind now finds itself. To this one might counter that precisely because of the external threat it seems necessary to swim against the current of widespread apocalyptic worldviews and, expressed in the form of a slogan, to divert for now our attention away from the bomb and direct it toward anxiety itself; for the possibility cannot be excluded that this objection is itself the expression of current apocalyptic inclinations at large whose presuppositions need to be investigated. For this reason the present study's methodological point of departure consciously proceeds with certain one-sided presuppositions; at the same time, it must be emphasized that its inquiry into the apocalyptic understanding of existence by no means stands opposed to the question concerning the causes that have brought our present situation to the edge of the abyss, which is why no false alternatives are permitted in the debate concerning apocalyptic.

I would like to thank all those who in their own way accompanied, supported, and aided my work on this book. Without both their human and their professional participation the book never would have been written. I am well aware of how much I owe to others—those who kept track of my own progress as well as those whose books I have read—and how many of their suggestions and ideas have found their way into my work. I would like to mention by name especially my friend and teacher Professor Dr. Alfred Jäger; he inspired this investigation, which was accepted as my Inaugural Dissertation in the Summer Semester of 1987 by the Kirchliche Hochschule Bethel, and followed its development with critical comments and suggestions. I would also like to mention Professor Dr. Michael Trowitzsch, who provided the second evaluation, as well as Dr. Arndt Ruprecht, who showed a great deal of interest in the work and accepted it for publication. Further, I would like to thank Professor Dr. Traugott Stählin and my friends at the Kirchliche Hochschule Bethel, in the Westphalian Evangelische Kirche, and in the Vereinigte Evangelisch-Lutherische Kirche of Germany, which provided funds considerably aiding the publication of the work. Finally, I would like to thank Verena Westermann, who helped me with corrections.

ULRICH H. J. KÖRTNER

Bielefeld
November 1987

Introduction

THE AGE OF ANXIETY

And children on the railing stare
at the evening crimson on the horizon
and they are afraid of the eternal night
that the sun will not return tomorrow morning
Odyssey Odyssey—
and no one knows where the journey is taking them
Odyssey Odyssey—
because insanity is at the helm.

—*Udo Lindenberg*

1. Awakening from Apocalyptic Blindness

Destruction is at the door, and the anxiety it elicits is growing. The end of the world is approaching into tangible proximity; the end of humankind, of history, of the earth. Although it is not just nuclear war that has evoked the notion of the end, such war has opened up the possibility that the myth of the end of the world might become historical reality. Nuclear war symbolizes this fear and anxiety in the face of destruction, destruction in which real danger and mythical menace converge, and the boundary between myth and reality disappears. The idea of such a war is both the object of such anxiety and its manifestation. The nuclear age, so called because of its dubious technical achievements, is the age of anxiety.[1] The unbearable fear of the end of the world is no doubt constantly being repressed; though at times it seems almost to have disappeared, after Hiroshima and Nagasaki it will never again fall completely silent. It continually rises up anew. This fear and anxiety elicited by the notion of the end has manifested itself in the past few decades as, e.g., fear of the Red menace during the Cold War, fear of the yellow menace, fear of the Third World War during the Cuban missile crisis, as the anxiety elicited by the population explosion at the beginning of the 1960s, as fear of Communist subversion during the period of student unrest and terrorism, as fear of the limits to growth prompted by the oil crisis at the beginning of the 1970s, or as fear of nuclear holocaust prompted by a new round of the arms race at the beginning of the 1980s. And now that the public has become aware of the extent of environmental destruction and of the irreversible damage to nature, the end of the world seems utterly unavoidable. The choice now no longer seems to be, as it was for Karl Jaspers,[2] between nuclear death or global change to reasonable behavior, but rather only between nuclear or ecological catastrophe. Despite politicians' assurances to the contrary, the future grows darker. "The lights are going out, and one feels oneself plunging into an abyss."[3]

Nothing seems able to stop this plunge into the abyss, certainly not so long as publicly expressed optimism represses the fear of destruction and obscures our view of the extent of the danger. Yet instead of tumbling blindly further into the abyss, more and more people seem to be awakening from this apocalyptic blindness, and despite their powerlessness they do not want to continue standing with closed eyes before the threatening end. Or is even this saying too much? Are ultimately even the admonishers and prophets struck by blindness? "These mass movements organized against the use of nuclear weapons do indeed confirm the acuteness of the danger, but they by no means attest any mass, anxious expectation of the end," remarked G. Anders some thirty years ago.[4] Even those who, through reasoned reflection, have become quite aware of the high probability of collective destruction are able to expose their feelings and especially their imagination at most for only a few moments to the threatening horrors. Karl Jaspers himself confessed: "I must shake myself out of a tendency to forget. Inside us, an original vitality resists and makes us live in fact as if that doom could not be."[5] Although we are all familiar with the fear and anxiety evoked by the thought of our own death, we have trouble identifying with the fear of death experienced by even ten other people. "The soul goes on strike at the thought of the Apocalypse. The thought remains a word."[6] Are we then in fact living not in an age of anxiety, but in an age incapable of anxiety, namely, of that specific anxiety which might be capable of sharpening our vision for the danger itself? Are we still illiterates of anxiety?[7]

Only anxiety can bring humankind out of this trance of the dance of death; this is anxiety of the end of the world, finding its necessary expression in apocalyptic thinking. This does not mean that carte blanche is given to those fearmongers who seek to dominate other people by making them pliable through artificially produced anxiety. What is needed today is not deadly, but rather liberating anxiety. What is needed is what S. Kierkegaard demonstrated in a different context, namely, to learn what anxiety is as did the young man in the fairy tale by the Brothers Grimm.[8] This does not mean that one needs to get caught up hysterically in medieval expectations of judgment and the terrors of hell. Yet we should remind ourselves that "this anxiety at the enormous dimensions of anticipated torment transcends everything a person is able to imagine in the way of 'innerworldly anxiety' in the face of this or that danger, including one's own death; and that it bears far more similarity to that particular anxiety appropriate today" than does anything human beings may have withstood in our century in the way of "reigns of terror and carpet-bombing."[9]

Apocalyptic blindness is the result of repressed fear of the end. To a large extent this fear has been repressed such that the imagination is unable to perceive the impending catastrophe in an undisguised form. This apocalyptic anxiety has been suppressed by contemporary belief in progress, an understanding of progress and growth recognizing no limits. It does not believe in an end, nor does it perceive any end. The notion of an end is itself inconceivable. Even the idea of one's own death is suppressed. The incessant process of continued development recognizes only the comparative of "higher, faster, farther" as celebrated every four years during the Olympic Games, the comparative of what is "better," recognizing neither what is merely good nor, especially, what is bad. What is bad is viewed as that which is less good, as something in need of and capable of improvement. A bad ending has not been figured in. The idea of progress has so inculcated itself into the culture of both the West and the East that all talk of an alleged end or of a collapse of this faith in progress remains superficial. Although temporary pessimism during a political crisis or economic recession may very well last for some years, it always vanishes after a while, like a case of the summer flu.[10] Doubtless the report of the Club of Rome concerning the limits to growth at the beginning of the 1970s set off considerable shock waves. Nonetheless, "generations of faith in the allegedly automatic advance of history has deadened our capacity to focus on an 'end,' even among those of us who no longer believe in progress at all."[11]

Now, however, a new form of apocalyptic thinking is emerging, articulating itself not just in the peace movement or in what is called the subculture, but also in art. Although this anxiety in the face of the end expresses itself openly on posters at demonstrations—"I am afraid"—it has in the meantime found a new language for itself, the ancient language of apocalyptic. The mythic language of apocalyptic is emerging in a new form, a form apparently suitable for addressing the idea of nuclear warfare, warfare that has made us into lords of the apocalypse, lords of the mythical end. The awakening from apocalyptic blindness is expressing itself in this new apocalyptic thinking. Nevertheless, critical vigilance should be exercised over against not only the massive threats to the earth and to humankind, but also over against the kind of apocalyptic thinking that focuses on such threats. The myth that sharpens our vision for the approaching catastrophe can just as easily cloud that vision and deaden our sense for reality. Both myth and thinking influenced by it remain ambiguous, capable not only of expressing justified anxiety but also of creating unreal anxiety. Apocalyptic focuses on what is inconceivable for those dominated by the spirit of progress. It seduces a person into thinking beyond what is conceivable, beyond the end, beyond life on "the day after." This is by no means limited to the religious-speculative sphere; it can also focus on completely worldly categories, manifesting itself in the cynical reflection of military leadership, which calculates beforehand the anticipated global human losses and figures into its strategic calculations the survival of a small elite. In such cases, focusing on the end suspends the incomprehensible idea of such an end and reverts momentarily to the insensibility of apocalyptic blindness. Apocalyptic thinking shakes a person out of sleep, scares, and then just as quickly calms that same person, in this way no longer disturbing the circle of believers in progress, and more likely even expanding their faith with a variation of the Hegelian dialectic of history. Or it flees before the reality it has just glimpsed and negates it in its own consciousness before the actual end. And who can say that this anxiety that awakens from apocalyptic blindness will not in the very same instant change into a kind of longing or inclination for destruction of the kind mentioned by F. Sieburg,[12] which in its cynical frenzy gives what is already falling into the abyss a shove and then even wants to leap into the abyss itself? It is not only the threatening Apocalypse itself that demands critical reflection, but apocalyptic thinking as well.

In its own turn, apocalyptic aids the imagination in reflecting on the end by offering images of horror. The visions of terror found in the New Testament book of Revelation have long been a classic theme of European painting.[13] Albrecht Dürer's Apocalypse cycle is one outstanding example standing at the beginning of modernity and constituting the standard model for many later portrayals of the end of the world. This tradition of apocalyptic painting has continued into the twentieth century under the influence of the horrors of two world wars.[14] It comes as no surprise, then, that the contemporary avant garde has discovered destruction and doom as a theme, e.g., in the works of the Italian Enzo Cucchi.[15] His pictures view the apparently normal world of daily life as being threatened from every quarter. Funeral processions, birds of death, and ghost ships permeate his works. Cucchi's pictures offer new nourishment for the impoverished imagination lamented by G. Anders, e.g., a city portrayed as already burning underneath, a black cloud overshadowing the infernolike scene like a mushroom cloud above; Anselm Kiefer's picture *Urd, Werdandi, Skuld,*[16] on the other hand, renders symbolically precisely this failure of our imagination in the face of the Apocalypse. Kiefer does not paint an apocalyptic scenario; the impending disaster appears in his gray-in-gray picture only in the features of the names of the three Norns from the old Norse saga who determine the destiny of gods and men. The world has burned to ashes, and all that remains are a few embers glowing in the waning fire, as if in the face of the impending cosmic conflagration the painter simply could think of nothing more: The imagination goes on strike.

Film as well as painting is attempting to render a picture of the end. In addition to several documentary films portraying the scenario of a nuclear strike as realistically as possible, commercial films such as *Malevil, Wargames,* and *The Day After* have stirred public interest.[17] Especially *The Day After* attempts to provoke the viewer on an emotional level to deal with the nuclear threat. The destruction of Kansas is brought close to home by the portrayal of the fates of individual families, bringing collective destruction uncomfortably close to the viewer.

Although apocalyptic speaks in images, it has long been a literary phenomenon, the impending end generating the production of literature of doom.[18] The Apocalypse has even found its way into children's books.[19] It is no accident that bestsellers have included Michael Ende's *Neverending Story,*[20] the fairy tale of the destruction of the land Fantasy (and its reemergence!), which many consider to be a symbol of our age, as well as the report to the President of the United States, *Global 2000,*[21] which prophesies with sober statistics and scientific prognostication nothing less than the end of history itself. Although the two publications may be worlds apart as far as style and genre are concerned, mythical imagination and scientific exactitude have always joined forces in apocalyptic.[22] The impending final, total destruction does admittedly recall both great and small occasions of destruction that have already occurred and that continue to occur. Thus H. Boehncke, R. Stollmann, and G. Vinnai address the theme of the end of the world in their literary, cultural-historical, and social-psychological essays, which understand themselves as the "disassembly of destruction."[23] The sediment of destruction, of the disappearance of reality, stored in the imagination, in films, historical images, in daily experience, or in the unconscious, are to be dissolved. "Otherwise we will drag them along with us, perhaps with the secret hope that they will be dissolved in the end of the world. 'Disassembly of destruction' might be called an attempt to disassemble the catastrophes that have been saved up before they are figured into the final settlement of accounts. And if not an actual disassembly of catastrophes, then at least an understanding or feeling of how they came about."[24] Yet an understanding of the origin of catastrophes has always been the explicit claim of apocalyptic.

The Apocalypse itself is to be approached through methodologically grounded apocalyptic. Christa Wolf also keeps alive the memory of past destruction and disaster. She is engaging in more than cultural history when she renders the past transparent for the imperiled present in her description of the destruction of Troy from the perspective of the prophetess Cassandra.[25] Wolf's story consists of a single inner monologue by Cassandra, a monologue illuminating in the fashion of a parable the structures of a society in demise, but at the same time bringing to consciousness the ambiguous position of the prophet. For it is precisely Cassandra, much later than the people around her, who illuminates the events that ultimately lead to Troy's destruction—basically always too late. On the one hand the prophetess warns us: "One can know when war begins, but when does the prewar begin? If there were rules for such things, one would have to pass them on. Etch them into clay, into stone, and pass them down to others. What would be etched there? There would be etched, among other sentences: Do not allow yourselves to be deceived by your own."[26] On the other hand, she confesses: "I derived pleasure from everything I saw—pleasure, but no hope!—and I continued to live in order to see."[27] Cassandra feels complicit guilt in the fall of Troy: "I, the terrible one, I, who wanted Troy to fall."[28]

This pleasure in collapse also motivates the thinking of U. Horstmann.[29] He philosophizes about humankind as a monster that never should have been created, and considers the only way out for this creature to be the transformation of our planet into a moonscape. Horstmann's pleasure in doom is the pleasure of the monster itself, indeed of all living things. Global Apocalypse would be the only humane deed performed by human beings in all of history. The *élan vital* of Bergson's philosophy of life is countered by Freud's death wish, and is thought through philosophically in the tradition of Schopenhauer, Klages, Foucault, and Cioran all the way to the hopeful, catastrophic end. This is why Horstmann views suicide "as the subjectively abbreviated reflex of apocalyptic yearning."[30] He suggests that "in the tradition of customary historical terminology" one might refer to our age as the "pre-apocalypse."[31] This apocalyptic end, however, brings deliverance for both humankind and the earth. "The history of the monster is fulfilled, and in all humility it awaits its double death—physical annihilation and the extinguishing of the memory of itself."[32] Horstmann's philosophy of doom is not an isolated case. Apocalyptic is finding its way into the new intellectual generation. J. Derrida, one of the intellectual precursors of the new spirit that calls itself postmodern, speaks "of an apocalyptic tone recently adopted in philosophy."[33] Apocalyptic is the spiritual home of those who feel the end has come for modernity.[34]

Ever since O. Spengler announced the demise of the West,[35] many Europeans have felt they were living in the age of the pre-Apocalypse. Spengler's portentous work, however, intended to keep the notion of demise free of any overtones of catastrophe.[36] He conceived of the disintegration of Western culture in organic categories strongly influenced by the thinking of Johann Wolfgang von Goethe. The rise and fall of the West is following the dying and rising of nature; the demise of the West is not the end of history, but rather the disintegration of one culture on which another will follow. Spengler's comparison of Western cultural history with the change in the seasons seemed to allow considerable time yet for the optimism of progress, his historical tables extending into the twenty-first century. Historical reality, however, caught up with such thinking. Spengler's work appeared in its first edition at the end of the First World War, which deeply and enduringly shocked all belief in progress and left contemporaries feeling they were living "between the times" in a permanent crisis.[37] In the face of current collapse and disintegration, it was impossible to keep from associating the element of catastrophe with the notion of the demise of the West.

The historical event, however, that became a symbol of the impending catastrophe, an event comparable to the Lisbon earthquake of 1755 and one presaging the collapse commencing in 1918, was the sinking of the *Titanic* on April 15, 1912. This steamer, considered unsinkable and with a name unabashedly announcing the self-consciousness of the culture of progress, took 1,563 people with it into the depths. The metaphor expressing the general understanding of existence even in the shadow of nuclear war is not the world tree, blooming and losing its leaves in the cycle of seasons, but the wreck of the *Titanic.* The sinking of the *Titanic* etched itself deeply into the consciousness of our century. Young Max Beckmann captured it in a monumental, gloomy painting in which the sinking ship itself can hardly be seen in the background; the center is occupied by the anxious, tormented shipwrecked passengers fighting for their very lives like animals and hardly standing out from the dark green waves pulling them to their deaths. Dietrich Bonhoeffer alludes to this catastrophe in his reflections on the role of Christians in the Third Reich: The disciples following Jesus without compromise

> mourn for the world, for its guilt, its fate and its fortune. While the world keeps holiday they stand aside, and while the world sings, "Gather ye rose-buds while ye may," they mourn. They see that for all the jollity on board, the ship is beginning to sink. The world dreams of progress, of power and of the future, but the disciples meditate on the end, the last judgement, and the coming of the kingdom. To such heights the world cannot rise.[38]

The thousand-year *Reich:* a sinking ship.

The sinking of the *Titanic,* however, continues to be a central metaphor for existence under the shadow of the nuclear threat, even to the point of providing the title for a satirical periodical. The sinking of this steamer was admittedly a "shipwreck with spectators," as H. Blumenberg titles his analysis of the shipwreck metaphor,[39] a metaphor with a long history. Threatened with nuclear disaster, however, the spectator relinquishes his position; or more precisely, he finally realizes that he has long since forfeited his role as spectator.[40] Disaster films that attempt to make this clear to him might actually suggest to him that he is, in fact, yet merely a spectator consuming such catastrophe as an aesthetic experience in the theater or on television, comfortably settled in his easy chair, his nerves pleasurably titillated. "Tush, tush, my dears, there is always someone who is simply a spectator, with the familiar twitching around the corner of his mouth, someone who rather than acting merely imagines his own role."[41] H. M. Enzensberger, from whose poem "Der Untergang der *Titanic*" ("The Sinking of the *Titanic*") these lines come, admittedly no longer views himself as such a spectator, but rather as one of the shipwrecked, "with water up to his neck." The impending world disaster no longer permits spectators.

Thus while the waters rise, the drowning person is ultimately left only with the "certainty of anxiety."[42] Apocalyptic blindness does not come to an end in anxiety, but rather through anxiety, albeit only through liberated anxiety. "Whoever lives, will see," Wolf's Cassandra assures us. "The thought occurs to me, and in the meantime I am secretly following the history of my own anxiety. Or more correctly, the history of its unleashing; or more precisely: of its liberation. Yes, anxiety, too, can be freed, and here we see that it belongs together with everything and everyone that is oppressed."[43] The freeing of anxiety means awakening from apocalyptic blindness. Whoever lives, shall see. Yet those who see, will they also live? Does this hope still exist? And how can those who see yet live in the face of what they see? How can one live with anxiety's conscious certainty of the end?

Theology must face these questions, and in its search for answers it will have to reflect on its own apocalyptic heritage and clarify its relationship to that heritage. The idea of an end is an integral part of theological tradition. Yet nothing would be more fateful than for theology to engage in the illusion that it might reflect on the end in the role of a spectator elevated above the situation itself. The theologian is included among those threatened. A theology of the end finds itself faced with that end. Before the theologian can find any answers to the desperate questions of the age, he or she must first pose the question of how theology itself is still possible in view of the impending end. Both Jewish and Christian apocalyptic can be understood as pastoral care for those in anxiety. The question is whether and how theology today is capable of such pastoral care, or whether the approaching end has rendered it speechless.

2. The Repression of Apocalyptic

"I see further than others," Oswald Spengler asserted in his apocalyptic voice.[44] Theology and the church, however, despite the prophetic understanding of their own proclamatory commission, have remained largely subject to apocalyptic blindness, and the history of apocalyptic is to a large extent the history of its repression. In 1832 F. Lücke,[45] drew on the work of K. I. Nitzsch in coining the term "apocalyptic," which derives from the superscription of the New Testament book of Revelation. And though Lücke provided the first comprehensive study of the religio-historical phenomenon called by this name, in theological consciousness at large apocalyptic remained for many years a merely historical phenomenon, relegated to the past; and though it was of religio-historical interest, it had no connection with contemporary theological concerns.[46] Although the discovery of apocalyptic features in the proclamation of Jesus and the discovery of the significance of apocalyptic for the faith of primitive Christianity by J. Weiss,[47] Albert Schweitzer,[48] and especially by F. Overbeck resulted in considerable alarm in theology, it left behind at most a profound perplexity in the face of apocalyptic.

This perplexity probably bothered no one more than Franz Overbeck, for in contrast to many of his fellow theologians, he rejected any attempt to soothe the uneasiness that emerged from primitive Christian apocalyptic. He considered his only task now to be that of mourning, which attempted to overcome the loss of a Christianity that in its original impulse had become alien and in which genuine full participation was no longer possible.[49] Long before Johannes Weiss, Overbeck recognized the basic eschatological tendency of primitive Christianity, and recalled that originally Christianity "came into this world announcing its imminent doom."[50] Apocalyptic negation of the world is an essential part of early Christianity, and "I doubt there can be a faith more incisive in its flight from the world than the earliest Christians' faith in the imminent return of Christ and the end of the present form of the world."[51] The Apocalypse of John, which occupies a unique form-critical position within the framework of early Jewish apocalyptic writings, thus does not constitute a fringe phenomenon within primitive Christianity; rather, by disguising his own name, the apocalyptist offers

> a witness to the energy of the faith, acknowledged to have existed elsewhere as well in the primitive Christian community, of still being called to prophecy. Such a case was no longer a possibility within Judaism during that period, and was perhaps *never* possible there, since among the Jews apocalyptic had replaced prophecy, i.e., presupposed its demise. In contrast, for Christians apocalyptic is the living form of prophecy which they still experience.[52]

In Overbeck's eyes, this thoroughly apocalyptic Christianity has been betrayed equally by both conservative apologetic theology and contemporary liberal theology and even modern nineteenth-century Catholicism.[53] Overbeck certifies all the variations of modern theology, despite the worlds that may well separate them, as the gravediggers of dying Christianity.[54] "The contradiction between primitive Christian eschatology and the future-orientation of the present is a fundamental one, and is perhaps the basic cause of the falling out between the present and Christianity. This began with the faith in an imminent end of the world. Nothing is more alien to the present than precisely this faith."[55] Faith in progress blocks access to apocalyptic. The falling out between the present and eschatology can no longer be overcome, least of all by theology, which in its essence is utterly alien to eschatological Christianity.[56] "One can call theology the *Satan of religion*,"[57] whereby one must keep in mind that Overbeck makes no distinction between true Christianity and genuine religion. There is no returning to apocalyptic Christianity and thus to true Christianity in general. "And this is the case because we are no longer and can no longer be the children which according to the original Christian directive we would have to be in order to be genuinely religious."[58] What is left is mourning for the lost childhood of humankind, a childhood to which no theologian can return us.

Overbeck counters both orthodox and modern liberal theology with his critical theology, which basically no longer claims to be theology. Even if critical theology can no longer awaken dying Christianity to new life,

> it can nonetheless serve as its protector against all those theologies claiming to represent it while accommodating it to the world, and which, as a result of indifference to its view of life, either dry it out into dead orthodoxy removing it from the world, or pull it down into secular existence, where it disappears. It is the task of critical theology to prevent such theologies from dragging, in the name of Christianity, an unreal creature through the world from which they have taken what is in any case its very soul, namely, negation of the world. Critical theology, even without identifying itself completely with the Christian view of life, and without underestimating the excessive consequences which Christian world negation means for human beings and for human existence—without the genuine acknowledgment of which there would never have been theology in Christianity—critical theology will nonetheless be able to empathize deeply enough with the view of life of Christianity to expurgate such an attempt completely . . . and is to be allowed to reject it in good spirits and with a good conscience."[59]

The fate that Christianity proclaimed to the world has overtaken Christianity itself. The *finis mundi* never occurred, and instead the *finis christianismi* came about,[60] leaving behind considerable confusion, the only way out of which Overbeck considers to be skepticism,[61] which admittedly is no real solution at all; rather, although it does "without hesitation leave Christianity as it is for the moment,"[62] it must admit to itself "that we do not know what we would like to know."[63]

Overbeck conducted the mourning rites for apocalyptic and for apocalyptic Christianity. The positive estimation of eschatology that emerged with early dialectical theology seemed then to disprove Overbeck. Eschatology now became the central focus of theology. "If Christianity be not altogether thoroughgoing eschatology, there remains in it no relationship whatever with Christ," Karl Barth formulated in a programmatic fashion.[64] The criticism of present Christianity and of disintegrating culture of the Christian West seemed to have found an ally in Overbeck. The new eschatology attempted to offer a solution to the "riddle he [Overbeck] has formulated so precisely"[65] by postulating a fundamental distinction between eschatology and apocalyptic in Christianity,[66] and of all people, Overbeck himself was called as the star witness for an unapocalyptic eschatology. Whereas in his own time

J. Weiss[67] had in any case spoken about the "eschatological-apocalyptic" sense of Jesus' proclamation of the kingdom of God—though he did take leave of this proclamation in the very next breath—continental exegesis now tried by any and all means to rescue Jesus from apocalyptic.[68] Whereas the consistent eschatology of Albert Schweitzer, M. Werner, and F. Buri[69] essentially eliminated eschatology, the rediscovery of eschatology in dialectical theology essentially resulted in the elimination of apocalyptic, with which one considered Overbeck's inquiries to be taken care of, inquiries still unaddressed even today.[70] This cannot, however, disguise the very real perplexity in the face of both apocalyptic and Overbeck; at best, this perplexity has merely assumed more subtle forms.

In addition to the suggestions of Barth or Bultmann, the axiological eschatology of P. Althaus illustrates in exemplary fashion the deapocalypticizing of Christian eschatology; Althaus, too, evokes the image of an unapocalyptic Jesus and an unapocalyptic Paul.

> The Bible doubtlessly does include all sorts of apocalyptic material, especially in its apocalyptic books. Measured against the standard of Jesus' and Paul's eschatological instruction, however, these apocalyptic elements in and of themselves prove to be not essential at all, and the biblical apocalypses prove to be by no means canonical based on their apocalyptic features as such. The words of Jesus and Paul concerning the end, in their economy and strict selection, are not only completely un-apocalyptic, but virtually anti-apocalyptic.[71]

The dogmatic conclusion drawn from this exegetical premise is that "eschatology is not concerned with the final history or with the end of history, but rather with that which is beyond history. It is not apocalyptic."[72]

So-called rigorous eschatology, chided in many quarters, also remains in its own way exegetically and dogmatically unsatisfactory. On the other hand, it functions as the beneficial thorn in the flesh of an unapocalyptic theology. Insofar as it views its own position in eschatological questions as a conscious and in its opinion necessary retreat from the primitive Christian expectation of the end, expectation described as apocalyptic, it in any event is conscious that apocalyptic is indeed a theological problem. Itself dogmatically unapocalyptic, it justifiably criticizes unapocalyptic eschatology, which no longer perceives its own antiapocalyptic attitude even as a problem.[73]

The alternative to theological repression of apocalyptic, however, is not merely its ill-considered acceptance. Uncritical appropriation of apocalyptic thought patterns remains basically just as uncomprehending in the face of apocalyptic as do attempts at unapocalyptic eschatology. Such theological reversion to apocalyptic ideas not infrequently constitutes a *sacrificium intellectus*, a sacrifice documenting theology's perplexity in the face of apocalyptic no less than do all those conceptions which postulate a fundamental antithesis between apocalyptic and Christianity.

Examples of ill-considered attempts at reception of apocalyptic abound. One need only recall the numerous attempts at interpretation focusing on world or church history that continue into the present.[74] As an example, J. A. Bengel recognized the pope in Rev. 14:6, 8, Johann Arndt and Philipp Jakob Spener recognized him in Rev. 13:1–10, then reckoned that the millennium foretold in Rev. 20 would begin June 18, 1836. Following in Bengel's footsteps, Jung-Stilling identified the sun-woman in Rev. 12 as the Moravian Brethren, and the first bowl of wrath in Rev. 16:2 as the French Revolution, while he found that the Antichrist exhibited features of Napoleon. Similar forms of apocalyptic are found among the representatives of Lutheran or Reformed orthodoxy in the nineteenth century, e.g., in E. W. Hengstenberg, J.H.A. Ebrard, and L. Harms. Hengstenberg thought the millennium of the messianic rule of peace to have already passed. His understanding was that it lasted from the time of the mission to the Germanic tribes to the end of the Holy Roman Empire of the German Nation in 1806. In contrast, Hengstenberg interpreted his own age from the perspective of Rev. 20:7–10: The demagogy of the revolutionaries of 1848 was allegedly the rebellion of Gog and Magog. L. Harms's exegesis seems even more adventurous. He interprets the Apocalypse of John as referring to the imminent deposition of the Guelfs (1866). In his interpretation apocalyptic degenerates into a restorative criticism of society and civilization, supported by a Lutheran-confessionalist, monarchical-Guelfic spirit that denounces Catholicism, Prussia, France, and democracy as satanic powers.

This kind of apocalyptic continues today in the view of history and the world within fundamentalist circles in Europe and particularly in the United States, the only difference being that today it is not the revolution of 1848, but rather the wars in the Near East that are identified as the rebellion of Gog and Magog, the battle of Armageddon as the future Third World War, and the Antichrist and harlot of Babylon as the Soviet Union.[75] Whereas the precipitate apocalyptic of nineteenth-century restorative circles was antidemocratic, fundamentalist apocalyptic is anti-Communist and politically ultraconservative. Its extensive and increasing influence on American politics shows how devastating the damage caused by apocalyptic can be. The fact that these are indeed precipitate attempts at appropriation of apocalyptic does not mean that they are not to be taken seriously. On the contrary, such ill-considered appropriation not infrequently has catastrophic effects and represents apocalyptic that has misunderstood itself and fallen prey to the power of its own rhetoric.

Other attempts at appropriation are thrown into positive relief against such precipitate apocalyptic. In addition to the interpretation of the Apocalypse of John from the perspective of the history of the kingdom and of the last things, as found in the work of J.C.K. von Hofmann and C. A. Auberlen, or in T. Kliefoth, C.H.A. von Burger, J. T. Beck, and T. Zahn, one should mention in connection with the twentieth century especially the work of K. Heim,[76] who tried to harmonize Christian eschatology with contemporary scientific thought. His eschatology is then an attempt at apocalyptic theology which thinks in scientific categories. Christian-apocalyptic thought is understood as the response to the desperate situation in which humankind finds itself as a result of the law of entropy. The scientific thesis of death as a result of global warming is associated with the apocalyptic notion of the end of the world. Heim considers New Testament eschatology to be the highest developmental stage of apocalyptic thought whose expectations are "attained out of the very depths of the misery of the world."[77] However, this insight does not prompt Heim to inquire concerning apocalyptic's own understanding of existence; instead, he sketches in his own turn a cosmological drama by integrating insights drawn from the physical sciences into cosmological speculation. Heim begins with the thesis that God's creation, as a result of the appearance of sin, "has thus received a different basic form, which it did not originally have at the time of its actual creation."[78] He describes this basic form as polar, and juxtaposes it with a future suprapolar form of the world. And when Paul compares divine judgment with a fire (1 Cor. 3:12f.), it seems to Heim "as if he [Paul] foresaw the coming heat-death [of the world]."[79] For Heim, faith in the resurrection becomes faith in an entry into a new dimension, that of suprapolar space in which the old world is sublated in the Hegelian sense: The *consummatio mundi* becomes a scientific hypothesis.[80]

Although Heim is indeed engaging in apocalyptic thinking in his own way, he does not view the characteristic feature of the present aeon, as does Jewish apocalyptic, to be the absence of God's justice, but rather the transitoriness and mortality of all existence, a position deriving ultimately from Greek ideas of the ancient church.[81] And it is no accident that some of the features of Heim's cosmological draft recall doctrines of emanation such as that of Origen.[82] In summary one can say that Heim correctly calls for a dialogue between Christian faith and scientific thinking, though he himself arrives at only insufficient solutions. His eschatology is insufficient because it places apocalyptic notions on the same level as theorems and hypotheses from the natural sciences. Significantly, apocalyptic expectation of the near end transforms itself in this interpretation into physical expectation of a distant end. Despite indisputable connections between Jewish apocalyptic and wisdom thinking, apocalyptic thinking is misunderstood from the very outset if it is held to be a quasi-scientific theory.[83]

Insufficiently grounded attempts at apocalyptic theology are incapable of genuinely overcoming the perplexity prompted by apocalyptic, something also seen in Old Testament exegesis, where one has tried in part to separate apocalyptic from Old Testament prophecy so as to appropriate all the more linearly its heritage for Christianity. In particular, apocalyptic has moved into proximity with theologically suspect wisdom literature.[84] Abandoned by all other theological disciplines, apocalyptic has been given over to peripheral church groups and sects outside the church, groups that have long administered this unwanted heir in their own fashion. "Apocalyptic has been appropriated and reformulated most effectively when it finds an entry point at the fringes of eschatological systematics—particularly within the narrower circles of what is already somewhat irregular theology."[85]

The crowding out of apocalyptic into sectarian circles has characterized church history since its beginnings. Even though the Parousia of the exalted Christ did not immediately occur, impatient expectation of his imminent return repeatedly flared up during the course of church history. Events in the year A.D. 70 were the first to generate a revivification of apocalyptic, a revivification finding expression in, among other places, the New Testament Apocalypse of John; then, in Montanism, the perpetuation of the expectation of the near end and the resistance to the emerging monarchical episcopate (initially in Asia Minor) toward the end of the second century led to the departure of organized prophecy from the church.[86] In its initial phase, Montanism anticipated the imminent end of the world and the descent of the heavenly Jerusalem onto a mountain near Pepuza and Thymion in Phrygia. Its prophetesses and prophets viewed themselves as mouthpieces of the paraclete foretold in the Gospel of John. This charismatic element brought the Montanist movement into opposition with ecclesiastical Christianity, which finally accused this Phrygian prophecy of heresy. Along with Montanism the church eliminated prophecy, whose remnants then became meaningless.

Apocalyptic expectation, however, remained alive, even if often only in the underground. Apocalyptic ideas are found in many of the leading theologians in the early church and in the medieval church, and its function during these periods shows how the attitude toward apocalyptic altered significantly.[87] Originally, Christian negation of the world expressed itself in apocalyptic language. The yearning for the end of the world comes to expression in the prayer from the Didache: "Let grace come, and let this world pass away" (*Did.* 10:6). This world, represented by the *Imperium Romanum*, was the kingdom of the Antichrist. With Eusebius of Caesarea, however, the court theologian under Constantine the Great, the decisive turning away from an apocalyptic interpretation of the Roman Empire began. The prophecy of the book of Daniel concerning the four world empires seemed to find its salvific fulfillment in the incorporation of the church into the Roman Empire.[88] Apocalyptic now became, in reverse fashion, the language of world affirmation insofar as Rome was declared to be the *katechon* of 2 Thess. 2:6–12, the power restraining Satan and impeding any premature end of the world. Hippolytus of Rome was the first to expound this apocalyptic interpretation of Rome[89] which replaced Revelation's view, which regarded Rome as the harlot Babylon and as the beast from the pit. This notion continued to be a factor in the Middle Ages especially in Jerome's version. Anxiety now focused no longer on the Roman state, but rather on the *defectio imperii*, which would have apocalyptic consequences. Whereas the disintegration of the Roman Empire seemed to inaugurate the rise of the Antichrist, the coronation of Charlemagne was interpreted by his theologians as *translatio imperii*, and both the emperor and his successors were venerated in the sense of 2 Thess. 2:6–12 as guarantors of the continuance of the world. Apocalyptic now stood in the service of worldly rule, and in this service its language degenerated into the ideological metaphor of the opposing parties in the investiture controversy.

On the other hand, apocalyptic blossomed anew in the prophetic vision of Joachim of Fiore (d. 1202), whose ideas were accepted within the Franciscan Order, among the flagellants, and with Fra Dolcino. Apocalyptic developed a kind of social-revolutionary power provoking the embittered opposition of both church and state, though in the struggle for worldly preeminence both political and ecclesiastical powers alternately tried to employ apocalyptically motivated heretical movements in their own interest.[90] For example, whereas the Cologne canon Alexander of Roes, in his *Memoriale* (1281), condemned as precursors of the Antichrist all those who worked for the destruction of the empire, apocalyptic features began developing among the Hussites and Taborites at the beginning of the fifteenth century. Apocalyptic thinking also played an important role during the Reformation, not least for Martin Luther;[91] yet the repression of apocalyptic was also a factor in circles of the Reformation, since the suppression of the enthusiasts and anabaptists also meant the suppression of the apocalyptic of Thomas Müntzer,[92] Hans Hut, and Melchior Hoffmann.[93] Although apocalyptic ideas were able to maintain themselves within certain parameters in the larger confessions, wherever they acquired theological significance, e.g., in Pietism, they were repressed by the Enlightenment and the emerging critical theology, which had no understanding of apocalyptic. Particularly Kant's destruction of the notion of a double reality and his description of "religion within the limits of reason alone" constituted a momentous event for apocalyptic thinking. Apocalyptic traditions were to a large extent able to maintain themselves only in the anti-Enlightenment theology of the eighteenth century and its successors, or was renewed in the revivals and awakenings of the Anglo-Saxon churches and in the German awakening movement. Yet here, too, apocalyptic currents departed the church insofar as they were not already forced out into the newly emerging apocalyptic sects.

The repression of apocalyptic equally damaged both theology and the church on the one hand, and apocalyptic itself on the other. Universal faith in progress, which also seized theological thinking, brought with it a blindness for the threats to humankind and history. Universal optimism, in whose concert Christian theology also joined, had along with apocalyptic also repressed its own anxiety at the notion of a possible end, and separated it literally from its own consciousness. Repressed apocalyptic, which has been able to maintain itself even into the present in sects and ecclesiastical fringe groups, is not the true Christianity which Overbeck missed in modern theology, though it presents itself as such, but is rather damaged apocalyptic. As little as the optimism accompanying universal faith in progress is ready to confront its own anxiety, just as little is repressed, traumatized apocalyptic ready to confront a hostile world and the radical intellectual-historical changes that began with Kant.

Just how traumatic the repression of apocalyptic is for both sides can be illustrated by the example of the Seventh-day Adventists.[94] This Christian movement emerged from the early nineteenth-century American Adventist movement. The leading figure in the beginning was William Miller (born 1782), who predicted that the return of Christ would occur in 1844. When Miller, a farmer and former chief of police, justice of the peace, mayor, and military officer, began preaching his message of the imminent end of the world as an itinerant preacher, a penitential and awakening movement was started. His preaching seized the masses, though also hundreds of preachers from the most varied denominations, and even extended to England and Australia. He by no means, however, intended to found his own community of believers. Rather, he was authorized as a preacher by the Baptist congregation of his hometown Low Hampton. Neither were his calculations concerning the end time based on mysterious revelations, but rather solely on his study of the Bible, especially on his interpretation of Dan. 8:14 and Dan. 9:24ff. He consciously avoided reading any commentaries, and used only a concordance. Although Miller was hoping to gain the attention of the churches, the churches themselves met Miller's movement with incomprehension. Because they correctly rejected his calculations of the return of Christ, they were at the same time not in a position to deal self-critically with the accusations brought by the Adventist awakening movement that they were too secularized and too much under the control of rationalist thinking, though this very thinking initially had an enduring influence on Miller himself.

The churches were unable to perceive in this emerging apocalyptic any justifiable concern which they themselves might have embraced. They remained blind for their own apocalyptic deficit in an age whose radical political and intellectual changes, commencing with the French Revolution, had awakened not only in Europe, but also in the United States a consciousness of the crisis situation of history. It is all the more noteworthy that the first general conference of the Adventists in 1840, in spite of everything, yet directed its members to remain in the churches, and to leave the churches only in those cases when a denomination unequivocally closed itself off from the doctrine of the return of Christ. The further reaction of the Adventists to the churches' lack of understanding shows how much this ecclesiastical rejection did nonetheless lead to a cramping of apocalyptic. The churches' apocalyptic blindness corresponded to the apocalyptists' own increasing blindness to reality. In 1842 the eighth general conference of the Adventists was already speaking about the "presence of widespread political and ecclesiastical powers of evil enduring until the Second Coming of Christ, at which time they will be destroyed."[95] The final general conference before the prophesied end of the world finally referred to the pope as a man of sin whose daughters were the Protestants. Millions were seized by the apocalyptic spirit. Some of the faithful let produce rot in the fields, left their place of work, or closed their businesses, and many gave away all their possessions. The disappointment was all the worse when the anticipated end on March 21, 1844, and, according to new calculations, on October 22, 1844, both failed to occur.

Miller gave up his calculations and officially confessed his error. He also regretted having given the order to leave the church. Many of his adherents, however, refused to believe the disaster, and held fast to their anticipation of the Second Coming; step by step a sectarian theology was developed by their remnants. One group under J. Bates, S. S. Snow, O.R.L. Crosier, and especially the husband and wife J. and E. G. White tried with all available means to rescue Miller's apocalyptic message. His calculations were elevated to the level of quasi-divine revelation, albeit in need of interpretation. "The first step that led away from scripture was by inner necessity followed by additional steps of the same kind. These were at the same time stages of development of a hoping community on its way to becoming a sect."[96]

In view of the expulsion of apocalyptic from church circles, it was left to outsiders such as S. N. Bulgakov and E. Bloch to pick up, each in a different way, the unused and unwanted apocalyptic inheritance. Guided by Marx and Hegel, whose philosophy of history inherited Jewish-Christian millenarianism, Bloch chose the principle of hope as the hermeneutical key to apocalyptic, and searched both in it and in culture and history at large for the utopian content that fires the hope in the

Omega, the salvific end of history. Behind all the distortions of reviled and repressed apocalyptic Bloch hears an "*explosive myth* of liberation," whose radical nature even dialectical theology, which had spoken constantly about eschatology, had not perceived.[97] Bulgakov attributed to apocalyptic the status of "a formal logic or doctrine of the fundamental 'categories' of the philosophy of history."[98] "And the accompanying interest in spiritually penetrating into the world of Jewish apocalyptic has appeared in our own age with considerable vitality, an age in whose consciousness the problem of the meaning of history, of its goal, and of its end arises with such force, an age seized by the anxious and fearful [!] feeling of a raging, inexorable, and involuntary forward movement, and by a vague feeling of historical germination."[99] Apocalyptic millenarianism becomes an important factor for Bulgakov, even though he criticizes historical millenarianism—which focuses on the historical realization of the messianic kingdom—and the socialist theory that carries it forward; he carries out this criticism by means of a spiritual, religious millenarianism, itself restricted or limited by an eschatology different from millenarianism.[100] The horizon of history is understood as an accomplishment of millenarianism, even if the concrete content of millenarianism may well change.[101] This historical horizon, however, is the utopian element, which remains an illusion, albeit a vital one. Just as the earth's horizon is actually a deception caused by our own vision and the spherical form of the globe, so also is millenarianism a projection dependent on perspective, "a deception of our vision." Yet just as we must live and reckon in a practical sense by taking into consideration the conditions of our planet and the earth's horizon, so also must we live with the horizon of history. "Millenarianism exists in this formal sense for all human beings, independent of their views."[102] The utopian spirit speaks from within apocalyptic, prompting Bloch to ask: "How can things be fulfilled without apocalyptically ceasing?"[103] "How could the world be perfected without this world being exploded and apocalyptically vanishing, as in Christian-religious pre-appearance?"[104]

Contrary to expectation, apocalyptic did enjoy a renaissance in theology, prompted especially by E. Käsemann's 1960 essay "The Beginnings of Christian Theology." He shook theologians with the assertion: "Apocalyptic was the mother of all Christian theology—since we cannot really class the preaching of Jesus as theology."[105] Systematicians such as W. Pannenberg and the circle around him,[106] G. Sauter,[107] and J. Moltmann[108] confront in completely different ways the challenge of apocalyptic and its heritage as represented by Bloch. The discussion of apocalyptic, which was by no means always viewed uncritically, was conducted largely from the perspective of hope. "It is a question of learning hope," Bloch reminded theologians, not even addressing his words primarily to them.[109] In view of the threatening end, however, one must ask just how capable this hope is today, of which theologians such as Moltmann and others have spoken.[110] What kind of hope can yet emerge from Bloch's utopia, which asserts that "this world will explode and apocalyptically vanish, as in Christian-religious pre-appearance," i.e., what kind of hope can emerge in a world in which this explosion is no longer the illusory horizon of history, but is being decisively prepared with all available means?

3. The Crisis of Hope

Although the utopian spirit does not simply hope intransitively or into the blue, it does allow itself to be enticed by that blue sky of the utopian horizon. "This blue, as a colour of distance, likewise designates in a graphically symbolic way the future-laden aspect, the Not-Yet-Become in reality, to which significant expressions, precisely because they are advancing, ultimately refer."[111] But where there is danger, rescue also arises for hope.[112] The principle of hope is not, however, cheap grace. If the *experimentum possibilis salutis* of the world is to succeed, it will require the incessant efforts of human beings. The salvific conclusion of the process of history is everywhere threatened by nothingness. Hope is actually militant optimism carrying a mourning wreath, forced to proceed without any certainty of success.[113] "Thus it definitely has the intentional content: There is still rescue—in the horizon."[114]

For many, however, the horizon is darkening. Heaven closes itself off and changes its color from azure to the yellowish gray of Orcus. Hope just does not seem to work anymore. The temporary feeling of awakening and the spirit of reform of the 1960s were able to hide the power of contemporary nihilism for only a short while, nihilism allowing for no hope. Nihilism involves thinking the ambiguous sentence "nothing matters," which with diabolical relentlessness steers toward global annihilation through nuclear war or through exploitation of the earth's resources.[115] At the same time, however, it is nihilism itself that in the face of the impending end that it has itself produced destroys all hope at its inception, unless one seizes on collective suicide as the nihilistic possibility of lending negative meaning to an absurd world: "Let us turn our metabolically ailing planet into a moonscape!"[116] The apocalypse is the great corrective that nihilism offers to the utopian spirit.

This is all the more terrifying considering that the philosophy of hope was anything but a philosophy forecasting sunny days, and understood itself rather as a declaration of war against the death wish of nihilism. Written between 1938 and 1947, the *Principle of Hope* addressed contemporaries living in a horrific age who had just lived through one epochal crisis and had to live through yet an additional apocalypse. "Who are we? Where do we come from? Where are we going? What are we waiting for? What awaits us?"[117] Coming from Bloch, these words are not simply the insipid questions of some vulgar philosophy of meaning, but rather the prelude to a determination of one's location within the age of dread: "Many only feel confused. The ground shakes, they do not know why and with what. Theirs is a state of anxiety; if it becomes more definite, then it is fear."[118] Bloch resists accepting nihilism as an unavoidable fate.

> Only in times of a declining old society, like modern Western society, does a certain partial and transitory intention run exclusively downwards. Then those who cannot find their way out of the decline are confronted with fear of hope and against it. Then fear presents itself as the subjectivist, nihilism as the objectivist mask of the crisis phenomenon: which is tolerated but not seen through, which is lamented but not changed.[119]

Bloch counters the resigned assertion "nothing matters" with hope—schooled in the thought of dialectical materialism—in the success of the material process. "Here, against all stale and static nihilism, it must be borne in mind: even the Nothing is a utopian category, though an extremely anti-utopian one."[120] Ontological philosophizing about omnipresent nothingness is countered by an ontology of "that which is not yet."[121] Insipid statistical nihilism is countered to a certain extent by a harsh-dynamic, dialectical nihilism of nothingness in the service of the all.

The principle of hope can be understood as a call, not to deny the nihilistically anticipated end through mobilization of hope, but rather to seize it in the name of hope as an opportunity. If the catastrophe comes, then what is worthy of coming to an end will come to an end. Hope, however, employs the objective tendencies leading toward destruction as a revolutionary weapon with which to negate nothingness.[122] Demise as an opportunity: This is the Jewish-Christian apocalyptic inheritance appropriated by the principle of hope in the middle of a disintegrating epoch. "Philosophy will have conscience of tomorrow, commitment to the future, knowledge of hope, or it will have no more knowledge,"[123] an assertion with which Bloch confronted especially Martin Heidegger, whose ontological illumination of existence Bloch considered to be guided by the spirit of anxiety, not getting beyond "the dull, depressingly stagnant, even shallow dimension that he has uncovered."[124]

Today, however, it seems as if Heidegger will have the last word. In his work "Overcoming Metaphysics," written during the same period as *The Principle of Hope*, Heidegger considers it a given that "man as *animal rationale*, here meant in the sense of the working being, must wander through the desert of the earth's desolation."[125] "The laboring animal is left to the giddy whirl of its products so that it may tear itself to pieces and annihilate itself in empty nothingness."[126] The "anarchy of catastrophes"[127] is the form in which the nihilistic will to power manifests itself, a will in which metaphysics—and that means Western thought in the larger sense—culminates and comes to completion. Nihilism, to our horror, also defeats Bloch's hope that we might yet be able to subdue raging nothingness. "The earth appears as the unworld of erring. It is the erring star in the manner of the history of being."[128] In any event, hope in a salvific *novum* beyond the catastrophe has become questionable, and the "prevalence of a positive prognosis—as soon as the dark possibilities have been closed off in a theoretical-practical sense, and the brighter ones propagated in a theoretical-practical sense"[129]—just does not seem able to assert itself.

If nihilism indeed allows us no more hope, then it seems only a theology of hope can shake us out of this unsteady tumble of death, a theology for which the prevalence of a positive prognosis acquires certainty through the power of divine promise. " 'Threatened by death' and 'subjected to vanity'—that is the expression of our universal experience of existence and the world. 'In hope'—that is manifestly the way in which Christian theology takes up these questions and directs them to the promised future of God."[130] Expressed in a single term, this expression of the universal experience of existence and of the world is thus anxiety. Moltmann's theology of hope grasps anxiety as the question to which hope in God's promise dares to offer an answer. Anxiety and hope are organized into a question-answer schema not unlike Paul

Tillich's method of correlation, which itself views the existential questions of human beings as being answered by the kerygma.[131] God's own promise leads our disturbing questions to an answer. Strikingly, anxiety is not developed further as a question in the theology of hope. Moltmann stopped precisely where his theology of hope, like Bloch's philosophy, finds itself subjected to massive questioning today, and the theological consideration of anxiety was never undertaken. Hope did not so much overcome anxiety as simply push it aside. Hope was not only conscious of being carried by divine promise, it was in any case also rendered more easy during the "golden" 1960s.[132] Hope no longer had to be secured through intense struggle, as was yet the case for Bloch, but rather was encouraged by the general public mood. Although the theology of hope was well aware of the ambiguity of the world and history,[133] it viewed itself as full of the optimism of God's promise and called to set sail for distant shores.

> This world is not the heaven of self-realization, as it was said to be in Idealism. This world is not the hell of self-estrangement, as it is said to be in romanticist and existentialist writing. The world is not yet finished, but is understood as engaged in a history. It is therefore the world of possibilities, the world in which we can serve the future, promised truth and righteousness and peace. This is an age of diaspora, of sowing in hope, of self-surrender and sacrifice, for it is an age which stands within the horizon of a new future.[134]

Hope corresponded to the future. Anxiety, as an ambivalent attitude toward that future, remained outside, and was mentioned, before one proceeded to the agenda of hope, as something that was basically already overcome.

The theology of hope of the 1960s cannot simply be reproduced in an unaltered fashion. Because it expelled anxiety from its hopeful consciousness, it is unable to offer any real response to contemporary fear of the end. Moltmann was himself already aware of this fact when he followed his theology of hope with a christological reflection on the cross which quite consciously picked up "the questions of 'negative dialectic' and the 'critical theory' of T. W. Adorno and M. Horkheimer, together with the experiences and insights of early dialectical theology and existentialist philosophy,"[135] for which Bloch in part had only contempt. Moltmann, who originally felt freed by the principle of hope from the culture of anxiety of the 1950s, already redirected attention some years ago to anxiety as an unaddressed theological problem: "Today it is necessary to recover the continuity between the *anxiety of 1978* and the *hope of 1968*. I think this is possible if we pick up again the *anxiety of 1948*, anxiety which has already been dealt with successfully."[136] For Moltmann this means reflecting concurrently on Bloch's principle of hope and Kierkegaard's seemingly antithetical concept of anxiety. If the future is indeed ambiguous and open, then both anxiety and hope are justified as equally possible attitudes toward it. If, however, anxiety is "the unavoidable and natural sister of hope" which makes spirited hope circumspect and cautious, then ultimately "the concept of anxiety" and "the principle of hope" are not antitheses, but are rather "completely capable of a complementary relationship."[137] Moltmann considers it the task of theology to view our own anxiety as being annulled in Christ's experience of anxiety on the cross, and to penetrate that experience in reflection.[138] In the final analysis, however, hope does still predominate. "The *depth* of Christ's experience of anxiety on the *cross*, if we follow the primitive Christian witness, is far surpassed by the experience of *breadth* in his *resurrection*."[139] Cross and resurrection by no means balance one another. "That is why in the end one must agree with Ernst Bloch: For Christian faith, too, hope 'is superior to fear.' "[140] Anxiety is met with hope that has grown cautious. It seems questionable today, however, whether Bloch's principle of hope, as moderate as its formulation may well be, can help at all, either in impeding the apocalypse itself, or at least in mastering the anxiety elicited by the idea of the end. When one speaks of "blessed anxiety upon which unconquered hope ignites,"[141] one is ultimately reverting to theological solutions which in view of the threatening apocalypse have already forfeited their persuasive power.

4. World Anxiety as a Theological Theme

Anxiety is in the air. What is needed in the shadow of such peril and threat is not the conjuring of hopes that have long since become fragile and cracked, but rather scrutiny and description of that anxiety. This is not least also a theological task, if in the face of the impending end theology still has anything to say. We must recognize anxiety as an eminently theological problem. If, however, theology is not to fail to address the contemporary situation, it must focus on anxiety with extreme precision. It is a mistake to speak in an undifferentiated fashion about an age of anxiety or to diagnose anxiety wholesale as a Western sickness,[142] a sickness that abides in a free-floating state because our world has changed from a hostile one filled with various external dangers into a cultural world.[143] What is spreading is anxiety in the face of doom, or even of the destruction of the world. This anxiety is not some vague, diffuse feeling, but is focused rather on a negatively colored future, on its end, the anticipation of which—as subjective as that anticipation may well be—is prompted by very real, external, threatening developments and dangers. The world of culture has eliminated a great many external dangers to which human beings in earlier centuries were subjected. Now, however, we realize that this same world of culture which has delivered us from such danger is itself massively threatened by external dangers, dangers that it has itself conjured and that make its continued existence a questionable proposition. The attitude or mood corresponding to the recognition of these threatening tendencies, though an attitude not identical with this recognition, is anxiety.

This anxiety is viewed too superficially if it is taken to be a psychological reflex of individually identifiable external sources of danger. It is rather an attitude or mood that in a certain way discloses to people their existence in the world. This anxiety is more than merely the perception of concretely identifiable threats. It is a way of experiencing the world, which is why one might refer to it as *world anxiety*. This anxiety, however, as we will see in detail later, discloses the world as one that must end. Anxiety disclosing the world as reality in demise can be called apocalyptic world anxiety. And it is this apocalyptic world anxiety with which theology must come to terms today.

What is called for, then, is a *theological theory of apocalyptic world anxiety.* The present study intends to develop such a theory. With its help a new understanding of apocalyptic can be acquired by inquiring concerning the apocalyptic understanding of existence. *The hermeneutical key to the apocalyptic understanding of existence,* according to our thesis, *is world anxiety,* and this thesis will be tested within the framework of an interpretation of selected examples from apocalyptic. A detailed examination of the phenomenon of apocalyptic, however, must come before any theological discussion, and in this respect theology has some catching up to do.

The first step will be to establish more precisely the methodological premise for an interpretation based on an analysis of existence. Then a phenomenological concept of world anxiety must be developed which makes it possible to interpret the center of apocalyptic thinking, namely, the expectation of the end of the world, as an expression of a particular experience of the world and of the corresponding understanding of existence. There exists, as will be seen, an inner connection between apocalyptic world anxiety and this expectation of the end of the world. *The end of the world is the quintessence of the experience of existence, of the world, and of time as disclosed by world anxiety.* This connection between world anxiety and the end of the world will be illustrated in the next step on the basis of selected examples of various types of apocalyptic and of notions of the destruction of the world. At the same time, we will investigate just how apocalyptic in varying ways tries to overcome the apocalyptic world anxiety concentrated in the expectation of an end of the world. *Apocalyptic,* this is our next thesis, *is the attempt to overcome apocalyptic world anxiety through an interpretation of our own existence, an interpretation that includes dealing with the expectation of the end of the world.*

The requisite theology of world anxiety, however, will have to be a critical theory of apocalyptic. The current apocalyptic spirit and the rediscovery of apocalyptic in the present cannot be permitted to mislead theology into an uncritical, ill-considered reception of apocalyptic thought. This would overlook the ambiguity of apocalyptic, an ambiguity requiring that one deal critically with apocalyptic itself and rendering wholesale judgments of apocalyptic impossible. Part of any circumspect investigation of the phenomenon of apocalyptic is also a description of its ambiguities and their causes.

The real theological question, however, is how Christian faith and apocalyptic thought are to relate. Consistent with the methodological premise of our investigation, the answer to this question will involve a comparison of the apocalyptic understanding of existence with the Christian understanding, whereby the central point of comparison will be world anxiety. As in the case of apocalyptic, we must inquire concerning the position of the Christian faith regarding apocalyptic world anxiety. A theology of world anxiety thus comprehends anxiety as a theological problem. *The theological problem in dealing with apocalyptic consists in world anxiety and in coming to terms with it.* The exposition of this problem necessitates establishing a *theological concept of anxiety.*

A theology of world anxiety thus inquires concerning the possibility of dealing in a theologically responsible way with apocalyptic world anxiety and with the apocalyptic understanding of existence. Its methodological premise will make it possible for theology to come to terms, in an age of threatened existence, with the apocalyptic heritage of Christianity. Only in such discussion will theology today be able to reflect on what is yet viable in the face of the impending end.

1

APOCALYPTIC: PHENOMENOLOGICAL DESCRIPTION

> Through the millennia, apocalyptic has been a living source for human beings in their encounter with crisis and their search for hope. It remains such today as well, albeit in an altered, "secular" way. The theme of apocalyptic transcends the limits of mere intellectual reflection and poses vital existential questions.
>
> —*Kurt Rudolph*

1. The Obscure Entity "Apocalyptic"

Dictionaries tell us that everything apocalyptic is "mysterious" and "dark."[1] At the same time, however, it appears as something abstruse. "Apocalyptic is a Greek borrowing and smacks not only of the weird and menacing; it also suggests the abstruse and fantastic."[2] Apocalyptic can be viewed in two different respects as an "obscure power," as K. Koch describes it[3]: Not only has no comprehensive, unequivocal interpretation of this phenomenon yet been put forward,[4] we are not even sure regarding the delimitation and parameters of what one should understand under the notion of apocalyptic. In the face of this obscurity, utterly different branches of scholarship have tried to gain access to apocalyptic, each defining the phenomenon in a different way.

Apocalyptic was discovered as a scholarly object of investigation by historical-critical exegesis in the first half of the nineteenth century. F. Lücke, who can be viewed as the founder of apocalyptic studies, picked up the superscription of the New Testament Revelation of John and referred to apocalyptic as a specific Jewish-Christian literary genre. "The name 'apokalypsis,' which most of the examples of the literature bear (though not all of them as an original part of the text), is the biblical designation for a peculiarly Jewish and Christian concept."[5] Accordingly, Lücke considered the task of scholarship to be twofold: "First, specify in an organized, scholarly fashion the concept and character of apocalyptic literature as illustrated by its extant historical manifestations; then portray the history of this literature in its primary representatives beginning with its source in the Jewish canon."[6] Since Lücke's time, apocalyptic has for long stretches been treated only as a literary-historical phenomenon, or more precisely, as a literary-historical phenomenon of Jewish and early Christian literary history; one must point out, however, that even the mere designation of such an independent genre and of its accompanying identifying characteristics has created not inconsiderable problems continuing up to the present.

From the existence of such apocalyptic literature in Judaism and early Christianity, whose flowering occurred in the five hundred years commencing with the third century B.C., scholars concluded what seemed apparent, namely, that there existed a corresponding spiritual-religious current in which these writings might have had their home. With good reason, then, apocalyptic can be viewed not only as a literary-historical phenomenon, but as a religio-historical one as well.[7] Attempts at proving the existence of this historical current, however, run into considerable difficulties insofar as historical evidence for its principles cannot be adduced. Until further notice, religious studies must depend here on clues and suspicions, which ultimately always depend on the literature classified as apocalyptic and on its possible historical development. Confusion is the result, and it is a serious problem, especially concerning the sociological locus of the presumed apocalyptic movements, e.g., in Judaism. In connection with early Christianity, as well, apocalyptic studies are on extremely insecure sociological footing.

The difficulties in analyzing this phenomenon increase as soon as the narrow confines of Jewish-Christian religious history are left behind. Here the inquiry limits itself first of all to the question whether Jewish and subsequent Christian apocalyptic originated exclusively on Old Testament ground, or whether extra-Jewish influences can be discerned, namely, from Iran. If such influences cannot be excluded, and if they prove in fact to be highly probable, the question arises regarding currents related to Jewish-Christian apocalyptic, doubtless first of all in the religious history of antiquity in the Mediterranean sphere and ancient Near East, and then also throughout the rest of religious history to the present. Whether such parallels can indeed be drawn, however, depends entirely on what criterion one acknowledges for apocalyptic. One must clarify whether the criteria for apocalyptic are to be derived exclusively from the corresponding Jewish-Christian literature up to the middle of the third century A.D., or whether other, more broadly conceived religio-phenomenological descriptive features are also applicable. In any case, any methodologically sound concept of apocalyptic established for religious studies presupposes a clarification of what is to be viewed as the constant identifying features of apocalyptic and of what determines the variables in these features.

To this point, we have discussed only problems relating to the study of religions in the stricter sense, and one can doubtless speak of apocalyptic—albeit not without considering the previously mentioned and in part quite serious difficulties—primarily as a religio-historical phenomenon. We must also inquire, however, whether secular parallels to this phenomenon exist, i.e., comparable phenomena offering an expanded notion of what is to be understood by apocalyptic, and that might exercise corresponding retroactive influence on the interpretation of the historical apocalyptic material. Within such a broadly conceived framework one might then also expect contributions from philosophy and psychology regarding the illumination of apocalyptic as a phenomenon not only deserving historical interest but also holding considerable significance in and for the present.

The extraordinary extent to which the questions discussed to this point are intertwined is obvious, and this makes it unusually difficult to establish a concept of apocalyptic satisfactory to everyone. Occasionally it seems more as if apocalyptic is in truth a nebulous entity that becomes increasingly more diffuse the more intensively one scrutinizes it,[8] though we should not let this discourage us from continuing to seek access to the apocalyptic phenomenon. Such entries might open up from completely different quarters, and attempts at understanding apocalyptic more closely can be undertaken from various perspectives: Apocalyptic can be conceived as a historical phenomenon whose origin one can attempt to *explain* historically in the widest sense. Apocalyptic can also be understood as the expression or manifestation of a quite specific understanding of existence, an understanding that we in our own turn can attempt both to illuminate and to *understand.* In what follows we will look for an access to such an *understanding* of apocalyptic and of the view of existence coming to expression in it.

2. Apocalyptic as a Literary Phenomenon

Apocalyptic thinking finds expression in apocalyptic literature. In view of the multilayered problems posed by a description of apocalyptic, some exegetes prefer to limit their dealings with this phenomenon to a purely literary-historical investigation of the apocalypses as an independent genre. J. Carmignac, for example, refuses entirely to speak of apocalyptic apart from the writings called apocalypses: "If we hesitate to speak of apocalyptic, it is because we would like to know whether it is a literary genre or more a theological pudding."[9] This kind of theologically prepared, historico-methodologically inedible "terminological pudding" can be avoided only by limiting the designation "apocalyptic" to the literary phenomenon. Here one must distinguish between the terms "apocalypse," "apocalyptic," and "apocalypticism." An "apocalypse" refers to a writing that can be classified as "apocalyptic" in the sense of a literary genre. "Apocalypticism," on the other hand, is used to refer to the attempt to systematize the characteristic features of apocalyptic literature.[10] Apocalyptic can be specified more precisely as "the literary genre which describes heavenly revelations through symbols."[11] Similarly, H. Stegemann understands apocalyptic exclusively as a "*literary* phenomenon, namely the production of 'revelatory writings' 'revealing' material which cannot be derived from innerworldly circumstances, e.g., from extant 'experiential knowledge,' but which are disclosed for the author and reader only through recourse to 'heavenly revelatory knowledge.' "[12] Some exegetes are inclined to view the form of apocalypses completely apart from their content,[13] content that continues to be a matter of dispute. In extreme cases, such analyses ultimately also disregard the possible historico-political and social background of apocalyptic literature.[14]

Now as before, the controversy continues whether we are justified in speaking of apocalyptic as an independent literary genre. In the first place, it seems problematic to apply, e.g., to pre-Christian Jewish literature classified as apocalyptic a term that established itself only in the second century A.D. as a *terminus technicus* for specific texts.[15] Even apart from any unified designation, the question arises concerning the formal unity of the postulated genre. G. von Rad, for example, was unable to discover such a unity. He believed his own studies had shown that apocalyptic does not represent an independent genre at all, but rather "from a form-critical perspective represents a *mixtum compositum* whose history of transmission suggests an extremely complicated prehistory."[16] On the other hand, certain peculiarities—in part regarding form, in part content—are discernible that recur at least in most Jewish apocalypses, peculiarities seeming to justify speaking of apocalyptic as an independent genre. Such a determination of genre is quite capable of responding to von Rad's objections by differentiating between the macrogenre, on the one hand, and the microgenres flowing into it on the other.[17]

The standard description of the genre of apocalypses is still that of P. Vielhauer,[18] which understands by apocalyptic first Jewish apocalyptic, then the Christian apocalyptic following upon it. The most important "stylistic features" of Jewish apocalypses[19] include[20]: pseudonymity; its frequent form as a revelatory account; extensive use of imagery and its decipherment, usually supplied by one or more interpretative angels; and an element of systematization of what is revealed, usually by means of organizational schemata, especially numerical speculation.

Jewish apocalypses are pseudonymous writings always claiming authorship by one of the great figures of the distant past, figures to whom secret revelations were given that have remained concealed until the present end time just commencing, and which were given in the form of visions, either as dreams or as visionary ecstasy. What is actually viewed, however, is imagery, either the anticipated events themselves or encoded symbols and allegories, which can in part be construed with extreme artificiality and thus solicit interpretation. On the other hand, such apocalyptic imagery can pick up extant traditions and symbols. Only rarely is the seer himself capable of the requisite interpretation, and usually an *angelus interpres*, if not God himself, appears to decode the revealed images. Although the language and imagery of apocalypses can be confusing in its profusion and variety, an inclination toward systematization permeates it. Numerical schemata and historical periodization are especially popular as devices through which the revelation is rendered accessible.

As a macrogenre, the apocalypses are a *mixtum compositum* of a series of smaller forms, including especially historical overviews in the future tense. For the most part, these overviews consist in *vaticinia ex eventu* rendered in the future tense from the perspective of the fictitious author from the distant past, dovetailing then into the eschatological prophecies intended by the actual author. These prophecies, however, foretell the imminent end of world history. In addition to such historical overviews, often presented in the form of periodizations, devices also include portrayals of the visionary rapture of the seer into the heavenly world, portrayals that in the later periods even became an independent microgenre. The high point of such raptures is the vision of the divine throne room, visions representing a form-critical connecting link between the call visions of the Old Testament prophets and later Jewish Merkabah mysticism. In addition to these characteristics, parenesis and prayers permeate Jewish apocalypses.

Regarding content, Vielhauer discerned four primary characteristics for the apocalyptic view of the world. In his opinion, the essential feature is a dualism dividing world history into two radically separate aeons. Before the new aeon—the kingdom of God—can emerge, the old world must pass away. There is no continuity between the two aeons. Furthermore, the apocalypses exhibit an inclination toward universalism and at the same time a higher estimation of the individual. Whereas on the one hand the entire history of the world, from creation to the end of the world, comes into focus in the historical overviews, on the other hand the kind of individualism already discernible in Ezekiel is developed further, according to which not mere membership in the people of God, but rather only the faithful keeping of the law decides the fate of the individual. As far as the estimation of history itself is concerned, Vielhauer suggests that apocalyptic is ambivalent. On the one hand, the present aeon is viewed as evil, so that one can speak of a fundamental attitude of pessimism in apocalyptic; on the other hand, this pessimism is eclipsed in intensity by the hope these apocalypses direct toward the new aeon. Considering the periodization of history, Vielhauer does not shy away from classifying the worldview of apocalyptic as deterministic. Apocalypses did not anticipate any changes in the divine will. Precisely from this unchangeable nature of the divine will, however, the apocalyptists derived their certainty concerning the imminence of the prophesied end.

While Vielhauer's form-critical classification of the apocalyptic literature of early Judaism still offers an important point of departure for further definitions,[21] it also shows the considerable extent to which the description and evaluation of the literary phenomenon intertwine, since terms such as "dualism," "universalism," and "individualism," "pessimism," and "determinism" already imply a clear judgment concerning apocalyptic. These thus also represent the most important points of contention in the theological debate concerning the classification of apocalyptic. Most recently, especially K. Müller has vehemently questioned all these wholesale judgments.[22] We will encounter these once again when we inquire concerning the relationship between Christian theology and apocalyptic, and thus also between Christian theology and the heritage of Christian apocalyptic.

Although at the level of fiction the Jewish apocalypses claim to portray authentic visionary experiences, one finds in fact that they are dependent on preceding traditions, symbols, and literary forms. This prompts the question concerning the origin of apocalyptic imagery, the corresponding basic conceptions of the world, and of literary models and sources. The solutions to these problems would also yield information concerning the authors and circles in which the apocalypses of early Judaism presumably originated. Although it is not disputed that specific elements of apocalyptic literature can already be found in the Old Testament writings before Daniel, the question is yet unresolved whether Jewish apocalyptic developed primarily from prophetic or from wisdom traditions. G. von Rad attempted to show that apocalyptic represented a body of writing rooted in wisdom literature.[23] Apocalyptic allegedly represented an "eschatologizing of wisdom."[24] Von Rad considered it likely that "at a certain, probably late stage, wisdom, which was in any case characterized by an encyclopedic inclination, opened itself to considerations of the last things," and that "this probably involved dealing with foreign, particularly Iranian materials."[25] He thought it appropriate to juxtapose antithetically the thinking of the prophets, directed toward salvation history, with the unhistorical thinking of apocalyptic. Admittedly, not only was von Rad's handling of the sources exegetically questionable, it was also clearly guided by theological premises constituting a theological disqualification of apocalyptic.[26] It is no wonder, then, that on the other hand apocalyptic has been viewed as a continuation especially of Old Testament prophecy, a view supported by references to individual features of apocalyptic, not least to features of the portrayals of visions,[27] which have parallels especially in Ezekiel and Zechariah, though also to ideas such as eschatological announcements of redemption, catastrophes prior to the time of salvation, or a historical plan, features recalling not only Zechariah but especially Isaiah.[28] Even if a relationship between the schools of apocalyptic and late prophecy does in fact obtain, one should not, on the other hand, overlook the influence of wisdom on apocalyptic literature; in this respect von Rad's thesis is to a certain extent correct.[29] It is also possible that Deuteronomistic legal doctrine played a role in apocalyptic circles.[30] All this taken together makes it difficult to offer an unequivocal answer to the question concerning Old Testament precursors of apocalyptic. "The basic problem thus remains: The Old Testament tradition has obviously served in a variety of ways as the testator for apocalyptic, a situation that would accord with its character as a product of the later period."[31]

One question that long has been a matter of debate is whether in the first place apocalyptic can be explained exclusively in the context of Old Testament traditions, or whether one must not also assume the presence of extra-Israelite influences.[32] Though objections have always been lodged against such an assertion of influence, on the other hand the thesis of influence from Iranian religion on Jewish apocalyptic has repeatedly been put forth. Attempts have been made, for example, to trace lines of tradition back to India for individual features of the apocalyptic worldview, such as the doctrine of the four monarchies or the periodization of history. It is relatively certain that the Hellenistic revelatory writings, which appeared contemporaneously with Jewish apocalyptic, do not constitute a source for the early Jewish texts. Furthermore, we can also say that as far as the resolution of the question of the development of Jewish apocalyptic is concerned, the Qumran writings played a far lesser role than has long been assumed.[33] For the rest, K. Koch is probably correct in his assessment of the religio-historical derivation of Jewish-apocalyptic literature: "Perhaps an either-or solution is completely inappropriate, and perhaps single-cause derivations simply will not yield what is needed."[34]

Nonetheless, the question of religio-historical influences on Jewish apocalyptic has opened up the investigation to comparable literature outside Judaism, such as the

Iranian *Avesta*-writings, though also Akkadian and Egyptian texts, Greek sources such as the Er-myth at the end of Plato's *Republic*, on up to Roman revelatory literature. Whereas Vielhauer still asserted that apocalyptic constituted a Jewish production of the Hellenistic period, or more precisely, "a *Jewish reaction to advancing Hellenistic culture*,"[35] it turns out that apocalyptic represents by no means merely a phenomenon of Jewish religious history. Accordingly, an expanded concept is necessary of what is actually understood by apocalyptic literature. K. Rudolph has suggested a cautious definition for this genre; according to this definition, apocalyptic includes

> essentially the following features: a linear, more or less periodicized course of history, "prophecy of the end time" (an eschatological element), a pessimistic worldview, doctrines of the beyond, polarization (dual or dualistic elements), notions of times of disaster and of salvation, esoteric knowledge concerning such events corresponding to revelations and visions of a special kind, deposited in written documents. All this presupposes a socio-religious situation of calamity or distress; the attempt to come to terms with this situation is actually the root of apocalyptic. It is probably wholly a phenomenon of the later period, and the product of an attitude of crisis. [Apocalypses are] revelatory writings (*apokalyptein!*) in which the previously mentioned features recur. They acquire their particular form through framed narratives, accounts of auditions and visions, celestial journeys, dialogues (*erotapokriseis*), and parenesis. The frequent use of images, metaphor, and symbols necessitates corresponding "interpretations." The author, legitimized by the cloak of pseudonymity involving a religious or divine person, is either associated with a person receiving a revelation or vision, or is identical with such a person. The sender of the revelation is a transcendent, "metahistorical" reality appearing in various guises (including ultimately *theologia negationis*).[36]

This kind of expanded concept of the literary genre of apocalyptic has the advantage of not completely sundering the form and content of apocalyptic literature from each other. Neither is this really possible in any case, and where it is nonetheless attempted, the framework of heavenly revelation asserts its independence over against the eschatological content, which is then in some cases even declared to be a merely contingent component.[37] In contrast, one can basically say of apocalyptic literature at large what Vielhauer said of Jewish apocalyptic specifically: "The main interest, however, does not lie in problems of cosmology or theodicy, but in eschatology."[38] On the other hand, it makes little sense to define the genre of apocalyptic literature only on the basis of its specific eschatological content, since in that case the most divergent texts from different epochs and cultural circles, though utterly dissimilar in form, would be classified as examples of one and the same form solely on the basis of the apocalyptic ideas represented in them. Ultimately, however, this means abandoning the idea of an independent genre of apocalyptic literature. As this kind of specific genre, then, one can recognize only that body of written apocalypses for which, as we have seen, identifying features of both form and content can be offered, features the description of which, however, must be allowed a certain breadth[39] within which specific variations of the apocalyptic genre (e.g., Jewish or Iranian) can be located. Finally, although apocalyptic thinking does manifest itself in apocalypses, i.e., in a literary genre by no means limited to the Jewish and Christian sphere, the occurrence at large of such thinking far transcends the sphere of apocalyptic literature in this narrower sense.

3. Apocalyptic as a Religio-Historical Phenomenon

As we have already seen, Lücke's artificial word "apocalyptic" is somewhat iridescent and in need of more specific differentiation. T. Olsson has spoken in this connection of an "umbrella term,"[40] and suggests distinguishing not only between apocalyptic as a literary-historical phenomenon (apocalypses) and as a religio-historical manifestation, but beyond this also between "*apocalypticism* as a speculative and verbal activity comprising more or less coherent systems of apocalyptic ideas" and "*apocalyptic ideas* which constitute the above systems but are also found in other contexts than apocalypticism."[41] This distinction recalls that between gnosis and gnosticism suggested in 1966 at the Gnosis-Congress in Messina,[42] a distinction, however, about whose usefulness scholars are not in agreement.[43] In any case, Olsson's assertion that apocalyptic thinking is by no means an exclusively religious phenomenon is certainly justified.[44]

If one bears in mind that apocalyptic thinking is not limited to a specific historical period, or to any single geographical, religious, or cultural sphere, then the definition offered by H. Ringgren is still useful, according to whom apocalyptic is "speculation claiming—usually in allegorical form—to interpret the course of the world and to reveal its end."[45] We can also speak with G. Lanczkowski of a "complex of ideas" relating to the "unveiling of future events occurring at the end of a world period," insofar as the reference is not only to the end of the world within the framework of a teleological historical conception but also to catastrophic events through which in regular recurrence an epoch of world history is brought to an end according to the notion of cyclical world ages.[46] Thus that which, as the word *apokalypsis* says, is unveiled, is not just something arbitrary, but rather the end of the world, though an end whose one-time nature need not be queried at this point. Picking up the fine formulation of J. Ellul[47] we can also speak of apocalyptic as the unveiling of reality, specifically of collapsing reality. Apocalyptic is the unveiling of reality in collapse.

Understood as this phenomenon,[48] apocalyptic is observed first of all in the Near East and Mediterranean sphere during the time of antiquity, where we must assume a certain measure of interdependence between the various manifestations. The Iranian apocalyptic mentioned earlier[49] developed the notion that three thousand years after Zarathustra, world judgment would be introduced by the appearance of an eschatological deliverer, the Saoshyant, and by the resurrection of the dead. This would be followed by the condition of a purified earth, called Frashokereti. Possibly these Iranian ideas have been influenced by Indian speculation, which portrays a sequence of four world ages called Yugas.[50] Such speculation was continued in Jainism and Buddhism. According to these conceptions, the final age of the world will end in the complete reversal of all present circumstances. Both the moral and the natural order will break down, ethical obligation will degenerate, sacrificial ritual will be neglected, and boundaries between castes will be breached. This catastrophic end, however, is enclosed within a great cycle in which the sequence of the four Yugas is continually repeated. The later Stoics also knew of a periodic end of the world and expected a world conflagration that would destroy the existing world and at the same time allow it to reemerge in its original form. In its own turn, the apocalyptic of Islam was probably influenced by Jewish and Christian sources, though Muhammad's own proclamation already had an essentially apocalyptic orientation.[51] The center of his message was the announcement of eschatological world judgment, preceded by natural catastrophes. Greek examples include Hesiod's doctrine of the world ages, Plutarch's *De genio Socratis*, and the Sibylline literature.[52] Even the Egyptian sphere attests apocalyptic ideas, though the Egyptian models did not, like those in Greek, develop an independent apocalyptic literature.[53]

Apocalyptic ideas are also attested in areas outside the Mediterranean basin, especially from the sphere of Germanic religion.[54] The end of the world is emphatically portrayed in the *Völuspá*, one of the texts of the *Edda*. A preliminary vision is given of the *Götterdämmerung* (the twilight of the gods, Ragnarokr or Ragnarok), which begins with the killing of the god Baldur. The eschatological drama culminates in a world conflagration, though hope remains for a new earth that will emerge from the waters of the sea. That apocalyptic is by no means bound to specific historical periods and cultural spheres is shown by the apocalyptically oriented religion of the Indians of the Tupi-Guarani tribe, who live from south of the Amazon to the border between Brazil and Paraguay.[55] Until 1912, when the Brazilian government enacted a prohibition, the Tupi-Guarani undertook journeys at regular intervals from the interior of the country to the seacoast. On each of these journeys the Indians wanted to reach the "land without evil," the dwelling place of the high god Nanderuvucu, before the end of the world, which they expected any day. They expected the earth to be plunged into the abyss and stars and human beings to be devoured by mythical creatures. This entire scenario would end with a world conflagration and a subsequent flood.

The apocalyptic of late antiquity also exhibits striking parallels with another intellectual-religious current in the Mediterranean sphere at that time, namely, gnosis, the investigation and understanding of which pose problems equal to those of apocalyptic studies. Astonishingly, Hans Jonas, who in his pioneer work *Gnosis und spätantiker Geist*[56] interpreted gnosis from the perspective of its understanding of existence, completely disregards the phenomenon of apocalyptic. In this way he was able to conclude that gnosis as such represented *the* expression of *the* spirit of antiquity. This thesis has not escaped criticism, nor can it, since it is global in a way rendering it incapable of explaining the contemporaneity of the variety of religions and intellectual currents of late antiquity.

At first glance, apocalyptic and gnosis seem to be separated by worlds. Cosmological speculation concerning the ontological nature of the world and the soteriological hope in redemption and the ascent of the heavenly sparks of light as souls in need of redemption, as developed by gnosis, seems as far removed as can be from the horizontal-historical and eschatological thinking of apocalyptic. For a long time it went unnoticed that apocalyptic and future eschatological notions also occupy considerable space within gnosis itself, something shown especially by the gnostic apocalypses among the finds from Nag Hammadi.[57] At its core, gnosis is doubtlessly "realized eschatology." Despite all this, however, gnosis is fundamentally focused on the end time and on the fate both of individual souls and of the totality of all souls culminating then. This fate is portrayed not only in cosmological-vertical speculation but also in what amounts to apocalyptic scenarios, which justify speaking about gnostic apocalyptic.[58] Features common both to apocalyptic and to gnosis include especially the microcosmic and macrocosmic dualism of two aeons and the low estimation of the present world period over against the future one, the development of an arcane discipline and the esoteric nature of knowledge guaranteeing salvation, the predominance of speculation concerning the primeval and end times, and a pessimistic view of historical development.[59] H. Jonas's conclusion is confirmed: "The gnostic myth is eschatological as regards both content and form."[60] This makes all the more pressing a clarification of the religio-historical relationship between gnosis and apocalyptic.

W. Schmithals has attempted such a clarification by inquiring concerning the apocalyptic understanding of existence. "That is to say, when this is done one suddenly discovers surprising areas of common ground between gnosis and apocalyptic, which make comprehensible Rudolf Otto's judgment which originated from H. Gressmann, 'Gnosis is of the very spirit of apocalyptic teaching,' a judgment which of course can be stated conversely as well."[61] Although at first glance it seems that "the gulf separating these two patterns of thought, each of which comprehensively covers the whole of human existence, is as great as that between Plato and Isaiah,"[62] Schmithals ultimately finds that gnosis and apocalyptic basically represent one and the same understanding of existence. The historical reference attested by apocalyptic is allegedly only an apparent one, so that as a matter of fact gnosis and apocalyptic are closely related and, to the same degree, "sharply separated from the Old Testament understanding of reality."[63] Historically, however, there is no interdependence, however articulated, between the two phenomena. Rather, the beginnings of both apocalyptic and gnosis were contemporaneous, so that according to Schmithals what we have is the historically parallel development of an identical understanding of existence.[64] This suggestion, however, is unsatisfactory, since it cannot explain why one and the same understanding of existence developed in such different directions. On the other hand, the traditio-historical and form-critical parallels also demand an answer addressing their historical development. If these two currents are traced back to a single, unified understanding of existence, then we lose all criteria for "distinguishing clearly between intellectual movements which in their essential features are as different as gnosis, apocalyptic, and Neo-Platonism."[65]

In his own critical evaluation of H. Jonas's work, H. Blumenberg defended the thesis that gnosis can be understood as a reaction to the disappointment of apocalyptic expectation of an imminent end and the attendant crisis into which the ethical demands of apocalyptic thought invariably were thrown, demands which "could be maintained, if at all, only under the premise that the time before the end was extremely brief."[66] This thesis is itself not without problems insofar as it is doubtful that apocalyptic ethics always constitute only interim ethics of the kind Albert Schweitzer thought applied to Jesus and the beginnings of Christianity. Nonetheless, one can legitimately ask whether gnosis must not be understood as a manner of thinking which realigns the horizontal apocalyptic view of history into a vertical view of cosmology. This suspicion seems all the more in order considering the interest apocalyptic thought has in cosmology. One need think only of the heavenly journeys and of the visions of the throne room. If, as H. Jonas suggests, gnosis is fundamentally eschatological as regards form and content, then one might view its eschatology as a radicalizing of apocalyptic eschatology.[67] This would mean, however, that R. Otto's assertion that gnosis is the very spirit of apocalyptic teaching[68] cannot be reversed.

Whereas H. Jonas characterizes late antiquity as the "gnostic age,"[69] in view of the tendency to trace gnosis back to apocalyptic roots[70] the impression might arise that late antiquity was ultimately an apocalyptic age.[71] This, however, goes beyond our present goal. In the first place, we must guard against single-cause derivations of gnosis. In the second, the differences and competing contemporaneity of apocalyptic and gnosis would again remain incomprehensible.[72]

The religio-sociological questions generated in this connection are not inconsiderable, and this applies equally to gnosis and apocalyptic. One must clarify in which strata of the populace or in which groups the various apocalyptic currents are to be located. This is an extraordinarily difficult question to answer as far as the historical manifestations of apocalyptic during late antiquity are concerned, since apart from apocalyptic literature itself historical information is almost entirely lacking. The failure, however, to clarify the sociological locus of apocalyptic constitutes a serious objection to any form-critical classification of apocalypses as a literary genre, since the concept of a genre implies sociological judgments concerning the life setting (*Sitz im Leben*) of literature belonging to that particular genre. To this point, however, there has been no satisfactory determination of the life setting of apocalypses, and studies in religion are to a large extent dependent on speculation in this respect.

As with so many areas of apocalyptic studies, in religio-sociological questions, too, both Jewish and subsequent Christian apocalyptic acquire paradigmatic significance. One must ask first about the authors of the apocalypses. Whereas early ages considered them to be visionaries, literary and form-critical studies showed that one must distinguish between the fictitious receiver of the revelation on the one hand, and the actual author on the other. In contrast to the fictitious visionaries, the actual authors of apocalypses are often considered to have been learned scribes, in which case the authors of the Jewish apocalypses probably should be sought in the circles of wisdom and exegetical learning. Today, however, scholars no longer exclude the possibility that the apocalyptic authors, in addition to a rich knowledge of prophetic and wisdom traditions, also had their own visionary experiences. K. Koch, for example, thinks it possible that the visionary accounts were composed by people "who practiced prayer, fasting, etc. in visionary meditation." Furthermore, Koch suspects the presence of a certain "school tradition." "When the apocalyptists pick up a prophetic linguistic model to recount secret experiences, and then independently alter that model, one must presuppose corresponding psychological practices. This suggests . . . that those interested in the 'spirit' of apocalyptic heroes (Daniel, Ezra) met in their own circles, perhaps in their own synagogues, and presented their scriptural interpretations and interpretative problems to one another."[73] For the time being, of course, these are nothing more than assumptions.

It is also unclear just how one is to conceive the circles of apocalyptists. Whereas W. Bousset or even E. Stauffer considered the Jewish apocalypses to be "folk books,"[74] others, such as O. Plöger and P. Vielhauer, sought the home of apocalyptic in "eschatologically-excited circles" which in Israel "were forced more and more by the theocracy into a kind of conventicle existence."[75] Apocalypses, then, were an esoteric literature of conventicles, read in circles with sectarian inclinations. Scholars have in part conceived the circles in which Christian apocalyptic blossomed to have been similar, specifically the readership of the New Testament Revelation to John.[76] A number of factors seems to confirm the existence of apocalyptically oriented conventicles.

A more difficult question is admittedly whether apocalyptic ideas were limited to such circles, or whether such conventicles themselves indicate the presence of a broader apocalyptic current. Caution is also advised regarding previous attempts to draw from apocalyptic literature conclusions concerning social tensions, though the question concerning such tensions is in principle a legitimate one. For example, some have assumed the presence of conflicts between Palestinian religious minorities and the ruling priestly caste.[77] One can by no means assert in a wholesale fashion that apocalyptic was a phenomenon of the lower classes. When criticism of the rich is occasionally heard in Jewish apocalypses, one might well assume behind such accusations circles of the older upper classes, whose power and influence were waning. Beyond this, there are no other indications of attacks directed specifically at priests.[78]

We can say with greater justification, however, that apocalyptic is a phenomenon of crisis. The present is experienced as a crisis situation, a situation to be interpreted with the aid of apocalyptic thinking and one with which one in this way hopes to come to terms. Apocalyptic is in this view less "scrutiny of the future"[79] than an attempt to deal successfully with the present. Radical changes of world-historical dimensions took place in antiquity with the rise and collapse of Alexander's empire, and later of the Roman Empire. For Israel, though also for other nations in the eastern Mediterranean sphere, these convulsions constituted national catastrophes politically, and intellectually-historically, also cultural alienation. In a comparable fashion, Zoroastrian apocalyptic can be understood as a reaction to the advance of the Romans, and later of the Arabs and Turks.[80] One must exercise caution, however, over against the inclination to limit such crisis situations to political events. In the area of Jewish apocalyptic, for example, it has been shown that sections of *1 Enoch* extend back to the third or even fourth century B.C., and thus originated prior to any situation involving persecution.[81] Similarly, a purely political explanation of apocalyptic in the case of the South American Tupi-Guarani would probably prove inadequate.

If, then, apocalyptic thinking can be understood from the sociological perspective as an attempt at dealing with crisis, one must ask further which strata of the populace experienced the present as this sort of crisis. If one bears in mind that the aristocratic stratum in Palestine cooperated with the Seleucids and later also with the Romans—to pick up the paradigm of Jewish apocalyptic again—one can hardly assert that all Israel felt repressed during these times.[82] J. J. Collins thus suggests that the affected circles included intellectuals of Jewish origin who were critical of the ruling class, "those who are wise" in Dan. 11:33, 35, who found adherents in the middle and lower classes.[83] G. Theissen draws a similar picture of the social structure of early Christianity.[84] This was allegedly an urban movement whose spokespersons possessed a certain level of education, while its adherents came from simple circumstances. Theissen also suggests that, like Jewish apocalyptic, early Christianity distanced itself from the political order. According to this view, apocalyptic thinking was a kind of "lay intellectualism" (M. Weber) flourishing in a social milieu corresponding approximately to that of gnosis.[85] This sociological description of apocalyptic, flourishing in circles of uprooted and politically disenfranchised intellectuals and their adherents, to the extent it can be maintained, does indeed find parallels in the composition of the Christian apocalyptic sects and conventicles that emerged in the nineteenth century. Regarding earlier apocalyptic movements, however, we are dependent on sociological assumptions.

If the comparison of Jewish, Christian, and gnostic apocalyptic reveals a similar sociological picture for all three movements, then the virulent question emerges whether the discernible ideological differences between the three currents can also be explained sociologically.[86] Whereas on the one hand repeated reference has been made to the revolutionary character of apocalyptic, one manifesting itself in the attitude of early Christianity and of the Revelation to John, on the other hand apocalyptic has been described as restorative and even reactionary.[87] Kippenberg believes one can discern the difference between Jewish, Christian, and gnostic apocalyptic in the ethical demands these currents make.[88] The Jewish apocalyptic notions of the end time correspond to the restorative, ethical demand for unerring faithfulness to the Mosaic law; in contrast, Christian apocalyptic demands innerworldly asceticism, and gnostic expectation, finally, demands asceticism that flees the world. If like Kippenberg one now interprets the decisions implied by apocalyptic in order, one finds that Jewish apocalyptic demands loyalty to the old traditions, early Christianity a break with these loyalties, and gnosis the complete negation of all institutions contributing to the support of this world. Accordingly, various ethical positions are conceivable within apocalyptic, among which according to Kippenberg the gnostic would represent the most radical. Let us disregard for the moment the question whether this model does justice to the complexity of Jewish, Christian, and gnostic apocalyptic and its history. What seems important to me is the realization that, viewed sociologically as a crisis phenomenon, apocalyptic can imply quite varied consequences for the life of society, consequences that in their own turn can mutually affect the various notions of the end time.

Many of the religio-phenomenological and religio-sociological questions raised in the preceding discussion still await definitive clarification. In many respects, from the perspective of religious studies apocalyptic yet remains an "obscure entity." Caution is advised over against retroactive conclusions regarding phenomena of earlier epochs from the perspective of contemporary experience and phenomena,[89] as well as over against the transfer of the interpretation of individual phenomena in one set of cultural circumstances to phenomena in completely different circumstances. Nonetheless, we are justified in speaking of apocalyptic as a universal phenomenon, albeit one certainly subject to multifarious transformations. The phenomenology of religion shows that the center of apocalyptic is the expectation of the end of the world. This variously developed expectation is the expression of a crisis consciousness, one deriving from a profound sense of powerlessness. As a universal phenomenon, apocalyptic is by no means limited to the religious realm, a fact shown by attempts at scrutinizing apocalyptic undertaken from perspectives other than those of religious studies.

4. Philosophical Approaches

We today are not the first to be somewhat perplexed by apocalyptic. As early as the Enlightenment, apocalyptic met with incomprehension, since, of course, the Enlightenment viewed itself as a liberation from precisely that particular worldview for which throughout the entire Middle Ages and into the time of the Reformation the end of the world was a familiar notion. These notions of the end of the world were now to be replaced by the active hope in the progress of humankind.

Like the philosophers of the Enlightenment, Kant shared the view that the enlightened person could make nothing of this kind of "mystical" or supranatural end of the world. Nonetheless, Kant is able to derive some sense from the idea of the end, sense able to maintain itself before reason not in a theoretical, but in a practical respect. For Kant, practical reason opened up new access to apocalyptic, which through the Enlightenment had become obsolete.

The notion of the end of the world occupied Kant in his treatise on *Religion within the Limits of Reason Alone*[90] (1793) and in an essay from 1794 entitled *Das Ende aller Dinge (The End of All Things)*.[91] Kant inquires not concerning the theoretical content of cognition, but concerning the moral function of eschatological perception. In this case one must thus speak of a functional view of apocalyptic. The decisive question for Kant is this: "Why is it that human beings expect an *end of the world in the first place?* And even if one grants them this possibility, why do they expect the end to come with terror (for the greater portion of humankind)?"[92]

The answer is that creation would appear purposeless or pointless if there were no ultimate or end purpose. Accordingly, all morality is teleologically oriented. For

Kant, however, the ultimate moral purpose consists in the "sovereignty of the good principle,"[93] which though incapable of being established by human beings, hindered as they are by evil, can nonetheless constitute the object of striving to the best of one's ability.[94] The "final object of practical reason" is "the realization of the idea of the moral end."[95] Despite the inability of human beings to realize the idea of the highest good, they discover within themselves the duty to work for this end, and thus find themselves "impelled to believe in the cooperation or management of a moral ruler of the world, by means of which alone this goal can be reached."[96] Faith in a judging, righteous God thus grounds teleologically oriented morality, and this faith is the source of the "wish of all well-disposed people," namely, that the kingdom of God come.[97] The coming of this kingdom is anticipated by the establishment of a commonwealth in the form of a church, whereby the infinite approach to the kingdom of God can only succeed if faith makes the transition from ecclesiastical faith to the exclusive sovereignty of pure religious faith, i.e., the religion of reason.[98] Teleologically oriented morality is supported by the presentation of "virtue striving toward holiness" in the form of salvation history.[99] Since salvation history and the kingdom of God, to which the former aims, are symbols with a moral function, then the end of the world can also be interpreted as a "symbolical representation."[100]

> This sketch of a history of after-ages, which themselves are not yet history, presents a beautiful ideal of the moral world-epoch, brought about by the introduction of true universal religion and in faith *foreseen* even to its culmination—which we cannot *conceive* as a culmination in experience, but can merely *anticipate*, i.e., prepare for, in continual progress and approximation toward the highest good possible on earth (and in all of this there is nothing mystical, but everything moves quite naturally in a moral fashion).[101]

Although according to Kant the moral value of the notion of the kingdom of God is thus immediately apparent, the idea of a catastrophic end time initially presents difficulties, since "the teacher of the gospel revealed to his disciples the kingdom of God on earth only in its glorious, soul-elevating moral aspect, namely, in terms of the value of citizenship in a divine state, and to this end he informed them of what they had to do, not only to achieve it themselves but to unite with all others of the same mind and, so far as possible, with the entire human race."[102] After further reflection, however, Kant finds that the idea of the end of the world has a moral-parenetical sense one can affirm, since "heroic faith in virtue does not seem, subjectively, to have as generally powerful an influence on the human disposition for conversion or repentance as does faith in a scenario accompanied by terrors conceived as preceding the last things."[103] Similarly, the notion of the Antichrist and the apocalyptic expectation of an imminent end can also be interpreted functionally.

> The appearance of the antichrist, *the* millennium, and the news of the proximity of the end of the world—all these can take on, before reason, their right symbolic meaning; and to represent the last of these as an event not to be seen in advance (like the end of life, be it far or near) admirably expresses the necessity of standing ready at all times for the end and indeed (if one attaches the intel-

> lectual meaning to this symbol) really to consider ourselves always as chosen citizens of a divine (ethical) state.[104]

A warning is issued especially by the idea of the appearance of the Antichrist, who symbolizes "the *anti-natural* (perverted) end of all things," an end consisting of the collapse of civil and religious order prompted by fear and selfishness.[105] We ourselves could possibly bring about this perverted end of all things, an end not inhering in the moral perspective itself, by "*misunderstanding* the end purpose."[106]

Kant gains new access to apocalyptic from the perspective of ethics. He interprets its content as "symbolical representations intended merely to enliven hope and courage and to increase our endeavors" toward the moral end purpose of the world.[107] For Kant, then, this access to apocalyptic is opened by teleological thinking which in its own turn can be traced back to Jewish-Christian apocalyptic, though Kant does not further develop any discussion of this apocalyptic origin, since he disputes any positive essential relationship between Christianity and Judaism.[108]

The connection between apocalyptic and universal-historical thinking was already recognized by F. Lücke in his first comprehensive presentation of apocalyptic literature. He found in biblical apocalyptic the "seeds of a world-historical perspective."[109] For Lücke, the apocalyptist enjoys a rank equal to that of the historian. "The historian has been called the prophet who directs his attention backward; hence the prophet or the apocalyptist can be called the historian who directs his attention forward."[110]

Inspired by Lücke, A. Sabatier thought a fundamental connection was discernible between apocalyptic and modern historical philosophy. Whereas Lücke always interpreted apocalyptic from the perspective of prophecy, Sabatier views the apocalyptists as historians who were not only wise, but were also philosophers.[111] "History oriented toward a goal, comprehensible laws, optimism": Sabatier believed these three essential, basic ideas of modern historical philosophy were already discernible in apocalyptic. His thesis is thus: "Messianism is the foundation of Jewish apocalyptic; it has remained the foundation of our own historical philosophy."[112] Sabatier even goes one step further and reckons the works of modern historical philosophy to the genre of apocalypses. The literary genus is the same, and has merely undergone repeated transformations during its history, which itself has gone through three stages: apocalyptic, theological, and philosophical.[113] The result is that all nineteenth-century philosophy of progress is viewed as apocalyptic, beginning with Hegel's philosophy: "Let us say this clearly and succinctly: This philosophy was our century's first apocalyptic, the bright revelation which has blinded three generations."[114] Sabatier draws this line out to A. Comte and the sociology founded by him all the way to the various forms of nineteenth-century socialism.[115]

At first glance it appears that Sabatier is trying to interpret nineteenth-century historical philosophy from the perspective of apocalyptic. The reverse, however, is more likely the case. Apocalyptic is interpreted from the perspective of historical philosophy, and then both are subjected equally to criticism.[116] Despite his critical stance, Sabatier is indeed concerned that while not overestimating apocalyptic and historical philosophy, neither is he interested in completely discounting them:

> Although these apocalypses doubtlessly do not reveal to us the mysteries of divine providence, they do represent a brilliant revelation of the ground itself of the human soul and of the incessant uneasiness constituting the dignity of that soul. Their value is precisely that of the human sciences in general, namely, the law concerning what one ought to do, the need for righteousness. The justification of such philosophy is found in this strengthening of conscience.[117]

The value of historical philosophy, and accordingly also of apocalyptic, thus resides in the sphere of morality. By evaluating positively apocalyptic thinking—and for him that means historical-philosophical thinking—as "strengthening of conscience," Sabatier is presenting an ethical-functional interpretation of apocalyptic in the same manner as Kant earlier.

The thesis of historical philosophy as a secularized form of salvation-historical thinking has become popular, and in the meantime questions have been raised from various perspectives concerning the influence of apocalyptic in the development of the modern historical consciousness. Influenced by the philosophy of Heidegger, W. Kamlah has defended the thesis that both the concept of history employed by historicism and the historical nature of modern human beings are a result of Christianity insofar as the "demystification" (Max Weber) and profanation of the world would have been inconceivable without the idea of the otherworldly orientation and desacralization of the world in Christianity.[118] Universal history appears as the secular transformation of Christian salvation history. Common to both is the teleological framework. Basically, universal history has been the object of attention "since we first conceived that unprecedented general consideration of the particular consisting in the fact that God became a specific, individual person, and that the history of human salvation was decided in specific historical events at a specific place and at a specific time."[119] The problem peculiar to the Western tradition consists in its binary root, namely, in the tension between its biblical and Greek origins.[120] The determining factor for the theme of universal history is, however, the Christian root. The Christian understanding of history was anticipated by "Israelite-Jewish historical thinking." Nonetheless, Kamlah follows Bultmann in asserting that Christianity cannot be derived causally from Judaism.[121] What Christianity brings is "the radical elimination of limits" attaching to Jewish faith in God, a faith restricted to the community of the people; this elimination thus also constitutes the overcoming of Jewish historical thinking. Over against Jewish nationalism, Jesus and the primitive church renounce any historic self-assertion.[122]

Though Christianity cannot be derived from Judaism in terms of historical development either, it is indeed anticipated by prophecy and apocalyptic in Israel. Admittedly, the historicness obtaining in these two is suspended in the eschatological *nun* of the *kairos*, and for just this reason Paul can proclaim Christ as a changing of the aeons. "Jewish apocalyptic expands political historicness into the aeonian historicness of creation. In Paul, this removal of limits has become radical."[123] Kamlah is aware that the Christian kerygma was initially proclaimed in apocalyptic and gnostic language. From this one might conclude that Christian faith is itself apocalyptic and mythical. By relativizing the mythical character of the primitive Christian proclamation, Kamlah tries to avoid the danger of losing Christianity in apocalyptic thinking by viewing it as a mere variation of that thinking:

> Compared with the multifariousness of "pagan" mythologies, Christian monotheism is unmythical, and only when compared with Greek reason does the thinking of primitive Christianity seem mythological in its incorporation of the colorful language of Jewish apocalyptic or of gnosis; it draws from this language because it conceives the suspension of all historical particularities not as the kind of recurrence described by reasoned, universal thinking, but rather as a cosmic, all-encompassing event happening but once.[124]

The thesis that modern historical philosophy emerged from the secularization of Christian eschatology culminates in the work of Karl Löwith.[125] Löwith subjects all of historical philosophy to radical criticism by negating the legitimacy of secular attempts to appropriate the inheritance of Christian eschatology.[126] In trying to illuminate the theological presuppositions of historical philosophy, Löwith questions the legitimacy of modernity.

For Löwith, historical philosophy means "a systematic interpretation of universal history in accordance with a principle by which historical events and successions are unified and directed toward an ultimate meaning." And from this he immediately concludes:

> Taken in this sense, philosophy of history is, however, entirely dependent on theology of history, in particular on the theological concept of history as a history of fulfillment and salvation. But then philosophy of history cannot be a "science"; for how could one verify the belief in salvation on scientific grounds?[127]

This kind of historical philosophy was fundamentally alien to Greek antiquity, since the identifying feature of universal-historical thinking, namely, the orientation toward a *telos* of history, presupposes an eschatological future as a temporal dimension. Such a future "exists for us only by expectation and hope . . . The ultimate meaning of a transcendent purpose is focused in an expected future. Such an expectation was most intensely alive among the Hebrew prophets; it did not exist among the Greek philosophers."[128] Basically, the events constituting the object of Christian faith, namely, creation, incarnation, judgment, and redemption, are admittedly "suprahistorical"; "the moderns elaborate a philosophy of history by secularizing theological principles and applying them to an ever increasing number of empirical facts," facts that question both the unity of world history as well as its progress.[129] All historical philosophy moves between the two conceptions of antiquity and Christianity without ever really getting beyond either.

Löwith tries to disclose the theological presuppositions of modern historical thinking by tracing the development of historical philosophy from J. Burckhardt past Marx and Hegel back to Augustine and Orosius and finally to its biblical origins. The system of Joachim of Fiore is especially important for the continuing influence of Jewish-Christian apocalyptic. According to his speculation, the age of the Holy Spirit was imminent, and was to last for a thousand years before the final end of the world. Löwith sees the influence of this speculation not only from Lessing, Fichte, Schelling, and Hegel on up to Marx and the positivism of Comte,[130] but even up to Hitler and the Third Reich. Though biblical thinking is on the whole futuristic, Löwith asserts that a fundamental distinction obtains between Jewish apocalyptic and the Christian view of the world. "The only antagonism which is not accidental but intrinsic to the message of the New Testament is that to Jewish futurism (expecting the Messiah in the future instead of recognizing him in the presence of Jesus) and to the apocalyptic *calculations* of the last events by Jews as well as by Christians."[131]

For Löwith, the appropriation of the inheritance of Christian eschatology by secular historical thinking is illegitimate because he views the salvific events, those believed by Christians, as completely unworldly events, events connected with history only insofar as the Redeemer himself was a historic person. "As an eschatological message of the Kingdom of God, the theology of the New Testament is essentially unconcerned with the political history of this world."[132] The thesis of the theological origin of modern historical consciousness must be qualified to the extent that for Christian faith in its inception world history no longer exhibited any positive meaning. "The 'meaning' of the history of the world is fulfilled against itself because the story of salvation, as embodied in Jesus Christ, redeems and dismantles, as it were, the hopeless history of the world."[133] Löwith considers modern historical consciousness basically illegitimate not because one is not *permitted* to translate Christian eschatology into the concepts of world history, but because one *cannot* so translate it.

Löwith's criticism of the modern conception of history leads him to take leave entirely of teleological thinking. The experience of the suffering of millions of persons, an experience characterizing the period during which Löwith's work was composed,[134] renders inadequate every teleological concept of history. And even a Christian concept of history could take only suffering—expressed theologically: the cross—as its standard.[135] "The problem of history as a whole is unanswerable within its own perspective. Historical processes as such do not bear the evidence of a comprehensive and ultimate meaning. History as such has no outcome. There never has been and never will be an immanent solution of the problem of history, for man's historical experience is one of steady failure."[136]

H. Blumenberg decisively rejects Löwith's criticism of modern historical thinking.[137] Whereas Löwith described modern historical consciousness as an escaped slave, Blumenberg defends the unqualified legitimacy of modernity and considers the thesis of the secularization of originally theological ideas to be not only historically inaccurate, but also a defamation of modernity. According to Blumenberg, those who speak about secularization not infrequently see something in modernity which "in essence" should not really exist at all. "To that extent the secularization theorem, insofar as it can be understood on the basis of theological premises alone, is (in its position in history) something in the nature of a final *theologumenon* [theological dictum] intended to lay on the heirs of theology a guilty conscience about their entrance into the succession."[138]

That is, according to Blumenberg's understanding modernity faced the task of appropriating the inheritance of those questions which theology had presented to the preceding epoch without ever answering them satisfactorily. It is thus also utterly false to assert that the modern notion of progress first originated through the secularization of Christian eschatology. On the contrary, Blumenberg finds the roots of the idea of progress outside theology. Originally, the idea of progress did not raise any claim to totality, but rather merely related "to the partial structure of the theoretical-scientific process, to the effects of the new methodological realization of knowledge as an undertaking transcending individuality and the present."[139] Still without comprehensive claims, this idea reappeared later in the literary and aesthetic sphere. Blumenberg explains this process, one described as secularization (not to mention it having been virtually proscribed), such that the idea of progress

> had to expand the scope of its originally regionally circumscribed and objectively limited assertions, then overextend this range into the generality of a historical philosophy; it did this in order to do justice to a question which, as it were, had remained stationary in space, unaddressed and unattended, after having been made virulent by theology. The idea of progress, as one of the possible answers to the question of the totality of history, was drawn into the function for consciousness that had been performed by eschatology, eschatology which itself had already been historicized. In the process, it was called upon to provide explanations, a task overburdening its rational capacity.[140]

In Blumenberg's view, the notion of progress appears as an *ersatz*-religion not on the basis of its origin, but of its function.[141] This *ersatz* became necessary after the failure of Christian theology.

Its ultimate failure was preceded by what can be called the "historicization of eschatology," of which Bultmann spoke with respect to Paul and John.[142] This kind of historicization became necessary because of the disillusionment of the early Christian expectation of a near end, expectation which itself can be understood only against the background of Jewish apocalyptic. Ultimately, Blumenberg thus views in apocalyptic the ground upon which Christian eschatology was able to flourish and upon which the developments leading to modernity could play themselves out. Over against Bultmann, Blumenberg does assert that Jewish apocalyptic was not a special form of cosmological-cyclical speculation, as it were a basic myth reduced to a single period within the cycle of eternal recurrence. Cyclical mythology, so Blumenberg, presupposes a positive estimation of the cosmos. "Jewish apocalyptics contains no cosmological interest of this sort whatsoever; rather it compensates for the failure of the historical expectations of a nation by prophesying a fulfillment beyond history. It is a theodicy that vindicates the Old Testament God of the Covenant by devaluing the innerworldly history of the people to whom His favor was supposed to have been assured."[143] At the center of Jewish apocalyptic we thus find the problem of theodicy, a problem that became determinative for the entire subsequent history of the West.

New Testament eschatology does not simply carry apocalyptic forward, but came about rather through a qualitative leap from the indefinite nature of apocalyptic notions of totality to early Christian expectation of a near end, one drawing the events of the end time into the life of the individual or at least of the present generation.[144] New Testament expectation of a near end meant not only a qualitative shift of eschatological notions, but no less a shift in the behavior of believers: "The Sermon on the Mount is typical of what can be expected in this situation."[145] At this point, the substance of Blumenberg's position coincides completely with that of Löwith: "If one takes this to be essential to the original core of Christian teaching, then it has nothing to do with the concept of history, or it has only one thing to do with it: It makes an absolute lack of interest in the conceptualization and explanation of history a characteristic of the acute situation of its end."[146] Although this expectation of the near end did indeed destroy the reference to the future nurtured by Jewish apocalyptic, this "exceptional condition of acute presence" could not be maintained in the long run,[147] and it is precisely this problem which both Paul and John seek to solve by proclaiming the decisive results of salvation history as having already occurred.

According to Blumenberg, this process leading to secular historical thinking was not at all set into motion by any secularization of eschatology, but rather by the secularization of Christianity *through* such historicized eschatology.[148]

> The quintessence of what has been portrayed is . . . that eschatology historicized *itself.* The exaggerated ethical demands made in the acute situation of expectation of a near end, the unavoidable refutation of the apocalyptic promise, and the necessary disillusionment of renunciation which could have triumphed only if the world had indeed passed away—all these factors forced answers to questions which had not been posed before, and in whose formulation theology did not have ample opportunity to exercise its skills. It was not the autonomous competition of modern historical philosophy that claimed to provide knowledge which previously had been accepted as revelation.[149]

Within the framework of his own criticism of modern historical thinking, criticism which Blumenberg had questioned, Löwith considered Marxism to be the secular offshoot of Christian eschatology. "For the secret history of the *Communist Manifesto* is not its conscious materialism and Marx's own opinion of it, but the religious spirit of prophetism."[150] Formulated even more incisively: "The real driving force behind this conception is a transparent messianism which has its unconscious root in Marx's own being, even in his race."[151] Bloch also accepts as a given that the roots of historical materialism are to be found in messianic thinking, though with the significant difference that he considers the appropriation of the inheritance of apocalyptic eschatology by Marxism to be not only legitimate, but historically necessary. His historical philosophy is thus not shy about carrying around "religion in its inheritance."[152] For Bloch, the present task is to render the liberating, hopeful potential of religion—and that means especially the Jewish-Christian religion—fruitful for the universal process whereby human beings become genuinely human. Only superficial Marxism can militantly present itself as being vulgar-atheistic. In fact, however, "implicit in Marxism—as the leap from the Kingdom of Necessity to that of Freedom—there lies the whole so subversive and unstatic heritage" which moves about in the Bible, long concealed, though not as a "binding-back."[153]

F. Engels was already convinced of the subversive and revolutionary character of early Christianity, and he considered one witness of revolutionary primitive Christianity to be the Apocalypse of John, which he held to be the earliest of the New Testament writings.[154] Engels believed the Apocalypse of John attested "Christianity in the crudest form in which it has been preserved to us." He viewed early Christianity as a Jewish sect, as "a mere average [sect], formed spontaneously out of the mutual friction, of the more progressive of such sects." "Christianity, like every great revolutionary movement, was made by the masses."[155] Whereas on the one hand Engels's diagnosis was that "wild, confused fanaticism"[156] could be found in the Apocalypse, he explained this fanaticism on the other hand by referring to the character of the mass movement that bore Christianity. "And mass movements are bound to be confused at the beginning."[157] For Engels, the Apocalypse of John belongs completely to Judaism; its Judaism is "a new stage in the development of the earlier one, but for that very reason it is the only true one." The movement standing behind the Apocalypse introduced "quite a new phase in the development of religions," one "which was to become one of the most revolutionary elements in the history of the human thought."[158] The radical apocalyptic coming to expression here is interpreted as the anti-Roman reaction to foreign rule and exploitation.[159] From this perspective Engels finds a certain measure of access to apocalyptic and primitive Christianity: "The history of early Christianity has notable points of resemblance with the modern working-class movement. Like the latter, Christianity was originally a movement of oppressed people."[160]

For E. Bloch, the heritage of this subversive apocalyptic religion discloses itself through the category of utopia. Although Bloch formulated his understanding of the utopian in his early work under the strong influence of mystical inspiration[161] in the spirit of revolutionary romanticism,[162] he develops it later in close connection with dialectical materialism and left-of-center Aristotelianism.[163] In summary, Bloch's initial "revolutionary gnosis" asserts: "The world is not true, but it does want to undertake its journey home through human beings and through the truth."[164]

Bloch's early piece, *Geist der Utopie* (The Spirit of Utopia), is more than an attempt at establishing and locating the concept of the utopian. There is some justification for calling this book itself an apocalypse, written as it was in its first version in 1918, "in these days when God's desperate evening crimson already sufficiently permeates all things, while neither Atlas nor Christ supports its heaven."[165] Bloch is addressing those who feel confined "within this prison, this insane asylum, this morgue that we call earth."[166] He reveals to them that the existing world cannot be saved, and that on the contrary, its doom means deliverance. This qualifies the present as an end time and as an eschatological situation demanding decision. "One cannot simultaneously seek or venerate the world, the lord of the world, and that which either heals it or is healed by it,"[167] for "the world is a tower in which a prisoner sits, and the tower itself cannot also be humanized."[168] The present is a time of extreme distress. "There is danger all about us, we who would like to break out of our darkness."[169] Bloch and his readers, however, are consoled by the realization that "only when what is false falls can what is genuine live."[170] Thus there is no hope for the existing world, "for this world is a mistake, and is nothing, and has no other rights before absolute truth than to come to an end."[171] At this point, the *kairos* enters; now is the time in which human beings are to decide concerning deliverance and disaster,

> now *Satan's* apocalyptic time rules, and for this premature, satanically arbitrary, but irrevocable conclusion nothing matters except the fullness of our own attained level of purity and preparedness, of our spiritual possessions and reflections, of *what we have become in the larger sense*, nothing matters except the proclaiming knowledge *of our name, of the name of God which has finally been found*, so that not everything will be futile, so that the journey is not robbed of its goal, and so that all the elements of its convalescence—lives, souls, works, and worlds of love—will not be doomed to destruction without even a germ remaining in the dust of cosmic waste. In this night of annihilation, only the good, mindful person can bring morning. [Now is the time] to devour in victory the crude, satanically breathtaking moment of conflagration of the apocalypse, and to overcome it.[172]

Not only the content, but also the self-understanding of Bloch's early piece itself is apocalyptic in this way: "But here, in this book, a specific beginning established itself, the unlost inheritance seized itself anew. . . . But this book, which concludes no peace with the world, leads us through for the first time to our as yet unused essence, to our secret head, our figure and germinating collection, to the center of our creative principle."[173] That is, this book not only claims to disclose and reveal the long obstructed knowledge of salvation, an inheritance full of utopian tendencies, it also attributes salvific capacity to itself, just as every apocalypse does. Bloch's *Geist der Utopie* is a thoroughly religious piece of writing, and one can justifiably ask at this point whether this is in any sense a search for a *philosophical* approach to apocalyptic, or whether apocalyptic is not being disclosed through apocalyptic itself.

In the *Principle of Hope* Bloch does try to analyze his category of the utopian with more philosophical differentiation and to attain conceptual clarity against the background of an ontology of "not yet being." Between the biblical heritage—meaning especially the "subversive *socio-apocalyptic* preaching" of the later Old Testament, of early Jewish apocalypses,[174] and of the *apocalyptic* Jesus[175]—on the one hand, and Marxist thought on the other, a hermeneutical circle emerges "so far as it is, in the end, possible to read the Bible with the eyes of the *Communist Manifesto*. For then it sees to it that no atheist salt shall lose its savor, grasping the implicit in Marxism with that *Meta* which prevents the salt itself from growing tasteless."[176] In this circle Bloch views apocalyptic as a "myth of promise,"[177] as a myth "with quite world-exploding signs."[178] Bloch turns against the creation myth and the static divine ruler governing it, and does so "behind the idea of an apocalyptic breakthrough into the Utopia of salvation,"[179] which he discerns in the Bible as its contrary principle.[180] This utopia provides motivation not only for the exodus in the concept of the God Yahweh, but also from within this concept itself.[181] What is truly unveiled in the apocalyptic sense is the human being who has not yet come to himself, the "*homo absconditus*."[182]

Bloch's explication of apocalyptic, especially as presented in the work *Atheism and Christianity*, is burdened by a historically extremely questionable interpretation of the biblical evidence.[183] Precisely in the matter of social-revolutionary impetus,

Bloch's understanding of Jewish-Christian apocalyptic stands up to historical evaluations, if at all, only with a great deal of qualification. One can also say this of E. Käsemann, whom Bloch occasionally cites as his exegetical authority, and who, driven by the question concerning the relationship between Christ and revolution, considers the Apocalypse of John, as did Engels before him, to be a revolutionary book.[184] Apocalyptic has doubtless also played an important role in revolutionary movements, such as that of Thomas Müntzer. But as little as one can accuse apocalyptic in a wholesale manner of restorative sentiments, just as little can its attitude—especially that of early Christianity and of the Apocalypse of John—be described precipitately as revolutionary. Admittedly, in the final analysis such criticism based on historical considerations does not really address Bloch's views, since his real intentions do not include the illumination of historical facts at all.

> For he is concerned here not with relative historical knowledge, acquired through the conscientious efforts and skill of the researcher, but rather with metaphysically unqualified knowledge which is to be demonstrated on the material of history. And when Bloch occasionally treats this material somewhat rigorously, artificially coercing it to fit these principles, one should not entertain petty doubts concerning historical veracity, but should rather ask whether a metaphysics of history in this sense is still possible at all.[185]

Precisely this is the real problem attaching to Bloch's attempt to inherit apocalyptic. Even granting that he emphasized the significance of the utopian and drew attention to apocalyptic as a positive phenomenon, it seems questionable whether apocalyptic can be inherited by historical philosophy, however articulated that philosophy may be, and whether in particular Bloch's own philosophy of the utopian, despite its undisputed significance for the thinking and theology of the present, is genuinely future oriented, or whether it rather constitutes a regression back to German Idealism.[186] Both the historical philosophy of German Idealism as well as every form of teleological historical thinking—something shown by Löwith and Blumenberg in their differing understanding of the legitimacy of modernity—have been plunged into a profound crisis situation, one accompanying the crisis in Western metaphysics. In view of the questionable nature of teleological thinking, the kind also determinative for Kant's own ethical reception of apocalyptic, the necessity arises for philosophy to seek a different approach to apocalyptic if it is not to continue to be an inaccessible obscure entity.

5. The Psychology of Apocalyptic

Apocalyptic is not conceptual thinking. It seeks expression in a flood of imagery. Apocalypses portray dreams and visions. It seems natural not only to explain this imagery in a traditio-historical and exegetical manner focusing on their possible inception, but also to look for psychological aids to understanding. The school of the history of religions already inquired concerning the psychic disposition of the unknown authors of Jewish apocalypses. Especially H. Gunkel, W.O.E. Oesterley, and

W. Bousset should be mentioned in this connection.[187] In the second edition of his main work on *The Religion of Judaism in New Testament Times*, Bousset devotes an entire section to the "psychology of the apocalyptists." Despite any traditio-historical dependency exhibited by the apocalyptic materials, Bousset is convinced of the authenticity of the visionary experiences of the apocalyptists, and declares the apocalypses to be the literary manifestation of disillusioned hope. "Under the excessive pain prompted by the increasingly gloomy fate of their people, and in the paroxysm of hope that was repeatedly deceived, and then repeatedly encouraged to the straining point again, these apocalyptists experienced dreams and visions."[188] And H. Gunkel remarks concerning 4 Ezra:

> The author wrestles for his God, he defends his faith against experience; the knowledge he seeks in prayer is to protect him from *despair*. . . . Yet when the author considers these problems, the shocking certainty forces itself upon him: He is convinced that he is asking for the impossible! . . . Thus 4 Ezra is a characteristic example of how Jewish-Christian eschatology came about: When this person utterly despaired of this world, the entire weight of religion threw itself upon the coming blessed aeon.[189]

What remains unclear in these explanations is why this disillusionment and despair found expression thus and not otherwise in apocalyptic imagery. In order to remove the suspicion of meaninglessness that might be prompted by apocalyptic, J. Metzner has recently suggested that one disregard for the moment the question concerning the "experience" of the apocalyptist and look rather for ways "to make the linguistic content of the apocalyptic accounts comprehensible."[190] At this level, psychoanalysis offers various contributions to the understanding of apocalyptic, contributions Metzner brings to fruition by not subscribing to a specific model of understanding, but rather by applying to the imagery of apocalyptic an entire ensemble of such models, models mutually in need of corrective, though also capable of being complemented.[191]

Research into psychosis has long found itself confronted by so-called experiences of the end of the world as a pathological symptom.[192] Psychopathology refers to the decisive stage of schizophrenia preceding the commencement of catatonia as the "apocalyptic stage."[193] The classic psychoanalytical explanatory model for such notions of doom comes from S. Freud, a model that originated with his study of the case of Daniel Paul Schreber.[194] Freud explains the schizoid's experience of the end of the world as a projection of his inner catastrophe, which itself consists in the withdrawal of the libido from the external world. The regressive withdrawal into the subject leads to the collapse of all connections with the external world, and at the height of psychosis this breaking off of all relationships is experienced as the end of the world. Freud later expanded his theory of psychosis to a two-stage model incorporating the temporal dimension, according to which the experience of the end of the world caused the separation of the stage of regression from that of restitution attempts. "This division, which *Freud* consciously employed as a model, can be characterized as the loss of world and the construction of world."[195] After the real, external world is lost from sight, a new world is created, albeit an illusory one. Indeed, the parallelism between such psychotic phenomena and the apocalyptic dualism of the two aeons is startling. What is important is that in Freud's school such experiences of the end of the world are explained only as the reflex of an inner-psychic process. This is also the case with M. Klein, though she does interpret the end of the world less as the withdrawal of the libido from originally positively possessed objects, explaining them instead as abnormal changes in the ego itself.[196]

In contrast, J. Gabel, whose own theory of psychosis was decisively influenced by G. Lukács,[197] explains the catastrophe coming to expression in schizophrenia as the collision between historically changing reality and a consciousness incapable of dealing with this reality, reality involved in the dialectical process. Notions of the end of the world, according to Gabel's view, are manifestations of a false, i.e., objectified and thus unhistorical, immovable consciousness.[198] Lukács explains the different variations of cultural pessimism and theories of decay as the false consciousness that declining classes have of the dialectical process of history. "The indisputable fact of change is reflected in the awareness of immediacy as a catastrophe, in other words, it appears in the form of a sudden change coming from outside and excluding all mediations."[199] Picking up this notion, Gabel's thesis is then "that the phenomenon described, probably for the first time, by Freud and known as the deranged experience of the end of the world . . . is the psychopathological homologue of this phenomenon of false consciousness."[200] According to Gabel, not only are these notions of the end of the world symptomatic of false consciousness, apocalyptic dualism is as well: "The dichotomizing Manichean perception of reality (the 'black-and-white' view) is characteristic of the collective and individual forms of egocentrism."[201] In other words: Dualism is a psychotic understanding of the world according to which everything is good that corresponds to one's own, deluded consciousness, and everything is bad that questions this illusory world.

J. Metzner now demonstrates the necessity of employing different models simultaneously in the psychoanalytical explanation of apocalyptic. While in Freud's view the experience of the catastrophic intrusion of the external world is not sufficiently explained, Gabel's own collision model excludes the temporal dimension brought into play by Freud's two-stage model. However, various models proposed by C. G. Jung also prove to be possible keys to the understanding of certain apocalyptic imagery, imagery that in part can symbolize "a threat to the unstable subject by repressed contents of the collective unconsciousness."[202] Metzner also shows that the various explanatory models are also limited in their scope. None of the models mentioned can serve as the single key to all apocalyptic imagery.

Common to all the attempts at explanation presented thus far is that their psychology of apocalyptic consists exclusively in a pathology of apocalyptic. Whether apocalyptic thinking is taken as the expression of an inner crisis or of false class consciousness, in any case it is always taken as a pathological symptom. In addition, both Freud's and Gabel's interpretations view not only the catastrophic but also the utopian features of apocalyptic thinking as delusions. If one applies Freud's model of the loss of world and the creation of a new world to biblical apocalyptic, then the heavenly Jerusalem is an illusory *ersatz*-world, one that furthermore does not even lie in the future, but is rather full of reminiscences of paradise lost in the past.[203] Similarly, Gabel describes utopia "as a typical product of spatializing ideology."[204]

A psychological explanation of apocalyptic would thus utterly contradict the philosophical appropriation of the inheritance of apocalyptic as represented by Bloch. Reception of apocalyptic under the category of the utopian would itself exhibit the character of an ideological consciousness, though this is by no means yet a given. In any event, psychoanalysis that takes utopia as a pathological symptom would itself have to be subjected to the criticism of being ideological. Bloch, at least, does try to ground his understanding of utopia with his own psychoanalytical theory,[205] a theory that has thus far received far too little attention for anyone to proclaim that psychology has spoken the last word concerning the significance of the utopian element for society and the individual. More penetrating questions still need to be asked concerning the relationship between utopia and ideology. The result would be, as Bloch in my opinion correctly asserts, that ideologies can by no means be classified exclusively as an example of false consciousness; rather, there inheres in them an element of cultural excess or surplus transcending any consciousness dependent on class or position, one that is actually active in the sphere of historical transformation precisely as a power bringing about change. "And now it becomes clear that this very surplus is produced by nothing other than the *effect of the utopian function* in the ideological creations of the cultural side."[206]

In another respect, too, it would be premature to dismiss apocalyptic thinking as false consciousness. A more broadly conceived understanding of delusion, of the kind employed by psychology involved in an analysis of existence, shows that the catastrophic notions of apocalyptic can indeed be the correct consciousness of what is to a certain extent a false situation.[207] G. M. Martin, who attempts to make fruitful for an understanding of apocalyptic those insights of psychology which are involved in an analysis of existence, comes to the conclusion: "Notions of the end of the world can be understood as appropriate, by no means merely fantastic expressions of an abnormal crisis, of an extraordinary threat to the subject."[208]

C. Kulenkampff employs concepts from existential philosophy, concepts he has in part himself developed, and in part taken over[209] (whereby especially J. Zutt's category of structures of existence should be mentioned[210]), in explaining schizophrenics' experiences of the end of the world as an element of abnormal conflicts, conflicts that, however, become possible only on the basis of what Kulenkampff identifies as the "general structural crisis of human existence."[211] The crisis situation, of which V. E. von Gebsattel already spoke[212]—the human situation of "standing in crisis"—asserts "that we are always in a state of transition" accompanied by continuing transformation and ongoing separation. On the one hand, existence is transformed quite imperceptibly. On the other, such changes can also come about incisively and in full view.[213] The crisis becomes abnormal, however, when a person confronts "an *existential dilemma* between being coerced into the impossible on the one hand, and the unyielding stance of the impossible on the other," a dilemma "whose dynamic as such is 'unbearable' because of its structural antinomy."[214] In such a situation, a person on the one hand loses all mobility. The horizon closes itself off, as it were. And yet that person is forced to proceed forward, since human existence, because of its inherent structure, cannot tolerate genuine stasis, or rather does so only in death. Yet because the possibility of going forward is closed off in reality, "illusion, as what might be described as 'possible unreality,' necessarily emerges in the face of the coercion to participate in what amounts to 'impossible reality.' "[215] Notions of the end of the world, then, can be traced back to the "dead-end structure of the world,"[216] a structure from which catastrophe appears to be the only means of escape.

According to this analysis of existence, notions of the end of the world emerge when the structures of existence, e.g., those of space and habitation described by J. Zutt,[217] collapse, and do so "in the sense of devastation, of *leveling destruction*," which Kulenkampff describes as an elimination of limits.[218] "The elimination of limits and boundaries, of any foundation, the collapse of structures—all these are accompanied by a loss of security, by an *elimination of security*. Unsecured and exposed in this way, with no possibility of recovering security, confidence collapses. A world in which trust and confidence have become impossible is a sinister world. Mistrust and anxiety rule rather than trust."[219] Since reality no longer seems to disclose an appropriate perspective, the person is subjected more and more to control by the surroundings. For Kulenkampff the salient feature of this situation is that "the physiognomic world has become both inescapable and untransparent *at the same time*."[220] According to this view, apocalyptic could be explained psychologically as the expression of what Kulenkampff calls the "loss of position." A person stands in his world in a posture offering resistance to that very world. When that person is no longer able to offer such resistance, he loses his position and footing. He collapses, as it were, and is overpowered and overwhelmed by the world.[221] And as the world crashes down upon this person, it collapses itself.

These various psychological approaches also demonstrate, however, that apocalyptic can be understood not only as a symptom of crisis, but also as an attempt at healing or resolution. In an abnormal case, the collapse is not only anticipated, but is experienced in an immediate sense as presumed reality. Although this experienced end of the world is paranoid, and although it is an illusion to imagine that the world has already ended, this does not justify the conclusion that all notions of the end of the world are paranoid. G. M. Martin has suggested the hypothesis "that not just the manifested illusion, but rather the notion itself of the end of the world preceding that illusion represents an attempt at healing and resolution,"[222] whereby he supports the view of depth psychology "that notions of the end of the world belong to the sphere of archetypal themes and motifs and derive from the realm of the collective unconscious."[223] Even if one cannot accord wholesale acceptance to this derivation based on C. G. Jung's depth psychology, one can nonetheless say that apocalyptic imagery represents "possible symbols for one's perception of reality" and simultaneously the attempt to bring about a "critical reconstruction through the catastrophe."[224]

More recently, E. Drewermann has also subjected apocalyptic to an interpretation based on depth psychology.[225] Against the one-sided juxtaposition of apocalyptic and hope, and against the understanding of apocalyptic as a form of utopian thinking, Drewermann objects that apocalyptic eschatology is "a regressive mythology of the future."[226] According to this view, the characteristic feature of this regressive inclination of apocalyptic is a "peculiar *forward return*,"[227] with anxiety and regression being the decisive factors generating apocalyptic notions. Drewermann objects to G. von Rad's thesis (of the origin of apocalyptic in wisdom) that the distinction between eschatology and apocalyptic—a distinction Drewermann also acknowledges—is not to be traced back to any differing degree of intellectualization of historical experience, but rather orients itself "essentially to the growth and dynamic of *anxiety*."[228] "The inner structure of *eschatology* prompts it to project the contents of the unconscious into history; *apocalyptic*, on the other hand, expands the psychic interior into the world itself."[229] Drewermann thus interprets apocalyptic as "*an introjected cosmology*."[230] Though the substance of his distinction between apocalyptic and eschatology is confusing, such distinction is unfortunately not an isolated instance in studies of this topic. Apocalyptic is a specific type of eschatology, not its alternative. Of enduring importance, however, is the significance Drewermann attributes to anxiety for the understanding of apocalyptic. According to this psychological analysis, apocalyptic notions serve as symbols for anxiety.

Thus whereas apocalyptic notions can be understood as completely meaningful symbolizations, nonetheless from the psychological perspective—quite apart from pathological manifestations—they remain ambivalent. The danger inheres in them that the ego can be completely swept away in their suction, and that consciousness finds no adequate connection with the experiential reality of the unconscious.[231] The possibility thus exists—one Kant already perceived in a different context—that the language of apocalyptic is misunderstood. For just this reason it is advisable to learn how to deal critically with apocalyptic thinking.

6. Anxiety and the Apocalyptic Understanding of Existence

The center of apocalyptic thinking is the expectation of the end of the world. As a "theory of catastrophe," about which G. Scholem has spoken,[232] apocalyptic is the expression of crisis consciousness, and the crisis symbolized in apocalyptic notions by no means plays itself out only in the interior life of the apocalyptist. It is also very much a crisis of the external world, or more precisely, a crisis into which the apocalyptist falls by virtue of events taking place between him and that external world. To that extent, apocalyptic is not merely one more description of the external world, but is rather the expression of an understanding of existence of those who share apocalyptic notions. The apocalyptic understanding of existence is rooted in a dead-end experience of the world, and the locus of such an experience is anxiety. Thus from the perspective of anxiety, apocalyptic can disclose itself to us anew apart from teleological historical thinking.

An understanding of this anxiety requires the cooperation of the history of religions, psychology, and sociology, though also of philosophy. Precisely the latter discipline offers aids to understanding the apocalyptic understanding of existence to the extent such philosophical analysis of existence is not isolated from the other interpretative approaches.

Such an analysis of the apocalyptic understanding of existence finds its model in the interpretation of gnosis undertaken by Hans Jonas, a model suggesting itself not least because, as the history of religions has shown, gnosis can itself be understood as radicalized apocalyptic. Furthermore, the determination of the relationship between literary, psychological, sociological, and philosophical interpretation that Jonas gives for gnosis might also yield results for an understanding of apocalyptic.

Jonas's interpretation, which attempts not only to explain gnosis historically[233] but to understand it, was influenced on the one hand by the philosophy of Heidegger,[234] while acknowledging on the other hand that psychology and sociology were also extremely valuable in explaining gnosis. In his own day, R. Reitzenstein traced gnosis back to the "pressure of horrific times." "So," as Jonas remarks, "at its inception we find external, though psychologically inverted powerlessness. On this ground, as it were as a means of reception, dualistic metaphysics allegedly arose" as a kind of "reflection of profound hopelessness and despair." Jonas immediately develops this suggestion further: "A refined *psychology* of sublimation and projection on the one hand, and a *sociology* of reference back to real circumstances on the other might offer legitimate points of interpretation here, though properly understood points."[235] Jonas views the legitimacy of these interpretative attempts in their tracing of ideal constructions back to a real or actual stimulus, one which, though developed in two different directions by psychology and sociology, in fact represents a unified phenomenon. Sociologically oriented psychology comprehends gnosis "not merely as a complex of imagery and ideas, but rather as such a complex giving expression to spiritual facts, i.e., to a motivated experiential totality, in a word: to causal subjective reality; it thus comprehends gnosticism primarily as a fact associated with life itself (rather than with doctrine)."[236]

According to Jonas, however, limiting the interpretation to sociology and psychology disregards the transcendental ground of psychological and sociological processes, and for precisely this reason the legitimacy of psychological and sociological explanations is understood correctly only if they are based on an analysis of existence. "It suffices to point out that psychological motivation always emerges only on the *ground* of an elementary and variously predetermined relationship with being, a relationship which does not consist only in the psychological element, but which contains rather its own 'transcendental' side."[237] Only from this perspective do the utterances concerning existence that are accessible to psychology and sociology become completely comprehensible. "Psychological, sociological, and even natural causalities exert influence only within the sense-*possibilities* of this transcendental aspect, possibilities encompassing a pre-empirical determination or decision concerning existence. This perspective determines which conclusions are drawn from experience, indeed, which experiences are 'had' in the first place."[238]

Given the significance of this transcendental aspect of which Jonas speaks, any interpretation falls short that insists on understanding gnostic thinking only as a reaction; "the simple reference to 'horrific times' will just not suffice."[239] There inheres in gnosis what amounts to a surplus that in its own turn continues to exert influence in generating history. "The element which in this way stands above mere concrete reaction and transcends in a unifying fashion the interchange of such impressionistic variations of disposition, constitutes the real truth and integrity of a historical—or even 'history-generating'—'world view.' "[240] As with psychology, so also with sociological analysis, one finds "an element fundamentally *transcending* all causal factors." Nonetheless, sociology retains its legitimacy, since an element of mutual influence obtains between an understanding of existence with its atemporal surplus on the one hand, and the historical situations in which such an understanding emerges or is appropriated on the other. That is, "the transcendental center at work here, because of the fundamental temporality and responsive receptivity of human beings, must first exert its influence—and this influence is brought about precisely by actual history, history without which human beings and human creativity cannot exist, and history possessing its own fateful coincidence of event and receptivity."[241]

Jonas has shown that an "enormous existential insecurity, human world anxiety, and anxiety before the world and before oneself" speaks from within gnosis.[242] Its texts are full of "evidence of being afraid, of being alone in the world, of terror in the face of its alien nature and hostility, and of yearning for home and anticipation of redemption."[243] Gnosis found a receptive audience among those who were oppressed by innerworldly hopelessness.

> The disinterest generated by powerlessness, intimations of death on the part of a civilization which quite justifiably no longer saw a future for itself after it eliminated for those who carried it any possibility of actively participating in shaping it, the collapse of the ideal of humanity, an ideal bound to the accessibility of proper conditions—all the hopelessness of this dying world contributed to this receptivity.[244]

In this situation the message of gnosis offered itself as a possibility of resolution, as an understanding of existence capable of dealing with and overcoming world anxiety.

It seems appropriate now also to inquire to what extent the apocalyptic understanding of existence might disclose itself as an attempt to deal with world anxiety. Within apocalyptic scholarship, both E. Schweizer[245] and W. Schmithals have recognized the task of disclosing apocalyptic through an analysis of its understanding of existence. Schweizer views Jewish apocalyptic as an analogon to gnosis, considering them to be "two variations of the same view,"[246] which he considers in need of considerable critical scrutiny. Both the Hellenistic gnostic and the Jewish apocalyptist devaluate the world in a problematical fashion:

> The paths of this world have become narrow and sorrowful, and the believer is able only to wait in anticipation of that completely other, coming world, a world which will commence in a completely miraculous and supranatural fashion without any contribution by human beings, and will do so from above. In this way, however, a person loses himself as well. He understands himself, after all, as merely a product of this evil world, a world grown old.[247]

The problem with Schweizer's view is that he levels a bit too strongly the distinctions between gnosis and apocalyptic, thus leaving unaddressed many questions posed by the apocalyptic understanding of existence. Furthermore, it is doubtful that in both gnosis and apocalyptic a person utterly loses himself and comprehends himself only as a product of the existing world.

In the case of gnosis, in any event, Jonas's assertion remains that "an ultimate core" is yet experienced within human beings "as alien over against the world, and at least this provides for human beings positive evidence of a higher, divine origin and home."[248] In this sense gnosis must be understood precisely as the attempt to regain oneself in the face of what is experienced as being lost within the world. The disposition contributing to the reception of gnostic thinking should not be confused with gnosis itself, which claimed to offer an attempt at resolution for what was experienced as a crisis of existence. Gnosis does also attest a very real element of fatigue in the face of life. "This does not constitute yielding" to the power of the old world and retreating "into the consolation of illusions and ersatz constructions which are in any case still derived within the old world's ontological horizon; it is rather an *attack* on that world from a different being, one that has awakened to itself—the birth of a new world. This sort of thing is not the business of worn down, passive, self-renunciating existence."[249] Nonetheless, the question Schweizer raises concerning a possible loss of self and of the world in gnosis and similarly in apocalyptic is still virulent, suggesting the possible presence of ambiguity within gnostic and apocalyptic thinking.

What Schweizer is actually describing is thus the disposition receptive to apocalyptic thinking. His interpretation of apocalyptic falls short, however, because it views the apocalyptic understanding of existence only as the reaction to changes that took place in the world of antiquity, changes put into motion by the rise and fall of the empire of Alexander the Great, and thus as a mere product of world anxiety. In contrast, Schmithals concludes that the understanding of existence common to both gnosis and apocalyptic is "the feeling of superiority to the vain world in the midst of this world."[250] As already seen, this judgment is supported by Jonas's analysis. Schmithals, however, who like Schweizer views gnosis and apocalyptic as two sides of the same coin and assumes a posture of rejection toward them both, is able to illuminate the apocalyptic understanding of existence only inadequately because he largely ignores its connection with world anxiety. His reference to the "pessimism" of apocalyptic[251] is wholly insufficient. The consciousness of superiority over the world is placed in the proper light only when it becomes transparent as a way of dealing with a profound experience of powerlessness. For this reason, Schmithals's analysis of the apocalyptic understanding of existence remains superficial.

The present study will inquire concerning the apocalyptic understanding of existence.[252] Our guiding question must thus be the same as that which H. Blumenberg posed with respect to gnosis: "What understanding of the world and of existence makes a situation comprehensible in which a kerygma of the end of the cosmos can be taken as *the* solution?"[253] Only that interpretation can provide a persuasive answer allowing apocalyptic to emerge in both its connection with and its difference from gnosis.

This opens up new philosophical access to apocalyptic from the perspective of the existential philosophy and thinking of Martin Heidegger. The task is to make fruitful for an understanding of apocalyptic the contributions of philosophy to the understanding of world anxiety. This reference to Heidegger may well seem somewhat odd in this connection, since it is generally recognized that apocalyptic, as K. Koch remarks, is utterly absent as a philosophical theme in Heidegger's work.[254] Although a preliminary view cannot challenge this assertion, a more thoroughgoing investigation into the thinking particularly of the later Heidegger shows that this thinking, especially Heidegger's theory of the "history of being," exhibits extensive affinity with apocalyptic thinking.[255] At the appropriate juncture we will address the question whether the course taken by the thinking of Martin Heidegger does not represent, next to Bloch's philosophy of hope, yet another manifestation of philosophical apocalyptic in our century.

Both E. Schweizer and W. Schmithals try to separate clearly the apocalyptic understanding of existence from that of the Christian faith. Although their theologically motivated defensive posture toward apocalyptic is not entirely undisputed today, it is nonetheless still representative. This kind of opposition is just as questionable as a precipitate appropriation of apocalyptic thinking by theology. Our task is rather to try to understand the apocalyptic understanding of existence in as unprejudiced a fashion as possible, and then to compare it with faith's own understanding of existence. We will find that neither an antithetical confrontational model nor a correlational model interpreting kerygma as an answer to the apocalyptic question can adequately illuminate the relationship between the apocalyptic and Christian understanding of existence. First of all one must recognize that both—apocalyptic as well as the Christian faith—try to provide an answer to that particular experience of the world as crisis deriving from world anxiety. It is precisely this world anxiety which apocalyptic seeks to overcome by disclosing anxiety-filled reality and its inherent inclination toward collapse.

2

WORLD ANXIETY

> Here, in the decisive moment of existence, when a person first becomes human and realizes his immense loneliness in the universe, world-anxiety reveals itself for the first time as the purely human fear before death, before the limit of the world of light, before rigid space.
>
> —*Oswald Spengler*

1. *Horror vacui*

The phrase "world anxiety" is a philosophical coinage of the twentieth century, one going back apparently to O. Spengler, in whose philosophy of history it plays a central role. Initially, this world anxiety—a theme that has in the meantime been repeatedly addressed—does not fear for the continued existence of the world itself. Not any threatening catastrophe of global dimension is what creates the anxiety in world anxiety, but rather existence in the world in the larger sense. It is not some danger in which the world might be caught, but rather the world itself that causes anxiety. In world anxiety both the world and existence seem equally obscure, questionable, alien, and strange.

World anxiety has been described in a variety of ways as the mood of the nineteenth and especially of the twentieth century, though Spengler himself uses "world anxiety" to refer to a phenomenon that he traces back into the early history of humankind. According to Spengler's understanding, it is the primal given and as such one of the main driving forces behind human history and cultural development. The moment the early human being becomes aware of the antithesis between self and world, "there arises in the soul—instantly conscious of its loneliness—the root-feeling of *longing*. It is this that urges 'becoming' towards its goal, that motives the fulfillment and actualizing of every inward possibility, that unfolds the idea of individual being. It is the child's longing, which will presently come into the consciousness more and more clearly as a feeling of constant *direction* and finally stands before the mature spirit as the *enigma of Time*—queer, tempting, insoluble."[1] Like Bloch, for example, one could view this yearning as a fundamental human drive.

> But this longing which wells out of the bliss of the inner life is also, in the intimate essence of every soul, an *anxiety* as well. As all becoming moves towards a having-become wherein it *ends*, so the prime feeling of becoming—the longing—touches the prime feeling of having-become, the anxiety. In the present we feel a trickling-away, the past implies a passing. Here is the root of our eternal anxiety of the irrevocable, the attained, the final—our dread of mortality, of the world itself as a thing-become, where death is set as a frontier like birth—our anxiety in the moment when the possible is actualized, the life is inwardly fulfilled and consciousness stands at its *goal*. It is the deep world-fear of the child—which never leaves the higher man, the believer, the poet, the artist—that makes him so infinitely lonely in the presence of the alien powers that loom, threatening in the dawn, behind the screen of sense-phenomena.[2]

Spengler considers this feeling of world anxiety to be "the most *creative* of all prime feelings." It finds expression in the symbols of extension, then also in the notion of causality, in the systematic search for knowledge, in numbers and in mathematics, in the formative language of art, and not least in human language itself.[3]

The characteristic feature of world anxiety in Spengler's understanding is the feeling of limitless loneliness, the *horror vacui*, or, in the words of E. Spranger, "the experience of being lonely and abandoned in the middle of finitude."[4] The term "world anxiety" has in our century come to describe an experience which not only repeatedly affects individual human beings, but which in the course of history has repeatedly been able to establish itself as the basic mood of the predominant spirit of an age.[5]

World anxiety emerged as a historically tangible mood at the end of antiquity, clearly discernible in gnosis. Precisely that feeling of being without a house of one's own, of not being at home, of which Spengler spoke, also characterizes the anxiety H. Jonas discovered in the texts of gnosis. The world generates anxiety in the gnostic in both its spatial and its temporal extension. "The anxiety caused by the enormous, immeasurable element of cosmic space is joined by that caused by the immeasurable element of cosmic time which one is called upon to endure . . . World anxiety is spatial-temporal anxiety, just as the Hellenistic concept of the *aeon* includes a temporal dimension."[6] In gnosis, this anxiety before the world turns back on the self, which is why world anxiety in this case is simultaneously self-anxiety. Thus in gnosis one finds an "enormous existential insecurity, human world anxiety," which is simultaneously "anxiety before the world and before oneself."[7] In gnosis there is thus a connection between world anxiety and that which one can call self-anxiety, a connection we will investigate more closely later.

World anxiety brought about the crumbling of trust and confidence in the world, trust which on the whole remained determinative for Greek philosophy. This mood of anxiety was to last through the entirety of the Western Middle Ages, and that despite the inclination of Christianity to assume an active posture toward the world quite contrary to its originally negative attitude.[8] In fact, this mood grew in intensity toward the end of the Middle Ages. "If one period deserves the name of the 'age of anxiety' it is the pre-Reformation and Reformation."[9]

This anxiety, which in the later Middle Ages focused especially on guilt and eternal damnation, yielded temporarily to newly awakened trust in the world during the Renaissance. W. Schulz suggests that this previously unknown trust in the world endured from Descartes and Galileo on down to German Idealism,[10] though one may well doubt whether this held true in as sweeping a fashion as the assertion implies. Furthermore, this trust in the world, insofar as in the modern age it is a reflex of the progress of the natural sciences and of mathematical thinking, is a thoroughly ambivalent phenomenon. One may ask with Spengler whether that mathematization of thinking which attempts to comprehend and master the world is not rather the expression of a profound insecurity in the face of being. Probably independent of Spengler, M. Scheler disclosed precisely this connection: "Anxiety gives birth to the calculability of the progress of life and is the emotional a priori of the proud 'cogito ergo sum.' "[11] On the one hand, the mathematization of thinking renders possible unimagined progress in the mastery and exploitation of nature, as well as in the economic sphere. On the other hand, this calculable world no longer offers the human being a genuine home. " 'World,' that is now the object of eternal anxiety, it is no longer some boldly and gleefully seized 'chance' . . . For such a person and for the accompanying sense of life, the world is no longer the warm, organic 'home,' but becomes rather a cold object of calculation and of the assault of one's work—no longer loved and contemplated, but rather something to be calculated and worked."[12]

World anxiety as the emotional a priori of modern philosophy becomes clearly discernible in the work of Blaise Pascal. Precisely this limitless loneliness of which Spengler spoke, that exposed condition, is the fundamental human feeling providing the point of departure for Pascal's thought in his *Pensées*. This work is a loquacious witness to the modern *horror vacui* seizing human beings in the face of calculable, infinite cosmic time and space. Both reflection on the macrocosm as well as a consideration of the microcosm causes Pascal to shudder,[13] for it shows how the human being stands in the middle between the two abysses of the Infinite and Nothing.[14] Whereas the infinite opens up into the expanses of the all, nothingness in Pascal's language functions to a certain extent as the ultimate value of all conceivable divisions, the "infinitely little."[15] The human being shudders upon realizing that "the whole visible world is only an imperceptible atom in the ample bosom of nature."[16] The expanse of the all causes anxiety to arise: "The eternal silence of these infinite spaces frightens me."[17] However, the discovery of finitude also causes a person to shudder: "When I consider the short duration of my life, swallowed up in the eternity before and after, the little space which I fill, and even can see, engulfed in the infinite immensity of spaces of which I am ignorant, and which know me not, I am frightened, and am astonished at being here rather than there; for there is no reason why here rather than there, why now rather than then."[18] Just as in gnosis earlier, so also is Pascal's own world anxiety a spatial-temporal anxiety, a shuddering before the spatial and temporal extension of the world, before its immeasurable scope and duration. Precisely this geometrically comprehensible world appears not as sheltering order in which the human being finds a home; it proves rather to be rejecting and mute, and virtually hostile toward human beings. "When . . . I regard the whole silent universe, and man without light, left to himself, and, as it were, lost in this corner of the universe . . . I become terrified, like a man who should be carried in his sleep to a dreadful desert island, and should awake without knowing where he is and without means of escape. And thereupon I wonder how people in a condition so wretched do not fall into despair."[19] For Pascal, world anxiety wavers between horror and astonishment, between *tremendum* and *fascinosum*. And as was the case earlier in gnosis, the human being seized by the *horror vacui* of the modern age shudders with astonishment as it were before the infinity and nothingness of the world as well as before himself.[20] Thus for Pascal, too, world anxiety and self-anxiety are intimately connected.

This world anxiety, which according to Spengler's words "never leaves the poet, the artist in his infinite loneliness," finds its poetic expression in Friedrich Schiller's poem "The Greatness of Creation," composed in 1782:[21]

The Greatness of Creation

Upon the winged winds, among the rolling worlds I flew,
Which, by the breathing spirit, erst from ancient Chaos grew;
Seeking to land
On the farthest strand,
Where life lives no longer to anchor alone,
And gaze on Creation's last boundary-stone.

Star after star around me now its shining youth uprears,
To wander through the Firmament its day of thousand years—
Sportive they roll
Round the charmèd goal:
Till, as I look'd on the deeps afar,
The space waned—void of a single star.

On to the Realm of Nothingness—on still in dauntless flight,
Along the splendours swiftly steer my sailings wing of light,
Heaven at the rear,
Paleth, mist-like and drear;
Yet still as I wander, the worlds in their glee
Sparkle up like the bubbles that glance on a Sea!

And towards me now, the selfsame path I see a Pilgrim steer!
"Halt, Wanderer, halt—and answer me—What, Pilgrim, seek'st thou here?"
"To the World's last shore
I am sailing o'er,
Where life lives no longer to anchor alone,
And gaze on Creation's last boundary-stone."

"Thou sail'st in vain—Return! Before thy path, Infinity!"
"And thou in vain!—Behind me spreads Infinity to thee!
Fold thy wings drooping,
O Thought, eagle-swooping!—

> O Phantasie, anchor!—The Voyage is o'er:
> Creation, wild sailor, flows on to no shore!"

Whereas world anxiety leads Pascal to humble astonishment and ultimately to the Christian faith, in Schiller it takes on virtually nihilistic features.

As already seen, the trust in the world that emerged during the Renaissance was by no means able to maintain itself unbroken into the period of German Idealism. Again and again, that particular world anxiety accompanying the history of the modern age as an undercurrent broke through this world-affirming optimism. In the end, it seized control of the collapsing philosophy of German Idealism itself, first of all in the later philosophy of Schelling,[22] whose insights into the structure of human drives generated doubt concerning the reasonable nature of the world. Hegel's assertion, "what is rational is actual and what is actual is rational,"[23] forfeits its absolute validity. The human being discovers within himself a dark, chaotic power which he fears might ultimately overpower both him and reason. The anxiety in the face of life of which Schelling speaks derives from the fact that "the true basic substance of all life and being is just what is terrible."[24] Though doubt in the reasonable nature of the world raises its countenance here in German Idealism itself, even the later Schelling struggles through to trust in the world, borne by the certainty that in the end reason will prevail after all and will lend meaning to history.

This doubt becomes radical, however, in Kierkegaard, for whom the world by no means still represents the ordered universe and home of the human being endowed with reason, but rather the fortuitous locus of the individual who has been thrown into existence, an individual whose being in the world eludes every reasonable explanation. The feeling of loneliness and of the blind fortuitousness of existence which we encountered in Pascal recurs in Kierkegaard:

> One sticks a finger into the ground to smell what country one is in; I stick my finger into the world—it has no smell. Where am I? What does it mean to say: the world? what is the meaning of that word? Who tricked me into this whole thing and leaves me standing here? Who am I? How did I get into the world? Why was I not asked about it, why was I not informed of the rules and regulations but just thrust into the ranks as if I had been bought from a peddling shanghaier of human beings? How did I get involved in this big enterprise called actuality? Why should I be involved? Isn't it a matter of choice?[25]

World anxiety becomes the driving motif of post-Idealistic philosophy. Schelling's insights continue to resonate in the thinking of Schopenhauer and Nietzsche, and, as shown by Scheler's anthropology and Freud's psychoanalysis, play an important role in the thinking of the twentieth century. On the other hand, under Kierkegaard's influence world anxiety becomes in various ways the key problem in the philosophical analysis of existence for Heidegger, Jaspers, and Sartre.

What we have seen in the fashion of an overview is to a certain extent a history of world anxiety, though we have only sketched in its contours. As already emphasized several times, the influence of the various historical, political, economic, cultural, and sociological circumstances on the emergence of this anxiety should by no means be underestimated. Yet it would be incorrect to view world anxiety for that reason as a historically fortuitous and temporary phenomenon whose final disappearance could be anticipated for the near or distant future. Spengler tries to exclude precisely this misunderstanding by referring to world anxiety as a primal feeling, one that amid all historical transformation and external influence is yet constitutive for existence. Heidegger interprets anxiety accordingly as a "state-of-mind," i.e., as an existential element disclosing existence as "being-in-the-world."

These initial remarks by no means resolve for us the problem of world anxiety, but rather actually only introduce it for the first time. In what follows we must endeavor to come to a phenomenological understanding of world anxiety, a phenomenon of which we have until this point only taken note. One may speak of world anxiety as a primal feeling only if it can be shown phenomenologically to be a basic state-of-mind of existence and can be illuminated as such. Within the framework of such an analysis particular significance attaches to the connection between world anxiety and self-anxiety, since, as we have already seen, precisely this connection is apparently constitutive for world anxiety, a suspicion in any case suggested by findings within the context of gnosis and in Pascal. Just what kind of relationship obtains between world anxiety and self-anxiety must yet be established by thorough investigation. The same applies to the relationship between world anxiety and what Spengler called longing or yearning. Precisely such yearning, as the drive which, as it were, seeks the light or is inclined to move forward, has from antiquity to Idealism to Bloch been viewed as the decisive fundamental human drive, whether referred to as entelechy by Aristotle, as *élan vital* in Bergson's philosophy of life, as the will to power by Nietzsche, or as the libido by Freud. Spengler then presents anxiety as a primal feeling of equal rank with yearning, though his determination of the relationship between the two remains conceptually unclear. On the one hand, he suggests that world anxiety develops from yearning,[26] and on the other, that the primal feeling of yearning itself is simultaneously anxiety. Spengler's remarks here suggest that world anxiety is characterized by a peculiar dialectic, and this is equally the implication when he draws a parallel with Luther's assertion that God is to be feared and loved equally.[27] This kind of dialectic of anxiety, as we have already seen, can be observed in Pascal, whose world anxiety is a shudder in which yearning and terror emerge simultaneously. However, this notion is only insufficiently addressed by Spengler's concept of world anxiety. Thus our own task is no less than to establish a concept of world anxiety that takes account of its apparently inherent dialectic.

2. Anxiety and Fear

Although in everyday language the word "anxiety" has in many cases the same meaning as the word "fear," anxiety and fear are frequently distinguished to varying degrees in philosophy and psychology. This differentiation goes back to Kierkegaard, who in a fashion different from many of his successors discerns not a quantitative difference between anxiety and fear (in the sense of differing grades), but a qualitative one. "The concept of anxiety is almost never treated in psychology. Therefore, I must point out that it is altogether different from fear and similar concepts that refer to something definite, whereas anxiety is freedom's actuality as the possibility of possibility."[28]

This distinction, cited and appropriated so frequently, needs explication. Kierkegaard describes human existence as a dialectical relationship within the self;[29] in the vocabulary of his work *The Concept of Anxiety* it is described as the synthesis of body and soul, mediated by the spirit.[30] Initially, however, the spirit is not yet posited in the human being, but rather is present only, as it were, dreamily. The state in which the human spirit is dreaming is specified more closely as the state of innocence and ignorance.

> In this state there is peace and repose, but there is simultaneously something else that is not contention and strife, for there is indeed nothing against which to strive. What, then, is it? Nothing. But what effect does nothing have? It begets anxiety. This is the profound secret of innocence, that it is at the same time anxiety. Dreamily the spirit projects its own actuality, but this actuality is nothing, and innocence always sees this nothing outside itself.[31]

The object of anxiety is thus "something that is nothing (linguistic usage also says pregnantly: to be anxious about nothing),"[32] whereas fear, according to Kierkegaard, always has a concrete object. Fear includes a relationship to a threatening object, anxiety, in contrast, to something that is nothing. This nothing of anxiety, however, is the actuality of the spirit, or put in another way: the actuality of freedom, something that can be seen when this nothing of anxiety becomes as it were concentrated.

Kierkegaard develops his concept of the self as a synthesis of body and soul, and his understanding of anxiety and freedom, within the framework of an interpretation of the biblical story of the Fall. In the narrative of the Fall, the nothing of anxiety becomes concentrated through the prohibition against eating from the tree of knowledge. Whereas the actuality of the spirit, as long as it dreams, is initially "the enormous nothing of ignorance" characterizing the state of innocence, now instead of nothing it has received an enigmatic word that it admittedly cannot understand.[33] As a word that Adam has not understood, the prohibition remains a nothing for Adam. As such, it "induces in him anxiety, for the prohibition awakens in him freedom's possibility. What passed by innocence as the nothing of anxiety has now entered into Adam, and here again it is a nothing—the anxious possibility of *being able.*"[34] The nothing of anxiety is thus one in which freedom has its possibility. Freedom, however, is the self, since for Kierkegaard freedom is synonymous with the self, which has a relationship with itself such that he can formulate: "The self is freedom."[35] The nothing of anxiety is thus not the not-yet of an object or an external event or something not yet actual, but is rather the wholly undetermined possibility "to be able." For just this reason anxiety has no object, and can be characterized as the actuality of freedom.

It is not just the absence of an object that constitutes for Kierkegaard the qualitative distinction between anxiety and fear. Although Kierkegaard does not develop this point further, it follows from his exposition of anxiety that fear is an unequivocally negative relationship to a specific object, an undialectical defensive posture. In contrast, anxiety is characterized by a peculiar *dialectic:* "Anxiety is a *sympathetic antipathy* and an *antipathetic sympathy.*"[36] Thus according to Kierkegaard anxiety is precisely not an unequivocal defensive attitude over against a threat, an attitude that in contradistinction with that of fear merely lacks an object, but is rather a dialectical attitude whose ambiguity Kierkegaard conceptualizes by juxtaposing two conceptual paradoxes. The phenomenon Kierkegaard calls anxiety by no means refers first of all to that limitless, undetermined horror, the shuddering before nothingness; rather, it is that which everyday language calls "pleasing anxiety, a pleasing anxiousness," or occasionally also "a strange anxiety, a bashful anxiety, etc."[37] Here we encounter ambiguity resembling that experienced in the face of the numinous, which in religious studies has been called *tremendum et fascinosum,* though the object of anxiety is not the wholly other of the divine, but rather the nothing of the possibility of freedom.[38] Kierkegaard also compares anxiety and its dialectic with a case of dizziness. "Hence anxiety is the dizziness of freedom, which emerges when the spirit wants to posit the synthesis and freedom looks down into its own possibility, laying hold of finiteness to support itself. Freedom succumbs in this dizziness."[39] Thus anxiety is simultaneously the kind of powerlessness associated with fainting on the one hand and self-assertion on the other. The qualitative leap that Kierkegaard calls sin "stands outside all ambiguity. But he who becomes guilty through anxiety is indeed innocent, for it was not he himself but anxiety, a foreign power, that laid hold of him, a power that he did not love but about which he was anxious. And yet he is guilty, for he sank in anxiety, which he nevertheless loved even as he feared it."[40] Because anxiety is a pleasing disquietude, in the state of innocence it is "in the first place no guilt, and in the second place it is no troublesome burden, no suffering that cannot be brought into harmony with the blessedness of innocence."[41]

It is above all this dialectical character of anxiety which according to Kierkegaard's understanding makes the terminological differentiation between fear and anxiety necessary, something frequently overlooked by those who raise objections against such differentiation. It has been asserted that the phenomenological separation of fear from anxiety does not accord with linguistic findings.[42] Not only everyday language, but even poetry and elevated prose often use the words "fear" and "anxiety" synonymously. Reference is also made to the fundamental etymological meaning of the word "anxiety," which is associated with the physical sensation of oppression or anguish and goes hand in hand with other physical reactions coming to expression in terms such as Latin *terror* (trembling and the chattering of teeth), *horror* (hair standing on end), the Indogermanic stem *bhi* (trembling of the lips), or German words such as *Schrecken* (to jump, spring up) or *Entsetzen* (loss of balance). No qualitative physiological distinction can be discerned between such symptoms of fear and the reactions of anxiety ("anxious," from Latin *angere,* to trouble, to choke; the German word *Angst* also is related etymologically to the German word *Enge,* "narrowness, tightness, constriction"), i.e., sensations such as a tightening of the chest or constriction of the throat with accompanying shortness of breath, eyes opened wide in terror, a racing pulse, paleness of skin, and anxious sweat. M. Wandruszka thus suggests subsuming the entire realm of such psychophysical reactions under the Greek term *phobos.* "This large area is delimited on the one side by the most brutal form of alarm, which we call horror, and on the other side by the weak but incessant warning issued by worry. Between the two extremes of the sudden violence of horror and the nagging torment of worry lies the broad field of *fear, uneasiness, anxiety, dread, shock,* of *phobos.*"[43] And indeed, from a biological perspective there is no difference between object-bound fear and free-floating anxiety, so that reactions of anxiety can be explained as transferred behavior involving flight, behavior emerging originally as a protective mechanism over against an actual threat.[44] Those who nevertheless do maintain the distinction between fear and anxiety do not ascribe any necessity to it in principle, but rather only heuristic value.[45]

This criticism of the special status of anxiety seems evident enough as long as anxiety is interpreted from the perspective of fear. Anxiety is then understood as a particular form of fear characterized only by the absence of an immediate object. Indeed, a clear distinction between anxiety and fear is extremely difficult in this case, since a person in a situation apparently void of any danger might in thought or imagination anticipate future dangers and react to them in precisely the same way as to immediate physical threats. In order to differentiate between anxiety and fear, the legitimacy of such anticipatory anxiety-fantasies would have to be evaluated. Anxiety would then ultimately be equated with pathological fear. Or one speaks about anxiety as long as it remains somewhat diffuse, which means nothing more than that anxiety is free-floating fear, triggered in most cases by a concrete occasion or a concretely conceivable danger; again, this renders it only relatively distinguishable from object-bound fear.

If anxiety is interpreted from the perspective of the phenomenon fear, then it, like fear, is to be viewed as a disposition or attitude of flight or as a solicitation to such behavior. The criticism of the Kierkegaardian distinction between fear and anxiety resulting from this view promoted precisely the analysis of anxiety undertaken by Heidegger. It is striking that the debate concerning the concept of anxiety in the past few decades has focused on the distinction between anxiety and fear made by Heidegger. Since then, Kierkegaard's *Concept of Anxiety* has frequently been read from the perspective of Heidegger and understood as a substantive counterpart to Heidegger's interpretation of anxiety in *Being and Time.* This is the only explanation for the fact that Heidegger's and Kierkegaard's terminological distinctions can be either supported or rejected in the same breath.

Although Heidegger on the one hand distinguishes between anxiety and fear, he does on the other hand view them as being "kindred phenomena."[46] Heidegger considers both phenomena to be states-of-mind disclosing a given *danger,* and both states-of-mind lead to a *reaction of flight,* i.e., to fleeing. Although Heidegger asserts that anxiety is the ontologically prior phenomenon which in its own term makes fear possible in the first place,[47] as a matter of fact anxiety is, in quite the reverse fashion, described in analogy with fear.

With respect to fear Heidegger distinguishes that in the face of which we fear, and that about which we fear.[48] That in the face of which we fear is "something which we encounter within-the-world" exhibiting the character of threat. As something we encounter within-the-world it belongs to the realm of what Heidegger calls readiness-to-hand, to the realm of the presence-at-hand, or to the realm of the *Dasein*-with ("being there with"). Fear discloses this innerworldly threat as something detrimental to me which approaches or is coming close. "In *fearing as such*, what we have thus characterized as threatening is freed and allowed to matter to us."[49] That about which we fear, however, is the threatened, fearing person, *Dasein* itself, or another person for whom we fear. "Yet when viewed more strictly, fearing-about is 'being-afraid-for-*oneself*.' Here what one 'is apprehensive about' is one's Being-with the Other, who might be torn away from one."[50] Fear discovers the detrimental element, the threatening loss from which *Dasein* seeks to flee.

Like fear, anxiety in Heidegger's view also discovers a threat, and here, too, one can inquire concerning that in the face of which one has anxiety and that about which one has anxiety. "*That in the face of which one has anxiety is Being-in-the-world as such*,"[51] i.e., *Dasein* itself. That in the face of which one has anxiety cannot be localized. " 'Nowhere,' however, does not signify nothing: this is where any region lies, and there too lies any disclosedness of the world for essentially spatial Being-in."[52] That in the face of which one has anxiety is nothing and nowhere. In everyday language, after anxiety has subsided, we are thus accustomed to saying, "it was really nothing." This nothing, however, before which anxiety is anxious, Heidegger does delimit over against the *nihil pure negativum*. The nothing of anxiety "is grounded in the most primordial 'something'—in the *world*,"[53] and is thus the world as such. That in the face of which one has anxiety is at the same time that about which one has anxiety. "Being-in-the-world itself is that in the face of which anxiety is anxious."[54] "Anxiety discloses Dasein *as Being possible*," and "makes manifest in Dasein its *Being towards* its ownmost potentiality-for-Being—that is, its *Being-free for* the freedom of choosing itself and taking hold of itself. Anxiety brings Dasein face to face with its *Being-free for (propensio in . . .)* the authenticity of its Being, and for this authenticity as a possibility which it always is."[55] Precisely this possibility of authentic being is perceived in anxiety as a threat before which individuated *Dasein* flees into what Heidegger calls falling into the "they." "Dasein's absorption in the 'they' and its absorption in the 'world' of concern, make manifest something like a *fleeing* of Dasein in the face of itself—of itself as an authentic potentiality-for-Being-its-Self."[56] Fleeing, however, is a reaction to threat. Accordingly, that in the face of which *Dasein* shrinks back, action that Heidegger characterizes as falling, "must, in any case, be an entity with the character of threatening; yet this entity has the same kind of Being as the one that shrinks back: it is Dasein itself."[57] If, however, *Dasein* falls into the "they," then situations can now arise in which an entity within-the-world can be perceived as an individual threat. "Fear is anxiety, fallen into the 'world,' inauthentic, and, as such, hidden from itself."[58]

The proximity of Heidegger's thinking to Kierkegaard's own analysis of anxiety is obvious despite the fact that Heidegger refers to Kierkegaard in only a single annotation.[59] Like Kierkegaard, Heidegger also draws attention to the fact that anxiety lacks an object, and is related to a "nothing." Whereas in Kierkegaard's eyes, however, this nothing remains highly ambiguous, both repelling and irresistibly attracting anxiety, in Heidegger's view it manifests itself exclusively as a threat. And accordingly, *Dasein* flees from that nothing, whereas for Kierkegaard in contrast it vacillates between flight and surrender. In other words, *the anxiety described by Heidegger is not dialectical.* Heidegger comes closest to Kierkegaard's dialectic of anxiety in his lecture "What Is Metaphysics?": "In anxiety occurs a shrinking back before . . . which is surely not any sort of flight but rather a kind of bewildered calm."[60] "Bewildered calm" is indeed a good description of the antipathetic sympathy which is simultaneously a sympathetic antipathy of the sort Kierkegaard's *Concept of Anxiety* addresses. In the final analysis, however, anxiety as described by Heidegger is not involved in dialectic, since anxiety one-sidedly "finds itself precisely in utter *impotence* with regard to beings as a whole."[61] In contrast, for Kierkegaard anxiety is simultaneously the weakest and most selfish phenomenon.[62] The fact that Heidegger is nonetheless able to describe anxiety as bewildered calm, however, is related to his new description of that in the face of which one has anxiety: "Anxiety reveals the nothing."[63] The nothing in question, however, is no longer grounded in the something that is the world, as was yet the case in *Being and Time*, but rather in Being itself. "For human existence the nothing makes possible the openedness of beings as such. The nothing does not merely serve as the counterconcept of beings; rather it originally belongs to their essential unfolding as such. In the Being of beings the nihilation of the nothing occurs."[64] The nothing "induces the slipping away of beings as a whole," which is why we "hover" in anxiety.[65] And only when brought before beings as such in this way does *Dasein* have freedom.[66] Thus whereas Heidegger like Kierkegaard relates anxiety and freedom, the concept of nothing in Heidegger is an ontological one. Though this already implies a significant difference from the way Kierkegaard formulates his own philosophical question, as far as the problem of anxiety is concerned, it is important to remember that this hovering of anxiety in Heidegger is not dialectical.

This sort of undialectical view also predominates to a large extent among those who would like to follow Kierkegaard and Heidegger and thus differentiate between anxiety and fear. Thus in Tillich, for example, fear and anxiety are qualitatively basically the same: "Anxiety and fear have the same ontological root but they are not the same in actuality."[67] Though Tillich thinks it necessary to distinguish between fear and anxiety, they are not to be separated. "They are immanent within each other: The sting of fear is anxiety, and anxiety strives toward fear."[68] Anxiety before the threat of nothingness, which manifests itself in a threefold form as fate and death, guilt and condemnation, and emptiness and meaninglessness,[69] has the tendency to construct objects of fear with whose help then anxiety can be transformed into fear, which in its own turn and in a manner different from anxiety itself can be confronted defensively in some way. This transformation from anxiety to fear, however, as described by psychoanalysis, does presuppose that anxiety, like fear, is a reaction to a threat.

O. Haendler has described anxiety as a "primal phenomenon."[70] Despite the pronounced psychoanalytical points of departure in his work, Haendler emphasizes that "anxiety is not intensified fear."[71] Although a qualitative distinction does obtain between the two, Haendler finds this distinction not in the dialectic of anxiety, but rather in a dialectic of fear. "Anxiety is characterized by the feeling we describe with the adjectives 'senseless,' 'gnawing.' In some way a person loses himself in anxiety, and is simply in a state of flight, 'in anxiety,' and within the parameters in which anxiety rules, it rules completely. In contrast, fear is associated with a feeling of being drawn to something, and the person simultaneously remains connected with the object of fear."[72] This feeling of being drawn in, a feeling that for Kierkegaard induces precisely the phenomenon anxiety to become dialectical, characterizes fear according to Haendler. In contrast, he finds that anxiety exhibits not a dialectical, but an "ambivalent character": "It perpetually has two sides, and is able to exert its influence in either direction, and under certain circumstances in both at the same time: It can be fruitful or unfruitful, constructive or destructive, it can strengthen or weaken, be meaningful or meaningless."[73]

There is, to be sure, a trace of the Kierkegaardian dialectic of anxiety in Haendler's more specific description of the phenomenon of anxiety, namely, in his differentiation between the various forms of anxiety[74] as the anxiety of flight on the one hand and incapacitating anxiety on the other.[75] Whereas the anxiety of flight compels the subject away from the threat, the person seized by incapacitating anxiety, in contrast, is as if lamed. Thus Haendler separates into two undialectical forms of anxiety that which in its dialectical relationship constitutes in the first place the phenomenon Kierkegaard describes as anxiety. Haendler's linguistic usage makes it quite clear just how difficult it is to carry through the terminological differentiation between anxiety and fear if the former is not conceived dialectically. If one follows Haendler's own terminology, his examples of anxiety are basically better suited as examples of fear.[76]

Karl Jaspers's understanding of anxiety undeniably involves a certain dialectic. Jaspers does not, to be sure, differentiate between fear and anxiety, but rather between the anxiety of being (i.e., with regard to existence as such) and existential anxiety. Anxiety, described in the Kierkegaardian tradition as dizziness, is for Jaspers the awareness "that I can be extinguished,"[77] the "horror of *not being*."[78] Anxiety is first of all the perception of the threat to naked existence posed by nonbeing. This "anxiety for existence" is ultimately the same as the anxiety about death. "From the point of view of *existence* all anxiety [Angst] derives from an underlying anxiety of death. Freedom from that would free me from all other anxiety."[79] Initially, then, Jaspers describes anxiety as a wholly undialectical phenomenon. Since in reference to this threat to existence he speaks not of fear, but rather of anxiety regarding one's existence, the first thing one notices with respect to Jaspers's concept of anxiety is that a differentiation between fear and anxiety against the background of an undialectical understanding of anxiety remains extremely problematical. As a matter of fact, Jaspers really does not address this differentiation. Although he does speak of objectless anxiety as the "all-pervasive consciousness that everything finite will pass away,"[80] this makes no assertion concerning any qualitative difference over against object-related anxiety.

In addition to the anxiety associated with existence or death, Jaspers acknowledges a second basic form as well which he calls existential anxiety. In addition to the anxiety prompted by the notion of physical nonbeing, human beings experience yet another, namely the "*anxiety of existential nonbeing*," a despair that "may befall it [the human being] despite its vital existence and in contrast to its simultaneous vigor and abundance."[81] This anxiety before existential nonbeing is the anxiety of not existing "authentically." It is the anxiety of losing oneself in freedom and thus becoming guilty. Insofar as anxiety does make me choose to seize my own, authentic being, Jaspers does view it dialectically: "What may destroy me is at the same time my way to Existenz. Without the threat of possible despair there is no freedom."[82] That is, existential anxiety for Jaspers, insofar as self-loss and self-gain are at risk, is indeed dialectical, but not—and this is the decisive difference over against Kierkegaard—insofar as it is based on a dialectical self-relationship of existence.

Jean-Paul Sartre's analysis of anxiety comes closest to Kierkegaard's dialectical concept of anxiety. Sartre picks up Kierkegaard's distinction between anxiety and fear such that "anxiety is distinguished from fear in that fear is fear of beings in the world whereas anxiety is anxiety before myself."[83] Fear arises through external threats, anxiety in contrast through mistrust over against myself. "In this sense fear and anxiety are exclusive of one another since fear is unreflective apprehension of the transcendent and anxiety is reflective apprehension of the self,"[84] whereby in this context the transcendent refers to the external world. According to Sartre, the phenomenon of anxiety encompasses two types of anxiety, on the one hand anxiety in the face of the future, and on the other hand anxiety in the face of the past, with the two types being dialectically related.[85] The specifics of this peculiar dialectic will concern us later during our inquiry into the relationship between self-anxiety and world anxiety. At this point it is important to remember that Sartre's analysis of anxiety represents in a certain respect a repetition of Kierkegaard's description of the phenomenon, though on the other hand Sartre understands his own explication as a synthesis of the respective concepts of anxiety presented by Heidegger and Kierkegaard: "These two descriptions of anxiety do not appear to us contradictory; on the contrary the one implies the other."[86] Anxiety in Sartre's understanding, however, is not, as with Heidegger, a human state-of-mind, but rather a reflexive concept whose reflexive content goes beyond that of Kierkegaard. Whereas according to Kierkegaard existence is a *dialectical* relationship of the self, a synthesis of body, spirit, and soul, for Sartre it is a *reflexive* relationship of the self in which the body plays a wholly subordinated role. Sartre's understanding completely displaces anxiety to the level of the reflexive:[87] "Anxiety then is the reflective apprehension of freedom by itself."[88] In a critical sense the question needs to be posed whether the sort of synthesis envisioned by Sartre between the concepts of anxiety of Kierkegaard and Heidegger is possible in the first place.

We have seen that an undialectical understanding of anxiety is able to justify only with some qualification its delimitation over against fear. In contrast, especially

Kierkegaard's dialectic of anxiety yields a qualitative distinction between anxiety and fear, though even his differentiation is not without its problems. An understanding of his treatise is hindered particularly by the fact that the meanings of his various terms—as is also the case elsewhere in his work—alter during the course of his own thought processes. That is, Kierkegaard's concept of anxiety is dynamic rather than static. What is actually described is not a condition of anxiety that is equally possible at any given time, but rather the process in which the character of anxiety itself as a condition changes. The particular dialectical anxiety of which Kierkegaard initially speaks does not already represent the entire phenomenon of anxiety in the larger sense, but rather only that particular anxiety which as an ambiguous state precedes the leap of the first sin. Kierkegaard's concept of anxiety thus cannot without qualification be delimited as dialectical over against one that is not dialectical, e.g., in Heidegger, as W. Schulz has attempted to do.[89] Kierkegaard's intention is to sketch the progress of sin. Under the influence of this progressing sin, however, so Kierkegaard's thesis, anxiety is robbed of its dialectic. Already in Adam's descendants—i.e., in each of us—anxiety takes on different coloring because the history of the race's entanglement in sin precedes them. "In each subsequent individual, anxiety is more reflective. This may be expressed by saying that the nothing that is the object of anxiety becomes, as it were, more and more a something."[90] This, it is true, involves not a qualitative, but rather a quantitative difference between anxiety and the nothing it perceives, on the one hand, and the anxiety of Adam on the other, as long as the later individual has not yet sinned. The assertion that this nothing becomes more and more a something does not mean, however, that a concrete object moves into the place of the nothing such that anxiety now becomes fear. Rather, the nothing of anxiety in the later individual before the individual falls into sin is "a complex of presentiments, which, reflecting themselves in themselves, come nearer and nearer to the individual, even though again, when viewed essentially in anxiety, they signify a nothing."[91] Thus in the later individual, too, anxiety initially remains dialectical. That particular anxiety is also dialectical which is no longer the presupposition, but rather already the result of sin, as long as that sin consists in the absence of a qualified consciousness of sin. Kierkegaard still describes that anxiety resulting from sin as being dialectical, on the one hand in the direction of fate, and on the other in the direction of guilt.[92]

In contrast, that particular anxiety that as a result of sin is aware of the difference between good and evil is an undialectical state-of-mind. That is, now "the object of anxiety is a determinate something and its nothing is an actual something, because the distinction between good and evil is posited *in concreto*—and anxiety therefore loses its dialectical ambiguity."[93] Anxiety is now an undialectical perception either of evil or of good as a threat; now indeed it is anxiety before or about something, be that something evil[94] or good (the demonic).[95] And here, though admittedly here only for the first time, in my opinion a conceptually strict distinction between fear and anxiety in Kierkegaard becomes difficult. When the anxious person imagines life's every conceivable terror,[96] or when that person knows that no matter how deep he has sunk, he can sink still deeper,[97]—in cases such as these one also might speak with some justification about fear.[98] This should not be misunderstood to mean that Kierkegaard is interpreting all fear as anxiety that has become undialectical, or as inauthentic anxiety, to use Heidegger's term again. For as we have already seen, right at the beginning of his investigation Kierkegaard distinguishes fear in the face of finite things from the original phenomenon of anxiety. One must thus probably understand Kierkegaard such that certain forms of fear are to be considered as undialectical derivatives of what he has described as anxiety. While many types of fear thus represent the perception of a concrete and immediate threat to which a person can react defensively in some way, other forms of fear derive from underlying anxiety which in its original form is a dialectical perception of human freedom.

The ambiguity of anxiety of which Kierkegaard speaks consists in its dialectic. Understood properly, however, anxiety is not only dialectical, but also—and in this respect, O. Haendler, for example, is correct—ambivalent. It can, as Haendler demonstrates, be fruitful or unfruitful, we might also say life-promoting or life-hindering. This ambivalence of anxiety has been mentioned especially by those who perceive something forced precisely in Kierkegaard's differentiation between anxiety and fear.[99] Similarly, psychology and medicine have criticized Heidegger's estimation of anxiety as an existentiale by asserting that anxiety is primarily a pathological phenomenon. The pathology of anxiety finds itself forced to pose critical questions concerning Kierkegaard's concept of anxiety, but also concerning the psychological disposition of its author. The suspicion has arisen that Kierkegaard's concept of anxiety not only does not stand up to the evidence of reality, but is itself a pathological symptom: "Never has the neurosis of the scrupler been more stirringly portrayed than in the self-tormenting anxiety broodings of Kierkegaard."[100] There is no question that Kierkegaard suffered psychological damage as a result of his upbringing. He himself wrote in his journals about the enormous melancholy against which he struggled futilely his entire life and which tormented him virtually every day.[101] It is doubtful, however, whether psychopathological diagnoses have provided any definitive determination concerning the validity of Kierkegaard's theory of anxiety.

In any event, Kierkegaard himself is quite conscious of the ambivalence of anxiety, anxiety which for him is in a certain respect the same as melancholy. He is able to equate anxiety and melancholy with an explicit reference to his work *Either/Or*, whose second part allegedly explains precisely that particular melancholy which the first part portrays.[102] In that second part of *Either/Or*, Judge William interprets the melancholy of the aesthetic A as "hysteria of the spirit," hysteria that comes about when the spirit tries to break through a person's immediacy and come to itself, yet is repressed by the aesthetic.[103] For Vigilius Haufniensis, too, the root of melancholy discloses itself as anxiety. Anxiety and melancholy, however, are highly ambivalent. On the one hand, freedom is to find its way to itself in anxiety; on the other, however, Kierkegaard, too, acknowledges pathological forms of anxiety. What one might classify as a pathological form of anxiety and accordingly treat medically, Kierkegaard calls the demonic, the significance of which we will address later on.[104] In any case, anxiety as a pathological phenomenon is not unknown to Kierkegaard, namely, as a life-hindering phenomenon or as the loss of freedom. He also emphasizes that such life-hindering anxiety can be virtually life-threatening and drive a person to suicide.[105] Insofar as it leads to faith, anxiety is according to Kierkegaard's understanding life-promoting. Otherwise, that is, insofar as it drives a person to suicide or to a complete loss of freedom, it is destructive. Thus Kierkegaard explicates the ambivalence of anxiety and tries to show how such anxiety—which perpetually runs the risk of becoming a hindrance to life—can be made fruitful.

Karl Jaspers draws attention to the ambivalence of anxiety in a different way: "Without anxiety there will be none of the precautionary activities required by existence, while excessive anxiety will impede them." For Jaspers the characteristic feature of the healthy person is that such a person lives "in naïve fearlessness but utter dependence upon this vitality." Thus ultimately even the healthy person experiences anxiety. "Not surmounting but forgetting anxiety" is what manifests itself directly in situations of danger or crisis.[106] While O. Haendler distinguishes between fruitful and unfruitful anxiety, Paul Tillich distinguishes between natural (or existential) and pathological anxiety. Whereas natural anxiety is "the state in which a being is aware of its possible nonbeing," or, expressed differently, "the existential awareness of nonbeing,"[107] pathological anxiety drives a person into neurosis, namely, into "the way of avoiding nonbeing by avoiding being."[108]

In the realm of psychoanalysis, Sigmund Freud similarly distinguished neurotic anxiety from so-called realistic anxiety.[109] "Real danger is a danger that is known, and realistic anxiety is anxiety about a known danger of this sort. Neurotic anxiety is anxiety about an unknown danger. Neurotic danger is thus a danger that has still to be discovered. Analysis has shown that it is an instinctual danger."[110] Whereas in his initial theory of anxiety Freud interpreted neurotic anxiety as transformed, accumulated energy of the libido which as a result of repression could not be released in any other way,[111] in his later theory of anxiety[112] he evaluated it in analogy with realistic anxiety as a signal indicating danger deriving from one of the drives of the id. With the aid of a reaction of anxiety following upon such a signal, the ego defends itself against this danger deriving from the drives, whereby, however, "this line of defensive activity eventuates in a neurosis owing to an imperfection of the mental apparatus."[113] To be sure, Freud's second theory of anxiety both underpins and relativizes the distinction between so-called realistic anxiety and neurotic anxiety to the same extent. "We know what the distinction is. A real danger is a danger which threatens a person from an external object, and a neurotic danger is one which threatens him from an instinctual demand. In so far as the instinctual demand is something real, his neurotic anxiety, too, can be admitted to have a realistic basis."[114]

Although the distinction between realistic anxiety and neurotic anxiety is thus virtually obscured, Freud does now introduce a further distinction. To this end he distinguishes, within the affect of anxiety,[115] "preparedness for anxiety" from the "generation of anxiety."[116] The decisive factor in evaluating anxiety is not the origin of the danger, i.e., that anxiety might be evoked by this or that actual external danger or by an inner drive, but rather the purposiveness of the reaction elicited by the anxiety signal. Viewed in this way, realistic anxiety according to Freud can itself be a highly unsuitable form of behavior.

> For the only expedient behavior when a danger threatens would be a cool estimate of one's own strength in comparison with the magnitude of the threat and, on the basis of that, a decision as to whether flight or defence, or possibly even attack, offers the best prospect of a successful issue. But in this situation there is no place at all for anxiety; everything that happens would be achieved just as well and probably better if no anxiety were generated.[117]

Insofar as in anxiety a traumatic experience and corresponding behavioral modes are reproduced in a completely different situation of danger, it is actually counterproductive or inexpedient. In contrast, only the disposition capable of enlisting anxiety is expedient or appropriate in this sense, or expressed differently, the signal function of anxiety. Instead of distinguishing between preparedness for anxiety and the generation of anxiety, Freud is also able to mention two reactions which we develop in situations of danger. "One is an affective reaction, an outbreak of anxiety. The other is a protective action."[118] Anxiety is purposive or expedient in the case of cooperation between the two reactions in effectively confronting the danger, "the one giving the signal for the other to appear," and inexpedient in the case of "paralysis from anxiety," when the one reaction spreads at the cost of the other.[119]

These and similar distinctions admittedly do not yet completely explicate the ambivalence of anxiety we have encountered thus far. We must point out first of all that the attempts at distinguishing between healthy or normal anxiety on the one hand, and pathological anxiety on the other, proceed on the basis of an undialectical understanding of anxiety. This concurs with the fact that the phenomenon of the demonic disclosed by Kierkegaard, a phenomenon within whose parameters anxiety becomes a medical problem, presupposes that the originally dialectical phenomenon of anxiety has become undialectical. That the psychoanalytical theory of anxiety also lacks dialectic is shown by Freud's assertion that anxiety is characterized by "a specific character of unpleasure."[120] Under closer scrutiny, then, the affect which Freud's theory describes as anxiety is strictly speaking actually fear. Whereas in the first place according to Freud the distinction between fear and anxiety consists only in anxiety's alleged lack of an object,[121] his theory of anxiety also entangles itself in contradictions. If, namely, the actual danger is one that a person recognizes and that emerges from an external object, then basically so-called realistic anxiety is nothing other than fear, whereby now also neurotic anxiety—given its inner connection with realistic anxiety—would represent fear prompted by one of the drives of the id. It is not that the phenomenon described by Kierkegaard as anxiety has received merely a different interpretation in psychoanalysis. Rather, it is never really addressed correctly in the first place. Although the diagnosis and treatment of pathological fear doubtless represents an important task, such fear resides on a different level than does the ambivalence of anxiety we are addressing here.

If we now summarize our observations to this point, we must agree with Kierkegaard that there is indeed a dialectical phenomenon that we can call anxiety. This dialectic was already evident in various historical manifestations of world anxiety, and this above all else is the feature distinguishing anxiety from fear. Whereas fear is the perception of an unequivocal threat and leads to a defensive posture over against this threat, anxiety perceives something the significance of which remains ambiguous for us and over against which it assumes a dialectical posture. Fear is basically related to an object. When such an object is not discernible, it is strictly speaking not objectless, but rather diffuse. In contrast, anxiety basically has no object. Anxiety's lack of an object, however, constitutes a qualitative rather than merely a relative difference from fear. Furthermore, we have also noticed the ambivalence of anxiety, an ambivalence that presents an important question concerning apocalyptic, namely, whether that particular world anxiety coming to expression in apocalyptic is fruitful or unfruitful anxiety. Put a bit differently, the problem is whether apocalyptic causes world anxiety to become fruitful or life-hindering, and whether it masters anxiety or incites it. First of all, however, one must inquire regarding just what connection obtains between the dialectic of anxiety on the one hand, and its lack of an object on the other. From what we have said thus far it seems likely that the objectless character of anxiety is grounded in its dialectic, but that this dialectic itself derives from what anxiety perceives. We must now determine just what it is that anxiety discovers.

3. The Discovery of the Future

Fear is the disposition that discerns threat; in contrast, anxiety is the disposition in which we discover the future. Anxiety is the discovery of the future. It discerns the questionability of the future.

The future that anxiety discovers, however, is different from that about which we normally speak in the sense of the usual concept of time. Whoever speaks these days about the doubtful nature of the future is usually thinking of the time yet remaining to the individual or to humankind. If one inquires concerning the future as the time yet remaining for us, the future appears as a calculable quantity. The future as outstanding time is calculated in seconds, hours, days, weeks, months, and years just as is the past. We conceive future and past as being separated by the forward moving boundary of the present moment, shrinking to a single point. The future as temporal duration is the object of the prognosis. Past and future are reduced to nonextendable points of principally equal value conceived as lying upon a sequentially ordered line of time comparable to a similar line of numbers. Viewed in this way, the future associated with the normal concept of time is infinite, which is why its end is the actually inconceivable interruption of an infinitely progressing series of points of time. In fact, however, this understanding of time only seemingly accommodates our experience of time.[122] We experience time as our own temporality, which moves in an irreversible direction. The irreversibility of time, however, is only seemingly expressed adequately by the physical measurement of time and the idea of linear time. If, that is, time is understood as an infinite sequence of moments, then quite contrary to our actual experience of temporality there is in principle no distinction between past and future.[123] Both past and future moments are in principle interchangeable, since the line of time of physical temporal measurement can be read just as easily forward as backward. In this way, contrary to our existential experience of time, the sequence of past and future becomes reversible. Such a reversal of temporal stages is conceivable because the concept of time rendering it possible is mathematical. Mathematical thinking is essentially spatial, comprehending "what has already become," with its attendant relationships, rather than "becoming." What has already become, however, is the past. The common understanding of time thus equates present and future with the past and recognizes time only as past time.[124] An adequate understanding of that particular future which anxiety discovers is utterly impossible on the basis of such a concept of time. The future discovered by anxiety is not a yet outstanding, chronologically calculable span of time, but is rather something that we might call the space of freedom or the arena of the possible.

In what follows we will explicate more specifically what is to be understood by this future disclosed by anxiety, though we are not concerned with developing a philosophical theory of human freedom or with offering an exhaustive discussion of the concept of the possible. Rather, we will investigate both the phenomenon of freedom and the concept of the possible only insofar as this is indispensable for understanding the relationship between anxiety and the future.

To this end let us first recall Heidegger's analysis of the concept of being in *Being and Time*. Heidegger destroys the philosophical notion of an isolated self conceived in and for itself, one that only in a second conceptual act is placed into the world, so that one might conceive the world as empty space which by and by is filled with objects. We exist, as Heidegger has shown, only insofar as we have a world and sojourn and react in that world. Without the world the self is inconceivable, which is why Heidegger, as is well known, referred to "being-in-the-world in general as the basic state of Dasein."[125] Being in a world is something belonging "essentially," as Heidegger puts it, to *Dasein*,[126] and that means to entities such as those which we are ourselves.[127] Conversely, according to Heidegger the world can be described only in the context of the unitary phenomenon of being-in-the-world,[128] only from the perspective of the In-being of *Dasein*, a description Heidegger undertakes in *Being and Time* in the chapter on the worldhood of the world.[129] Now, apparently it is part of our own manner of being that on the one hand we are in the world, and yet on the other are simultaneously separated from it. Our own being in the world consists in our having a certain leeway or space enabling us to react to the world in one way or another. Something steps in between us and the world which first allows us to experience the world as such. We can perhaps best refer to this phenomenon of dependency between self and world as the "between."

With varying usage this concept of a between already appears in M. Buber as well as in Heidegger. Buber's category of the between stands in correlation to that of relationship, whereby Buber understands the relationship as the enduring latency of meeting or encounter.[130] Buber critically responds to individualism and collectivism with the assertion that "the fundamental fact of human existence is human being with human being."[131] It is rooted in the fact that "one being refers to another as an other, as this specific other being, in order to communicate with that other in a sphere common to both but transcending each individual sphere. I would call this the sphere of the between, a sphere posited with the existence of the human being as human being, though conceptually not yet grasped."[132] According to Buber, the between is not an "auxiliary construction," but rather a "primal category" localizing the relationship between human beings neither in the inwardness of those standing in the relationship, nor in the external world at large, "but rather factically between them."[133] Buber illustrates this between in examples of conversation as well as in the silent, fleeting encounter of two glances, or of the momentary sharing that takes place listening to music.[134] More specifically, Buber occasionally specifies the between as love,[135] though he guards against mistaking the between as motives of feeling: "What appears here is inaccessible to psychological concepts, it is something ontic."[136]

Though Buber also discounts any psychological misunderstanding of the category of the between, a category that he discovered and G. Marcel called "something much more mysterious,"[137] its identification with love does nonetheless result in a personalistic constriction of the concept. The between as the free space of encounter is exclusively an interpersonal, human phenomenon. Regarding the extrapersonal realm, however, Buber's determination of the between obtains only when ultimately the communication with the nonhuman world—with what Buber calls the It—can be comprehended as a personal occurrence. However, it is probably best to exercise caution regarding Buber's assumption that human beings and nature can enter into an I-thou relationship.[138]

The notion of the between is conceived differently by M. Heidegger, for whose philosophy the significance of the phenomenon has long been overlooked.[139] Buber's personal category of the between initially finds a certain correspondence in what Heidegger in *Being and Time* calls "distantiality." The fundamental existentiale of *Dasein*, namely, care, also characterizes Being-with. "In one's concern with what one has taken hold of, whether with, for, or against, the Others, there is constant care as to the way one differs from them," even if one only wishes to even out this difference. This Being-with-one-another consists in this distance, and is, without our being conscious of it, disturbed by the care about this distance; "if we may express this existentially, such Being-with-one-another has the character of *distantiality*."[140] This distantiality, it is true, belongs to the mode of everyday being, that which Heidegger calls the "they." It is noteworthy, however, that for Heidegger, too, such distantiality presents the problem of an interpersonal between, even if the latter is not designated as such. However, whereas Buber considers this between to be filled out especially by love, and classifies it as part of full, we might even say, authentic personal relationships, for Heidegger it belongs to the realm of inauthentic *Dasein* and offers space for competing behavior.

It is in the context of his analysis of temporality, however, that Heidegger explicitly comes upon the problem of a between. *Dasein* is something temporally extended out. It moves along positioned between birth and death. "The 'between' relating to birth and death already lies *in the Being* of Dasein."[141] Heidegger conceives past, present, and future, however, not as what is no-longer or not-yet in the sense of the usual understanding of time, but rather as "*ecstases* of temporality."[142] In accord with Heidegger's concept of temporality, birth and death are equally present in the unity of *Dasein*.

> Factical Dasein exists as born; and, as born, it is already dying, in the sense of Being-towards-death. As long as Dasein factically exists, both the "ends" and their "between" *are*, and they *are* in the only way which is possible on the basis of Dasein's Being as *care*. Thrownness and that Being towards death in which one either flees it or anticipates it, form a unity; and in this unity birth and death are "connected" in a manner characteristic of Dasein. As care, Dasein *is* the "between."[143]

Hence the between of which Heidegger speaks in *Being and Time* is temporal, though it coincides not with the future as one of the ecstasies of temporality, but rather with *Dasein* itself.

In a renewed fashion, though differently, Heidegger encounters the problem of the between in the cognitive-theoretical realm. Concluding a lecture on Kant given in 1935/36, Heidegger inquires concerning the conditions making possible our perceptions of things which we do not actually produce or create ourselves. He finds "that we must always move in the *between* between man and thing." On the one hand, this between exists "only while we move in it"; on the other, however, it is independent of human beings. The between extends "as an anticipation beyond the thing and similarly back behind us"; for that reason, it is what encompasses both person and thing equally.[144]

At this point we may perhaps go one step further. If, that is, the between of which Heidegger speaks obtains or is only in that we human beings move about within it, yet *Dasein*, as Heidegger emphasizes on the other hand, is temporal through and through, then it seems likely that the between is also to be understood as characterized by the element of time. And it is precisely this between characterized by the element of time that we wish to call the future. Future in the sense of a temporal between is the fundamental condition of human freedom, or, as already formulated, the leeway given our freedom. As such, the future is a free space for encounter, specifically for the encounter not only between the I and its world, but also for the encounter between an I and a thou.

This leeway for encounter and movement can be described ontologically as the space of the possible. Now, the concept of the possible is philosophically ambiguous, and its entire semantic history cannot be presented within the parameters of the present context. If the future is conceived as the leeway given to freedom or as the free space for encounter, then "possibility" is in any case not to be understood as a concept of logic separating the conceptually possible from the conceptually necessary. Just as little is possibility to be conceived as that which is not yet actual. The notion that the possible is what is not yet actual derives, as is well known, from Aristotle, who formulated the ontological principle: *hoti proteron energeia dynameōs estin* (Metaph. Θ.1049.b.5).[145] For Aristotle, then, actuality enjoys ontological priority over possibility. In contrast to the former, being is not attributed to the latter. This kind of ontology concedes to the future a rank ontologically inferior to that of the past. If possibility is what is not yet actual, then the future is that which can be prognosticated, that which can be planned and which in that planning is already one remove from its futurity. "Future actuality is actually eliminated thus for the sake of the present of the plan itself,"[146] and present actuality is eclipsed by actuality such that in the end, as K. Rahner suggests, the future can be described as "plans plus formally empty time as measured by the clock,"[147] but also that the future can no longer be perceived as futurity. It is the philosophy of E. Bloch that intercedes here on behalf of the primacy of the future. However, by taking up arms explicitly with left-of-center Aristotelianism[148] in order to establish a mooring for its future-oriented notion of hope in an "ontology of the Not-yet,"[149] Bloch's philosophy itself fails to escape the fate just mentioned afflicting any ontology modeled on Aristotle. Only such thinking takes seriously the futurity of the future which questions the primacy of actuality. Here one must mention especially Heidegger. Heidegger distinguishes Being-possible, which *Dasein* is existentially in every case, from logical or modal possibility. "Ontologically," the modal category of the possible "is on a lower level than actuality and necessity. On the other hand, possibility as an *existentiale* is the most primordial and ultimate positive way in which Dasein is characterized ontologically."[150] Heidegger concisely reverses the Aristotelian ontological principle: "Higher than actuality stands *possibility*."[151]

Possibility, we must continue this train of thought, is not what is not yet actual, and is not what comes from out of actuality, but rather what is approaching or coming toward actuality. Possibility in this sense is what K. Rahner distinguished from the planable future as the "absolute future."[152] Over against the future that can be made, one which strictly speaking is an actuality or reality that can be made—a kind of transformation of reality—the absolute future is, we might say with E. Jüngel, "external" to actuality. Of future possibility one can say that "its external mode is futurity."[153] Such futurity is what makes possible in the first place that particular transformation of actuality normally referred to as the future. It is not actuality that sets free the possibility of future, but rather, vice versa, the future that creates the possibility for actuality. Future is the rendering possible of actuality. The possible in the sense of what is not yet actual has its ontological ground in the possibility of the absolute future. Put another way: Internal possibility is made possible by external possibility. One can thus say with A. Jäger that the possibility discussed here as future is "foundational possibility."[154]

It is then anxiety in which this temporal between of the future discloses itself to us, and in this sense one can speak of the discovery of the future through anxiety, though one admittedly cannot say that the future constitutes the object of anxiety. Rather, the future is entwined with the freedom of the anxious person such that the discovery of the future is nothing other than the discovery of human freedom, which in its own turn does not constitute an object. Thus although anxiety does make a discovery, it has no object. It discovers the space of freedom and thereby allows us to become aware of ourselves as free. In anxiety, then, we discover ourselves and the world. In anxiety we become certain of ourselves, and do so such that we experience ourselves and the world as positioned in possibility. By being an effective experience of future, anxiety is simultaneously an effective experience of the self and the world. This will become even more clear when in what follows we inquire concerning basic forms of anxiety.

4. Basic Forms of Anxiety

In anxiety we discover the world and ourselves. Thus self-anxiety and world anxiety are the basic forms of anxiety. "World anxiety" and "self-anxiety," it is true, are ambiguous concepts. Just as one can differentiate between anxiety before (or in the face of), in, and about something as aspects of anxiety,[155] so also can one speak of the various meanings of world anxiety and self-anxiety. There is much talk about the two basic forms in the sense of anxiety before (or in the face of) something. In this view, self-anxiety and world anxiety would be anxiety *in the face of* myself or the world, whereby this usage easily runs the risk of obscuring the difference between anxiety and fear insofar as the self or the world is taken as a phenomenal object, something inappropriate not only for anxiety, but also for the phenomena of the self and the world. In the more recent history of philosophy one uses the term "world anxiety" to describe above all the locus of anxiety. World anxiety conceived in this way is anxiety *in* the world. Though not customary, the term "self-anxiety" can also be used in an analogous fashion, indicating clearly that the self is to be viewed as the locus or bearer of anxiety. Emphasizing this through the concept of "self-anxiety" can be meaningful especially in connection with psychoanalytical anthropology. Thus Freud emphasizes that it is not the id, i.e., the unconscious, but rather the ego that is the bearer of anxiety.[156] Self-anxiety would thus be another expression for the "ego-anxiety" of which Freud speaks.[157] A person speaking today about world anxiety, however, is usually referring less to anxiety as the mood of Being-in-the-world than to the threats to the continued existence of the earth and of humankind. In popular parlance, world anxiety not infrequently refers to anxiety in the face of destruction, i.e., anxiety *about* the world and its future. Accordingly, one can also speak about self-anxiety as anxiety about the existence of the self. All three aspects resonate in anxiety, and should not really be isolated from one another.

We must now ask about the connection between self-anxiety and world anxiety. The answer seems to come quickly. It is obvious that all anxiety before the world is at the same time anxiety about the self, just as anxiety about the world is above all anxiety about the possibilities of the existence of the self. And finally it is obvious, since the self is always in a world, that the ego-anxiety of which Freud speaks has its locus in the self and thus simultaneously in the world. As obvious as these conclusions seem, they are equally as problematical, for they by no means explain the inner connection between world anxiety and self-anxiety, but rather merely point out that world anxiety as anxiety in the face of something and about something is nothing other than anxiety about the self; thus the distinction between self-anxiety and world anxiety becomes at times difficult or even superfluous. The conclusion would be that as a matter of fact there are not two basic forms of anxiety at all, but rather only one.

Since the self and the world are not objects like a dog that is about to bite me or a car rushing toward me, we must indeed be careful, since Being-in-the-world is an all-encompassing phenomenon, not to separate world anxiety and self-anxiety completely from one another. We are nonetheless constrained, however, to keep self-anxiety and world anxiety apart, since any reference to anxiety in the face of myself evokes something in the face of which one has anxiety that is not necessarily involved in world anxiety or even in anxiety about myself. At precisely this point, however, the question concerning the inner connection between self-anxiety and world anxiety becomes urgent for the first time. The question is now just what relationship obtains between, on the one hand, anxiety in and in the face of the world that is yet anxiety about the self, and, on the other, anxiety in the face of just this self. Treatments of the problem of anxiety have in part lost sight of precisely this connection. "Formulated somewhat crudely: World anxiety is taken as a theme in existential philosophy, while anxiety before myself is taken as a theme in anthropology and its related disciplines,"[158] whereby mutual accusations of one-sidedness are exchanged and encounters are characterized by mistrust or lack of understanding. Not only does such division of labor by no means facilitate finding the answer to the question we have posed, it sooner impedes access to the problems in the first place.

Freud's theory of anxiety is an exemplary illustration of such concentration on self-anxiety within the context of anthropology. Just as Kierkegaard develops not a static concept of anxiety, but rather follows anxiety in its forward development, as it were in its movement, so also does Freud—though without even mentioning Kierkegaard—present a life history of anxiety. In Freud's view, every state of anxiety experienced by the ego is a reproduction of the trauma of birth.[159] In the developmental stage of early childhood anxiety appears initially as the ego's reaction to the absence of the beloved object, i.e., the mother. According to Freud, anxiety as a reproduction of the birth experience signals the danger of separation, and is thus essentially anxiety of separation. The birth experience can be reactivated in such situations because birth itself is a separation process, namely, separation from the mother. In that case "the earliest anxiety of all—the 'primal anxiety' of birth"[160] would itself exhibit the character of separation anxiety. Conflict with the awakening sexual instinct leads at a later stage according to Freud's view to castration anxiety, which again fears separation from a highly valued object. At a later stage of development, however, castration anxiety is transformed into moral anxiety or social anxiety, i.e., into anxiety before the superego. Finally, the last transformation of this anxiety before the superego Freud calls the anxiety of death (or of life), anxiety before the powers of destiny, which are nothing other than projections of the superego.[161]

Freud directs his attention primarily to neurotic anxiety. One might call this self-anxiety if one disregards the fact that Freud's concept of anxiety is fundamentally a psychological concept of fear. The actual driving force in its explication resides in the origination and displacement of instinctual conflicts. These take place in a person's interior, though on the other hand they are related to conflicts with the external world; this is true because "an instinctual demand often only becomes an (internal) danger because its satisfaction would bring on an external danger—that is, because the internal danger represents an external one. On the other hand, the external (real) danger must also have managed to become internalized if it is to be significant for the ego. It must have been recognized as related to some situation of helplessness that has been experienced."[162] It is thus corporeality, we might say, which in the form of instincts becomes a danger to the ego. A person threatens himself through his own corporeality insofar as through the gratification of those instincts he provokes conflicts with the external world. The instinctual body is thus the seam between self and world, and the self perceives itself as threatened by that body insofar as it indirectly provokes threat through the world. The latter is admittedly an initially isolated external danger. As hard as Freud tries to include the ego's relationship with the world in his considerations, anxiety before the "real danger" is not world anxiety in the sense we have discussed.

World anxiety as the discernment or perception of the future in its relation to the world means something different from the reaction to threat posed by external factors as described by Freud. Even in the larger sense precisely the future reference of the self and the world remains unclear in Freud. According to him, the decisive element in the development of anxiety is "the first displacement of the anxiety-reaction from its origin in the situation of helplessness to an expectation of that situation—that is, to the danger situation."[163] The question arises concerning just what makes this displacement possible. Freud's explanatory model leaves open the question of why a person is capable of expectation in the first place, i.e., what the ground is of the capacity for anticipation. In expectation we turn toward the future. Freud's theory of anxiety does not further address the theme of this relation with the future and thus the connection between anxiety, future, and freedom. His inclusion of corporeality in the analysis of anxiety, however, does take us further. Even though his concept of anxiety remains unsatisfactory in many respects, Freud's treatment of anxiety proves to be significant in its assertion that corporeality constitutes the decisive bridge between self-anxiety and world anxiety.

One decisive insight of Heidegger's analysis of anxiety is that self and world are not objects of anxiety to be separated from one another. He underscores the connection between self-anxiety and world anxiety by presenting as that in the face of which one has anxiety neither the self nor the world as such, but rather Being-in-the-world as an indivisible phenomenon. Since Being-in-the-world as such is actually that before which a person has anxiety, anxiety is at once both world anxiety and self-anxiety. Anxiety as world- and self-anxiety, however, is at the same time anxious both in the face of and about Being-in-the-world. World and self in their total manifestation are simultaneously that in the face of which and about which one has anxiety. According to Heidegger, anxiety is anxious in the face of a nothing grounded in the world. This nothing as that in the face of which one has anxiety is the world as such in its nonobjective nature. *Dasein* is anxious in the face of itself and about itself because the perception of the nothing places it before the possibility of its own authentic potentiality-for-Being. Placed thus before the choice of either seizing or missing itself, *Dasein* experiences its fundamental unsecured status. This insecurity, however, comes about through the pure fact of Being-in-the-world, and not through any component in the self, and this is the decisive difference between this theory of anxiety and those of both Freud and Kierkegaard. Corporeality, through which the self is not only in the world, but also of the world, plays no role in the problem of anxiety as conceived by Heidegger.[164] The body and its instincts do not appear as unpredictable quantities plaguing *Dasein*. Anxiety is thus reduced to the state-of-mind in which I perceive myself and my possibilities. Although Heidegger succeeds completely in working out the connection between self-anxiety and world anxiety, the price he pays is that corporeality and thus also the dialectic of anxiety are removed from his field of vision.

Like Heidegger, Tillich also "ontologizes" anxiety. A person experiences anxiety in the face of nonbeing. That in the face of which one has anxiety is for Tillich thus nothingness as negation of being. As the negation of being, this nothingness is ontologically inferior to being.[165] If nonbeing is dependent on the being it negates, then this is also true with respect to human existence threatened by it. "The character of the negation of being is determined by that in being which is negated. This makes it possible to speak of qualities of nonbeing and, consequently, of types of anxiety."[166] Tillich discovers three types of anxiety "according to the three directions in which nonbeing threatens being. Nonbeing threatens man's ontic self-affirmation, relatively in terms of fate, absolutely in terms of death. It threatens man's spiritual self-affirmation, relatively in terms of emptiness, absolutely in terms of meaninglessness. It threatens man's moral self-affirmation, relatively in terms of guilt, absolutely in terms of condemnation."[167] Accordingly, Tillich distinguishes the anxiety of fate and of death from the anxiety of emptiness and meaninglessness and the anxiety of guilt and condemnation.[168]

As anxiety before the threefold threat of nothingness, the disposition Tillich describes is world anxiety. It is anxiety in the face of the world and about the self. As anxiety before death, this world anxiety corresponds to what Jaspers called anxiety for existence.[169] In Tillich's explications, anxiety of guilt and condemnation, in the sense of anxiety in the face of myself, is distinguished as genuine self-anxiety over against this world anxiety in the form of the anxiety of death and anxiety of meaninglessness. In the context of anxiety of meaninglessness Tillich does point out that in the context of the death instinct a person can under certain circumstances become a danger to himself, wanting to throw away his existence because it suddenly seems meaningless to him.[170] However, only the anxiety of guilt and condemnation really constitutes genuine anxiety in the face of myself. A person experiences himself as "finite freedom," i.e., as "free within the contingencies of his finitude."[171] Within these limits imposed by finitude, a person finds himself challenged to choose himself, i.e., "to make himself what he is supposed to become, to fulfill his destiny." This decision, however, is overshadowed by "a profound ambiguity between good and evil" permeating everything a person does because "it permeates his personal being as such." The anxiety of guilt and condemnation perceives this ambiguity. "The awareness of this ambiguity is the feeling of guilt." It can intensify into "the despair of having lost our destiny."[172] The self-anxiety of condemnation corresponds thus to existential anxiety in Jaspers.[173]

For Tillich, a relationship obtains between self-anxiety and world anxiety because the anxiety of any one type inheres in the anxieties of the other types. As illustrated by Paul's assertion concerning sin as the sting of death, the anxiety of guilt can inhere in the anxiety of death, though also in the anxiety of meaninglessness. In a reverse fashion, the threat of death and destiny can strengthen the consciousness of guilt, and the collapse of all meaning can render impossible any affirmation of myself. The relationship between the forms of world anxiety and self-anxiety consists according to Tillich in mutual immanence. Yet as with Heidegger, corporeality as a dimension of self-anxiety is not included in Tillich's investigation; at most, it might be intimated behind the catchphrase "contingencies of his finitude."

We have already noted the proximity of Tillich's analysis of anxiety to Jaspers's concept of anxiety. For Jaspers, anxiety for my existence is anxiety before ontic nonbeing, and existential anxiety is fear in the face of existential nonbeing. However, unlike Tillich, Jaspers views the two forms of anxiety not as mutually immanent, but rather as "essentially different."[174] The connection between the two is a negative one. The emergence of existential anxiety suspends or annuls anxiety for my existence. The moment anxiety before existential nonbeing emerges, anxiety before ontic nonbeing disappears. "I stop worrying about my existence, stop being sensibly afraid of death, and begin to feel the crushing fear of culpably losing myself. I come to see the emptiness of being and of my being. My vital despair in the situation of having to die is no more than a parable, then, for the existential despair of being unsure of self-being."[175] In a reverse fashion, existential death, the losing of one's authentic being, first causes the anxiety for one's existence to intensify to the point of despair in face of one's unavoidable biological end.[176]

One must say that this self-anxiety, appearing in Jaspers's explications as existential anxiety, does, like that of Kierkegaard, involve a certain dialectic. Like Kierkegaard, Jaspers compares existential anxiety with dizziness:[177] "The frightened movements of dizziness and shuddering become a turning point in fear. I am aware that I can be extinguished. Anxiety is the vertigo and trepidation of freedom facing a choice."[178] Existential anxiety is dialectical insofar as a person can choose and find himself only if he accepts the risk of losing himself and engaging in existential self-destruction. Although Jaspers does not *expressis verbis* address the theme of the role of corporeality in the dizziness of anxiety as does Kierkegaard, this dimension does not appear to have gone wholly unnoticed, as shown to a certain extent by Jaspers's comparison of anxiety with the dizziness experienced on the brink of a precipice.

> Vertigo *on the brink of a precipice*—when I feel the urge to hurl myself down, and draw back, shuddering—is the parable for a destructive tendency I come across in the motion of absolute consciousness, like a seductive voice whispering in my ear that everything must go to wrack and ruin. What operates in that voice is the attraction of plunging into the dark; what marks the tendency is the aimlessness of a daring born of desperation rather than exuberance.[179]

Although he does not clarify the origin of the seductive voice and destructive tendency, the mention of the darkness does perhaps give us a clue. The power of attraction of this darkness refers back to the primal ground of being itself of which Schelling had spoken in his own time. It seems appropriate to trace this destructive potential which in anxiety pushes toward the surface of consciousness back to corporeality, or more precisely, to the unconscious and its instinct structure. In this case, the dialectic of anxiety in Jaspers would under certain circumstances correspond to that of Kierkegaard, and a certain proximity would obtain between Jaspers and both Schelling on the one hand, and Freud's psychoanalysis on the other. As a theme unto itself, it is true, corporeality is alluded to in Jaspers only in this parabolically encoded fashion.

Although one must definitely speak of a dialectic of anxiety in Jaspers, on the other hand self-anxiety and world anxiety here represent two essentially different types of anxiety. There is some question whether the anxiety of death as a source of all anxieties in the face of finite threats, as Jaspers understands it, is not better described as fear, so that one's point of departure in Jaspers would actually be an antithesis between self-*anxiety* on the one hand and world *fear* on the other. In that case, Jaspers's concept of anxiety would correspond to a certain degree to that of Sartre, who does indeed differentiate between self-*anxiety* and world *fear:* "First we must acknowledge that Kierkegaard is right; anxiety is distinguished from fear in that fear is fear of beings in the world whereas anxiety is anxiety before myself."[180] As in the case of Jaspers, so also in Sartre do world anxiety and self-anxiety mutually exclude one another. Sartre similarly explicates this negative relationship using the example of dizziness. "Vertigo announces itself through fear."[181] Such fear obtains to the extent that the precipice represents mortal danger deriving from an external source. As far as the possibilities are concerned that approach me from outside, I am completely passive, and "in so far as I am also an object in the world, subject to gravitation, they are not my possibilities."[182] The more I become aware of myself and of my own possibilities for encountering this danger, fear gives way to anxiety. My future behavior, however, is possible behavior. That is, it does not derive from the context of causality. "In this case the effect defined as my possibility *would be strictly* determined. But then it would cease to be *possible;* it would become simply 'about to happen.' "[183] In reference to the self, then, according to Sartre a qualitative distinction obtains between futurity and possibility. Anxiety constitutes the situation at the abyss because I discover my possibilities without knowing whether in the future I will indeed realize them. And this in its own turn I cannot know because I as freedom am removed from the causal nexus, and accordingly no cause can be presented from which my future acts might be derived beforehand. In a way I am simultaneously both the person I will be and yet also not that person. "Anxiety is precisely my consciousness of being my own future, in the mode of not-being."[184] Thus in Sartre's sense anxiety is anxiety before myself, anxiety in which I mistrust myself with respect to my own future behavior.

For Sartre self-anxiety appears on the one hand as anxiety in the face of the future, and on the other as anxiety in the face of the past. Sartre illustrates this anxiety using the example of the gambler who has sworn never to gamble again, and yet who at the sight of the gaming table is thrust into temptation anew.[185] Anxiety in the face of the past is the anxiety at the prospect that past possibilities will catch up with me anew in the future; or vice versa, that nothing will hinder me from abrogating former resolutions or positively accepted values. What connects anxiety in the face of the future with that in the face of the past is the "nihilating structure of temporality" of which Sartre speaks: "Consciousness confronts its past and its future as facing a self which it is in the mode of not-being."[186]

Self-anxiety in Sartre is dialectical because it can be traced back to the demonstrated dialectic structure of the temporality of our existence. Like Kierkegaard, Sartre also presents a dialectical structure of the self, though this structure applies to its temporal nature, and not to any antithesis between body and spirit. Although corporeality does occupy considerable space in Sartre's philosophy, it is significant only for fear, or more precisely, for fear before the world. In contrast, any influence of the dimension of the body on anxiety is excluded. Although Sartre does indeed point out that I am a part of the world, yet as such a thing I stand completely alien over against myself. The possibilities of this thing are according to Sartre not *my* possibilities.[187] Sartre also rejects all psychological determinism based on the structures of the unconscious. "In the latter case anxiety would come from that of which we have a presentiment, a screen deep within ourselves for monstrous motives which would suddenly release guilty acts. But in this case we should suddenly appear to ourselves as *things in the world;* we should be to ourselves our own transcendent situation. Then anxiety would disappear to give way to *fear.*"[188] The body is thus not something belonging to existence, or something oppressing existence, but is rather something alien and purely contingent that cannot be mediated with existence. With directness inconceivable for Kierkegaard, one can only say the following: I am my body, whereby in this case I become a mere thing.[189]

Although Sartre deviates at this point from Kierkegaard, on the whole he stands considerably closer to Kierkegaard's interpretation of anxiety than to that of Heidegger. Nonetheless, Sartre asserts that Heidegger's and Kierkegaard's descriptions of anxiety, instead of contradicting one another, actually mutually contain one another. According to Sartre's understanding, Kierkegaard characterizes anxiety as anxiety in the face of freedom, Heidegger as the apprehension of nothingness.[190] Evidence that Heidegger's and Kierkegaard's concepts of anxiety mutually imply one another appears for Sartre to be provided by his own demonstration that the nihilating structure of temporality is constitutive for freedom. It is true, the nothingness which in Sartre separates me from my future or past corresponds precisely to the moment in Kierkegaard's dialectic of time and eternity,[191] but not to the nothing in *Being and Time* which for Heidegger is nothing other than the world as such. Heidegger's and Kierkegaard's respective concepts of nothingness, however, cannot be simply reckoned together with no further elaboration. Considering in any case the additional, in part serious, differences between their two descriptions of anxiety, one must remain skeptical over against any synthesis of these two concepts of anxiety.

The dialectic of anxiety before the future and before the past in Sartre finds its correspondence in the dialectic of time and eternity in Kierkegaard.[192] Kierkegaard describes existence as a dialectical relationship of the self in the sense of a synthesis of the temporal and the eternal.[193] The purely temporal and the eternal, which initially exist unmediated next to one another, are mediated in the moment. "The moment is that ambiguity in which time and eternity touch each other, and with this the concept of *temporality* is posited."[194] In other words, the dialectical structure of existence itself is temporality, in which the division of time into present, past, and future is grounded. Here one is reminded of Heidegger's concept of the ecstasies of temporality. In a fashion different from that of Sartre later, Kierkegaard now traces the dialectical structure of temporality back to the existential dialectic of body, psyche, and spirit. "The synthesis of the temporal and the eternal is not another synthesis but is the expression of the first synthesis, according to which man is a synthesis of psyche and body sustained by spirit."[195] Thus Kierkegaard describes the dialectical structure of existence in a twofold fashion without allowing us to equate the two formulations of the synthesis.[196] Rather, temporality, the temporal synthesis of existence, emerges from the antithesis between body and spirit.[197]

Kierkegaard develops his concept of the synthesis of body, spirit, and psyche (soul) by offering a somewhat willful interpretation of the Old Testament story of the Fall (Gen. 3). The Fall is preceded by a state of innocence in which the human being constitutes a unity of the psychical and the physical. In innocence, although the spirit is already present as that which grounds the synthesis between the body and soul, it is only present as dreaming.[198] The spirit posits itself—and thus also the synthesis between body and soul—by pervading these two differentiatingly,[199] i.e., by negating the state of the union of soul and body. Even the dreaming spirit in the state of innocence is according to Kierkegaard "in a sense a hostile power, for it constantly disturbs the relation between soul and body," though on the other hand it is also a friendly power, since it is precisely that which constitutes the relation between body and soul in the first place.[200] By positing itself, and for Kierkegaard that means through the fall into sin, the spirit takes the place formerly occupied by the soul in the state of dreaming innocence. Only through this process does a person's body become a truly human body, but that means, however, a sexually determined body fixed in its sex as either female or male.[201] From now on, however, the spirit is oppressed by precisely this body which it posits as real for the first time by pervading the synthesis of body and soul differentiatingly. This synthesis is created as a contradiction consisting in the fact that a complete, perfect spirit has neither sexuality nor a history, though in the synthesis represented by the existing person this spirit is bound to the sexuality and resulting history of the body.[202]

With profound horror at the "discrepancy of intellectuality and sexuality," Kierkegaard, as W. Schulz remarks, "outlines thematically the possibilities of the modern form of the 'unhappy consciousness,' and does so concretely even to the point of providing details."[203] The dialectic of anxiety emerges for Kierkegaard from within this discrepancy. On the basis of the negative dialectic of his structure of existence, the human being's relationship to the world as well as to himself is characterized by an element of profound insecurity. The human being shudders upon realizing that he can depend neither on the world nor on himself.

> Human structure is fundamentally absurd. I as a body am part of the world, or more precisely of the natural world, and am so in a quite concrete sense, since as a sexual body I am involved in the existence and continuation of this world; and as spirit I simultaneously transcend the world. I cannot undo this contradiction, and that means that I must suffer from it. The human being is not only

> damned to anxiety, but also obligated, for only in anxiety does a person experience and confirm his own absurd structure of being. Thus the wound of negativity is to be kept open.[204]

The question does, to be sure, arise for us whether human self-consciousness must necessarily be unhappy. For Kierkegaard's thesis is based, as W. Schulz points out, on the dogma deriving from the metaphysical tradition according to which absolute priority is to be given to our spirit and faculty of reason.[205] One must thus ask critically whether the metaphysical postulate of the independent, pure spirit can be maintained at all. All the same, Kierkegaard's insight retains its validity that the human being is a dialectical unity of body, soul, and spirit of which we become aware in anxiety.

The various questions raised both at the beginning as well as during the course of this chapter have found a certain measure of clarification. Anxiety, we found, is the discovery of the future. The future itself, however, opens up before us as the space of freedom. Within anxiety the future illuminates that which has become, and illuminates it in its movement and communicative encounter. In anxiety we discover ourselves and the world as positioned in possibility. One particular characteristic of anxiety as the discovery of the future is the peculiar dialectic of yearning and dread, the dialectic of shuddering and of dizziness. This dialectic can be traced back to the structure of our existence, a tension-filled synthesis between the physical-psychical and the spiritual. Because of the particular structure of our existence, this emerging future, disclosing itself before us only in the completion or fulfillment of our own existence, also appears in a kind of twilight. That is, its effect on us is at once both liberating and threatening, dangerous as well as threatened. What is perceived only dialectically in this way, however, is not something objective, but rather a nothing that renders possible Being-in-the-world as something equally lacking the qualities of an object. For just this reason anxiety has no object. The result of that particular dialectical structure of our existence, however, is that there is anxiety not only as world anxiety but also as self-anxiety. An inner connection obtains between the two basic forms because the self-world relationship, as a result of the dialectic of body and spirit, goes straight through each of us. Securely connected in this fashion, self-anxiety and world anxiety are the basic forms of anxiety.

5. Anxiety, Fear, and Hope

Anxiety discovers the future. Yet the future is open. Must one not for that very reason argue against the assertion that anxiety alone discloses the future? Does not the future also give one just as much occasion for hope? Does not hope, in addition to anxiety, also give us access to the future? Is hope not a fundamental experience of equal rank with anxiety, or even of higher rank? "Does not all of being," M. Wandruszka asks, "hope just as profoundly as it is anxious? . . . Without hope there is no anxiety. In the total hopelessness of ultimate despair, anxiety, too, is extinguished."[206] And W. Jens assures us that "a person is just as inhuman in having no anxiety as in having no hope."[207]

Similarly directed toward the future, anxiety and hope seem to be mutually interrelated.[208] It seems the two must either exist together or perish. Or, as K. Schwarzwäller summarizes: "Anxiety is the stimulus of hope."[209] Thus not just anxiety alone, but rather anxiety and hope as two sides of the same coin would in their correlation be the discovery of the future. In any event, J. Moltmann is of this persuasion: "Anxiety and hope seem to me to be the two sides of our experience of freedom."[210] For just this reason Moltmann considers both Kierkegaard's concept of anxiety and Bloch's principle of hope to be capable of mutually complementing one another. What allegedly connects Kierkegaard's anxiety and Bloch's hope is "a sensibility for *the possible*,"[211] whose ambiguity is constituted by the juxtaposition of anxiety and hope.

We need to examine the possibility of such a mediation of the positions of Bloch and Kierkegaard. According to Bloch's understanding, all anticipations of the future have the character of a wish. Thus he raises philosophical objections against Heidegger's analysis of existence because "here then from the mood, because it announces itself solely as a mood of expiring life, i.e., here: of a declining class, the wishful character is completely missing, without which even this diffuseness of emotions" discerned by Heidegger, "as one of *emotions*, cannot exist; unless, as Heidegger must himself say, it is 'moodlessness.' "[212] Bloch points out that anxiety, too, looks to the future quite in the fashion of a wish, albeit as an "unwish." Oriented toward the future in this way, it stands alongside hope, which itself inclines in the fashion of a wish toward possibility. For Bloch, both anxiety and hope belong to the "expectant emotions," constituting a category next to the "filled emotions."[213] The expectant emotions, such as anxiety, fear, hope, and belief, are distinguished from the filled emotions, such as envy, greed, or admiration, "by the *incomparably greater anticipatory character* in their intention, their substance, and their object."[214] As already for Heidegger, so also for Bloch the future is the primary phenomenon of temporality.[215] All emotions refer to the future as the genuinely temporal aspect in time, "but whereas the filled emotions only have an unreal future, i.e. one in which objectively nothing new happens, the expectant emotions imply a real future; in fact that of the Not-Yet, of what has objectively not yet been there."[216] All emotions, though especially the expectant emotions, refer to the horizon of time. For Bloch, this horizon coincides with the mode of the future. It is the utopian Omega of a salvific conclusion to the history of that Not-yet to which the expectant emotions wholly open themselves. This is why ultimately hope receives priority among all the emotions even though in the face of the yet undecided future both hope and anxiety can occasionally become equally powerful.

> For the negative expectant emotions of anxiety and fear are still completely suffering, oppressed, unfree, no matter how strongly they reject. Indeed, something of the extinction of self announces itself in them, and something of the nothingness in which ultimately the merely passive passion streams. Hope, this expectant counter-emotion against anxiety and fear, *is there the most human of all mental feelings and only accessible to men, and it also refers to the farthest and brightest horizon.*[217]

Bloch conceives anxiety as the emotion of the unwish, i.e., as the negation of hope, or vice versa—as we just saw—hope as the negation of anxiety. Here an interesting parallel with Heidegger emerges. Whenever Heidegger occasionally speaks of hope, he describes it as a derivative mood running counter to anxiety and fear. "To say that hope *brings alleviation* from depressing misgivings, means merely that even hope, as a state-of-mind, is still related to our burdens, and related in the mode of *Being*-as-having been. Such a mood of elation—or better, one which elates—is ontologically possible only if Dasein has an ecstatico-temporal relation to the thrown ground of itself."[218] All the same, there can be no talk of any equal ranking of anxiety and hope with respect to the disclosure of the future in Heidegger, just as although the necessity of an existential analysis of hope and other emotions is acknowledged in *Being and Time*, such is never undertaken.[219]

Bloch grounds his doctrine of the emotions in his own theory and psychology of instinctual drives as well as in a corresponding ontology. For him, anxiety and hope are related in the manner of pleasure and unpleasure. However, the fact that hope ultimately must maintain the upper hand in the conflict between the emotions derives from the inherent structure of instincts and in the final analysis from the ontological disposition of human being and world. That which drives human beings and to which the various human drives can be traced back is the *appetitus*, the hunger or also drive for self-preservation. Hunger "is the self-preservation drive, it alone might be so fundamental—no matter what changes occur—as to set all the other drives in motion in the first place."[220] This hunger seeks satiation. It is the feeling of lack that must be addressed. A *negativum* manifests itself in lack, the Not of the Not-yet which demands fulfillment and overcoming. "Not having, lack, is thus the first *mediated* emptiness of Now and Not. With hungering as the first designated sign of Not, with questioning as the first designated appearance of X, of the riddle, of the knot in the Not which it cannot stand."[221] Although human hunger seeks satiation, it is insatiable. The stomach is only "the first lamp into which oil must be poured."[222] Physical hunger is merely the first manifestation of that *appetitus* in human beings. A certain urge is at work in hunger. "The urging expresses itself *first* as 'striving,' craving to go anywhere. When the striving is *felt*, it becomes 'longing,' the only honest state in all men."[223] The appropriately human expression of this longing, however, is hope. Yet hope, and the *appetitus* underlying it, find their corollary in the Aristotelian notion of matter as the substratum of a world dialectically stretching itself out processively toward an *ultimum* and *optimum*. Just as in the human being, however, so also in the world itself as wholly unfinished a powerful longing is at work. Bloch expressly refers to the Aristotelian definition of matter, which has come to him by way of left-of-center Aristotelianism.[224] Matter is "not only *kata to dynaton*, according to possibility, and therefore the respectively conditioning element according to the given measure of the Possible, but it is *to dynamei on*, *What-is in possibility*, there the—in Aristotle admittedly still passive—*womb of fertility from which all world-forms inexhaustibly* emerge."[225] It is "the substratum of possibility within the dialectical process."[226] This *appetitus* driving hope thus corresponds to Aristotelian entelechy.

This notion of longing as the driving force of human life and of the world process connects Bloch not only with Aristotelianism but also with German Idealism. Let us first recall Schelling. In his own work on human freedom Schelling emphasizes the necessity of developing a philosophy of nature. Only within that framework can the problem of freedom be addressed adequately.[227] Nature, however, is traced back to the ground of God, a ground that is God himself. God is the ground of his own existence, a ground that is at the same time separate from God. "He is *nature*—in God; a being inseparable and yet different from him."[228] Nature, things for which only the concept of becoming is adequate, have their ground in "that which in God is *not God himself* . . . i.e., in that which is the ground of his existence. If we wish to make this being more humanly understandable, then we might refer to it as the yearning which the eternally One experiences to beget itself." This longing is will, a will of the understanding, namely, its longing and desire; "not a conscious, but rather an intimating will whose intimation is the understanding."[229] "As the yet dark ground" it represents "the first stirrings of divine existence."[230] Insofar, however, as that longing strives "to maintain the view of life inherent within itself and to close itself off within itself, so that a ground may always remain,"[231] it is "simple passion or desire, i.e., blind will."[232] Such will is an individual will or also a "particular will" over against the "universal will." This emergence of the particular will, however, is for Schelling the evil that is in conflict with the spirit.

In God two principles inhere unseparated which in human beings can be sundered: "The beginning of creation is the yearning of the One to beget itself, or the will of the ground. The second is the will of love, through which the word is uttered into nature and first makes itself personal through God."[233] Only through the disunion of the two can the revelation of God come about in the world. In order to render possible its own revelation, God's will to revelation must call forth the particular will and the antithesis. Placed before the free choice between good and evil, the human being, driven by the temptation to evil and yet free, chooses evil with the freedom of necessity that cannot be contradicted, evil that reverses the relationship of the undivided principles in God.

> The anxiety of life itself drives human beings away from the center into which they were created; for this center, as the purest essence of all will, is for every particular will a consuming fire; in order to live within it, a person must die to all individuality, which is why it is an almost necessary attempt to step out of this into the periphery in order to seek there a measure of peace for one's selfhood. Hence the universal necessity of sin and of death as the actual dying off of individuality, a dying off through which all human will must go as through a fire, in order to be cleansed.[234]

Necessity must be attributed to evil and to sin if the process directed toward the revelation of the divine spirit is to be completed. And yet according to Schelling the choice of evil remains a person's own, free act. Even the unconscious and irresistible inclination to evil is already characterized as the "*actus* of freedom."[235] Without following Schelling's explications here in detail, we should bear in mind that the world process is set into motion and maintained by striving or longing, and then passes through a stage of alienation from its origin in order in the end to attain completion in the revelation of God.

For Hegel, too, the emergence of evil seems to be a necessary transition stage of the world process. Hegel interprets the biblical Fall narrative commensurate with his own philosophy of the developing spirit that comes to itself. Hegel rejects the understanding of many representatives of the Enlightenment according to which the condition of primitive peoples, comparable to that of the innocence of childhood, is allegedly a condition of paradisiacal perfection, since in such a condition nature and the human spirit are not sundered. "The truth is that original natural unity in its form as existence is not a state of innocence, but rather of barbarism, of passion, of savagery or wildness, in fact."[236] What the biblical story of the Fall actually portrays in mythical form is "the everlasting necessary history of mankind."[237] The human being is predestined to be spirit. It is the spirit itself, however, that presses into the disunion with nature and then just as quickly reconciles with it, coming only through this dialectical mediation to itself. "We may therefore say that it is the everlasting history of the freedom of man that he should come out of this state of dullness or torpor in which he is in his earliest years; that he should come, in fact, to the light of consciousness; or to put it more precisely, that both good and evil should exist for him."[238] If paradise symbolizes the condition of the immediate unity of spirit and nature, then the loss of this immediacy "must rather be considered as a divine necessity."[239] "The relationship [of man to nature] in which man is a natural essence and behaves as such, is one that ought not to be. Spirit is to be free and is to be what it is through itself."[240]

Kierkegaard deals critically with both Schelling's and Hegel's interpretation of the Fall. Although we cannot undertake such here, a comparison of the specifics of Kierkegaard's interpretation of Gen. 3 with those of Schelling and Hegel would be highly informative. Like Schelling, Kierkegaard deals with the myth of the Fall in a treatise on freedom. Kierkegaard's *Concept of Anxiety* is a counterpart to Schelling's investigation *On the Nature of Human Freedom*, dealing with the nature, loss, and reattainment of human freedom. Kierkegaard shares the conviction of Idealism that the human being is predestined to be spirit. And for him, too, the human process of becoming human, the positing of the spirit, is equated with the Fall. Kierkegaard, however, is most concerned with excluding a rational explanation of sin. Sin remains inexplicable. For Kierkegaard the entire content of the biblical myth of the Fall is concentrated in the one sentence: "*Sin came into the world by a sin.*"[241] Thus the leap from innocence into guilt is excluded from every reasonable explanation. It neither occurs with necessity in the sense of Hegel's philosophy, nor can it be traced back to the power of longing or in the sense of the ecclesiastical tradition to the impulses of the desires, "concupiscence." As Schelling already in his treatise on freedom, so also does Kierkegaard describe the condition preceding the Fall as dizziness and anxiety. This anxiety, however, remains completely ambiguous and is unable to explain the Fall, whereas in contrast Schelling seems to imply that it does when he asserts that the anxiety of life drives a person almost with necessity away from the center of being to the periphery. In anxiety there is no irresistible inclination to evil at work whose superior power might explain sin causally. For Kierkegaard, the place of undialectical longing is taken by anxiety which is ambiguous because it is dialectical. "One easily sees, I think, that this is a psychological determination in a sense entirely different from the *concupiscentia.*"[242]

In comparison, anxiety in Bloch's understanding is not only completely undialectical, it also coincides with fear as the emotion of the unwish. Compared with Kierkegaard's analysis of anxiety and its dialectic of existence—itself doubtless yet dependent on the thinking of Idealism—Bloch's ontology of Not-yet-being constitutes a regression back to German Idealism, though we cannot in the present context explicate the specifics of Bloch's relationship to either Hegel or Schelling. Bloch's anxiety, as an undialectical, negatively charged emotion, moves together with hope, as its positively charged counteremotion, on a different plane from the anxiety disclosed by Kierkegaard. What Bloch has in mind is the mutual relationship between fear and hope. As little as his classification of expectant emotions is able to refute Heidegger's insight into the disclosure of *Dasein* alone through anxiety, just as little are Bloch's philosophy of hope and Kierkegaard's phenomenology of anxiety capable of mutually complementing one another.

Nonetheless, an inner connection obtains between anxiety, fear, and hope. Fear, as we saw, is the discernment or perception of threat. In contrast, hope perceives what aids and benefits. Whereas in Kierkegaard's sense anxiety can be described as antipathetic sympathy and sympathetic antipathy, fear behaves antipathetically, and hope sympathetically. Fear and hope emerge, one might conclude, when dialectical anxiety becomes undialectical. It then dissociates into positively or negatively directed emotions. Hence anxiety is the condition enabling fear and hope to arise. Both have their ground in anxiety. Fear and hope, as emotions of expectation, are not only directed toward objects, they also fill out the empty space of the future with finite expectations and ideal images. Not only do we construct images of ourselves and the world, we also imagine the future itself. These expectations are images the ego outlines of itself and its world in the future. They are fear or hope that has been molded and shaped. In the future discovered by anxiety, "in possibility all things are equally possible, and whoever has truly been brought up by possibility has grasped the terrible as well as the joyful."[243] In an undialectical manner fear grasps the terrible, hope the joyful.

In the space of the future, hope and fear can thus be the advance guard preceding us before we finally enter the space of freedom and grasp possibility in action. They are ambivalent, however, insofar as they are able to hinder us from engaging in the future. "In possibility everything is possible. For this reason, it is possible to become lost in possibility in all sorts of ways, but primarily in two. The one takes the form of desiring, craving; the other takes the form of the melancholy-imaginary (hope/fear or anxiety)."[244] Hope can *entice* us to decision. Just as easily, however, it can hinder the ego in that final decision in which it might completely enter into the future; it constitutes such a hindrance by viewing the future as an experimental field without any binding force. (In such hope gone astray, hidden fear can even be at work: the fear of obligation.) Fear in its own turn can *drive* a person into decision, though it can just as easily hobble a person by perceiving the free space as a naked abyss. (Hence incapacitating fear can be nourished by the secret hope of rescuing the ego through just such abiding immobility.)

Although both hope and fear can *lead* us to decision, they cannot make the decision for us. Although we might be transported by hope or driven by fear, the decision with which we enter the future remains an underivable act of freedom. In the end, however, such an act needs neither hope nor fear, but rather courage. Courage is the emotion of acting freedom discovered in anxiety. Courage, not hope, is what overcomes anxiety. We must undertake a thorough investigation into how courage is able to overcome anxiety and what its ground is.

3

WORLD ANXIETY AND THE END OF THE WORLD

> . . . that deep-seated world anxiety, the concern that large parts of our world will perish and that there will be no future . . .
> —*Horst-Eberhard Richter*

> Everything that lives both affirms and negates itself to the point of frenzy.
> —*E. M. Cioran*

1. Apocalyptic Anxiety

The apocalyptist is anxious. His anxiety discloses to him both the world and his own existence. As just this sort of original disclosure of world and existence, however, the apocalyptist's anxiety is to be distinguished from the attempt to come to terms with existence in the form of apocalyptic itself. By apocalyptic we understand that particular complex of notions and ideas which attempts to deal with a specific kind of anxiety which we can call apocalyptic anxiety. In other words, apocalyptic refers to that particular interpretation of our existence that claims to overcome apocalyptic anxiety. Apocalyptic anxiety is a specific configuration of world anxiety and self-anxiety manifesting itself in the expectation of the end of the world. Our present task is thus to discover the connection between the idea of an end of the world on the one hand, and anxiety as a disclosure of existence on the other.

As we saw in the previous chapter, anxiety is the discovery of the future and thus simultaneously the disclosure of world and self. In the leeway or open space of the future—as we called the discovery of anxiety—the appearance of the world, I, thou, and we is such that these are discovered to be temporal. Their temporality, however, is finitude. Just as we say that anxiety discovers the future, so with the same justification can we assert that anxiety is the discovery of finitude. This is the sense of P. Tillich's assertion that "anxiety is finitude, experienced as one's own finitude."[1]

Tillich defines finitude as being which is limited by nonbeing. "Being, limited by nonbeing, is finitude. Nonbeing appears as the 'not yet' of being and as the 'no more' of being. It confronts that which is with a definite end (*finis*)."[2] Thus anxiety discloses existence as threatened by the possibility of nonbeing. It evokes the possibility of death.

The experience of finitude, however, does not imply any intuitive knowledge of death, as has been variously postulated by M. Scheler or M. Heidegger. From the discovery of the possibility of our nonbeing there does not follow any certainty regarding the necessity of one's own death, but rather only the realization that we do not exist of necessity. Neither Scheler nor Heidegger has been able to make such intuitive certainty of death philosophically persuasive. Hence Heidegger's notion of an anticipation of death is problematical because he views *Dasein* as determined by the certainty of one's own death. "As long as Dasein is, there is in every case something still outstanding, which Dasein can be and will be. But to that which is thus outstanding, the 'end' itself belongs. The 'end' of Being-in-the-world is death."[3] A precise analysis shows that it remains an open question just how from the experience of finitude in the sense of merely possible nonbeing there should emerge the certainty of one's own end as a reality that will occur with absolute certainty in the future.[4]

Precisely this question, however, brings us to the phenomenon of apocalyptic anxiety. Although not every perception of finitude can be called apocalyptic anxiety, such a perception does doubtless occur as an independent phenomenon. Anxiety becomes apocalyptic precisely when the certainty of one's own end is derived from the experience of finitude. *Apocalyptic anxiety, so our thesis, is the perception of finitude as inescapability, as a situation from which there is no way out.* To that extent Heidegger's analysis of death can be interpreted as an individualization of what is sooner collective apocalyptic anxiety, an individualization in which individual death takes the place of the end of the world.[5]

Many justifiably refer to apocalyptic as a crisis phenomenon. The crisis of apocalyptic, however, does not consist simply in catastrophic social or political circumstances, though on the other hand it should not be evaluated disengaged from the temporal circumstances in which it is imbedded. The real crisis of apocalyptic consists rather in the anxiously perceived inescapability of Being-in-the-world, one resulting in a profound sense of powerlessness. Precisely because there appears to be no way out of finitude, apocalyptic anxiety precipitates enormous feelings of powerlessness. The experience of apocalyptic anxiety is one of powerlessness.

The thesis that apocalyptic anxiety is the hermeneutical key to apocalyptic thus does not assert that apocalyptic is attempting to overcome general, purely atemporal world anxiety, a kind of anxiety of being or existence in and for itself. Of course, this thesis equally contradicts any interpretation that understands apocalyptic merely as the reflex to social or political repression. Rather, apocalyptic takes us back to a specific form of world anxiety, namely, to its most extreme form. To this form of world anxiety the future as the space of freedom appears hopeless because the world provides no way out for existence. This does not assert that in the case of apocalyptic anxiety the future and finitude do in fact offer no way out. What is decisive, rather, is that in the mood of apocalyptic anxiety they seem to offer no way out. Although we do reject precipitate sociological or sociohistorical interpretations of apocalyptic, this does not mean that apocalyptic takes us into the realm of pure inwardness. It is not some timeless *memento mori*. Apocalyptic anxiety and its corresponding powerlessness do indeed have points of contact with the cultural, political, and social circumstances of the time. The world and the self disclosed by anxiety in the light of the future do not simply appear in and for themselves, but rather always as already formed in a certain way and mediated by the concrete corporeality and historical circumstances in which we live. It would, however, be utterly false to conclude that apocalyptic anxiety results from a rational analysis of historical circumstances, one that comes in some quasi-objective manner to the conclusion that present circumstances are so inescapable that for quite cogent reasons it seems reasonable to be plagued by anxiety. Quite the reverse, it is rather apocalyptic anxiety itself that with immediate access allows the future and thus also the world to appear completely lacking any way out. Thus a mutual relationship obtains between the anxious person and his world. Apocalyptic anxiety does not emerge within an individual completely disengaged from external circumstances that can be described sociologically. It is able to emerge, however, only on the basis of the possibility inherent in existence of considering Being-in-the-world as such to be completely hopeless and without prospect. It is thus the possibility of anxiety itself, given with the general disposition of our existence as described in the previous chapter, that makes possible this kind of disclosure of circumstances, which are described in a thoroughly rational manner as threatening or repressive, such that these circumstances seem to us utterly inescapable.

Representatives of analytical psychology have demonstrated that such world anxiety can intensify into apocalyptic anxiety. To the structure of Being-in-the-world disclosed by apocalyptic anxiety we can apply the phrase "dead-end world structure" coined by C. Kulenkampff in connection with schizophrenics' experiences of the end of the world.[6] A person arrives at a dead end because the world as the horizon of the future shows itself to be closed off and repulsing at every point. It does not yield, as it were, when we try to utilize the leeway the future opens up to us for intervening formatively in the world. The future, as the space of freedom moving along with us, threatens to get lost because the world does not yield to our movement toward that future. In this way a person loses mobility and falls instead under the power of his repulsing environment.

The result of this kind of dead-end world structure is the loss of what Kulenkampff calls "resistance."

> A person *stands* in a world, and depending on the manner of that standing, and on his and thus also the world's movement into that position, that world appears differently, develops itself differently, and thus represents itself differently. In the midst of overwhelming physiognomies, then, our position, our standing, as one of in-sight and in-spection essentially has the character of resistance, of standing against. This means that the situation within physiognomic space is essentially pathic as far as the subject is concerned. That subject must resist (stand against) in order to endure at all (to continue to stand). As a condition of *remaining* standing, the movement of the subject within this space is also essentially pathic. Because the subject loses itself, exposes itself, and gives itself up and

> surrenders itself, it is in a peculiar sort of entwinement simultaneously both activity and pathic passivity.[7]

Kulenkampff's train of thought here can easily be continued with respect to apocalyptic anxiety. When the energy for "resistance" dissipates, we are overcome by powerlessness or weakness. Apocalyptic thinking is sated with such experiences of powerlessness. We advisedly refer to the fundamental experience of apocalyptic as an experience of powerlessness, and not, for example, as one of repression. For as we saw in the first chapter, we encounter apocalyptic by no means only in the lower social classes; apocalyptic anxiety is by no means the fundamental mood of the underprivileged in times of societal and political crises. Neither do experiences of powerlessness result only from radical changes of a political nature. They can arise just as well in confrontation with aspects of nature which prove to be overwhelmingly powerful. Neither does the apocalyptic experience of powerlessness limit itself to specific areas of life or of societal circumstances; rather, it is able to convulse the entire existence of the person seized by apocalyptic anxiety. At the same time, however, this experience of powerlessness does not occur beyond political and societal circumstances, but is rather the experience of powerlessness over against the historically concrete world inclusive of its societal and political power relationships. Apocalyptic powerlessness as an all-encompassing experience of existence includes the experience of political and societal powerlessness, since the world disclosed by anxiety is always also a politically formed or no longer formable world. Not being limited to the political realm, however, apocalyptic powerlessness means the loss of any possibility of having a formative impact on the world, and that means the loss of all communicative encounter with the world in the larger sense.

Finally, the mood of apocalyptic anxiety releases the expectation of the end of the world, an expectation that as a result of this profound powerlessness intensifies into certainty. The psychological analysis of existence makes an important contribution to the understanding of such an anticipation of the end of the world as well. Taking Heidegger's treatment of "violence" as the point of departure, C. Kulenkampff has illuminated psychotic experiences of the end of the world as necessary manifestations resulting from radical powerlessness. In his *Introduction to Metaphysics*, Heidegger describes the human being as a violent creature. As *to deinotaton*, the most powerful being, the human being asserts itself over against the overwhelming unhomely, unnerving element, as Heidegger calls it, which does not allow us to feel at home. "But man is the strangest of all . . . because he departs from his customary, familiar limits, because he is the violent one, who, tending toward the strange in the sense of the overpowering, surpasses the limit of the familiar <das Heimische>."[8] From this perspective Heidegger describes what he calls human violence: "Man is the violent one, not aside from and along with other attributes but solely in the sense that in his fundamental violence <Gewalt-tätigkeit> he uses power <Gewalt> against the overpowering <Überwältigende>."[9] With respect to psychotic experiences of the end of the world, Kulenkampff now explains:

> *No longer capable of being "violent" means being overwhelmed oneself.* In other words: From every quarter the fullness of physiognomic phenomena overruns "fallen" existence, which is now defenselessly exposed to the onslaught. This process of *being overpowered* is also decisively facilitated by the fact that the loss of oversight and in-sight necessarily accompanying one's loss of position or footing removes from existence the possibility of further trusting things, of making the physiognomic world, as the accustomed world, habitable and stable: Not only the ubiquitous superiority and inescapable onslaught of physiognomies casts the overwhelmed person to the ground, filling him with anxiety, but also their impenetrability, their puzzling character. The impossibility of getting to the real essence of things deters any stabilization of physiognomic space as such, and any possibility of gaining a foothold within that space. The world thus flooded by physiognomies shows itself in all its ambiguity and fluctuating, unfathomable character, i.e., in all its bottomlessness.[10]

Kulenkampff's psychological interpretation of experiences of the end of the world with the aid of existence-analytical categories derives from pathological cases in which patients believe they are now experiencing or even have already experienced the end of the world. In contrast, the apocalyptist anticipates the end of the world as an event that is yet outstanding. This distinguishes him from the schizophrenic. Nonetheless, Kulenkampff's analysis aids our attempt to understand apocalyptic expectation of the end of the world as an expression of a specific understanding of existence. The decisive insight we gain from Kulenkampff's interpretation of psychotic cases is that notions of the end of the world result from a feeling of total powerlessness.

The connection between the experience of powerlessness and the end of the world can, it seems to me, also be demonstrated within the context of our analysis of world anxiety. My suggestion is that we try to formulate this connection in the terminology with which we have already experimented in the previous chapter. Anxiety, so one of our most important conclusions, is the discovery of the future, though at the same time the discovery of the finitude of world and self. We will call that particular anxiety apocalyptic for which finitude appears completely inescapable, offering no way out. This kind of inescapability in all areas of life, however, eliciting a feeling of complete powerlessness, radically threatens the future itself, which we have described as the space of freedom without which the human being is unable to exist. The self and the world, in their own turn, endure only as long as the future, the "between," remains open. In this situation offering no way out the loss of the between is the only expectation remaining for apocalyptic anxiety. *If the between disappears, then the world collapses in on me. Hence the world collapses.* The sublation of the between is the true end of the future. If, however, the world collapses in on me as soon as the future ends, then the expectation of the threatening loss of future is the same as the expectation of the end of the world, which necessarily includes the demise of the self. Thus the end of the world does not consist in the destruction of objects or of portions of the external world, as all-encompassing as such destruction may well be. This kind of external understanding of the idea of the end of the world would additionally presuppose a world concept according to which the world would actually be merely the totality of all existing individual things. In the previous chapter, however, we already saw that such an understanding of world is wholly insufficient. *Rather, the end of the world anticipated by apocalyptic consists essentially in the sublation of the between.*

This conclusion seems to have brought us to the very center of the apocalyptic understanding of existence. If apocalyptic anxiety is that mood which discovers the inescapability of finitude and thus the radical endangerment of the future, then we can define apocalyptic as that particular complex of ideas in which the expectation of the end of the world comes to expression. Accordingly, those multifarious notions of the end of the world or of portions of that world, notions we have yet to evaluate individually, are not so much futuristic prognoses for the future or prophetic pronouncements as the metaphorical expression of present experience, namely, of a present experience of the future: The future that encroaches into the present is experienced as being radically threatened.

The numerous images of the end of the world are projected into the future as the metaphorical expression of the present experience of the future, though without for that reason one being able to equate them with future reality itself. This does not mean, however, that such notions of the end of the world have no connection with our experience of reality. Rather, they employ catastrophic experiences from the realms of nature and history. The destruction of reality in the form of natural or historical catastrophes is by no means merely an arbitrary illusion, but is rather a formative factor of the experiential world. The world itself, which we always encounter only as concretely formed and historical, has acquired what is for us its perceivable form in part through catastrophes. A certain element of the catastrophic inheres within the world. Thus we can also say that apocalyptic anxiety is the perception of this catastrophic element, which then flows into its imagery of the end of the world. Nevertheless, its images of the end of the world may not be mistaken for future reality. This would amount to a misunderstanding of apocalyptic itself, a misunderstanding to which admittedly even the apocalyptists themselves not infrequently succumb. On the other hand it must be said that the end of the world as the sublation of the future is the logical expectation of anxiety intensified into totality.

2. The End of the World and World Negation

Apocalyptic not only lends expression to apocalyptic anxiety, it also attempts to overcome it. The nature of this attempt at overcoming is what concerns us now. An initial illumination is provided by the psychopathological interpretation of psychologically abnormal experiences of the end of the world as already discussed in chapter 1, section 5. As we have already seen, from the perspective of psychoanalysis various interpretations can be given to experiences of the end of the world. Common to all these interpretations, however, is that they view psychotic experiences of the end of the world as an extreme defensive reaction of the ego against what is perceived as a mortal threat. The end of the world does not itself constitute the threat, but rather a wishful fantasy with which the ego undertakes an enormous act of repression. " 'End of the world' is thus the extreme form of defense, to the point of denial: What I love and cannot attain, what I for that reason hate, and what for that reason threatens me, simply does not exist."[11] J. A. Arlow and C. Brenner discover in such fantasies of the end of the world a "projective defense of destructive wishes."[12] In other words, these fantasies of the end of the world function as world negation. The psychotic attempt at overcoming anxiety consists in world negation. G. M. Martin is correct in asserting that it is not just the manifest illusion that the end of the world has already occurred, but also the fantasies preceding that illusion that represent an attempt at solving psychological conflicts.[13] This observation seems to me to be helpful in understanding apocalyptic, which after all does not assert that the end of the world has already taken place, but rather speaks about an impending end of the world. We initially said that the end of the world as the annulment of the future is the immediate expression of world anxiety intensified into totality. To this we can now add that the verbalization of this anxiety already constitutes an initial attempt at overcoming it. Simply by giving apocalyptic anxiety a voice and rendering the end of the world in imagery, apocalyptic is already trying to overcome world anxiety. This attempt, however, like all other attempts of apocalyptic at overcoming apocalyptic anxiety, consists in *world negation.* Put succinctly, our thesis is that *apocalyptic is an attempt at overcoming total world anxiety through world negation.*

The concept of world negation is, of course, in need of some explanation. In the language of psychoanalysis one would have to address world negation as an act of repression, specified further as a defensive reaction.[14] Freud interpreted some defensive actions "analogous to flight, by means of which the ego avoids a danger threatening from without."[15] Here he is thinking especially of repression, "at bottom, an attempt at flight."[16] Freud's definitions here might suggest that the world negation of apocalyptic is also to be understood as such an attempt at flight. In this sense M. Laubscher[17] speaks of the "escapism" not only of apocalyptic, but of all those movements which W. La Barre[18] summarized some time ago under the collective term "crisis cults." "These function as an escapist valve."[19] First of all we agree with Laubscher's criticism of the concept "crisis cult," which in ethnological studies[20] is also applied to apocalyptic: "The term 'crisis cult' is imprecise, too weak, and palliative. The expression *catastrophe* suits the various situations."[21] The term "escapism," however, is probably just as questionable. We need to establish whether every form of world negation is to be interpreted as an act of flight.

In the realm of philosophy, especially Karl Jaspers addressed the phenomenon of world negation. His expositions seem to support equating world negation with escapism. According to Jaspers, there is "a most intimate nexus between religion and world denial,"[22] whereby a distinction is made between magic, superstition, and mythologies of peoples on the one hand and religion on the other. This is why Jaspers can also suggest that world negation is primarily religiously motivated. The premier example of religious world negation which Jaspers adduces, however, is not, e.g., apocalyptic, but rather "the phenomenon of total asceticism, of monasticism," appearing not only in Christianity, but equally, for example, in the Chinese and Indian sphere.[23] Jaspers traces world negation back to being seized by essential being and its absolute claims. "At the crucial point . . . denial is a *negative resolution*."[24] By "resolution" Jaspers understands first of all the self's choice of freedom. "In this choice I *resolve* to be myself in existence."[25] As a choice with unqualified existential character, this resolution is identical with self-being. "Resolution and self-being are one."[26] According to Jaspers, however, such self-being includes the capacity for communication. Only as communicative is the self really itself. Thus the resolution also aims at communication. "This resolution in choice is originally *communicative*. I choose myself as *I choose another*."[27] Every breaking off of communication thus means that the self collapses and its transcendent origin is abrogated.[28] Now, world negation is negative resolution because precisely for the sake of conscious self-choice it pushes for the breaking off of communication. "I do not identify myself with any objectivity of mundane existence, nor with any subjectivity of my merely personal existence; I do not enter into any unconditional communication. Wordlessly and uncommunicatively, relating to nothing but transcendence, I deny everything for this."[29] Jaspers interprets world negation as a paradoxical act of flight. "For objectively it is impossible to leave the world in the world. A taxing *negative existence* of Existenz—'so lost, so lonely' with a deity that will not talk to us directly after all—occurs beside the world, in which Existenz has to remain after all."[30] For Jaspers, this paradoxical character makes world negation ambivalent. It can slip into fateful entanglements. "Negative resolution is like an analogue of suicide."[31] On the other hand, properly understood it does fulfill a positive function. It is "an unceasing memento, addressed to the mundane existence of possible Existenz when its good fortune would make it self-righteous."[32]

With respect to apocalyptic, the role of communication in Jaspers's analysis of the phenomenon of world negation should be emphasized. According to Jaspers, world negation is the attempt—albeit one doomed to failure—to exist authentically without communication. As we have seen, the breaking off of communication with one's surroundings also plays a central role in pathological cases of experiences of the end of the world. Hence as a characteristic feature of world negation, the breaking off of communication or at least the tendency to do so deserves special attention. At a later point, we will investigate in detail just how apocalyptic tends toward a breaking off of communication with the seemingly inescapable and sinister world.

Jaspers's—and Laubscher's—identification of world negation with an act of flight, however, is questionable. Freud's distinction between defense and repression proves to be helpful in carrying forward our treatment of world negation. With respect to the concept of defense—a more general concept over against "repression"—Freud suggests: "We believe it may well be that there are defensive processes which can with justice be compared to an attempt at flight, while in the case of others the ego offers resistance of a far more active kind, undertaking vigorous counteractive measures."[33] Precisely in view of gnosis, which is related to apocalyptic, Hans Jonas rejected the identification of world negation with world flight, and spoke, not of an avoidance of the world in gnosis, but rather of an assault on that world.[34] Similarly, an understanding of world negation limited to asceticism, as seems to be the case with Jaspers, is also too narrow.

A thorough study of the phenomenon of world negation shows that it appears in various basic forms. Flight from the world or asceticism are not simply identical with world negation, but represent rather one possible manifestation of it. Under the rubric "flight from the world," to linger for a moment with this particular form of world negation, one can subsume not only the various forms of monastic asceticism which in part constitute a very real withdrawal from human society, as, e.g., in the case of hermits or the cenobites in the ancient church, but in a certain respect also what M. Weber described as the "inner-worldly asceticism" of Christianity, especially of Puritanism. Flight from the world, however, also doubtless includes the attempts at breaking out in the form of itinerant movements which, as we have seen, can in part also be apocalyptically motivated. The counterpart of world flight is world indulgence. World indulgence negates the world by consuming it. Here one can think not only of the extreme forms of hedonistic lifestyles but also of contemporary forms of production and economy oriented toward growth and consumption. On the other hand, I prefer to distinguish world flight from contempt or hatred of the world, which with nihilistic confidence would simply let the world go to the devil without developing any strategies for hope. World improvement can be understood as one further basic form of world negation. Whether the focus is on evolutionary or revolutionary attempts, in either case the existing world appears as one that should not be or remain thus. A final basic form of world negation is world denial. Two types can be distinguished: Acute world denial denies the material existence of the given world or asserts that a different world actually lies behind this given world. Latent world denial anticipates the sublation, removal, destruction of the world in the near or distant future, either through divine judgment or in the form of historical, global, or cosmic catastrophes.

This division of world negation into several basic forms is, as one can easily see, based on ideal types, and remains for the moment no more than a suggestion. One might suggest a different and more appropriate classification schema. It is imperative to note, however, that world negation can be not only flight but also assault. Although it can assume resigned, passive features, it can also act as a stimulant, breaking through to new possibilities for actively coming to terms with existence. Furthermore, the suggested basic forms of world negation do not mutually exclude one another, but rather can be combined. World contempt, for example, can just as easily turn into world indulgence as into ascetic world flight. By the same token, certain forms of asceticism contribute to world improvement. On the other hand, every attempt at improving the world is nourished by a utopia, an image of a world that as yet has no place in the given world. It thereby presupposes world denial such that it will, if not hate the present world, at least under certain circumstance and to a certain extent despise it. World denial may tend toward world flight and the formation of conventicles. Such conventicles, however, can be as reactionary and world-fleeing as future-oriented and avant-garde. Finally, acute world denial can lead to flight before the world in meditation or mysticism, though possibly also to libertine ethics, which throws itself into a kind of world indulgence, leaving the spiritual person, the soul, and the real world untouched while seeking to accelerate the passing of the devalued material world.

Following these distinctions by way of experiment, one might describe *apocalyptic* more specifically as essentially *world negation in the form of world denial.* If psychotic experiences of the end of the world can be described as the process of acute world denial, then apocalyptic thinking can in general be seen as a form of latent world denial. The existence of the oppressive and inescapable world and the existential experience of complete powerlessness are not denied as present reality, but on the contrary are illuminated with a crass and harsh light. What is denied is the durability of this dead-end world structure. The nonexistence of the world is displaced into the future. When the latent denial of the world disclosed by apocalyptic anxiety is radicalized, apocalyptic itself approaches acute world denial. As already seen, gnosis distinguishes itself from apocalyptic through just such radicalization. Christian apocalyptic, however, also comes close to such acute world denial insofar as it believes that the final battle between God and the hostile powers has in principle already been fought, and that this hidden reality has not yet become revealed before all the world. By remaining for the most part latent, however, the world denial of apocalyptic represents the attempt to overcome apocalyptic anxiety through world negation *without transcending present reality*, whence arises the peculiar existential tension in apocalyptic between the present experience of reality on the one hand and the desire for its annulment on the other.

This now circumscribes the center of apocalyptic thinking. As we will yet see in some detail, it can assume quite varied forms, can develop as world-fleeing or world-formative, as reactionary or revolutionary, and can gain access into the most varied forms of life. We need to make the fundamental distinction, however, between apocalyptic that simply verbalizes the end of the world, i.e., the inescapability of finitude in the sense described above, and apocalyptic that negates complete inescapability through the design or draft of a future counterworld or through some other opening to new hope, apocalyptic which to that extent moves beyond the notion of the end of the world. Drawing on more recent studies of utopian notions we will suggest distinguishing between negative and positive apocalyptic.

Such a distinction not only applies to the ensemble of various apocalyptic notions; it also is made necessary by the transformations apocalyptic anxiety itself can undergo. A look at O. Haendler's theory of anxiety is helpful at this point. Haendler distinguishes three types of anxiety: anxiety before . . . , catastrophic anxiety; anxiety in . . . , crisis anxiety; and anxiety for . . . , love anxiety.[35] In the context of apocalyptic, Haendler's description of catastrophe anxiety and crisis anxiety are of interest. The mood Haendler describes as catastrophe anxiety "is characterized by the fact that a catastrophe, i.e., an external event, is impending or is feared. The characteristic feature of the catastrophe before it actually occurs is the threat it represents, not its irrevocability."[36] In the situation of catastrophe one hopes up till the very last moment. One hopes for a way out, "but the door becomes more and more narrow. The greater the catastrophe, the closer it leads toward complete annihilation. Essentially, the catastrophe leads ultimately to an end, and then there is nothing left. If this end does not come, then the catastrophe itself as such has not completely occurred."[37]

This clearly negative tendency distinguishes catastrophe from crisis. Accordingly, catastrophe anxiety, in contrast to crisis anxiety, is condemned to complete passivity and helplessness. "Where even the tiniest bit of defense is possible, a bit of crisis enters into catastrophe, and one breathes a sigh of relief."[38] Catastrophe is in the final analysis inescapable, and delivers those affected over to utter powerlessness. "The catastrophe itself is hostile to any encouragement and contains no trace of assistance within. As soon as such is present, the catastrophe is no longer pure as such, but rather has already turned into a crisis."[39] The crisis is characterized by the fact that "one does not really know what outcome it will have."[40] The radical threat is taken very seriously indeed, but the decision regarding the outcome remains open and may even take a turn for the better and bring about something new. "The anxiety is accordingly not simply danger anxiety, but rather decision anxiety, transformation anxiety,"[41] anxiety that does not exclude action and is thus comparable to "birth anxiety."[42]

On the basis of Haendler's expositions, it seems both possible and helpful to distinguish between negative and positive apocalyptic. On the basis of our own observations we can in Haendler's sense say that apocalyptic anxiety is first of all catastrophe anxiety. Admittedly, the danger that threatens it comes not merely from external sources, as Haendler suggests in the case of catastrophe anxiety, but because of the dialectical self-relationship of our own existence also from an internal source. The tension-filled relationship between self and world, as we saw in the previous chapter, runs directly through our very being. For just this reason, not only the world as such seems sinister and uncanny to the apocalyptist, he seems equally strange to himself. Wherever catastrophe anxiety is merely verbalized, with no element of hope, we are dealing with negative apocalyptic. From this perspective, however, the essence of positive apocalyptic becomes comprehensible. Positive apocalyptic, we suspect, emerges when apocalyptic thinking is able to transform catastrophe anxiety into crisis anxiety. Just how appropriate Haendler's expression "birth anxiety" is in this context is shown by the comparison frequently made in apocalyptic between the travails of the end time on the one hand, and birth pains on the other.[43] Whereas in the case of negative apocalyptic the attempt at overcoming apocalyptic anxiety consists in its verbalization, in the case of positive apocalyptic it consists first of all in the transformation of this anxiety, by means of apocalyptic thinking, from catastrophe anxiety into crisis anxiety.

We will be able to evaluate more extensively the juxtaposition of negative and positive apocalyptic only later in our study when we look at the various forms in which apocalyptic thinking manifests itself. Only then will we also be able to determine whether apocalyptic on the whole succumbs to the danger threatening other attempts at world negation, namely, the negation of the worldly self along with the world. In that case, loss of world and loss of self emerge as the result of world negation.

First, however, let us summarize the findings of this chapter thus far. World anxiety and self-anxiety as the perception of the future are simultaneously the perception of the finitude of self and world. They can intensify into apocalyptic anxiety, which we have described as the perception of finitude as being inescapable. This anxiety discloses to us the "between," the term we have used to refer to the future, such that it appears threatened by annulment. The annulment of the between, however, has proven to be the center of the notion of the end of the world. In its own turn, this annulment does not emerge wholly without connection with experiences, but rather is itself related to experiences of catastrophe, which is why we can also evaluate apocalyptic anxiety and the resulting powerlessness as a perception of a certain catastrophic element. Apocalyptic, as that particular complex of ideas in whose center stands the expectation of the end of the world, tries to overcome apocalyptic anxiety through world negation, which we described more specifically as latent world denial. Apocalyptic can, however, be limited to taking the inescapability of finitude as a theme and verbalizing the apocalyptic feeling of powerlessness, though it can also, in the midst of utter inescapability, negate inescapability itself by opening up new hope. Negative and positive apocalyptic can be distinguished from one another accordingly.

3. Collective World Anxiety

Apocalyptists tend to form groups. Their thinking blossoms not only in sects, but repeatedly spreads in the form of mass movements. Apocalyptic is a collective phenomenon. Wherever it breaks out, apocalyptic anxiety is often shared by many people. It is collective world anxiety.

As logical as this conclusion may be, just as thoroughly does it seem to contradict our entire previous analysis. For it is widely considered a given that anxiety is never collective, but rather to the highest degree always individual. As an example, let us recall Heidegger's view of this complex. According to Heidegger, anxiety is that state-of-mind through which I break through to the authenticity of my unique existence. In a reverse fashion, he asserts: "But in anxiety there lies the possibility of a disclosure which is quite distinctive; for anxiety individualizes."[44] Hence according to Heidegger, collective anxiety is self-contradictory. Rather, collective moods belong to the realm of existential inauthenticity, to the everydayness of the "they." In Heidegger's language, the "they" is "the 'subject' of everydayness."[45] "They" live in the everyday world, which means "that the 'who' of everyday Dasein just is *not* the 'I myself.' "[46] Now, this does not exclude the possibility there is such a thing as collective moods; the subject of such moods, however, is the "they," which is why such moods cannot be anxiety. They arise rather through a "falling" into inauthenticity. What Heidegger describes as "falling" "has mostly the character of Being-lost in the publicness of the 'they.' "[47] Whenever I succumb to a collective mood, I am no longer authentic: "The dominance of the public way in which things have been interpreted has already been decisive even for the possibilities of having a mood."[48] Accordingly, one might at most say that the mood underlying apocalyptic is actually collective fear, "anxiety, fallen into the 'world,' inauthentic, and, as such, hidden from itself,"[49] but in no way anxiety in the sense discussed.

P. Tillich's treatment of this problem takes us a bit further. Tillich comes upon the question of the possibility of collective anxiety by distinguishing not only between types of anxiety but allegedly also between various "periods of anxiety."[50] Tillich's presentation goes beyond that of Heidegger insofar as it does not one-sidedly ontologize anxiety, but rather presents it within its historical context and relates the concrete manifestations of anxiety to specific sociological factors. Admittedly, Tillich, too, finds it problematical to speak of collective anxiety (or of collective courage), since he holds fast to the self as the actual locus of anxiety. Tillich has to argue against the existence of a collective subject. "Self-hood is self-centeredness. Yet there is no center in a group in the sense in which it exists in a person . . . Therefore it is neither adequate to speak of a we-self nor useful to employ the terms collective anxiety and collective courage."[51] Tillich emphasizes on the other hand that only in an encounter with other persons does an individual become a person. "His self-affirmation is a part of the self-affirmation of the social groups which constitute the society to which he belongs."[52] From this perspective it now seems justifiable, while rejecting the notion of collective anxiety in this sense, to speak instead of collective in the sense of universal anxiety. "There is no collective anxiety save an anxiety which has overtaken many or all members of a group and has been intensified or changed by becoming universal."[53] In this sense, according to Tillich, collective or universal anxiety is a crisis symptom inseparable from social and political circumstances. "The anxiety which, in its different forms, is potentially present in every individual becomes general if the accustomed structures of meaning, power[!], belief, and order disintegrate."[54]

Tillich's exposition is extremely revealing with respect to apocalyptic, a topic he does not discuss more specifically. Picking up Tillich's more specific definitions, one can say of apocalyptic anxiety that it is collective or universal anxiety. Though it is not the anxiety of Heidegger's "they" or of some collective subject of a given group, it is nonetheless genuine anxiety; it can arise first of all in an individual, then in times of crisis can seize many people, become modified thereby, and increase in intensity.

As an expression of the *Zeitgeist*, apocalyptic can, to use Heidegger's words, degenerate into "idle talk," which as an external factor determines the feelings and thoughts of the individual. On the other hand, it constantly threatens to immunize itself over against the world in elite conventicles. The danger of "ghettoization," as H. E. Richter has doubtless ascertained with justifiable concern, also exists regarding the contemporary psycho-scene in which people today try to formulate and overcome their apocalyptic anxiety.[55] It can also, however, portend crisis developments already being anxiously perceived by sensitive individuals, while others yet linger in what they believe to be complete security. The apocalyptist senses the very first, faintest vibrations of approaching convulsions under which the world threatens to collapse, and does so long before the catastrophe becomes a common topic of discussion. Apocalyptic anxiety shows itself not least in this sense to be genuine anxiety insofar as it initially drives the apocalyptist very much into an isolated state, since his own understanding of existence so contradicts the predominating view of the world. In his powerlessness he poses the question of power, becoming thereby an uncomfortable contemporary. And even when this anxiety is no longer limited to the individual, it usually affects only a minority. The host of apocalyptists remains small. Yet precisely in this minority a kind of thinking can grow whose message is understood when the catastrophic element can no longer be denied and apocalyptic anxiety becomes truly collective.

4

NOTIONS OF THE END OF THE WORLD

Both Professor and prophet depress,
For vision and longer view
Agree in predicting a day
Of convulsion and vast evil,
When the Cold Societies clash
Or the mosses are set in motion
To overrun the earth,
And the great brain which began
With lucid dialectics
Ends in a horrid madness.
—*Wystan Hugh Auden*

I would like to put it simply thus:
A book is closed.
—*Ray Bradbury*

Do I love this world so well
That I have to know how it ends?
—*Wystan Hugh Auden*

1. The End as Idea and Reality

A certain element of the catastrophic inheres within the world. Human beings not only harbor catastrophic expectations that can become concentrated into the totality of the end of the world, they also share catastrophic experiences. It is our experiences of catastrophes and destructive ends, experiences of catastrophic reality, that are precipitated in apocalyptic imagery. The annihilation of reality proves to be a formative factor in the experiential world of nature and history. We may or may not be moving toward new catastrophes or toward complete annihilation. What is certain is that we have always been coming from catastrophes. Even if apocalyptic anticipates the end as something that is yet impending, we nonetheless also know that ruin and destruction already lie behind us in various forms. The end, demise, is not just an idea, but reality. In what follows this will be illuminated in the realm of nature by a look at geology, paleontology, and biology, in the realm of history by reference to the interpretations of history as crisis history, and in the realm of individual existence by a recalling the problem of death as addressed in philosophy. In order to understand better the notion of demise or of the end, we will search for the exemplary "sediment of endings"[1] which have already occurred or which are continually repeated.

Geology, astrophysics, and paleontology constitute as it were the counterpart to the apocalyptic scenarios of cosmic catastrophes. "If the geohistorical remembrance of catastrophes is not in our brains, it is in any event in the various sedimentary strata in the earth; and if there have been profound and extensive catastrophes in the past, it is indisputable there can also be such in the future."[2] Ending in the form of geological catastrophes or of the extinction of entire species is an integral part of the evolutionary thinking generally accepted in biology, thinking which in the meantime has been developed into an integrated comprehensive theory.[3] Paleontology, in addition to biogeography, comparative anatomy and morphology, embryology, molecular biology and biochemistry, offers empirical evidence for the modern theory of evolution.[4] G. de Cuvier (1769–1832) is to be considered the real founder of scientific paleontology. He discovered the differences between temporally sequential plant types in the history of the earth and recognized fossils as the remains of extinct plant and animal species.[5] Cuvier supported the idea of evolution in the form of a theory of catastrophe according to which the organisms of the earth were destroyed several times by catastrophes and created anew later according to different plans. Of course, according to this understanding various individual living beings did manage to survive the numerous catastrophes.[6] Even if Cuvier's theory of catastrophe could not be maintained scientifically, the extinction of entire species and lines cannot be doubted as a fact of evolutionary history. Furthermore, modern paleontology does not exclude the possibility that the transition from the earth's middle period to that of modernity was accompanied by a catastrophe of enormous magnitude responsible for the extinction of numerous species such as, e.g., the dinosaurs. Although the dimensions, causes, and effects of this geohistorical catastrophe are yet disputed within the scientific community, this is of no further importance for our present context. What is of significance for our topic is especially the results of what was formerly called natural history:

> Human beings live not only from the beginning forward, and not only toward the end, inquiring about them both, but rather as participating observers of geohistory they are already living from other endings forward, and are surrounded by endings and catastrophes, those that have already occurred and those that are yet anticipated. This is the concrete paleontological and eschatological horizon of human cosmic-apocalyptic existence.[7]

Various experiences of destructive natural phenomena are reflected in the different nature motifs used in portrayals of the end of the world. A. Olrik has summarized the most important of these in his study of the Nordic Ragnarok.[8] For example, recollections of earthquakes or of volcanic eruptions underlie the motif of a hidden mythic monster that breaks out of the earth, such as a dragon, the bound giant in the Caucasus, or the Tartar or Estonian dogs in the mountain. Similarly, the notion of a world conflagration derives from experiences with nature. The basis for this motif in India, for example, is the drought which has repeatedly afflicted the land. The same holds true for the notions of the end of the world in Peru. Several Indian tribes in North America also anticipated a world conflagration. Their expectations are understandable considering the enormous forest and plains fires there. The same applies to the motif of the world conflagration in South America. While the primary apocalyptic motif of the end of the world for many peoples in the equatorial region consists in fire, northern portrayals of the end of the world sooner reflect a great flood. The motif of the toppling of the earth derives from earthquakes, and this motif appears variously as a collapse or as overturning. The freezing of the world is a less frequent motif. Although it does occur as *Markusawinter* or Fimbal winter in Nordic and Persian portrayals, it occurs with astonishing infrequency, not even—as one might expect—among Eskimos. Motifs accompanying the end of the world can also be traced back to natural phenomena, such as the widespread motif of the eclipse of the sun or of the moon, often taken as a portent of the end of the world, and finally also the falling of the stars or of the moon, recalling the appearance of meteorites and comets.

As one can easily see, apocalyptic motifs taken from nature derive in part from physical and regional sources, though they do migrate and, in mythical guise, find acceptance in regions that are themselves unaffected by such natural phenomena. Furthermore, various individual motifs from nature are combined with others in different combinations, e.g., when in Parseeism, Hinduism, or in Jewish and Christian apocalyptic a plunging comet ignites the earth or, according to Peruvian notions, the moon falling to earth brings about the flood of the end time. It is the task of comparative religious studies to pursue the interweavings, migrations, and transformations of these motifs in their specifics, and cannot be undertaken here. What should be remembered, however, is that natural phenomena and experiences in the realm of nature have become the point of crystallization for apocalyptic nature motifs. This does not mean that reference to such phenomena suffices to explain the phenomenon of apocalyptic. This is the inclination of Olrik's study when he asserts that "the impressions from nature, in their immediate power, create Ragnarok."[9] Although Olrik does indeed recognize anxiety as a decisive moving force in apocalyptic thinking, the world anxiety of apocalyptic we have analyzed extends ontically deeper than the anxiety elicited by natural forces.

We are surrounded by endings and catastrophes not only in the realm of nature but also in the arena of human history. We are thinking not only of the creeping demise and downfall of cultures, described, e.g., by Spengler in organic terms, and of the disintegration of past empires and centers of power, but also of the countless victims of historical catastrophes. History as a series of wars and genocide, as a slaughterblock of humanity, is a permanent story of destruction about which Friedrich Schiller said: "World history is the last judgment." Here we do see that history is more than a mere accumulation of brute facts. The occurrences of the past and historical consciousness stand in a multilayered mutual relationship. The experience of history generates a certain historical consciousness and historical methods, which in their own turn first allow history to emerge in a specific way. Thus history is not only full of crises and catastrophes. Rather, these come into view as such because in the modern age they are recollected and maintained within recollection by crisis consciousness. Experiences of destructive endings on the one hand, and what amounts to apocalyptic crisis consciousness on the other, go hand in hand in modern historical writing. It is modern historical consciousness as crisis consciousness that allows the past to emerge as the history of crises and catastrophes. "The modern consciousness of history is a consciousness of crisis, and all modern philosophy of history is in the last analysis a philosophy of crisis."[10] Whereas even Augustine's historical thinking in *De civitate Dei* cannot be understood without considering the element of crisis experience, in modernity it was above all the French Revolution which generated the image of history as an ongoing crisis, as "a permanent state of crisis,"[11] with the result that crisis became the center of historical philosophy and research for Hegel, Ranke, Burckhardt and Droysen, Saint-Simon or Comte. To that extent history is not merely the arena of human experiences of downfall and endings, but also of apocalyptic thinking, hoping, and fearing, whose traces we want to follow in this chapter in several examples.

Not only history confronts us with experiences of demise and the end, the problem of death does as well, and in modern philosophy a peculiar connection can be observed between the problem of death and the notion of the end of the world. Here it is not world history that is interpreted as the last judgment, but rather individual death as the end of the world. However, whereas Kierkegaard, Heidegger, and even Schopenhauer view one's own death as the end of the world, for G. Marcel, P. L. Landsberg, and F. Wiplinger it is the death of the other person that comes to represent the demise of the world for me.[12]

Demise and endings—this much becomes clear in the context of the problem of death in the realms of nature and history—exist not only in the human imagination, but are integral parts of our reality. Apocalyptic is not only the intensified perception of the catastrophic, but simultaneously its anticipation. As such it is based on human experience and yet must be viewed critically insofar as it runs the risk of equating its own images of that possible catastrophic future with future reality itself. Finally, the connection between apocalyptic thinking and human experiences of endings is also recognizable in the fact that this expectation of the end of the world can assume various dimensions. Just as catastrophes and endings can attain different dimensions, so also can one distinguish between partial, global, and cosmic notions of the end of the world. It may be the fall of Troy, of the Roman Empire, or of the West itself which appears subjectively as the end in the larger sense. Nevertheless, such partial expectations of the end can also quite legitimately be referred to as apocalyptic, and it would be shortsighted to consider only the scenarios of enormous cosmic catastrophes as genuine apocalyptic ends of the world. Just as individual death can already appear as the end of the world itself, so also partial endings. To do justice to the phenomenon of apocalyptic it is thus necessary in what follows to describe—albeit only in an exemplary fashion and by no means exhaustively—notions of the end of the world in the broadest sense.

2. Successfully Endured Ends of the World

The catastrophes from which we human beings have always been moving forward have left deposits not only in the sedimentary strata of the earth's crust but also in myths. Numerous myths of the most diverse peoples and cultures concerning the beginning of the world speak of a primal catastrophe. In these myths, a consciousness of living after the catastrophe comes to expression. Those who are alive today view themselves as the descendants of those who once escaped with their lives. Behind them lies the successfully endured end of the world.

This successfully endured end is the subject of the countless flood narratives familiar both from early cultures as well as from highly developed ones on all continents. The biblical myth of the great flood[13] (Gen. 6:5–8:22)[14] has hundreds of parallels in the history of religions.[15] The suspicion is justified that such mythical flood stories are dealing with recollections of catastrophes. "In addition to dim reminiscences of the so-called pluvial age, severe *local* water catastrophes in the distant past probably also contributed to the emergence of such legends."[16] It is true that such myths also gained acceptance in areas that were never afflicted by these sorts of catastrophes. A more temporal-historical interpretation of the flood stories fails to recognize their mythical character. The flood narratives portray "a primeval happening, not a historical event."[17] The myth expresses a contemporary understanding of existence: "The flood is the archetype of human catastrophe, and as such has been formed into narrative. What the flood narrative aims at expressing is derivation as a result of the preservation of the one amidst the demise of all others. It is precisely this that is the goal of the flood narrative."[18]

The mythical catastrophe is recalled for the sake of the present, and often the flood narratives have an etiological conclusion. Those who were rescued are the ancestors of the present inhabitants of a country, of two peoples, or of people of all skin colors.[19] Such etiology does not constitute historical derivation, but is rather the expression of one's self-understanding. The understanding of existence expressed in the flood stories can be summarized as follows: Existence means having survived and escaped. The human being is one who escaped.

This understanding of existence and the notion of the successfully endured end of the world still resonate today. Thus, e.g., C. G. Jung's 1945 essay, which dealt with the problem of German collective guilt, is entitled "After the Catastrophe." Jung does indeed use apocalyptic language here: "This is the first time since 1936 that the fate of Germany again drives me to take up my pen. The quotation from the *Voluspo* with which I ended the article I wrote at that time, about Wotan 'murmuring with Mimir's head,' pointed prophetically to the nature of the coming apocalyptic events.

The myth has been fulfilled, and the greater part of Europe lies in ruins."[20] The Second World War is the successfully endured apocalypse, in this case the twilight of the gods.

C. G. Jung considers the catastrophe to be not only behind us, but before us as well, certain "that the German catastrophe was only one crisis in the general European sickness":[21] "The phenomenon we have witnessed in Germany was nothing less than the first outbreak of epidemic insanity, an irruption of the unconscious into what seemed to be a tolerably well-ordered world."[22]

Thus in the final analysis the great flood would indeed be merely the prelude to the apocalyptic drama. The New Testament source Q already sees a connection between the great flood and the last judgment: "As it was in the days of Noah, so will it be in the days of the Son of man. They ate, they drank, they married, they were given in marriage, until the day when Noah entered the ark, and the flood came and destroyed them all" (Luke 17:26–27). The end time will break in as suddenly and unexpectedly as did the catastrophe of the primeval time.[23] Apocalyptists live "before the flood."[24] Such apocalyptic reminiscences of the flood can degenerate into cynical defeatism: "After us, the deluge," was the philosophy of life of the fading nobility before the French Revolution. This is the apocalyptic of those who have previously lived at the cost of others, and who know that they are about to get their just due. However, the world anxiety and experiences of powerlessness of the genuinely powerless also prompt the image of the flood to arise. The great flood becomes the cipher for crisis consciousness: "The floods are rising—the dams are bursting."[25]

3. Periodic Ends of the World

In Goethe's *Faust*, Mephistopheles confesses: "I am the Spirit of Eternal Negation, and rightly so, since all that gains existence is only fit to be destroyed; that's why it would be best if nothing ever got created."[26] This eternal cycle of "dying and becoming" and the hope in its fundamental revocability characterize the apocalyptic thinking of Hinduism. Cyclical thinking acquires its form in a doctrine of the four ages of the world constituting the indispensable background for the messianic expectations of the Vishnu faith.

Indian cosmology develops a doctrine of four sequential ages called Yugas. At the beginning of the world there was the golden age, the Krita Yuga, lasting four thousand years. This was followed by the Treta Yuga, extending over a period of three thousand years and followed by the Dvapara Yuga of two thousand years. The present world age, the dark epoch of the Kali Yuga, is to last one thousand years and culminate in the end of the world itself. Yet even that catastrophe will be followed by a new golden age, with which the cycle of the world ages, which continues ad infinitum, begins again anew.

The division of world history into periods is familiar to us from Parseeism, though it divides history into epochs of equal duration and does not develop the view of the eternal recurrence. A periodization of history is also familiar from Jewish apocalyptic, which was probably influenced by Eastern thought. We find such periodization in Indian traditions of North and South America as well as in Hesiod and the Pre-Socratics Anaximander, Empedocles, and Heraclitus. Such periodization of history is not in every case associated with the notion of an eternal recurrence of the same. This connection does not even represent an original part of Indian thought, where the sequence of the four Yugas initially encompasses the entire course of the world. Only later did the continuing repetition of this cycle, which including the times of crisis at the end of the epochs lasts twelve thousand years, replace the one-time sequence of four world ages.[27] Furthermore, Vedic literature was by all appearances yet unfamiliar with the doctrine of the four world ages.[28] In this context, however, we cannot discuss the specifics of the developments of these Indian ideas.[29]

The cyclical thinking of Hindu apocalyptic is the expression of profound world negation. Although most portrayals of the doctrine of the eternal cycle of the four world ages do presuppose the continuation of humankind, this does not mean that the cycle of "dying and becoming" is extolled in the sense of the modern philosophy of life as the victory and power of life. In one passage of the Mahabharata the turn to the good is virtually grounded by the annihilation of humankind: Through its destruction, the emotions and thus the source of suffering and evil are also extinguished.[30] This culmination reveals a development in Indian thought. Whereas in many archaic conceptions of cyclical thinking the view of the reactualization of the golden primeval age is to provide consolation for human beings, who are suffering under the terrors of history, the fully developed doctrine of the four Yugas no longer finds in this regeneration of the beginning any real solution to the problem of suffering. "It is not any impulse for deliverance motivating the Indian end of the world," A. Olrik writes, "but rather the impulse to vanish into the all of the deity. The repetitions, the numerous sequential world periods have no other goal than to show the deity to be the enduring one, and to underscore the infinite insignificance of the present world."[31]

Thus precisely in the Indian doctrine of the world ages, the consoling function of apocalyptic becomes recognizable. This theory is "invigorating and consoling for man under the terror of history."[32] It articulates the world anxiety precipitated or at least intensified by the various invasions of foreign peoples from the second pre-Christian century to the sixth century of the common era, as well as by the competition between Brahmanism and Buddhism;[33] this world anxiety expresses itself in the consciousness of belonging to the end time, the Kali Yuga. At the same time, however, Indian speculation concerning the world ages also tries to overcome this anxiety by urging its contemporaries to understand the age of darkness as an opportunity to come to know the causes of all suffering and, through such knowledge, to enter the path to freedom from all misery and all the horrors of history. On the other hand, this justifies the continuing sufferings of those who culpably close themselves off from such knowledge and thus from the possibility of deliverance from suffering.[34]

Although Indian speculation regarding the world ages in its fully developed form is driven by profound world negation that basically assumes a negative posture over against reality, other notions of cyclically recurring ends of the world are characterized by genuine optimism: It is precisely this apocalyptic world negation which ultimately opens up to them the possibility of world affirmation.

At this point one must recall the cyclical understanding of history of the Stoics, whose speculations concerning the eternal recurrence of all things and of all events stands in a certain relationship with the periodicized cyclical historical understanding of India. It is dependent on Eastern, at least on Iranian influences, as well as on the thinking of the pre-Socratics, in particular that of Heraclitus. The Stoics combined the idea of the eternity of the cosmos with the notion of the growth and passing away of all individual phenomena. Not the present world, but rather the cosmos itself, conceived as a perfect living being endowed with reason, is eternal. The present world must have come into being at one time, and will for that reason also pass away. Zeno presented four arguments for this view of the transitoriness of the present world: The structure of the earth's surface, whose differences in elevation would long have been evened out by wind and rain if the world really endured eternally; alterations in the coastline evidenced by the presence of mussels in the interior of the country; the transitoriness of all things, including the hardest rocks; and finally the young age of the human race, something demonstrated by the youth of its culture.[35]

The cosmos develops from the primal ground of the world, the fiery primeval substance. It is eternal insofar as it is conceived as substance, yet transitory as *diakosmēsis*, as the development of this substance in concrete individual phenomena. The course of the world proceeds in periods to a turning point from which it returns to its point of departure. At the end of the final world age is the world conflagration, the *ekpyrōsis*, which causes all multiplicity to fall back again into the unity of the original source and at the same time functions as a catharsis in which the world is cleansed from all the slag of imperfection. In some cases, e.g., in Cleanthes, whose views probably served as the model for those of Dion, this end of the world can be portrayed in richly imaginative imagery.[36] This is followed by the palingenesis.[37] Out of the fire of the world conflagration, however, arises not a new, unknown world, but rather the same one in which human beings presently live. If, that is, the present world is interpreted as a product of the all-encompassing logos, there is no reason to believe that the logos, after once having created the best of all possible worlds, should in the case of new creation bring forth a different world, which would only be a less perfect one. What holds true for the logos in the larger sense, however, must also be the case for the *logos spermatikos*. From this the Stoics concluded that not only the world itself in its totality eternally recurs, but also individuals. Similarly, every single individual event will recur in eternity.

It is not possible to discuss the specifics of the later influence exerted by the Stoic understanding of the world. The influence of the Stoics, as is well known, becomes evident in the philosophy of life toward the end of the nineteenth century, in particular with Nietzsche, who picked up the idea of the eternal recurrence of the same and formulated it anew.[38] Stoic thinking was also influential in the philosophical historical views of Spengler, to which we will devote a special discussion in what follows. Spengler picks up the notion of a periodization of history and of recurring endings. On the one hand, he applies this idea to the historical development of individual cultures, relocating it from cosmogony into history; on the other hand, he tries to keep it free of the apocalyptic element of the catastrophic. Here his philosophy of the end recalls the numerous attempts during antiquity to defuse the myths of the end which periodically alarmed the inhabitants of Rome in times of external threat. Whereas one basic myth asserted that the duration of Rome's existence was limited by a mythical number, another myth associated Rome's fall with the universal world conflagration at the end of the "great year." Again and again during times characterized by the mood of demise, the hope arises that the transition from one world age to the next might occur without catastrophe.[39] According to this understanding, "the wars, the destruction, the sufferings of history are no longer the premonitory signs of the transition from one age to another, but themselves constitute the transition."[40] Precisely this idea, as suggested above, characterizes modern historical philosophy as a whole, which can be understood as crisis philosophy. What U. Horstmann remarked concerning the cyclical understanding of catastrophe of the Anahnac religion of central Mexico[41] also applies to this historical philosophy, namely, that it is not the end of history, but rather history itself that constitutes the permanent, cyclically structured catastrophe.

Such cyclical reproduction of the end, however, rather than intensifying world anxiety, tries to overcome it, albeit at the price of the sublation of history. The various versions of cyclical notions of the end of the world ultimately represent attempts to exorcise apocalyptic world anxiety with the help of archaic thought patterns going back to archaic myths and rituals. The connection between archaic thinking and periodic historical speculation becomes tangible in the division of the world course into four periods, patterned after the change of the seasons, stages of life, or phases of the moon. The analogy with the seasons of the year, whence especially Wundt and Abegg would derive the Indian doctrine of Yugas,[42] can be followed all the way into Spengler's work on the decline of the West. However, neither can the analogy with the cycle of the moon be overlooked.[43] M. Eliade, who has studied the connection between cyclical historical imagery and "archaic ontology,"[44] speaks appropriately of the "lunar structure" or perspective of periodicized historical speculation.[45] Such lunar-structured thinking, however, keeps apocalyptic consolation at the ready, since precisely the consciousness of the normalcy of the cyclically recurring catastrophe negates the element of the inescapable experienced in apocalyptic anxiety. It is annulled in the negation of the irrevocability and finality of the end of the world. New optimism emerges from this negation, and corresponds to the certainty that the catastrophe "has a meaning and, above all, that it is never final."[46]

4. The One-Time End of the World

In contrast, the one-time end of the world is definitive, and it is to this complex of ideas that we will now turn our attention. In addition to Jewish apocalyptic, which will constitute the main focus of our study, one should also mention especially the ideas of Parseeism and of Germanic religion.[47] In addition to the Indian doctrine of the world ages, it is generally thought that the religion of Iran in particular provided fertile soil for the apocalyptic of antiquity. The apocalyptic of Parseeism went through a long development.[48] The proclamation of the prophet Zoroaster already contains typical apocalyptic ideas, and he expected the last judgment and the establishment of the kingdom of God during his own lifetime. After his death, his views underwent numerous modifications. The younger literature of Parseeism, known as the Pahlavi literature, offers a broad portrayal of the course of world history containing extended descriptions of heaven and earth, death and the beyond. As in Parseeism, Hinduism, the Stoics, Judaism, or Islam, an especially well developed apocalyptic is also found in Germanic religion. Its most important document is the Völuspá ("Prediction of the Prophetess"), a text from the *Edda* that has occasionally been called the "nordic Sibyl."[49] Its views of the end of the world betray in part clearly Christian influence,[50] as well as possibly connections with the apocalyptic of Iran.[51] We will not discuss the content of the Völuspá more specifically here.[52]

2 Apoc. Bar. 85:14 offers what is virtually a one-sentence programmatic summary of the notion of the one-time end of the world: "On this account there is *one* law by one, *one* age and an end for all who are in it." This programmatic thesis from the realm of Jewish apocalyptic already exhibits an important consequence of the notion of the one-time end of the world: the dualism of two worlds. The great catastrophe of the end time separates two antithetical worlds. Although the present world is consecrated to its ineluctable end, a new one is being prepared for those who will be rescued from the catastrophe. As final as this anticipated end of the world is, it seems questionable just how definitive it is in reality. Before we address this question, however, let us examine the connection between world anxiety and the end of the world using the example of Jewish apocalyptic.

In his analysis of the Ragnarok, Olrik determined that anxiety is the decisive motif in all notions of the end of the world. As far as the developmental history of the idea is concerned, Olrik's point of departure is that "at lower stages of culture the predominating feature is the *anxiety* that the end of the world *might* occur; at higher stages, however, it is the *conviction* that it *will* occur."[53] The anxiety back to which Olrik tries to trace apocalyptic, however, is not what we have described as world anxiety, but rather merely the exaggerated fear of natural catastrophes.[54] In contrast, in what follows we will interpret the notion of the one-time end of the world as a reflex of apocalyptic world anxiety, and to this end we choose the example of Jewish apocalyptic.

The assertion that world anxiety is the real key to understanding Jewish apocalyptic as well is not universally accepted. Considering the portrayals of the messianic kingdom occupying such a large space in apocalyptic literature, it seems more appropriate to look for the real driving force behind Jewish apocalyptic rather in the motif of hope. In what follows, the significance of hope for Jewish apocalyptic is by no means denied; our thesis, however, is that this apocalyptic hope is comprehensible only if one interprets it as an attempt at overcoming apocalyptic world anxiety. Just as the colors used to portray the kingdom of God stand out brightly only against the dark background of the horrors of the end time and of the end of the world, so also is hope thrown into relief as the new, though not original mood against the background of the preceding anxiety. For this reason it seems justified to concentrate the investigation initially not on the various Jewish utopias of the messianic kingdom, but rather on the notions of the one-time end of the world and the end time immediately preceding it. These can be interpreted as an expression of the world anxiety to which the apocalyptic hope of a counterworld tries to provide a response.

An interpretation of Jewish apocalyptic accordingly needs to begin with the phenomenon of anxiety in the apocalyptic texts. The world anxiety in question here, however, does need to be distinguished from the *tremendum* which seizes the visionary in the face of God or of his angel.[55] In addition to this anxiety before the holy, we do encounter in apocalyptic literature expressions of yet another convulsive emotion which in the sense of our preceding discussion can be called world anxiety. We can distinguish the anxiety of the visionary before what is actually seen in the vision, the anxiety of the apocalyptist before the future, the anxiety of those oppressed during the end time and before the final judgment, and finally the anxiety of God's enemies on the day of judgment and as divine punishment.

Several times we find in Jewish apocalypses utterances concerning the anxiety that overcomes the fictitious figure of the visionary in the face of the images he sees. "In the first year of Belshazzar king of Babylon," we read in the Old Testament book of Daniel,[56] "Daniel had a dream, and the visions of his head which he saw as he lay in his bed made him anxious."[57] Anxiety penetrates into Daniel to such an extent that his face changes color.[58] For a time he is even sick with anxiety.[59] In Nebuchadnezzar, too, the dream of the four world kingdoms causes anxiety.[60] The fictitious Ezra quite similarly concludes the account of his own vision of the son of man: "Then in great fear I awoke" (4 Ezra 13:13).[61]

In order to understand this phenomenon of anxiety properly, one must recall the pseudonymous character of Jewish apocalypses. Although they address the contemporaries of their actual author, they work with the literary fiction of having been composed in the distant past by a significant figure. The time of the actual author and readers of the apocalypses as well as past history are portrayed in the future tense, as the object of fictionalized prophecy. What the fictitious visionary of the distant past views as a dream image and receives interpreted as the reflection of future events is in fact a metaphorical or symbolic description and interpretation of the reality experienced by the author and readers of the apocalypses as well as of their expectations, fears, and hopes regarding the future. Thus any interpretation of the anxiety prompted by what is viewed in the vision must take into account the pseudonymity and literary fiction of apocalypses. Hence I would suggest that the anxiety of the alleged ancient visionary in the face of the vision itself is in fact the fictitiously anticipated world anxiety of those to which the apocalypses are actually addressed. The anxiety in the face of the dream images of the visionary thus reflects the anxiety of the apocalyptic authors and their readers.[62]

This thesis is supported by a series of examples from apocalyptic literature. Enoch enlightens his readers: "But not for this generation, but for a remote one which is to come" (*1 Enoch* 1:2). "And all shall be smitten with fear, and the Watchers[63] shall quake, and great fear and trembling shall seize them unto the ends of the earth" (*1 Enoch* 1:5).[64] The ancient visionary foretells future world anxiety. In other words: The present world anxiety of the contemporary readers is referred to in the future tense. Apocalyptic anxiety is the subject of *vaticinia ex eventu.* Hence Ezra also realizes that those in the future "shall see great dangers and much distress, as these dreams show" (4 Ezra 13:19). The fictitious figure from the past, however, not only prophesies the world anxiety of future generations, but is himself seized by this anxiety. For example, the angel Ramiel admonishes Baruch, who is quite disturbed, to get hold of himself: "Why does thy heart trouble thee, Baruch, and why does thy thought disturb thee? For if owing to the report which thou hast only heard of judgement thou art so moved, what [wilt thou be] when thou shalt see it manifestly with thine eyes? And if with the expectation wherewith thou dost expect the day of the Mighty One thou art so overcome, what [wilt thou be] when thou shalt come to its advent?" (*2 Apoc. Bar* 55:4–6).

Whereas in some instances the figure of the ancient recipient of the revelation is seized by anxiety in the face of the vision itself, in others the reverse is true, and it is the anxiety in the face of an uncertain future that prompts them to demand revelation in the first place: "In the thirtieth year after the destruction of our city, I Salathiel, who am also called Ezra, was in Babylon. I was *troubled* as I lay on my bed, and my thoughts welled up in my heart, because I saw the desolation of Zion and the wealth of those who lived in Babylon. My spirit was greatly agitated, and I began to speak anxious words to the Most High" (4 Ezra 3:1–3).[65] The experience of the present world is so distressing that the future itself seems radically called into question. The experiences of evil, of powerlessness, and of Israel's own desolate condition, as well as the absence of divine help and justice can no longer be dealt with within the horizon of the previous interpretation of the world. For Israel and the individual believers there no longer seems to be any future. The world anxiety of the apocalyptist is the experience of a world that at every quarter appears hostile and inescapable. In this exponentially intensified anxiety the seer pleads for enlightenment, revelation, unveiling, *apokalypsis.* The example of 4 Ezra[66] clearly shows that apocalyptic is the expression of—though especially the attempt at overcoming—world anxiety. The divine revelation of the events of the end time is to relieve Ezra's anxiety in the face of the future. For that reason, so the angel Uriel explains to Ezra, God sent him "to show you all these things, and to say to you: 'Believe and do not be afraid! Do not be quick to think vain thoughts concerning the former things, lest anxiety overtake you in the last times' " (4 Ezra 6:33f.). Like Ezra, Baruch is also seized by anxiety in the face of the future. And like Ezra, Baruch, too, is consoled by God: "Why, then, are you disturbed about that which you do not know, and why are you restless about that of which you do not possess any knowledge? . . . For truly, my salvation which comes has drawn near and is not as far away as before" (*2 Apoc. Bar.* 23:2, 7). It is not difficult to see that from within the anxiety before the future, anxiety experienced by a fictitious Ezra or Baruch, there speaks the world anxiety of those for whom the apocalypses are actually intended. Their powerlessness and despair is to be overcome through the unveiling of the events of the end time.

The apocalyptically intensified world anxiety of the readers is reflected not just in the anxiety of the fictitious recipients of the revelation, but rather is in its own turn the content of fictitious prophecies. Anxiety itself acquires salvific-historical significance. That is, the exponential intensification of that anxiety is itself the decisive feature of the time portending the proximity of the end and thus of salvation. "This therefore shall be the sign. When a stupor shall seize the inhabitants of the earth, and they shall fall into many tribulations, and again when they shall fall into great torments. And it will come to pass when they say in their thoughts by reason of their much tribulation: 'The Mighty One no longer remembers the earth'—yea, it will come to pass when they abandon hope, that the [new] time will then awake" (*2 Apoc. Bar.* 25:1–4).[67] *2 Apocalypse of Baruch* speaks in the future tense of the world anxiety of its own readers. That this anxiety is the object of an alleged prophecy being painfully fulfilled in the presence of the readers themselves is intended as an initial consolation for those who are overpowered by this anxiety, anxiety which is itself to be overcome by being declared a part of the eschatological drama.

For this reason, admittedly, the apocalyptists do not view the events of the end time in an exclusively positive emotional light. Anxiety can be intensified to the point that not only does the world seem hostile and inescapable, but even God's own judgment seems to be a crisis with an uncertain outcome. Precisely this last judgment, announced as an event of deliverance, can become the object of anxiety regarding the future.[68] Anxiety generates insecurity to the point that despite apocalyptic disclosures a tormenting uncertainty regarding salvation settles in the heart of the apocalyptist.

Next to the expressions of anxiety discussed to this point, those in which the world anxiety of the apocalyptic authors and their readers is reflected, we also encounter in the apocalypses expositions concerning the anxiety of God's enemies on the day of judgment. Just as already the fallen angels in the primeval time are seized by fear and trembling in the face of impending punishment,[69] so also will it be with sinners at the end of days: "And the children of the earth shall seek to hide themselves from the presence of the Great Glory, and shall tremble and quake; and you sinners shall be cursed for ever, and shall have no peace" (*1 Enoch* 102:3).[70] The anxiety of the godless is the content of a cry of woe in the parenetic book of *1 Enoch*: "Woe to you, you obstinate of heart, who watch in order to devise wickedness: therefore shall fear come upon you and there shall be none to help you" (*1 Enoch* 100:8). On that day of world judgment the sinners will be seized by boundless anxiety, while the righteous, those currently so afflicted, are freed of all anxiety. This observation leads us to the thesis that fear and terror on the part of the godless on the day of judgment are related in the manner of a mirror image to the world anxiety of the apocalyptists. The present world anxiety of the powerless becomes through apocalyptic projection a phantasy of punishment. Just as the apocalyptists are full of anxiety now, so also will the enemies of God be filled with it in the sense of equalizing justice at the end of days. The measure of anxiety as punishment for the wicked is the same as that of the world anxiety of the apocalyptists.

Additional observations seem also to support the thesis that the anxiety of the wicked during the events of the end time is a projection of the anxiety of the apocalyptists. 4 Ezra speaks of an intermediate condition of souls after death in which sevenfold pain and sevenfold joy anticipate the reward and punishment of the last judgment. The wicked are to suffer sevenfold torments, including "the *seventh* way, which is worse than all the ways that have been mentioned, because they shall utterly waste away in confusion and be consumed with shame, and shall wither with fear" (4 Ezra 7:87). In a reverse fashion, we read the following about the highest joy of the righteous: "The seventh order, which is greater than all that have been mentioned, because they shall rejoice with boldness, and shall be confident without confusion, and shall be glad without fear" (4 Ezra 7:98). Whereas freedom from anxiety is counted as the highest joy of the blessed, so also can the anxiety potential of the apocalyptists in the present be measured against this hope. It is in fact the apocalyptists who are consumed by anxiety and enervated by fear. The anticipated anxiety of the wicked is a reflex of one's own powerlessness. Although the author of *2 Apocalypse of Baruch* assures us that "the souls of the wicked, when they behold all these things, shall then waste away the more; for they shall know that their torment has come and their perdition has arrived" (*2 Apoc. Bar.* 30:4f.), it is in fact first of all the readers of this and other apocalypses who are about to expire from anxiety. And it is they in whom the apocalyptic anxiety has intensified into the expectation of the end of the world.

We can now demonstrate how world anxiety is intensified in Jewish apocalyptic into the expectation of a one-time end of the world, i.e., we can demonstrate that the notion of the end of the world is the consequence of apocalyptically intensified world anxiety. We will take as our point of departure the apocalyptic descriptions of the catastrophic tendencies of the present.

"The central idea of apocalyptic is the announcement of what is at least a temporary distancing of God from history, one allowing a free unfolding of evil."[71] One can pick up this definition offered by J. Lebram and modify it in the sense of our investigation to this point: Jewish apocalyptic addresses the problem of the experience of God's absence, an absence whose consequence must be the end of the world. The fundamental experience of apocalyptic can be described, picking up an unnerving expression coined by Martin Buber, as the darkness or eclipse of God.[72] Because God is absent, darkness spreads over the earth. The eclipse of God causes the earth to grow dark. "For the world lies in darkness, and its inhabitants are without light" (4 Ezra 14:20). Because God is absent, the present age has neither direction nor promise: "And we are left in the darkness, and amid the trees of the forest, and the thirst of the wilderness" (*2 Apoc. Bar.* 77:14). This darkness is sinister and alien. The dark forest and the waterless desert are sinister regions, zones of death, and serve as symbols of a world that has become inhospitable, hostile to life, alien, and threatening.

The contemporary world of experience is not only threatening and frightening, it is also old and tired. "For the youth of the world is past, and the strength of the creation already exhausted, and the advent of the times is very short, yea, they have [almost already] passed by; and the pitcher is near to the cistern, and the ship to the port, and the course of the journey to the city, and life to its consummation" (*2 Apoc. Bar.* 85:10).[73] The certainty that the world is becoming increasingly old results not only from observation of natural phenomena, such as was the case among the Stoics in connection with the doctrine of the world ages, but is also a reflex of Israel's own catastrophic condition. The fatigue of the world reflects the exhaustion of the people of Israel, who are suffering under historical convulsions. When Ezra asks whether the world is yet young or has already grown old, the angel Uriel responds: "Those born in the strength of youth are different from those born during the time of old age, when the womb is failing. Therefore you also should consider that you and your contemporaries are smaller in stature than those who were before you. And those who come after you will be smaller than you, as born of a creation which already is aging and passing the strength of youth" (*4 Ezra* 5:53–55). In the angel's response the age of the world serves to explain the enervation of those living now. In fact, however, this advanced exhaustion is to be discerned in the enervation of the people. The experience of one's own enervation and powerlessness, exhibiting nothing more of the former glory of the Davidic kingdom and of the power of the Yahweh faith, issues into the notion of the advanced age of the world. "And so the entrances of this world were made narrow and sorrowful and toilsome; they are few and evil, full of dangers and involved in great hardships" (4 Ezra 7:12).[74]

According to the estimation of the apocalyptists, Israel is in a catastrophic position. "And now, O Lord," Ezra laments in prayer, "behold, these nations, which are reputed as nothing, domineer over us and devour us. But we your people, whom you have called your first-born, only begotten, zealous for you, and most dear, have been given into their hands" (4 Ezra 6:57f.). And the fictitious Baruch comes to the bitter realization: "Our fathers went to rest without grief, and lo! the righteous sleep in the earth in tranquillity; for they knew not this anguish, nor yet had they heard of that which had befallen us. Would that thou hadst ears, O earth, and that thou hadst a heart, O dust: that ye might go and announce in Sheol, and say to the dead: 'Blessed are ye more than we who live' " (*2 Apoc. Bar.* 11:4–6). The living will envy the dead. Israel's catastrophic situation provokes the question of theodicy: "Why has Israel been given over to the gentiles as a reproach; why the people whom you loved has been given to godless tribes, and the Law of our fathers has been made of no effect and the written covenants no longer exist; and why do we pass from the world like locusts, and our life is like a mist?" (4 Ezra 4:23f.). In the imagery of this vision Zion appears as a wife in mourning with torn clothing and ash-covered head.[75]

It should be remembered that the apocalyptic portrayals of Israel's catastrophic situation come from different epochs in the history of the people. The oldest apocalypse from the sphere of the Old Testament itself, the book of Daniel, was probably composed between 166 and 165 B.C. and reflects the situation of the people after the prohibition of the Jewish cult and the temple desecration of December 167 B.C. under Antiochus IV Epiphanes (176/5–163 B.C.).[76] These events, commencing with the murder of the high priest Onias III in the year 170 B.C., are portrayed in the future tense in the form of a fictionalized revelation reinterpreting the saying of the prophet Jeremiah concerning Israel's seventy-year exile[77] into a prophecy concerning the entire course of history:[78] "And after the sixty-two weeks, an anointed one shall be cut off, and shall have nothing; and the people of the prince who is to come shall destroy the city and the sanctuary. The end shall come with a flood, and to the end there shall be war; desolations are decreed. And he shall make a strong covenant with many for one week; and for half of the week he shall cause sacrifice and offering to cease; and upon the wing of abominations shall come one who makes desolate, until the decreed end is poured out on the desolator" (Dan. 9:26f.).[79]

The so-called parenetic book in *1 Enoch* (*1 Enoch* 92, 94—104)[80] takes us into the period of the dynasty of the Hasmoneans, reigning after the Maccabean revolts possibly alluded to in Dan. 11:34.[81] While an ideology of dominion and of the state regarding the actualized salvation of Israel develops under the militarily and politically successful Hasmonean dynasty established in the year 140 B.C., the Hasidaean opposition portrays a rather gloomy picture of the present in the parenesis of *1 Enoch*, holding fast to an expectation of the end, albeit an end that is being delayed: "For I know that the state of violence will intensify upon the earth; a great plague shall be executed upon the earth; all (forms of) oppression will be carried out; and everything shall be uprooted; and every arrow shall fly fast. Oppression shall recur once more and be carried out upon the earth; every (form of) oppression, injustice, and iniquity shall infect (the world) twofold. When sin, oppression, blasphemy, and injustice increase, crime, iniquity, and uncleanliness shall be committed and increase (likewise)" (*1 Enoch* 91:5f.). Only God's own judgment will bring these wicked conditions—conditions which the Hasmoneans have not overcome either—to an end. The apocalyptists believe they are living in "evil times," not in days of actualized salvation.[82] This diagnosis is supported by reference to numerous grievances. Cries of woe concerning sinners and their transgressions occupies considerable space in the parenetic book.[83] In part, these accusations recall the social criticism of the Old Testament prophets.[84]

With 4 Ezra and *2 Apocalypse of Baruch* we enter the period after the destruction of Jerusalem in the year A.D. 70. To a certain extent the assertion in 4 Ezra 3:1, namely, that 4 Ezra was composed "in the thirtieth year after the destruction of our city," is accurate.[85] Israel's situation toward the end of the first century A.D. is compared with that of the Babylonian exile. *2 Apocalypse of Baruch* was composed during the same time of distress as 4 Ezra.[86]

Any detailed analysis of the adduced texts would have to consider thoroughly both the differing historical circumstances and the literary strata and various prehistories of the texts in their present form. Our own investigation, however, can neglect to a certain extent the questions addressing historical circumstances, since we are concerned more with analyzing the understanding of existence of the apocalyptic witnesses. That is, our question is not concerned primarily with which historical circumstances individual texts may be alluding to, but rather with which understanding of existence comes to expression in the apocalyptic literature. The understanding of existence in these texts, however, claims to be living in a catastrophic present. "O Lord, my God! Behold, the present years are few and evil" (*2 Apoc. Bar.* 16).

Because world anxiety is intensifying into apocalyptic proportions, the apocalyptist assumes that the future will also bring an intensification of the catastrophic. Although the catastrophic present yet allows a certain measure of leeway for one's own actions, the future will become increasingly inescapable, and the world will press in ever more closely on the afflicted. One type of anxiety that becomes especially noticeable is that of being completely overwhelmed in the end by the hostile world. That means, however, that the world will collapse in upon the apocalyptist and thus itself disintegrate and perish. The intensification of the catastrophic, insofar as nothing stops it, is the preliminary stage of the inexorably approaching end of the world. Thus God announces to Ezra in 4 Ezra 14:15–17:[87] "For evils worse than those which you have now seen happen shall be done hereafter. For the weaker the world becomes through old age, the more shall evils be multiplied among its inhabitants. For truth shall go farther away, and falsehood shall come near." In rabbinic tradition one also encounters this expectation that the catastrophic present will intensify to the point of the most extreme inescapability, to the point that even the God-fearers despair of redemption, and Israel sinks down to the lowest level of misery.[88] This intensification of the catastrophic will not even leave the natural order untouched. The present world is sinister, rejecting, and hostile. The world of the most extreme end time, however, will be a perverted world in which all order is turned upside down. The cycle of sowing and reaping, growing and bearing fruit will be utterly confused, the stars will deviate from their normal course, the alternation of sun and moon will be untracked, and astronomical disorder will result in the complete disorientation of the inhabitants of the earth.[89] The ideas of Jewish apocalyptic coincide in this point with those of Indian speculation concerning the Kali Yuga.

The apocalyptic historical surveys confirm that history appears no less catastrophic than the present, a present that already gives one occasion to fear the worst. One might think especially of the vision of the four world kingdoms in Dan 2; 7,[90] of the animal vision in *1 Enoch* 85—90, the apocalypse of weeks in *1 Enoch* 93; 91:12–17, the eagle vision in 4 Ezra 11f., the vision of the forest, vine, fountain, and cedar in *2 Apoc. Bar.* 35ff., the vision of the cloud and the black and white waters in *2 Apoc. Bar.* 53; 56ff., but also of *1 Enoch* 106f. or 4 Ezra 3:4ff. It is not just Israel's history that is being illuminated here; the history of other peoples is also brought into focus. F. Lücke already believed one could observe in Jewish apocalyptic the expansion of historical consciousness into a concept of universal history,[91] and since then such universal-historical consciousness has repeatedly been adduced as a characteristic feature of apocalyptic.[92] To be sure, one can justifiably speak of the universal-historical consciousness of apocalyptic only if one bears in mind that universal history appears not as the universalism of salvation, but rather as the totality of perdition. World anxiety, precisely because of the narrowing of its own angle of vision to the threatening end, brings about a universalization of historical vision. The expansion of historical consciousness results from the perspective concentration on the end. It is Israel's catastrophic fate that makes necessary this expansion of historical consciousness.

According to the vision of the cloud in *2 Apoc. Bar.* 53; 56ff., world history is a series of cloudbursts breaking in upon Israel. The apocalyptist literally sees black: "And it happened that before the cloud disappeared, behold, it rained black waters, and they were darker than had been all those waters that were before, and fire was mingled with them, and where those waters descended, they wrought devastation and destruction" (*2 Apoc. Bar.* 53:7). The world history represented by the cloud is the history of disaster since the days of Adam. 4 Ezra views it the same way: "For the first Adam, burdened with an evil heart, transgressed and was overcome, as were also all who were descended from him. Thus the disease became permanent; the law was in the people's heart along with the evil root, but what was good departed, and the evil remained" (4 Ezra 3:21f.). In view of this disastrous experience, then, there is no more talk about God's earlier promises to his people. Only the evil remained. Apocalyptic is no longer able to adduce the recollection of earlier salvation history to counter the anxiety and hopelessness of the present. This is shown, e.g., by the Hasidaean apocalypse of weeks at the beginning of the parenetic book in *1 Enoch*. "The only things one should remember are the promising [!] beginnings of human beings in a 'universal history' of 'unrighteousness,' at whose end the 'law for sinners'—binding for all people without distinction—merely admits that God is unable to attain his goals with humankind."[93] The animal vision of *1 Enoch* 85ff. also suggests that universal salvation for all the peoples of the world lay completely outside the horizon of expectation. It is not the anticipation of a divine plan for salvation, but rather the realization of the utter inescapability of the present, as disclosed by world anxiety, that leads to universal-historical thinking.[94] Not universal redemption, but universal, divine catastrophic judgment ineluctably awaits the entire world. Accordingly, the learned attempts at reckoning the end[95] are the

> historically influenced expression of a theology no longer able, in view of a totally gloomy experiential horizon, to understand history as the permanent field of tension between the reception of divine promises on the one hand, and actualized fulfillment on the other; rather, in the question of life and salvation, this theology is now able to apply only the standard of a divine determination of the "end" to the overall horizon of what is for Israel a wholly unsuccessful course of history, a determination reserving justice for itself.[96]

These abysmal experiences plunge believers into profound despair regarding the goodness and righteousness of God, something one can discern toward the end of the first century A.D. in 4 Ezra: From Adam, who sinned, "there sprang nations and tribes, peoples and clans, without number. And every nation walked after its own will and did ungodly things before you and scorned you, *and you did not hinder them*" (4 Ezra 3:7f.). History is the result of human action, of human transgressions and evil. That God did not put a timely stop to this human activity as it proliferated into catastrophic proportions is a tormenting puzzle to which apocalyptic tries to provide an answer.

First of all, however, the end of the world does not appear as a salvific act of intervention on the part of God, but rather as the logical end of the course of history, as the necessary goal of the threatening tendencies of the present protracted into the future. One possible objection to this assertion is that Jewish apocalyptic anticipated the end of the world as God's delivering intervention in history, and that it views the end not as a fate inherent in the world itself, but rather as a breaking off of history both determined and caused by God. This objection, however, is unsound, since it presupposes that Jewish apocalyptic to a certain extent develops the notion of an end of the world spontaneously in order to counter, with its help, the preceding anxiety and hopelessness. This would mean, however, that anxiety is to be overcome by a notion which in many people itself creates anxiety, the result being presumably not an amelioration, but rather an intensification of anxiety. It is difficult to imagine that this sort of connection between world anxiety and the end of the world was the case in Jewish apocalyptic. Our thesis, on the other hand, is that the interpretation of the end of the world as a beginning of new salvation represents a transformation of already extant notions of demise and end. It is the attempt at critically appropriating previous images of the end of the world. Jewish apocalyptic, so our suspicion, picks up already extant notions of the end, notions prompted by world anxiety, and transforms this imagery of anxiety into that of hope.

This connection between world anxiety and the end of the world, already given for Jewish apocalyptic, seems yet discernible in *1 Enoch* in what remains of the book of Noah. One fragment of this writing describes the announcement of the great flood by Noah's grandfather Enoch:

> In those days, Noah saw the earth, that she had become deformed, and that her destruction was at hand. And (Noah) took off from there and went unto the extreme ends of the earth. And he cried out to his grandfather, Enoch, and said to him, three times, with a bitter voice, "Hear me! Hear me! Hear me!" and he said unto him, "Tell me what this thing is which is being done upon the earth, for the earth is struggling in this manner and is being shaken; that I not perish [myself] with her!" (*1 Enoch* 65:1–3).

Noah must experience the ever worsening circumstances on earth. The earth's fatigue and convulsed condition fill him with anxiety intensifying into an expectation of the end. The passage just cited illuminates like a spotlight the real center of the notion of the end of the world: The collapse of the world would be the equivalent of the end of the person overwhelmed by the world. Anxiety before the end of the world is ultimately anxiety before the loss of self. This is why Noah's anxious question concerning the fate of the earth concludes with the words: "that I not perish [myself] with her!" Noah—and this observation seems important to me—does not acquire the certainty of the end of the world from any divine revelation. The end of the world is not the object of an *apokalypsis*, but rather Noah's own preliminary fear before he receives any information concerning the end time.

In this anxiety, which of itself becomes concentrated into the certainty of the end, Noah cries out to his grandfather Enoch, who does not declare Noah's anxiety to be unsubstantiated and unfounded. Rather, he confirms both its justification as well as Noah's conviction that the end of the world is imminent. By the power of divine revelation, however, Enoch is able to unveil the events of the end time and to lend meaning to them. Furthermore, he reveals to his grandson that God will deliver him from the judgment of the flood and will bless his descendants. In his anxiety before the end, Noah embodies almost typologically the Jews afflicted by Israel's catastrophic situation, those who believe that the only thing lying before them is the end. Enoch, on the other hand, the mediator of revelation, is the prototype of the apocalyptist in the truest sense of the word, namely, the unveiler who reinterprets the certainty of the imminent end of all things into the ground for hope for those who despite the experience of disaster and God's absence nonetheless hold fast to the Yahweh faith. Not the end in and of itself is the theme of consoling apocalyptic, but rather the end reinterpreted as a transition.

The preliminary connection between world anxiety and the end of the world is also discernible where the notions of Jewish apocalyptic are substantively in contact with Iranian and Indian speculation regarding the world ages. Such is the case, for example, in the portrayal of the reversal of the natural order in the astronomical book of *1 Enoch*. The confusion in nature culminates in the disintegration of every trace of order among the celestial bodies. "All the orders of the stars shall harden (in disposition) against the sinners and the conscience of those that dwell upon the earth. They (the stars) shall err against them (the sinners); and modify all their courses. Then they (the sinners) shall err and take them (the stars) to be gods. And evil things shall be multiplied upon them; and plagues shall come upon them, so as to destroy them all" (*1 Enoch* 80:7f.). There is no mention of any supranatural intervention on God's part. It is the course of things themselves, left over to itself, which inexorably leads to the end of the world. In a different context, we read in the angelology concerning the demons[97] that they will cause trouble "until the day of the great final judgment, until the great(?) age is consummated" (*1 Enoch* 16:1). The course of the world is consummated in the final judgment.[98] A similar idea resonates in 4 Ezra. The end will come unavoidably, as the harvest follows sowing. "Because the age is hastening swiftly to its end" (4 Ezra 4:26). Different than in Iranian or Indian speculation, however, the waning age is not one of four or even more world ages, but encompasses rather all of world history. The end of the world is a one-time event that is not repeated.

Jewish apocalyptic does not abide with the notion of the end of the world. It anticipates rather the end as the commencement of a new beginning, and wants to awaken hope in God and in a condition of hitherto unknown good fortune. Both Hasidaean as well as rabbinic apocalyptic expand the view to include the Messiah, a figure of deliverance sent by God, and his kingdom.[99] One misunderstands the hope of Jewish apocalyptic, however, insofar as one overlooks the dark underground of redemption. Jewish messianism, as G. Scholem formulated it, is also and precisely in its expectation of redemption a "theory of catastrophe," in which "the catastrophic and destructive nature of the redemption on the one hand and the utopianism of the content of realized Messianism on the other" are inextricably bound together.[100] The yearned for day of the Lord is "a day of catastrophe,"[101] so that one finds the decisive characteristic of Jewish apocalyptic in the "*catastrophic nature of redemption,*" "which is then complemented by the utopian view of the content of realized redemption."[102] Only "beginning at the moment of the deepest catastrophe [does] there [exist] the chance for redemption."[103]

Jewish apocalyptic interprets the most extreme culmination of the world crisis as the precondition for final deliverance. Dan. 12:1 already prophesies: "And there shall be a time of trouble, such as never has been since there was a nation till that time; but at that time your people shall be delivered, every one whose name shall be found written in the book [of life]." *2 Apocalypse of Baruch* also predicts a time of extreme distress before God's intervening deliverance. "And it will happen that they will say in their thoughts because of their great tribulations, 'The Mighty One does not anymore remember the earth'; it will happen when they lose hope, that the [new] time will awake" (*2 Apoc. Bar.* 25:4). Similar pronouncements are found in rabbinic literature. "The son of David will not come before the denouncers have increased, or until the pupils have decreased, or until every penny has disappeared from the purse, or until one despairs of redemption" (*Sanh.* 97a, 41 Bar.). "The Israelites spoke before God: Lord of the world, when will you redeem us? He answered them: When you have sunk to the lowest level, in that hour I will redeem you" (*Midr.* Ps. 45 sect. 3 [135a]).[104]

In Jewish apocalyptic, although hope in redemption does not pass over the catastrophic nature of the present, it does argue against the inescapability of the catastrophe by teaching its readers to understand it as a crisis. As far as the world anxiety of the apocalyptist is concerned, this means that Jewish apocalyptic tries to transform catastrophe anxiety into crisis anxiety.[105] In Jewish apocalyptic, so our thesis, there is a transformation of apocalyptic anxiety.

The introductory chapters of what is known as the historical book of *1 Enoch* illustrate how Jewish apocalyptic tries to overcome catastrophic world anxiety by transforming it into crisis anxiety. Enoch describes for his son Methuselah a vision of the coming judgment which he had a long time ago. "I was sleeping in my grandfather Mahalalel's house, and I saw in a vision the sky being hurled down and snatched and falling upon the earth. When it fell upon the earth, I saw the earth being swallowed up into the great abyss, the mountains being suspended upon mountains, the hills sinking down upon the hills, and tall trees being uprooted and thrown and sinking into the deep abyss. Thereupon a word fell into my mouth; and I began crying aloud, saying, 'the earth is being destroyed' " (*1 Enoch* 83:3–5). Enoch's vision of the end of the world is noteworthy in two respects. First, it illustrates quite well the phenomenon which Kulenkampff had called "being overwhelmed" in connection with schizoid experiences of the end of the world.[106] Heaven collapses, the world caves in—initially only in Enoch's dream. Second, this dream of the end of the world provokes terrible anxiety. The fictitious Enoch's visionary experience of the end of the world is pure nightmare. Enoch is utterly overwhelmed by anxiety and is without hope. His apocalyptic anxiety can be called catastrophe anxiety in Haendler's sense, anxiety that condemns a person to complete passivity and powerlessness. There is not the slightest possibility of defense against the threat of total destruction. Enoch's account, however, continues in a manner highly significant for our investigation. Enoch tells how his grandfather woke him from his nightmare and asked about the reason for his cries. After Enoch has recounted his dream, his grandfather responds:

> How terrifying a thing have you seen, my son! You have seen in your dream a powerful vision of great significance for all the sins of the whole world: it must

> sink into the abyss and be destroyed with great destruction. Now, my son, rise and pray to the Lord of glory, for you are a man of faith, so that a remnant shall remain upon the earth and that the whole earth shall not be blotted out. My son, all the things upon the earth shall take place from heaven; and there will occur a great destruction upon the earth (*1 Enoch* 83:7–9).

Although Mahalalel confirms Enoch's dream, and thus initially strengthens his grandson's world anxiety and his expectation of the end of the world, he does—and this is the decisive feature in his discourse—charge Enoch on behalf of his faith in Yahweh and enjoins him to pray that God might not allow the end to be utterly final and complete. That is, the prayer is an entreaty that the catastrophe be transformed into a crisis. Within that prayer itself, however, catastrophe anxiety can be transformed into crisis anxiety, and Mahalalel accordingly embodies the real concern of Hasidaean apocalyptic, which consists in overcoming apocalyptic catastrophe anxiety by transforming it into crisis anxiety. And on the level of literary fiction such a change does indeed take place. Enoch does initially pray in the way his grandfather has advised him, and even writes down the wording of his prayer "for the generations of the world" (*1 Enoch* 83:10). This prayer issues in the petition:

> Now, O God, and Lord and Great King, I pray and beg so that you may sustain my prayer and save for me (a generation) that will succeed me in the earth; and do not destroy all the flesh of the people and empty the earth (so that) there shall be eternal destruction. Do now destroy, O my Lord, the flesh that has angered you from upon the earth, but sustain the flesh of righteousness and uprightness as a plant of eternal seed; and hide not your face from the prayer of your servant, O Lord (*1 Enoch* 84:5).

In this prayer for the transformation of what is to be a total catastrophe into a crisis yet allowing for a future beyond the horror, the petitioner's mood changes: "When [after the prayer] I descended underneath and saw the sky, the sun rising in the east, the moon descending in the west, the diminishing of the stars, and the whole earth, and everything as he had determined it in the beginning, I blessed the Lord of judgment and extolled him. For he made the sun to come out from the windows of the east; so it ascended and rose upon the face of the sky, starting to go the way that it was shown" (*1 Enoch* 83:11). The view of the rising sun contrasts the collapse of heaven in Enoch's vision. Just as night yields to the sun, so also does anxiety yield to newly germinating hope. Although the darkness of night is the locus of apocalyptic anxiety, the apocalyptist directs his gaze to the dawn of a new day, underscored by the accumulation of verbs describing the sunrise. The horizon reappears in the new light.

A similar transformation process can be observed in *2 Apoc. Bar.* 1ff. God announces to Baruch the impending fall of Jerusalem and of the kingdom of Judah. The fall of Jerusalem announced in the year 585 B.C. on the level of literary fiction, however, stands in fact for the destruction of the city in the year A.D. 70. The historical events toward the end of the first century B.C. are accommodated to the situation at the time of the prophet Jeremiah. Baruch reacts with great consternation and fear to the announcement of the catastrophe and the instructions to leave the city. In his despair he petitions God: "If I have grace in your eyes, take away my spirit first that I may go to my fathers and I must not see the destruction of my mother" (*2 Apoc. Bar.* 3:2). He is tormented by the question:

> What will happen after these things? For if you destroy your city and deliver up your country to those who hate us, how will the name [of the people] Israel be remembered again? Or how shall we speak again about your glorious deeds? Or to whom again will that which is in your Law be explained? Or will the universe return to its [original] nature and the world go back to its original silence? And will the [great] multitude of the souls be taken away and will not the nature of man be mentioned again? And where is all that which you said to Moses about us? (*2 Apoc. Bar.* 3:5–9).

Baruch's tormenting questions reflect the despair of the Jews after the catastrophe of the year A.D. 70. Israel's hopeless situation calls into question the faith of the fathers and makes it impossible to derive from the salvation history of the past any hope for the future. Consideration of this bleak situation of the people of God causes the idea of the end of the world to emerge. The present seems so inescapable that there no longer can be any future or world beyond the destruction of Jerusalem. In the perspective of the apocalyptist Israel's catastrophe expands into the end of the world, and the destruction of the holy city is equated with the beginning of the end of the world. There is no hope beyond this end, and the anxiety before this end can be called catastrophic. At this point, however, God's response to Baruch is directed to the anxious apocalyptists who share such thoughts: "The city will be delivered up for a time, and the people will be chastened for a time, but the world will not pass away" (*2 Apoc. Bar.* 4:1). It is not world anxiety in and for itself that is disputed here, but rather apocalyptic anxiety in the form of catastrophe anxiety. The catastrophe is reinterpreted into a crisis. Although there is admittedly no more hope for the earthly Jerusalem, a heavenly Jerusalem is yet offered as a counterpart to the city given over to destruction. Not even this apocalyptic filled with new hope is able to maintain the continuity with past salvation history.[107]

In a different context, O. Haendler used the expression "birth anxiety" to refer to what he describes as crisis anxiety.[108] The image of birth and of birth pains is also employed in Jewish and Christian apocalyptic. Mark 13:8 describes the emergence of pseudo-messiahs, the outbreak of wars, earthquakes, and famine as *archē ōdinōn.*[109] The turn of phrase "this is the beginning of the messianic woes," however, originally derives not from Christian sources, but rather already occurs as a term in rabbinic Judaism.[110] According to Haendler, crisis anxiety as birth anxiety differs from catastrophe anxiety, among other ways, in that it does not exclude, but rather can include activity. Here, too, a parallel can be drawn with Jewish apocalyptic, since precisely the question of the extent to which the birth of the new world needs human cooperation generated a dispute within Judaism between Hasidaean apocalyptists on the one hand, and Hasmonean circles on the other, between quietistic and zealot circles.

The image of birth is essentially related to that of a constricted or narrow exit that must push through to a new world, and the essential notion of the end of the world might be compared with a birth canal. Although apocalyptic literature does not attest this specific comparison, it does contain the imagery of a narrow passage:

> There is a sea set in a wide expanse so that it is broad and vast, but it has an entrance set in a narrow place, so that it is like a river. If anyone, then, wishes to reach the sea, to look at it or to navigate it, how can he come to the broad part unless he passes through the narrow part? Another example: There is a city built and set on a plain, and it is full of all good things; but the entrance to it is narrow and set in a precipitous place, so that there is fire on the right hand and deep water on the left; and there is only one path lying between them, that is, between the fire and the water, so that only *one* man can walk upon that path. If now that city is given to a man for an inheritance, how will the heir receive his inheritance unless he passes through the danger set before him? (4 Ezra 7:3–9).

The message of these two examples, however, is the following: "Therefore unless the living pass through the difficult and vain experiences, they can never receive those things that have been reserved for them" (4 Ezra 7:14). The passage cited interprets not only the events of the end themselves, but the entire present aeon as a narrow passage through which one must pass. These images bring to expression an experience of the narrowness of the world, a narrowness experienced as a threat. In the sense of our discussion in chapter 3, this experience can be interpreted as a calling into question of the future by the threatening loss of the "between" between self and world. As the world approaches increasingly closer, the between making possible both life and activity, a between without which there is no longer either world or self, becomes increasingly smaller. Anxiety discloses this endangerment of the between, the threatening narrowness of the world. At this point one might recall the inner connection between anxiety and narrowness extending even into the realm of the physiological. Anxiety is the feeling of narrowness in which it seems I am about to suffocate. Anxiety discloses existence as a condition of being in an increasingly narrow world.

Jewish apocalyptic, however, as a response to world anxiety, does not consider this narrowness to be the end, but rather a transitional stage, albeit a necessary one. "This present world is not the end; its glory does not abide in it. . . . But the day of judgment will be the end of this age and the beginning of the immortal age to come" (4 Ezra 7:112f.). Just as crisis anxiety is actually transformation anxiety, so is the day of judgment not expected as a day of annihilation, but rather as one of transformation. "On that day, I shall cause my Elect One [the messiah] to dwell among them, I shall transform heaven and make it a blessing of light forever. I shall [also] transform the earth and make it a blessing, and cause my Elect to dwell in here" (*1 Enoch* 45:4f.).[111] "In those days, there will be a change for the holy and the righteous ones" (*1 Enoch* 50:1). A change will also take place for the dead, and they will receive a new form at the resurrection.[112]

Just as the countenance of the earth will be transformed, so also, however, will anxiety yield to joy, a change in mood brought about by the certainty of imminent salvation. Thus does God console Baruch, who is extremely disturbed because of the uncertainty of the future: "Why, then, are you disturbed about that which you do not know, and why are you restless about that of which you do not possess any knowledge? . . . For truly, my salvation which comes has drawn near and is not as far away as before" (*2 Apoc. Bar.* 23:2, 7).[113] The joy of the righteous is the content of one of Enoch's visions of the last judgment: "The hearts of the holy ones were filled with joy, because the number of the righteous was near, the prayers of the righteous ones heard, and the blood of the righteous avenged before the Lord of the Spirits" (*1 Enoch* 47:4). The anticipatory joy of the apocalyptist grows from the certainty that such salvation is imminent.[114]

The preceding discussion has shown how one can gain access to Jewish apocalyptic by way of the phenomenon of world anxiety. Although this hermeneutical key proves to be useful for witnesses from various periods of Jewish history, its validity would have to be evaluated more thoroughly for specific cases, and the methodology of an interpretation from the perspective of an analysis of existence would have to be refined. Our previous results should not give the impression that Jewish apocalyptic actually constitutes thinking that remained unchanged through the various centuries, or any essentially unified system of ideas. In fact, the apocalyptic thinking of Judaism during the postexilic period remained constantly in flux and generated extremely disjunctive notions of judgment, the end time, and the salvific messianic age, and allowed such notions to exist beside one another. This lack of unity attaching to apocalyptic notions in Judaism is by no means to be denied by the preceding presentation, and the reference back to the phenomenon of apocalyptic world anxiety does not serve to press retroactively and, ultimately, arbitrarily into a timeless systematic framework what is actually unsystematic.[115] The concept of world anxiety is thus not to be elevated into the basis of an ideal or typical system of Jewish apocalyptic. Rather, as already pointed out, it fulfills the role merely of a key that fits various locks and opens doors to various conceptual worlds characterized by apocalyptic notions. As a kind of brief supplement, we will in what follows recall the most important conceptual elements of Jewish apocalyptic and thus round out the picture we have already acquired.

Common to all types of Jewish apocalyptic is the notion that a catastrophic event will bring about a one-time, decisive turn from disaster and affliction to salvation. The thinking of Jewish apocalyptic is thus fundamentally dualistic at the outset. Cautiously formulated, the dualism of Jewish apocalyptic consists in the irreconcilable antithesis between a present condition of disaster and affliction on the one hand, and a future condition of salvation on the other. As far as specifics are concerned, of course, what we are calling dualism here can be developed in extremely different ways. It frequently appears as the juxtaposition of two world periods of the aeons. The idea does interject itself, though by no means persuasively, that the future aeon constitutes a world completely different from the present world and history. The sublation of history is by no means the generally predominating understanding of the precondition of future salvation.

1 Enoch 71:15 speaks of a "world that is to come," Hebrew *habbā' hā'ôlām*. The counterconcept "this world" is, however, not found in *1 Enoch* 71. In contrast, the book of similitudes (*1 Enoch* 37:70), does refer to the present world as "this world of unrighteousness" without explicitly coining a term for the future world, though such is certainly present in substance. *2 Apocalypse of Baruch* clearly delineates this antithesis between two worlds. "This world,"[116] "this age,"[117] "this world of affliction,"[118] "this world that passes away,"[119] and "that world,"[120] "the world that is to come,"[121] or the "new world"[122] all stand antithetically juxtaposed. The situation in 4 Ezra is similar. "For this reason the Most High has made not *one* world but *two*" (4 Ezra 7:50). The present world is the "corrupt world" (4 Ezra 4:11),[123] separated by a "dividing of the times" (4 Ezra 6:7ff.) from the "age to come,"[124] the eternal "world to come."[125] Whereas in *2 Apocalypse of Baruch* the setting of the future aeon is in heaven, 4 Ezra localizes the new world on earth. Finally, the apocalypses also differ in their understanding of the character and duration of the kingdom of the Messiah and its relationship to the final new aeon.[126]

No less contradictory are the apocalyptic ideas of rabbinic Judaism, though with respect to the two aeons and the messianic period the substance of their views largely coincides with that of 4 Ezra.[127] Rabbinic sources also distinguish between the two aeons,[128] reckoning with the commencement of a salvific messianic age, either with God bringing redemption or a messiah inaugurating the new world.[129]

The path to the new aeon leads through a judgment of catastrophe. With respect to tradition history, messianic judgment of the nations is to be distinguished from universal judgment of the world, though apocalyptic literature often mixes these two notions of judgment with one another. Whereas the judgment of the nations or even the universal judgment of all the wicked is carried out by means of natural forces, fire, war, epidemics, or the divine hosts,[130] according to other sources a forensic trial will be convened at the end of days. This motif, too, is frequently associated with the notion of universal catastrophic world judgment.[131]

Various expectations were attached to the messianic kingdom during the course of Israel's postexilic history. On the one hand, such expectations are more of the nationalistic sort: Israel is reestablished within its original boundaries; the Jewish Diaspora returns to the promised land; Jerusalem becomes the capital of a theocratic world kingdom in which the Messiah reigns as the prince of peace; or the temple is rebuilt in unimagined splendor. On the other hand, the messianic kingdom takes on features of paradise itself in which the greatness of the human being and the splendor of his countenance are reestablished. Additionally, it is occasionally anticipated that the messianic kingdom will bring with it heretofore unknown fertility of the earth, plants, and human beings. Furthermore, the celestial bodies will shine with great luminosity. Some traditions' hopes for the salvific messianic age involve an end to all suffering and weeping as well as the elimination of death.[132] Insofar as the period of the messianic reign is distinguished from the new aeon, the interim kingdom will ultimately be succeeded by the new world. Not in every case, however, is the new world the future aeon of human history. In rabbinic literature the new world can also refer to the heavenly dwelling place of souls after death.[133] Insofar as the new aeon is conceived as the conclusion of world history, it is introduced by a resurrection of the dead[134] and world judgment, occasionally also separated from the past world by a world sabbath, a silent phase.[135]

The salvific messianic age is preceded by a period of great affliction. Revolution and war, plagues and famine, a reversal of the entire moral order, disregard for the Torah, and the suspension of all natural laws are conceivable as signs of the end time.[136] In the course of the postexilic history of Judaism various attempts were made to reckon the end of these afflictions and thus the commencement of the salvific messianic age. In this connection various conjectures concerning a periodization of world history were developed. Sources attest a division of the course of history into twelve,[137] ten,[138] seven,[139] or only two periods.[140] Other attempts at reckoning the end time reinterpret the seventy years from the prophecy of Jeremiah concerning the duration of the exile. The first to engage in such an interpretation is Dan. 9.[141] In its own turn, this text became the basis for further attempts at reckoning which apply the seventy year-weeks from Dan. 9 to world history in the larger sense.[142] In addition, attempts were made to derive statements concerning the time of the end from individual passages from the Old Testament.[143]

Such periodization of the course of history and the determination of the end take us back to the question we posed at the beginning, namely, just how definitive this one-time end of the world in the thinking of Jewish apocalyptic really is. Those who attribute definitive character to the one-time end of the world frequently associate their evaluation with a fundamental criticism of apocalyptic historical thinking. The determinism to which history is allegedly subjected, coupled with the dualism of the aeons, is allegedly the equivalent of a sublation of history[144] or a "dehistoricization of history."[145] This accusation will be discussed again later in connection with a critical evaluation of the overall phenomenon of apocalyptic.[146] As a sweeping judgment—let this much be said here—it is in any case unable to do justice to the textual findings of Jewish apocalyptic. The cosmic end here is definitive insofar as it brings about a decision that is final and irrevocable for all the world. On the other hand, it is not in every case asserted that all history in the future will break off or be destroyed. This sort of sublation of history is, however, intimated when heaven rather than the earth is declared to be the setting of the future aeon. At least the older tradents of Jewish apocalyptic, however, do not intend for history to be brought to an end. "Actually the exact opposite is intended: History is to be set into motion anew, beyond judgment, by a convulsive and universally efficacious intervention on the part of God."[147] Even *2 Apocalypse of Baruch* yet reassures its readers: "The city will be delivered up for a time, and the people will be chastened for a time, but the world will not pass away" (*2 Apoc. Bar.* 4:1). The various attempts at reckoning the time of the end encountered criticism already within rabbinic Judaism.[148]

This so-called determinism, however, is misunderstood insofar as it is interpreted as an anticipatory sublation of history. As an example, in the case of the animal vision in *1 Enoch* 85ff. one can say at most that the end is determined, "but again not as the end of history in the larger sense, but rather as the end of Israel's own history of disaster, brought about by God."[149] To that extent the image of the line of time cut vertically from above at the end of history, one often applied to the apocalyptic concept of time, leads to misunderstanding. A more suitable image is the "notion of a long stretch of time at whose quickly approaching zenith [!] one expects a single and final manifestation of God which will open up a salvific dimension whose proportions and application transcend the norm of all canonical historical deeds of God that have previously constituted Israel's understanding of history."[150] "The goal of Hasidaean apocalyptic in the face of a violently convulsed historical terrain of extreme religious and political exigency was nothing less than a disavowal of that particular linear stretch of history which tradition had constructed over long periods of time through a gradual accrual of past salvific deeds of God, deeds which only and ultimately in their full sum were able to call Israel into existence."[151]

The end of the world, we have asserted, is definitive in Jewish apocalyptic insofar as it brings about a one-time decision. It is judgment, crisis, a breaking off as well as a new beginning. This, too, reflects the transformation of world anxiety in Jewish apocalyptic from catastrophe anxiety into crisis anxiety. Parseeism and Germanic religion similarly did not anticipate the end of the world necessarily as a complete destruction of history as such. The one-time end of the world as a total sublation of history is the expression of apocalyptic catastrophe anxiety. Jewish apocalyptic, however, reinterprets the threatening catastrophe into a crisis and mediates the consolation that the crisis of history must not necessarily mean its sublation.

5. *Annihilatio* and *Renovatio Mundi*

The sublation of history is first really radically thought through in the notion of the *annihilatio mundi* as developed by Lutheran orthodoxy in the seventeenth century.[152] Already for Johann Gerhard, who developed the thesis of the *annihilatio mundi* and exercised a lasting influence on Lutheran eschatology as late as Buddeus,[153] the *annihilatio*-concept serves to counter Reformed ideas concerning the end of the world. The notion of the *annihilatio mundi* also understands itself clearly to be occupying a position at the front in the battle against contemporary millenarian currents which later were to exercise influence within both Calvinism and Pietism. Extreme world negation, behaving on the surface like an extreme radicalizing of apocalyptic thinking, is at its apex actually antiapocalyptic.

Despite condemnation during the Reformation age,[154] a plethora of millenarian currents can be observed during the seventeenth century with expectations vacillating between pronounced materialistic and wholly spiritualized notions of an innerworldly salvific age.[155] A phenomenon not easily distinguished from the various types of millenarianism, types not easily subsumed under a common denominator, was the widespread conviction that the end of the world was imminent. This imminent expectation is the inheritance of the Reformation, and is more strongly rooted in Lutheranism than in Reformed circles. Luther himself thought that the "dear last judgment" was even now at the door. He understood the Reformation itself as an eschatological event, just as in a reverse fashion he interpreted numerous events of his own time, in particular the differing reactions to the Reformation movement itself, as signs of the end time; this is the case, e.g., in his *Suppulatio annorum mundi* of 1545 (1541).[156] Despite his rejection of millenarianism, apocalyptic was an integral part of Luther's eschatology.[157] Reformed theologians were more reserved with respect to near expectation, e.g., Calvin.[158] Within Lutheranism, however, near expectation continued without interruption into the seventeenth century, propagated in apocalyptic writings and church hymns. The mood accompanying such expectation was also widespread in Catholic regions. Only during the course of the seventeenth century—astonishingly despite the Thirty Years' War—did faith in the end time lose significant ground.

Johann Gerhard shares the near expectation of his age: "Just as all the prophecies of scripture extend no further than about fifty more years . . . the sixth millennium of the world hastens to its end . . . We will soon see Christ coming."[159] On the other hand, his "Tractatus de consummatione seculi"[160] constitutes a counterpart to contemporary millenarianism, the critique of which occupies considerable space in the *Loci Theologici*.[161] Gerhard argues against the justification of a literal interpretation of key biblical passages such as Isa. 65:17ff., and does so with the help of a hermeneutic of eschatological salvation explaining the worldly imagery of future glory as a metaphorical portrayal of worldless salvation.[162] Admittedly, this hermeneutic can only with great difficulty draw support from Luther—despite Luther's rejection of millenarian eschatologies—since Luther does not espouse any eschatological annihilation of the world.

The worldly or unworldly character of eschatological salvation on the one hand, and the nature of eschatological human corporeality on the other, are points of contention not only in the dispute Lutheran orthodoxy carries on with millenarianism, but also with Reformed theology.[163] Here Reformed eschatology, with its notion of the *renovatio mundi*, remains wholly "under the influence of ancient church tradition,"[164] whereby millenarianism is also rejected in principle on the Reformed side. The cosmic end of the world, the *consummatio mundi*, analogous to individual death, is not conceived as total destruction, but rather as a culmination and renewal of the world. Although the view was widespread that God would bring about the cosmic catastrophe presumably by means of fire, this world conflagration would exhibit purifying and cleansing power.[165] The world is given over to annihilation not according to its substance, but rather merely with respect to its nonessentials.[166] In substance, however, the end of the world does not mean the annihilation, but rather the completion of the world: "Consummatio seculi *synteleia tou aiōnos* est."[167] From the fire of the catastrophe, however, the renewed earth emerges: "Conflagrationis mundi effectus non substantiae annihilatio sed a vitiis agnatis per peccatum purgatio et renovatio erit; non annihilatio sed purgatio est."[168] The notion of a *renovatio* and *purgatio* by means of a world conflagration recalls the Stoic motif of the *ekpyrōsis*. In contrast, however, Reformed eschatology emphasizes both the initiative and the freedom of God's actions. The world conflagration and thus also the *renovatio mundi* is not a natural law, but rather an act of God himself, who is superior to the world: "Mundo deus non natura finem imponet."[169] This thesis clearly delimits the dogmatic doctrinal piece *De consummatione mundi* over against world-pessimistic theories of decline that view the end of the world as unavoidable fate.

Both over against Reformed theology as well as over against Luther and the Lutheranism of the sixteenth century, a serious break in eschatological thinking takes place in the idea of the *annihilatio mundi* developed by J. Gerhard. The world will be given over to complete destruction. This *annihilatio* affects the substance of the world, and not merely its nonessentials. Gerhard summarizes this thought: "Consummatio seculi sive destructio mundi est Dei actio, qua per ignem coelum, terram, mare et omnes creaturas, quae in eis sunt, solis angelis et hominibus exceptis, in nihilum rediget ad veritatis, potentiae ac justitiae suae manifestationem et piorum hominum liberationem."[170]

Annihilatio mundi thus means the destruction of all creatures not endowed with reason. Angels and human beings are expressly excepted. By "world" in this context Gerhard understands "tota rerum universitas cum omnibus partibus et contentis, exceptis solis angelis et hominibus."[171] Gerhard, too, does not trace the end of the world back to any innerworldly development, but rather to a sovereign act of God, "Dei actio." The goal or *causa finalis* of this intervention is on the one hand the glorification of divine power and righteousness, and on the other the deliverance of the faithful.

Gerhard attempts to ground the idea of the *annihilatio mundi* biblically. Among other passages, he adduces and interprets 2 Peter 3:5ff. and Rom. 8:19–22. All the same, Gerhard's concept of the *annihilatio* is not biblical.[172] It derives rather from the philosophical discussion of ontological questions, and in Gerhard takes a turn constituting a fundamental contradiction of Aristotelian metaphysics and the subsequent scholastic eschatology dependent on it. Gerhard's idea of the *annihilatio mundi* is "the theologically motivated objection to philosophically grounded eschatology, eschatology extrapolated from knowledge of the given structure of the world."[173] This objection is itself grounded in the doctrine of God, a peculiar understanding of the world, and a concept of eschatological salvation that breaks with ecclesiastical tradition. In this context, as K. Stock has shown, the real background of Gerhard's eschatology is not, as, e.g., P. Althaus supposed, "to be found in any penetration of medieval mysticism into Lutheran theology,"[174] but rather in the Lutheran understanding of the bodily presence of Christ in the Eucharist.[175] The idea of the *annihilatio* draws ontological consequences from the Lutheran doctrine of omnipresence, a doctrine that in its own turn must presuppose a nonspatial, yet for that very reason worldless nature regarding the eschatological corporeality of Christ.

From the perspective of the doctrine of God, the notion of the *annihilatio mundi* is a necessary consequence of God's permanence. The essence of the world consists precisely in its impermanence and finitude. Impermanence and corruptibility, however, refer not only to its nonessentials, but also to its substance. The final and total destruction of the world is to be conceived for the sake of God's own permanence. This destruction, however, remains an act of divine freedom. To that extent Gerhard's concept of the *annihilatio mundi* can be understood as "the metaphor of the freedom and permanence of God."[176] For this reason, the world can have no part in eschatological salvation. On the other hand, it is essential for human beings to have a world and to be in that world, so that the question must arise just how the eschatological corporeality of human beings is conceivable as a condition for participation in divine salvation without any reference to a world. Gerhard's solution to this problem is that in the eschaton God himself will replace the world for human beings. "Put metaphorically: Just as the heavenly Jerusalem is conceived without either temple or other edifices, and just as the inhabitants of the holy city can do without either sun or moon . . . so also will God himself replace the world for the eschatologically identical human being . . . *By destroying the world, God himself becomes the world for human beings.*"[177]

Gerhard's conception of eschatology comes across like a radical intensification of apocalyptic thinking in an age shaken by a variety of end-time expectations. And indeed, the idea of the *annihilatio mundi* results not only from theological postulates or the need for legitimation in the Eucharist dispute. Gerhard's *annihilatio* concept finds support in experiences of the catastrophic side of nature and history. The great flood illustrates typologically both the fundamental impermanence of the world constitution and its future destruction.[178] Natural and historical catastrophes are manifestations of God's anger at human sin. Accordingly, in Gerhard's understanding the *annihilatio mundi* encompasses all the previous particular tendencies toward destruction into one universal destruction.[179] In this way, all innerworldly and innerhistorical catastrophes are disclosed by an apocalyptic hermeneutic.

Insofar as the worldliness of future salvation is rejected, Gerhard's *annihilatio* concept does admittedly acquire antiapocalyptic tendencies. Since we are first of all asking only phenomenological questions concerning the apocalyptic understanding of existence, we do not need to discuss more closely at this point the innertheological criticism of Gerhard's eschatology. Viewed phenomenologically, however, the world negation expressed in Gerhard's concept of the *annihilatio mundi* seems to be a radicalizing which turns apocalyptic into its opposite. The *salto mortale* of apocalyptic world negation takes place in the concept of the *annihilatio.* This interpretation of the *annihilatio* idea accords well with the observation that Gerhard's concept of world destruction goes back to what are ultimately gnostic sources such as are encountered in the eschatological design of Valentinus and, with altered presuppositions, also in Origen.[180] Gnosis, however, as we have already seen, can be understood as a radicalizing of apocalyptic thinking.[181] Precisely this radicalizing resonates in Gerhard's eschatology, though as the paradigmatic settlement of accounts with millenarianism in the *Loci Theologici* shows, it acquires an antiapocalyptic tendency. Any attempt at combating millenarian apocalyptic with the aid of eschatology variously influenced by gnostic ideas is like trying to drive out the devil with Beelzebub.

The real problem attaching to the thesis of the *annihilatio mundi* is that it is able to conceive world negation only at the price of a total sublation of history. Here it clearly differs from Jewish apocalyptic. One must admit that the *annihilatio* idea does conceptualize and harshly illuminate the elements of negativity and the catastrophic; or that it even overdraws them, though through such exaggeration it is able to make quite clear the negative tendencies of reality itself. Nonetheless, the question needs to be directed to the concept of the *annihilatio mundi* whether precisely in the idea of world negation it does not capitulate before the catastrophic nature of history. As we saw, Jewish apocalyptic reinterprets the threatening catastrophe of history into a crisis, and in this way is able to transform catastrophe anxiety into crisis anxiety. This possibility does not seem to exist any longer for the Lutheran eschatology of the seventeenth century, for whom the *consummatio seculi* is the equivalent of surrendering the world. Surrendering the world in notions of total destruction defines it with respect to its negativity and catastrophic nature. Precisely the irreconcilable protest against the given world is the equivalent, in this instance, to a capitulation over against the world. If anywhere, the accusation of the dehistoricization of history seems justified when directed against the idea of the *annihilatio mundi.*

6. Scientific Theories of the End of the World

"One widespread notion we encounter among various peoples is that of a *great destructive power* whose intervention means the end of humankind and of life associated with it. This power can be conceived (1) as purely physical (flood, collapse, conflagration), (2) as mythical (living beings), though connected with a natural phenomenon, or (3) as purely mythical."[182] This division of prescientific notions of the end of the world[183] presented by A. Olrik brings into focus in an introductory fashion the inner connection between apocalyptic thinking and scientific theories of the end of the world. Just as prescientific apocalyptic by no means develops merely mythical notions of threatening dangers, but rather does indeed also entertain natural, physical explanations of the anticipated end of the world, so also in a reverse fashion does apocalyptic potential inhere in scientific theories of the end of the world. And just as, for example, Jewish apocalyptic develops the notion of the end of the world with scientific exactitude—prompting the thesis that the origin of apocalyptic is to be found in wisdom—genuinely apocalyptic motifs occasionally provide the background to the scientific question regarding the possible end of the world.

The connection between apocalyptic and science does not mean that scientific theories of something like an end of the world are to be dismissed as modern myth. Rather, an inner relationship obtains between the two quantities such that on the one hand a latently or manifestly apocalyptic anxiety can prompt the question from a scientific perspective concerning something like an end of the world in the first place, just as in a reverse fashion scientific theories of the end can generate or even soothe apocalyptic anxiety. It is not enough to take scientific statements concerning the end of the world merely as the cosmological counterpart or mere consequence of scientific theories of origins. Insofar as they deal with the future of humankind, of the earth, or even of the entire cosmos, theories of the end of the world exhibit the character of prognosis. Neither should one forget that some of the scenarios of catastrophe under discussion today are commissioned prognoses in which the apocalyptic dimension of scientific theories of the end become perhaps most clear. It is not the scenarios of scientists that are first able to generate what amounts to apocalyptic anxiety, but rather quite the reverse, it is anxiety before and for the future that first sends science down the path of its investigations.

Over against this fundamental and mutual relationship between anxiety and scientific scenarios of the end time, the fact that many of these images of catastrophe coincide with the imagery of prescientific apocalyptic is of secondary significance. At the same time, this fact is noteworthy.

Our own task can be neither a complete presentation of the history of scientific theories of the end of the world, nor especially any scientific analysis and critical evaluation of the various scenarios and their probability. Rather, in what follows we will merely seek out the apocalyptic theme in scientific dealings with the end of the world and illustrate its variations paradigmatically in several examples.

Consistent with our previous division of notions of the end of the world, here, too, we can distinguish between partial, global, and cosmic scientific theories of an "end of all things." Partial or global scenarios deal with catastrophic developments on the earth or with its total destruction. Possible causes include geological or climatic changes, a cosmic catastrophe such as a collision with a comet, the slowing of the earth's rotation, or the extinguishing of the sun, the exhaustion of resources, or the population explosion. Cosmic theories of the end address the question of a possible end of the entire cosmic development. These include especially the cyclical theory of the oscillating universe on the one hand, and the thesis of the heat death of the cosmos, based on the Second Law of thermodynamics, on the other.

As we have already seen in connection with the Stoics,[184] the question whether the earth is subject to a progressive aging process already possessed great significance in antiquity. The observation of changes in geological formations, in particular alterations in coastlines and general erosion through wind and rain, made this question unavoidable.

In the eighteenth century, to take a modern example, it is Immanuel Kant who in an essay from the year 1754 addressed from the perspective of the physical sciences the question whether the earth is aging.[185] Right at the outset Kant rejects those popular assertions concerning the age of the earth already sufficiently familiar to us from apocalyptic literature: the alleged worsening of the climate, the diminishing life expectancy of human beings, the decline of morals. In contrast, Kant subjects to serious and critical analysis[186] the scientific scenarios of the aging process of the earth presented during his own age. Like its advocates, Kant, too, is prompted by his own observation of nature "to suspect with some probability a subtle substance, everywhere efficacious, a so-called world spirit, though also to be concerned that incessant procreations consume more and more of the same quantity of material than the destruction of natural constructions leaves behind, and that nature, through such consumption of the same material, does forfeit some measure of its power."[187] The possibility considered here by Kant anticipates basically the law of entropy formulated in 1863 by Clausius, though Kant admittedly was not in a position to provide sound arguments for his suspicion of a universal running out and end of all natural processes. Nonetheless it remains noteworthy that, in the age of the Enlightenment no less, Kant reckons with the possibility of an irreversible process of the decline of nature. Significantly, he sees signs of such not least in the course of the development of human culture. At this juncture at latest, thinking derived from the physical sciences on the one hand, and existential experience of the world on the other, come into contact:

> When I compare the drive of ancient peoples toward great things, the enthusiasm of ambition, of virtue and of the love of freedom, an enthusiasm that inspired them with high ideals and elevated them above themselves—when I compare this drive with the ameliorated and indifferent character of our own age, although I do find reason to wish our centuries luck in undergoing such a change equally tolerable to moral doctrine and the sciences, I nonetheless am tempted to believe that these are signs of a certain cooling down of that particular fire which animated human nature, a fire whose intensity was so fruitful in its excesses as well as in its beautiful results.[188]

The fact that Kant ultimately does not give in to resignation and pessimism derives from the hope he brings to the Enlightenment. Quite possibly the "cooling down of the fire" may well be the result not of any unchangeable destiny of nature, but rather of societal conditions, the state constitution, and education, all of which could be decisively improved through the influence of the Enlightenment.

In contrast, over against such weighty questions Kant attributes completely subordinated significance to the possibility of global catastrophes which might be precipitated by the collision with a comet or by volcanic activity in the earth's interior. In Kant's opinion, no meaningful prognoses can be presented regarding such chance occurrences. "There are other causes which through a sudden convulsion of the earth could bring about its destruction . . . However, these sorts of chance occurrences pertain as little to the question of the aging of the earth as does the consideration of earthquakes or conflagrations to the question of how a building might age."[189] Although this does not imply that such global or cosmic catastrophes are to be fundamentally excluded, Kant does distinguish between corresponding catastrophe anxiety on the one hand, and a general, scientific theory of decline on the other. Such a theory finds no support in the possibility of catastrophic accidents.

The fear of a collision between the earth and a comet, or of the consequences of particular planetary constellations, has in the course of history repeatedly held sway over human beings. Frequently the appearance of such celestial bodies has been understood as the divine announcement of the approaching end of the world and of the last judgment. When the possibility of a meteorite catastrophe is discussed with scientific arguments, one is not infrequently dealing—as is well known—with apocalyptic prophecies in scientific garb. Examples continue even into recent history.[190] From an astronomical perspective, however, the probability of such a collision is extremely slight, just as the possibility of a collision between stars or planets is very slight.

In contrast, theories of destruction deriving from the physical sciences[191] which in the Kantian sense anticipate an ongoing disintegration of global proportions include the older assumption that the earth will plunge into the sun, as well as the theory of the freezing death of the earth resulting from a cooling and extinguishing of the sun. It is also conceivable that before the sun is extinguished, it will expand one final time, thereby destroying all life on earth and finally the earth itself. One certain expectation is that the sun will one day share the fate of the other stars. On the other hand, the time periods within which this development will take place are so astronomical that in the case of these astrophysical considerations one should probably speak of an extremely distant expectation of the end of the world.

The "lunarizing" of the earth has also been variously considered. This hypothesis suggests that because of increasing loss due to friction the rotation of the earth will one day be brought to a standstill, so that afterward the earth will like the moon revolve with one side constantly turned toward the sun, and one side constantly turned away from the sun. Kant investigated this possibility as early as 1754 in a treatise prompted by an open competition sponsored by the Royal Academy in Berlin.[192] In his treatment, Kant develops the theory that the rotation of the earth on its axis will—albeit in inconceivably distant time periods—be braked by the gravitational pull of the moon, which causes high and low tides whose movement is contrary to the rotation of the earth. The result would be that after the rotation is brought to a standstill one side of the earth would constantly be illuminated by the sun, while on the side turned away from the sun eternal night and cold would rule. It is noteworthy how in the nineteenth century the renewal of this scientific theory[193] results in the moon later being accorded apocalyptic symbolic content. Through the medium of thinking based on the natural sciences it becomes the metaphor of apocalyptic future expectation: "Hence the moon, whose entire surface structure as viewed through a telescope does not offer any favorable surface for organic living beings at least according to our understanding, would be the reflection of the future threatening the earth after several millennia."[194]

Other scenarios begin with climatic changes. Their prognosis constitutes, for example, part of the American study *Global 2000*. In such scenarios the inner connection between scientific prognosis and anxiety before an uncertain future becomes especially clear. It is the consciousness of present danger which in this case first prompts the search for scientific prognosis. Futurology is questioned from the perspective of a wide-ranging crisis consciousness. It is anxiety before the threat of destruction that asks for scientific scenarios of the future of our earth. These scenarios deal primarily with factors dependent on human beings, and summarize in a single, comprehensive world model the anticipated changes in population density, natural resources, and the environment; in these scenarios, however, climatic developments also play a role, developments conceived as being dependent on human beings only in a limited fashion.[195] In addition to the prediction of stable temperature conditions, other scenarios concerning the climate anticipate strong or moderate global cooling or a moderate or strong warming.[196] At least the extremes on the scale of climatic scenarios, albeit with certain qualification, can be described very well as theories of catastrophe whose visions of a future characterized by extreme aridity, violent storms, or increasing icing, find parallels in the apocalyptic imagery of prescientific notions of the end of the world.

Such astrophysical, geological, and meteorological theories of catastrophe are joined by the more biologically oriented ones. These include the scenario of a global collapse precipitated by the population explosion.[197] The problem of the alarming growth of the world's population is connected with problems such as the shortage of food, exhaustion of natural resources, and environmental destruction. The complex associated with the catchphrase "limits to growth" as well as that concerning possible nuclear catastrophe with its attendant ecological consequences will be treated later for reasons yet to be discussed.[198]

We are interested first in conceptual models based on the theory of evolution which develop a concept of the end history and of the end itself either globally, referring to all earthly life, or particularly, referring to the fate of the human species. Within the framework of evolutionary thinking, P. Teilhard de Chardin outlines a scientifically grounded—or should one rather say scientifically "disguised"?—history of salvation.[199] The development of the cosmos strives from inanimate material, driven by spiritual energy inherent in all material, to the origin of the biosphere and then to the noosphere, the dimension of consciousness, and finally finds its fulfillment and completion in the Omega Point, in which all developmental lines, after initial differentiation, converge.[200] Teilhard's nature philosophy has cosmic dimensions. So, also, does he not wish to exclude a completion of the evolution of the spirit at the cosmic level. According to Teilhard it is conceivable that earthly life, mediated by the human spirit, might one day break through to other planets and branch out there as well, or that life "gets into psychical touch with other focal points of consciousness across the abysses of space . . . Consciousness would thus finally construct itself by a synthesis of planetary units. Why not, in a universe whose astral unit is the galaxy?"[201] These hypotheses, however, are not central for Teilhard, since he "considers their probability too remote for them to be worth dwelling on."[202] Despite its cosmic horizon, Teilhard de Chardin's vision of the future remains a theory of the global end time, mindful of the basic assumption "that our noosphere is destined to close in upon itself in isolation, and that it is in a psychical rather than a spatial direction that it will find an outlet, without need to leave or overflow the earth."[203]

What comes about in this way is nothing less than a modern apocalypse. It inquires not concerning the fate of the earth; rather, the earth itself becomes the symbol of its own salvation history. The prophesied eschaton, what Teilhard calls the Omega Point,[204] is compared with one of the poles of the globe to which all meridians strive and in which they converge. The curving of the earth's surface is the prototype of the cosmic convergence of the spirit. On this foundation Teilhard draws on the terminology of the theory of evolution to describe an eschatological drama in which human beings, as the apex of all biological development, have a key role.[205] The actual end is preceded by what Teilhard called the "ultimate earth," to be distinguished from the presently existing "modern earth." "Thus in all probability, between our modern earth and the ultimate earth, there stretches an immense period, characterized not by a slowing-down but a speeding up and by the definitive florescence of the forces of evolution along the line of the human shoot."[206] Unmistakable "signs"[207] precede the end of the earth, including the slowing down and ultimate cessation of biological evolution accompanied by simultaneous hastening of intellectual development, a unification of humankind transcending nations and races, the global organization of research and its concentration on the human being as its object, and finally the conjunction of science and religion. The end, however, is the goal for the collective "spirit of the earth."[208] This Omega Point is reached when "mankind, *taken as a whole*, is obliged—as happened to the individual forces of instinct—to reflect upon itself at a single point."[209] As Teilhard explains, one can speak of this actual end of the world only in allusions:

> The end of the world: the wholesale internal introversion upon itself of the noosphere, which has simultaneously reached the uttermost limit of its complexity and its centrality. The end of the world: the overthrow of equilibrium, detaching the mind, fulfilled at last, from its material matrix, so that it will henceforth rest with all its weight on God-Omega. The end of the world: critical point simultaneously of emergence and emersion, of maturation and escape.[210]

The path to this end of the world leads according to Teilhard de Chardin either through a peaceful convergence or through a final planetary crisis inaugurated by a final polarization of good and evil.[211] At this point Teilhard himself refers to the convergence of his own system with apocalyptic thinking. The first hypothesis, the assumption of a peaceful final condition of the earth preceding the end of the world, stands in clear proximity to millenarianism. Teilhard, whose inclinations favor this hypothesis,[212] is able only with some effort to distinguish the assumption of a final convergence in a condition of world-encompassing peace from millenarianism.[213] On the other hand, the second hypothesis is admittedly "more in conformity with traditional apocalyptic thinking."[214] In the language of evolutionary theory, the apocalypses can be read as follows:

> We may perhaps discern three curves around us rising up at one and the same time into the future: an inevitable diminution in the organic possibilities of the earth, an internal schism of consciousness ever increasingly divided on two opposite ideals of evolution, and positive attraction of the centre of centres at the heart of those who turn towards it. And the earth would finish at the triple point at which, by a coincidence altogether in keeping with the ways of life, these three curves would meet and attain their maximum at the very same moment.[215]

According to this biological apocalypse, the path of evolution leads through death to true life: "The death of the materially exhausted planet; the split of the noosphere, divided on the form to be given to its unity; and simultaneously (endowing the event with all its significance and with all its value) the liberation of that percentage of the universe which, across time, space and evil, will have succeeded in laboriously synthesising itself to the very end."[216] If one formulates the two hypotheses developed by Teilhard de Chardin in the language of Christian dogmatics, we find juxtaposed here all-encompassing reconciliation on the one hand, and double judgment on the other. And just as very little of substance can be said from the perspective of dogmatics about the end of the world, so also in the biologically influenced language of Teilhard. At Teilhard's conclusion the place of the dogmatic concept of the last judgment is taken by that of ecstasy: "Ecstasy in concord; or discord; but in either case by excess of interior tension: the only biological outcome proper to or conceivable for the phenomenon of man."[217]

Like Teilhard de Chardin, so also does H. von Ditfurth develop an eschatological concept based on the theory of evolution, though Ditfurth does draw contrasting consequences from the insights of biology and argues against the guarantee of survival for the human species postulated by Teilhard.

> Here the great man unquestionably drew his conclusions from an all-too-geocentric perspective. The guarantee of survival for humankind he derives is a beautiful dream. The history of the universe will not stand still if humankind disappears from it. From the countless beginnings we must presuppose in addition to the one on earth, cosmic evolution will in the future bring forth ever new, ever greater and ever more wonderful manifestations of the spiritual and intellectual principle, a principle which in us, in an initial flickering of self-consciousness, had just begun to become embodied. No one will even notice that human beings have disappeared from history. The future of the cosmos will not even contain a trace of our memory.[218]

Similar to Teilhard de Chardin, Ditfurth also rejects all types of monistic thinking and reckons with a dimension of consciousness independent of material substance.[219] Yet Ditfurth concludes from the laws of selection and mutation that the human species does not constitute an exception in the process of evolution, and is like countless other species before and contemporaneous with it threatened by extinction. There is no escape from the threatening catastrophe of ecological crisis or nuclear holocaust. Rather, the exit of our species, an exit unavoidable according to the laws of biology, will take place in these catastrophes. "Of all the species that have existed in the more than four-billion-year history of the earth, according to paleontological estimates at least 99.9 percent have become extinct. No biological species lives forever. This also applies to the species whose members have with no false modesty given themselves the name *homo sapiens.*"[220] It is the human being himself who conjures the danger of his own destruction and at the same time causes a "fauna cut" of unimagined proportions.

Ditfurth does not, to be sure, draw from this insight the conclusion that one must issue the call for repentance and an appeal to human reason. Because of their inherited biological characteristics and their biologically preprogrammed behavioral models, human beings are allegedly not at all seriously in a position to avert either their own fate or that of the earth.[221] Their biological hereditary factors, above all the mechanism of anxiety, are what drive human beings inexorably—albeit as a result of biologically explainable factors—into self-destruction. The extinction of the species *homo sapiens* is thus preprogrammed. Despite his admittedly predominantly pessimistic tone, Ditfurth's scenario does not dissolve into gloomy colors. Rather, Ditfurth feels his way along the scientific path toward eschatological hope based on Plato's doctrine of ideas, Schopenhauer's philosophy, yet also on Martin Luther.[222] Although Ditfurth rejects the notion of life after death,[223] he nonetheless raises the question "whether death will be identical with our *destruction.*"[224] He contests this and opens up to his reader the possibility "that a reproduction or model does not exist without its original, that the world in which we find ourselves rests on a transcendent foundation both supporting and rendering it possible . . . and that thus, when we in death fall out of this world, do not fall into nothingness."[225] Thus Ditfurth can pray with Luther: "Come, dear last judgment."[226]

Ditfurth's book fulfills thereby all the important criteria of an apocalypse. In an age filled with world anxiety it claims to unveil reality. The future appears threatened by serious dangers. For critical contemporaries, the situation seems virtually hopeless. Ditfurth's apocalypse crassly illuminates this inescapability. For the apocalyptist the possibility of the end of the world becomes a certainty. At the same time, however, a path of escape emerges. In the midst of closing horizons a glimmer of hope shines. The catastrophe of collective death is reinterpreted as a crisis, and the ultimate exit becomes a transition. From this perspective the catastrophe facing us presents itself "as a wholesome event of 'awakening.' For the person who genuinely takes it seriously it presents no reason for despair. This, by the way, is also the central point of my response to those who will accuse me of taking away all hope from human beings by referring to the inescapability of our situation."[227] Ditfurth's book claims to offer consolation, not hopelessness, joining thereby the literature of traditional apocalypses, which has always been literature of consolation. This scientifically organized work is a book of consolation for those afflicted by anxiety. In this apocalypse the scientific theory fulfills ultimately the function of pastoral care.

Ditfurth's thesis of the dying out of the human species, with its attendant criticism of anthropomorphic interpretations of evolution, formulates under altered theoretical conditions an idea which Paul Thiery d'Holbach already articulated in a different form. "Nature, considered in its whole," Holbach writes in his anonymous *System of Nature* of 1770, "shows us beings . . . born to die, and exposed to those continual vicissitudes from which no one of them is exempt. The most superficial glance of the eye will suffice, then to undeceive us as to the idea that man is the final cause of the creation, the constant object of the labours of nature."[228] With that, Holbach is already considering the possible extinction of the human species: "What absurdity, then, or what want of just inference would there be to imagine, that man, the horse, the fish, the bird, will be no more! Are these animals so indispensably requisite to nature, that without them she cannot continue her eternal course?"[229] Far from being the crown of creation or the king of the universe, human beings are actually merely an episode in the history of nature, an "ephemeron."[230] Here Holbach anticipates Darwinistic insights, though without the apocalyptic consolation H. von Ditfurth offers us.

Whereas the previously selected examples of theories derived from the natural sciences (or from the philosophy of nature)—despite occasional cosmological references—develop a concept of the partial or global end, the following examples deal with cosmological theories of the end. Visions of the beginning of the world, "despite considerable rational exactitude, nonetheless exhibit a thoroughly mythical format," as E. Drewermann accurately remarks. "And the same applies to the various notions concerning the end of the world."[231] They exhibit, we might add, not only a mythical format but also an eschatological quality. E. Dubois-Reymond was thus able to refer to the theory of the heat death of the cosmos, a theory based on the Second Law of thermodynamics, as "scientific eschatology."[232] While the theory of heat death anticipates an irreversible process of decay in the cosmos, the critics of this theory speak of a universe cyclically oscillating between the primal beginning and the end. From a physical perspective, the assumption is that even protons will decay in 10^{31} years.[233] And the universe, currently still expanding, will either revert back to the conditions of its primal beginning, or will continue to expand until it decays into increasingly colder radiation,[234] depending on whether the total mass of the universe either exceeds or falls short of the critical mass density of 10^{-29} grams/cubic centimeter.[235]

The assumption of an irreversible cosmic end is based on the law of entropy, a law with which, significantly, the concept of historicity enters into physics and astronomy. Thus C. F. von Weizsäcker asserts: "There is a theorem of physics, the Second Law of thermodynamics, according to which events in nature are fundamentally irreversible and incapable of repetition. This law I should like to call the law of the historic character of nature."[236] The law of entropy,[237] as we know, asserts that the entropy, i.e., the measure of heat of a body which is no longer available as kinetic energy, can remain constant or increase within a closed system, but cannot decrease. Expressed differently, what one calls heat is a disordered movement of atoms. The transition from movement into heat is accordingly a transition from ordered to disordered movement. The Second Law of thermodynamics states "that ordered motion can be converted completely into disordered motion, but that disordered motion cannot be converted completely into ordered motion."[238] This physical law is based on considerations of probability. Since the condition of ordered movement is less probable than that of disordered movement, the assumption is that every body goes from a condition of lesser probability to one of greater probability, and that means a condition of highest possible entropy. This maximum of disordered movement or entropy is called heat death. For the universe this means:

> Nature is a unique course of events. The final state would be one in which all motion has come to rest, in which all differences in temperature have been equalized . . . But given enough time, no structure in the universe should be able to escape heat death. It is conceivable, of course, that certain forms of energy, such as the energy of atomic nuclei or the kinetic energy of stellar bodies moving in empty space, would never be converted into heat at all. But even then, there would be in the end no longer any conversion of energy.[239]

The inclusion of the law of entropy in scientific cosmology has serious consequences, e.g., with respect to the problem of the origin of time. The theory of the heat death of the universe means nothing less than a denial of the idea of the eternal nature of the cosmos, an idea that with the emergence of modern science took the place of the myths of the creation of the world. Just as a universal end of the world is conceivable on the basis of the law of entropy—albeit not as a sudden event, but rather as a creeping process—so also does the Second Law of thermodynamics render possible the idea of a temporal beginning of the universe. With that, modern physics is overtaken by the problems of myth.[240]

Just as theories of the heat death of the cosmos (or its cold death) on the one hand, and of an oscillating universe on the other[241] exhibit clear affinities with the various apocalyptic notions of a one-time or a periodic end of the world, so in a reverse fashion do scientific scenarios of a possible planetary or cosmic end of the world exercise their own influence on apocalyptic thinking, first of all insofar as scientific prognoses can be transformed into new apocalyptic imagery. We have seen paradigmatic examples of this in the theory of the braking of the earth's rotation or in the thesis of the extinction of the human species. The same applies to the aforementioned cosmological theories of contemporary physics.

One can also observe the effects of scientific theories on apocalyptic thinking insofar as such scenarios constitute a challenge to our understanding of existence which apocalyptic tries to address. This is most likely to occur in the case of the assumption of an oscillating universe. Analogous to the previously discussed notions of a cyclical end of the world, this theory does offer the consolation that there will be no definitive end of the world, and that the end can never be total. Admittedly, the idea of eternal return, e.g., as developed by Nietzsche, can also lead to nihilism, since it includes the recurrence not only of fulfilled moments in life but of suffering as well, such that the cosmic process becomes a cycle of eternal meaninglessness.

The cosmological consequences of the Second Law of thermodynamics represent a serious challenge to our understanding of existence, since they are in a position to evoke complete hopelessness. The law of entropy results in a concept not only of a one-time but of a genuinely definitive end of the world. This definitive cosmic end is not even—as was the case with the idea of the *annihilatio mundi*—to be conceived as a sublation of history, but rather quite clearly as its utter elimination, leaving no hope whatever. "The real situation of the universe," K. Heim suggests, "is like the situation of a man condemned to death, who still has a fair interval of time between the verdict and the execution."[242] This sort of heat death also constitutes the great corrective for any philosophy of hope, such as that of E. Bloch, a corrective confounding every notion of a salvific Omega. K. Heim tries to counter the nihilistic consequences of the law of entropy by working out a connection between the view of the physical sciences with biblical eschatology.[243] In view of the immeasurable suffering of the world, Heim finds precisely this idea of an oscillating universe to be lacking any consolation, whereas in contrast the thesis of the heat death in connection with New Testament eschatology gives him occasion for new hope.

> For us there are only two possibilities. The first is that the world will in fact go on as at present. Then life is not worth living. The other possibility is the *hope* that history is not an eternal cycle, but a course which had a beginning and moves toward a goal, and that all the situations of the Cross through which we have passed are only a transitional stage on the way to this destination. But this destination must not be annihilation if everything is not to be utterly meaningless, but must be what the New Testament calls a *telos* (goal, end), in which not merely will some things in this world be improved and the gravest abuses find an end but in which the whole basic form of this world will be abolished to make way for a new form.[244]

The end becomes a culmination, the concluding point a *telos*, destruction transformation, and the catastrophe a crisis. Despite different priorities and presuppositions, this theological attempt at a solution and Bloch's philosophy of hope stand astonishingly close at this point. Bloch's ontology of the Not-yet also does not consider itself contradicted by the law of entropy, but believes rather that this law must be read dialectically as the sublation of the negative through negation, so that at the end the path leads through absolute nothingness to totality:

> But the dialectic through Nothing has even included world-annihilation within itself, has certified temporariness for the universe, by using the Nothing. The Orcus which is described in physical terms as freezing death, in mythological terms conversely as world-conflagration, physically contains the birth of another cosmos or universe, utopianly even the birth of a totally fulfilling All. New heaven, new earth, the logic of the apocalypse presuppose the dialectical functional change of the fire of annihilation which is otherwise considered to be satanic; *every advent contains nihilism as something utilized and defeated*, death as something devoured in the victory.[245]

For Bloch, too, the end appears as a transformation and the catastrophe as a crisis such that scientific thinking takes a utopian turn. The elimination of history is transformed dialectically into the sublation of history.

7. The Decline of the West

Examples of theories of decline can be adduced not only from the natural sciences and the philosophy of nature but also from the philosophy of history. Just as do many scenarios from the natural sciences, so also do historico-philosophical theories of decline exhibit various degrees of congruency with mythical models of one-time or cyclical ends of the world. The most significant example of this sort of historico-philosophical theory of decline in the twentieth century is Oswald Spengler's work *The Decline of the West*. In his philosophy of decline, which actually constitutes a philosophy of life[246] and which with some justification can be called "metaphysics of decline,"[247] three larger sweeps from the history of philosophy emerge. The first runs from Kant to Hegel and Dilthey, the second from Herder and Goethe to Schlegel and Burckhardt, while the third shows Rousseau, Schopenhauer, and Nietzsche to have been important precursors of Spengler.[248]

Spengler's philosophy of decline continues on the one hand the series of historical models extending back into antiquity that understand history as the history of decay, and on the other hand the Western cultural criticism of the nineteenth century. The real significance of Spengler's understanding of decline lies in his continuation of this line of cultural criticism, which is carried by a metaphysics of world anxiety, and not in his disputed historico-scientific accomplishment or his attempt at providing the foundation for a philosophy of life.[249]

Like Spengler, so also did Burckhardt, Baudelaire, and Nietzsche, though also Dostoyevsky and Tolstoy, not anticipate the kind of future progress greeted by, e.g.,

Proudhon, Comte, Condorcet, or Turgot each in his own way;[250] rather, they anticipated the decay of Western culture.[251] Just as Spengler, especially in his political writings, understood himself to be the prophet of impending political and military catastrophes,[252] so also did Nietzsche see himself as the herald of a gloomy future, a "spirit of daring and experiment," a "soothsayer-bird spirit":[253]

> What I relate is the history of the next two centuries. I describe what is coming, what can no longer come differently: *the advent of nihilism.* This history can be related even now; for necessity itself is at work here. This future speaks even now in a hundred signs, this destiny announces itself everywhere; for this music of the future all ears are cocked even now. For some time now, our whole European culture has been moving as toward a catastrophe, with a tortured tension that is growing from decade to decade: restlessly, violently, headlong, like a river that wants to reach the end, that no longer reflects, that is afraid to reflect.[254]

What the "soothsayer-bird spirit" Nietzsche says of himself also applies to Spengler, namely, that he "*looks back* when relating what will come."[255] The prophetic gaze back into history enables one to interpret the future.

What Baudelaire, for example, whose work Spengler read, diagnosed with loathing as the Americanization and decay of European culture,[256] Spengler affirms without reservation as the course of the will to power in the history of the West. His diagnosis of the age yields what is in part a grippingly relevant portrait of political and economic circumstances. This diagnosis is characterized by a fateful ambivalence. On the one hand, its perspicacity and extreme sensibility regarding the catastrophic tendencies of the present age are attractive; on the other, it lends expression to the contempt that the conservative revolutionary feels toward the Western democracies and in particular toward the Weimar Republic, the contempt of someone who is prepared to give a push to what is already falling and destined for demise, becoming thus a spiritual forerunner of the Third Reich. Spengler, who sees the advent of the Second World War,[257] despised the peace that held sway in Europe after 1918, a view he shared with conservative circles in Germany:

> This all too long peace over a period of growing excitement is a fearful inheritance. Not a statesman, not a party, hardly even a political thinker is today in a safe enough position to speak the truth. They all lie, they all join in the chorus of the pampered, ignorant crowd who want their tomorrow to be like the good old days, only more so—although statesmen and economic leaders at least ought to be alive to the frightful reality. Only look at our leaders of today! Once a month their cowardly and dishonest optimism announces the "up-branch of the cycle" and "prosperity," on the strength of a mere flutter on the stock exchange caused by building-speculations: the end of unemployment, from the moment that a hundred men or so are given jobs, and as the climax the achievement of "mutual understanding between the nations," as soon as the League—that swarm of parasitic holiday-makers on the Lake of Geneva—has formulated any sort of a resolution. And in every conference and every paper the word "crisis" is bandied about in connexion with any passing disturbance of the peace. And

> thus we deceive ourselves, blind to the fact that we have here one of those incalculable great catastrophes that are the *normal* form in which history takes its major turns.[258]

Spengler is more than some cultural philosopher calmly outlining the course of history. It is no exaggeration to call him a prophet of decline[259] whose own writings themselves constitute a symptom of the prophesied end, a sign of the times.[260] The present is revealed as the end time, as reality in decline. Catastrophe—not crisis—is the normal form in which the course of history progresses. "History recks nothing of human logic. Thunderstorms, earthquakes, lava-streams: these are near relatives of the purposeless, elemental events of world history. Nations may go under, ancient cities of ageing Cultures burn or sink in ruins, but the earth will continue to revolve calmly round the sun, and the stars to run their courses."[261] In a certain sense Spengler's work, at least the writings of his later years, can be called apocalyptic literature of unveiling. What is disclosed is the catastrophic disposition of reality. History is not some string of crises, but rather a series of catastrophes whose meaninglessness is comparable to that of natural catastrophes. The philosophy of history becomes a theory of catastrophe. However, the true nature of human beings is also allegedly unveiled: "Man is a beast of prey. I shall say it again and again. All the would-be moralists and social-ethics people who claim or hope to be 'beyond all that' are only beasts of prey with their teeth broken, who hate others on account of the attacks which they themselves are wise enough to avoid." Rather than condemning the predatory nature of human beings, quite the contrary, Spengler, like Nietzsche before him, basically affirms it. Spengler speaks in favor of "predatory ethics": "If I call man a beast of prey, which do I insult: man or beast? For remember, the larger beasts of prey are *noble* creatures, perfect of their kind, and without the hypocrisy of human moral due to weakness."[262] However, not only does Spengler's work lend itself to apocalyptic interpretation, so also does its author himself. During the period following the composition of his main opus on the decline of the West, Spengler himself assumed more and more the role of the apocalyptic prophet—albeit an unwilling prophet who was himself finally overtaken by the prophesied events.[263]

With that, an explicitly catastrophic notion of decline acquires contours in Spengler's political writings which Spengler himself originally had rejected. In his writing on pessimism, which tries to refute the accusation of defeatism, Spengler tries to eliminate the misunderstanding that the philosophy of history presented in his *Decline of the West* was actually a theory of catastrophe.

> Its understanding was . . . made more difficult by the disturbing title of the book, even though I had expressly emphasized that it had already been decided years before and that it is the strictly objective designation of a historical fact whose accompanying features are among the best-known phenomena of history. There are those, however, who mistakenly understand the decline of antiquity to have been like the sinking of an ocean liner. The word does *not* contain the idea of catastrophe. If instead of "decline" one says "consummation" or "completion," an expression associated with a quite specific sense in the thinking of

> Goethe, then the "pessimistic" aspect is eliminated for the time being without altering the real meaning of the term.[264]

Spengler then precisely defines the concept of pessimism in this sense. He rejects the blanket implications of pessimism.[265]

> However, as far as the "goal of mankind" is concerned I am a radical and resolute pessimist. For me, mankind is a zoological expression. I see no specifically human progress, goal, or path except in the imagination of western Philistines of progress. I do not even perceive any spirit, and much less any unity of striving, feeling, or understanding in this naked mass of people. Only in the history of individual cultures do I perceive any meaningful direction of life toward a goal, what amounts to unity of soul, will, and experience. This is something limited and factual, though it does contain something willed, attained, and then further new tasks consisting not in ethical slogans and generalities, but rather in tangible *historical* goals.[266]

Spengler's work aims not at passivity and fatalism but rather at action and innercultural activity, and one can accordingly refer to his basic attitude[267] as active, "*brave* pessimism."[268]

Spengler explicitly denies that history has any ultimate goal. His understanding of decline, rather than advancing the notion of the one-time end of the world, embraces—mediated by a philosophy of life—Stoic thinking and the age-old idea of periodic decline.[269] As far as Spengler's cultural philosophy is concerned, this cyclical thinking admittedly does not manifest itself as metaphysics of the world as a whole, but rather as the metaphysical foundation and explanatory principle of individual cultures. Within this framework, however, the histories of those cultures cannot be viewed synoptically within an overall developmental history of a single, unified human culture. Rather, according to Spengler the great cultures grow and decay quite isolated and independently of one another.[270] In contrast, world history is nothing but a "phantom."[271]

Accordingly, Spengler rejects the traditional division of history into ancient, medieval, and modern.[272] The familiar scheme is replaced by a new paradigm operating with organic concepts offering a fundamental critique of the Eurocentrism of Western historical writing[273] and accordingly presented by Spengler as "the *Copernican discovery* in the historical sphere."[274] This discovery consists in Spengler's "method of comparative morphology."[275] It views cultures as self-contained organisms subject to natural growth and decline. Each culture, however, has "its *own* image," "its *own* idea, its *own* passions, its own life, will, feeling, its *own* death."[276] As the medium of its description of the developmental history of individual cultures, Spengler's comparative morphology draws comparisons from the world of plants:

> Here the Cultures, peoples, languages, truths, gods, landscapes bloom and age as the oaks and the stone-pines, the blossoms, twigs and leaves—but there is no ageing "Mankind." Each Culture has its own new possibilities of self-expression which arise, ripen, decay, and never return. There is not *one* sculpture, *one* painting, *one* mathematics, *one* physics, but many, each in its deepest essence differ-

> ent from the others, each limited in duration and self-contained, just as each species of plant has its peculiar blossom or fruit, its special type of growth and decline. These cultures, sublimated life-essences, grow with the same superb aimlessness as the flowers of the field. They belong, like the plants and the animals, to the living Nature of Goethe, and not to the dead Nature of Newton. I see world-history as a picture of endless formations and transformations, of the marvelous waxing and waning of organic forms. The professional historian, on the contrary, sees it as a sort of tapeworm industriously adding on to itself one epoch after another.[277]

On the one hand, Spengler's method of comparative morphology subdivides the history of the great cultures into periods analogous to the four seasons spring, summer, autumn, and winter, or into an early period, culture, and civilization; and on the other hand, it correlates analogous sections of cultural development into cross sections.[278] In this way Spengler discloses an analogous sequence of "contemporary" "spiritual epochs" in Indian, classical, Arabian, and Western culture. Furthermore, he compares the sequences of "cultural epochs" and "political epochs" in Egyptian, classical, Arabian, and Western culture. Each culture passes sequentially through the phase of antiquity, the phase of culture subdivided into early and late periods, and finally through the stage of civilization. While the early and late periods of the cultural phase correspond to summer and autumn of the culture in question, civilization, which is to be distinguished from them, is the equivalent cultural-historic winter. According to Spengler, intellectual-historic characteristics of civilization include the emergence of a materialistic world-outlook, the advance of philosophical skepticism, "inner completion" of mathematical theories, the degradation of abstract thinking into "professional, lecture-room philosophy," and the "spread of a final world-sentiment." In contrast to the stage of culture, that of civilization lacks any real formative power. In an analogous fashion, civilization is characterized in the artistic sphere by what Spengler criticizes as "modern art" and by the slipping of art and architecture into commercialism, by an end of formative development and the prevalence of ornamentalism and imitation as well as by a representative artistic style in the service of power and mass appeal. Finally, from a political perspective civilization is the epoch of the masses, of the metropolis, and of cosmopolitan sentiment. Its characteristic features include first of all the dominance of money in politics and with that the emergence of democracy (!), and finally the development of Caesarism, i.e., the victory of power politics over financial power and democracy. In this period nations degenerate into formless populations which ultimately are united in an empire bearing despotic features. At the end of civilization, however, private and familial politics of individual rulers predominates. The world is distributed as booty or is conquered more and more by new, younger peoples. Ultimately, primeval-human conditions penetrate into the behavior and outlook of high civilization.

Far from being "the highest point of an ascending straight line of world-history," the nineteenth and twentieth centuries are rather the beginning of the end, the initial centuries of the cultural-historic winter of the West which is to come to an end after the year A.D. 2200. The present represents merely a "transitional phase which occurs with certainty under particular conditions." For Spengler it is a given that "there are well-defined states (such as have occurred more than once in the history of the past) *later* than the present-day state of West Europe, and therefore that the future of the West is not a limitless tending upwards and onwards for all time towards our present ideals, but *a single phenomenon of history, strictly limited and defined as to form and duration, which covers a few centuries and can be viewed as, in essentials, calculated from available precedents.*"[279] The decline of the West is thus not a future catastrophe, but rather a present occurrence,[280] not an individual event, but rather a process, albeit one concerning which calculations concerning the end time are made. The decline of the West is identical with the process of civilization.[281]

We will not in the present context evaluate Spengler's outline regarding its cogency and historical validity.[282] For our investigation of apocalyptic thinking and understanding of existence, Spengler's philosophy of decline is especially significant in its disclosure of the inner connection between world anxiety and the end of the world. At this point we can recall Spengler's analysis of world anxiety.[283] In the phenomenon of anxiety Spengler discovers the hermeneutical key to understanding all cultural development. Anxiety, which is simultaneously longing, stands at the beginning of every individual development. Longing and anxiety are the primal feelings of every emerging ego; these are the feelings of becoming and having become. The world anxiety of the soul of the child, "anxiety of the irrevocable, the attained, the final, of mortality, of the world itself as a thing-become,"[284] stands as "the most *creative* of all prime feelings" at the beginning of all cultural development as well. Spengler's exposition concerning world anxiety—which, astonishingly, he nowhere develops further—contains *in nuce* the metaphysics underlying his cultural critique. It contains "the seeds of almost every one of Spengler's fundamental ideas in concentrated form, and it would have taken merely their continued exposition and systematic development to bring to light also his hidden metaphysics both in its possibilities and its contradictions."[285]

As we have already shown,[286] such contradictions impair Spengler's concept of world anxiety. Whereas on the one hand Spengler classifies world anxiety as a primal feeling of equal rank with longing, on the other hand he interprets it as a feeling derived from longing. The tensions attaching to Spengler's metaphysics, tensions permeating his work and never satisfactorily resolved,[287] are perpetuated in these inconsistencies. Longing and anxiety correspond on the level of feeling to the ontological statements concerning on the one hand the world as becoming, and on the other the world as being which has become. This antithesis between becoming and having become intensifies ultimately into that between time (becoming) and space (having become), both of which threaten to be sundered from one another such that the world as a whole can no longer be conceived metaphysically. Spengler tries to deflect this disintegration of world into becoming and having become as two independent quantities by means of the concept of direction. Although this concept of direction is supposed to express the interrelationship between becoming and having become, between time and space, in Spengler's exposition it unfortunately remains ambiguous. Time is directed time, and through its directed lapse, according to Spengler, space emerges. Spatial depth is the result of lapsed time. Spengler's use of this idea, however, is not successful in conceiving the spatial character of temporal existence and its accompanying dialectic of space and time. Rather, first of all this absolutizes the spatial character (including the character of having become, causality, and rigidity) as the negative side of the world, and temporality (including the character of becoming, fate, and life) as the positive side. Finally, both sides are laboriously brought together into a unity by means of the mediating concept of direction. It is precisely this difficulty in Spengler's ontology which is advanced in his description of world longing and world anxiety. Whereas on the one hand these primal feelings exist in juxtaposed isolation like time and space, and ultimately are fused again through the concept of direction, on the other hand the origin of all feelings in a unified primal phenomenon is asserted such that anxiety is to develop from longing, analogous to the origin of space from directed time.[288] Like his ontology, Spengler's concept of world anxiety is also unsatisfactory.

Nonetheless, Spengler's cultural morphology is an informative example illustrating the relationship between world anxiety and apocalyptic. World anxiety as described by Spengler is the primal feeling of having become, of mortality, of space, of causality, and of death. According to Spengler, it is precisely those characteristics associated with the concept of space that predominate in a cultural-historical sense in the phase of civilization and thus of decline. Spengler's comments on the phenomenon of world anxiety are found, significantly, in his chapter on the "Meaning of Numbers."[289] The primal feeling of anxiety comes to expression "in the intellectual, understandable, outlinable symbols of *extension*."[290] These symbols ultimately serve to combat the sense of the uncanny and to overcome anxiety. "At the zeniths of the great Cultures those formations, though retaining inwardly the mark of their origin, the characteristic of binding and conjuring, have become the complete form-worlds of the various arts and of religious, scientific and, above all, *mathematical* thought. The method common to all—the only way of actualizing itself that the soul knows—is the *symbolizing of extension*, of space or of things."[291] With reference to mathematics, this means the following as far as numbers are concerned: Only what has already become can be counted, not becoming. One of the characteristic features of civilization, however, is "the completion of the mathematical form-world." Art develops a rigid inventory of forms used more for commercial artistic purposes. Architecture and the plastic arts develop an inclination to ornamentalism, and the development of political constructions strives toward "anorganic" forms. Advancing imperialism degenerates into ahistoric rigidity.

His description of this decline, then, employs terms deriving from the category of space. Winter, the decline of the West, is like every cultural decline the phase of having become, a phase in which spiritual formative powers are extinguished. Life itself becomes problematical. Space, however, symbolizes death. "A deep relation, and one which is early felt, exists *between space and death*."[292] All symbols of space symbolize dreaded death. "Every great symbolism attaches its form-language to the cult of the dead, the forms of disposal of the dead, the adornment of the graves of the dead."[293] The ornamental element in all spheres of culture is thus the cult of the dead of a declining civilization.[294] And with that the circle closes: The decline of the West is the object of world anxiety, just as in a reverse fashion that particular world anxiety comes to expression and is to be banished in those manifestations which have proven to be dependable signs of decline. Those symbols of space represent the death of the individual as well as that of culture itself, and thus symbolize precisely what anxiety fears. In a reverse fashion, however, it is precisely this anxiety which creatively evokes these symbols in the first place. The decline is thus not only the object but also the result of world anxiety. This insight from Spengler's work, however, accords with our own determination of the relationship between world anxiety and the end of the world,[295] which revealed that the end of the world is to an equal extent both expectation of world anxiety and, as an idea, the expression of and thus attempt at overcoming world anxiety.

Spengler's thesis of the decline of the West was extraordinarily influential and vehemently discussed. Spengler's greatest influence was exercised by the first volume of the *Decline of the West*, which appeared in 1919. "In 1919 everyone read and discussed Spengler: the educated world in the broadest sense, young people who had returned from the war, and the specialty disciplines—these, too, in the broadest sense, since which discipline was not affected?"[296] Although Spengler's preliminary work extended back as far as 1911–1914, his work was not originally conceived as a response to the catastrophe of the First World War, though for the readers in 1919 the impression had to arise that *The Decline of the West*, as E. Spranger put it, "appended a theoretical confirmation to the events."[297] W. Wolfradt noted laconically in the *Weltbühne:* "Spengler was the man of the year in 1919."[298] Neither did the second volume of Spengler's main opus fail to exercise such influence.[299] Spengler, who did not occupy a professorial position but rather led the life of an independent scholar, exercised enormous influence on the subsequent academic generation,[300] though Spengler's preference for self-isolation, which actually accorded better with his personality, prevented the formation of a school.[301] In scholarly circles Spengler's cultural philosophy largely encountered rejection and criticism.[302] "The men who concerned themselves with him most and who probably also stood closest to him were leading representatives of German business,"[303] e.g., especially Paul Reusch, the head of the *Gute-Hoffnungshütte* in Oberhausen, and the Hamburg overseas merchant Roderich Schlubach.[304] Spengler's fundamental insights were, however, accepted by authors such as H. Freyer, Martersteig, P. Lensch, or Moeller van den Bruck,[305] and not least by M. Schröter.

Spengler's theses also attracted attention in theological circles. The criticism of the young movement of Dialectical Theology toward the cultural protestantism of the nineteenth century found a conservative counterpart in Spengler's cultural critique. In the convulsive situation following the First World War there was a great temptation to appropriate naively Spengler's thesis concerning the decline of culture and at the same time to advocate one's own conviction concerning the unused creative energies of Christianity. Thus W. Elert wrote in 1921:

> There is for the time being no disputing Spengler's insight that none of the culturally formative powers is in a position any longer to find a unified style void of reflection, not to speak of imprinting on such a style the spirit of the age as a whole. If despite his prognosis the future does nonetheless someday offer us this kind of cultural unity, that still would not constitute a refutation of his judgment concerning the present. Hence anyone in the present who would tie Christianity to one of the decadent powers as its ally of deliverance . . . is tying the skiff of Christendom to a ship bound for destruction. Thus at this moment there is but a single great commandment for those whom Christendom has appointed to be its spokespersons: to extricate Christianity from the snares of a declining culture to avoid its being pulled down into the whirlpool . . . The more a person is convinced of the liberating, clarifying, sublime power of Christianity, all the more dispassionately will that person view the collapse of false supports. Only when Christianity once again has become completely alone, i.e., completely free of the present "culture," will it demonstrate again the power it has already evidenced more than once in its history to generate a new one.[306]

Thus theologically motivated cultural critique also flourished in the ground of Spengler's philosophy within the Lutheranism critically opposed to Dialectical Theology.

Spengler's influence on the eschatology of P. Althaus also becomes clear where Althaus critically disputes the notions of the end of history advocated by biblicism and in response tries to emphasize the relevance of the last things.

> The last things are perpetually relevant. To that extent every age is the last age. There are, however, "last" ages in a special sense. Here, too, history corresponds to the individual life. Just as in the latter every hour is directed toward death and carries within it the possibility of death, nonetheless in special hours, such as those of sickness, life is "closer" to death than otherwise, and is more actively reminded of it than in daily life—so also are there historical hours which are closer to the end than others, the times of a dying culture, epochs of degeneration and catastrophe experienced as a powerful testimony and parable of the *dies irae, dies illa.* Great historical decisions (which do not confront every generation!) remind us of the final decision and are an intimation of its proximity. Such hours of history again and again give birth to imminent expectation. And even if as the anticipation of the temporal proximity of the end this expectation is not fulfilled, it still is correct in sensing the coming end—for it is precisely because of the death and evil effective in history, whose emergence one has experienced, that the end will indeed certainly come and is indeed certain in its proximity. The lightning of the final day flashes in every innerhistoric collapse.[307]

Althaus tries to connect conceptually eschatological imminent expectation and the idea of historically inherent decay. In the process, the element of the catastrophic within history stands clearly in the foreground, whereby Althaus is thinking primarily of the experience of the First (and in later editions also of the Second) World War.[308] The historical catastrophes confront Luther's *deus absconditus.* All the same, Althaus refers just as emphatically to "times of a dying culture," i.e., to the experience of general decline of which Spengler spoke.[309] And this experience, too, is associated with the biblical notion of judgment. Althaus carries forward Spengler's ideas when he views the culture of the West as unique and considers the fate of all peoples to be tied to its further course.[310] Similar reflections are found in the cultural critique of Albert Schweitzer, though not without between-the-lines criticism of Spengler's cultural morphology,[311] and in M. Schröter's concluding remarks, composed in 1948, to his Spengler-study.[312] According to Althaus:

> The western rationalization of life through science and technology contains the dynamic of continual progress; in such progress, however, it increasingly releases the powers of death. Will not this our own fate simultaneously be that of all of humankind? . . . Has humankind outlived its possibilities? Although any definite prognosis would be impertinent, the *question* itself is certainly legitimate and should be posed—and this kind of "historico-philosophical" reflection does doubtlessly concern theology to a certain extent, even if we are charged in a different way with looking for the signs of the time both in history and in individual lives.[313]

Even where theological criticism was directed at Spengler's work,[314] the idea of cultural decay elicited strong fascination. D. Bonhoeffer, for example, criticized Spengler's biological point of departure;[315] nonetheless, in the fragments of his own ethics and from the perspective of his experiences with the Third Reich and the ecclesiastical struggle, Bonhoeffer chides Spengler not for painting too gloomy a picture, but rather quite the contrary for making this decay seem too harmless:

> By the loss of the unity which it possessed through the form of Jesus Christ, the western world is brought to the brink of the void. The forces unleashed exhaust their fury in mutual destruction. Everything established is threatened with annihilation. This is not a crisis among other crises. It is a decisive struggle of the last days. The western world senses the uniqueness of the moment at which it stands, and it throws itself into the arms of the void, while the Christians talk among themselves of the approach of the Day of Judgement. The void towards which the west is drifting is not the natural end, the dying away and decline of a once flourishing history of nations. It is, once again, a specifically western void, a rebellious and outrageous void, and one which is the enemy of both God and man. As an apostasy from all that is established it is the supreme manifestation of all the powers which are opposed to God. It is the void made god. No one knows its goal or its measure. Its dominion is absolute. It is a creative void, which blows its anti-god's breath into the nostrils of all that is established and awakens it to a false semblance of new life while sucking out from its proper essence, until at last it falls in ruin as a lifeless husk and is cast away. The void engulfs life, history, family, nation, language, faith. The list can be prolonged indefinitely, for the void spares nothing.[316]

Far from being the winter of a culture upon which in keeping with the cycle of nature a new spring will follow, the decline of the West issues rather into nihilism, nihilism of unimagined dimensions and with horrible consequences for humankind, nihilism that can be described adequately only with the help of apocalyptic categories.[317]

Nihilism undergoes an interpretation that can be called apocalyptic not least in the middle and later philosophy of Martin Heidegger. The history of Being outlined in his later work proves to be a history of decay and of forgetfulness of Being whose virtually apocalyptic consequences manifest themselves in nihilism, though also in the worldwide advance of technology, of conditions hostile to human beings, of the cult of power, and of brute force. It may seem doubly offensive to mention Heidegger at this point. The students and appointed interpreters of his work will presumably oppose both the classification of Heidegger's later philosophy as apocalyptic as well as the mention of Heidegger's name in the same breath as Spengler's. From both the theological and the philosophical perspective, however, various references have been made to the affinity between Heidegger's later work and apocalyptic thinking, just as attention has occasionally been drawn, despite the differences of thought and especially of philosophical niveau, to substantive points of contact between the work of Spengler and Heidegger. In Heidegger's philosophy, in its concern with Being toward death and with the meaning of care, though also in its ontological distinction between Being and beings, Günther Anders, for example, sees an example of "apocalyptic prophecy" with significance for the present.[318] In fact, not only the later philosophy, but already the conception of *Being and Time* and its phenomenological analysis of "Being-toward-the-end" is allegedly "a transfer of apocalyptic expectation into the language of the lonely individual," "replacing the apocalypse with a person's own death,"[319] albeit such that "the catastrophe automatically becomes something positive: the chance for humankind to 'become authentic.' "[320] With reference to Heidegger's later work, G. Sauter speaks of an "eschatology of being" whose schema is allegedly "a symptom of philosophical apocalyptic."[321]

A. Jäger similarly seeks the roots of Heidegger's understanding of Being and of the notion of a history of Being "in the realm of late-Jewish apocalyptic."[322] Jäger also, however, sees the substantive proximity of Heidegger to Spengler: "The feeling of decline and demise, of having come to the dangerous limits of western possibilities, clearly enough breathes Spengler's cultural pessimism."[323] Although this does not mean that Heidegger's thinking is directly dependent on Spengler's cultural morphology, it does mean that in Heidegger's construction of the destiny of Being we are encountering historical speculation "in the spirit of Nietzsche, in analogy and close proximity to Oswald Spengler's *Decline of the West*," "even if the differences and uniquely new elements in this conception are visible from all sides."[324] While Jäger perceives Heidegger's intellectual kinship with Spengler primarily in Heidegger's later work, A. Baeumler believes one can discern "a hidden kinship" between the points of departure for the questions of both Heidegger and Spengler already with respect to *Being and Time*.[325] Both allegedly share—without assuming any immediate connection—the philosophical turn to *Dasein*, a renunciation of representative terms such as "human being" or "humankind," as well as a turning away from the philosophy of the spirit of German Idealism. Ultimately these observations indicate the proximity of both Spengler and Heidegger to the philosophy of life, though such philosophy is inherently so multilayered and lacking unity that such a thesis must of necessity remain imprecise. Nonetheless, the considerations of G. Anders do prompt us to ask whether a certain parallel does exist between Spengler's discussion of decline in the context of cultural philosophy dealing with cultures as individuals on the one hand, and Heidegger's talk of Being toward death within the framework of an analysis of *Dasein* on the other.

The analogies between Spengler's main work and Heidegger's construction of the history of Being are admittedly much more clear-cut. It is not without some pathos that Heidegger speaks of the "West" (with the resonating element of the setting sun and evening, German *Abendland*). In metaphysics, i.e., ultimately in the thinking of Western philosophy beginning with Plato and extending up till the present, he sees "the necessary fate of the West and the presupposition of its planetary dominance."[326] Like Spengler, Heidegger speaks about decline, albeit it not that of the West, but rather of the "truth of beings"; "the decline of the truth of beings means: the openness of beings and *only* beings loses the previous uniqueness of their authoritative claim."[327] Thus for Heidegger such talk about decline is ontologically rather than cultural-philosophically anchored. Explicitly, however—and this is extremely noteworthy—Heidegger finds that Spengler's thesis of the decline of the West proves itself in the decline evidenced in the history of Being: According to Heidegger, we are living "in a thought-provoking time," the expression "thought-provoking" referring to "what must be thought."[328] "*Most thought provoking in our thought-provoking time is that we are still not thinking*,"[329] "not even yet, although the state of the world is becoming constantly more thought-provoking."[330] This "judgment on the present age," however, coincides with Spengler's own philosophy of decline. "If people today[331] tend once again to be more in agreement with Spengler's proposition about the decline of the west, it is (along with various superficial reasons) because Spengler's proposition is only the negative, though correct, consequence of Nietzsche's words: 'The wasteland grows.' We emphasized that these are words issuing from thought. They are true words."[332] Since Western metaphysics culminates in Nietzsche's philosophy, Zarathustra's assertion "the wasteland grows"[333] is the expression of a real idea holding true with reference to the history of Being.[334] Spengler's own thesis of decline participates in this truth to the extent that the cultural catastrophe he diagnoses is the consequence or subsequent symptom of a catastrophe of Being.

What has happened in the twentieth century cultural-historically and world-politically, and what is continuing to happen, is not, as with Spengler, the actual decline of the West, but rather the result of a much more deeply convulsive decline. "The decline has already taken place. The consequences of this occurrence are the events of world history of this century."[335] With Hegel's philosophy of the "absolute knowledge as the Spirit of will" there began the "completion" of metaphysics[336] which reached its apex in Nietzsche's critique of metaphysics. Nietzsche's talk about the will to power does not mean the end, but rather "the final entanglement in metaphysics."[337] The decline of which Heidegger is speaking, however, "occurs through the collapse of the world characterized by metaphysics, and at the same time through the desolation of the earth stemming from metaphysics."[338] The key role in this desolation of the earth inheres in the "will to will," to which Nietzsche yet refers as the "will to power." It does not mean, as Nietzsche supposed, the overcoming, but rather the completion of metaphysics.[339] This will to will, however, which wills nothing but itself, is nihilistic, and in it the true essence of the history of Western thinking emerges. Nihilism, as Heidegger explains in his treatise on Nietzsche's assertion that "God is dead," is "a historical movement, and not just any view or doctrine advocated by someone or other."[340] It is "the fundamental movement of the history of the West. It shows such great profundity that its unfolding can have nothing but world catastrophes as its consequence."[341] The will to will is "the anarchy of catastrophes."[342] Its movement exhibits an unyielding inclination toward the abyss. "The question is whether the individuals and communities are in virtue of this will, or whether they still deal and banter with this will or even against it without knowing that they are already outwitted by it."[343]

The catastrophic consequences of the predicted end can be summarized under the concept of technology, whereby "technology" is not limited simply to machinery, but is conceived rather as widely as possible, similar to Greek *technē*. As used by Heidegger, the word means "completed metaphysics,"[344] and encompasses equally dealings with nature, the development of culture, political circumstances, and thinking. "Technology" circumscribes "objectified nature, the business of culture, manufactured politics, and the gloss of ideals overlying everything."[345] The parallel to Spengler at this point is also striking, since he also developed a critique of technology.[346] One must add the qualification, however, that Heidegger does not in this context invoke Spengler, but rather the "worker" of Ernst Jünger.[347] By his own admission, Heidegger was strongly influenced by Jünger's writings.[348] One must point out further that Spengler's critique of technology[349] by no means attains the depth of Heidegger's.[350]

Politically, technology according to Heidegger means the degradation of human beings into "laboring animals,"[351] their transformation into masses and objectification into "the most important raw material" in politics and business.[352] Additional resulting phenomena associated with nihilism mentioned by Heidegger include the totality of world wars, the ultimate removal of any distinction between war and peace, the suspension of any distinction between "national" and "international," the leveling and resulting uniformity of the masses, and, as a pendant, the totality of planning and the necessity of "leadership" and "leaders."[353] The political problems attaching to this latter idea became sufficiently clear in connection with the events surrounding Heidegger's rectorship in Freiburg during the academic year 1933/34, and should be neither underestimated nor suppressed. Of significance in our own context, however, is at this point again the parallel with Spengler. Just as Heidegger aimed at leading the leader (the *Führer*) and in this way understanding the "movement" of National Socialism better than it understood itself, so also did Spengler believe he was to purify and ennoble the rising movement of nationalism.[354] In both cases the attempt ended with those involved falling into disfavor with the leaders.[355] Above all, however, Heidegger's statements concerning the necessity of leadership and of leaders constitute the substantive counterpart to Spengler's talk of Caesarism as a political symptom of cultural decline.[356]

According to Heidegger, technology takes possession equally of both politics and culture. Like these, so also does the human being ultimately become the object of planning.

> The way in which artificial insemination is handled corresponds with stark consistency to the way in which literature is handled in the sector of "culture." (Let us not flee because of antiquated prudery to distinctions that no longer exist. The need for human material underlies the same regulation of preparing for ordered mobilization as the need for entertaining books and poems, for whose production the poet is no more important than the bookbinder's apprentice, who helps bind the poems for the printer by, for example, bringing the covers for binding from the storage room.)[357]

A characteristic feature of technology is "the consumption of all materials, including the raw material 'man,' for the unconditioned possibility of the production of everything."[358] In its dealings with nature, modern technology proves to be a way of "revealing" what is concealed in beings, and for Heidegger this means revealing the truth of things, which in contrast to earlier forms of technology does not produce in the sense of *poiēsis*, but is rather "a challenging, which puts to nature the unreasonable demand that it supply energy which can be extracted and stored as such."[359] Nature becomes an object, something placed externally opposite us. It is "set upon" [*gestellt*] like a pursued animal, "in the sense of challenging it,"[360] becoming thus a victim of the will to power. Even though Heidegger invokes Jünger rather than Spengler, one must at this point nonetheless point out anew the substantive parallel with Spengler's critique of technology, a parallel involving Heidegger's notion of en-framing [*Ge-stell*] as the essence of technology. Already in *The Decline of the West*, Spengler similarly identified "determination" [*Feststellen*] as the essence of human dealings with nature, whereby in connection with Spengler's own ontology of world anxiety such "determination" is to be understood as a means of control: The threatening element is controlled when one "determines" it in its form and disposition. According to Spengler, science and technology are related like myth and cult. Like science, so also is technology a way to determine nature. "The decisive turn in the history of the higher life occurs when the *determination* [*Fest-stellen*] of Nature (in order to be guided by it) changes into a fixation [*Fest-machen*]—that is, a purposed alteration of Nature. With this, technology becomes more or less sovereign."[361] Thought emancipates itself from sensation, and the alienation from nature comes about when direct experience is replaced by "a *picture*" of the world.[362] The determination associated with technology is fundamentally violent, and this violence intensifies to an unimagined degree in the modern technology of the West. In contrast to earlier forms of technology, it is "Faustian technology."[363] This kind of technology commenced with the Gothic epoch and is characterized by a violence toward nature fueled by virtually religious ardor. The religious origins of all technical thought are manifested in the

> happy research of the early Gothic monks . . . These meditative discoverers in their cells, who with prayers and fastings *wrung* God's secrets out of him, felt that they were *serving* God thereby. Here is the Faust-figure, the grand symbol

> of a true discovering Culture. The *Scientia experimentalis*, as Roger Bacon was the first to call nature-research, the *insistent* questioning of Nature with levers and screws, began that of which the issue lies under our eyes as a countryside sprouting factory-chimneys and conveyor-towers.[364]

The parallel with Heidegger's critique of technology is obvious, and extends so far that both Heidegger and Spengler understand technology not as the result, but as the cause of modern science. Like Bergson before him, Spengler is also of the persuasion that the *homo faber* precedes *homo sapiens*. Scientific theory is "a *picture* which detaches itself from the technology of the day, and not vice versa—whether this be a day of high-level Civilized technology or a day of simplest beginnings—by way of *abstraction*, as a piece of waking-consciousness uncommitted to activity."[365]

Heidegger later advocates a remarkably similar view, namely, that technical knowledge precedes theoretical science: "One of the essential phenomena of the modern age is its science. A phenomenon of no less importance is machine technology. We must not, however, misinterpret that technology as the mere application of modern mathematical physical science to praxis. Machine technology is itself an autonomous transformation of praxis, a type of transformation wherein praxis first demands the employment of mathematical physical science."[366] However, whenever modern technology "determines" nature, the relationship with the world also changes insofar as the world is now re-presented, i.e., becomes a picture. For just this reason, according to Heidegger, the age of technology is the "age of the world picture."[367] In contradistinction with Spengler's thesis, however, Heidegger does distinguish modern technology from the essence underlying it; it is the latter that precedes modern science.[368] The presupposition of modern science, however, and of its exact research, is the process whereby the world is turned into an object, a process of the sort commencing with Descartes,[369] whose philosophy is the beginning of what Heidegger describes as the culmination or completion of metaphysics. Bacon's *scientia experimentalis*, contrary to Spengler's understanding, is located not this side, but rather on the other side of the decisive turn.[370] Despite significant differences, one can nonetheless enumerate clear correspondences between the critiques of technology advanced by Heidegger and Spengler, both of whom yet await rediscovery in connection with the ecological crisis of the present.[371]

In the realm of thought, finally, technology consists in the production of ideas with which to control the masses. "The signs of the ultimate abandonment of Being are cries about 'ideas' and 'values,' the indiscriminate back and forth of the proclamation of 'deeds,' and the indispensability of the 'spirit.' "[372] True thinking is replaced by ideologies.

As we have already seen, Heidegger's discussion of decline does not constitute cultural critique in the narrower sense, but stands rather in the context of his ontology. The focal point of Heidegger's philosophy is the question concerning Being, which has its own history, and for that reason Heidegger's exposition is intended to be read first of all "in the manner of the history of Being" rather than of culture.[373] According to Heidegger, however, the history of Being exhibits eschatological features, and he thus speaks of an "eschatology of Being."[374] However, not only Heidegger's cultural critique, but also the ontology underlying it exhibits apocalyptic features. Technology and the catastrophic developments of the twentieth century do not simply lie in human hands. They are the "destining" of Being. The essence of modern technology "is an ordaining of destining, as is every way of revealing," though admittedly not "a fate that compels. For man becomes truly free only insofar as he belongs to the realm of destining and so becomes one who listens and hears, and not one who is simply constrained to obey".[375] Being, however, which is to be distinguished from all beings, is hidden from human beings, and the entire history of the West and of its thought, of metaphysics, is permeated by the "oblivion of Being."[376] To that extent the catastrophic element in modern history is the consequence of the oblivion of Being as an epoch in the history of Being. And not only that: It is a sign not only of the oblivion of Being, but also of the "abandonment of Being."[377] The revealing of Being, which alone could prevent the final catastrophe, has not yet occurred. It would, to be sure, possess the quality of revelation. "*But nowhere do we find such experiencing of Being itself* . . . The history of Being begins, and indeed necessarily, *with the forgetting of Being.*"[378] Metaphysics does pose the question of Being, albeit wholly inadequately, but that is not all. "Metaphysics is an epoch of the history of Being itself."[379] In its very essence, however, it is nihilistic. "Thought from out of the destining of Being, the *nihil* in 'nihilism' means that *Nothing* is befalling Being."[380] To that extent the abandonment of Being is the real catastrophe "in that age."[381]

The structural analogy between Heidegger's history of Being on the one hand, and apocalyptic, e.g., Jewish apocalyptic, on the other, is clearly discernible. The entire previous history of the West constitutes a single epoch, a single world age corresponding to the *ho aiōn houtos* in Jewish apocalyptic. Just as the latter is stigmatized by the absence or eclipse of God, so the former by the abandonment of Being. In both cases, however, the apocalyptic revelation is yet outstanding and is reserved for the future. The parallels to Jewish apocalyptic are thus greater than Heidegger's consciously pagan tenor and borrowings from Greek culture would have us believe.

They extend even further than previously suggested. The figures of apocalyptic seers also find their counterpart in Heidegger's later work. They are replaced by the singers and poets who keep watch for the revelation of Being and search for a new, nonmetaphysical way of thinking. "The unholy, as unholy, traces the sound for us. What is sound beckons to the holy, calling it. The holy binds the divine. The divine draws the god near. The more venturesome experience unshieldedness in the unholy. They bring to mortals the trace of the fugitive gods, the track into the dark of the world's night. As the singers of soundness, the more venturesome ones are 'poets in a destitute time.' "[382] The premier figure among these seers is Friedrich Hölderlin. "Hölderlin is the pre-cursor of poets in a destitute time. This is why no poet of this world era can overtake him."[383] Heidegger openly confesses: "I think Hölderlin is the poet who points toward the future, who expects the god, and who therefore cannot remain simply a subject for Hölderlin research in the literary historical imagination."[384] However, not only poets such as Hölderlin, but Heidegger himself is one of the seer-figures "of this world era": "Only a god can still save us. I think the only possibility of salvation left to us is to prepare readiness, through thinking and poetry, for the appearance of the god or for the absence of the god during the decline; so that we do not, simply put, die meaningless deaths, but that when we decline, we decline in the face of the absent god."[385] As a successor of Hölderlin in a destitute time, Heidegger is one of the few—and does he perhaps even consider himself the only one?—who "struggle with building narrow and not very far-reaching footbridges for a crossing."[386]

For this, however, there must be some hope in the darkness of the world night. Such hope emerges from Hölderlin's promise, one Heidegger often cites: "But where danger is, grows / The saving power also," a verse coming significantly from the poem entitled "Patmos," which deals with the figure of the New Testament apocalyptist John.[387] The way in which Heidegger understands these verses as a "beckoning," i.e., as a word of promise, justifies referring to it as apocalyptic. In the context of his conception of the history of Being, Heidegger diagnoses an epoch of the greatest danger, greater even than critics of cultural and technological development would admit. It is part of the essence of Being that its revealing will occur only amid the greatest danger. "The destining of revealing is as such, in every one of its modes, and therefore necessarily, *danger*."[388] And even more: "The destining of revealing is in itself not just any danger, but danger as such. Yet when destining reigns in the mode of Enframing [*Ge-stell*]," and that means in the mode of the essence of modern technology, "it is the supreme danger," and "[man] comes to the very brink of a precipitous fall."[389] It is not technology itself that is dangerous, but rather nothing less than the destining of Being. At the same time, however, this allows rescue to draw near, even if one cannot say positively just what the nature of this rescue will ultimately be. At this point the apocalyptists of earlier ages were able to say more than Heidegger. Nevertheless, the comforting idea is maturing, namely, that precisely this hidden, forgotten Being which occasions the greatest danger will also bring deliverance. Rather than the human being, it is in the best case Being itself that guarantees this deliverance. "Human activity can never directly counter this danger. Human achievement alone can never banish it. But human reflection can ponder the fact that all saving power must be of a higher essence than what is endangered, though at the same time kindred to it."[390]

At the moment of highest danger, a new beginning is heralded. This, however, is an apocalyptic notion. Like all apocalyptic, so also does Heidegger's construction of the history of Being claim to unveil reality, and what is unveiled is the catastrophic nature of reality. This nature seems at first to be an inescapable fate insofar as it does not exhaust itself in the sufficiently familiar catastrophes and catastrophic tendencies of the twentieth century, but derives rather from the deepest ontological roots. The catastrophic nature of reality is total. The insight into the destining of Being, however, teaches us to understand the catastrophe of decline and end as a planetary crisis. The end becomes a transition, and "only after this decline does the abrupt dwelling of the Origin take place for a long span of time."[391] Such unveiling of the catastrophic nature of reality and the interpretation of this catastrophe as both crisis and opportunity, however, are, as we have already seen on several occasions, central themes of apocalyptic thinking. The notion of waiting for the revelation of the mystery is also apocalyptic. Whereas the Jewish apocalyptist, for example, awaits the revelation of the mysteries of the Most High, Heidegger knows about "the mystery of Being."[392]

As already in other types of apocalyptic, so also, finally, do we encounter anxiety in Heidegger. Heidegger seeks to get to the bottom of "what is happening in that age."[393] What he tries to unveil is the "self-deception, forever gaining the upper hand in relation to genuine nihilism," going deeper than even Nietzsche himself had thought insofar as it constitutes the essence itself of metaphysics. The self-deception over against genuine nihilism consists in doing away with thinking and replacing it with idle chatter. It corresponds thus to the inauthenticity which Heidegger analyzed in *Being and Time*. Self-deception attempts "in this way to talk itself out of its anxiety in the face of thinking. But that anxiety is anxiety in the face of anxiety."[394] Thus anxiety, or more precisely, anxiety before anxiety, is the stigma of the present world age. Genuine thinking begins where this anxiety is exposed and its roots in the destining of Being, in the oblivion of Being and abandonment of Being, are identified. In this way Heidegger's unveiling thought leads initially into a confrontation with anxiety and to its intensification. At the same time, however, singers and poets such as Hölderlin and Heidegger, who are currently on the trail of a new kind of thinking, offer eschatological consolation to the anxious human beings now confronted for the first time with anxiety which until now may perhaps have been concealed, consolation in whose light the planetary-wide catastrophe is now transformed into crisis: "But where danger is, grows / The saving power also."

As we have seen, Heidegger's phenomenology of the decline of the metaphysically determined world constitutes an independent counterpart to Spengler's theory of the decline of the West, a counterpart also far superior in its ontology. In addition to such analogies, the direct influence of Spengler can be discerned up to the very present. As an example we might mention H. Friedrich's thesis of "cultural catastrophe."[395] Friedrich's "obituary for the west," in particular his "notes concerning the psychopathology of modernity,"[396] explicitly invoke Spengler's insights.[397] These are paired with the sufficiently familiar warnings of more recent date concerning global ecological collapse. The hubris of *homo sapiens* consists in the modern idea of progress. "And this hubris means suicide through progress."[398] "Under the premonitory sign of perspective thinking directed primarily toward profit and appropriation," it acquires an "apocalyptic character," and does so through the alienation of "this particular being from its origin and thus from the root of its being."[399] Like Spengler before him, H. Friedrich also develops the thesis of cultural catastrophe with the help of biological categories, except that the place of Goethe's nature philosophy is taken by statements of ethology, especially those of the behavioral scientist Konrad Lorenz.[400]

A new variation of Western cultural pessimism is emerging from the thinking of those intellectuals who under a term taken from architecture are beginning to establish themselves as the "postmoderns." Spengler's gloomy prediction of the decline of the West is replaced by the oracle of the "death of modernity."[401] References to "catastrophic modernity" are postmodern.[402] The future is negatively cast: "World history is either openly or covertly catastrophic."[403] All hope is lost and all utopias collapse: "The year 2000 will not take place."[404] Heidegger and Nietzsche are rediscovered under the influence of Foucault, Bataille, Baudrillard, and Derrida, and the proximity to Ludwig Klages or Oswald Spengler is in many instances overly obvious, e.g., in Horstmann's work: "We, all of us, are already the final human beings, participants in the end time, afterbirth, those who cover both ourselves and our traditions."[405] The causes of the threatening, occasionally even morbidly yearned for end are sought in human rationality, the logical result being that one bids farewell to critical reason, e.g., in the work of P. Sloterdijk.[406] What has previously been understood as rationality is now unmasked as rational cynicism, as the thinking of a schizoid society with a "catastrophile complex."[407] This society virtually seeks out the end, driven by the desire for decline and the end and governed by "the latent will to catastrophe."[408] According to Sloterdijk, "the hour of kynicism" is arriving,[409] advocating happiness here and now. The great political utopias are replaced by "happiness—the ultimate impudence,"[410] and critical reason by a "philosophy of cheekiness"[411] claiming to be the answer to the omens of a new prewar period; it is the "life philosophy of crisis."[412]

J. Derrida, one of the spokespersons for the postmoderns, diagnoses "an apocalyptic tone recently adopted in philosophy."[413] As part of a "rereading" of Kant's similarly entitled polemic "On a Newly Arisen Superior Tone in Philosophy,"[414] which is viewed together with the New Testament Apocalypse of John and engaged in tense discussion, Derrida seeks to outbid all eschatologically colored discourse concerning the end of philosophy or the decline of the West by disclosing apocalyptic as the transcendental condition of all discourse. Derrida sees an affinity between the postulate of the Enlightenment on the one hand, and apocalyptic on the other with its claim to unveil reality. Just as apocalyptic claims to unveil the truth about reality, so also does all Enlightenment claim to unveil the truth. Derrida concludes that ever since Kant's critique of references to the end of philosophy, all of modernity has been permeated by apocalyptic discourse. Each succeeding Enlightenment outbids the preceding one, deriving from its claim to discover the truth ever new discourse concerning the end outbidding all preceding discourse. Like the apocalyptic of, for example, Judaism, so also does the continuing Enlightenment assume, in the name of reason, various forms of

> going-one-better in eschatological eloquence, each newcomer more lucid than the other, more vigilant, and more prodigal too, coming to add more to it: I tell you this in truth; this is not only the end of this here but also and first of that there, the end of history, the end of the class struggle, the end of philosophy, the death of God, the end of religions, the end of Christianity and morals (that, that was the most serious naïveté), the end of the subject, the end of man, the end of the West, the end of Oedipus, the end of the earth, *Apocalypse Now*, I tell

> you, in the cataclysm, the fire, the blood, the fundamental earthquake . . . and also the end of literature, the end of painting, art as a thing of the past, the end of psychoanalysis, the end of the university, the end of phallocentrism and phallogocentrism, and I don't know what else.[415]

If, however, apocalyptic is a "transcendental condition of all discourse, of all experience even, of every mark or every trace," then the genre of "apocalyptic" writings in the strict sense seems to be merely "an example, an *exemplary* revelation of this transcendental structure."[416] Furthermore, the desire for a demystification of the apocalyptic tone, the "enigmatic desire for vigilance, for the lucid vigil, for elucidation, for critique and truth,"[417] is according to Derrida also a mode of the apocalyptic.

Postmodern thinking, which in this way synoptically conceives the pathos of the Enlightenment in modernity on the one hand, and classical apocalyptic on the other, suspends the boundary established in modernity between the rational and the irrational.[418] "Each of us is the mystagogue *and* the *Aufklärer* [enlightener] of an other."[419] In Derrida's schema, neither the mystagogue nor the enlightener escapes apocalyptic as the transcendental condition of all discourse. It is a matter of following the better apocalyptic traditions and of denouncing the false ones.[420] Postmodern thinking denounces the false enlightenment pathos of modern rationality and claims for itself the better apocalyptic tradition. And indeed, even the insistence on apocalyptic as the transcendental condition of all discourse is apocalyptic, an unveiling, since "all language on apocalypse is also apocalyptic and cannot be excluded from its object."[421] Derrida's postmodern thinking, however, does not open up discourse concerning the end of modernity as a cultural period, but rather denounces in an apocalyptic fashion the claim to truth raised by enlightened rationality. There is no truth, but rather "only *truths*, effects of apocalyptic events." And precisely this constitutes "the truth of what can first be called post-modernism."[422] For just this reason, postmodern discourse is "an apocalypse without apocalypse, an apocalypse without vision, without truth, without revelation."[423] However, the capacity of this apocalypse to unveil reality, i.e., the disposition of its critical consciousness, will need to be evaluated just as is that of other forms of apocalyptic.

The idiomatic expression of the postmoderns appears as a variation of the notion of the decline of the West, which itself Derrida views in a reverse fashion merely as an individual example of the apocalyptic discourse of modernity as a whole, discourse culminating in the scenario of nuclear "apocalypse now." Again in an apocalyptic fashion, Derrida claims to unveil the apocalyptic structure of the global nuclear scenario in a series of seven sections called "missiles/missives" taking their literary model from the seven letters of the Apocalypse of John.[424] And such discussion of nuclear holocaust does indeed constitute apocalyptic discourse. The same applies to the theorem of the limits to growth. Both envision a planetary end by combining the notion of cultural decay, represented in our own century primarily by the idea of the decline of the West, with scientific theories of the end of the world. Now that we have discussed scientific theories of the end on the one hand, and the complex of ideas associated with the decline of the West on the other, we will conclude this chapter by discussing the theorems of the limits to growth and of nuclear holocaust, theorems that in a certain way combine these two ideas.

8. The Limits to Growth

"The project was not intended as a piece of futurology. It was intended to be, and is, an analysis of current trends, of their influence on each other, and of their possible outcomes. Our goal was to provide warnings of potential world crisis if these trends are allowed to continue, and thus offer an opportunity to make changes in our political, economic, and social systems to ensure that these crises do not take place."[425] With these words the executive committee of the Club of Rome explicates the intentions of its study *The Limits to Growth* (1972), a study commissioned by the Massachusetts Institute of Technology and conducted by Dennis L. Meadows and other scientists.[426] Its object is not to provide "prognoses" concerning the course of the future, but rather a world model with whose help one can better estimate and analyze dominant "tendencies" and their possible consequences for the fate of the earth and of humankind. "We would not expect the real world to behave like the world model in any of the graphs we have shown, especially in the collapse modes."[427] The participating scientists did not want to be understood as prophets, and certainly not as prophets of doom, but rather merely as "systems analysts."[428] They were concerned only with elucidating "valid basic behavior modes for the world system"[429] and with illuminating the structure of the affected feedback loops.[430] "It [the report] advances tentative suggestions for the future state of the world."[431]

Despite this reserved tone and the anticipatory response to alleged misunderstanding or unwanted interpretations, the formula of the "limits to growth" has in the meantime had the same effect as Spengler's own dark statement concerning the decline of the West in its own day. The eschatological substance of the scenario of the limits to growth was quickly recognized by both advocates and critics of the study of the Club of Rome. Both critics and adherents of the new world formula read the Meadows report as an apocalypse. "Its information and content was propagated and perceived through the screen of personal and technical nimbus of mystery and unveiling."[432] The uneasiness with technical civilization which was in part expressed by the report of the Club of Rome itself, and in part precipitated by it, "has intensified into a new apocalyptic mood and crystallized into a cybernetic world model which is both tangible and subject to the criticism of numbers, functions, and computer printouts, a model that can be praised, criticized, and castigated. Our age has made it possible to comprehend the end of the world in terms of calculations."[433]

It does not seem entirely inappropriate to read Meadows's study on the limits to growth as an apocalypse. "We believe," so the opinion of the executive committee of the Club of Rome, "that it contains a message of much deeper significance than a mere comparison of dimensions, a message relevant to all aspects of the present human predicament."[434] Whereas in many quarters the message was taken as a call to repentance to humankind, and in particular to the industrialized nations,[435] critics chided the MIT scientists for engaging in "negative utopia"[436] and heard in their words merely "the old saw of the decline of the West,"[437] or, even worse, thought they had encountered "pre- or post-fascist" tendencies.[438]

The reference to Spengler's *Decline of the West* raised by critics of the Club of Rome was intended as a denunciation. Their criticism is unfortunately defective insofar as although it does quite justifiably fault the authors of the study for neglecting political and societal factors,[439] it then presents its own critique of the critique of growth, yet does so in the name of a utopia which is itself permeated by the idea of progress.[440] This prognosis concerning the future and societal progress counters the vision of doom evoked by the limits to growth with the vision of a humane society which will master the technological problems and problems of provisioning foreseen by the Club of Rome; of course, this countervision is no less eschatological than the vision it replaces. Unfortunately, the eschatology of the critics has come into question itself because it is based on a pathos of progress which in the meantime finds itself challenged from every quarter and overtaken by the very crisis developments foreseen by, among others, the Club of Rome.[441]

Despite all the scientific and perhaps also political problematic attaching to the study of the Club of Rome, the dangers facing humankind which it illuminates, including the reckless exploitation of nature and of its nonrenewable resources, as well as pollution and destruction of the environment, the population explosion, and exponential growth of the world economy—these dangers simply can no longer be denied.[442] The theorem of the limits to growth is confirmed in a depressing fashion by the extensive material collected for the American President in the report *Global 2000.*[443] The analysis presented in *Global 2000* is based on a world model[444] which in comparison with that of the Club of Rome is much more sophisticated.[445] Nonetheless, reference to Spengler's thesis concerning the decline of the West is by no means exhausted by the admission of the threat. In many instances the idea of the limits to growth have taken the place of Spengler's ideas. The decisive factor affecting the change in consciousness at the beginning of the 1970s in the Western industrialized nations was not even the immediate experience of ecological crises, but rather the purely politically motivated oil boycott undertaken by the Arab countries, an economic consequence of the fourth Israeli-Arab war (Yom Kippur War) in October 1973 and the economic recession it precipitated, a recession painfully applying the brakes to economic growth. Since then, whenever the theorem of the limits to growth has held sway over public consciousness, it can be understood as an association of the idea of the decline of the West with scientific prognoses of an end of the world. A critique of civilization on the one hand, and scientific eschatology on the other, enter into a new apocalyptic association in the idea of the limits to growth. The factors allegedly leading to the decline of the West are expanded by the addition of the ecological component. The cosmological assumption of heat death based on the law of entropy is replaced by reference to "growth death."[446] Accordingly, C. Amery reads the diagram from the Meadows study as the "end-time curve of this earth."[447] And just as on the one hand the theorem of the limits to growth was able to take the place of the idea of the decline of the West, so also in the meantime has in many instances the debate concerning ecology been enriched by material from the critique of civilization, material clearly breathing the spirit of Oswald Spengler even though for various reasons his work is no longer cited by name. The attempt to draw parallels between the notion of the limits to growth and the idea of the decline of the West should not be misunderstood as a denial of the presence and dimensions of the global ecological crisis. In view of the actual threat, however, one should inquire concerning the apocalyptic potential of the theorem of the limits to growth.

Read as an apocalypse, the report of the Club of Rome says less about *when* and *how* the end will occur than *that* it will occur. Exponential growth is moving toward a certain end. Like all apocalyptic, the study of the limits to growth also contains an inherent claim of enlightenment. Reality is allegedly being unveiled, and is being unveiled with the help of extensive statistical material which from a distance recalls the gematria of apocalyptic influenced by wisdom, e.g., in Judaism. This represents a quantification of the catastrophe. What is actually revealed is not the course of future events, but rather the basic catastrophic structure of reality itself. For the authors, "the model's feedback loop structure is a much more important determinant of overall behavior than the exact numbers used to quantify the feedback loops."[448] Despite the use of computers as a technical aid for enlightenment, the parallel to the visionary gift of the apocalyptist is also present. The world model underlying the study is an "intuitive model"[449] and allegedly serves to expand our "intuitive capabilities."[450] There is an urgent need for enlightenment and for the development of intuitive capabilities because the temporal horizon in which for the most part human beings plan, live, and set priorities, no longer stands in any connection with the dimensions and urgency of the problems of survival facing humankind.[451] Time is growing short, and precisely the deception regarding the time yet remaining for humankind is accelerating the outbreak of the catastrophe itself. In this eschatological situation, the MIT research group now appears, a group that sees further, is able to think in terms of larger periods of time, and is able to disclose the true structure of catastrophic reality.

Although its message is gloomy, it is not an apocalypse without hope. "In any event, our posture is one of very grave concern, but not of despair," since there is yet "an alternative."[452] It consists in a counterutopia to the world of exponential growth. The goal envisioned by the Club of Rome is the counterworld of global equilibrium and poststabilized harmony.[453] In this world, one coming into view when the turn from quantity to quality, i.e., from quantitative to qualitative growth takes place,[454] the eschatological ideal of the equality of all will be realized. "In a long-term equilibrium state, the relative levels of population and capital, and their relationships to fixed constraints such as land, fresh water, and mineral resources, would have to be set so that there would be enough food and material production to maintain everyone at (at least) a subsistence level. One barrier to equal distribution would thus be removed. Furthermore, the other effective barrier to equality—the promise of growth—could no longer be maintained."[455] The promised counterworld, however, is distinguished from other eschatological utopias in that it is not conceived to be without pressures.

> An equilibrium state would not be free of pressures, since no society can be free of pressures. Equilibrium would require trading certain human freedoms, such as producing unlimited numbers of children or consuming uncontrolled amounts of resources, for other freedoms, such as relief from pollution and crowding and the threat of collapse of the world system. It is possible that new freedoms might also arise—universal and unlimited education, leisure for creativity and inventiveness, and, most important of all, the freedom from hunger and poverty enjoyed by such a small fraction of the world's people today.[456]

In view of the threatening collapse of the world system, there is despite everything yet hope. Such hope depends on the successful mobilization of all political and socially relevant powers and on winning over these powers to the idea of voluntary growth limits in the economy and in population development.[457] It is a matter of turning the catastrophe aside and in perceiving the crisis as a last chance. Differently than in most examples of apocalyptic, this yearned for counterworld appears not after the catastrophe, but rather precisely and only if the prophesied catastrophe does not take place at all. The study of the Club of Rome concerning the limits to growth is thus an example of self-destroying prophecy. As G. Picht remarked, it was written with the expressed goal that it might be proven false, and to that extent constitutes a "negative utopia."[458] On the one hand, then, a plethora of catastrophic tendencies is unveiled which thus far have allegedly been concealed from our everyday consciousness; on the other hand, hope is expressed that we might succeed in countering these tendencies. The deterministic character of the catastrophe is allegedly reversible. This hope of self-destroying prophecy seeks support in salvific tendencies which in their own turn have until now been concealed and are to be unveiled. Incisive changes are necessary. "This change is perhaps already in the air, however faintly."[459] The apocalypse of salvation takes a position portentously next to the apocalypse of disaster.

Carl Amery subjects the numbers and statistics of this apocalypse to an extensive cultural-historic interpretation. The roots of this lethal understanding of growth—this is one of the main findings of his treatise *The End of Providence*—are to be found in the creation faith of the Jewish-Christian tradition. The "Jewish program"[460] taken forward by Christianity[461] allegedly created the foundation for unbridled growth with its accompanying exploitation of nature by believing in a divine guarantee of survival, "the firm promise of a future corrective to the unbearable condition of the world, a collective promise for the world of human beings in the larger sense"[462] and "the assurance of a balance of the planetary biosphere in favor of human beings."[463] The understanding of progress supported by this religiously anchored faith, an understanding whose basic structure was preserved even in its completely secularized variations, led to total success. Precisely this total human success in the struggle for existence, however, has led to total crisis. "The final terror, the alarm in the spaceship earth, a spaceship whose system of self-provision is in acute danger, is itself also merely the result of a victory in a struggle in which the only goal was to snatch away the largest possible quantity of spoils from the hostile biosphere."[464] "Summarized briefly, one can say that total crisis is the result of total success."[465] The threat has reached apocalyptic proportions. "The handwriting of disaster is on the wall."[466] The ecological crisis amplifies as an additional threat the traditional dangers already threatening the survival of humankind, namely, the Cold War and the possibility of nuclear self-annihilation. The internal decay of culture goes hand in hand with the external threat.[467]

In Amery's view the situation appears even more gloomy than at the end of the report of the Club of Rome. Not even the discovery of new sources of raw materials and energy and the complete throttling of population growth could prevent the catastrophe "if the favorite child, the pampered central idea of active humankind is not surrendered: perpetual growth, ever more optimistic expansion toward ever rosier horizons."[468] This involves equally a renunciation both of the philosophy of growth cherished by the West on the one hand, and of the optimism of progress advocated by socialism on the other.[469] The most disturbing finding from Amery's analysis, however, is "the most recent and most fateful discovery . . . namely, the discovery that our common raft is edible."[470] What is new in the new apocalyptic is that it no longer recognizes any guarantee of survival after the catastrophe. Those plagued by anxiety are no longer addressed by the—albeit distant—God who might promise salvation beyond the catastrophe, salvation that might turn the catastrophe into a crisis. The new type of apocalyptist hears only the "words of the absent God": "Why are you crying for help, you fool? I'm not going to help you. You've already helped yourself."[471]

Whereas Amery's critique of civilization is consciously indebted to modern traditions of enlightenment, the author Herbert Gruhl combines the theorem of the limits to growth with cultural-critical ideas clearly connected with the notion of the decline of the West.[472] Gruhl's report concerning the situation of humankind is also based on the study of the Club of Rome, though it believes the catastrophe can be limited in its effects, nonetheless now considers it unavoidable. In broad strokes Gruhl outlines a doctrine of stages for human history. The present is a historical crisis whose name is "the planetary turn,"[473] a stage without any analogy, preceded by three historical stages.[474] The first was characterized by "isolated, extensive tribal territories," the second by "colonial superimposition," and the third by "expansion in depth and height." Now, however, humankind stands at the decisive turning point from the third to the fourth stage.[475] This fourth stage stands completely under the auspices of struggle. The struggle for naked survival, for mineral wealth, water, and basic foodstuffs breaks out between peoples, leading to what Nietzsche called the "revaluation of all values" and Gruhl the "total shifting of potences."[476] What Gruhl develops as the scenario of the future corresponds in substance fairly closely to the stage of Caesarism in Spengler's cultural morphology. But the parallel goes even further. The more the catastrophic situation of humankind comes to a head, the more severe will in Gruhl's view the East-West conflict become, the "dual" between East and West.[477] Only the one prepared to accept renunciation in the material sphere and to accept a simple lifestyle will survive the catastrophe. The Western industrialized nations will be affected especially hard by the planetary turn. Not the countries of the third world, but rather the industrialized nations who are spoiled in their prosperity and highly vulnerable in their infrastructure will be the first to plunge into the abyss.[478] This would constitute the ecologically caused decline of the West. In the dual between East and West, however, the East is in a better position regarding the outcome in the age of ecological priorities than is the West. Since the people of the East have long been accustomed to a low standard of living, they will be more capable of adaptation than the people of the Western world in times of ecologically enforced renunciation of growth. In other words, the East Bloc, under the leadership of the Soviet Union, will from the perspective of power politics profit from the ecological crisis. The scenario Gruhl outlines of the fall of the West and the rise of the East again recalls Spengler's historical philosophy. One of Spengler's central ideas was that the decline of the West would be followed by the rise of Russia, whose drive toward the West was precipitated by an "asiatic restoration" in the form of the October Revolution.[479] According to Gruhl, too, the future belongs to Asia to the extent that the West does not undergo a radical change in thinking. In Gruhl's opinion, China is even better equipped than the Soviet Union for the time of ecological crisis and struggle.[480] The struggle of the West against destruction acquires features of the end time.[481]

In this eschatological "boundary situation"[482] the clairvoyant also finds only meager hope. This hope attaches especially to the succeeding generation, who will perhaps grow up from the very beginning with an ecologically aware consciousness.[483] Yet even this hope is actually merely optimism with a mourning wreath: "As soon as the first collapse is reported, the only possibility remaining for us will be perpetual catastrophe response, year in and year out. Even if it seems highly improbable—especially for us in Europe [sic!]—that the catastrophe might be prevented, we should at least prepare for rescue operations."[484] This attitude recalls that of Noah in the Old Testament, who in the calm before the great storm continued unperturbed in the building of his ark: The building of the ark anticipates the catastrophe, and ecological admonishers such as Gruhl are also concerned with precisely this kind of active anticipation of the catastrophe, though their hope is considerably weaker than that of Noah. Gruhl expresses his own agreement with a quote of Eugene Ionesco: "I am one person among three billion others. How can my voice be heard? I am preaching in an overpopulated desert. Neither I nor others can find any way out. I believe there is no way out."[485] The use of this citation is revealing. The "systems analysts" such as Meadows are replaced by the "preacher." As a preacher in the desert he also stands in the line of biblical eschatological traditions, of the preacher in Deutero-Isaiah and John the Baptist—who is interpreted from the perspective of that preacher—as well as of Nietzsche's Zarathustra and his prophecy: "The wasteland grows: woe unto him that harbors wasteland." The ecological prophet of doom lives "in an overpopulated desert." But Nietzsche's statement can also be understood literally. Only then it must read: "The forest is burning—the desert grows."[486]

The ecological admonisher changes from a systems analyst to a preacher in the desert. He is a solitary individual and is able to reach only a negligible number of others. This has always been the situation of the apocalyptist. Today he confronts the "prophets" of a futurology dedicated optimistically to the future and to progress.[487] Futurologists such as H. Kahn are unmasked as false prophets of salvation whose message is countered by the dark words of decline and the end. Admittedly, the initial self-destroying prophecy of the limits to growth ultimately turns into a pure ecology of doom which surrenders all hope. For as Ionesco says, when there is no way out, it is no longer possible to interpret the threatening catastrophe apocalyptically as a crisis and to understand this crisis as a chance. The horizon darkens. World history drives on toward its end, an end that is actually "total death" devouring both humankind and the earth itself.[488]

9. The Nuclear Holocaust

Anxiety before the global ecological catastrophe pushed into the background that particular danger which after the Second World War evoked apocalyptic anxiety and demanded apocalyptic answers: the nuclear threat. The danger of a nuclear holocaust has not diminished in the meantime; in fact, quite the contrary is the case. Despite increasing potential for destruction, however, the nuclear danger has been overshadowed by the ecological debate. The truly apocalyptic dimensions of damage to the environment has caused the bomb to seem like one of several dangers now threatening humankind. In this way "the absolute threat represented by nuclear weapons has in the eyes of many become merely a relative threat."[489] Of course, although the avoidability of ecological collective death is yet being debated scientifically and politically, no serious denial is possible concerning the absolute character of the nuclear threat. Although we cannot yet predict whether one day, because of the inner logic of developments since 1945, nuclear holocaust will be unavoidable, we can say that the possibility of the nuclear annihilation of both humankind and of the earth does indeed exist, and that this danger, as a pure possibility, can never be eliminated. Human knowledge of the technical possibility of nuclear arms makes the threat irreversible and to that extent into an absolute danger. Hence when for this reason nuclear holocaust as a possibility and as an apocalyptic idea is discussed at the end of this chapter about various notions of the end of the world, this actually involves a double climax: On the one hand, the nuclear threat, as an absolute danger over against the decline of the West or the limits to growth, constitutes a qualitative leap; on the other hand, given the consequences nuclear war would have on the overall ecological constitution of the earth, it can be understood not only as an ecological threat, but as the actual center of the environmental crisis.[490] Finally, another climax in the course of the previous sections occurs where the nuclear threat is made responsible for the decay of culture and of human relationships. Where this is the case, such as by way of suggestion in J. Schell,[491] the idea of the decline of the West undergoes a final intensification. And at least for certain parts of the European peace movement the question arises whether in their ranks the nuclear holocaust has not taken the place of Spengler's decline of the West.

What more recently in Western countries is articulating itself as new apocalyptic or as "neo-apocalypticity"[492] represents a reaction to the rediscovery of the absolute nature of the nuclear threat precipitated by the renewed arms race. The absolute nature of the threat represented by nuclear war corresponds to the inescapability of the end of the world in older types of apocalyptic. Nuclear arms put humankind into a position to actualize traditional apocalyptic imagery. They make possible a historicization of apocalyptic imagery, which at the same moment means the end of all history. "In the past," so Karl Jaspers, "there have been imaginative notions of the world's end . . . But now we face the real possibility of such an end."[493] Nuclear arms lend to apocalyptic terminology such as that concerning the end of the world a "serious, unmetaphorical meaning."[494] This alteration of the status of apocalyptic imagery, of nuclear danger, and of reality in the shadow of the nuclear threat seems adequately addressed now only by the language of apocalyptic. In what follows we will evaluate apocalyptic language and apocalyptic thinking in connection with the nuclear threat in various examples, and will inquire concerning their understanding of existence.

In the work of Karl Jaspers the affinity between intellectual discourse concerning nuclear weapons on the one hand and earlier forms of apocalyptic on the other already becomes clear. In his view, nuclear weapons represent not only a previously unknown danger, they also force us to reflect upon the end: "to *think:* to look around us; to observe what is going on; to visualize the possibilities, the consequences of events and actions; to clarify the situation in the directions that emerge."[495] As an actual possibility, the end of the world conjured by nuclear weapons lags far behind the cosmic end of the world envisioned by traditional apocalypses as far as actual dimensions are concerned. The end rendered possible by nuclear weapons would no longer be "a fictitious end of the world. It is no world's end at all, but the extinction of life on the surface of the planet."[496] The end of the world conjured by nuclear weapons would at most be global, and at least by cosmic standards even partial. From the perspective of human existence, of course, such an end would involve the same measure of totality as the mythic end, e.g., in Jewish or early Christian apocalypses.[497]

Jaspers does deviate from both apocalyptic and gnosis insofar as he disputes the unavoidability of the end. According to Jaspers, "the thesis concerning the end constitutes an uncritical leap from the aspect of a phenomenon to the alleged fundamental process itself, from an orientation within what actually can be known to a condition of total knowledge."[498] Such total knowledge would fail to recognize the basic disposition of human existence by negating human responsibility.[499] "For one thing is certain: The annihilation of life by nuclear weapons would in no way be the unavoidable end to what in and of itself is a destructive underlying process, regardless of whether such a process is allegedly discerned empirically or gnostically and mythically. It remains an uncoerced human act, one that up till it actually takes place is dependent upon human freedom."[500] Precisely because the possibility of actualizing apocalyptic imagery does exist, such imagery should not be taken literally, but rather must in Jaspers's sense be understood as "symbols" whose language takes as its theme the truth of human existence.[501] Reflection upon the end made necessary by the nuclear threat can make critical use of such symbols.

Reflection upon the end does not recognize its unalterable necessity, but rather considers itself charged, in the context of the possibility of the end, with rethinking the fundamental situation of human existence. The threatening end prompts us to reflect upon what Jaspers calls the origin. The global threat "forces human beings to see the end, so that they must choose: Rebirth from their origin, or destruction. We are challenged to carry out extreme, even human-all-too-human measures against this most extreme threat; this is no longer merely an accomplishment of the sort in which human beings have excelled thus far, but rather a transformation of our entire appearance from depravity back to ourselves, to the origin of our essence."[502] The origin of human nature, however, lies according to Jaspers in the freedom to make responsible decisions, which in this case is to be a freely made decision against destruction. For Jaspers, however, reflection upon the end goes one step further than is the case with many warnings and other forms of self-destroying prophecy. Reflection upon the end seeks not only to be an appeal to prevent the end, but also goes beyond this in posing the question of meaning for the case that the end does indeed come about. This total threat "becomes the pivot of our lives"[503] and poses the question of meaning for a Being which in the end will quite possibly be surrendered to total annihilation after all.[504] In its search for an answer to the question of meaning, reflection upon the end conceives "being at the end."[505] Although "being in the end" is subject to annihilation by nothingness, "absolute nothingness is inconceivable."[506] On this basis Jaspers attempts to understand the notion of "being in the end" as a symbol allowing for the belief in an absolute meaning of human existence that cannot be destroyed by even the most total of catastrophes. This thinking of absolute meaning, making use of the symbols of immortality and eternity,[507] is grounded in trust in what Jaspers calls the ground of our existence, in the confidence that one is affirmed in one's own existence, "a confidence that no temporal failure can quench, not even that of reason."[508] Such reflection upon the end dares to "build even if we cannot know how long our building will stand."[509] The possibility of the end prompts Jaspers to rethink our understanding of existence. Nuclear weapons lead to an understanding of existence from the perspective of doom.[510]

According to Jaspers, anxiety plays a fundamental role in existence.[511] In his own determination of anxiety, Jaspers distinguishes anxiety for existence, whose primal form is death anxiety, from existential anxiety, which sees the threat not in physical annihilation, but rather in existential nonbeing, in the disintegration of authentic existence. According to Jaspers, anxiety for existence, as anxiety before physical nonexistence, assumes a key role in the situation of possible total destruction. People in the nuclear age have anxiety before anxiety: "Aghast, we want to draw back from extremity. It cannot be. It must not be. No panic! we cry. We want calm. In an atmosphere of calm, we think, this can be handled."[512] It is precisely the apparent calm in public life and the surface optimism that are signs of profound anxiety, anxiety in the face of anxiety for existence disclosed by reflection upon the end. Anxiety denies anxiety before the horrific, before potential destruction. At the same time, however, anxiety for existence is consciously employed as a political device, since nuclear scare tactics are based on limitless anxiety. Jaspers rejects this form of anxiety as a device of politics. "Anxiety alone cannot bring lasting peace. Is it not illusory to build a world on fear, on negotiations and agreements resting on fear alone? The way out of evil is not that cheap."[513]

Nevertheless, it is precisely in anxiety, or more precisely, in anxiety for existence, that Jaspers sees the decisive presupposition for political action in the face of nuclear weapons. The threatening situation requires not a repression, but rather on the contrary an intensification of anxiety. Such intensification of anxiety serves not as a means of political extortion, but rather as a condition for renewed existential reflection and change of ethos. As such, anxiety is initially ambiguous. Although it can have a destructive effect and amplify the impulse toward destruction, it can also lead to deliverance. "What needs increasing is the anxiety of the people; this should grow to overpowering force, not of blind submissiveness, but of a bright, transforming ethos that will bring forth appropriate statesmen and support their actions, for anxiety is ambiguous. As sheer anxiety it merely cries for help at any cost and is in vain. It must turn into a power that compels men to save themselves in the sphere of reason; then it can evoke the will that grasps its meaning before Transcendence, transforms man, and makes him true."[514] That is, anxiety can become a positive power when it prompts reflection on one's own existence, and changes from pure anxiety for existence into existential anxiety. In that case, it is anxiety "that may make us save ourselves."[515]

According to Jaspers, "senseless" and "illuminated" anxiety are juxtaposed. "If panicky anxiety drives us into irrationality, enlightened anxiety frees us for reason. We must take the unlimited risks of knowledge and anxiety if we want to remain truly human."[516] "Illuminated" anxiety is thus a saving power. Jaspers's own reflection upon the end has as its goal an enlightenment of anxiety. The disclosure, intensification, and enlightenment of anxiety for the sake of rendering it fruitful are decisive concerns of all apocalyptic, which understands itself as an unveiling of reality. Even if Jaspers assumes a negative posture over against both apocalyptic and gnosis as forms of unsubstantiated total knowledge, his own reflection upon the end does exhibit an affinity to apocalyptic insofar as its presupposition and object of unveiling is, if not the irrevocability of the catastrophe itself, at least the irreversible nature of its possibility. This reflection upon the end exhibits an impulse of enlightenment akin to that of apocalyptic. It is concerned not with an unveiling of the end itself, but rather with the unveiling of the possibility of that end, the goal being its prevention.

The end threatens. According to Jaspers, however, the danger comes not only from nuclear weapons. Jaspers considers totalitarianism to be of equal rank and equally catastrophic. The threat that "forces human beings to view the end" derives from both phenomena.[517] Like nuclear holocaust, so also does totalitarianism appear as annihilation. "By one, we lose life; by the other, a life that is worth living."[518] In the case of worldwide totalitarian rule[519] "history would end, though existence would continue. The atom bomb and total rule are the two terminal forms of destruction."[520] Much more decisive than the question of physical survival of humankind, according to Jaspers, is "the basic question . . . what makes life worth living?"[521] Jaspers rejects absolutizing Albert Schweitzer's demand to revere life.[522] "But it [faith in life] is not the last thing. It becomes untruthful, untrue, and ruinous when life as such is made the sole, the absolutely highest good. Then man takes the place of Transcendence, expressing an actual lack of faith."[523] Reason, love, and human freedom are not permitted to be sacrificed for the sake of preserving physical existence. Jaspers suggests that there is "truth that makes the ultimate effort and, if it fails, lets us meet the end without fear."[524]

For Jaspers, the problems of nuclear weapons and of totalitarianism are "fatefully" linked. "In practice, at least, they are inseparable. Neither one can be solved without the other."[525] This relationship can be understood if one considers the source from which Jaspers sees the danger of totalitarianism emerging: Russia. For Jaspers, whose book appeared during the period of the Cold War, "Russia and total rule seem to be identical."[526] Jaspers does, however, understand the distinction between the antithesis between political freedom and totalitarianism on the one hand, and between the Soviet power bloc and the Western world on the other. "*Totalitarianism* and *freedom* are conflicting principles, *Russia* and the *West* are conflicting historical realities. In the long run, the two conflicts need not coincide."[527] In the present situation of humankind, however, they do coincide thus, and that is why the danger of nuclear weapons and that of totalitarian rule are related. For the unilateral renunciation of nuclear weapons on the part of the West would be the equivalent of a surrender of the free world to totalitarianism, and would thus conjure, for the sake of preserving physical existence, the danger of the annihilation of any existence worth living. In a reverse fashion, Western self-assertion over against the East involves the possibility of nuclear holocaust, the annihilation of physical existence. And only now, according to Jaspers, is the global dilemma really described accurately. "How shall we preserve ourselves in the rising tide of chaos?"[528]

In retrospect, Jaspers's dilemma appears as a philosophical mirror-image of Western anxiety during the period of the Cold War. This dilemma arises especially through the association of the notion of the nuclear end of the world with the older idea of the decline of the West. Jaspers's portrayal of Russia's greatness, its future, and its danger for Europe can refer explicitly to Nietzsche, Max Weber, and Oswald Spengler as its precursors.[529] Jaspers speaks with pathos about the West, whose adversary is Russia. "Yet Russia is Western and Asian at the same time. She is not a part of the Latin-Germanic West."[530] The West of those peoples, including its associate America, is threatened with destruction. "Unless Europe and all of the West can be firmly united in time, Europe will be overrun and America lost in short order."[531] In certain respects the shadow of destruction has already overtaken the West insofar as it "no longer stands on her own feet," but rather is able to play its political role only within the field of tension between the superpowers.[532] In this extremely dangerous situation the West can assert itself only in alliance with the United States of America. Jaspers understands the kind of "western solidarity" demanded in the hour of greatest danger to be the "unconditional coalition of all free European countries with America"[533] (whereby Jaspers tacitly equates Europe with Western Europe, no longer conceiving the West within the boundaries familiar to Spengler!). Nuclear weapons and totalitarianism confront Western Europe "with a necessity that may be salutary. . . . [making] it impossible for the West to preserve itself unless an act of self-regeneration places it purely and truthfully upon the road that would enable all to have world order in freedom."[534]

In the final analysis, the central focus of Jaspers's exposition is the destruction or preservation of the West, the fate of which will decide that of the entire world. Jaspers's work concerning nuclear weapons and the future of human beings turns out to be a variation of the notion of the decline of the West in the nuclear age, to a certain extent its nuclear version. Although Jaspers thinks he has adequately demarcated his own reflection upon the end over against apocalyptic, we find that his analysis, despite all its efforts at providing a critique of ideology, suffers from apocalyptic blindness: It fails to realize that it itself has incubated an apocalyptic conceptual model with proven staying power in the twentieth century, namely, that of the decline of the West. Jaspers becomes an unwilling apocalyptist by submitting, under the influence of the Cold War, to the fascination of this theorem.

Jaspers's thesis of the double danger of the end of the world, apostrophized by G. Anders as the "two-hell axiom,"[535] encountered justified criticism. In more recent scholarship, J. Schell has emphasized "that doom can never be a human purpose at all, truly serious or otherwise, but, rather, is the end of all human purposes, none of which can be fulfilled outside of human life."[536] The assumption that the highest good is not life itself, but rather moral life—an assumption that first actually establishes the thesis of the double danger of destruction—is thus to be rejected. Schell's objection seems justified that Jaspers has applied "to the species as a whole a canon of morality that properly applies only to each individual person."[537] A qualitative distinction obtains between the question of the survival of or the sacrifice of an individual on the one hand, and the question of the survival of the species on the other, within which the death of an individual might possibly serve a purpose and acquire meaning. Accordingly, the main objection G. Anders raises against the alternative presented by Jaspers—an alternative that he insists is "simply beyond discussion"—is also that Jaspers equates the absolute danger of nuclear holocaust with a relative danger, in this case that of the Soviet threat.[538] "The final alternative today is not 'totalitarianism or nuclear threat,' but rather 'either a power makes use of the nuclear threat because it is totalitarian in any case, or a power becomes totalitarian by making use of the nuclear threat.' "[539] Jaspers's alternative cannot be maintained, since the "threat of nuclear war, i.e., of liquidation, is itself totalitarian by nature."[540]

Although Anders allows that Jaspers perceived the qualitative difference between the nuclear threat and the danger of totalitarianism, he accuses him of not taking this counteridea seriously. If one considers the significance the theorem of the decline of the West had for Jaspers's book—a role of which Jaspers apparently was not aware and which led him to become an unwilling apocalyptist—then one can agree with Anders's criticism that Jaspers became "a prisoner of his own mythologizing two-hell axiom."[541] Once one recognizes the apocalyptic quality of the idea of the decline of the West, then the historical objections Anders justifiably raises against the exaggeration of the Russian threat are of much less significance than the ideological-critical observation that one is dealing in Jaspers's analysis with "a virtually Manichaean division of the world into a bright and dark half."[542] The real problematic attaching to Jaspers's book consists in the surrender over against a fundamental apocalyptic idea that acquires mythical features. Though Jaspers did indeed wish to distance himself critically from apocalyptic as ungrounded total knowledge, this gives Anders the occasion to unmask Jaspers as an apocalyptist, albeit as a "lecture-hall apocalyptist" who, although intent on preventing the catastrophe, nonetheless shrinks back not only from undertaking the necessary action, but also from issuing the call to such action or even supporting such a call.[543]

In all of this, Anders significantly does not intend the title of apocalyptist to be derogatory. Quite the contrary, it is for him basically an honorific title, since Anders's own philosophical discourse with the nuclear threat quite consciously employs apocalyptic conceptual and linguistic models. The object of Anders's philosophizing is "the danger of total catastrophe."[544] According to Anders, it is only through apocalyptic that this catastrophe can be, if not overcome, at least battled, and for just this reason, Anders considers the use of the language of traditional apocalyptic, e.g., of Christian apocalyptic,[545] to be anything but sacrilegious. Quite the contrary, for him the justification of an apocalyptic means of expression has at no point in world history been greater than today in the shadow of nuclear war. "The present danger of the end is the first to be objectively serious—so serious, in fact, that it could not be more so."[546] The nuclear threat robs apocalyptic language of its metaphorical status, rendering it thus the only adequate description of reality.[547] Hence Anders does not in any way wish to distance himself from apocalyptic. Rather, he understands himself quite explicitly as an apocalyptist,[548] though as a "new type of apocalyptist"[549]: "Since we believe in the possibility of the 'end of time,' we are apocalyptists; yet because we battle against the very apocalypse we have ourselves made, we are—and this type has never before existed—*enemies of the apocalypse.*"[550] This new type is the "prophylactic apocalyptist," one who "has no other purpose than to thwart the apocalypse."[551]

The new apocalyptic in the shadow of the nuclear threat interprets the present as the end time, albeit as an end time that remains without end as long as the nuclear catastrophe is successfully thwarted. Although the most important thing to the prophylactic apocalyptist is that the end time might have no end, one can clearly identify the beginning of this end time. The "epochal threshold" to the end time was crossed in the year 1945. The dropping of the atomic bombs on Hiroshima and Nagasaki introduced a new and at the same time the final stage of the history of humankind. "A new age began on August 6, 1945, the day of Hiroshima."[552] August 8, 1945, a day rich with associations, the day on which, precisely between the bombing of Hiroshima and Nagasaki, the Charter of the International Military Tribunal in Nuremberg against crimes against humanity was signed—this day is the "most monstrous date,"[553] monstrous like the entire new age. Furthermore, the crossing of this epochal threshold also changed the metaphysical status of humankind: "We passed from the condition of *genus mortalium* into that of *genus mortale.*"[554]

Like earlier types of apocalyptic such as that in India, Iran, or in Judaism, so also does nuclear apocalyptic, taking the epochal threshold of 1945 as its point of departure, present a periodization of history. Anders subdivides the history of humankind into three ages. The point of comparison against which they each are distinguished in a characteristic fashion from the previous epoch is human mortality. "The titles ascribed to the individual ages would thus be:

1. All human beings are mortal.
2. All human beings can be killed.
3. Humankind as a whole can be killed."[555]

As one quickly sees, the parallel with classical forms of apocalyptic consists not only in the fact of a periodization of history, but also in the fact that such periodization is developed from the perspective of the present, finding its criterion for subdivisions in a contemporary experience of catastrophe.

The new and final epoch of history is distinguished from the preceding ones in that it contains the possibility of a historicization, as it were a demythologization (to alter slightly a familiar hermeneutical catchword) of apocalyptic notions. Anders considers the real danger in the nuclear age to be "annihilism."[556] "The place of the *creatio ex nihilo*—an expression signalling omnipotence—is taken by the antithetical power: the *potestas annihilationis*, the *reductio ad nihil*—a power now presented as residing in our own hands."[557] This juxtaposition of *creatio ex nihilo* and *potestas annihilationis* is revealing, recalling the theologumenon of Lutheran orthodoxy regarding the *annihilatio mundi*, which we have already discussed in depth.[558] The annihilation of humankind and of the earth by means of nuclear weapons would constitute the historicization of the theological idea of the *annihilatio mundi*. In fact, it would constitute in a perfidious way—to continue for a moment Anders's exposition—the retroverification of Lutheran orthodoxy and the refutation of the Reformed understanding of the *renovatio mundi*. In the event of nuclear holocaust, the latter would no longer take place. The Lutheran conception of an eschatology of *annihilatio mundi*, a conception largely rejected during the subsequent history of theology, has in an utterly unexpected fashion become a real possibility as a result of the nuclear threat.

According to Anders, annihilism is a syndrome in which nuclear weapons and philosophical nihilism come together. Anders summarizes nihilism in the formula "nothing matters," a formula expressing metaphysical monism on the one hand, and a radical, pragmatic amoralism on the other.[559] According to Anders, both these basic features of nihilism characterize nuclear weapons. "*The secret maxim of the bomb is identical with that of monism or nihilism; the bomb behaves like a nihilist.*"[560] In a reverse fashion, it holds that "*the masters of the bomb are nihilists in action*"[561] insofar as the possession of the bomb, i.e., having it, is identical with an act, and accordingly "*the bomb*" must be understood as "*act.*"[562]

This threat in the form of annihilation involves not only the annihilation of humankind and of all life on earth, but beyond this also the annihilation of all memory of what was, of history, of that which is no more. What threatens us—to use an expression from the Apocalypse of John[563]—is the second death: Even those who are already dead would die yet again in the nuclear firestorm. "For with our own end they, too, must go to ruin—as it were for the second time and this time once and for all. Although today, too, they already 'merely have been,' through their second death they will 'have been' in a way as if they 'never were.' "[564] J. Schell is thinking along the same lines when he considers the possibility raised through nuclear weapons that death itself, insofar as it, too, is a part of life, now threatens not only humankind but even itself. Different than the death of the individual, the annihilation of humankind would constitute "the death of death," which would not only bring about the second death of those already dead, but would also prevent the as yet unborn and unconceived from entering life in the first place. The second death would constitute the end of history itself, not only of the past, but of the future as well.[565]

G. Anders considers even mere possession of nuclear weapons already to constitute an act. And with that the nuclear holocaust encroaches into the present not only as a possibility, but also as a conceptual and above all a politically anticipated totalitarian reality. We may continue this idea and say that the *annihilatio mundi* has proleptically already become reality, and it is in this sense that J. Schell's statement can be understood, namely, that we are already experiencing the reality of annihilation. According to Schell, "we are similarly 'in extinction' while we are in life, and are after extinction when we are extinct."[566] Being toward death, as Heidegger expressed it, has become Being toward annihilation.

As far as the threat of a historicization of the *annihilatio mundi* through nuclear weapons is concerned, on the one hand it represents a qualitative leap over against all previous threats, a leap which can be circumscribed with the apocalyptic metaphor of second death; on the other hand, it is absolute insofar as it can never be eliminated as a possibility. Not even complete nuclear disarmament could eliminate the nuclear threat, since the physical and technical knowledge required to build nuclear weapons can never be removed from the collective memory of humankind.[567] "The modern equivalent of Augustine's *non possumus non peccare* is *non possumus non posse*."[568] In other words: "The reality of this danger consists not only in the existence of actual, physical weapons, but rather in the status of our technical development, in our 'know how' . . . The danger of the apocalypse can never be eliminated."[569]

The nuclear and prenuclear ages are separated by a qualitative leap in potential threat, something already clear with Anders. Although he identifies a periodization of history, the first two epochs he mentions are separated from the nuclear end time by the qualitative leap associated with the year 1945. Despite any continuity regarding the intensification of human cruelty, this leap does insert an element of discontinuity into human history. This discontinuity resonates when Schell describes contemporary human beings as citizens of two worlds: "We live with one foot in each of two worlds. As scientists and technicians, we live in the nuclear world, in which whether we choose to acknowledge the fact or not, we possess instruments of violence that make it possible for us to extinguish ourselves as a species. But as citizens and statesmen we go on living in the pre-nuclear world, as though extinction were not possible and sovereign nations could still employ the instruments of violence as instruments of policy."[570] G. Anders would disqualify the term "as" in Schell's exposition, since every "as" classifying human beings according to their functions and making them into citizens of several worlds has according to Anders been discredited by the dropping of the atomic bombs in 1945.[571] This is why he also must reject the thesis of the simultaneous existence of a prenuclear and nuclear world. Accordingly, for Anders the prenuclear and the nuclear world do not appear in juxtaposition, but rather in temporal sequence. In contrast, the temporal discontinuity of the two worlds becomes quasi-spatial for J. Schell. Both conceptions, however, recall the old apocalyptic notion of the two aeons. These two aeons also appear organized partly in a temporal sequence, as is the case in Jewish apocalyptic, and partly in spatial juxtaposition, as, e.g., in the case of gnosis. There is admittedly a significant difference between nuclear apocalyptic on the one hand and the doctrine of the two aeons on the other insofar as the new aeon in the shadow of the bomb is an age of enormous cataclysm. This qualitative leap, which originally separated the two aeons from one another in the form of world judgment, no longer concludes the end time in the new apocalyptic, but rather precedes it. If there ever was an age or world of salvific conditions, then it was the prenuclear world or epoch. The nuclear threat reverses the sequence of the two aeons. Beyond the coming aeon into which we have already entered, only the negative prevalence of nothingness obtains.

Just as the nuclear threat in and of itself is irrevocable, so also is the end time which commenced in 1945, at least within time itself, since the end of the end time would for humankind be identical with the end of time as such. Thus the eschatological moment is as permanent as is the nuclear danger. J. Schell illustrates this idea in the image of a "doomsday clock":

> Since 1947 the *Bulletin of the Atomic Scientists* has included a "doomsday clock" in each issue. The editors place the hands farther away from or closer to midnight as they judge the world to be farther away from or closer to a nuclear holocaust. A companion clock can be imagined whose hands, instead of metaphorically representing a judgment about the likelihood of a holocaust, would represent an estimate of the amount of time that, given the world's technical and political arrangements, the people of the earth can be sure they have left before they are destroyed in a holocaust.[572]

What is significant about Schell's doomsday clock is that its hands move not only forward, but also backward. The flow of time in the usual sense seems suspended, including the fact that the twelfth hour cannot be passed; if it were, time itself would be suspended. Thus the end time seems at once both limited and infinite. As long as the bombs are not detonated, it is always so many minutes before twelve. The eschatological moment, the proverbial "five minutes till twelve," becomes our eternal present, and the condition of being annihilated, of "being in annihilation," becomes an existentiale.

This is also the case in the analysis of the end time offered by G. Anders. In his view, the nuclear end time is qualitatively different from all previous epochs because of the endless (if not eternal) *nunc stans* of the eschatological *kairos*. The nuclear threat has created a permanent apocalyptic *kairos*. Apocalyptic near expectation turns into the perpetual expectation of secular, present eschatology.

On the one hand, the perpetually present apocalyptic moment renders possible the historicization of apocalyptic imagery and allows it to become actual in an unmetaphorical fashion. In addition, it becomes the "*kairos* of ontology." According to Anders, "the apocalyptic moment, or, more correctly: the perilous moment of possible apocalypse, since this moment offers to us the chance of encountering nonbeing, can be viewed as that particular moment in which ontological reflection first really comes into its own; that is, we may view it as the '*kairos* of ontology.' "[573] Thus Anders considers it not at all coincidental that the nuclear threat coincides temporally with intensified ontological inquiry regarding nothingness. Especially Heidegger's early philosophy, its inquiry concerning nothingness and its emphasis on the ontological difference between Being and beings is interpreted by Anders as the philosophical reflex to the fact that "the possible catastrophe had already cast its cold shadow into that period" after the First World War.[574]

Time is also qualified and structured by the apocalyptic *kairos*. The apocalyptic moment divides times into past, present, and future. "What lies behind us—in the sense of what is valid once and for all—is the presupposition on the basis of which the catastrophe is possible. What lies before us is the possible catastrophe itself. What is always present is the possibility of the catastrophic moment."[575] This structure differs once again from Anders's apocalyptic periodization of history. The temporal structure based on the apocalyptic moment refers to our existential experience of time as such. As a presupposition of the catastrophe, valid once and for all, the past is perpetually present, just as in a reverse fashion the future in the form of the catastrophe encroaches into the present, the perpetually present moment of the possibility of catastrophe. The temporal structure described by Anders recalls the ecstasies of time in Heidegger's analysis of time. The apocalyptic ecstasies of time in Anders's model disclose a new understanding of existence. Temporality, qualified by the apocalyptic moment, becomes an apocalyptic existentiale.

Because Anders speaks of time not only in the sense of a history of salvation, or rather of disaster, but also in analogy to existential temporality, one can now also understand the peculiar temporally limited character of the end time in his thinking. The end time in the shadow of nuclear threat is not temporally limited in the usual sense, i.e., in the sense of the usual understanding of time. Rather, it is, as it were, "eternally temporally limited," seemingly a paradox. This resolves itself as soon as one evaluates the understanding of this temporal limitation as an expression of an apocalyptic understanding of existence: According to this understanding, existence is temporal limitation. Since the dropping of the first atomic bombs, however, our consciousness of this temporally limited character is no longer bound to a calendrically determinable point in time. The element of temporal limitation has become an existentiale. This is why according to Anders there is no longer "our time" in the sense of "our age." "Unless we define this age as that time which is constantly in danger of coming to an end and in so doing taking *time* in the larger sense along with it. Put theologically, it is *end time*." "End time," however, also means that as a result of the nuclear threat our own time "is always 'at the end,' " yet is at the same time "endless in the sense of 'final.' "[576] Put theologically, Anders's apocalyptic is thus a kind of present-tense eschatology.

According to Anders, the nuclear threat qualifies the present as *kairos*. The *kairos* is a situation of decision of eschatological quality in which a decision is made concerning the preservation or destruction of humankind. To be sure, Anders does vacillate concerning the extent to which a decision for salvation is even possible now. The *kairos* plunges the nuclear apocalyptist into the schism between the certainty of salvation and the certainty of disaster. At the end of the 1950s, in the middle of the Cold War, we read in Anders that the chance to fight for peace is greater than ever: "We are currently at a good moment within a frightening time. In a dead calm."[577] Of course, he insists that one must seize the opportunity and not be seduced into inactivity by the apparent calm on the surface. A mere few years later, pessimism begins to permeate Anders's writings. Contemporaneously, as we recall, Hölderlin's verses, "But where there is danger, rescue also grows," plays a central role in Heidegger's thinking. In the midst of the drama of the history of Being, Hölderlin's words open up for Heidegger a timid perspective of salvation. Despite all abandonment by Being, there arises a faint glimmer of hope in the advent of a God and the unveiling of Being, and thus in a new age of salvation. Anders rejects this hope nourished by Hölderlin's verses. In fact, he considers Hölderlin's lines to be fatal. "The citing of these words should be prohibited."[578] They have already been exposed insofar as they are cited in what amounts to a cynical fashion as a device of appeasement by advocates of nuclear armaments. But Anders's criticism is more fundamental: "One can argue whether Hölderlin's solemn words were ever true; I personally believe that they had already long been unbelievable even as they came out of the poet's mouth."[579] For Anders this also cuts off Heidegger's path of understanding the threatening catastrophe as a crisis and chance. Hope for deliverance exists only as long as we successfully prevent the end from occurring and are able to draw out infinitely the end time. This, however, excludes once and for all the possibility of any final deliverance.[580]

Our earlier findings suggested that apocalyptic is not only the expression of world anxiety, but above all an attempt at overcoming apocalyptic anxiety already present. Hence we must now also inquire concerning the connection between world anxiety and apocalyptic in the nuclear age as well as concerning the particular function of apocalyptic in the thinking of G. Anders.

For G. Anders, apocalyptic in the nuclear age clearly functions as enlightenment. The same holds true, as we have just seen in the case of Jaspers, for other types of nuclear apocalyptic, though this cannot be asserted for every apocalyptic, as we will see in the following chapter. For Anders, the opposite of apocalyptic enlightenment is the condition of "apocalyptic blindness."[581] Humankind is not only apocalyptically blind, but also "*apocalyptically obtuse*,"[582] and is afflicted not only with apocalyptic blindness, but also with "*apocalyptic laziness*."[583] Despite all efforts at enlightenment, "apocalyptic indifference" has become widespread.[584] The dimensions of the threat and its discernibility stand in an inverse relationship to one another:

"The universality of the threat makes recognizing it more difficult; no, actually it prevents it from being recognized at all."[585] Furthermore, recognition of the danger is even consciously prevented. According to Anders, apocalyptic blindness has not only historical roots, roots associated primarily with modern faith in progress, it also has roots in power politics. The decisive means of concealing the danger consists in the multifarious disavowal of the threat it represents.[586] Hence, the catastrophic nature of reality—this is a classic feature of apocalyptic—is allegedly hidden and requires special unveiling.

This conceptual field includes Schell's thesis of the illusory character of the world in the shadow of nuclear threat. The normalcy of daily life is merely apparent, and deceives us concerning its true catastrophic substance. Because the nuclear holocaust has not yet occurred, "we have begun to live *as if* life were safe, but living *as if* is very different from just living."[587] The day-to-day world of *as if* is a fictitious world with only alleged stability. "In its apparent durability, a world menaced with imminent doom is in a way deceptive. It is almost an illusion."[588] According to Schell, too, the catastrophic nature of reality is concealed and requires unveiling. At this point one is reminded of W. Benjamin's 1938/39 statement: "The real catastrophe is that 'things go on in this way.' "[589] This apparent normalcy should be seen as the real catastrophe, since it blurs our vision for the danger of destruction. It is itself catastrophic reality.[590] What seems to be real is in truth unreal, and what is undiscernible—because it is concealed—is the true reality.

Apocalyptic in the age of nuclear weapons should lift the veil of reality, or, better, should rip it to shreds. It is "the work of enlightenment."[591] It brings light into the world of the blind, into a world in which humankind is in danger of "surrendering itself to absolute and eternal darkness."[592] And indeed, the nuclear apocalyptic of G. Anders and other authors does provide a persuasive example of the affinity J. Derrida asserts obtains between apocalyptic and enlightenment. *Apokalypsis*, unveiling, does understand itself as a kind of enlightenment. Just as every enlightenment "at the same time keeps within itself some apocalyptic desire,"[593] so also is apocalyptic the bearer of light whose metaphor has influenced the modern age of enlightenment.[594]

The new type of apocalyptic represented by Anders also seeks to provide enlightenment in the political sense by posing the question of power. Apocalyptic becomes a political factor, and its unveiling of reality subjects itself to the suspicion of political treason. Addressing those with political power, Anders writes: "Go ahead and call the international character of this populist movement *treason*. That doesn't bother us. On the contrary: We embrace this word, since *what we are doing consists exclusively in betraying to the world just how things stand with it*."[595] What is actually unveiled is not only the true dimensions of the threat, but also the fact that although all people are actively entangled in its preparation,[596] the actual power to bring about the nuclear holocaust resides in the hands of only a few. The politically powerful among the nuclear powers are the real "lords of the apocalypse."[597] This is why the nuclear holocaust would not constitute collective suicide, but rather the murder of billions of innocent victims.[598] Apocalyptic which poses the question of power is actually an outcry of powerlessness. At least according to Anders, apocalyptic always originates in groups "which are condemned to powerlessness by the nearly absolute, or at least extremely absolutistic pressure of a worldwide power."[599] In the idea of the end they try to overcome powerlessness through hope in a counterpower superior to the threatening power. In the shadow of the bomb this powerlessness assumes unsuspected dimensions. The widespread absence of any apocalyptic mood in public consciousness is no counterargument, but rather can be explained according to Anders by the fact that under the nuclear threat "the disempowerment is *too great.*"[600] Nuclear apocalyptic becomes the voice of the powerless in their fight against a superior power. "Prophylactic apocalyptic" is active consolation for the powerless in the nuclear age.

Nuclear apocalyptic not only tries to counter the undiscernible character of the catastrophe or of its possibility through political enlightenment, but also puts equal emphasis on mobilizing the imagination.[601] Our traditional power of imagination fails before the dimensions of this danger. The nuclear holocaust cannot really be imagined. "If this is indeed the case, then if everything is not to be lost the *decisive moral task today consists in the development of our moral imagination.*"[602] Both feeling and imagination must develop a new sensibility through appropriate "exercises."[603]

Meditation on the bomb is variously recommended as such an exercise. "An old dependency" again and again draws a philosopher such as P. Sloterdijk[604] to the atomic bomb "because its nuclear mode of operation challenges contemplation most of all. Nuclear fission is in any case a phenomenon that invites meditation, and even the nuclear bomb gives the philosopher the feeling of here also really touching on the nucleus of what is human. Thus, the bomb basically embodies the last, most energetic enlightener."[605] For Sloterdijk the bomb unites the European tradition of enlightenment with the essence of Far-Eastern meditation. It is "the real Buddha of the west," in fact "the only Buddha that western reason could understand."[606] Sloterdijk even understands the politics of deterrence as a kind of meditation. On the other hand, "meditation on the bomb" seeks out "the urge to build bombs in us" and tries to make the atomic detonation into our own experience: "One must have put oneself in its interior [i.e., into the interior of the bomb] in order to feel what it means to explode into the cosmos with a complete dissolution of the self."[607] Not only philosophers, but also psychologists are prompting us today to meditate on the bomb, on the one hand in order to sound out one's own participation in the nuclear threat, and on the other to accommodate one's imagination to the dimensions of the potential catastrophe.[608]

In the meantime, numerous attempts have been made to balance the catastrophe-deficit of our imagination in the age of nuclear threat through the medium of film, literature, and the plastic arts.[609] Although any sharpening of the sensibilities of the individual for the danger of catastrophe is doubtless welcome, I. Riedel does legitimately raise the question "whether meditative, self-critical discourse with apocalyptic imagery can suffice, given the actual danger in which our world presently hovers."[610] One would have to ask further whether some of the exercises today, instead of healing apocalyptic blindness, do not rather contribute to false appeasement or even accommodation to the catastrophe, so that the apparently enlightened condition—one abiding in utter inactivity—would in truth be merely an enlightened blindness, and the apocalyptist paradoxically a blind person who can see.[611] Quite justifiably, then, Anders thus demands not the development of a voyeuristic or consumer imagination capable of inventing stories, but rather of a moral imagination, i.e., the power of imagination capable of mobilization for the sake of responsible action against the nuclear threat. These questions, however, already take us into the next chapter.

The exercising of the imagination consists in the anticipation of the catastrophe, and in this point, too, nuclear apocalyptic corresponds to the structure of apocalyptic thinking in general. *Apokalypsis* as the unveiling of reality unveils its catastrophic character by anticipating its culmination point, namely, the catastrophe. For G. Anders, the prototype of the apocalyptist who anticipates the catastrophe is the figure of Noah.[612] The anticipation of the catastrophe reverses the ecstasies of temporality, and thus Anders has his Noah say: "Turn time around—the voice said to me—anticipate the pain even today, cry your tears beforehand! And the prayer of mourning you learned as a boy for speaking at the grave of your father, pray it today for the sons who will die tomorrow and for the grandchildren who will never be born! For the day after tomorrow it will be too late!"[613] Just as in earlier times, so also is the new type of apocalyptist in the nuclear age—to pick up a formulation of J. Schell—a "historian of the future,"[614] i.e., someone who anticipates as already having happened what has in fact not yet happened and will perhaps never happen.

In addition to the development of a moral imagination and the anticipation of the catastrophe, the work of enlightenment undertaken by the new apocalyptic includes in Anders's view also unveiling and dealing with anxiety in the age of the bomb. That is, anxiety is just as undiscernible as the danger itself. Although the danger is indeed as great as it is, there seems to be no anxiety before it. In fact, however, the age of nuclear threat is an age of anxiety. The new apocalyptic unmasks apocalyptic blindness as a consequence of an "anxiety before anxiety, before one's own and that of others."[615] Anxiety before anxiety characterizes the world age of abandonment of Being already in the thinking of Heidegger.[616] We encounter it again in nuclear apocalyptic. In both cases it characterizes the epoch of realized nihilism. Because people remain "powerless *for* anxiety," the end time is the "age of the incapacity for anxiety."[617] The incapacity for anxiety is anxiety before anxiety.

The apocalyptic unveiling of reality generates anxiety. This must be so, since in fact anxiety is the only appropriate disposition in the face of the danger of absolute annihilation. Thus first of all the new apocalyptic does not seek to master anxiety, but rather to overcome inappropriate anxiety before anxiety in order to free from its repressed condition appropriate anxiety before the end. The apocalyptic of the nuclear holocaust fights for the right to anxiety.[618] It expressly fosters the "courage for anxiety":[619] "The commandment to expand our imagination thus means *in concreto:* We must expand our anxiety. Postulate: *Do not have anxiety before anxiety, have courage for anxiety. Also the courage to foster anxiety. Foster anxiety in your neighbor as in yourself.*"[620] By unveiling the dimensions of the catastrophic nature of things, apocalyptic thus heightens anxiety. It does not, of course, try to evoke anxiety merely for the sake of spreading panic. What is to be intensified is "*appropriate anxiety.*" This apocalyptic is not involved in the business of the kind of anxiety that makes people unfree, but rather of "*having anxiety in order to become free;* or in order to survive at all."[621] World anxiety is thus the condition for freedom. In this estimation Anders agrees with Jaspers, whom he otherwise criticizes. Like Jaspers, Anders thus also distinguishes between fruitful and unfruitful anxiety, and only the former counts as a condition of freedom and of survival. According to Anders, fruitful world anxiety is "(1) fearless anxiety, since it excludes all anxiety before those who could deride us as anxiety-cowards; (2) vivifying anxiety, since it drives us out into the streets instead of into the corners of our rooms; (3) a loving anxiety which should be anxious *about* the world, not only *before* what might happen to us."[622] While the concept of world anxiety largely understands the world as the locus of anxiety, as that wherein I am anxious, or that before which I have anxiety, it refers in connection with the exposition of Anders to anxiety about the world.[623]

The anxiety about which nuclear apocalyptic speaks, however, is not only world anxiety in the general sense, but also genuine apocalyptic anxiety. As far as apocalyptic anxiety is concerned, we observed earlier that it is the perception of finitude as inescapability.[624] Apocalyptic anxiety is the perception of a dead-end world structure expressing itself in the imagery of closed space and ultimately concentrated in the certainty of the end of the world. Such spatial enclosure can also be observed in the image of the end time offered by G. Anders, though here the space is simultaneously closed insofar as the possibility of the end appears irrevocable, and yet potentially infinite insofar as from generation to generation it might be possible to prevent destruction. Although in this way, and despite the enclosed nature of the space of freedom,[625] a certain "*leeway or free space for our freedom*" is preserved,[626] nonetheless the preliminary apocalyptic experience over against the nuclear threat consists in utter powerlessness and the loss of precisely this free space. Just as older forms of apocalyptic try to break through the enclosed, inescapable nature of finitude, so also now the new apocalyptic of the nuclear holocaust. Thus we read the following illuminating comments in J. Schell: "By acting to save the species and repopulating the future, we break out of the cramped, claustrophobic isolation of a doomed present, and open a path to the greater space—the only space fit for human habitation—of past, present, and future."[627] In Schell's experience of the "cramped, claustrophobic isolation of a doomed present" we find once again precisely that particular understanding of existence which in a different context we already learned to understand as an expression of apocalyptic world anxiety.

According to Schell, this apocalyptic claustrophobia can be overcome through opening up a new path and through entry into the free space of history. At this point we do encounter a decisive difference over against older forms of apocalyptic which considered the catastrophe to be a necessary transition stage, the only way out of the enclosed space of the gloomy present. The new apocalyptic wagers everything on preventing the catastrophe, and to that extent the impression that might arise in Schell's work is deceptive, namely, that this enclosed space in which apocalyptic anxiety finds itself might yet be exited. Since the end is not to occur, and yet its possibility is irrevocable, this means that in principle one can no longer break through its inescapable nature. The boundaries of this space can now only be expanded from time to time; they can no longer be passed, as G. Anders explicates. The end can at most be delayed, perhaps even for an infinitely long time, but it can no longer be entered as a door to a new space, and under these conditions the catastrophe can in no way be interpreted as a crisis. For that reason, however, apocalyptic anxiety must also in principle be irrevocable. This irrevocability qualifies the nuclear age as the age of anxiety.

The new apocalyptic, then, anticipates the catastrophe with the single and expressed goal of preventing it. "Our task is to insure that the *end time*—despite the fact that it might at any moment turn into the *end of time*—become *endless.*"[628] Nuclear apocalyptic is thus self-destroying just as is the apocalyptic associated with the idea of the limits to growth. These "prophylactic apocalyptists" are more than traditional pacifists. "There have already been people before us who were anti-war. We, however, are a new generation. Since today war means annihilation, we are *anti-annihilation.* We are the first generation of those opposed to annihilation, a generation which must be followed, as long as there are human beings, by further generations opposed to annihilation. Since the threat itself will never disappear, so also may the chain of our successor generations never be broken."[629] As long as the knowledge of nuclear weapons exists, the pre-apocalyptic condition of humankind will continue. To the extent prophylactic apocalyptic does anticipate the end, that end lies behind it in an anticipatory fashion, giving rise to the paradoxical situation that the pre-apocalyptic age of the end time is at once also the post-apocalypse. "Our age," M. Wetzel explains, "is *post-apocalyptic* insofar as the nuclear apocalypse has always already taken place—in literature, the media, simulation-centers, etc., all of which are full of its tangibly perceptible presence."[630] Thus we may go beyond G. Anders and say that on the one hand the end may no longer—as was the case in older apocalyptic—be traversed, yet on the other that it has already been traversed and is constantly being traversed, though without leading out of the inescapability of finitude.

The apocalyptic of nuclear holocaust results in absurdities. The goal of prophylactic apocalyptists' self-destroying prophecy clearly differs from that of classical apocalyptic with its hope for the end. This new goal "has never before existed in the history of eschatologies, and against the background of apocalyptic attitudes familiar to us from religious history they presumably seem absurd. Yet they seem so precisely because we are reacting to something which is itself absurd."[631] The absurdities of nuclear apocalyptic are the reflex to a situation in which collective self-destruction "takes the form of a spiritual sickness."[632] In this absurd situation, apocalyptic also behaves crazily in the truest sense of the word. Such apocalyptic excesses are the subjective reflection of objective excess, and this objective excess is the nuclear threat.[633]

The apocalyptic of nuclear holocaust exhibits crazy behavior in U. Horstmann's philosophy of flight from human beings. At the end of an "escalation ladder" outlined by H. Kahn and cited by Horstmann, there is "spasm or insensate war."[634] Horstmann's anthropofugal thinking anticipates in its absurdity the convulsion and madness of nuclear holocaust. Horstmann's essay is the *salto mortale* of nuclear apocalyptic. The question whether his philosophy of contempt for human beings is to be understood as serious or ironic cannot be decided.[635] In view of the screaming absurdity to which this pamphlet is reacting, any decision would in any case be of no consequence. The cynicism of which Horstmann is variously accused actually derives from the bomb itself, in which the history of the human desire for annihilation and of the requisite potential for destruction culminates. It is the bomb which in a cynical fashion gives the lie to the idea of humanity. In view of catastrophic reality and of humankind which with great perseverance, tenacity, and obstinacy is working toward its own destruction, Horstmann, like M. Foucault, is able to respond to all such talk of humanism only with philosophical laughter.[636] Horstmann's essay on the monster is nothing but bitter laughter recalling British "black humor," after which one is unsure whether to laugh or to cry. Yet nothing would be more fateful than to dismiss Horstmann's fulminant treatise as black humor. "To mock philosophy," so the motto Horstmann uses for his book, a motto coming from Pascal, "means to engage in genuine philosophizing." Although the essay is "*dedicated to the as yet unborn and to those yahoos able to distinguish science from satire*," this kind of clear distinction no longer seems possible in the shadow of nuclear holocaust.

For Horstmann, the term "human being" is a "euphemism."[637] As a matter of fact, the human being is the monster, something it until now has been willing to admit to itself only in the rarest of cases. Horstmann's anthropofugal thinking is indebted to the tradition of Holbach, L. Klages, Freud, Nietzsche, and not least Schopenhauer, and in the present finds itself in agreement with the philosophy of M. Foucault and E. M. Cioran. According to Horstmann, the endless trail of blood running through human history and already intimating the end in a global holocaust can be explained only by the assumption of a death instinct outstripping all other needs in human beings. Following Schopenhauer's lead, Horstmann assumes that this death instinct is a basic and universal characteristic of all life, so that we human beings, because of our capacity for self-consciousness, "are the pariahs of creation, since we are the only ones who sense that the organic is nothing but a great, mutual choking and devouring, an ingesting without end, without meaning, and without purpose."[638] A "simple philosophical imperative" speaks from within this anthropofugal thinking: "The suffering must end!"[639] Horstmann thus develops an annihilistic consciousness of calling: "The monster . . . which *comprehends* the ubiquity of suffering can derive from this comprehension the unspoken commission, the challenge, to act not only for its own species, but for all of life."[640] Humankind thus does not merely have the capacity, but also virtually the moral obligation to bring about the nuclear holocaust. Rather than being prevented, the event of the nuclear catastrophe is rather to be forced to take place. Thus at most, the end may for a time yet be delayed, since because nuclear technology has not yet matured sufficiently, in addition to the liquidation of humankind, which is already possible, we cannot yet guarantee the complete annihilation of all other life as well on earth, all the way to the tiniest microbe. "Patience and discretion for just one more generation; then the apocalypse will no longer be merely a treasonously private one, but rather the apocalypse of all creatures! The last judgment of all organic matter! The return of undefiled matter! The inbreaking of the kingdom of heaven on earth!"[641] The lunarization of the earth, which Kant considered as a physical possibility in a completely different context (namely, in reference to the earth's rotation), is an image we encountered as a symbol of earlier apocalyptic anxiety;[642] for Horstmann it embodies all apocalyptic hope: "Let us turn our metabolically anemic planet into a moon!"[643]

In Horstmann's philosophy of flight from human beings, the anxiety before the nuclear holocaust changes into hope for the catastrophe. Here hope in the end, which G. Anders excludes, becomes possible again even in the nuclear age. Accordingly, both peace research and the peace movement are treated with biting derision,[644] and the publications of G. Anders mentioned with sarcasm.[645] Horstmann's hope in the end of the world in the firestorm of nuclear war seems absurd, though it does uncover the hope in the end without which the strategy of nuclear deterrence would collapse. That is, whereas the apocalyptic of, e.g., G. Anders is characterized by fear before the end, distinguishing itself thus from traditional apocalyptic, it is precisely in the philosophy of deterrence that the hope in the end originally at home in apocalyptic is preserved. Although the nuclear powers threaten each other in the hope that by keeping nuclear weapons ready they can prevent the nuclear holocaust, such nuclear deterrence presupposes on the other hand the hope that if things get serious the end really will come about. Hope in the end is thus the foundation upon which it allegedly will be possible to turn aside the end. This kind of logic is doubtless no less absurd than Horstmann's promotion of the nuclear final solution.

Whether intentionally or not, Horstmann entangles himself in contradictions. His anthropofugal thinking takes as its point of departure the thesis that this monster is "exiled, alien, a refugee from the totality of creation,"[646] a foreign body inside living nature. Later, however, the human being appears as the fellow creature and companion sufferer of all other living beings: "Are we not all children of that first cell which failed in the business of dying? Are we not all *one*, pain-permeated, quaking, squealing flesh whimpering for redemption?"[647] Whereas on the one hand the human being is an outcast and mischief-maker of nature whose disappearance would reestablish the paradisiacal primeval condition of nature, on the other hand it is to be charged with universal responsibility for the entire biosphere.[648] Horstmann's dealings with the model of humanism are no less contradictory, since in any case the humanism he secretly denounces supplies the standard against which he gauges the inhumanity of the monster. And what else is this universal solidarity with suffering creatures than the formulation of a humane ethics with the highest moral claims? Without this ideal of humanism in the background the legitimacy of the annihilistic consciousness of being called would collapse, and there could be no talk of any obligation for universal sympathy or of global responsibility. And finally, Horstmann participates in the striking contradiction of all apocalyptic, namely, that of "prolonging thinking and the world, and creation in the larger sense, even while and by dealing with the end itself. For books about the end of the world must be written *before* the event itself, since in a fashion different from most other literature, they are inexorably drawn into precisely that about which they provide us something to read."[649] Hence in every respect Horstmann's essay is philosophical, absurd theater, theater which—and in this respect it is truly apocalyptic—unveils the absurdity of our reality in the shadow of the nuclear threat.

In the face of this absurdity, it is difficult to separate fact from fiction, and this is why several questions yet remain concerning the views especially of G. Anders. Similar to K. Jaspers before him,[650] Anders believes it is possible to distinguish between apocalyptic fiction and nuclear reality. In his view, older apocalyptic notions of the end time were "let us call a spade a spade—*fiction*."[651] The apocalyptic of nuclear holocaust, on the other hand, is allegedly describing an actual threat, and this distinguishes in particular the primitive Christian apocalypse from the nuclear apocalypse. "The expectation of the end nourished by that age, one which after all did not become actualized, was, put somewhat crudely, unfounded. In contrast, that of today is objectively justified. Compared to the expectation of the end today, all apostolic talk of apocalypse is a mere product of the imagination."[652] Such delimitation of new and old apocalyptic seems questionable. It constitutes what J. Derrida called an example of apocalyptic critique which in the name of enlightenment is itself directed toward a preceding form of enlightenment.[653] Manifestly, however, the *world anxiety* at the time of Jewish apocalyptic or of primitive Christianity was *no less real than the world anxiety of those who fear the nuclear holocaust.* In a reverse fashion, the nuclear holocaust has as yet been anticipated only in the imagination, and is thus no less unreal or fictional than the end of the world of primitive Christian or Jewish apocalyptic. Derrida justifiably finds that

> for the moment, today, one may say that a non-localizable nuclear war has not occurred; it has existed only through what is said of it, only when it is talked about. Some might call it a fable, then, a pure invention: in the sense in which it is said that a myth, an image, a fiction, a utopia, a rhetorical figure, a fantasy, a phantasm, are inventions. It may also be called a speculation, even a fabulous specularization. The breaking of the mirror would be, finally, through an act of language, the very occurrence of nuclear war.[654]

Whenever this state of affairs is not appreciated, that particular apocalyptic which fights against apocalyptic blindness becomes apocalyptically blind itself. In such cases it fails to push through to an inquiry concerning the structure of the apocalyptic language it has itself appropriated from tradition and concerning its moorings in the human understanding of existence, an inquiry of the type we undertook in the first chapters. If indeed the apocalyptic imagery of earlier ages were allegedly mere fiction with no correspondence in actual external danger, then we should be all the more astonished that earlier centuries were able to develop a language that as a matter of fact only today has really begun to speak. If, however, as is the concern of the present investigation, one asks about the roots of the notion of the end of the world in world anxiety and the apocalyptic understanding of existence, then the analogy between prenuclear apocalypses and nuclear apocalyptic is much less astonishing. Both forms of apocalyptic express a comparable understanding of existence, and the decisive roots of this end-time thinking reside in both instances not in objective dangers deriving from the external world, but rather in subjective experience. Both forms of apocalyptic are the expression not of any objective description of the world residing on the plane of scientifically verifiable statements, but rather on that of an existential experience of the world. No matter how extensively the apocalyptic of nuclear holocaust is based on facts and numbers—therein comparable to the theorem of the limits to growth—what characterizes it is this: Under changed historical conditions it repeats an earlier possibility of existence.

It is not the existence of the bomb itself, but rather already the ineradicable knowledge necessary for its construction which makes the apparently clear boundary between reality and fiction indistinct. The " 'reality,' let's say the encompassing institution of the nuclear age, is constructed by the fable, on the basis of an event that has never happened."[655] The dissolving of the boundary between reality and the imagination, as is well known, is a psychotic symptom, and it thus does not seem an exaggeration when Schell apostrophizes the strategy of nuclear deterrence as a "spiritual sickness." From this perspective a revealing light falls on Schell's assertion that we are simultaneously citizens of two worlds, the nuclear and the prenuclear. It constitutes not only a religio-historical analogy to gnostic eschatology, but can just as easily be interpreted as the description of collective schizophrenic symptoms. That is, the bomb is the cause and symbol of collective schizophrenia: Nuclear fission both causes and symbolizes a collective cleavage of consciousness. Apocalyptic excesses would accordingly be the symptom of collective psychosis, and not every form of apocalyptic would really constitute a form of enlightenment. Instead of unveiling reality, apocalyptic can just as easily conceal it, or can distort reality through an unreflected exchange of reality and fiction. That is why an ideological-critical look at apocalyptic is now needed. The uncritical repristination of an apocalyptic understanding of existence can turn into a fateful detriment to existence. Any understanding of apocalyptic thus includes not only an interpretation of its understanding of reality of the sort we have undertaken to this point in our investigation, but also an articulation of the ambiguity of apocalyptic. This describes the task of the following chapter.

5

THE AMBIGUITY OF APOCALYPTIC

> Apocalyptic thinking always contains the elements of horror and consolation interwoven together.
>
> —*Gershom Scholem*

> Anxiety and violence are moving toward their own destruction. World conflagration is to extinguish its own fire.
>
> —*Friedrich Kümmel*

1. Positive and Negative Apocalyptic

Apocalyptic thinking arises out of apocalyptic anxiety. All apocalyptic tries to master that specific form of world anxiety which we have called apocalyptic world anxiety. Common to all apocalyptic is a preceding experience of being enclosed in a world hostile on all sides. The only perspective allowed by the inescapability of the present world and the threatening loss of future associated with it is the end of the world. As we have already seen, not all forms of apocalyptic deal in the same way with apocalyptic world anxiety and with the attendant expectation of the end of the world. Whereas some types of apocalyptic thinking merely verbalize the experience of the catastrophic and the anxiety before the end, others provide hope in an ultimate escape from the dead-end structure of the world as disclosed by apocalyptic anxiety. To this extent, the apocalyptic understanding of existence is thus not unified, and accordingly, differing religious, ethical, and political intentions can be at work in apocalyptic. This disunity constitutes the ambiguity of apocalyptic.

Taking the phenomenon of world anxiety as our point of departure, we have already distinguished two basic forms of apocalyptic, namely, negative and positive apocalyptic.[1] Whereas negative apocalyptic is capable only of verbalizing apocalyptic world anxiety, positive apocalyptic is able to nurture hope in the face of the end. Insofar as one understands apocalyptic world anxiety as catastrophe anxiety, one can also describe the distinction by saying that negative apocalyptic is the verbalization of such catastrophe anxiety, while positive apocalyptic tries to change catastrophe anxiety into crisis anxiety, to interpret the threatening or anticipated catastrophe as crisis, and to understand the end as a passage or transition.

Our distinction between positive and negative apocalyptic needs a bit of additional explication, since we must clarify its relationship to the distinction between positive and negative utopia discussed in utopian studies. First of all, we must emphasize that the terms "positive" and "negative" are not to be associated with any value judgments; that is, "positive" does not stand for "good," nor "negative" for "bad." So also in utopian studies, the distinction between positive and negative utopia is not of necessity identical with a valuation of good and bad utopia. This latter distinction involves particularly conservative criticism of utopian thinking, which in different variations believes one can distinguish between utopia and utopianism, considering the latter to be morally and politically dangerous because of its ideological inclinations.[2] In this case utopianism manifests itself as the ideological falsification or distortion of authentic utopia and of its best intentions.[3]

In contrast, the use of the concepts of positive and negative utopia in utopian studies serves first of all a formal distinction within utopian literature. Negative or anti-utopia[4] then does not refer to some naive utopia characterized by faith in progress which might be the object of conservative utopian criticism, but rather to a literary form which with the playing rules of utopia turns its intentions and hopes into their opposites.[5] One might sooner assert the reverse, namely, that the anti-utopia represents utopian criticism carried out by means of utopia, though viewed formally it constitutes a "subspecies of utopia."[6] Negative utopias in this sense include A. Huxley's *Brave New World* and G. Orwell's *1984*.

According to K. H. Bohrer, the causes of the emergence of anti-utopias are to be sought in a crisis in utopian thought commencing in the second half of the nineteenth century, one that was simultaneously a crisis in the notion of progress.[7] Similarly, with respect to the twentieth century mention has been made of a reality shock that has undermined the conviction that things might be improved.[8] As parallel causes of such reality shock for utopian thinking one might mention on the one hand the French Revolution of 1789, and on the other the Russian October Revolution of 1917, whose claim of historically actualizing utopian ideas stands in stark contrast to the actual results of the revolution. Strikingly, one encounters not only conservative criticism of utopian ideas, but also a kind of iconoclasm forbidding the portrayal of eschatological conditions, and thus a distancing from utopian tradition among the political left. Wherever the content of utopian thinking is no longer mediated, but rather only its presuppositions and mechanisms, Bohrer speaks of "damaged utopia,"[9] which leads equally to a radicalizing and political weakening of utopian thinking.

A consideration of utopian studies and the distinctions regarding the concept of the utopian are of significance for us insofar as Bloch understands apocalyptic, primarily Jewish-Christian apocalyptic, under the rubric of the utopian.[10] Whenever in utopian studies one inquires concerning the utopian potential of apocalyptic,[11] it is generally classified as positive utopia. Despite the notion of a radical and catastrophic break between the aeons, apocalyptic is interpreted as a form of positive utopian thinking, since it anticipates a new heaven and earth or speaks in a millenarian fashion about the hope for better times.

Of course, occasionally the connection is also made between apocalyptic and negative utopia, e.g., when S. A. Jørgensen explains the emergence of anti-utopian thinking since the nineteenth century as a result of the fact "that the history of modern humankind has become increasingly more apocalyptic."[12] Apocalyptic, in whose essence an element of positive utopian potential is inherent, moves in Jørgensen's view and from the perspective of twentieth-century conditions into proximity with the anti-utopia; for Jørgensen does not employ the concept of apocalyptic in a unified fashion and, in view of modern dystrophies in the vulgar sense of the word, equates it with the catastrophic. The identification of the apocalypse with catastrophe also underlies R. Koselleck's concept of "anti-apocalyptic."[13] According to Koselleck, eschatological elements are progressively reinterpreted in the antiapocalypse.[14] One example of such an antiapocalypse is for Koselleck *Memoirs of the Year Two Thousand Five Hundred* by L.-S. Mercier.[15] Mercier's novel, which appeared in 1771, initially raises the possibility that the future "will end in ashes, wreckage, and ruins. Despite this prophetic threat, however, we find at the end that it is only Versailles which lies in ruin."[16] The novel anticipates the French Revolution, though not as a complete catastrophe, but rather as a necessary and beneficial crisis.

For the sake of dialogue between utopian studies and apocalyptic studies, it seems helpful to define precisely and to distinguish not only the concept of the utopian, but also that of apocalyptic. In this way we can eliminate several unclear notions entertained by utopian studies in their dealing with apocalyptic. According to Koselleck, for example, what makes Mercier's utopia an antiapocalypse is precisely the transformation of the anticipated catastrophe into a crisis. The hope in revolution replaces the aristocratic resignation of "after us, the deluge." Such an understanding of catastrophe as crisis, however, as our previous investigation has shown, is precisely not a characteristic of antiapocalyptic, but rather of apocalyptic. More precisely, Koselleck's antiapocalyptic corresponds to what we have called positive apocalyptic. Although the reference to connections between apocalyptic and negative utopia is also justified, it is negative apocalyptic, with its ability only to verbalize the catastrophe, which stands especially close to negative utopia.

Negative contemporary apocalyptic corresponds to the emergence of negative utopia in the closing years of the nineteenth century and in the twentieth century. Just as one can call the visions of Aldous Huxley or George Orwell negative utopias, so also can one use the expression negative apocalyptic to refer to the scenarios concerning the limits to growth provided by the Club of Rome or to G. Anders's apocalyptic interpretation of the nuclear threat. Neither case entertains any hope in the eschaton. To the extent that negative utopia and negative apocalyptic do entertain hope, it consists precisely in preventing the eschaton. In the one case, it is utopia which is to be prevented, in the other, the end. Whereas positive apocalyptic confronts world anxiety by placing its hope in the end, an end that apocalyptic anxiety views as negative, negative apocalyptic at most hopes in the possibility of preventing that end from ever coming about, that is, if such apocalyptic does not simply resign itself to anticipating the impending end. The escapability of the end is everywhere negated.

In inquiries concerning the social effects of apocalyptic, blanket judgments regarding whether it is conservative or negative are equally inappropriate.[17] No less inappropriate, however, are attempts to label positive apocalyptic as progressive, and negative apocalyptic as restorative or reactionary. J. Moltmann undertakes such a classification of progressive and conservative tendencies as two basic forms of apocalyptic, except that instead of speaking about positive and negative apocalyptic, he claims to distinguish progressive messianism from reactionary apocalyptic.[18] On the one hand, Moltmann rejects, as it were, as bad apocalyptic the apocalyptic orientation toward signs of the time interpreted as signs of the end, exemplified by the apocalyptic confessionalism of the nineteenth century;[19] on the other hand, he confirms as good apocalyptic the messianic orientation toward signs and wonders of the spirit.[20] In this way, Moltmann quite justifiably draws attention to the ambiguity of apocalyptic. Yet it is doubtful that socially progressive and restorative tendencies can be classified this unequivocally as two basic forms of apocalyptic. As G. Scholem emphatically reminds us, the effects of messianism are also ambiguous, and precisely the messianism of, e.g., Judaism can have a clearly restorative function.[21] Indeed, the price of messianism which devalued the present for the sake of the eschaton was according to Scholem the endless powerlessness in Jewish history.[22] Similarly, G. M. Martin justifiably questions whether Christian messianism really was always as progressive and activist as Moltmann asserts, and whether the effects of Christianity did not also remain ambiguous insofar as the history of its expansion—"perhaps also because it always transmitted apocalyptic modes of expectation and action—resulted in crises, and even catastrophes."[23]

Analogously, the assertion of A. Neusüss must also be rejected according to which the antithesis between utopian and anti-utopian is identical with that between progressive and conservative.[24] In contrast, M. Winter's understanding is more helpful according to which negative utopia is defined as utopia containing a critique of utopia. Winter points out that a critique of utopia delivered in the form of anti-utopia can clearly exhibit progressive tendencies: "Utopian-critical utopia discloses not only the conflicts of the society in which it emerges, but also the conflicts of the society which appears to solve these conflicts in a utopian fashion. It always points us one step further."[25] Winter discerns a socially necessary function of negative utopia precisely in the "skepticism over against linear utopian optimism and faith in progress." Winter's thesis is that "utopia is complete only when it conceives its own critique as well. This dialectic keeps it from succumbing to shallow faith in progress. The ability to think about both utopia and its negative counterpart could keep us from becoming the heirs of Frankenstein."[26]

Negative apocalyptic also occasionally exhibits a comparable critical function. Precisely its consideration, through the medium of negative apocalyptic, of the possibilities of ecological catastrophe or of nuclear holocaust must be understood as inner-apocalyptic critique or as apocalyptic-critical apocalyptic. It forces apocalyptic as a whole to be accountable concerning the content and basis of its hope in the age of nihilism. What Kant's critique of traditional metaphysics meant for religion and theology, negative apocalyptic accomplishes for its positive counterpart. If positive apocalyptic is yet to be possible in the age of nihilism, it must submit to the trial by fire of negative apocalyptic. Any positive apocalyptic incapable of giving an adequate account, over against nihilism, concerning its own hope subjects itself to the justified criticism of metaphysical escapism. In this case, however, the relationship between progressive and restorative is reversed. It is not negative, but rather positive apocalyptic which, viewed sociologically, becomes a reactionary force, while in a reverse fashion negative apocalyptic promotes progressive tendencies. Apocalyptic consideration of the nuclear threat provides a vivid example for this state of affairs. Whereas on the one hand the new apocalyptic in the tradition of G. Anders is able to forge a socially critical movement, on the other a rigorously positive apocalyptic in the form of fundamentalism, one putting its hope precisely in nuclear doom and a Third World War,[27] openly commits itself, e.g., in the United States, to extremely conservative politics.

With respect to their social or political implications, not only apocalyptic in the larger sense, but also positive and negative apocalyptic viewed in and for themselves remain ambiguous. Although hope in the end and a reinterpretation of the catastrophe into a crisis can indeed free up socially critical and progressive potential, they can just as easily mislead one into flight before and from reality, i.e., into avoiding social problems instead of confronting them. In a reverse fashion, negative apocalyptic can express a social-political fatalism which actually sanctions the status quo insofar as it is convinced of the necessity that everything continue on as before—even up to a bitter end at which everything is judged. Just as negative apocalyptic is able to frustrate all hope in social or inner-historical change, so also can it, as self-destroying prophecy, summon its contemporaries to be absolutely sure that things do not in fact go on as before. In this case, it develops as a critical force directed toward social change.

Thus the ambiguity of apocalyptic cannot be overcome by playing out one of its two basic forms against the other and by one-sidedly taking the side of either positive or negative apocalyptic. What is required is rather an equally critical discourse with both manifestations of apocalyptic. The dialectic of positive and negative apocalyptic leads to an inner-apocalyptic critique of apocalyptic, i.e., to a self-critique of apocalyptic, one promoting critical discourse with apocalyptic in the larger sense.

2. The Unveiling of Reality

Semantically, *apokalypsis* does not mean catastrophe and doom, but rather uncloaking, unveiling, disclosure, uncovering, or revelation.[28] Revelation in the sense of *apokalypsis* is understood quite generally as "the disclosure of what is veiled, the opening up of what is hidden," as R. Bultmann formulated it.[29] K. Barth explicated the concept of revelation in the following way: "A closed door is opened, a covering removed. Darkness becomes light, a question finds its answer, a riddle its solution."[30]

This is both a fine and an appropriate description actually quite accurately describing the genuinely apocalyptic element within apocalyptic.

Apocalyptic *apokalypsis*, however, is revelation only in this general semantic sense, not in the sense of the Christian-dogmatic narrowing of the concept of revelation. The translation of *apokalypsis* by "revelation" in connection with apocalyptic easily leads to misunderstanding insofar as the apocalyptic understanding of revelation is not clearly distinguished from the dogmatic use of this term in the sense of God's self-revelation. Taking the concept of God's self-mediation as the point of departure only blocks access to an appropriate interpretation of the phenomenon of apocalyptic;[31] such a concept became common theological currency especially through K. Barth's doctrine of God's self-revelation,[32] which he developed in connection with and delimitation over against W. Herrmann's understanding of revelation.[33] Yet even quite apart from its dogmatic intensification in Dialectical Theology, the concept of revelation is a problematical interpretative category for apocalyptic, since theologically it is burdened by inflationary use.[34] The concept of unveiling proves to be more helpful.

Apocalyptic seeks to unveil, to enlighten. This says nothing yet, however, concerning just what the content or object of its unveiling is. Insofar as the concept of *apokalypsis* is not used in a completely formalized fashion as the designation of supranatural mediation of knowledge regarding arbitrary content,[35] those involved in religious studies frequently mention the end of the world or catastrophic events lying in the future as the objects of apocalyptic unveiling.[36] Numerous examples might be adduced for this understanding of the element of unveiling. Let us examine several paradigmatic passages from the apocalyptic literature of Judaism. In the book of Daniel the *angelus interpres* says to Daniel: "Behold, I will make known to you what shall be at the latter end of the indignation; for it pertains to the appointed time of the end" (Dan. 8:19).[37] Similarly, Baruch has been shown "the course of times, and that which will happen after these things" (*2 Apoc. Bar.* 14:1). The book of Daniel itself refers to the content of disclosure as "mystery" or "mysteries," Aramaic *rāz*,[38] which the Septuagint translates as *mysterion*. The term *mysterion* is also familiar elsewhere in Jewish apocalyptic literature as an apocalyptic *terminus technicus*.[39] In the eyes of the book of Daniel, God's prominent characteristic is to be the revealer of mysteries: "But there is a God in heaven who reveals mysteries" (Dan. 2:28). The God of Israel is "the God of gods and Lord of kings, and a revealer of mysteries" (Dan. 2:47); it is he "who reveals mysteries" (Dan. 2:29).[40] The book of Daniel, however, speaks of mystery with respect to the end time. Its content is "what will be in the latter days" (Dan. 2:28). Apocalyptic would then be the unveiling of a distant future, as we read in Dan. 8:26: "But seal up the vision, for it pertains to many days hence."[41] Such an understanding of apocalyptic as the unveiling of the future, however, disregards the fictional framework of Jewish apocalypses. Although the prophesied events are indeed distant from the perspective of the fictitious recipient of the revelation, they are not so for the actual readers of the apocalypses. In this connection, we may for a moment disregard at least in part the difficult problem whether the apocalypses are in every case documents of eschatological imminent expectation.

What is decisive is that the prophesied events of the end time, though their actual commencement may well lie in the distant future, do intrude into the present of the readers. To the extent the present is not already qualified *as* the end time, it is at least qualified *by* the prophesied end time. This is also evident in other examples of apocalyptic.

In this case, of course, the assertion often made in religious studies is yet unsatisfactory according to which apocalyptic intends to unveil the end of the world or future events of the end time. The real problem with which apocalyptic is dealing is not the prediction of future events, but rather the threatening loss of future as the constitutive element of human existence.[42] Not prophecy, but rather the opening up of the future is the central theme of apocalyptic unveiling. In the sense of a concept of the future providing an analysis of existence, G. Sauter referred to "*apokalypsis* as the unveiling of the future."[43] According to Sauter, the various imagery of Jewish apocalyptic seeks "each in its own way to open up the future and yet at the same time to close it off again—but 'future' not in its grammatical and temporal sense, but rather as the theological datum through which the world as a whole is to be disclosed."[44] The unveiling of the future thus means rendering the future possible. According to the evidence of Jewish apocalyptic, however, the future is opened up by God. In Jewish apocalyptic, the *apokalypsis* unveils equally the divine reality and the world which is viewed in the light of that reality. With the same justification with which Sauter calls *apokalypsis* the unveiling of the future, he can also say of it: "Revelation dis-covers history."[45] This assertion recalls the interpretation of apocalyptic offered by W. Pannenberg, who speaks of the "accessibility of reality as history through the biblical revelation of God."[46] "History," so Pannenberg, "is reality in its totality."[47] One can speak of an unveiling of reality as history with respect to Jewish apocalyptic, as Sauter justifiably critically qualifies this idea, only insofar as one remembers that history in its totality is not the indirect self-revelation of God,[48] but rather remains radically separated from God and is given over to destruction. One can call Jewish apocalyptic the unveiling of reality as history only if it remains clear that in its understanding revelation can never be a predicate of history.[49]

According to the evidence of Jewish apocalyptic, the divine reality unveils the future or reality as history. Admittedly, the divine revelation, as we have seen, is not a constitutive part of all apocalyptic. Furthermore, we should avoid any precipitous theologizing of our topic and any mingling of a phenomenological interpretation of apocalyptic with the theological problems of the dogmatic concept of revelation, especially with the problem of revelation and history. All the examples of apocalyptic we have investigated thus far, however, have been concerned with the problem of the future, with the threatening loss of the space of freedom which is constitutive for human existence. Apocalyptic unveils present reality in the light of this threatening loss. Apocalyptic, we may say with an expression coined by J. Ellul, is the unveiling of reality.[50]

With this formula of the unveiling of reality, Ellul claims to interpret not the phenomenon of apocalyptic, but rather only the New Testament Revelation of John. That is, according to Ellul the Apocalypse of John is not to be viewed together with

Jewish or extra-Jewish apocalypses. His point of departure is rather "that there is a world of difference between the Apocalypse of John and the others."[51] Hence Ellul also interprets the concept of revelation exclusively with reference to the Apocalypse of John. "If the Apocalypse is revelation, that means an act of God who intervenes in the course of history, and the book is not a description of this intervention, contrary to what it has too often been considered, nor is it a potential revelation that the Holy Spirit could come to animate (as all the rest of Scripture). As revelation, the book is propelled by an internal movement and the attempt must be made to recover this movement."[52] "The whole Apocalypse is an allegory of God and of his work; nothing more!"[53] In this way the concept of "unveiling reality" is unnecessarily limited in its scope for the interpretation of apocalyptic insofar as the concept of *apokalypsis* is bound, in a one-sided theological fashion, to the dogmatic concept of God's self-revelation in Christ.

Here, however, precisely Ellul's concept of the unveiling of reality provides an appropriate description of the apocalyptic interpretation of the world insofar as it is freed from its exclusivity and theological limitations. Essential structural features which Ellul discloses with regard to the Revelation of John, as might be demonstrated on the basis of the material we have already discussed, characterize not only this one New Testament writing, but also apocalyptic in the larger sense. Just as according to Ellul the Revelation of John, so also does apocalyptic on the whole develop a specific reference framework of reality and truth: "The real provides the truth with the means for expressing itself, the truth transfigures the real by giving it a meaning that it obviously does not have in itself."[54] The substance of this understanding of the relationship between reality and truth corresponds to Sauter's own assertion that "revelation thus unveils, discloses a being which cannot be discovered by demonstration, one which does not manifest itself on its own because it does not appear in the world of demonstration and construing."[55] Metaphorically speaking, apocalyptic interprets reality in a light not universally accessible, and opens up an interpretation of reality that reality does not make accessible of its own accord. To that extent, not only the Revelation of John, but every form of apocalyptic is "a key to the interpretation of a present event."[56]

Apocalyptic carries the light of enlightenment into a world perceived as dark. "For the world lies in darkness, and its inhabitants are without light" (4 Ezra 14:20).[57] The apocalyptic *apokalypsis* lifts the veil of darkness, and in its light reality can be recognized as it really is and as it previously could not be known. "Then the wise people shall see the truth" (*1 Enoch* 100:6).[58] One can thus speak with J. Derrida of an apocalyptic claim to provide enlightenment, one we have demonstrated clearly in several varieties of apocalyptic. Viewed in this way, an affinity does indeed obtain between enlightenment and apocalyptic. However, one misunderstands the phenomena if one denies any distinction between philosophical enlightenment and the apocalyptic interpretation of the world and, with Derrida, declares the apocalyptic element to be the transcendental condition of all discourse.[59] This kind of philosophical formalization of the concept of apocalyptic is no less confusing than its formalization in religious studies. The differences become clear as soon as metaphorically speaking one inquires concerning the origin of the light of enlightenment in apocalyptic.

Metaphorically speaking, the source of light in apocalyptic is the end of the world. The apocalyptic understanding of existence interprets reality from the perspective of the end of the world, the anticipation of which is the consequence and verbalization of apocalyptic world anxiety. The apocalyptic experience of the world is concentrated in the expectation of the end. Apocalyptic interprets both the present and history from the perspective of that end. The end of the world disclosed by anxiety qualifies the present as "end-time," and apocalyptic is thus enlightenment concerning the qualification of reality by the end.[60] From the perspective of the notion of the end, the world becomes accessible to experience and interpretation in a way not possible apart from the disposition of apocalyptic world anxiety. For just this reason, *2 Apoc. Bar.* 27:15 can say that "those who live on earth in those days will not understand that it is the end of times." From this perspective, the notion of the concealment of what has just been revealed in Jewish apocalyptic now becomes comprehensible. In various ways, the recipients of revelation on the fictional level are charged with sealing the apocalyptic message for a later age. Although one might take this fiction of the long concealed message to be an expression of apocalyptic elitism and conventicle inclinations, such an interpretation would not penetrate deeply enough. On the level of the understanding of existence, such fictional cloaking of the message of unveiling can be interpreted as the literary expression of the experience that, apart from the disposition of apocalyptic world anxiety, access to the idea of the end of the world and thus to an apocalyptic interpretation of the world necessarily remains closed.

We already saw earlier that the end of the world of which the apocalyptic understanding of existence speaks is not a future event in the sense of the ordinary understanding of time, but rather in a certain way intrudes as a possibility into the present itself.[61] The end of the world is not a historical event of the near or more distant future, but rather a metaphor for the catastrophic nature of present reality. It is the summary, formulated as expectation, of all the catastrophic tendencies of the currently experienced world. According to the apocalyptic understanding of existence, the end is, as it were, the depth dimension of reality and as such is always present. The end is equally the conclusion, breaking off, crisis, and *telos* of all reality, and to that extent one can say that the apocalyptist construes the world as reality in decline. *Apocalyptic is the unveiling of reality in decline.* This implies an interpretation of the world that views everything in reference to the end and illuminates its participation in the catastrophic nature of the world. The unveiling of reality in decline involves structuring one's world experience through the idea of the end of the world.

It should have become clear that the assumption of the end of the world does not result from a situational analysis undertaken by the apocalyptist, but rather quite the reverse constitutes the precondition for an apocalyptic interpretation of the present. The end of the world is not the end result, but rather the point of departure for the apocalyptic unveiling of reality. In a reverse fashion, apocalyptic is not an interpretation of the world emerging directly from apocalyptic anxiety. As the attempt at mastering anxiety, apocalyptic should be distinguished from the apocalyptic anxiety preceding it. The interface between apocalyptic as the attempt at mastering anxiety and apocalyptic world anxiety is the notion of the end of the world. This notion is on the one hand the result of apocalyptic world anxiety and understanding of existence; in apocalyptic as a developed complex of ideas, however, it is the hermeneutical basis for a secondary interpretation of the world. The apocalyptic unveiling of reality as reality in decline is thus the result of a hermeneutic of the end of the world. The interpretation of the world by apocalyptic is to that extent one mediated by the notion of the end of the world: The unveiling of reality in the form of apocalyptic becomes possible through the fact that the notion of the end of the world, which is first of all merely the logical expectation of exponentially intensified world anxiety, acquires a new function as the medium of the interpretation of the world.

Apocalyptic seeks to unveil reality in order to provide deliverance from world anxiety. Here, too, the claim of enlightenment manifests itself, since the unveiling of reality has the goal of liberation, liberation both from anxiety and from the world provoking that anxiety. The potential of liberation inherent in apocalyptic consists in its negation of the totally closed quality of reality. Initially, the end of the world is the conceptual consequence that anxiety draws from its experience of the complete inescapability of reality. Negative apocalyptic verbalizes this experience of the inescapability of finitude and of the totally closed quality of reality by anticipating the end of the world. In contrast, positive apocalyptic is able to go one step further and comprehends the end of the world as the sublation of this inescapability. The end of the world is a crisis. "And this crisis, in the etymological sense, discloses an *egress* from the radical closure of the present time."[62] Yet not only the Apocalypse of John, as J. Ellul believes, but also all positive apocalyptic "is the discovery of the egress of history, which implies a possible emergence for the present time."[63] In this context the word "egress" is used with twofold meaning, namely, both spatially and in the sense of finality. Positive apocalyptic interprets the end as a transition and understands reality from the perspective of the end of the world interpreted thus. Understood correctly, however, even negative apocalyptic interprets the end as an egress; even if in its eyes the end is neither a passage nor a transition of any sort, an element of liberation does inhere in it. Even the simple collapse of the world would break through the totally closed quality of the world, albeit at the price of its complete destruction. Even the end of the world as pure destruction constitutes the negation of inescapability. The notion of the end of the world entertained by negative apocalyptic also negates the irrevocability of the totally closed nature of the world. Insofar as it, too, is a type of world negation,[64] its anticipation of the end makes possible a distancing of oneself from the world, and thus also liberation. Although the collapse of the world as anticipated by negative apocalyptic would indeed mean the irrevocable loss of future and the destruction of the ego, it would, precisely as the end of the world, also simultaneously be the end of its inescapability. Hence for both positive and negative apocalyptic, the unveiling of reality means the discovery of the egress out of the totality of closed reality.

The reaction among intellectual circles to Jakob von Hoddis's poem "The End of the World" (1912) illustrates in an exemplary fashion just how existentially liberating apocalyptic can be. This and other poems and letters from early expressionistic poets before the First World War combined cultural pessimism "with hope in the end of an age moldy with bourgeois narrowness and prudery, and with hope in the beginning of a new phase of human development."[65] The poem reads:

The End of the World

The burgher's hat flies off his pointed head,
Everywhere the air reverberates with what sounds like screams.
Roofers are falling off and breaking in two,
And along the coasts—the paper says—the tide is rising.

The storm is here, the wild seas are hopping
Ashore to squash thick dikes.
Most people have a cold,
The trains are dropping off the bridges.[66]

The impending cultural catastrophe is conceived as an act of liberation and provides the occasion for apocalyptic . . . cheerfulness. The two strophes of this poem, Johannes R. Becher recalls,

> seemed to transform us into completely different people, to lift us out of a world of deadening bourgeois values which we despised and from which we did not know how to escape [!]. These eight lines abducted us. We discovered ever new wonders in these eight lines; we sang them, hummed them, murmured them, whistled them, went to church with them on our lips, and whispered them to ourselves while bicycling. We called them to one another across the street like a secret watchword, sat with one another with these eight lines, freezing and hungry, spoke them to one another, and hunger and cold no longer existed. What had happened? At that time, we did not know the word: transformation. We felt like new people.[67]

The unveiling of reality: The apocalyptic poem contains a message of liberation in its promise of the bursting of the dams of a reality closed off on all sides, and points the way to an egress out of the unbearable world of obtuse bourgeois values. The discovery of an egress in the double sense of the word has a liberating effect.

To be sure, prewar expressionism also illustrates the ambiguity of apocalyptic. At the outbreak of the First World War, this yearning for the end of all security also plunged expressionistic artists and intellectuals into a delirium of enthusiasm and made them blind to the un-"spirit of 1914." The alleged unveiling of reality by apocalyptic does not protect it from portraying reality ideologically and in this way virtually concealing it.

Apocalyptic enlightenment also extends into the political realm. As we have already seen on several occasions, it poses the question of power and functions as a mouthpiece for the politically powerless. Classic examples of such unveiling of political structures include the visions of the world empires in Dan. 2 and 7 as well as the identification of Rome with the beast from the abyss in Rev. 13. However, precisely this kind of apocalyptic claim to illuminate political conditions can be ideological. The ideological distortion and thus obscuring of political reality is by no means merely the result of a misuse of apocalyptic, but is rather one of its inherent possibilities.[68] One must thus guard against the blanket judgment "that apocalyptic literature is resistance literature,"[69] nor can one in every case speak of the "subversive power of apocalyptic,"[70] unless one admits that resistance and subversiveness in and of themselves do not yet imply anything regarding the political understanding of the apocalyptist, nor about his social standing or the progressive or conservative nature of his sociopolitical options.[71]

Apocalyptic harshly illuminates reality with the light of the end of the world. "Just as El Greco's lightning illuminates Toledo, so also does the catastrophe anticipated in the imagination cast a fantastically sharp light onto the course of the world. What is important emerges, and what is unimportant recedes into the shadows."[72] In this way, structures of reality and structures of power are uncovered, not least those which are enhanced and embellished by the powerful. However, to take the metaphor a bit further, these structures are not only brought to light, but are overexposed such that the complexity of the structures of reality are reduced to a dualism of black and white, good and evil, light and darkness. Precisely the simplification resulting from the light of the possible catastrophe can be extraordinarily illuminating. What seems black to our usual consciousness is according to the vision of apocalyptic actually white, what one thinks is good is in truth evil; and the present order of things is in reality a perverted world that has become untracked, a world up to which apocalyptic holds a mirror and which it confronts with a counterworld.[73] Whenever its metaphorical character is forgotten, however, apocalyptic of necessity becomes a distortion of reality and degenerates into ideology. Apocalyptic ideology mistakes its own imagery for reality and obscures consciousness.[74]

The ambiguity of all apocalyptic unveiling of reality is occasionally taken as a theme within apocalyptic itself. Thus *2 Apocalypse of Baruch* reads: "And there will be many tidings and not a few rumors, and the works of the phantoms will be visible, and not a few promises will be told, some idle and others affirmed" (*2 Apoc. Bar.* 48:34). According to *2 Apocalypse of Baruch*, this ambiguity of the apocalyptic interpretation of the world is one of the signs of the end time, and is thus the object of an inner-apocalyptic critique of apocalyptic of the sort we discussed earlier. The apocalyptic unveiling of reality in its own turn requires enlightenment; otherwise, it remains incapable of self-critique and becomes immune to the necessary ideological criticism. Sooner or later, apocalyptic ostracized by the world or isolated of its own accord becomes ideological. Such ideological or ideologized apocalyptic, however, is what in our Introduction we already referred to as damaged apocalyptic.[75] Such damage threatens apocalyptic not only from external sources via the repression of apocalyptic anxiety from general consciousness; it is equally a danger inhering within apocalyptic itself, one deriving from the fact that apocalyptic anxiety and the apocalyptic experience of the world, even though these constitute a universal existential possibility, do not represent an understanding of existence that is easily or always accessible. For just this reason, sociologically apocalyptic is overwhelmingly a minority phenomenon.[76] The tendency to sectarian existence and thus to ideological hardening is not only forced onto apocalyptic from external sources—something that doubtless is often the case—but rather already inheres as a possibility in the source of its understanding of existence in apocalyptic world anxiety.

Apocalyptic becomes capable of the necessary self-criticism when it renders fruitful for an inner-apocalyptic critique of apocalyptic the dialectic between positive and negative apocalyptic. Beyond this, it remains dependent on criticism from external sources, and that means on communication with nonapocalyptic experiences of existence and interpretations of the world. It is not least the degree of its capacity for communication exercised by apocalyptic thinking that is decisive for securing apocalyptic against ideological hardening.

3. Hope in the End

The discovery of an egress from a reality closed off on all sides liberates a person from world anxiety and provides hope. This is the substratum of apocalyptic hope. Apocalyptic does not direct its hope aimlessly into the blue, nor does it merely erect a series of disordered wishful images. Rather, apocalyptic hopes in the end which it has discovered as an egress, and this end can become equally the goal as well as the ground of apocalyptic hope. In this twofold respect apocalyptic hope is hope in the end. Both positive and negative apocalyptic, each in its own way, entertain hope in the end. Although the latter's vision of something beyond the catastrophe remains blocked, it is nonetheless still able to hope in the end insofar as destruction is the final and only possible act of liberation. An element of hope also inheres in negative apocalyptic.[77] Its hope directs itself toward the end as its goal. For positive apocalyptic, the end is the ground of hope rather than its goal, and the content of hope is above all the utopian counterworld beyond the catastrophe. Admittedly, the ground of such utopian hope consists in the unveiled catastrophe. The end is the necessary condition of future glory; precisely because the end is conceived as a passage or transition, it functions as the ground of apocalyptic hope for better conditions and times. In the case of positive apocalyptic, the end can be compared with the lens of a magnifying glass. It concentrates the light of the content of hope and illuminates present reality with its help. To that extent, however, according to positive apocalyptic one cannot simply hope past the end, as it were; without this end, the ground disappears from under apocalyptic hope. As the ground of hope, the end is for positive apocalyptic, too, the necessary, albeit not the only object of hope, and its preliminary if not ultimate goal. Although both positive and negative apocalyptic seek to awaken hope in the end, the two assign a different value to the end itself.

In positive apocalyptic, hope is to overcome anxiety. The apocalyptist approaches the end full of confidence: "For the righteous justly have good hope for the end and go away from this habitation without fear because they possess with you a store of good works which is preserved in treasures. Therefore, they leave this world without fear and are confident of the world which you have promised to them with an expectation full of joy" (*2 Apoc. Bar.* 14:12f.). What is overcome is the anxiety both before the end of the world as well as before death, which anticipates that end. Positive apocalyptic is tuned to the key of hope, and thus to a certain extent those particular attempts at interpretation are justified which interpret apocalyptic from the perspective of hope and inquire concerning the hope inherent within it. Positive apocalyptic seeks to be a message of hope, something overlooked whenever unfamiliarity with the phenomena or imprecise use of language results in *apokalypsis* being equated with destruction and catastrophe.

One accomplishment of utopian studies, especially those of Bloch and, similarly, Bulgakov, is their disclosure or at least recollection of the central significance of hope in apocalyptic.[78] Bloch understands apocalyptic as one manifestation of utopian thinking. According to him, utopias are wishful images of anticipatory consciousness which detects the tendencies of matter in the direction toward an *ultimatum* of their process and tries to accommodate them.[79] They are "outlines of a better world"[80] or "wishful images of the fulfilled moment."[81] "At the same time, one must distinguish between utopianism and the utopian as such. The one approaches circumstances only immediately, abstractly, in order to improve them in a purely conceptual fashion; the other, in any case, always secured its construction materials from external sources as well."[82] Bloch's theory of the utopian is not only a rehabilitation of utopia, but no less also a critique of utopian thinking, albeit a critique from a perspective "which is commensurate, and which does not condemn, and certainly not replace, e.g., skimming over by factical creeping."[83] Only the concrete-actual utopia stands up to criticism, i.e., utopia mediated with the process of matter itself. "*Concrete* utopia, however, i.e., precisely this sort, is such because it is mediated with the historical index of historical-process-oriented matter. And as *actual* utopia it is in the world in the first place only because the matter of the world has itself not yet reached closure, because the process of this matter is neither thwarted (which would suffocate utopia) nor already achieved (which would make utopia into advent)."[84] The motivating impetus behind concrete-actual utopian thinking, however, i.e., of anticipatory consciousness, is hope, which Bloch conceives as an emotion of wish or of positive expectation. On the one hand, this expectant emotion is subsumed under an extensive doctrine of impulses, and on the other bound back, by means of Bloch's ontology of Not-yet-being, to matter, which is itself conceived as process-oriented.[85]

Although Bloch locates apocalyptic in the wide field of the utopian, the particular character of apocalyptic hope nonetheless does not escape him. On several occasions Bloch emphasizes the catastrophic element in apocalyptic, which he refers to as "explosion." According to Bloch, Jewish-Christian apocalyptic is an "*explosive myth* of liberation,"[86] a "myth of promise,"[87] "with quite world-exploding signs,"[88] a manifestation of "the idea of an apocalyptic breakthrough into the Utopia of salvation."[89] Although Bloch does place his emphasis on hope and promise, the hope of apocalyptic also directs itself in his view precisely toward this "explosion" as a liberating event. Here Bloch is describing the substance of what we have also found, namely, that apocalyptic hope is hope in the end, whereby Bloch's description would be limited to positive apocalyptic. Not only does Bloch perceive such hope in the end as egress and liberation in the writings of Jewish-Christian apocalyptic, he would also like to mediate such hope to his own contemporaries. Hope in the end is a powerful apocalyptic motif already in his writing on the *Geist der Utopie* [*The Spirit of Utopia*], a persistent motif also characterizing his *Principle of Hope.*[90] Bloch's question, "how might things come to completion without in an apocalyptic fashion ceasing to be,"[91] "without this world being exploded and apocalyptically vanishing,"[92] lends virtually classical expression to apocalyptic hope in the end.

Utopian studies largely emphasize hope when dealing with apocalyptic,[93] and this is also the case in those theological attempts at interpretation which view apocalyptic against the horizon of the problem of future and history and employ as their hermeneutical key the theological category of promise instead of the category of utopia. Differently than in Bloch's work, the catastrophic element of apocalyptic hope largely recedes into the background in the writing of Moltmann or Pannenberg. Only G. Sauter, within the framework of his own theological investigation into the problematic attaching to notions of the future, interprets apocalyptic as a theory of catastrophe following the lead especially of G. Scholem.[94]

As is well known, apocalyptic occupies a central position in Pannenberg's theology of history. Pannenberg derives the concept of history from the biblical understanding of revelation and defends the thesis that apart from biblical faith in revelation there can be no general concept of history.[95] As history, reality is disclosed through the categories of promise and fulfillment. "History is event so suspended in tension between promise and fulfillment that through the promise it is irreversibly pointed toward the goal of future fulfillment."[96] Pannenberg follows especially the exegetical work of D. Rössler,[97] which itself was prompted by U. Wilckens's discussion of New Testament apocalyptic.[98] According to Pannenberg, Jewish apocalyptic expanded the Old Testament understanding of history into the notion of universal history. He asserts that "the expansion of salvation history into universal history, apart from the lists in Chronicles, was first carried through systematically in apocalyptic."[99] In Pannenberg's view, apocalyptic universal history is thus redemptive history, just as his own theology of history is "a conception of history based on revelation," i.e., a continuation of "redemptive-historical thinking" in theology.[100] This redemptive-historical understanding of apocalyptic screens out the catastrophic features of Jewish apocalyptic for the sake of the theological greatness of promise, overlooking that promise and hope in salvation in apocalyptic are constituent parts of a theory of catastrophe.

Taking the category of promise as its point of departure, Moltmann's theology of hope presents the future as a theological problem, but rejects Pannenberg's understanding of history as the indirect self-revelation of God, an understanding that allegedly does not take seriously enough the structure of biblical faith in the God of promise, moving instead within the parameters of Greek cosmology and of the cosmological proof of the existence of God, ultimately never moving beyond the understanding of revelation as theophany.[101] Of course, according to Moltmann, too, faith in the divine promise is the point of departure for the Old Testament understanding of history. Like the message of the Old Testament prophets, so also, according to Moltmann, does Jewish apocalyptic wrestle with the problem of the future and for the Israelite "hope for history": "If, as we might say, in the message of the prophets the Israelite 'hope for history' was struggling with the experiences of world history, and if in this struggle world history was understood as a function of the eschatological future of Yahweh, so it is also in apocalyptic: historic eschatology is here struggling with cosmology and in this struggle makes the cosmos understandable as a historic process of aeons in apocalyptic perspective."[102] In this view, apocalyptic would be "the beginning of an eschatological cosmology or an eschatological ontology for which being becomes historic and the cosmos opens itself to the apocalyptic process."[103] Its central focus is "the expectation of the future victory of the righteousness of God over dead and living."[104]

Moltmann places hope at the center of his interpretation of apocalyptic. His understanding of Jewish apocalyptic as the beginning of an eschatological cosmology or ontology implies the conclusion that an inner relationship obtains between apocalyptic thinking and Bloch's philosophy of hope and its ontology of Not-yet-being. Precisely in comparison with Bloch, however, one notices the considerable extent to which the catastrophic features of Jewish apocalyptic recede into the background for Moltmann. Although in *The Crucified God* Moltmann does understand apocalyptic as an attempt at mastering the problem of theodicy within a universal-historic perspective,[105] and thus as the locus of discourse with the negative features of history, nevertheless the idea of the catastrophic nature of redemption plays no significant role in Moltmann's understanding of apocalyptic. What is important for Moltmann in apocalyptic is that in it the cosmos opens itself to the category of process. Yet here one must object that according to apocalyptic thinking this opening is a catastrophic event, an act of explosion, to use Bloch's expression. The cosmos is in fact not opened up to any apocalyptic process, but rather is exploded apocalyptically.

A reading of apocalyptic documents from the perspective of hope is certainly justified, since apocalyptic does indeed seek to be a message of hope. Such an interpretation of apocalyptic witnesses as documents of hope, however, misses the mark if it takes a general concept of hope as its point of departure and fails to consider that the hope of apocalyptic is actually hope in the end. The content of apocalyptic hope is characterized by the catastrophic nature of this yearned for redemption.[106] For this reason, apocalyptic hope in the end can be understood only from the perspective of apocalyptic anxiety, to which it seeks to provide an answer. World anxiety proves to be the real hermeneutical key to understanding apocalyptic hope.

At this point, let us recall the relationship between anxiety, fear, and hope.[107] Anxiety, we found earlier, is a dialectical mood. As the discovery of the future, it stands in a dialectical relationship with that future. In a manner different from that of Bloch, who takes the *appetitus* (hunger), an undialectical basic impulse, to be the psychological root of hope, we took as our point of departure a dialectical basic emotion that we found in anxiety. Anxiety is the key to understanding hope because hope emerges when dialectical anxiety becomes undialectical and the positive element comes to the forefront which in anxiety is associated dialectically with a negative element. Thus hope does not reside on the same level as anxiety, but rather as fear, which in contradistinction to anxiety is always an undialectical mood. Anxiety is thus equally the condition for both fear and hope. Fear and hope emerge from anxiety as soon as anxiety becomes undialectical. For this reason, apocalyptic hope can also be derived from a preceding mood of anxiety. Apocalyptic world anxiety precedes apocalyptic hope as its precondition.

In apocalyptic, hope in the end is largely associated with the certainty that the end is indeed near. Such imminent expectation comes to expression, e.g., in *2 Apoc. Bar.* 85:10: "And the pitcher is near to the cistern, and the ship to the port, and the course of the journey to the city, and life to its consummation." 4 Ezra illustrates the proximity of the end with the imagery of an extinguishing fire which at the end smolders for only a short while, and of a heavy downpour at whose end a few drops fall for only a short while. "Consider it for yourself; for as the rain is more than the drops, and the fire is greater than the smoke, so the quantity that passed was far greater; but drops and smoke remained" (4 Ezra 4:50). The proximity of the end is not only metaphorically circumscribed in apocalyptic, it frequently is also reckoned temporally. One classic example of such reckoning of the end time is the book of Daniel, which proposes a period of three and a half times until the end of the world,[108] and at the end proceeds on the concrete assumption that 1,290 or at most 1,335 days remain yet before the end of the world.[109] End-time reckonings of this sort permeate the entire history of the church and of sectarian movements, and precisely their refutation by the course of history has not infrequently resulted in negative assessments of apocalyptic near expectation.

At this point, however, apocalyptic deserves to be understood better than it occasionally even understands itself. Reckonings concerning the end time, which even the apocalyptist himself reads or presents as a map of world history, constitute a self-misunderstanding of apocalyptic imminent expectation. Such reckonings express in temporal categories the proximity of the end, proximity which in fact is not to be understood temporally at all. The end is near not in the sense of the grammatical concept of time, but rather in the sense of perpetual presence, of ultimate urgency and unavoidability. The end is near as the catastrophic quality of the currently experienced world. It is near as the catastrophic dimension of depth of reality. The end is near because it pressures and oppresses the apocalyptist in each and every aspect of reality, reality that in its own way participates in the catastrophic nature of the world and thus in the end of the world. Apocalyptic imminent expectation must thus be understood as the immediate consequence of an understanding of reality that conceives this reality as reality in decline. If the end is near as a pressing dimension of reality, then hope in the end must be imminent expectation. Yet because imminent expectation at its source is not a temporal prognosis, but rather a statement concerning present reality, imminent expectation—as, e.g., in the case of the parenetic book in *1 Enoch*—can be transformed into perpetual expectation.[110]

This state of affairs can be observed not only in Jewish apocalyptic but also, to take another example, in Bloch's philosophy of hope. One's initial impression is that its eschatology actually constitutes a philosophy of distant expectation. The *Principle of Hope* concludes with the words:

> *True genesis is not at the beginning but at the end*, and it starts to begin only when society and existence become radical, i.e., grasp their roots. But the root of history is the working, creating human being who reshapes and overhauls the given facts. Once he has grasped himself and established what is his, without expropriation and alienation, in real democracy, there arises in the world something which shines into the childhood of all and in which no one has yet been: homeland.[111]

This homeland of identity which is the object of Bloch's hope lies historically in the far distance. It cannot even be equated with the already quite distant realm of freedom for which Marx yearns, but rather at best only emerges in an even more distant future, so distant, in fact, that unavoidable heat death might in the end even thwart the advent of the Omega. Yet even if existence and society in some infinitely distant future were to become radical in the sense of the concluding words of the *Principle of Hope*, this would still only be the beginning of the genesis of the Omega, and homeland would still only be in the incipient stage. To be sure, the picture does change when one considers that matter, even according to Bloch, exhibits a utopian quality. "Process matter . . . is itself pure utopia."[112] To that extent one must say that the utopian Omega and salvific *totum* in the process of matter is already present, i.e., imminent. On the level of the acting subject, this perpetual proximity of the home of identity corresponds to Bloch's idea of the extraterritoriality toward death. According to this view, the human being carries within an "extraterritorial core" of existence which, undiscernible, pushes forward like processual matter and promotes the process of transitoriness, toward the Omega, yet without itself being subject to transitoriness and death because it has itself not yet entered into the process and thus subjected itself to death.[113] Thus according to Bloch, on both the objective and subjective side of the world the Omega is perpetually near despite the furthest distance imaginable. Bloch then quite logically understands his philosophy of hope as present eschatology which attempts to "negate the near and distant goal in an equally gentle and wise montage of stages and goal."[114]

> For *only distant and high goals*, passing over all interim members and proximate goals, are proclaimed by abstract utopia, and not by the concrete utopia immanently associated with the epoch. The kind of bound *incipit vita nova* evoked here thus honors proximate goals in a theoretical-practical fashion: both by falling within the experiential span of a single human life and also by keeping a society without self-alienation in view as a distant goal.[115]

Thus every concrete-actual utopia is an intimation of the home of identity, and in every proximate goal the distant goal is also intimated. And every attempt to actualize proximate utopian goals is an attempt undertaken "with singularly 'present eschatology,' called creative expectation."[116]

If we have correctly identified the origin of apocalyptic imminent expectation, then one cannot derive it psychologically from the pressure of overwhelming torment compensated by an ardent longing for redemption. Rather, imminent expectation is already implied in the idea of the end itself. Apocalyptic anxiety unveils the end as one inherent in all things. Apocalyptic imminent expectation is not primarily an expectation of hope, but rather one of anxiety. This imminent expectation of anxiety is first transformed into imminent expectation of hope only in apocalyptic as the attempt at mastering anxiety.

Apocalyptic hope can admittedly intensify into a longing for the end. 4 Ezra 5:43 impatiently inquires of God: "Could you not have created at one time those who have been and those who are and those who will be, that you might show your judgment the sooner?" Because the apocalyptist finds the present unbearable, and "because the only consolation he sees for this life is the end itself, he yearns for the end with passionate ardor."[117] 4 Ezra tries to apply the brakes somewhat to this apocalyptic haste by pointing out that God has established "a certain progression" in the world.[118]

Although this yearning for the end can be reflected in a quietistic attitude, it can also turn into apocalyptic activism which tries to push what is already falling and assist the advent of the end. While Jewish apocalyptic—to remain with this example for a moment—largely attributes to God and his actions alone the initiative for bringing about the end of the world, and excludes the possibility of any human participation in the establishment of the messianic kingdom, there is also a kind of messianic activism that clearly answers in the affirmative the question "whether one may 'press for the End,' that is to say, force its coming by way of one's own activity."[119] "This is the Messianic activism in which utopianism becomes the lever by which to establish the Messianic kingdom."[120] Although such activism may well seem socially desirable and courageous over against the widespread political quietism of apocalyptic, it represents a problematical consequence of the apocalyptic world experience,[121] problematical because this hope for the end can quite possibly change into pleasure in the end.

This potential pleasure in decline and the end places apocalyptic hope into an ambivalent light and occasions criticism of the sort Nietzsche formulated in his aphorism about the "destroyers of the world": "When some men fail to accomplish what they desire to do they exclaim angrily, 'May the whole world perish!' This odious feeling is the height of envy which reasons thus: because *I* cannot have one thing the whole world in general must have *nothing!* The whole world shall not *exist!*"[122] Nietzsche identifies envy as the source of this pleasure in decline and the end, and his criticism of apocalyptic thus coincides with his genealogy of morals, which traces the Jewish-Christian ethos back to the envy of the rabble, of the socially lower classes.[123] Although feelings of envy can doubtlessly not be excluded in every instance as the source of this pleasure in decline, the roots of apocalyptic pleasure are sooner to be found in despair. Such despair in the inescapability of reality changes into virtually orgiastic pleasure, pleasure which G. Vinnai associates with the death impulse discerned by Freud.[124] "Someone with nothing to lose may perhaps prefer an end with terrors rather than terrors with no end, especially if a completely new salvific period is to commence after the end with terrors."[125] However, wherever hope in the end is reversed, as it were, and becomes pleasure in the end, then apocalyptic which actually is seeking to overcome apocalyptic world anxiety and find an egress from a world full of destructive tendencies itself becomes a potential element of destruction.

This constitutes the ambiguity of apocalyptic hope, namely, that by hoping for the end it actually constitutes hope for destruction.

Both positive and negative apocalyptic hope for the end, and in this point earlier forms of apocalyptic, whether positive or negative, seem to differ from the various forms of negative apocalyptic in the age of nihilism. These latter, contemporary forms of apocalyptic, forms we have come to know as self-destroying prophecy, fear the end because contemporary criticism of metaphysical thinking destroys all hope in anything beyond the catastrophe. Apocalyptic that understands itself as antimetaphysical is not only incapable of hope in the end, but must even combat such hope. This seems to constitute a qualitative leap in the history of apocalyptic, a leap that, e.g., G. Anders has described by suggesting that apocalyptic becomes paradoxical or absurd.[126] The apocalyptic both of nuclear holocaust and of ecological catastrophe understands itself as "prophylactic" apocalyptic (G. Anders), as apocalyptic of those opposed to destruction and prepared to prevent the end at any price. This apocalyptic is negative, though no longer in the sense that the complete end is understood, if not as crisis and transition, then at least as the last means of liberation. Consequently, this apocalyptic is neither resigned nor intent on accelerating the end, but rather struggles with all its energy to preserve the apocalyptically understood world. Although politically quite progressive, viewed in this way it nonetheless fights for the preservation of the status quo: The end time from which there is no escape is to be perpetuated indefinitely.

This sort of prophylactic apocalyptic is not without analogy, as G. Anders believes, since as we have already seen in a different context the history of the Middle Ages does indeed sufficiently attest the phenomenon whereby precisely apocalyptic forms of thought, which constitute a mode of world negation, are put to use as the language of world affirmation. In the Middle Ages this occurred where Christians no longer understood the state as the beast from the abyss according to Rev. 13, but rather as the *katechon* from 2 Thess. 2:6f. This apocalyptic was also prophylactic, since it supported the emperor and worldly dominion for the sake of hindering or delaying the end.[127] Of course, this prophylactic apocalyptic was inherently ambiguous insofar as on the one hand it did seek to impede the end and affirmed the existing world, yet on the other held fast to the traditional Christian hope in the end and thus to apocalyptic world negation. This remnant of hope in the end, however, actually constituted an inherited and domesticated notion, and is completely absent in the newer type of prophylactic apocalyptic. The collapse of traditional metaphysics does not even allow for hope in the end as a vestigial notion.

Of course, the ambivalence of apocalyptic hope emerges in the fact that the fear before the end characteristic of antimetaphysical apocalyptic is indeed occasionally transformed into destructive and self-destructive inclinations toward destruction. In this case, the age of nihilism does allow for—admittedly absurd—hope in the end. One example of this transformation of apocalyptic fear before the end into the craving for destruction is U. Horstmann's "monster."[128] Horstmann diagnoses this craving for destruction as a fundamental impulse in human history, one explaining "the extremely early, occasionally manic concern with world-catastrophe and one's own decline."[129] Horstmann himself surrenders "with anthropofugal glee" to this craving.[130] He repeatedly associates the collective craving for the end with the problem of suicide, "which appears as the subjectivistically abbreviated reflex of apocalyptic yearnings."[131] He rejects suicide as a selfish negation of the individual allowing the species itself to continue to exist.[132] Suicide is, however, accepted as an act of apocalyptic prolepsis and anthropofugal protest. Horstmann acquires the "anthropofugal insight that the suicide anticipates the ultimatum act of species annihilation in a kind of impatient symbolism, and every person who takes his own life, casting thus an ostentatious vote for nonbeing, erects with his own soulless body a monument against the dim humanistic notions of survival and the sated torpor which would guide the collective away from its path toward Armageddon."[133] Horstmann presents suicide as the impatient and premature enactment of collective craving for destruction and the end. His praise of the end of the world and his critique of suicide are themselves admittedly ambiguous. "There are people," F. Hebbel once said, "who would like to precipitate the end of the world in order to spare themselves suicide."[134]

Nonetheless, one should not overlook the danger that contemporary prophylactic apocalyptic can also be or become a latent form of craving for the end, and in this sense A. Glucksmann has directed critical inquiries toward the European peace movement. "The idea that fear can be driven out by fear seems absurd. 'Onward! Let's go!' cried earlier enthusiasts of war. 'Down with weapons! Save yourself if you can!' is the recommendation today of the no less numerous manifestations. These contradictory attitudes also encourage avoidance. The same leitmotif guides their cadences: better an end with terror than terror with no end."[135] Glucksmann is extremely critical of the West German peace movement: "Germany became an enthusiast for pacifism in the quiet rejoicing of a reacquired 'we.' In the idea of its own death it discovered proof of its existence; from the foam of infinite dissolution it returned to the sweet feeling of finding itself."[136] Although this critique of the peace movement is admittedly rather one-sided, an uncritical affirmation of the peace movement would overlook the danger inherent in the apocalyptic craving for the end latent in certain parts of that movement. H. Nagel's reference to the Hiroshima bomb, "a bomb actually intended for Germany, which capitulated too early and ever since has been searching for the fulfillment of its destiny,"[137] should prompt reflection not only over against administration politics, but also over against certain tendencies within the peace movement itself. In a reverse fashion, prophylactic apocalyptic can be just as ambiguous as is this hope for the end, and a critical posture must be established over against this type of apocalyptic as well.

In his story "Der Untergang," H. E. Nossack has described how apocalyptic hope in the form of craving for the end can become potentially destructive and self-destructive. The story deals with the destruction of Hamburg in 1943. Nossack's self-critical illumination of his own relationship with catastrophe is even today still able to guide us to a critical attitude toward apocalyptic hope and to remind us of its ambiguity.

> Was this hatred [Nossack confesses in the story] not familiar to me, I who paced back and forth somewhere in nothingness, corporeally and utterly lacking the energy for even a single idea? Have I not guarded against it for decades and resisted its outbreak? Have I not known that one day it would break out, and have I not yearned for just this day because it would finally relieve me of the task of guarding? Yes, I have, just as I now know, and have always known, that the fate of the city would be my own fate. And if it is so, namely, that I yearned for the destiny of the city to come about in order to force my own destiny into decision, then I must stand up and confess my own guilt in the destruction of the city.
>
> All of us toyed with the idea of a great flood; the events of the time forced us to. Did that not already amount to leaving the past in the lurch? And what witty chatter, what boasting, for when we seriously confronted the question regarding just what we would want to rescue from an imminent flood, something to preserve for the survivors, where indeed did we find anything that seemed so important and necessary that we would have risked everything for it, up to our last breath? In what did we believe so strongly that the powers of destruction were reluctant to touch this faith so as not to confer eternal life upon precisely that which they destroyed? Of all the things which we used and which burdened us, what was still ours? Today I would dare to question the purity of the motives of those who warned of the catastrophe and exhorted us to make preparations. Did they not perhaps want the catastrophe to occur in order to force others down to their knees, while they themselves felt at home in the chaos? And were they not driven by a craving to test themselves, though at the cost of familiar existence?[138]

4. Pastoral Care for Those in Anxiety

Positive apocalyptic is a message against anxiety. Its intention is to console those overwhelmed by world anxiety. Its hope, and thus also the apocalyptic utopia, functions as consolation. This consoling function of apocalyptic also includes a parenetic goal. While on the objective side apocalyptic to a certain extent understands the end of the world as a liberating event, on the side of the subject it exhorts one to adopt a manner and form of living corresponding to insights into the catastrophic nature of reality. The structuring of one's life and behavior, structuring that draws moral consequences from the unveiling of reality in decline, is for apocalyptic often the presupposition for the end of the world genuinely becoming an act of liberation for the individual rather than constituting the certain end both for the individual and for the world. Consolation and parenesis are central components of pastoral care.[139] In summary, then, one can say that apocalyptic is pastoral care for those plagued by anxiety.

Apocalypses are literature of consolation. This consoling function of apocalyptic literature is occasionally expressly taken as a theme within apocalyptic itself, as is the case in several passages within Jewish apocalypses. In this context, *1 Enoch* 104:10–13 reads:

> And now I know this mystery: For many sinners shall alter the words of truth and many sinners will take it to heart; they will speak evil words and lie, and they

> will invent fictitious stories and write out my Scriptures on the basis of their own words. And would that they had written all the words truthfully on the basis of their own speech, and neither alter nor take away from my words, all of which I testify to them from the beginning! Again know another mystery!: That to the righteous and the wise shall be given the Scriptures of joy, and cause much joy, righteousness, and wisdom. So to them shall be given the Scriptures; and they shall believe them and be glad in them; and all the righteous ones who learn from them the ways of truth shall receive their reward.

Committing the apocalypse to written form serves to console those plagued by anxiety: "Therefore," we read in the letter of the fictitious Baruch, "I have been the more diligent to leave you the words of this letter before I die so that you may be comforted regarding the evils which have befallen you" (*2 Apoc. Bar.* 78:5). Baruch emphasizes the misfortune of the brothers and the righteousness of divine judgment: "Therefore, if you think about the things you have suffered now for your good so that you may not be condemned at the end and be tormented, you shall receive hope which lasts forever and ever" (*2 Apoc. Bar.* 78:6), though admittedly only presupposing a corresponding change in behavior. However, the parenesis is also intended as consolation.[140]

"Consolation" and "exhortation" are rendered in Greek by *paraklesis or parakalein.*[141] This word group also occurs in the apocalyptic and rabbinic literature of Judaism.[142] One striking example of the central significance of consolation for apocalyptic is the fourth vision of 4 Ezra.[143] Zion's lament amid its present misfortune is compared with the dirge of a woman for her son. Her neighbors cannot comfort her. Ezra finally tries to comfort the woman by referring to Zion's misfortune: "Let yourself be persuaded because of the troubles of Zion, and be consoled because of the sorrow of Jerusalem" (4 Ezra 10:10).[144] While Ezra consoles her thus, the woman, a symbol of Zion, turns into "an established city."[145] In his own turn, the consoler is to be consoled by God by means of this initially terrifying vision: "And behold, you saw her likeness, how she mourned for her son, and you began to console her for what had happened. For now the Most High, seeing that you are sincerely grieved and profoundly distressed for her, has shown you the brightness of her glory, and the loveliness of her beauty" (4 Ezra 10:49f.). The apocalyptist, himself a consoler, requests such consolation yet again after the fifth vision: "Strengthen me and show me, your servant, the interpretation and meaning of this terrifying vision, that you may fully comfort my soul" (4 Ezra 12:8). Already half consoled by the vision of the glory of Zion and its interpretation, Ezra is thus requesting that this consolation now be made complete.

The positive apocalyptist is a consoled consoler.[146] He considers himself sent to those threatening to fall into despair in apocalyptic world anxiety: "Go, therefore, now during these days and instruct the people as much as you can so that they may learn lest they die in the last times, but may learn so that they live in the last times" (*2 Apoc. Bar.* 76:5). Ezra, having been comforted, speaks at the end of the fifth vision to his people: "Take courage, O Israel; and do not be sorrowful, O house of Jacob; for the Most High has you in remembrance, and the Mighty One has not forgotten you in your struggle" (4 Ezra 12:46f.). In his own turn, Ezra is himself consoled by the interpreting angel with quite similar words: "Therefore he [God] sent me to show you all these things, and to say to you: 'Believe and do not be afraid! Do not be quick to think vain thoughts concerning the former things, lest you be anxious concerning the last times' " (4 Ezra 6:33f.).

Like the interpreting angel who consoles the apocalyptist,[147] so also is the revelation itself consolation. The unveiling of the mysteries of the course of history provides consolation amid affliction. The fictitious Baruch writes: "And the Mighty One did according to the multitude of his grace, and the Most High according to the magnitude of his mercy, and he revealed to me a word that I might be comforted, and showed me visions that I might not be again sorrowful, and made known to me the mysteries of the times, and showed me the coming of the periods" (*2 Apoc. Bar.* 81:4). The God who unveils reality is praised as a consoler: "You are the one who reveals to those who fear that which is prepared for them so that you may comfort them" (*2 Apoc. Bar.* 54:4).

However, not only the revelation itself, but also its content, namely, messianic salvation, can be called consolation. Although this is not the case in the Jewish apocalypses, it does occur in rabbinic literature, where "the word *nḥmh*, 'consolation,' 'consoling,' became a comprehensive term for messianic salvation."[148] Picking up on Isa. 40:1f., writers speak of "Zion's consolation," the "days of consolation," the "years of consolation," or the "consolation of Jerusalem," whenever the reference is to messianic salvation.[149]

We become aware of the consoling function of apocalyptic not only in the case of Jewish apocalyptic, but in other contexts as well. This is the case, e.g., with the various notions of a cyclical end of the world. Thus M. Eliade finds that "the Indian theory of the four ages is . . . invigorating and consoling for man under the terror of history."[150] The same applies to the myth of the world conflagration. "Strange as it may seem, the myth was consoling."[151] To recall an example from the sphere of scientific theories of the end of the world, H. von Ditfurth's portrayal of the anticipated global catastrophe is also intended as consolation. Amidst catastrophic developments, the reader is to be consoled that in death we do not fall into nothingness, but rather participate in a spiritual dimension transcending the world we find before us [152] For K. Heim, on the other hand, the Second Law of thermodynamics provides a consoling idea. Entropy breaks through the law of the eternal recurrence of meaninglessness and suffering.[153] The consoling element in Heidegger's later philosophy also became clear. Amidst the apocalyptic abandonment of Being, the consoling notion matures that the most extreme danger is simultaneously the commencement of rescue. This is the consolation mediated by Hölderlin's verse: "But where there is danger, there grows also what saves."[154]

The other aspect of the apocalyptic confrontation of anxiety can be called parenesis. Exhortation to repent or to transform one's behavior and life so as to be found worthy of future redemption occupies an important position in apocalyptic literature. One classic example from the sphere of Jewish apocalyptic is the so-called parenetic book in *1 Enoch*.[155] Enoch's admonitions and warnings, his words of consolation to the believers, and his cries of woe over the wicked[156] are introduced by the historical survey of the ten-week apocalypse,[157] a passage added later to the parenetic book. From this subsequent insertion of the ten-week apocalypse "we see that the parenesis seeks its theological foundation in this only slightly older historical portrayal, and that this historical portrayal itself is to find its goal in the parenesis."[158] In apocalyptic, the unveiling of the course of history, in a broader sense the unveiling of reality, is not an end in itself, but rather serves the end of consolation and parenesis.

A survey of Jewish apocalyptic cannot fail to notice the key position the law occupies in its parenesis. Jewish apocalyptic tries in its own way to preserve the belief of postexilic Judaism that the law is the source of life. "Whoever chooses this law has chosen life."[159] Admittedly, such faith in the vivifying power of the law already experienced a deep crisis even in the pre-Christian period. The experience of a world disclosed by apocalyptic world anxiety casts doubt on the validity of the law. The crisis of wisdom already discernible in Ecclesiastes continues insofar as the law no longer appears as the quintessence of divine order and righteousness in this world, and the result is "that the law is no longer able to carry the burden placed upon it in wisdom theology."[160] The findings of 4 Ezra 14:21 are unnerving: "For your Law has been burned, and so no one knows the things which have been done or will be done by you."[161] Yet Ezra is portrayed as a second Moses who, illuminated by divine wisdom, has the law written down anew.[162] In the case of 4 Ezra, apocalyptic exhorts to hold unwaveringly to the law in the hope that both the fruits of loyalty to the law and God's justice will be revealed in the coming aeon. This holding fast to the law will determine not only individual salvation but also the time of the final judgment and of the renewal of the world. The answer to the question of just when the end will come is: when the number of the righteous is complete.[163] "In this way the present, which with its experience of the world evokes doubt in the law, acquires a basically positive qualification."[164]

History becomes the locus of proving oneself in which the individual decides concerning his participation in future salvation by means of his own loyalty to the law. Something similar applies in *1 Enoch*. According to this apocalypse, too, one's eschatological fate "by no means rests on an act of divine arbitrariness, but rather only and alone on the individual's own responsible decision over against the individual commandments of the law, which always demands a specific 'act' . . . in the sense of concrete fulfillment of the commandments."[165] Since one's eschatological fate depends on one's position over against the law, *1 Enoch* is not "indifferent toward the history which actually precedes judgment; rather, this history is given an eminently positive qualification insofar as it becomes the decisive locus of the eschatological-critical function of the Torah in its concrete individual demands."[166] *Apokalypsis*, the unveiling of reality, renders possible both a new grounding of the law and its reestablishment as the "Law of life" (4 Ezra 14:30), though this law admittedly no longer contains a collective promise to Israel. The eschatological people of God is now comprised of those individuals who remain faithful to the law, and those will be only a few. Precisely that which has been called the universal history of Jewish apocalyptic now proceeds with an individualization of salvation. The apocalyptically disclosed sphere of history is now the individual's locus of self-authentication where faithfulness becomes the deciding factor affecting one's personal eschatological fate.

This parenetic orientation is also attested by other types of apocalyptic, and this applies in a certain respect, e.g., to Heidegger's conception of the history of Being.[167] It finds Hölderlin's consolation unsatisfactory, and instead sets out to follow the traces of a new manner of thinking which is to prepare the way for an eschatological unveiling of Being. Yet Heidegger does not develop any real ethics as such. In contrast, those particular variations of apocalyptic classified as self-destroying prophecy do clearly exhibit the character of appeal, beginning first of all with the various conceptions emerging from the idea of the limits to growth. The study of the Club of Rome—the same can be said of *Global 2000*—appeals to all socially and politically influential powers to become advocates of alternatives to the threat of death resulting from excessive growth.[168] The apocalypse issues in insights, formulated as an appeal, concerning the absolute necessity of incisive alterations in economic life, and thus ultimately also in the behavior of the individual, if the goal of poststabilized harmony on earth is to be attained. Similar appeals include C. Amery's renunciation of the insistence on growth[169] or H. Gruhl's demand for rethinking, material renunciation, and a simple lifestyle.[170] Changing one's own behavior or that of entire groups and societies becomes the precondition for eschatological salvation.

Parenetic inclinations are also exhibited, however, by apocalypses of nuclear holocaust sharing the goal of preventing nuclear catastrophe while yet advocating completely differing political agenda. K. Jaspers's parenesis exhorts us to reverse our course and to reflect on the origin of the human essence. The entire threat is understood as an appeal to a renewed consideration of the question of meaning. Furthermore, apocalyptic anxiety is to be made fruitful and redirected toward political strategies for preventing both nuclear cataclysm as well as totalitarianism.[171] G. Anders's prophylactic apocalyptic also exhibits the character of appeal. The prophylactic apocalyptist is not merely a passive opponent of destruction in the role of a spectator, but rather views himself as charged with acting in a way that works actively against destructive tendencies.[172] Prophylactic apocalyptic issues the challenge to become actively engaged in preserving the world, and pursues the goal of developing a moral imagination encouraging such action.[173] It transforms apocalyptic anxiety into vivifying anxiety which "drives us out into the streets instead of into the corners of our rooms."[174] Precisely this contemporary prophylactic apocalyptic in all its manifestations is parenetic through and through.

Consolation and parenesis constitute the pastoral side of apocalyptic, though this pastoral dimension does also participate in the ambiguity of apocalyptic. The ambiguity of its consolation can be formulated thematically with the catchphrase "consolation and assuagement." Critical dealings with apocalyptic also include the question of the possible assuaging effect of apocalyptic hope. We will raise this question especially in the following section, which examines the problem of the loss of world inherent in apocalyptic. Apocalyptic hope can serve to compensate in an assuaging fashion this loss of world.

Apocalyptic consolation is also ambiguous because it occasionally nourishes itself from craving for decline and the end. A few examples can suffice to illustrate this point. According to *1 Enoch*, God will deliver the kings and the mighty of the earth into the hands of his elect at the end of times; "like grass in the fire and like lead in the water, so they shall burn before the face of the holy ones and sink before their sight, and no trace will be found of them" (*1 Enoch* 48:9).[175] Enoch calls out to the believers: "Be hopeful, you righteous ones, for the sinners shall soon perish from before your presence. You shall be given authority upon them, such authority as you may wish to have" (*1 Enoch* 96:1). The threat to the wicked, however, is quite frank: "Do know that you shall be given over into the hands of the righteous ones, and they shall cut off your necks and slay you, and they shall not have compassion upon you" (*1 Enoch* 98:12). Such words express hatred, vindictiveness, and the craving for destruction and the end, craving that can intensify into sadism. Occasionally, however, masochistic tendencies can also be observed, such as those in *2 Apoc. Bar.* 52:5–7: "And concerning the righteous ones, what will they do now? Enjoy yourselves in the suffering which you suffer now. For why do you look for the decline of your enemies? Prepare your souls for that which is kept for you, and make ready your souls for the reward which is preserved for you." The pleasure derived from the future torments of one's enemies, however, can clearly be discerned in that particular scene in which Enoch views all sorts of instruments of torture. "And I asked the angel of peace, who was going with me, 'For whom are they preparing these chains?' And he answered me, saying, 'They are preparing these for the kings and the potentates of the earth in order that they may be destroyed thereby' "(*1 Enoch* 53:4f.).

It was especially Nietzsche who mercilessly denounced these fantasies of vengeance found in apocalyptic, fantasies continued in the Christian portrayals of the end of the world, e.g., in Tertullian and Augustine, and summarized in Thomas of Aquinas's thesis that in heaven the blessed would view the punishments of the damned so that their, the blessed's, happiness would be complete.[176] For Nietzsche such vindictive fantasies offer conclusive proof of the slave morality of Jewish-Christian ethics: "These weaklings!—they also, forsooth, wish to be the strong some time."[177] This anticipation of the final judgment of the wicked is according to Nietzsche the reflex of an unquenchable hatred for the strong and for the ruling social class. He describes the Apocalypse of John as "that most obscene of all the written outbursts, which has revenge on its conscience." And he adds the additional note: "One should also appraise at its full value the profound logic of the Christian instinct, when over this very book of hate it wrote the name of the Disciple of Love, that selfsame disciple to whom it attributed that impassioned and ecstatic Gospel—therein lurks a portion of truth, however much literary forging may have been necessary for this purpose."[178] As early as our investigation into the sources of apocalyptic hope it seemed questionable to view hatred and envy as the primary motivating factors behind apocalyptic thinking. Apocalyptic results first of all from an experience of powerlessness, and to that extent—here we can agree with Nietzsche—it does articulate the understanding of existence of the weak and the inferior. Although this weakness is not to be summarily rejected out of moral considerations, Nietzsche does correctly see how an experience of powerlessness in the form of eschatological fantasies can be transformed into a craving for vengeance. And although this insight should not in our opinion lead to a fundamental rejection of apocalyptic, it does disclose the ambiguity of apocalyptic which makes a critical attitude in one's dealing with it a necessity.

This ambiguity results from the fact that "the anticipation of the 'postmortem tribunal' participates in the very history of violence against which it protests."[179] Thus J. Ebach follows Nietzsche in objecting "that in the opposition of the apocalyptists we yet find the same value system and standards of those whom they would overcome."[180] Here we encounter once again the potential for violence inherent in hope for the end, potential that can prompt apocalyptic hope to change into a craving for the end.[181] The apparent overcoming of anxiety by the comforting prospect of the final judgment can in this case express what is actually unmastered anxiety. F. Kümmel has drawn attention to this connection between violence and unmastered anxiety.[182] "Unmastered anxiety leads to violence, and violence is at its core anxiety and itself generates anxiety."[183] Hence precisely this craving for the end is a symptom of unmastered world anxiety, and apocalyptic is an attempt at mastering that anxiety which doubtlessly can and often enough has foundered. This once again throws new light on apocalyptic activism. The transformation of apocalyptic into both fantasies and acts of violence can result from a foundering of apocalyptic: "Anxiety and violence are moving toward their own destruction. World conflagration is to extinguish its own fire."[184] The potential foundering of apocalyptic in its attempt at overcoming world anxiety, however, settles neither those questions addressed to it nor those generated within it. Hence "a pacifistic criticism of the dimensions of violence and vengeance," for example, "must also be evaluated according to whether it, like apocalyptic, holds fast to the demand for justice."[185]

No less ambivalent than apocalyptic consolation are the parenetic goals of apocalyptic. Parenesis which calls for repentance can anticipate the eschatological division of humankind into two groups, effecting thus a division between those within and those without, and concentrating only on the deliverance of those who in a certain measure are already within. Instead of portraying the gruesome fate of the wicked, apocalyptic parenesis in this case screens out the fate of those outside. Ezra is admonished: "But think of your own case, and inquire concerning the glory of those who are like yourself . . . Therefore do not ask any more questions about the multitude of those who perish" (4 Ezra 8:51, 55). *2 Apoc. Bar.* 48:48 reads similarly: "But now, let us cease talking about the wicked and inquire about the righteous." Such parenesis exhorts its listeners to persevere. Rather than the deliverance of humankind it is now exclusively one's own deliverance that moves to the center of apocalyptic. Among others, J. Moltmann has criticized this sort of "exhortation to persevere." The object of his criticism is the determinism inherent in apocalyptic parenesis. Through this exhortation to persevere, "faith and unbelief, good and evil, election and reprobation, righteous and unrighteous are firmly established, and what matters is to abide by what we are."[186] Moltmann understands this attempt at perseverance not as a sign of a strengthening of identity, but rather quite the reverse as a symptom of a weakness of identity: "He who is of little faith looks for support and protection for his faith, because it is preyed upon by fear."[187] The apocalyptic inclination to conventicle existence can accordingly be precisely the result of unmastered apocalyptic anxiety, the symptom of a failure of apocalyptic, and can conceal within it the danger of a loss of identity arising when the apocalyptic negation of the world leads to a total loss of world.[188] The ambiguity of apocalyptic culminates in the danger of such loss of world.

5. Disengagement from the World as Loss of World: A Critique of Apocalyptic

World negation is apocalyptic's answer to apocalyptic world anxiety.[189] What is negated is an inescapable world threatening to pull the anxiety-plagued person along with it down into destruction. The apocalyptic understanding of existence negates the world in order to rescue existence. As we have already seen,[190] apocalyptic can be described more precisely as a mode of latent world denial. Hence apocalyptic world negation is not without further qualification to be equated with flight from the world and loss of world. Quite the contrary, it is precisely apocalyptic which can be a way of confronting the world and its negative elements instead of avoiding them. The reality of the oppressive and inescapable world as disclosed by apocalyptic anxiety is not denied, but on the contrary uncovered and sharply delineated. As latent world denial, apocalyptic tries to overcome world anxiety without passing over present reality. This form of world denial is latent because it at once takes present reality seriously and negates it by anticipating the future end of the world. This anticipation of the end of the world, however, leads in apocalyptic to an existential tension between the present experience of reality on the one hand, and the wish for its sublation on the other.

This negation of the world by apocalyptic is ambiguous. It vacillates between the possibilities of an attack on the world, flight from the world, and a complete loss of world. Its world negation can equally be a protest of the powerless against a world that is overwhelming in its inescapability, as well as an expression of utter resignation. Just as it can issue in an existential attitude of quietism, so also in a reverse fashion in an attitude focused on actively mastering existence and reshaping the world. On the other hand, precisely this will to reshape the world in apocalyptic can change into the will to take an active role in its destruction. The negation of world need not be limited to the conceptual anticipation of the end of the world, but can under certain circumstances become the goal of apocalyptic activism. Hope in the end fluctuates between protest and assuagement.

In view of such ambiguity, unequivocal statements concerning apocalyptic world negation are problematical. Interpretations are questionable which without justification equate world negation with world flight and thus accuse apocalyptic *in toto* of a loss of world, loss of history, or loss of reality and escapism. Although this criticism of apocalyptic is to a certain extent justified, as the following concluding discussion shows, it does not address the complete truth of apocalyptic ambiguity. On the other hand, neither are those interpretations sound which view the apocalyptic understanding of history one-sidedly as salvation-historical thinking. Where apocalyptic is alleged to be involved not in a loss of history, but rather in the first real acquisition of a concept of history, i.e., where apocalyptic is not accused of the "dehistoricization of history,"[191] but rather is extolled for conceptualizing for the first time a real understanding of history,[192] one easily overlooks the fact that the apocalyptic notion of universal history encourages the negation of any salvation within history and stands thus completely in the service of world negation.[193]

By no means does apocalyptic world negation in every case mean a loss of world. It need not evade the world, but rather can very well constitute an attack on that world. What H. Jonas asserted for gnosis is essentially true of apocalyptic, namely, that it was not resigned flight from the world, but rather an assault on the world and an energetic attempt at mastering existence.[194] Hence the one-sidedness of Bultmann's objection is problematical according to which apocalyptic was the equivalent of a dehistoricization of history. Jewish apocalyptic in any case is an assault against a world whose inescapability in its own turn threatens to lead to a loss of history. It is not apocalyptic, but rather the constitution of reality that leads to the possibility of a cessation or sublation of history. Over against this, Jewish apocalyptic, for example, hopes precisely for the deliverance of the historical disposition of the world or for its reestablishment through God's intervention. It is not history as such, but rather the previous history of disaster which is to be sublated or brought to an end, history that in the eyes of apocalyptic of necessity leads to the sublation of all historical movement as a result of a loss of the dimension of the future.[195] Neither does apocalyptic in every case enter upon a flight from history, since at least in the case of Jewish apocalyptic the individual is directed to history as the locus of confirming one's faithfulness.[196] The apocalyptist focused on proving his faithfulness in the sphere of history hopes for a new future and thus for a new historical existence beyond the catastrophe.

The cost of this apocalyptic attack on the world is, to be sure, "that one may now speak of the world in which we live only in eschatological negation."[197] For just this reason, apocalyptic means not only an attack on the world but also "life in deferment" or in a condition of abeyance. The fact that apocalyptic speaks of the world only in eschatological negation can result in a hindering of one's final engagement in history as the locus of proving oneself. Within Judaism, the "price of messianism" according to G. Scholem thus consists in the weakness of "something preliminary, something provisional," something unable "to give of itself entirely."[198] The ambiguity of apocalyptic world negation corresponds to the ambivalence of apocalyptic existence. "There is something grand about living in hope, but at the same time there is something profoundly unreal about it. It diminishes the singular worth of the individual, and he can never fulfill himself, because the incompleteness of his endeavors eliminates precisely what constitutes its highest value. Thus in Judaism the Messianic idea has compelled a *life lived in deferment*, in which nothing can be done definitively, nothing can be irrevocably accomplished."[199]

This condition of abeyance is also where hope abides in Bloch's thinking, hope which is the heir to Jewish-Christian apocalyptic. The world appears as *experimentum*, as *laboratorium possibilis salutis*[200] in which new procedural instructions are constantly being tested and discarded without ever claiming to be definitive. Human existence and world history are merely an experiment in the case of whose failure the attempt can be repeated or improved, with nothing lost. "Such knowledge-conscience as the inherited substratum of religion cited above, i.e., as the mindfulness that it is *hope in totality*, at the same time grasps the essence of the world in tremendous suspense, towards something enormous which hope believes is good, which active hope works to ensure is good."[201] This hope in totality thus denies the finality of historical existence and the irrevocability of life that has been lived and history that has taken place. For Bloch, its finality is negated by the idea of the extraterritoriality of an as yet unilluminated core of existence to death.[202] "But where and by what means does there enter into this perpetually preliminary, i.e., hoping messianic life and thinking something that is final, an engagement in concrete actuality without reservation and without the possibility of evasion, a complete surrender to being able to die?"[203] This is a question we should, with Moltmann, direct critically to Bloch's philosophy of a hope in totality.

Quite independently of Bloch, G. Anders has in a different context also leveled criticism against any understanding of the world as an experimental field. "What one calls 'experiments' are . . . pieces of our reality; of our historic reality . . . For history acknowledges no joking, no 'once does not necessarily mean always.' It refuses to retract or recant, the word 'attempt' is unknown to it. There is no free experimentation in it, since everything announcing itself with the modest asseveration of only taking place as an experiment immediately occurs 'once and for all,' and thus takes place as 'the real thing.' "[204] In this point, criticism of apocalyptic can be summarized as the assertion that the notion it presents of a world in a state of suspension is an illusion deceiving us concerning the historic constitution both of reality as well as of our own existence.

The place of life in deferment can also be taken by flight before or out of the world. The ambiguity of apocalyptic includes the possibility that world negation in it can be a mode of world flight. For example, *2 Apoc. Bar.* 2:1 issues a call to flight. The faithful are to leave Jerusalem. The admonishment of the Apocalypse of John is quite similar: "Come out of her [Babylon], my people, lest you take part in her sins, lest you share in her plagues" (Rev. 18:4).[205] The prototype of this flight from a city condemned to destruction is the withdrawal of Lot and his family from the city of Sodom, which has been given over to divine judgment.[206] We can for the moment leave unanswered the question whether the Apocalypse of John is summoning to an emigration from the Roman Empire, or whether the reference is an "inner emigration."[207] Both forms of world flight—actual withdrawal and flight into inwardness—are attested in the sphere of apocalyptic.

We can recall the wanderings of the Tupi-Guarani as an example of actual flight.[208] At periodic intervals they tried to reach the ocean in order to be taken up there into paradise before the end of the world. Like such journeys, the inner emigration of the apocalyptist can also be questionable escapism.[209] Literary parallels include under certain circumstances the heavenly journeys and throne visions familiar from apocalyptic literature.[210] One also encounters variations of such mythical or conceptual escapism in contemporary types of apocalyptic. Examples can be found in connection with the expectation of nuclear catastrophe. For this case some people reckon with the existence of alien intelligence on other planets. "There the course of reason which founders for us continues forward in a different reality. There beings live which, within time, continue or begin anew or complete or also fail in what did not succeed for us here on earth."[211] Although the existence of alien intelligence is a scientific hypothesis quite possibly worthy of consideration, in an apocalyptic context it serves—as K. Jaspers criticizes—the attempt at evading the totality of the threatening end.[212] Recourse to God can also derive from escapist tendencies. Instead of intelligent extraterrestrial beings, God emerges as the representative of our selves. "By setting up an intelligence that itself escapes extinction and looks down upon the event, and by endowing that intelligence with suspiciously human characteristics, we in effect deny or evade the reality of extinction, for we have covertly manufactured a survivor."[213] In this respect we will in our final chapter pose the question concerning the extent to which the Christian faith and Christian theology are in fact in a position to confront the idea of the end, and the extent to which their attempt at mastering anxiety is more than an escapist strategy of assuagement.

Finally, we should not overlook the fact that apocalyptic escapism also has a political dimension. Hanson criticizes apocalyptic's "lavish use of myth" as "a tempting escape" and views it as an "escape from this fallen order" meant for those who had lost social power.[214] The mark of every apocalyptic movement is allegedly a "world-weariness" which seeks in myth the "source of repose from a reality which they find too brutal to integrate into their apocalyptic vision."[215] With an eye on the Apocalypse of John, D. Bonhoeffer warned the church of the political questionability of apocalyptic. "The complete fulfilment of its mission will always be gravely endangered if the congregation supposes itself too directly to be placed in the situation of Rev. 13. The apocalyptic proclamation may well be a flight from the *primus usus* [*legis*]."[216] Apocalyptic—to expand this warning somewhat—can mislead us into flight from political responsibility. This by no means asserts that political escapism drives apocalyptic—as, to be sure, can often be observed—into a politically conservative camp.[217] Politically progressive movements can also constitute this sort of "flight-movement."[218]

Ultimately, this flight before the world leads to a loss of world. Although apocalyptic parenesis does indeed direct one to the present world as the locus of proving oneself, as parenesis of perseverance it constitutes a demand for disengagement from the world, and the loss of world is the final consequence of apocalyptic disengagement from the world. P. D. Hanson observes in this respect a development within Jewish apocalyptic. "Their [the postexilic descendants of the prophets] attitude toward the historical realm as the arena of Yahweh's saving acts first became one of indifference, finally of hostility."[219] If this view of the world in abeyance on the one hand, and life in deferment on the other are based on a deception concerning the actual disposition of history, then hope in a complete sublation of history is decidedly antihistorical. As M. Eliade has pointed out (albeit too sweepingly), some—but admittedly only some—notions deriving from the sphere of Jewish apocalyptic, notions that reckon with a complete annihilation of the existing world and the emergence of a completely different one while not mentioning any real history beyond the catastrophe, do "indicate an *antihistoric* attitude."[220] The diagnosis of R. Bultmann (again, too unspecific) also applies to some apocalyptic hopes, namely, that "the end is not the completion of history but its breaking off."[221] Similarly, P. D. Hanson's thesis is also too sweeping and thus problematical: "Prophetic eschatology is transformed into apocalyptic at the point where the task of translating the cosmic vision into the categories of mundane reality is abdicated."[222] Although this thesis must be rejected as an overgeneralization, it does draw attention to the possible loss of reality in apocalyptic. Such loss of reality causes apocalyptic to become ideological, and becomes possible because "apocalyptic includes a return to a mythopoetic view of reality."[223] Finally, the possibility cannot be excluded that the loss of world in apocalyptic is not the culmination of the experience of an inescapable world, but rather quite the reverse the manifestation of an inflexible consciousness incapable of confronting a reality caught in the process of historic changes.[224]

In this case we are fully justified in speaking of an ideologization of apocalyptic, though if this estimation is not to remain exclusively pejorative, the concept of ideology must at this point be specified more closely. We speak of a possible ideologization of apocalyptic in the sense of the sociological definition of K. Mannheim, according to which a consciousness is ideological "when it fails to take account of the new realities applying to a situation, and when it attempts to conceal them by thinking of them in categories which are inappropriate."[225] Sociologically, then, such apocalyptic can be interpreted in Mannheim's sense as structural ideology, though we also have seen examples in which apocalyptic is enlisted as functional ideology in the service of particular interest and power groups.[226] Its necessary criticism is of political significance.

As the highest intensification of the expectation of the end of the world and of apocalyptic hope in the end, the idea of the *annihilatio mundi* anticipates the potential loss of world in apocalyptic. Or better: It is the expression of what is at least a latent loss of world that has already occurred. Precisely the most extreme escalation of apocalyptic world negation allows its ambiguity to emerge in exaggerated clarity. On the one hand, the anticipated sublation of history uncovers mercilessly and with unsurpassable clarity the negative elements and the catastrophic dimension of our reality. Yet on the other hand, apocalyptic consciousness capitulates in this case before the facticity of reality. In this final consequence apocalyptic leads to a surrender of the world, a world that together with the greater portion of humankind is given over to its fate. Apocalyptic is then no longer an assault on the world, but rather resignation that capitulates before the catastrophic nature of history and before the reality of unveiled evil. In its most extreme forms, the world negation of apocalyptic is thus transformed into a sanctioning of the status quo. It is precisely the most radical hope of which apocalyptic is capable—namely, that history be sublated and the world

6

CHRISTIAN FAITH AND THE APOCALYPTIC WORLD EXPERIENCE

> The essence of Christianity is world affirmation which has passed through world negation.
>
> —*Albert Schweitzer*

> Hope is justified only through faith, and faith justifies itself. Perhaps both flourish only on the ruins of all-too-human hopes and expectations, on the fertile ground of despair in everything that is subject to illusion and disappointment.
>
> —*Karl Löwith*

1. Theology in View of the End

Apocalyptic is a theological challenge. It challenges theological thinking because the latter itself harbors an apocalyptic heritage, a scandalous and largely unpopular heritage. The relationship between the Christian faith and apocalyptic is not only a historical, but with increasing urgency also a systematic-theological problem. The question arises concerning just what relationship obtains between an apocalyptic understanding of existence on the one hand, and the Christian understanding on the other. This question becomes the more urgent in a historic situation situated completely in the shadow of global threat. If Christian theology has any reference to reality, and if statements of faith are to be relevant in the dispute concerning what is real,[1] then the danger of the nuclear annihilation of all life on earth must be taken seriously as a theological problem. Even a person who does not consider himself among the modern apocalyptists of the nuclear holocaust cannot avoid the realization that the technical knowledge alone of how to construct an atomic bomb constitutes a threat to humankind which can never be eliminated, not even with the total elimination of all nuclear weapons at our disposal today. The nuclear threat, at very least, constitutes not a temporary, but rather an irrevocable global threat. The actual possibility of an end to all life is now a constituent part of our reality. Any theology claiming to make relevant statements concerning reality has to confront the possibility of the end. Any theological dealing with apocalyptic today can thus take place only in view of the threat of such an end.

One must take seriously the insight that humankind has no guarantee of survival, and that the Christian faith cannot provide such a guarantee. This realization shocks theological thinking, and thus far very few theologians have mustered the courage to confront this fact. Not a few people yet believe that the God of hope assures the continuation of human beings and nature. Such a theological guarantee of survival, however, comes extremely close to a kind of supranaturalism which today can no longer be considered theologically responsible. On the other hand, anyone who confronts the fact that the Christian faith can also not guarantee the continuation of earthly life, finds, in view of this conceivable end, that the truth itself of the Christian message is now at stake. One of the few who summoned the courage to state this truth was Paul Tillich. He dared to raise the unavoidable question: "Would the suicide of mankind be a refutation of the Christian message?"[2] The threat of the end forces us to reconsider both the essence of faith as well as its doctrine of God as the creator, reconciler, and redeemer. The question is not only what meaning the eschatological statements have, but also what meaning statements concerning creation, especially the doctrine of preservation, can yet have in view of the possibility of the annihilation of all life. Any theology refusing to draw the consequences inherent in this realization that the Christian faith does not offer humankind any guarantee of survival has failed to perform its task.[3]

Apocalyptic, at least positive apocalyptic, can be understood as pastoral care for those afflicted by anxiety in view of the end. The question arises whether and how the Christian faith is capable of such pastoral care today, and whence that faith itself draws support in view of the threatening catastrophe. Accordingly, we need to ask what role apocalyptic thinking plays in the Christian faith's understanding of reality. We will consider this first with regard to the New Testament. This relationship, however, must be reconsidered with respect to the contemporary situation of humankind. To this end, the question concerning the relationship between faith and apocalyptic must be expanded through a theology of world anxiety that comprehends world anxiety as a theological problem. Theology in view of an end that has now become quite conceivable must inquire concerning the significance anxiety has for faith. The Christian faith will be capable of providing sincere pastoral counseling for those afflicted by anxiety, however, only if it gives an account of just what it is that lends support to its own attitude toward existence in view of the threatening end. Otherwise it runs the risk of being mistaken for a leap into the irrational or the supranatural, leading not to a mastering of reality, but rather to flight before it. The serious consideration of apocalyptic can protect theology from religious escapism and lead to a reflection on what is required today and what can yet be said theologically in view of the end.

2. Apocalyptic and Christian Faith in the New Testament

The relationship between apocalyptic thinking and Christian faith is a cardinal question within New Testament exegesis, one whose answer has remained extremely controversial even into the present. Historical and systematic-theological arguments are interwoven in the various attempts at a solution. Just as every religio-historical explanation of this relationship generally implies a systematic-theological judgment, so also in a reverse fashion do systematic-theological interests not infrequently influence exegetical judgments. "Exegesis often betrays more of what scholars do not want to see than what they do see."[4] This applies not least to the evaluation of the relationship between apocalyptic and Christianity within New Testament exegesis.[5]

The perplexity and aversion over against apocalyptic documented throughout the course of the history of research reveals a substantive problem. The question concerning the nature and form of the relationship between Christianity and apocalyptic in the New Testament cannot be addressed simply by classifying certain texts, textual groups, or elements of transmission as apocalyptic, or by excluding the same from apocalyptic. Texts such as the Apocalypse of John, Mark 13 par., 2 Thess. 2, Jude, or 2 Peter 3 attest at most that apocalyptic can be found *in* the New Testament. In fact, that there is apocalyptic *in* Christianity, and that there has been since its beginnings, is undisputed, so that in this respect one might argue merely concerning the scope of apocalyptic traditions in Christianity. This, however, is not the real problem. The decisive question is whether Christianity is itself a form of apocalyptic, i.e., whether one must speak not about apocalyptic *in* Christianity, but rather about Christianity itself as a form of apocalyptic and thus about the apocalyptic essence of Christianity.

This question cannot be decided, however, simply by adducing in an isolated fashion apocalyptic traditions and notions found in New Testament texts.[6] In those instances when clearly apocalyptic views are represented in New Testament texts, it is not infrequently—especially in more recent texts—a matter of isolated *topoi* not exhibiting any specifically Christian basis. Relatively independent of basic Christian ideas, various passages address among other things the delay of the Parousia[7] or details of the tribulations of the end time[8] and of the last judgment.[9] Like such discussions, so also did primitive Christian prophecy probably hardly go beyond the traditional framework of apocalyptic thinking.[10] Such references, however, hardly answer the essential question, a question whose solution demands rather an investigation of New Testament texts at large from the perspective we have formulated.

For a specific reason, New Testament texts have largely been omitted from our preceding discussion. The inclusion of New Testament writings in our analysis of the apocalyptic understanding of existence would have anticipated the answer to the question concerning the relationship between apocalyptic and Christianity, a question that only now can really be raised, i.e., after we have exhaustively dealt with apocalyptic as such.

A comprehensive treatment of the question concerning the inner relationship between apocalyptic and Christianity in the New Testament transcends the parameters of this study. Instead, we can deal with the problem only in a summary fashion on the basis of a few examples—relevant ones, to be sure. For this reason it is advisable not to limit this question too exclusively to the Apocalypse of John. Instead, we will look briefly at the general problem in Paul, the Synoptics, and in the Johannine circle, and then finally draw some more general conclusions.[11]

In his letters, Paul employs numerous terms and concepts deriving traditiohistorically from Jewish apocalyptic.[12] One can mention the doctrine of the ages,[13] discussions concerning righteousness and judgment,[14] the idea of a new creation,[15] and Paul's understanding of the Parousia, the resurrection of the dead, the rapture of the congregation, and the final judgment.[16]

Although the influence of apocalyptic notions on Paul's theology is unmistakable,[17] its significance for Pauline thinking is exegetically disputed. As is well known, Bultmann advocated the thesis that ultimately Paul stood outside apocalyptic and "interpreted the apocalyptic view of history on the basis of his anthropology."[18] J. Becker emphatically defended Bultmann's thesis particularly against E. Käsemann's interpretation of Paul.[19] And G. Delling, for example, concedes an extensive, albeit not exclusive influence of Jewish apocalyptic on Pauline theology,[20] although in his view apocalyptic merely constitutes the "background" of Paul's theology, "in particular of its basic eschatological line,"[21] and by no means can be taken as the hermeneutical *passe-partout* of primitive Christian or Pauline theology.[22]

In contrast, E. Käsemann's investigations have shown that Pauline theology on the whole does exhibit a fundamental apocalyptic character, even if in his letters Paul does not develop any apocalyptic system. Put succinctly and initially with a bit of exaggeration: "Even when he became a Christian, Paul remained an apocalyptist."[23] What Bultmann called anthropology leads not to a dissolution of apocalyptic, but quite the reverse, like soteriology, is developed within the framework of apocalyptic thinking. Not only Paul's eschatology and his understanding of history,[24] but also his doctrine of justification[25] and finally his ethics[26] prove to be a specific continuation of apocalyptic. Among other things, the battle against the present eschatology of the enthusiasm predominating in Corinth is fought under the auspices of this apocalyptic.[27]

Admittedly, one is justified in speaking of Paul's apocalyptic only if one remembers that his theology no longer moves within the traditional framework of Jewish apocalyptic, but rather pushes forward to its own type of apocalyptic. Paul was not an apocalyptic theologian in the sense that he merely interpreted the Christian faith and its message within the framework of thinking that otherwise remained unaltered, thinking to which in this form he would have adhered even in his pre-Christian period.[28] Rather, a reciprocal relationship obtains for Paul between the Christian message and its apocalyptic interpretation. On the one hand, the kerygma, more generally the message of the salvific significance of Jesus, is interpreted in apocalyptic categories. On the other hand, however, this apocalyptic thinking is modified christologically.

At the center of this reciprocal influence stands Christology. Especially the understanding of Easter as an eschatological event, referred to as a resurrection from the dead, is decisively influenced by Jewish apocalyptic.[29] This faith in the resurrection of Jesus, however, decisively altered the content of the notion of resurrection. In Paul, this process leads to a christological functionalization and transformation of apocalyptic ideas. His Christology transcends the traditional framework of Jewish apocalyptic. This explains "Paul's active role over against the traditional apocalyptic material," something especially evident in 1 Cor. 15. "Paul is not merely a tradent, he is a reinterpreter, indeed a re-former of traditional eschatology" who occasionally shows himself to be a "creative apocalyptist."[30] Actually, the plethora of apocalyptic material is sooner reduced. The Pauline reworking of apocalyptic materials exhibits a tendency toward reduction with the goal of concentrating on the Christ-statement.[31] Except for larger textual passages such as 1 Cor. 15, Paul's individual future-apocalyptic statements stand only loosely connected, and are never worked into a closed apocalyptic system. Whenever Paul speaks about his own personal hope, he by no means does so in a decidedly apocalyptic fashion.[32]

Apocalyptic traditions are familiar to Paul not only from Judaism, but are also already found in pre-Pauline primitive Christianity. Texts such as 1 Thess. 4:13ff. or 1 Cor. 15 show us that Paul understands the apocalyptic hope in the future as an interpretation of the Christian kerygma. Generally one can say that "through reference back to and a reinterpretation of primitive Christian apocalyptic Paul expounds faith as hope in view of the experience of the world from a christological perspective."[33] In its own turn, this christological perspective now exercises considerable influence back on the apocalyptic sources. In the case of Paul's theology, it is a matter of "apocalyptic modified by faith in Jesus."[34] This christological modification raises the question concerning the extent to which the Christian understanding of existence in Paul really is apocalyptic or has already left the apocalyptic understanding of existence behind. We will address this question later from a systematic-theological perspective. For now at least we find that the apocalyptic notions found in Paul are neither rudimentary and thus theologically insignificant remnants of his Judaism nor a mere variation of apocalyptic thinking which might be understood as a linear development within the history of Jewish apocalyptic.

As in Paul, so also are apocalyptic influences discernible in the Synoptic Gospels. The occurrence of apocalyptic motifs, however, does not necessarily allow the conclusion that the authors of the Gospels were apocalyptists. The composers of the Gospels extract apocalyptic material from the primitive Christian tradition and work it into the new genre of the Gospels, a genre that in and of itself is not an apocalyptic literary form. The significance which the material from the apocalyptic tradition might have at the level of the Gospels themselves, i.e., at the redactional level, needs to be examined in each individual case.

The sayings source Q, which served as a source for the Gospels of Matthew, Luke, as well as of Mark,[35] might have been a document of primitive Christian apocalyptic.[36] Q was read in congregations in which primitive Christian prophecy and apocalyptic had entered into "an indissoluble union."[37] Q represents a kind of compendium of the teachings of Jesus, with its interest clearly focused on the eschatological element of this teaching. Jesus' proclamation is according to Q that of the eschatological judge foretold by John the Baptist. The emphasis is on the idea of judgment. Furthermore, Q implicitly develops a Christology preferring the title of the Son of Man deriving from Jewish apocalyptic, even though both messianic and wisdom influences are discernible in Q's Christology in addition to the apocalyptic influence. As far as the significance of apocalyptic in the New Testament is concerned, it is doubtless significant that both Matthew and Luke used the sayings source extensively. On the other hand, one should not overlook the fact that although Q did apparently enjoy its own independent history of influence after the composition of the Gospels of Matthew and Luke, it was not canonized as an independent writing, but rather in the long run remained acceptable within the later church at large only as incorporated into the genre of the Gospels.[38]

That apocalyptic is of considerable significance not only within the so-called sayings source, but also within the framework of the Gospel of Mark, is attested not so much by individual sayings or christological titles such as that of the Son of Man, which Mark employs more frequently than other titles of majesty,[39] as by what is known as the Little Apocalypse in Mark 13. E. Brandenburger has recently shown that Jesus' eschatological discourse in Mark is from a form-critical perspective indeed an apocalypse.[40] Mark 13 is probably based on a written source[41] which was presumably not a Jewish, but rather a Jewish-Christian apocalypse from the time of the Jewish War,[42] one interpreting contemporary events as a sign of the end time and of Christ's imminent Parousia. However, not only the source, but also the Markan composition itself is structured according to apocalyptic motifs, genre elements, and conceptual patterns. "The overall form is . . . not simply a sum of individual genres. Rather, everything is influenced at a higher level by the latent interest in clarifying a problem, one conceived in the apocalyptic conceptual framework, through the unveiling of eschatological mysteries, and in mediating behavioral rules on the basis of such clarification. To that extent one can very well, indeed one must call Mark 13 an apocalypse."[43] The Markan redaction is by no means, as has often been asserted, antiapocalyptic, but rather reworks the problem of disillusioned hopes in the Parousia very much within the conceptual framework of central apocalyptic presuppositions. What is genuinely new over against Jewish apocalyptic, however, is that now it is not a mythical angelic figure or a fictitious person from early history, but rather Jesus of Nazareth who reveals the events of the end time. This involves more than a merely formal shift. Its basis is rather the confession to Jesus as the exalted Son of Man. The apocalyptic teacher of revelation "is marked by christologically informed knowledge. Thus the peculiar conception emerges that the departing and returning *kyrios*, the Son of Man from heaven and the earthly revelatory mediator Jesus constitute essentially a unity."[44] The Gospel as a portrayal of the life of Jesus, comparable from the perspective of genre history to the biography of the suffering righteous person,[45] supplies the framework for a christologically based apocalypse. Furthermore, within the overall composition of the Gospel the apocalypse Mark 13 occupies a prominent position. Placed before the passion story, it appears as the legacy the Son of Man leaves to his disciples.[46]

Both Matthew and Luke appropriate Jesus' apocalyptic eschatological discourse from Mark 13,[47] and in Luke it even reappears in a doublet deriving from Q.[48] To be sure, varying shifts in emphasis can be observed in Matthew and Luke not only in comparison with Mark 13, but regarding eschatology in general.

The Gospel of Matthew begins with a view of history divided into periods reminiscent of apocalyptic notions of history (Matt. 1:2ff.), extending the curve following Mark 13 as far as the *synteleia tou aiōnos*,[49] which coincides temporally with the Parousia of the Son of Man and is associated with the *katabolē tou kosmou*.[50] Admittedly, the question of the exact time remains unresolved, and both imminent expectation as well as distant expectation can be accommodated to the eschatological views of the Gospel of Matthew. On the one hand, Matthew maintains characteristic formulations of imminent expectation,[51] while on the other hand a situation of uncertainty concerning the date of the Parousia takes the place of the pressing end-time catastrophe. As a result, the eschatological reveille as found in the pre-Matthean tradition is replaced by a "vigilance parenesis"[52] issuing a call to perpetual preparedness in the face of the end of the world expected at any moment.[53] To a large extent the motif of the pressing imminence of the Parousia is replaced by that of severe judgment, a motif also promulgated in connection with the post-Easter church.[54] On the other hand, the eschatological events are portrayed with more detail in the Gospel of Matthew than in his sources, with statements concerning the events of the end time coming into a certain tension with the complex of statements concerning the kingdom of God.[55] The kingdom of the Son of Man, about which one can also speak in the present tense, is conceived together with the kingdom of God, which according to Matthew is already present.[56]

The shifts in emphasis over against Mark 13 are even more noticeable in the Gospel of Luke than in Matthew. The introductory question to Jesus in Luke 21:7 already no longer speaks about eschatological fulfillment as does Mark 13:4, but rather about innerworldly events. According to Luke 21:7, the prophecy concerning the imminent Parousia is a misunderstanding. The persecution of the Christian community is separated from the eschatological events of the end, which thereby are deferred into the future. The destruction of the Jerusalem temple and the events of the Jewish War are not interpreted as signs of the imminent Parousia, which lies rather in the distant future. The Q doublet Luke 17:20f. explicitly rejects the question concerning the time of the Parousia and instead asserts that the kingdom of God is already in the midst of us.[57] The Gospel of Luke clearly reflects an experience of prolonged time which refuted the initial imminent expectation of primitive Christianity. In Luke, Jesus appears as the caesura between two epochs (Luke 16:16), and the position occupied by the end time is taken by the time of the church, qualified positively as a time of salvation. The thesis according to which Luke completely replaced the Parousia expectation with a concept of salvation history is problematical.[58] Passages such as Luke 3:9, 17; 10:9, 11; 18:7f.; 12:45f.; and 21:32 sooner suggest that despite his qualification of the present as a time of salvation, Luke does nonetheless hold fast to the expectation of the Parousia. Although the time till the end of the world is prolonged, it is still perilously short.[59] The theme of the Parousia also plays a role in Acts, here in connection with the ascension in Acts 1:1–12. The ascension anticipates the commencement of the time of the church and, in the fashion of a mirror image, also Christ's Parousia: "This Jesus, who was taken up from you into heaven, will come in the same way as you saw him go into heaven" (Acts 1:11).[60] Like the Gospel, Acts also shows that despite the aforementioned—in part considerable—modifications, Luke basically did not leave the framework of traditional primitive-Christian eschatology.[61]

It may seem odd that we have until now excluded the question concerning the position of the historical Jesus over against apocalyptic. Several objective considerations, however, support this exclusion. In the first place, this question can be discussed only on the basis of the Synoptic Gospels, which can be considered as historical sources for questions concerning the historical Jesus. Any investigation of the position of Jesus over against apocalyptic implies a distinction between authentic original sources, the post-Easter tradition, and written redactional activity, a distinction requiring extraordinary methodological effort.[62] Most importantly, however, the question we raised in the preceding discussion concerning the relationship between the Christian faith and apocalyptic thinking in the New Testament is a theological question that actually must be put not to the Jew Jesus, but rather to the witnesses of post-Easter faith. This insight, formulated especially by R. Bultmann, has encountered considerable resistance without ever really being refuted. The debate surrounding the historical Jesus, a debate carried on since the 1950s with the goal of getting beyond Bultmann's "fact that" Jesus came, has not really demonstrated persuasively that Jesus and his message belong not to the presuppositions of the Christian proclamation, but rather to Christianity itself.[63]

To a large extent, representatives of the thesis of the unity of the historical Jesus and the Christ of the New Testament message have confused the question concerning the historical continuity between Jesus' activity and the primitive-Christian proclamation with the question concerning the substantive-theological relationship between these two entities. A positive response to the question concerning the historical continuity between the proclamation of Jesus and that of the primitive church, a response of the sort variously offered by E. Fuchs, G. Ebeling, E. Käsemann, H. Conzelmann, or G. Bornkamm, by no means resolves the question concerning the substantive unity of the two. J. M. Robinson and H. Braun have seen this problem most clearly. Proof of historical continuity does not answer the question why the proclaimer become the proclaimed, and why the Christian message is something more and different than the mere repetition of the preaching of Jesus. The Christian faith does not repeat what one might call the faith of Jesus, but rather is faith in Jesus as the Christ. In this sense one can say in any case that Jesus was not a Christian, just as presumably he did not demand from others faith in himself as the Christ. For just this reason, however, an objective discontinuity obtains between the Christian proclamation and that of the historical Jesus. The question concerning the relationship between Jesus and Jewish apocalyptic is historically naturally just as legitimate as that concerning Jesus' influence on the post-Easter theology of the primitive church. Despite all of this, however, it plays a subordinate role for our topic systematically, and for that reason Jesus' position over against apocalyptic needs to be addressed only in the form of an indication of the problem itself.

Whether Jesus was indeed an apocalyptist, and to what extent his proclamation of the imminent *basileia* was influenced by apocalyptic views is a central problem within the framework of the question concerning the historical Jesus. The picture A. Schweitzer drew of the apocalyptist Jesus is not without its problems; according to this view, the apocalyptist Jesus preached the imminent end of the world and finally sought to force the advent of the kingdom of God by provoking his own death in Jerusalem.[64] On the other hand, the widely observable and labored effort of New Testament exegesis is no less problematical which seeks to rescue Jesus from apocalyptic and to present a counterimage of an unapocalyptic Jesus.[65] One possible direction that might offer a solution to the historical problem is that Jesus' proclamation represents a peculiar *variation* of apocalyptic.[66] According to this view, Jesus' proclamation of the imminence of the kingdom of God is in both its agreement and its differences very much indebted to apocalyptic. "His originality *as* an apocalyptist would consist in this variation, not in some abstract, unprecedented new revelatory message (kerygma) deriving its authority only from within itself and demanding obedience and faith. This variation manifested itself especially in a new qualification of the present."[67] One must keep in mind, however, that the question concerning the relationship between Christianity and apocalyptic is to be directed not to the historical Jesus, but rather to the texts of the New Testament.

As was the case with the writings of the New Testament discussed to this point, so also can one not simply label as unapocalyptic or even antiapocalyptic those of the so-called Johannine circle, although especially the Gospel of John seems to be as far removed as possible from anything apocalyptic. One searches for the most part in vain in this peculiar eschatology—usually described as present eschatology—for any future statements about the coming events of the end time. Instead, the present is qualified as a time of judgment as well as of salvation. Nonetheless, one does find within the Gospel of John several statements relating to the future,[68] statements probably belonging to the original textual material and not, e.g., to a later redactional hand,[69] though they play a fairly subordinate role in the eschatology of the evangelist.[70]

This notwithstanding, the thesis is worthy of consideration according to which Johannine eschatology also stands in some relationship with Jewish and then also early Christian apocalyptic. It is possible that apocalyptic constitutes at least one of the religio-historical backdrops for the dualism pervading the entire Gospel. Of course, the extraordinarily difficult problem of the religio-historical position of Johannine theology cannot be discussed here with the necessary thoroughness.[71] At this point, however, one should guard against sweeping solutions and false alternatives. Following J. Becker one can distinguish in the Gospel of John three series of dualistic statements suggesting different religio-historical parallels or perhaps also sources.[72] On the one hand, we find the notion of a vertical division of humankind into two groups. This coincides with the antithesis between light and darkness, the latter arising when human beings close themselves off from the light.[73] One can refer to this as historic dualism of decision. In addition, there is talk of a fundamental division of humankind into good and evil,[74] which might be described as predestinate-ethical dualism. And finally, one finds in the Gospel of John also a separation of church and world,[75] which one can describe as ecclesiastically informed dualism. Because these variations of dualism exhibit quite different emphases, we must label as unsatisfactory the religio-historical alternative of a monocausal derivation of the Johannine conceptual world either from Jewish, specifically Qumran eschatology, or from a form of gnosis, e.g., heterodox Jewish gnosis. Whereas the predestinate dualism of the Gospel of John recalls gnosis,[76] its dualism of decision recalls the eschatology of the writings from Qumran.[77] Furthermore, one must consider that an inner relationship obtains between apocalyptic and gnosis and that the eschatology of gnosis can be interpreted as a radicalizing of apocalyptic eschatology.[78] For this reason, one should view with some reservation any one-sided solutions to the religio-historical problem of Johannine theology.

The separation of light and darkness and the division of humankind into two groups based on behavior toward the revealer and the revelation recall the doctrine of the two aeons in Jewish apocalyptic.[79] The idea of the *thlipsis* under which the believers have to suffer in the *kosmos* (John 16:33) also recalls Jewish apocalyptic. In the Gospel of John, however, the separation of two temporal epochs has become an inner-historic one. Apocalyptic future hope is fulfilled in the present, the end-time drama is a perpetually present occurrence. One can perhaps say that the Gospel of John has simultaneously both radicalized and broken through apocalyptic thinking by displacing the end of the world and the final judgment into the historic situation of decision of the individual. Apocalyptic conceptual models and terms are reinterpreted within the framework of present eschatology.

The apocalyptic topos of the resurrection of the dead is a striking example of this; the Gospel of John treats this topos in the story of the resurrection of Lazarus. Martha, the sister of Lazarus, confesses in conversation with Jesus the traditional apocalyptic notion of the general resurrection of the dead at the end of the present age (John 11:24). Jesus responds to her: "I am the resurrection and the life; he who believes in me, though he die, yet shall he live, and whoever lives and believes in me shall never die" (John 11:25f.). In my opinion, Jesus' conversation with Martha illustrates the dialogue between Johannine theology and apocalyptic, and reveals something about its view of the inner relationship between the apocalyptic understanding of existence and Christian faith. Faith in Jesus as the Christ does not simply lead to a relinquishing of apocalyptic thinking, but rather to its christologically based reinterpretation, one that to the same extent can be understood as its radicalizing.

The theological confrontation between Johannine theology and apocalyptic, both in agreement and in antithesis, is continued in the later writings of what is known as the Johannine circle. Compared with the Gospel, the letters of John exhibit in part a re-apocalypticizing. The present eschatological dualism is understood temporally again in 1 John.[80] While for the composer of the Gospel light and darkness to a certain extent reside on the plane of existential temporality, their parallel in 1 John 2:8 becomes a temporary dualism which again better approximates the apocalyptic notion of the two temporally sequential aeons: "The darkness is passing away and the true light is already shining." The darkness is about to pass away, and thus increasingly becomes something belonging to past history, whereby in contrast light belongs to the present. Christ divides history into two epochs. Until his coming, darkness ruled in the world. Christ's appearance, however, inaugurated a new epoch, that of expanding light. In addition, the Johannine understanding of the *hōra* , the perpetually eschatologically qualified hour of decision, is re-apocalypticized when 1 John 2:18 speaks of the present as the *eschatē hōra.* The eschaton becomes a historical period in which the Antichrist also now appears, albeit in the form of many different Antichrists: The mythic-apocalyptic figure of the Antichrist is identified with theological adversaries. Finally, because a temporal component is reintroduced into eschatology, the concept of hope acquires new meaning, an expression the author of the Gospel uses in not a single passage. In 1 John, the *elpis* directs itself toward the future, for which a definitive revelatory event is expected.

We can summarize our observations concerning Paul, the Synoptics, and the Johannine circle by pointing out that influences of apocalyptic thinking by no means manifest themselves only in marginal writings or in remote passages of the New Testament. The New Testament as a whole stands under a strong apocalyptic influence, and apocalyptic has substantively influenced the theology of the most important New Testament writings. The reasons for this can be found in earliest Christianity. We find that the theology of primitive Christianity temporally preceding the New Testament writings cannot be understood without taking into account its relationship to apocalyptic thinking. The center of the Christian faith is not the expectation of the end of the world, but rather faith in the salvific significance of Jesus of Nazareth. Precisely this salvific significance, however, was in earliest Christianity interpreted by means of apocalyptic terms and concepts. This applies not least to statements concerning the resurrection. Primitive-Christian Christology interpreted apocalyptically Jesus' fate and his salvific significance. Structural elements of apocalyptic determine the structure of the Christology of the earliest church.[81]

Hence much can be said in support of E. Käsemann's thesis that apocalyptic is "the mother of all Christian theology."[82] This metaphor means "that post-Easter [!] apocalyptic represents the oldest variation and interpretation of the kerygma."[83] Käsemann's thesis thus does not assert that Christian theology stands in an unbroken line of continuity with Jewish apocalyptic, but rather that primitive-Christian theology represents in Käsemann's view a unique kind of apocalyptic, i.e., christologically modified apocalyptic.[84]

Unfortunately, we cannot be satisfied with this explanation of the relationship between apocalyptic and Christianity, particularly since Käsemann's concept of apocalyptic is on the one hand too narrowly conceived, and on the other is in a certain respect polemical. That is, Käsemann employs the term "apocalyptic" in order, among other things, to criticize the inflationary use of the word "eschatology" and the one-sided preponderance of present eschatology in the dogmatic thinking of the twentieth century.[85] On the other hand, in my opinion Käsemann interprets the concept of apocalyptic too narrowly. As the central motif of post-Easter Christian apocalyptic he presents "the hope in the epiphany of the Son of Man coming to his enthronement."[86] That is, he speaks of apocalyptic actually only "in order to grasp the imminent expectation of the Parousia."[87] The question arises whether this says too little about apocalyptic, even in Käsemann's own sense.

The overview in this section has shown that apocalyptic conceptual models play a theologically significant role in the New Testament. Even though apocalyptic topoi do appear relatively isolated in some passages, this should not prompt the false conclusion that the New Testament on the whole employs apocalyptic language more as an aside. Neither can the interpretation of the Christian kerygma through apocalyptic means be dismissed as historically fortuitous. Early Christianity apparently considered such language and concepts substantively appropriate and even theologically necessary. Although the attempt at separating these apocalyptic conceptual forms, as ultimately external and arbitrary form elements, from some timeless content, namely, the kerygma, corresponds to the notion of liberal theology concerning the husk and kernel of Christianity, it nonetheless fails to take account of the New Testament evidence. Apocalyptic language is for early Christianity not merely an external accommodation to the conceptual world of the addressees of its proclamation. Hence neither can one say that Käsemann's thesis concerning apocalyptic as the mother of Christian theology, while holding true historically, does not do so theologically, since the *ductus* of primitive-Christian thinking was unapocalyptic.[88] Apparently, according to the understanding of early Christianity, Jesus was not simply "*the end of apocalyptic theology, since he was the beginning of eschatological salvation in the midst of the 'old' world*, i.e., under the conditions of the continuing history of the world and of humankind."[89]

If indeed one must object to the assertion that primitive-Christian theology was basically *un*apocalyptic, then on the other hand one must also be hesitant to portray it merely as a variation of apocalyptic. Käsemann's definition of primitive-Christian theology as *christologically modified* apocalyptic also offers no satisfactory solution, but points out rather the decisive theological problem. That is, the question arises concerning just what influence in its own turn the apocalyptic interpretation of the kerygma of Jesus as the Christ had on the interpreting apocalyptic itself. Why is the application of apocalyptic conceptual models in Christology theologically appropriate? To what extent is apocalyptic thinking itself modified by the application of such models? And can one yet use the term "apocalyptic" to refer to the kind of thinking resulting from such modifications? We will now expand these questions in the direction of a theology of anxiety.

3. A Theology of Anxiety

If the apocalyptic understanding of existence appears as a theological problem, then so also anxiety, which has proven to be a hermeneutical key to this understanding. The theological treatment of the relationship between the Christian faith and apocalyptic must include a theological determination of the relationship between faith and anxiety. That is, we find that anxiety in its own turn is not only a psychological or philosophical but also a theological problem. This insight prompted O. Haendler's "demand for a theology of anxiety: One cannot fully explicate the problem of anxiety without viewing it from a basically theological perspective."[90] Haendler precisely defines the task of a theology of anxiety: "The determinative meaning of a theology of anxiety is that it views anxiety basically and comprehensively as a reality within existence before God."[91] The demand for a theology of anxiety is based on the thesis, to be presented discursively in dialogue with other disciplines, that "reality can be definitively and fully understood and lived only as reality before God."[92] If anxiety is the real key to an understanding of the apocalyptic understanding of existence, this means that apocalyptic as a theological problem can be explicated in a manner appropriate to the subject matter only within the framework of a theology of anxiety. Apocalyptic world anxiety is a theological problem.

In order to explicate theologically the apocalyptic understanding of existence, we must first find a suitable theology of world anxiety. In our search we find that various theological theories of anxiety are in several respects problematical or even useless. Numerous theological interpretations of anxiety develop less a real understanding of anxiety than theological anxiety before anxiety, i.e., to a certain extent a theological "phobophobia."[93] A theology of anxiety serving merely to ward off anxiety through dogmatic means, and to repress anxiety instead of providing a guide to mastering it theologically, blocks access at the very beginning to any theological understanding of apocalyptic world anxiety and thus of apocalyptic as such.

We must thus distance ourselves from any theological theory of anxiety that relates anxiety and faith in the sense of a questionable question-answer schema and presents faith as the solution to all of life's problems, including world anxiety.[94] As profound as such a theology of anxiety might well seem, it nonetheless can be "summarized in the single, quite familiar sentence: 'You, too, need Jesus.' "[95] In this way, anxiety appears as a symptom of unbelief, while faith is confused with the feeling of being free from anxiety. Such a theological construction is not only possibly quite disastrous from a psychological perspective, it is also theologically in need of critique. This sort of theology of anxiety is actually an apologetic theology that considers the message of Christianity to be the answer to unsolved questions of life. Here one is advised to recall Bonhoeffer's theological objection that God is not a "stopgap," and seeks to be acknowledged and believed not on the periphery, but rather in the middle of our lives.[96] "The reason for this lies in God's revelation in Jesus Christ. He is the center of life and has by no means come 'in order' to answer our unsolved problems."[97] Hence any attempt at presenting faith as the solution to the problem of anxiety is problematical. "As far as the concept of 'solution' is concerned, the Christian answers are just as unpersuasive—or just as persuasive—as other possible solutions."[98] Hence one must remain critical toward any apologetic theology of anxiety that tends toward a more or less clearly formulated "methodism,"[99] though admittedly no less critical toward secularized variations of such methodism in manifestations such as existentialism or psychotherapy.[100]

An apologetic theology of anxiety in the sense described makes anxiety the presupposition of faith and equates the latter with freedom from all anxiety. In the interest of self-criticism, one must confess with respect to the ecclesiastical and theological tradition of Christian dealings with anxiety that the Christian proclamation has proclaimed faith not only as a path to the elimination of anxiety, but in many cases has misused anxiety as a means to its proclamation. In its history, the church has been not only the locus of overcoming anxiety, but no less one of generating it as well.[101] "One presupposes anxiety, one generates it and even strengthens it, all merely so as to be able to overcome it through Christianity."[102] This kind of theological "anxiety business," including its fairly sublime forms, should be summarily rejected.[103]

Criticism should be directed not only toward the use of anxiety by the Christian proclamation as a means of applying pressure, or as a mission strategy of anxiety, but also toward the misunderstanding of faith as a condition of freedom from anxiety. This way of construing faith misunderstands the New Testament statement 1 John 4:18a: "There is no fear in love, but perfect love casts out fear." The first letter of John is precisely not asserting that the Christian faith is fundamentally free from anxiety, something shown by the often omitted continuation of the sentence: "For fear has to do with punishment, and he who fears is not perfected in love" (1 John 4:18b). According to this statement from 1 John, faith by no means frees a person from anxiety as such, but rather from fear before divine judgment. Thus we read also in 1 John 4:17a: "In this is love perfected with us, that we may have confidence for the day of judgment."[104] Thus 1 John 4:17f. may not be read as a continuation of John 16:33, where the Johannine Christ says: "In the world you have anxiety; but be of good cheer, I have overcome the world." Such an interpretation is inappropriate because 1 John 4:17f. speaks of *phobos*, while John 16:33 speaks of *thlipsis*.[105] The word *thlipsis*, however, which in the Gospel of John reappears only in John 16:21, refers to something like misery or affliction, and does not mean primarily anxiety, and certainly not anxiety as a fundamental condition of human existence, but rather the kind of affliction into which the Christian community falls because its faith provokes the hostility of the world, of the *kosmos*.[106] In a manner similar to that of John 16:33, other passages in the New Testament also speak of the tribulation or affliction into which the Christian community falls because of its faith.[107] Consequently, the Gospel of John is not describing anxiety as a general possibility inherent in existence, but rather as a specific experience of anxiety associated precisely with faith. In contrast, in 1 John 4:17f. the alleged freedom from anxiety associated with faith refers not to one's relationship with the world or experience of the world, but rather to the believers' relationship with God. As little as John 16:33 is dealing with anxiety as an existential condition associated with Being-in-the-world in the sense of Heidegger, just as little is 1 John 4:17f. asserting that the Christian faith is completely free of anxiety.

If the thesis concerning the fundamental absence of anxiety in faith is not justified by the evidence of New Testament texts, then it must now also evoke fundamental theological reservation. If the capacity for anxiety is a basic anthropological constant, then it seems any theological anthropology that denies or questions the inner connection between this capacity and our disposition as created beings will be extremely problematical. The theological negation of anxiety is the equivalent of the negation of what it means to be genuinely human. "By causing anxiety to disappear, correct faith is also equally extinguishing the human being as such."[108] The thesis of faith's freedom from anxiety is not only questionable from the perspective of creation theology, but also from that of soteriology. "Simply to take the overcoming of anxiety as a goal is both contrary to the gospel and inhuman."[109]

For this reason, O. Pfister's concept of a theology of anxiety proves to be untenable. Pfister maintains that a principle antithesis obtains between anxiety and faith. The point of departure for his reflections is an interpretation of 1 John 4:17f., which admittedly fails exegetically because it levels the conceptual distinction between *phobos* and *thlipsis* and also completely ignores the context of the passage.[110] This is the only way to explain how Pfister is able to elevate to the status of timeless anthropological truth the verses 1 John 4:17f. as "words which sound like a formula in neurological theory, transporting us to the highest admiration."[111] Pfister qualifies the Christian faith more specifically as "faith of love" which overcomes anxiety, whereby anxiety is declared to be the result of blocked libido in the sense of Freud's early theory of anxiety. According to Pfister, 1 John already basically anticipates this theory of anxiety: "Thus according to 1 John 4:18, anxiety derives from disrupted love."[112] Not only is the manner questionable in which psychoanalysis functions as an auxiliary discipline to theology in Pfister's thesis,[113] but also the thesis of the "fundamental resolution of the problem of anxiety through Christianity,"[114] whose gospel Pfister articulates as "power through love."[115] The challenge to faith should not be misunderstood as a "call to anxiety-free life."[116]

O. Haendler's view of anxiety is more sophisticated. He emphasizes "that anxiety as such does not necessarily have to constitute a contradiction to faith."[117] Haendler also corrects the misunderstanding according to which John 16:33 is taken to mean that anxiety is a sign of lack of faith. According to Haendler, "this statement is not saying that you will have anxiety in the world as long as you do not believe, but rather: The world is in any case such that, viewed either with or without belief, it causes anxiety; indeed, in faith new causes of anxiety come to life which previously had not entered into the picture at all."[118] On the other hand, according to Haendler the solution to anxiety is by no means in every case the goal of faith. "What is more important than that anxiety is resolved is that it becomes fruitful."[119] Now, however, according to Haendler faith has in God nonetheless the decisive promise that all anxiety can be resolved.[120] "And all anxiety moves toward its resolution when the soul which it has pervaded enters into a union with the powers coming to it from God."[121] According to Haendler's theological estimation, "faith lives from truth, anxiety from a phantom."[122] For just this reason, Haendler, too, is now able to declare the final overcoming of anxiety through faith, whereby the resolution and classification of anxiety "are the two possibilities of its transformation in faith."[123] Although Haendler intentionally does not speak of the absence of anxiety from faith, on the other hand he can say: "Anxiety can pass away before the correct faith in the true God."[124]

And the fact that faith lives from truth means: "The truth of eternity is the strongest, the final, and the only complete overcoming of ultimate anxiety."[125] Although this thesis presupposes that all anxiety is ultimately anxiety before God, Haendler does not oversimplify this argument such that he equates anxiety with unbelief and sin. Rather, according to Haendler anxiety occupies an ambivalent position over against God: "Anxiety is so tenacious precisely because all anxiety, which does seek resolution in God, is in the final analysis anxiety before this very God."[126] The person befallen by anxiety flees to God and at the same time shrinks before him. In contrast, overcoming anxiety in faith does not mean freedom from anxiety, but rather the transformation of anxiety before God into the fear of God.[127] Although some of Haendler's formulations do encourage the misunderstanding that all anxiety disappears through faith, other parts of his concept genuinely do point beyond the position of what is initially an apologetic theology.

In contrast, other theological contributions—in a fairly unsophisticated and, in their apologetic tendencies, all-too-transparent fashion—identify anxiety with sin. It is both dangerous and shameful when questionable theologies hold up their contemporaries' anxiety before them "with more or less concealed gloating,"[128] and interpret it as the result of (or even the justified punishment for) their secularization and godlessness. Thus according to H. Thielicke, anxiety is the consequence of the disconnectedness of modern human beings,[129] "anxiety before the abyss of nothingness gaping on the horizon of a world depopulated of its gods."[130] It is allegedly the *horror vacui*, anxiety before the vacuum left behind after the dethronement of the God of judgment.[131] Proceeding from the undiscussed presupposition that all human beings strive to be without anxiety, Thielicke presents the alternative between the nihilistic and believing absence of anxiety. The former, however, is allegedly identical with the absence of anxiety experienced by an animal,[132] so that the twentieth-century human being is challenged to decide between degenerating into an animal or preserving one's humanity, the latter of which the Christian faith alone makes possible.

One cannot fail to notice E. Brunner's malicious pleasure in the anxiety of human beings after the Second World War: "They no longer have the faith in God which Christians have; they have traded this faith, like the character in the folk tale did his lump of gold, for the cheap light metal of self-confidence, and with this trade they lost all certainty, and that is why they are living in anxiety."[133] Brunner's presentation also illustrates how a theology of anxiety with this proclivity "is attempting nothing less than to load onto the concept of anxiety the burden of a kind of psychological proof of the existence of God."[134] To this end, Brunner compares the modern human being to the lost son in Jesus' parable in Luke 15:11ff. "The anxiety of the European is like the first feelings of homesickness for the father's house he left behind."[135] Anxiety is interpreted as yearning for God. "Anxiety always contains an element of a desire for trust. This distinguishes anxiety from despair."[136] The latter was first attained in existentialism, the "philosophy of despair,"[137] and in nihilism. In contrast, the person plagued by anxiety is yet open to the message of faith. For Brunner, anxiety is the point of contact and departure for an apologetic theology culminating in the call to penance: "There is still time: Anxiety can be overcome through Christ."[138]

Anxiety stands in extremely close proximity to sin in the theology of anxiety presented by H. U. von Balthasar as well,[139] though Balthasar does avoid the theological mistake of identifying all anxiety with sin. Rather, anxiety is accepted as a basic human condition and defined as a structural component of our disposition as created beings. "In view of the word of God, anxiety is first something like a general and neutral, basic state-of-mind of human existence."[140] In fact, however, the neutrality of anxiety is suspended in the condition of the sinful world, so that now one speaks about the anxiety of the wicked on the one hand, and that of the good on the other. Balthasar develops this thesis on the basis of an investigation of the Old Testament.[141] While the anxiety of the wicked is the immediate result of sin, the good are anxious concerning their relationship with God. Balthasar views the Old Testament as being permeated by a "promise of the absence of anxiety" into which God seeks to force human beings "with all the means of anxiety."[142] According to Balthasar, this promise of the absence of anxiety is fulfilled in the New Testament.[143] This means first of all that anxiety undergoes an essential transformation. The word of God takes anxiety merely "as one of the basic states-of-mind of human existence, so as to revaluate it from God's lofty position, just as all that is human is actually clay in the hand of the creator and redeemer."[144] The transformation takes place such that anxiety is first deepened.[145] This intensification culminates in the anxiety of Jesus Christ. "In the literal and strict sense of the word," this anxiety is "absolute anxiety, which by eclipsing and encompassing every other, becomes the standard and judgment for all anxiety."[146] The Old Testament promise of an absence of anxiety is fulfilled in the fate of Jesus; hence it means "the complete and final conquest of human anxiety through the cross."[147] This has serious consequences for the theological interpretation of anxiety.

According to Balthasar, anxiety *post Christum* is not a legitimate possibility for our existence, not even the anxiety of the good, which in the Old Testament was yet "an anxiety both allowed and desired by God, a correct and serious anxiety."[148] For the Christian, the absence of anxiety "before God, before the world, before every other power except that of Christ in the New Covenant is a strict commandment."[149] Accordingly, world anxiety is also to be equated with unbelief. "The Christian has absolutely no permission and no access to anxiety."[150] It must have grievous consequences for pastoral care when Balthasar continues: "If he is nevertheless a neurotic and existentialist, then he lacks Christian truth, and his faith is sick or weak."[151] In this sense, Balthasar speaks of world anxiety only as a disease. When he nonetheless ultimately does come to speak of a legitimate form of anxiety, it is "a new anxiety, an atoning anxiety in grace, one coming from Catholic solidarity."[152] It is participation in the cross of Christ, "participation in the anxiety of the cross,"[153] owing itself to grace and to the permission "to co-experience anxiety, to the extent bestowed by grace, within the anxiety of Christ."[154]

Balthasar's theology of anxiety, intended as a Catholic response not only to existentialism, but especially to Kierkegaard's concept of anxiety,[155] is based ultimately on a Thomistic understanding of nature and grace which comprehends grace as a transformation and completion of human nature, and decisively distances itself from Luther's understanding of the existence of the Christian as *simul peccator et iustus.*[156] Only against the background of an ontologizing of grace can redemption be comprehended as the "path of sinful anxiety to redemptive anxiety," between which is situated a "zone of absence of anxiety characterized by the radiance of faith, love, hope."[157] Equally as problematical as the ontologizing of grace is Balthasar's assertion that the path from sinful anxiety to redemptive anxiety leads "to complete faith and thus to true indifference."[158] Here we find that the postulate of faith's freedom from anxiety is not really biblically founded at all, but represents rather the Christianized version of the Stoic ideal of *apatheia.*[159]

Although Balthasar insists that "anxiety for the word of God is not a shameful thing,"[160] he nonetheless does ultimately inveigh against it with a prohibition binding for the believer, equating then the locus of salvation with a zone of freedom from anxiety. In contrast, D. Bonhoeffer is much more reserved in his consideration of the question whether, viewed theologically, anxiety is a shameful thing. In a letter of November 27, 1943, one written during his incarceration and just after an air raid, Bonhoeffer writes:

> The people here speak quite openly about the anxiety they have experienced. I don't quite know what to make of it, since anxiety is actually also something of which a person is ashamed. I have the feeling that one could really only talk about it in confession. Otherwise it can so easily contain an element of shamelessness. But this is by a long shot no reason yet to call a person heroic. On the other hand, naive openness can be quite disarming. But there is also a cynical, what I would almost call godless openness, one which then also lets loose in the arena of excessive drinking and wenching, and which makes such a chaotic impression. Does anxiety also belong to the "*pudenda*" which should remain hidden? I must consider all this further . . .[161]

Bonhoeffer continues his reflections in a letter from the second Sunday of Advent, 1943, critically evaluating his considerations of his own anxiety: "I believe that under the guise of honesty something is being presented here as 'natural' which in fact is basically a symptom of sin; it is really quite analogous to open talk about sexual things."[162] So after all, Bonhoeffer does ultimately reckon anxiety among the shameful things, though this does not mean—his further reflections show this—that anxiety is to be counted as a sin and prohibited to the Christian. It is not anxiety as such, but rather the trafficking with it which for Bonhoeffer is a pastoral and then also dogmatic problem. His theological questioning directs itself to our relationship with anxiety "*in statu corruptionis.*"[163] The banishment of one's admission of anxiety into the confessional underscores just this theological ambivalence of anxiety.

The theological problem of anxiety—this is our preliminary finding—is much more complex than it appears for an apologetic theology of anxiety or for a theology in search of a point of departure. Anxiety does not occupy the role of a psychological proof of the existence of God which might serve the Christian proclamation as a point of departure; nor is anxiety to be equated in an undifferentiated fashion with sin, and faith confused with the absence of anxiety. Rather, a theology of anxiety must theologically illuminate the ambivalence of anxiety, which consists in the fact that on the one hand it is a given part of our existence and as such belongs to the disposition of human beings as created beings, yet on the other stands *in statu corruptionis* in an ambivalent relationship with sin.

This is the appropriate place to reflect upon Kierkegaard's understanding of the relationship between anxiety and sin. According to Kierkegaard, it is not anxiety that is the equivalent of sin, but rather despair, which Kierkegaard's pseudonym Anti-Climacus diagnoses as the "sickness unto death."[164] Over against this despair, anxiety stands in an ambiguous relationship with sin. Kierkegaard's treatise on anxiety, or that of his pseudonym Vigilius Haufniensis,[165] is subtitled "a simple psychologically orienting deliberation on the dogmatic issue of hereditary sin." According to Kierkegaard, anxiety is a psychological concept, sin in contrast a term taken from Christian dogmatics. His investigation, however, is not intended to explain psychologically the phenomenon of sin, but rather to approach by way of a psychological route—psychological in the sense of a philosophical psychology—a phenomenon that escapes scientific explanation regardless of what sort of explanation it might be. "Sin does not properly belong in any science, but it is the subject of the sermon, in which the single individual speaks as the single individual to the single individual."[166] Different than anxiety, sin is "no subject for psychological concern."[167] Anxiety interests Kierkegaard with respect to the problem of hereditary sin, and does so insofar as in it he finds the ultimate psychologically describable presupposition, though without this description of the state immediately preceding sin in any way explaining sin itself. The state of anxiety, "this abiding something, this predisposing presupposition, sin's real possibility, is a subject of interest for psychology. That which can be the concern of psychology and with which it can occupy itself is not *that* sin comes into existence, but *how* it can come into existence."[168] Kierkegaard's central thesis underscores the impossibility of explaining sin scientifically-psychologically: "*Sin came into the world by a sin.*"[169] Anxiety is accordingly the precondition of sin, but not its cause. For Kierkegaard, psychology analyzes the possibility of sin and then leaves its further treatment to dogmatics, though in its own turn the latter is just as incapable of explaining the phenomenon of sin as is psychology: "dogmatics must . . . rather explain it by presupposing it, like . . . a moving something that no science can grasp."[170] Kierkegaard considers the psychology of anxiety to be placed into the service of Christian dogmatics, whereby a psychology of the possibility of sin remains a questionable and ambiguous undertaking.[171]

The sort of dogmatics in whose service Kierkegaard places the psychology of anxiety is a continuation of Schleiermacher's doctrine of faith, which Kierkegaard highly regards and whose work he studied intensively.[172] Kierkegaard's own critique and reinterpretation of the doctrine of hereditary sin agrees in its point of departure with that of Schleiermacher and coincides with the latter's critique of the traditional understanding of the fall into sin.[173] With the thesis that sin came and repeatedly comes into the world only through sin, Kierkegaard is nonetheless rejecting not only Hegel's, but ultimately also Schleiermacher's interpretation of Gen. 3 as a "myth of the understanding."[174] Specifically, Schleiermacher considers the presupposition of sin to be found in sinfulness.[175] Kierkegaard's critique of Schleiermacher's solution leads to several characteristic shifts over against this doctrine of sin, shifts which need not be discussed further in our present context. According to Schleiermacher, what connects us with the first human beings is on the one hand the "idiosyncrasies of sex," and on the other being subject to "changes of mood amid which such shortcoming of will-power showed itself intermittently on various sides. In the light of all this, the origin of sin and the consciousness of it became quite intelligible."[176] Although Kierkegaard argues against the possibility of this sort of explanation, he does, like Schleiermacher, assert that mood is involved in the presupposition of the Fall. According to Kierkegaard, however, this presupposition does not consist in any changes of mood—which for Schleiermacher means changes of pleasure and pain[177]—but rather in a mood dialectically supporting both pleasure and pain, i.e., in anxiety. Anxiety as a dialectical mood is a state, and sin is not a smooth transition into a different state, but rather a qualitative leap that cannot be derived causally from the preceding state.[178] In contrast, Schleiermacher's derivation of sin from changes of mood is a myth of the understanding which fails to recognize the character of sin as a leap.[179] For Kierkegaard, then, anxiety replaces this change of mood.

Anxiety already appears in Schelling's treatise on freedom as the mood preceding the fall into sin.[180] According to Schelling, the "anxiety of life" forces the individual will away from the center of the universal will and thereby into sin. Although Kierkegaard follows Schelling's assertion that anxiety is the precondition of sin, he does not agree that there is a continual and ultimately unavoidable development from anxiety or by way of anxiety into sin. Since anxiety is ambivalent according to Kierkegaard, and the concept of anxiety a "mediate determination," it in no way prejudices a person's decision and thus the leap of sin. As an ambiguous mood of this sort, anxiety in Kierkegaard's view is also to be distinguished from concupiscence. By rejecting any explanation of sin from concupiscence, since the latter in its own turn already must presuppose sin as its explanation, Kierkegaard is also criticizing the Idealist assumption of an undialectical fundamental impulse in human beings. This objection to such a fundamental impulse, however, is the presupposition for the criticism implied in the *Concept of Anxiety* of both Schelling's and Hegel's understanding of sin.[181]

Hence according to Kierkegaard, anxiety is not identical with sin, though it does stand in a special relationship with it insofar as on the one hand it constitutes its presupposition, and on the other is itself altered by sin first quantitatively, and ultimately even qualitatively. That is, on the one hand sin came into the world with anxiety, and on the other sin in its own turn brings anxiety along with it. "Consequently, anxiety means two things: the anxiety in which the individual posits sin by the qualitative leap, and the anxiety that entered in and enters in with sin, and that also, accordingly, enters quantitatively into the world every time an individual posits sin."[182] This is saying first of all that in a later individual anxiety can be more reflective than in Adam and as sin quantitatively increases in the world.[183] Furthermore, according to Kierkegaard one must distinguish between objective and subjective anxiety. This distinction implies "that subjective anxiety signifies the anxiety that is present in the individual's state of innocence . . . By objective anxiety we understand, on the other hand, the reflection of the sinfulness of the generation in the whole world."[184] Whereas subjective anxiety is that which is posited in the individual, the notion of objective anxiety picks up Paul's statement regarding the anxious longing of creation.[185] Kierkegaard emphasizes, however, that even under this presupposition there is no transition from anxiety to sin, or—to use Hegel's terminology—from quantity to quality. "Therefore, although anxiety becomes more and more reflective, the guilt that breaks forth in anxiety by the qualitative leap retains the same accountability as that of Adam, and the anxiety the same ambiguity."[186]

In broadly conceived analyses, Kierkegaard explains the progress of sin and the accompanying further development of anxiety, and does so up to the point at which anxiety, which has come into the world with sin, is qualitatively altered by sin. According to Kierkegaard, sin annuls possibility and posits actuality, albeit "an unwarranted actuality, and as such, anxiety can relate itself to it."[187] According to Kierkegaard, however, by relating itself to sin, anxiety also loses its dialectical ambiguity, "because the distinction between good and evil is posited *in concreto.*"[188] Henceforth, anxiety is either anxiety before evil or anxiety before good, the latter sort involving the loss of freedom. Even now, however, anxiety is not identical with sin. The "anxiety of sin" is more precisely "anxiety as the consequence of sin," and is distinguished from the latter insofar as, in a manner different from sin, it is a state. "Ethically speaking, sin is not a state. The state, however, is always the last psychological approximation to the next state. Anxiety is at this point always present as the possibility of the new state."[189] Accordingly, Kierkegaard views this as the distinction between anxiety and despair. "In contrast to anxiety, despair is *not a state*, but rather an *act* which I in each instance perform."[190] Hence Kierkegaard's thesis in *The Sickness unto Death* is: "Sin is: *before God, or with the conception of God, in despair not to will to be oneself, or in despair to will to be oneself.* Thus sin is intensified weakness or intensified defiance: sin is the intensification of despair."[191]

As little as Kierkegaard identifies anxiety with sin, just as little does he identify faith with a state free of anxiety. Faith does not extinguish anxiety, but rather overcomes it. "When salvation is posited, anxiety, together with possibility, is left behind. This does not mean that anxiety is annihilated, but that when rightly used it plays another role."[192] Whereas anxiety under the dominion of sin entangles a person ever more deeply in sin, ultimately causing that person to lose the consciousness of freedom, anxiety under the auspices of faith becomes a redemptive power bestowing freedom.[193] A characterizing feature of faith according to Kierkegaard is the ability to be anxious in the right way, while the absence of anxiety would be a sign of inhumanity or of a destroyed personality. "That there may be men who never experience anxiety must be understood in the sense that Adam would have perceived no anxiety had he been merely animal."[194] "If a human being were a beast or an angel, he could not be in anxiety. Because he is a synthesis, he can be in anxiety; and the more profoundly he is in anxiety, the greater is the man."[195] Faith that extinguished anxiety would at the same time extinguish the person, who according to Kierkegaard is a synthesis of body and spirit. According to Kierkegaard, however, the disposition of the

Christian faith consists in allowing anxiety—which is not a defect, but rather a constituent part of our humanity[196]—to become fruitful, and in helping us in dealing with anxiety in a new way.

The task of faith with respect to anxiety is compared with one of Grimm's fairy tales in which a young man sets out to learn what it is to fear.

> In one of Grimm's fairy tales there is a story of a young man who goes in search of adventure in order to learn what it is to be in anxiety. We will let the adventurer pursue his journey without concerning ourselves about whether he encountered the terrible on his way. However, I will say that this is an adventure that every human being must go through—to learn to be anxious in order that he may not perish either by never having been in anxiety or by succumbing in anxiety. Whoever has learned to be anxious in the right way has learned the ultimate.[197]

Kierkegaard is presupposing, of course, that only in faith can anxiety help a person to freedom and become fruitful for life. "Anxiety is freedom's possibility, and only such anxiety is through faith absolutely educative, because it consumes all finite ends and discovers all their deceptiveness."[198] All the same, anxiety remains ambiguous because it can be misunderstood and drive a person to suicide.[199] Yet it can just as well lead to faith, and by the power of faith bring up a person "to rest in providence."[200] Anxiety thereby enters into a correlation with faith, something that cannot be said of despair.[201] The anxiety of faith is liberating in that it destroys all false security. According to Kierkegaard, from faith there emerges the power to bear the fundamental insecurity of human existence. By confronting and withstanding anxiety instead of repressing it or dismissing its seriousness, faith acquires the courage to live, while unbelief despairs. "From finitude one can learn much, but not how to be anxious, except in a very mediocre and depraved sense. On the other hand, whoever has truly learned how to be anxious will dance when the anxieties of finitude strike up the music and when the apprentices of finitude lose their minds and courage."[202] The Christian faith—thus Kierkegaard's probable meaning here—overcomes anxiety by courageously living through it. Even though Kierkegaard does not employ the term "courage" in this context, his statements can nonetheless be interpreted to mean that faith is a mode of courage. Faith is the courage to be in anxiety.

Kierkegaard's description of the relationship between anxiety, sin, and faith provides guidance for a theology of anxiety, though such a theology cannot without further reflection follow his understanding of sin, which remains problematically tied to the thinking of German Idealism, specifically to Hegel's concept of sin.[203] Precisely through the declared opposition to Hegel does the latter's philosophy gain influence over Kierkegaard's thinking. This opposition manifests itself in the case of the concept of sin first of all in the fact that Kierkegaard emphasizes the inexplicability of sin and turns critically against Hegel's understanding of the story of the Fall, according to which the human being must sin with divine necessity, since he cannot otherwise follow his divine determination and attain his true being. For Hegel, the Fall coincides with the divinely willed act of becoming human.[204] Kierkegaard argues vehemently against the necessity of the Fall. Against Hegel's interpretation of the Fall as the necessary loss of immediacy, Kierkegaard objects that one must distinguish between immediacy and innocence, and that the Fall is by no means to be understood as a necessary loss of innocence.[205] "Innocence is a quality, it is a *state* that may very well endure, and therefore the logical haste to have it annulled is meaningless."[206] By trying to prepare the dogmatic doctrine of sin by a psychology of anxiety, however, Kierkegaard devalues—contrary to his own declared intentions—the substance of the Christian estimation of sin.[207] The fall into sin, as a decision made in anxiety, is the generalized form of the ethical self-choice which Kierkegaard considers an unalterable demand. Through the fall into sin, the spirit is posited. According to Kierkegaard, however, it is precisely the determination of human beings to be spirit, an assumption Kierkegaard shares with German Idealism.[208] Hegel's critic thus ultimately agrees with Hegel that the fall into sin is the act of becoming human. Under this presupposition, the question concerning the necessity of the Fall is unavoidable. Its affirmative answer in Hegel is not without its consequences, and the question is whether these consequences—which run contrary to a theological understanding of sin as disobedience to God—can be thwarted[209] by a mere veto.[210]

Under problematical philosophical presuppositions, Kierkegaard develops the notion—one theologically apparent after all—that anxiety behaves ambiguously over against sin and faith. The distinction Kierkegaard makes between the anxiety of sin and that of faith can be compared with that which Blaise Pascal makes between true and evil fear: "Evil fear; fear, not such as comes from a belief in God, but such as comes from a doubt whether He exists or not. True fear comes from faith; false fear comes from doubt. True fear is joined to hope, because it is born of faith, and because men hope in the God in whom they believe. False fear is joined to despair, because men fear the God in whom they have no belief: The former fear to lose Him; the latter fear to find Him."[211] In his own turn, Pascal hits here upon a decisive issue insofar as not only according to the Old Testament is fear of the Lord the beginning of wisdom,[212] but especially for Paul, faith in the specifically New Testament sense—Christian *pistis*—is characterized by the correlation of hope and fear, *elpis* and *phobos*.[213] Although according to Paul faith does indeed free a person from the anxiety of sin—or, to use Pascal's and Kierkegaard's expression, from the anxiety of despair—faith for Paul must nonetheless be mindful that the grace (*charis*) liberating it from the anxiety of despair is that of the God of judgment. Precisely because faith is *elpis*, it is also *phobos* and vice versa. Thus in both a positive and negative respect anxiety according to the Pauline understanding plays a central role in a person's relationship with God.[214]

The thesis asserting faith's freedom from anxiety thus cannot be based on the New Testament. Rather, John 16:33 confirms as a fact the anxiety (*thlipsis*) precisely of believers. Paul speaks quite openly about his own anxieties (*phoboi*) in 2 Cor. 7:5. And actually, according to the New Testament understanding faith is exempted neither from fear nor from anxiety as distinguished by Kierkegaard, something underscored by the Gospel portrayals of Jesus' own mortal anxiety in the Garden of Gethsemane.[215] Jesus' anxiety is not annulled, but rather suffered through. It intensifies into such immensity that according to Luke 22:43 God even sends an angel to strengthen Jesus in his agony.[216] It is not the statement that faith is free of all anxiety that is commensurate with the New Testament, but rather Paul's assertion that anxiety (*stenochōria*), too, is unable to separate the believer from Christ's love.[217] When Kierkegaard goes beyond this and speaks positively about the anxiety that saves through the power of faith, this idea finds a certain parallel in Paul's own statement about the ambiguity of grief (*lypē*) in 2 Cor. 7:10: "For godly grief produces a repentance that leads to salvation and brings no regret, but worldly grief produces death." Similarly according to Kierkegaard, anxiety, which is a constituent part of our existence, is not extinguished in faith, but rather made fruitful, i.e., it becomes a power serving not only life, but also faith itself.

Of course, the New Testament uses the linguistic equivalents for "anxiety" and "fear" without, like Kierkegaard, distinguishing conceptually between the objectless, dialectical mood of anxiety on the one hand, and the object-bound, undialectical mood of fear on the other. Hence, the New Testament writings by no means speak of anxiety or fear only in the sense of the fear of God or anxiety before God. Neither is it even remotely a New Testament notion that every anxiety or every fear is to be equated with anxiety before God. This sort of misunderstanding of New Testament statements is not found in Kierkegaard either; rather, he just manages to thwart it by going beyond Pascal and introducing the conceptual distinction between anxiety and fear as two different phenomena. Insofar as Kierkegaard's treatise on anxiety, according to its subtitle, is to be understood as a psychological—psychological in the sense of a philosophical psychology—preliminary treatise to the doctrine of sin of Christian dogmatics,[218] one can say that Kierkegaard's distinction between anxiety and fear—despite all its faithfulness to the phenomena themselves—does serve theological interests.[219]

A theological theory of anxiety must take account of anxiety as a fundamental given in our lives. References to the anxiety of faith, however, should not be misunderstood as a Christian attempt to gloss over anxiety. Courage to be in anxiety should not be confused with the acceptance of everything that spreads fear and makes people anxious. Faith is an experience of liberation that includes the liberation from anxiety under the auspices of sin and from the fear that makes a person unfree. Hence the task of faith consists not only in having the courage to be in anxiety where anxiety cannot be annulled, but equally in enlightenment concerning anxiety mechanisms hostile to life, in driving out false anxieties, and in combating any and all anxiety mongering. Faith is charged with liberating people psychologically wherever the spread of fear makes them dependent or keeps them captive in such dependency. It must confront those who incite anxiety in order to make people pliable and docile.[220] This critical task of a theology of anxiety must be seen as going beyond Kierkegaard.

Anxiety—to summarize our findings to this point—is a fundamental state-of-mind of human life. Put theologically, being in anxiety is part of the creature aspect of human beings. Anxiety, which should be distinguished from fear, is constitutive for human existence, since it is the mood in which a person discovers the future as the space of freedom, and because with this discovery it at the same time discloses both the world and our mode of being as Being-in-the-world. Although anxiety is to be affirmed theologically as a structural part of our existence as creatures, it is at the same time an ambiguous phenomenon. Anxiety *in statu corruptionis* participates in the reality of sin. It participates in sin insofar as anxiety becomes the locus of missed freedom, or put theologically: of sinning. In the wake of missed freedom, anxiety changes into anxiety before the loss of freedom and of the future determining that freedom. This is anxiety as a consequence of sin, with an unfree relationship to freedom. In contrast, the anxiety of faith can be comprehended as liberated anxiety,[221] as a liberated relationship to freedom rather than as a relationship free in and of itself. Christian faith is a mode of courage. It is courage to be in anxiety, courage that has a liberated relationship to freedom and thus to the future as the space of freedom and to the world constituted through this space. From this liberation to be in anxiety there ultimately grows faith's obligation to counter every artificial generation of anxiety and fear. The artificial generation of anxiety is sin, because it represents the attempt to rob people of their freedom. If anxiety is indeed a distinguished locus of sinning, then anyone who artificially generates anxiety is leading others into the temptation of sin. Faith that is to witness the liberation from sin is obligated to thwart every attempt at tempting others to sin by means of artificially generated anxiety. At the same time, however, such faith is to affirm anxiety as a state-of-mind accompanying newly gained freedom.

Now that we have established the framework of a theology of anxiety, we can turn our attention to the phenomenon of apocalyptic world anxiety as viewed from a theological perspective. Based on our previous findings, Balthasar's estimation according to which world anxiety is allegedly merely a disease to be fought, something illegitimate and thus sinful, proves to be theologically false.[222] Neither world anxiety nor its apocalyptic intensification can be disqualified as sin. Theologically one must counter with the assertion that apocalyptic world anxiety is a consequence of sin. It is anxiety—to use Kierkegaard's words—that came into the world with sin. As we have shown within the context of an analysis of existence, it discloses the future as radically threatened, or, put differently, it discloses the inescapability of finitude. This inescapability, however, must be interpreted theologically as a result of sin. The world disclosed by apocalyptic world anxiety, a world with a dead-end structure, is a world under the dominion of sin. The threatening end of the world is the consequence of the unbroken dominion of evil. Apocalyptic anxiety unveils this dominion and anticipates its consequences, namely, the threatening loss—resulting from sin—of future, freedom, and world.

That apocalyptic world anxiety is to be interpreted theologically as a result of sin is confirmed by the fact that apocalyptic understanding counts it among the eschatological afflictions (*thlipseis*).[223] These afflictions, however, are the necessary result of a world left over to itself and to its own evil and sin. Apocalyptic world anxiety is thus not merely a given structural feature of the creature aspect of human existence, but rather one possible variation of the fundamental disposition of anxiety under the influence of the reality of sin.

The *thlipseis*, including anxiety, belong according to the apocalyptic understanding to the unavoidable signs of the end time. Apocalyptic world anxiety belongs to the tribulations of those who hope for deliverance. In Jewish apocalyptic, for example, this is the anxiety of the righteous, of believers, those who although assailed and tempted nonetheless hold unerringly fast to the Yahweh faith and to the divine law. Drawing once again from Kierkegaard's language, in Jewish apocalyptic this world anxiety becomes the anxiety of the good before the evil. This perspective casts theological light on the ambiguity of apocalyptic we have already explicated in several contexts. As pastoral care for those in anxiety, apocalyptic, as we have seen, is not only consolation, but also parenesis. Those in anxiety are exhorted to undertake a change in their way of living, a change that endures in the face of the threatening end and promises participation in possible deliverance. Apocalyptic exhorts to persevere and to avoid all evil. That particular anxiety, however, which is anxious about salvation and endeavors with every ounce of energy to stay away from evil, is not the anxiety of faith, but rather anxiety as a result of sin.[224] Put theologically, the ambiguity of apocalyptic derives from the fact that its anxiety, precisely insofar as it is anxious before evil, stands under the dominion of sin.

Against the background of this insight, we must now determine the relationship between apocalyptic world anxiety and the anxiety of faith. Our thesis is that the anxiety of faith is the anxiety of newly acquired freedom. With reference to apocalyptic, this means that the anxiety of faith is not a result of the inescapability of finitude, but rather of having overcome this inescapability. Yet precisely because faith is a liberated relationship to freedom and to anxiety, it is now also courage to be in apocalyptic world anxiety.

This notion must be explained further. Numerous New Testament statements concur in their assertion that believers will have to suffer tribulations characterizing the eschatological situation. To that extent, apocalyptic world anxiety also belongs to the situation of believers. The idea that the *thlipseis* of the church are the beginning of the eschatological tribulations is thus moving apparently completely within the framework of apocalyptic views. Even the statement in John 16:33 could be interpreted as an apocalyptically directed statement, i.e., that the *thlipsis* does not constitute a fundamental feature of human existence in and of itself, but rather is to be comprehended as a characterizing feature of Christian reality, reality completely ruled by sin. Paul makes it quite clear in Rom. 8:22ff. that even the believer is no stranger to apocalyptic world anxiety. According to Paul, believers participate in apocalyptic world anxiety as expressed in the anxious waiting of creation. The believer is not exempt from apocalyptic world anxiety, and thus also not from the apocalyptic understanding of the world. Insofar as faith knows that nothing can separate it from the love of Christ (Rom. 8:35f.), it is rather the courage to be in apocalyptic anxiety.

This courage admittedly comes according to the New Testament understanding from overcoming the inescapability of the world in the fate of Jesus of Nazareth. Faith endures apocalyptic world anxiety in the belief that the structure of reality disclosed by that anxiety has been broken through in the fate of Jesus. The courage of faith to be in anxiety results from its belief in the overcoming of this inescapability.

Thus we read in John 16:33: "In the world you have anxiety; but be of good cheer, I have overcome the world."

Here we encounter a difference between the apocalyptic and Christian understanding of existence whose causes and significance we will examine more thoroughly later in this chapter. For the moment let us say only that according to the understanding of the Christian faith it is not apocalyptic world anxiety, but rather the cross of Christ that unveils reality. However, the cross does initially confirm world anxiety insofar as the cross is to be understood as breaking through the inescapability of the world, to which apocalyptic refers as inescapability that is as yet unbroken. Yet faith not only deepens apocalyptic world anxiety that is already present, it also leads a person into such anxiety in the first place. That is, according to the New Testament estimation the eschatological *thlipseis* are not only a world experience already present, one that believers quite possibly share with other people; rather, they are understood as a consequence of the cross and of the believers' participation in Jesus' fate. These *thlipseis* are the necessary result precisely of the salvation event. According to John 16:33, Christians must have anxiety in the world, in the *kosmos*, because Christ's coming provokes the hostility of the world in the first place against God and against those who believe in him for Christ's sake. Hence, the overcoming of the world is what first creates an apocalyptic situation, albeit one that is immediately annulled. For just this reason, apocalyptic world anxiety from the Christian perspective is not merely tolerated; rather, faith itself is led into apocalyptic world anxiety. The overcoming of the world, however, is not visible; it is believed. The only thing visible is the cross. Thus faith, as coparticipation in the crucifixion, remains tempted. Its temptation, however, includes the experience of apocalyptic world anxiety.

To be sure, the Christian faith is not the unbroken continuation of the apocalyptic understanding of existence. Rather, apocalyptic world anxiety can be taken up into faith's understanding of existence only because it is both provoked and simultaneously altered through the fate of Jesus, which culminates in the cross and resurrection. Through the power of faith, apocalyptic world anxiety—originally a result of sin—becomes the anxiety of faith.

Let us summarize the findings of our investigation to this point. We have developed the basic features of a theology of anxiety enabling us to treat apocalyptic world anxiety as a theological problem. Our attempt at a theological evaluation of apocalyptic world anxiety has led to an initial theological determination of the relationship between the apocalyptic world experience on the one hand, and the Christian understanding of existence on the other. Within the framework of our question as expanded over against the previous section, our exegetical findings from the New Testament have been confirmed. From the perspective of anxiety, too, we have found that the Christian understanding of existence neither is unapocalyptic, nor does it appropriate in an unbroken fashion the apocalyptic understanding of existence. These findings can now be subjected to systematic-theological clarification. The first question is how faith can be understood theologically as a mode of courage both in concurrence with and antithesis to apocalyptic. On the basis of the insight that humankind is threatened with complete annihilation, however, this question must be pushed even further. We must ask just what the foundation of faith's courage in the face of such a threat is, and whether it can yet stand up to world anxiety in the shadow of the end.

4. The Sublation of Apocalyptic

The thesis of unapocalyptic Christianity has a long tradition. Kierkegaard already supports the view that a fundamental distinction obtains between the Christian faith as an attitude toward existence on the one hand, and the apocalyptic understanding of existence on the other. In his *Christian Discourses* of 1848 one reads that "it is the believer who is nearest the eternal, while the apocalyptic visionary is farthest from the eternal."[225] According to Kierkegaard, what separates the apocalyptist from the Christian is care and anxiety. While the believer takes to heart the exhortation of the Sermon on the Mount not to be anxious,[226] apocalyptic thinking derives from just such anxious care. Care directs itself toward the future, while in contrast faith lives completely in the present. Precisely in turning away from the future, the believer allegedly is turned toward the eternal, like someone rowing a boat with his back toward the goal, who nonetheless only in this way comes closer to that goal.[227] In contrast, the apocalyptist turns toward the future and thus away from the eternal. For him, "the next day becomes a prodigious confused figure such as fairy-tales describe. Just as those demons of whom we read in the book of Genesis begat children by earthly women, so is the future the monstrous demon which of men's womanish imagination begets the next day."[228] For Kierkegaard, apocalyptic is a fantastic world of the imagination emerging from care and anxiety.

While for Kierkegaard a fundamental antithesis obtains between the apocalyptic and Christian understanding of existence, our previous findings point in a different direction. Christian courage is courage to be in apocalyptic world anxiety, courage that employs apocalyptically influenced language. The thesis of unapocalyptic Christianity thus cannot be maintained.

Käsemann has described Christianity as a peculiar modification of apocalyptic, the Christian theology of primitive Christianity allegedly representing christologically modified apocalyptic. The question arose, however, just how far this modified apocalyptic moves yet within the framework of apocalyptic thinking. It has become clear that the courage to be in anxiety within the Christian faith brings about a change in the understanding of existence over against that of apocalyptic. The Christian faith is more or something different than a mere variation of apocalyptic. Perhaps the modification of apocalyptic by the Christian faith can be described best as its sublation. Sublation means that the Christian understanding of existence neither merely negates the apocalyptic understanding of existence nor shares it wholly without contradiction. Hence in our context the concept of sublation has a dialectical meaning, and we thus want to understand the Christian faith in a dialectical sense as the sublation of apocalyptic.[229]

The sublation of apocalyptic accordingly means something other than its end,[230] as if apocalyptic and Christianity might be related in a fashion analogous to the schema of prophecy and fulfillment. In that case, the end of the world would have to have already taken place according to the Christian understanding. Now, early Christianity did indeed associate the fate of Jesus with the end of the world. The cross and resurrection of Jesus were interpreted apocalyptically such that the conclusion of Jesus' life allegedly represented the beginning of the end of the world. According to Matt 27:45ff., darkness, earthquakes, and the resurrection of the dead accompanied Jesus' death. Jesus' death was the signal introducing the end of the world, whose final collapse was yet expected during the lifetime of the first generation of Christians. Even when this hope proved deceptive, Christianity nonetheless basically held fast to the assertion that Jesus' fate was associated with the end of the world. Despite the outstanding Parousia, according to primitive-Christian understanding "the apocalyptic drama was in a certain way concluded."[231] Hence one might say that according to the Christian understanding the end of the world has indeed already occurred. Whereas apocalyptic anticipates the end of the world, faith allegedly sees it already actualized in the fate of Jesus. This assumption is supported by the fact that the early Christian communities did not expect a further messiah, but rather the Parousia of the crucified Jesus.

Against the background of the schema of prophecy and fulfillment, R. Bultmann and E. Fuchs altered the Pauline thesis about Christ as the end of the law[232] and interpreted the fate of Jesus theologically as the end of history.[233] If the end of the world has already taken place, however, then apocalyptic has basically also come to its end. Thus precisely because Jesus' fate is associated apocalyptically with the end of the world, *post Christum* it should no longer be possible to interpret the world apocalyptically. In this view, Christianity would constitute the end of apocalyptic because it is its fulfillment. The thesis of Christ as the end of history parallels history focused theologically on the law. Like the law as interpreted by Pauline thinking, so also, according to the view of Fuchs and Bultmann, does history entangle human beings in a nexus of disaster in which they seek to realize themselves and yet can only lose themselves. The end of history, like the end of the law, means the possibility of a new freedom and of liberation to a new life and a new understanding of existence. Liberation from history is understood as disengagement or disentanglement from the world, as liberation from the nexus of disaster which is the historical world, as a call out of decayed history and into the true historicness of human existence.

The thesis of Christ as the end of history correctly sees that faith understands the nexus of disaster perceived by apocalyptic to be sundered at its decisive point. The critical question, however, is whether this conceptual model takes sufficient account of the actuality of extant and, today, even escalating tendencies of disaster. In view of the present global danger the thesis of the end of history falls under the suspicion of religious escapism, just as the concept of disengagement from the world unmistakably exhibits an escapist tenor, even if it does not wish to be perceived or understood as such. The question also arises why the New Testament, despite its faith in the inbreaking of salvation, now as before is capable of speaking apocalyptically if, after all, the end of the world has already come about. The assertion that the thesis of Christ as the end of history is referring not to the historical Jesus as an event of the past, but rather to his perpetually new eschatological evocation, cannot really refute this objection, since the New Testament authors employ apocalyptic linguistic devices in reference not only to the past, but also to the present and future. Significantly, the thesis about Christ as the end of history finds itself forced to marginalize completely the apocalyptic influences in the New Testament or to view them as an accommodation to its addressees' conceptual horizon. This does not, however, take sufficient account of the substance of the New Testament evidence.

In order to understand better the concurrence and antithesis of the Christian faith over against apocalyptic, let us first reconsider the basic features of the apocalyptic understanding of the world. The apocalyptist experiences the world as the locus of wickedness or of disaster. Existence offers absolutely no experience of salvation, whereby the world itself is conceived as a self-enclosed sphere of life. This applies in both present and historical respects. The world is an enclosed time-space nexus of disaster, and for just this reason history is also an enclosed continuum of disaster. Since the world itself is without salvation, salvation can only reside outside it or come from outside it. For this reason, apocalyptic directs its attention away from a present of darkness and into a future of light. Its hope, however, cannot be derived from its experience of the world. Since according to apocalyptic understanding the present and past utterly lack any experience of salvation, then the inbreaking of salvation can only be anticipated as a future *possibility*, and not derived from any salvation-historical recollection. Thus, apocalyptic hope is essentially the *anticipation* of possible deliverance. This deliverance for which it hopes is to lead to the destruction of the closed, dead-end structured world. Just as the experience of a dead-end structured world becomes concentrated in the certainty of inevitable catastrophe, so also is apocalyptic hope convinced of the catastrophic nature of future redemption. The path to salvation leads through catastrophe. New life possibilities lie beyond the end.

A comparison of apocalyptic and Christian world experience based on these basic features reveals both common features and differences. According to the Christian understanding also, the world is the locus of wickedness, an enclosed continuum of disaster. Like apocalyptic, faith also hopes for future deliverance, and both are convinced of the catastrophic nature of redemption, something sufficiently attested by the New Testament scenarios of the end of the world. Unlike apocalyptic, however, the Christian faith views an event in history that has already occurred as the inbreaking of salvation, and believes that in that event the enclosure of the world of disaster and the history of disaster have been fundamentally sundered or broken through. What separates apocalyptic and the Christian faith from one another is faith in the cross and resurrection of Jesus as a salvific event.

This is saying far more than that the Christian faith varies or modifies apocalyptic thinking. Of course, it is true that the fate of Jesus is interpreted with the help of apocalyptic notions, since the idea of the resurrection of the dead is, after all, apocalyptic. While faith in the resurrection of Jesus makes possible an understanding of his death as a salvific event, the Christian faith shares with apocalyptic the conviction concerning the catastrophic nature of redemption. The event of redemption stands under the sign of the cross and is a catastrophe. With this application of apocalyptic conceptual models to Jesus' death, however, there now occurs a decisive change over against apocalyptic. If Jesus' death is to be understood as the inbreaking of salvation, then history is no longer a self-enclosed continuum of disaster, but rather in addition to the experience of wickedness and calamity also the locus of an experience of salvation. Whereas apocalyptic is exclusively the *anticipation* of the *possible*, faith is the *recollection* of the *reality* of salvation. In contradistinction to apocalyptic, faith has access to salvation-historical recollection. Since the Christian faith is able to speak in the manner of recollection about the *reality* of salvation instead of anticipating salvation only as a possibility, it breaks through apocalyptic thinking at a decisive point.

However, the Christian faith is not the end of apocalyptic, but rather must be understood as its sublation, since the believer, too, finds himself now as before placed into a world rich with experiences of disaster and trouble. The certainty that in the fate of Jesus the world's nexus of disaster has been broken through should not mislead one into denying present experiences of disaster, or to confuse the historically contingent inbreaking of salvation with its total realization. Wherever this occurs, as was the case with the Corinthian enthusiasts, we are reminded, e.g., by Paul, that final deliverance is given to us in the present only in the form of this recollection of the cross. Christian faith does not call into question the apocalyptic experience of disaster, but rather consists precisely in enduring the tension between the confession to Jesus' fate as a salvific occurrence—i.e., the recollection of salvation as the object of faith—and the apocalyptic experience of the world.[234] Like the apocalyptist, the believer also experiences wickedness and the failure of deliverance to arrive. Faith describes this as the experience of temptation. Like the apocalyptist, the believer also hopes for future deliverance and for the inbreaking of salvation. Yet whereas apocalyptic hope consists exclusively in the anticipation of the possible, faith anticipates that future possibility by recalling past reality. Christian hope is hope that remembers, or hoping remembrance of the fate of Jesus of Nazareth. This remembrance yet remains apocalyptic in that the recollected inbreaking of salvation in the form of the cross is a catastrophe.

Faith remembers the fate of Jesus as God's salvific intervention. Where death seems to have the upper hand, in truth life actually is victorious. Where unrighteousness triumphs, righteousness cuts a path for itself. Where utter despair rules, life finds new meaning. Where life is robbed of all hope, the fate of Jesus opens up new life possibilities. In the midst of the most extreme powerlessness and remoteness of the divine, God's vivifying power cuts a path for itself, breaking through the inescapability of a world left over to itself and surrendered to destruction. In the midst of the catastrophic nature of reality there is the experience of a counterworld of love, righteousness, and life.

Jesus' life was determined by the proximity of God, whereas the apocalyptic world experience could speak only of God's absence and remoteness. Jesus' "real secret is that he is open even where everything around him blocks openness. He is open for the near God and for his near fellow human being and for the moment, open doubtlessly also for suffering, without which such openness is not possible."[235] The openness that the near God makes possible is the result of this new freedom. Jesus' openness owes itself to a leeway or space of freedom opening up where the apocalyptically understood world loses that very space. Put differently, the openness characterizing Jesus' life results from the inbreaking of future into a world of inescapability and enclosure, into a world of a threatening absence of future. It is the near God witnessed by Jesus who grants such future.

In order to formulate this idea as a theological concept, however, we must define more precisely the concept of future. Until now, we have distinguished merely between the future as a planable future and the future as absolute future or as a fundamental possibility. Future as the not-yet of reality and future in the sense of fundamental possibility were distinguished from one another as internal and external futurity.[236] The Christian faith's experience of future, however, requires beyond this a distinction between *futurum* and *adventus.* Whereas *futurum* refers to the time following the present, deriving from the present itself what is future as the not-yet-actual, *adventus* is speaking of the future as an eschatological entity. Precisely this eschatological future, however, is the concern of the inbreaking of salvation as the object of Christian faith.

Especially E. Brunner and A. Rich have pointed out that into the eighteenth century the German word *Zukunft*, "future," was an eschatological term in the sense of Latin *adventus* and Greek *parousia.*[237] The *Zu-Kunft* (*ad-ventus*) is that which "comes toward" the present, not that which proceeds out from the present. Future in this sense, as "coming toward," is the coming or approaching of God, his arrival or his Parousia. This sense of "future" is what is meant when we say that salvation consists in the Christian understanding in the inbreaking or opening up of future. The inbreaking of salvation consists in the Parousia or in the arrival of God.[238] According to Christian understanding, this advent is the Christ event; the *adventus* of God, however, opens up a new future in the sense of *futurum.* Because God comes toward or approaches the present in the sense of *adventus,* future can proceed in the sense of *futurum* out from the present.

In order to express in an appropriate theological fashion the inbreaking of salvation in the fate of Jesus of Nazareth, we must understand the God of Jesus as the god of the future. The Christian God, however, is not, as Bloch believes, a God with *futurum* as the essential quality, but rather *adventus.*[239]

By recollecting the fate of Jesus, faith, too, reckons with the nearness of God. Its recollection is thus more than a historical recollection. It is rather an evocation of God's nearness. The recollection of the fate of Jesus has the power in its own turn to open up the future where apocalyptic world anxiety finds our future blocked. By remembering the fate of Jesus as a salvific event, faith in its turn experiences God's nearness and his *adventus.* In this way, faith experiences in a perpetually new fashion and in the midst of the catastrophic nature of reality the fact that future is granted to it. Its own experience of God's nearness is reason for hope in a counterworld of love, righteousness, and life.

God's Parousia is thus neither an exclusively future event, nor is it in the Christian understanding merely a historical event of the past, but rather an event in the sense of *adventus.* Mindful of the fate of Jesus as the Parousia of God, apocalyptically tempted faith lives within the horizon of the *adventus* of God. Its hope expects the near or imminent God. Hence it is imminent expectation. As is well known, early Christianity expressed this imminent expectation in chronological categories as future hope. One expected the imminent return of Christ yet during the lifetime of the first or at least the second generation of Christians. Despite the disillusionment of this imminent expectation, temporally understood imminent expectation has been revived repeatedly throughout the course of church history even into the present. Theologically one must say that future imminent expectation is a vulgar form of Christian imminent expectation, vulgar because it describes the *adventus* of God as a *futurum*. In its essence, however, Christian imminent expectation is not future hope, but rather hope focused on *adventus*. To that extent, the changes that have come about in Christian eschatology in the course of time after the disillusionment of future imminent expectation are more than merely an accommodation to disillusioning reality. They are profoundly connected and commensurate with the issue at hand. Faith assailed and tempted by the experience of a world that now can be understood only apocalyptically hopes in the near or imminent God, who inevitably will overcome the world. This eschatological "imminence" is the expression of the certainty of this inevitability.

It is theologically problematical to interpret the *adventus* of God in the fate of Jesus of Nazareth as prolepsis, as W. Pannenberg has done.[240] That is, Pannenberg's concept of prolepsis is actually not to be understood eschatologically at all, but rather historically-teleologically.[241] The prolepsis prefigures in an inner-historical fashion the *telos* of history which first constitutes history as a cosmos or as a meaningful totality. From the perspective of the end, history is conceived as "reality in its totality."[242] Hence the prolepsis basically exhibits only the quality of *futurum* rather than *adventus:* It prefigures the end of the *futurum* which stands in continuity with the present. Although Pannenberg does emphasize the eschatological character of the Christ event, his concept of the future remains unclear. Pannenberg calls God "the power of the future,"[243] which is simultaneously the "power of being,"[244] and differentiates between the "realization of the historical future at a given time" on the one hand and the "power of the ultimate future" on the other, referring to God's "own eschatological futurity."[245] In contradistinction to the innerworldly future, God's future is also referred to as the "essential future" establishing the meaningful totality.[246] Nevertheless, God's future is not distinguished clearly enough from innerworldly futurity, e.g., when Pannenberg says that in each past age, too, God was the future,[247] or explains the difference between apocalyptic and Christianity merely by pointing out that in Christianity "that which is future is conceived as already present not only for God himself, but is also already experienced by the believer as being present, since in a hidden fashion it is already commencing in the present world as well, beginning with the presence of the coming reign of God in the appearance of Jesus."[248] In the same vein, Pannenberg refers to God's future as the "dimension of depth of the temporal present,"[249] this dimension of depth referring, however, to the presence of the *telos* of the *futurum*.

On the basis of this unclarified understanding of the future, Christianity in

Pannenberg's view must appear as a modification of apocalyptic which does not fundamentally transcend the framework of apocalyptic thinking. As a result of his teleological understanding of the prolepsis of the end which constitutes history as totality, Pannenberg's program of revelation as history is transformed into a program of history as—albeit indirect—revelation.[250] If in this way history in its totality—and that really must mean inclusive of all disastrous events and absurdities—becomes a revelation of God, then the understanding of revelation itself as a salvific event must become murky. Over against this one must recall with K. Barth that from the Christian perspective "revelation is not a predicate of history, but history is a predicate of revelation."[251] Neither has Pannenberg's historico-theological conception made the program of a history of salvation more persuasive.[252]

Above all, however, Pannenberg's concept of apocalyptic theology fails to take into account the fundamental difference between *futurum* and *adventus*. The Christ event is not the *telos* of the *futurum*, but rather the *adventus* of God, which simultaneously is the *archē* of a new *futurum*. If at all, the concept of prolepsis can be used not teleologically, but at most eschatologically.[253] In that case, however, it represents substantively precisely what we have called the *adventus*. Given the difference between *futurum* and *adventus*, Christianity can accordingly not be understood in unbroken continuity with apocalyptic, as the circle around Pannenberg has tried to do.[254]

In contrast, J. Moltmann has demonstrated the discontinuity between apocalyptic and Christianity much more incisively. "Between the expectation of late Jewish apocalyptic and of Christian eschatology stands the cross of Jesus," as Moltmann summarizes his criticism of Pannenberg's understanding of apocalyptic.[255] Christian eschatology is "*eschatologia crucis*,"[256] and thus "not to be understood as a special case of general apocalyptic. Christian eschatology is not Christianized apocalyptic."[257] All the same, in addition to this discontinuity Moltmann also sees the inner relationship between apocalyptic and the Christian faith. He tries to do justice to this situation by differentiating in a different context between apocalyptic and messianism, interpreting Christianity not as a form of apocalyptic, but rather as a form of messianism.[258] Conservative, reactionary apocalyptic oriented toward the signs of the time is juxtaposed with messianism directed toward the signs and wonders of the divine spirit.

Compared with the understanding of apocalyptic of the Pannenberg group, that of Moltmann has the advantage that it takes into account the ambiguity of apocalyptic and articulates it as a theological problem.[259] To be sure, it is probably not possible to play apocalyptic and messianism off against one another the way Moltmann does. Moltmann reserves the name "apocalyptic" for those particular versions of apocalyptic thinking which he rejects. Over against this, one must point out that messianism is also a form of apocalyptic. Hence a messianic Christology or ecclesiology would be no less a variation of apocalyptic theology than the historical theologies of the nineteenth century indicated by Moltmann. One will have to say, however, that in the New Testament the step from messianism to Christology is completed,[260] so that with respect to messianism, too, Christianity proves to be the sublation of apocalyptic.

No less problematical is the way in which Christ as a sign of hope is conceived in Moltmann's view as a sign of crisis.[261] According to Moltmann's understanding, "the point at issue is in the first place the 'signs and wonders' which accompany the messianic exodus in the history of the Spirit . . . Only afterwards and in addition, and therefore to a secondary degree, can 'the signs of the end' then be perceived as well—the signs of the growing crisis in world history."[262] Moltmann's decisive theological insight asserts that the signs of crisis and of danger are provoked through the liberating events associated with the figure of Jesus. Thus "these are not the portents of total crisis; they are always merely signs of particular and specific conflicts. For it is not world crisis that leads to Christ's Parousia; it is Christ's Parousia that brings this world with its crises to an end."[263] From this eschatological notion Moltmann draws the ecclesiological conclusion that "it is in its very character as the saving leaven that the church is also the opposite; and it is in its character as proclamation of the righteousness of God that the gospel also reveals the world under the divine wrath. Just because it proclaims that salvation is near it provokes crises."[264]

The notion of the hostility of the world provoked by faith is very much in keeping with the New Testament, though the New Testament does view the Christian's role as being far less active than does Moltmann. The "dark, gloomy side of Christianity's mission and expansion," as Moltmann calls it, consists according to the New Testament understanding primarily in apocalyptic suffering, not in the provocation of historical crises and catastrophes. Moltmann's eschatological understanding of the history of Christianity allows the conclusion—one he doubtlessly did not intend—that in retrospect one might legitimize theologically the occasionally devastating results of Christian mission activity. If the church understands itself as a leaven of disaster and of divine judgment, then it will fall into the whirlpool of apocalyptic ambiguities and become caught in the undertow of apocalyptic pleasure in demise and destruction, ambiguities that cannot be checked by mere denouncement.[265]

What is most questionable, however, is the assertion that the "signs of the time" are not the "portents of total crisis," but rather symptoms of particular and specific conflicts provoked by the reality of Christ in this world. Although Moltmann can very well draw support from the fact that the New Testament, too, associates catastrophic events with the appearance of the Son of Man, the New Testament conceives the Parousia as the end of the world and thus precisely as total crisis. In contrast, Moltmann tries to neutralize experiences of actual catastrophes by means of a christological thesis. The aspect of possible demise and destruction is relativized. One cannot say that Moltmann's eschatology evades the experiences of the negative; his theology of the cross impressively tries to confront the question of theodicy and experiences of the catastrophic. All negativities are taken panentheistically into God.[266] For Moltmann, God is the name of the process in which all negativities are overcome. The question, however, is whether the repristination of Schelling's ideas does not obstruct one's view of the possible foundering of the world process. As seriously as Moltmann does take the universality of suffering theologically, he nevertheless appears to evade the idea of an end whose actuality has become possible insofar as he interprets actual catastrophes in nature and history within the context of an ultimately Old Testament–prophetic understanding of judgment: From this perspective, these catastrophes are taken as merely limited crises which cannot really call into question the continuation of the world itself. It seems as if in the final analysis Moltmann's eschatology is not really prepared after all to confront without reservation the possibility of total catastrophe. Precisely this, however, is the central task of theology today.

At this point, we admittedly encounter yet a further problem. In view of the historical beginnings of Christianity, it is astonishing that the end of the world should be a problem for faith in the first place. One would sooner expect that the annihilation of the world would be affirmed theologically as the realization of both apocalyptic and primitive-Christian world negation. This idea, which at first glance seems cynical, touches on the questions raised by Overbeck, questions that concerned us earlier in our Introduction.[267] Anyone for whom the possible end becomes a temptation and problem, assumes—in whatever form—an attitude of world affirmation. If, however, as Overbeck and others have determined, the Christian faith was an attitude toward existence characterized by world negation, then one cannot so easily dismiss Overbeck's reproof that every form of world affirmation constitutes apostasy from true Christianity. One has to concede to Overbeck that primitive Christianity did expect a swift end of the world, and that the attempt at world affirmation represents from the historical perspective a change over against the faith of primitive Christianity.

Albert Schweitzer described this change as "an evolution from a Christian-pessimistic to a Christian-optimistic philosophy."[268] Schweitzer also characterizes the primitive-Christian understanding of existence as an attitude of world negation, an assertion picked up by both M. Werner and F. Buri. This transformation in Christianity from world negation to world affirmation is allegedly additionally furthered at the beginning of the modern age by the fact that "the world-view of Christianity changes, and becomes leavened with the yeast of world- and life-affirmation. It gradually begins to be accepted as self-evident that the spirit of Jesus does not renounce the world, but aims at transforming it."[269] Differently than Overbeck, however, Schweitzer considers this development to be legitimate. His point of departure for understanding this process, a process Overbeck radically criticized, is the ethic of the historical Jesus. That is, despite his pessimistic worldview, Jesus allegedly advocated an "activist ethic." "This activist ethic is what is wanted to provide the cardinal-point of an evolution from a Christian-pessimistic to a Christian-optimistic philosophy."[270] In other words, the transformation of the Christian faith from world negation to world affirmation is legitimate because Jesus' own ethic already contained an element of world affirmation.

In contrast, Overbeck identifies true Christianity with historical primitive Christianity in its attitude of world negation. Although he is doubtless successful here in sharpening our critical consciousness for the relationship between world affirmation and world negation, one must ask whether Overbeck's position is not one-sided insofar as he accepts as valid only a historical interpretation of Christianity. It is quite possible that in this point Overbeck succumbs to the fascination exercised by the historical method on the waning nineteenth century.[271]

Albert Schweitzer interpreted Christianity as world affirmation that has passed through world negation. What is problematical about this thesis is that its argumentation draws its support from the historical Jesus and his alleged ethic. Schweitzer's own criticism of research into the life of Jesus disclosed the limits imposed upon the question concerning the historical Jesus. Beyond this, M. Kähler has already demonstrated the questionable character of theological argumentation which believes it can draw its support from the historical Jesus.[272] Over against this, we have interpreted the Christian faith in its relationship to apocalyptic from the perspective of the fate of Jesus, which was understood as the *adventus* of God. With this presupposition one can very well transform Schweitzer's thesis into an idea that leads beyond Overbeck's aporia. It is then not the ethic of the historical Jesus, but rather his fate that unites within itself an element of world negation with one of world affirmation. Put theologically, the cross is God's judgment on a world remote from God, a world heading for destruction. As such, it is the quintessence of total world negation. Insofar as Jesus' fate is the inbreaking of God into this world, however, the cross is simultaneously the expression of God's affirmation of the world. The suffering and love of God embodied in Jesus breaks through the apocalyptic rigidity of the world. Hence neither is evil rigidly set in its wickedness, but rather is overcome by God's love. Faith is able to affirm the world despite its lost and catastrophic nature because precisely this world of wickedness and disaster has in the form of the cross become the locus of salvation. Viewed in this way, Christianity was able to find its way to world affirmation during the course of its historical development because such affirmation was already inherent in the message of the cross itself. Remembering the fate of Jesus, faith affirms with hope the world also as the locus of future salvation. All the same, faith is not simply an attitude of world affirmation. Jesus' fate is to be understood equally both as God's "yes" and as God's "no" to the world. Just as the path to the glory of resurrection must pass through the cross, so also can faith push forward to an affirmation of the world only through world negation. Faith is world affirmation that must repeatedly pass anew through apocalyptic world negation.

Because faith affirms the apocalyptically negated world simultaneously as the locus of possible salvation and of God's *adventus*, the annihilation of the world which today lies fully within the realm of possibility becomes a temptation and a theological problem for faith. Here faith is something other than hope in the continuation of the world or than the apocalyptic hope in a different world beyond the catastrophe. Rather, faith affirms the world in view of what is today the possibility of that world's very real negation. The Christian faith is courage for questionable existence.

5. Faith as Courage for Questionable Existence

The twentieth century is rich in experiences of the catastrophic and of meaninglessness. It is the age of terror. Even if this characterization can also be applied to earlier epochs in world history, the catastrophic and its possibilities have attained hitherto unimagined dimensions in our century. The tendencies of the catastrophic have not only fostered theoretical nihilism and a nihilistic feeling toward life, but have also smoothed the way for a kind of active nihilism, an annihilism that quite possibly might find its senseless fulfillment in an *annihilatio mundi* brought about by human beings themselves. Catastrophic has made progress, a kind of climax of terror profoundly calling into question all previous ideas of progress that direct their attention to a meaningful *telos* of history. Although it is too early to speak of an end of the idea of progress, we are justified in speaking of a shock to teleological thinking, one shaking its very foundations. The threatening end, the *annihilatio mundi* which has now become technologically possible, calls into question all teleological thinking in all its variations.

> The warm current of teleology which has carried our consciousness until now is increasingly drying up. The teleological confidence in an increasing reconciliation between human beings and nature is broken, and now that it is passing away we notice for the first time just how profoundly and abidingly it has shaped us—all the way into our philosophical and theological interpretations of the future. Now, suddenly, Sisyphus once again takes his place next to Prometheus, Nietzsche next to Marx, Camus next to Teilhard, Monod next to Whitehead.[273]

It is as if these words of J. B. Metz were becoming increasingly true. Nietzsche steps up beside Marx: This is one of the possible monikers for postmodernity, with whose philosophy we have become acquainted as the current form of apocalyptic thinking. Sisyphus next to Prometheus: Whereas Prometheus embodies for Bloch the attitude of utopian-teleological hope, Camus chooses the figure of Sisyphus as the symbol of a philosophy that courageously confronts the absurd. Whereas Bloch, the philosopher of hope, became the dialogue partner of theology under the auspices of departure and exodus, Camus might posthumously become the counterpart of a theology in the shadow of threat.

Teleological historical models are just as incapable of rescuing us from the terror of history as is archaic cyclical thinking. Such models serve ultimately only to intensify the despair of modern human beings who find themselves trapped in history. "It is a despair provoked not by his own human existentiality, but by his presence in a historical universe in which almost the whole of mankind lives prey to a continual terror (even if not always conscious of it)."[274] According to Kierkegaard, the only alternative to despair is faith. A variation of this idea recurs in M. Eliade, who considers modern human beings confronted by the either-or of faith and despair.[275] Only faith, Eliade assures us, liberates us from the terror of history, since it bestows freedom from history. According to Eliade, a person becomes free through faith in God, for whom in the biblical understanding everything is possible. Here, too, Kierkegaard's thinking resonates, since according to Kierkegaard's definition God is precisely this, namely, that everything is possible.[276] Kierkegaard's understanding of faith is admittedly yet governed by teleological thinking insofar as he comprehends existing as a movement, and holds fast to the notion that every movement needs a goal in order to be movement. Faith, too, has a goal, namely, God. Kierkegaard, however, understands faith as a movement whose goal is its ground.[277]

The crisis in teleological thinking has produced a crisis in theology, which is indebted to teleological thinking over long stretches wherever it in any way argues from the perspective of salvation history. In view of the threatening end, however, many of the previous theological answers become questionable. Theology can no longer avoid confronting without illusion the idea of the possible end, and in this situation the only theology that will be persuasive is one offering an alternative to teleological thinking. Of necessity, however, all teleologically directed theology becomes speechless in the face of this threatening end.

The experiences of the catastrophic and the tendencies toward demise and destruction cause any faith to become questionable whose appearance is primarily that of hope. Because hope is teleologically structured, the crisis in teleological thinking necessarily plunges every theology of hope into a crisis. The component of hope in the Christian faith cannot be seriously doubted. What is problematic, however, is Moltmann's assertion of the primacy of hope in Christian life. According to Moltmann, that is, "in the Christian life faith has the priority, but hope the primacy."[278] Moltmann even understands faith itself from the perspective of hope: "To believe means to cross in hope and anticipation the bounds that have been penetrated by the raising of the crucified."[279] Christian hope "constantly provokes and produces thinking of an anticipatory kind in love to man and the world."[280] According to Moltmann, theology is such anticipatory thinking. With that, however, theology like faith becomes caught in the teleological undertow.

It is not because hope can be ambiguous and illusory that the recourse to hope in this understanding of faith is problematical. It is no accident that the myth recounts that hope, too, was contained in Pandora's box. We, too, have seen that hope can lose itself in the future, as it were, without actively seizing that future.[281] One cannot level this reproach at Moltmann. He does not hope aimlessly into space, but speaks rather about hope that is established on the one hand, and active on the other, about an engaged hope of faith, about hope that is confidence.

What is questionable about Moltmann's understanding of faith is that despite its grounding in the cross of Jesus, it is nonetheless merely a Christian variation of a certain form of teleological thinking which has long since been overtaken by the incessant terror of history. The future is construed teleologically, a future into whose endless expanse and openness faith pushes the eschaton in anticipation. The theology of hope counts on an openness of the space of the future which is largely contradicted by the experience of the catastrophic and of the threatening end. And be the end deferred ever so far into the future, its possibility nonetheless cannot be eliminated. It is the limit of our future.

Eliade and, in his own way, already Kierkegaard speak about a faith that specifically cannot be given a teleological interpretation. This faith is not to be understood primarily as hope, but rather as courage. The juxtaposition of the apocalyptic and Christian understanding of existence has shown that the Christian faith can indeed be comprehended as a mode of courage, and it is quite possible that such an understanding of faith can open up new perspectives for theology in the shadow of the end.

Both P. Tillich and K. Rahner, each in his own way, have interpreted faith as courage, and it was Tillich who demonstrated how it is not hope, but rather courage that overcomes anxiety. He develops a history of anxiety in which the epochs of anxiety before death, before guilt, and before meaninglessness follow upon one another. Accordingly, Tillich tries to illuminate the various forms of courage through which the various forms of anxiety were overcome. According to Tillich, however, courage is not to be confused with freedom from anxiety. It does not extinguish anxiety, but rather takes it into itself.

We have already discussed in a different context the relationship between anxiety, fear, hope, and courage.[282] While fear and hope can be considered expectant emotions, we viewed courage in connection with decision, with the deed of active freedom. Tillich's considerations point in the same direction. "Courage," Tillich points out first of all, "is an ethical act." According to Tillich, however, its ethical significance reveals itself only within the framework of ontology. Courage "must be considered ontologically in order to be understood ethically."[283] Tillich defines courage as follows: "The courage to be is the ethical act in which man affirms his own being in spite of those elements of his existence which conflict with his essential self-affirmation."[284] Courage overcomes anxiety—and according to Tillich this means the "state in which a being is aware of its possible nonbeing"[285]—by means of the "in spite of" of self-affirmation.

More specifically, Tillich now defines faith as "the courage to accept acceptance."[286] The believer knows himself to be affirmed or accepted by being itself, by that which concerns us unconditionally. "Faith is the state of being grasped by the power of being-itself. The courage to be is an expression of faith and what 'faith' means must be understood through the courage to be."[287] As this state of being grasped thus, faith is "the character of accepting acceptance . . . Faith accepts 'in spite of'; and out of the 'in spite of' of faith the 'in spite of' of courage is born."[288]

For Rahner, too, faith is "the concreteness of something that we can describe as 'courage.' "[289] Whereas Tillich demonstrates the juxtaposition of courage and anxiety, Rahner focuses especially on the connection between courage and hope, bringing courage very close to hope. "For courage in the last resort is hope and hope is not hope if it is not courageous."[290] To be sure, Rahner's intent is to develop an understanding of hope from the concept of courage: "But in the light of the term 'courage' the term 'hope' can be understood better and more radically."[291] The result is that hope becomes an ethical concept, just as indeed that of courage is from the very start. Thus Rahner can finally say "that hope is decision, deed, venture, all of which are typical of the courageous person."[292] The source of hope is thus courage. Faith is such courage "when there is a question of *that* deed and *that* courage for the deed which are related to the totality of the one human existence."[293] Faith is the courage for an absolute hope grounded in God as the absolute future.[294] Faith hopes in God as the absolute future which is different from any planable future.[295]

Both Tillich and Rahner expand their understanding of faith considerably beyond the Christian concept. Tillich reckons with the possibility of an absolute faith similar in its formal structure to Christian faith, but with no particular content. "It is simply faith, undirected, absolute."[296] Its three components are "the experience of the power of being," "the dependence of the experience of nonbeing on the experience of being and the dependence of the experience of meaninglessness on the experience of meaning," and finally "the acceptance of being accepted."[297] According to Tillich, only this absolute faith can overcome the anxiety of meaninglessness. This faith recurs in the symbol of "the Crucified who cried to God who remained his God after the God of confidence had left him in the darkness of doubt and meaninglessness."[298]

While Tillich discusses the possibility of a latent church,[299] Rahner addresses the question of an anonymous Christianity.[300] Rahner maintains that courage, "if it is understood in its necessity and radicalness, is precisely what Christian theology describes as faith."[301] According to Rahner, the Christian faith differs from anonymous faith only through its explicit nature and reflexivity. It is related to the faith of anonymous Christians as an "explicit theory of action" does to the "spontaneous carrying out of this action instinctively and without reflection."[302]

Rahner's thesis about anonymous Christianity is problematical insofar as faith in the Christian sense moves into proximity with a kind of basic or primal trust which might be considered a universal anthropological structural element of every human being.[303] The faith associated with the cross and resurrection of Jesus is derived from a basic and universal attitude of trust to the point that even faith in the resurrection of Christ is derived anthropologically: "Since in his fundamental courage for life he believes in *his* 'resurrection' (that is, in being redeemed in his own death), he believes in the resurrection of Jesus."[304] The Christ event is merely "the historical happening of what he grasps for himself by hope," courage which Rahner has described previously as a universal possibility of existence.[305] This, however, largely screens out the peculiarities of Christian faith.

In contrast, Tillich speaks of absolute faith only where he perceives specific structural features of the Christian faith in a modified form within an existential model of trust. For Tillich, absolute faith is not to be confused with some unspecific basic trust, but rather structurally resembles faith in the justification of the sinner, though without any content formulated from the perspective of Christianity. Reference to the fate of Jesus is thus no longer constitutive for absolute faith. Even if for theological reasons one must remain reserved over against Tillich's thesis of absolute faith, it is worth noting that his interpretation of faith as a mode of courage points out a path to an understanding of the Christian faith that leaves teleological thinking behind.

Tillich identifies the power of being, being itself, as the source of courage, Rahner the absolute future. Despite any potential criticisms, Rahner's interpretation of faith does deserve consideration because it associates the courage of faith with God's future. In Rahner's sense, however, God's future is not to be understood teleologically. That is, the absolute future of which Rahner speaks refers to God's coming, God's approach, and is thus *adventus* or *parousia* in the sense explicated in our preceding discussion. In our understanding, however, the *adventus* of God is not to be separated from the fate of Jesus and formalized as an ontological entity. The *adventus* of God is primarily the fate of Christ, and faith is the courage that owes itself to this *adventus* of God in the cross and resurrection.

Faith does not hope teleologically for the end of the world as the annihilation of the extant world. It is grounded not in the future *collapse* of the world, but rather in God's *intervention*, as *adventus*, into this world, and hopes for the ever new intervention of the God which appeared in Jesus of Nazareth. As such, the Christian faith is the experience of the acquisition of space in the midst of apocalyptically experienced enclosure. The enclosure and inescapability of the world, the collapse of the world and of the individual in it are all essential elements of the apocalyptic experience of existence. Over against this experience, Paul writes in 2 Cor. 4:8f.: "We are afflicted in every way, but not crushed; perplexed, but not driven to despair; persecuted, but not forsaken; struck down, but not destroyed." In a paradoxical way, the apocalyptic experience of existence is both shared and negated in faith.

The *adventus* of God creates room for hope, and for this reason courage and hope cannot be played off against one another. Faith, however, is not only and not primarily hope. The *adventus* of God allows us to experience a new future in the midst of all absence of future. Faith is courage that includes the courage for hope against all hope. If faith liberates us to human existence in the midst of a world that is destructive both for and through human beings, then it also liberates us for hope, which is a fundamental feature of our existence. From courage, then, there grows the possibility of new hope in the midst of all hopelessness, but not vice versa. This is the perspective from which to interpret the Christian symbols of hope for humankind and the earth. They are the anthropological reflex of God's proximity. The hope of faith comes not from any *telos*, but rather from the experience of the *adventus* of God. While hope directs itself toward a *futurum*, it, like the *futurum* itself, is grounded in *adventus* and in courage. Over against apocalyptic, however, just as over against a teleological understanding of history, hope in the Christian faith is "*effectively indeterminate*," something seen perhaps most clearly in the fact "that Paul (Rom. 8:24) does not have to write, as would an apocalyptist, that we are delivered *only* in the direction of hope. In Jesus Christ the *particula exclusiva* for rescue in hope was eliminated."[306]

Faith is courage for questionable existence. Our existence is questionable because it is threatened by nonbeing, and, like the existence of the world, is called into question by the conceivable end. The certainty that there is nothing more to be expected from being and existence is concentrated apocalyptically in the expectation of the end. The annihilation of the world, should it take place, would ratify Western nihilism. The potential annihilation of being causes us to lose confidence in the meaning of existence. The end, which has now become fully conceivable, reveals the absurdity of our existence. Faith, too, experiences the absurd. It is tempted faith vacillating between the certainty of meaning on the one hand, and nihilism on the other.

Experiences of the absurd include the realization that humankind is threatened by destruction that would destroy all meaning. Faith participates in the anxiety before the nihilistically threatening end of humankind. As already emphasized on several occasions, the fate of Jesus as a salvific event does not offer any guarantee for the survival of human beings and nature. Hence both the believer and the nonbeliever find themselves confronted by the threat of the end. Certain theological conclusions can be drawn from this situation. Faith is precluded from relativizing the global catastrophe of nuclear holocaust—a catastrophe that has now become quite possible—through eschatology that speculates concerning the postmortem fate of humankind. Wherever this occurs—in a massive form, for example, in fundamentalist circles—one evades the totality of the threatening end, and in this case eschatology is merely a religious variation of speculation concerning "the day after." Such eschatology reflects on the end with the goal of annulling the end.

In view of this global threat, a problem arises analogous to the theological understanding of death. Collective destruction, like individual death, is to be taken seriously as a limit. As the limit of life it is also the limit of our thinking. Any thinking intent on transcending this limit fails to realize that the locus of our reflection is to be found only on this side of that limit. Just as individual death must be the limit for every individual eschatology, so also is the collective destruction of humankind the limit for every universal eschatology. Otherwise Christian eschatology becomes an attempt to evade the severity of the threatening end. If, however, the threatening end is accepted as the limit of eschatological thinking, then nihilism threatens to overwhelm theology.

It was especially Paul Tillich who reflected on the consequences of this situation for Christology. His argumentation presupposes that Jesus of Nazareth would not be the Christ without those who believe in him, since the Christian faith is bound to the transmission of the message of salvation. That is, the threatening end of humankind becomes a christological problem because it would destroy the historical continuity without which the universal validity of Christology is called into question. Tillich recalls first the New Testament statements according to which Christ will always be with those who believe in him, unto the end of the world, so that the gates of hell will not overcome his church and finally Christ will return as the judge of the world. But Tillich then immediately asks:

> How can such assertions be combined with the possibility that mankind may destroy itself tomorrow? And even if human beings were left who were cut off from the historical tradition in which Jesus as the Christ has appeared, one must still ask: "What do the biblical assertions mean in view of such a development?" One cannot answer in terms of ordering God not to allow such catastrophes. For the structure of the universe clearly indicates that the conditions of life on earth are limited in time, and the conditions of human life even more so.[307]

Tillich responds that God's revelation in Christ possesses absolute validity only for human beings as it addressees, and refers to their existence; this does not exclude other relationships between God and other parts of the universe, something valid both in a spatial respect—consider the possible existence of extraterrestrial beings[308]—and from a temporal perspective. According to Tillich, however, Jesus as the Christ is the center of human history:

> In faith it is certain that for historical mankind in its unique, continuous development, as experienced here and now, Christ is the center. But faith cannot judge about the future destiny of historical mankind and the way it will come to an end. Jesus is the Christ for us, namely, for those who participate in the historical continuum which he determines in its meaning. This existential limitation does not qualitatively limit its significance, but it leaves open other ways of divine self-manifestations before and after our historical continuum.[309]

Tillich's christological argumentation respects the potential end of humankind as a limit of thought insofar as Jesus is conceived as the Christ *pro nobis.* Tillich's Christology maintains the reference to our own existence instead of trying to appropriate a position outside our historical reality. If one inquires further just how he succeeds in conceiving Christology together with the possible end of humankind, the answer is that he does so by means of the idea of God. With the doctrine of God, however, he seems to have found a position outside our own historical situation after all, and beyond any conceivable catastrophe. Just as the end of humankind would not mean the destruction of the universe, and does not exclude the possibility of intelligent life on other planets, neither would the disappearance of Christ as the center of human history mean the end of God. The theological problem and temptation presented by the possible self-destruction of humankind is answered by hope in divine self-manifestations beyond human history.

Although Tillich is apparently quite prepared to entertain the notion of the end within the sphere of Christology, it seems that the idea of God is excepted from this questioning. This is in any case suggested by the fact that Tillich does not really pose the question of theodicy within the context of Christology. The questions raised push more forcefully to the forefront in connection with Tillich's eschatology, where he takes up the problem of theodicy by seeking its solution in Schelling's idea of essentialization. Tillich's fundamental assertion is: "The Divine Life is the eternal conquest of the negative; this is its blessedness."[310] Expressed metaphorically, God overcomes all negativity by eternally remembering the positive in all things while excluding the negative. "With a bold metaphor one could say that the temporal, in a continuous process, becomes 'eternal memory.' "[311] Through the idea of essentialization all catastrophes and negativity will ultimately acquire meaning: "The conflicts and sufferings of nature under the conditions of existence and its longing for salvation, of which Paul speaks (Romans, chapter 8), serve the enrichment of essential being after the negation of the negative in everything that has being."[312]

According to Tillich, it is the idea of God that can overcome nihilistic despair in the face of threatening destruction. Although Tillich's talk of essentialization is expressly intended to be understood not literally, but rather symbolically, the question does arise whether for Tillich the idea of God does not lead theology to evade reality. Both the hypothesis of extraterrestrial intelligence as well as the idea of God can be the attempt to elude in an escapist fashion the severity of the threat of destruction. The doctrine of God basically runs the risk of becoming flight from precisely the human dilemma we should be confronting. J. Schell critically objects to such attempts that "by setting up an intelligence that itself escapes extinction and looks down upon the event, and by endowing that intelligence with suspiciously human characteristics, we in effect deny or evade the reality of extinction, for we have covertly manufactured a survivor."[313] Now, the utmost concern of Tillich's doctrine of God with its reference to the God above God is to cleanse the doctrine of God of all suspiciously human characteristics. In the idea of essentialization as eternal memory, however, there nonetheless inheres in symbolic form the idea of a subject that survives the catastrophe, or of suprapersonal subjectivity, and it is significant that Tillich is well aware of having left behind in his eschatology the position on this side of the limit which we identified as the death and end of humankind. Thus Tillich admits with respect to his own eschatology: "Although most considerations given within the theological circle deal with man and his world in their relation to God, our final consideration points in the opposite direction and speaks of God in his relation to man and his world."[314] It seems that here the framework of Tillich's method of correlation is exceeded, and with it the limit imposed by the end.

The question thus arises concerning the extent to which Tillich's theology ultimately really does confront the experience of the absurd and of nihilistic despair, even though it claims to do so. Tillich speaks of faith which has the courage to accept being accepted. In his understanding, the source of this courage is found in being itself or in the power of being. Like the long metaphysical tradition of the West before him, Tillich conceives being and meaning together. Being, interpreted against the background of German Idealism, specifically the philosophy of Schelling, is once again called upon to establish meaning and thereby to overcome the anxiety of meaninglessness. One must ask, however, whether this solution still holds up after metaphysical reflection on being has come to its end in nihilism, which both theoretically and practically concludes that there is nothing to being and existence and thus no meaning to existence.[315]

The real danger of the destruction of humankind forces us to reconsider not only Christology, but also the doctrine of God. In doing so, we must take seriously the insight that we can speak not only about Christ, but also about God only on this side of the limit imposed by the end. We can still speak in a theologically responsible fashion only about the God *for us*, the God who stands in relation to our historical existence. In view of the threatening end, all speculation concerning God *as such* in his aseity is precluded. This means, however that the nuclear holocaust, which has now become fully conceivable, also constitutes the limit of every doctrine of God. Faith can hold only to the God for us, and cannot console itself with the idea of a God beyond or without humankind as the ground of the universe. Such a God would at most be conceivable as *deus absconditus*, one who, e.g., in Luther's sense is precisely not the guarantor of salvation and the ground of hope, but rather an abyss. The God for us, however, the *deus pro nobis*, is the God emerging in the fate of Jesus, the only one to whom faith can cling in recollection in the face of the horror. This God has not annulled panentheistically all negativity within himself, but rather himself falls, in the form of the cross, into the vortex of nothingness. We must dare to make the harsh assertion that the end of humankind would also mean the end of the God for us.

This sentence is saying something different than that God will no longer exist after the catastrophe. With such a negation we would again be speaking about God in and of himself, albeit in the form of a negative assertion. What is meant rather is that just as death is the limit for us, so also would the threatening annihilation of humankind be the limit of God for us. To use a slightly altered version of a formulation from the Revelation of John, the annihilation of humankind would be the equivalent of a second death of God.[316]

The theological meaning of these statements emerges from the notion of remembering and forgetting. According to the Old Testament understanding, what is actually terrifying about death is being forgotten, even with God. Being dead means to have been forgotten. The concept of forgetting can thus first of all serve our interpretation of elements of Christology, since the cross must be understood as the attempt to dislodge Christ and his message from human consciousness, and to surrender them to oblivion. The misunderstood reference to the death of God is to a certain extent justified within the context of Christology insofar as, along with Jesus of Nazareth himself, the God he preached was also to fall into oblivion. The death of God in the fate of Jesus of Nazareth consists in being surrendered to oblivion. This is all we mean by the otherwise quite problematic reference to the death of God. Within the framework of such an interpretation, the resurrection of Jesus now means that Jesus was snatched away from oblivion when God called him into living memory both for himself and for human beings. By recalling the living Jesus into memory, God also recalled himself into human memory. The overcoming of the death of God consists in the post-Easter remembrance of the crucified one.

The destruction of humankind constitutes a second death of God insofar as, together with every conceivable human subject of remembering, the memory of Jesus and thus that of God also would be extinguished. To conclude from this that there would be no more God after the annihilation of humankind would be to ignore the *extra nos* of the *deus pro nobis* and to declare God a product of human consciousness. However, theological reference to God's *extra nos* cannot overlook the consequence which the destruction of humankind would involve for the doctrine of God, namely, that, differently than in the case of the death and resurrection of Jesus, no subject would remain into whose memory God might recall himself. Here we come to the limit of what can be said. At this limit perhaps the last thing that can be said is that the God of Jesus proves to be the God for us precisely in the fact that at the end he would go down with us, would enter into destruction with us just as he entered into death with Jesus of Nazareth. For faith this constitutes a final consolation, albeit one itself bordering on the absurd.

Representatives of the new apocalyptic of nuclear holocaust have picked up this reference to a second death in order to express with its help the qualitative distinction between individual death and the destruction of humankind. This distinction would then consist in the fact that along with humankind all memory of the dead of the past would be extinguished. The dead would then have been as if they never were. The annihilation of humankind would be the equivalent of the annihilation of all memory. The nihilistic result would be that the distinction between perpetrators and victims of history, between justice and injustice would be leveled, and that guilt and forgiveness would become meaninglessness. Over against this, the Christian faith draws from the resurrection of Jesus the hope that the God who would go down with us would be able to overcome his own second death, and would himself nonetheless be able to recall into memory his own humankind, humankind who could no longer remember him. Over against contemporary apocalyptic under the sign of nihilism, the final hope of faith is: We will have been. And with this the hope remains that the distinctions between perpetrators and victims, justice and injustice, guilt and forgiveness will not lose their meaning. This has consequences for ethics and for one's personal life and actions in the shadow of threat. With this formulation of Christian hope we admittedly are coming a bit closer to Tillich's notion of essentialization and eternal memory, a notion we criticized earlier. In the version we are suggesting, however, this idea is modified from the perspective of Christ. The reference is now to a kind of tempted hope that acquires paradoxical features.

The attitude toward existence characterizing faith in the *deus pro nobis,* faith that takes seriously the limit of the end in the doctrine of God as well, resembles less Prometheus than Sisyphus, who confronts the absurd and rebels against it. Hence Christian theology in the shadow of the end finds an important dialogue partner in Camus's philosophy of the absurd.[317] The attitude toward existence assumed by Camus can also be called courage. It is the courage to affirm or accept oneself in the face of the absurd. This courage does not, however, annul the absurdity of our existence. All belief in the meaningfulness of our existence is negated. For Camus, hope stands on the same level as suicide. He considers both to be attempts at fleeing the absurd, and both are to be rejected.[318] In truth, however, there is no escape, and not even the possibility for flight through hope, since human beings "are deprived of the memory of a lost home or the hope of a promised land."[319]

The idea of the absurd emerges through alienating experiences, through the perception that "the world is 'dense,' " through the perception of the degree to which "a stone is foreign and irreducible to us," and of the intensity with which "nature or a landscape can negate us."[320] Similarly alienating is "this discomfort in the face of man's own inhumanity, this incalculable tumble before the image of what we are, this 'nausea,' as a writer [Sartre] of today calls it."[321] The world appears senseless. More precisely, according to Camus the experience of the absurd is that of the discord or contradiction arising through the simultaneous presence of ourselves and the world, so that "the Absurd is not in man (if such a metaphor could have a meaning) nor in the world, but in their presence together."[322]

It is not Camus's intention to evade the absurd, but rather to live it. Hence, he rejects not only hope and suicide but also the leap into faith in God, a leap Kierkegaard executed in an exemplary fashion. Over against other representatives of existentialism, Camus objects that they do take a leap into a kind of meaningfulness which distorts one's view of the real absurdity of the copresence of human being and world. According to Kierkegaard, faith is the only alternative to despair. Despair, however, is sin. Camus, however, rejects precisely this leap from despair into faith. "Seeking what is true is not seeking what is desirable. If in order to elude the anxious question: 'What would life be?' one must, like the donkey, feed on the roses of illusion, then the absurd mind, rather than resigning itself to falsehood, prefers to adapt fearlessly Kierkegaard's reply: 'despair.' Everything considered, a determined soul will always manage."[323] If according to Kierkegaard despair is sin, then according to Camus the monstrous assertion must be risked: "The absurd is sin without God." Camus does not, however, seek redemption from this sin, but rather takes it upon himself to "live in that state of the absurd."[324]

In his attitude toward existence, Camus is able to identify with Sisyphus: "Sisyphus is the absurd hero. He *is*, as much through his passions as through his torture."[325] Sisyphus symbolizes an attitude of revolt. He revolts against the absurd. "That revolt gives life its value."[326] He also revolts against death. The person in revolt[327] understands himself as someone condemned to death who does not accept his fate, but rather rebels against his execution even up to his last breath. "It is essential to die unreconciled and not of one's own free will."[328]

This revolt against the absurd, however, creates new meaning in the midst of all meaninglessness. "The absurd has meaning only insofar as it is not agreed to."[329] To that extent, however, life acquires meaning through this revolt.

The myth of Sisyphus represents an attitude of courage. The courage of the absurd spirit is the courage to affirm oneself bravely despite all experience of the absurd. Faith comes quite close to this attitude. It is, however, to use Tillich's words, the courage to accept oneself as accepted in the face of the absurd. Camus neither can nor wants to take this step as well. The faith in being accepted implies an *extra nos*, the notion of which Camus considers to be merely an excuse. The courage of faith, however, reckons with the *adventus* of God for us, i.e., with his coming-to us. In the midst of the absurd, the *adventus* of God is the coming of meaning. Without denying the differences here, theology today should listen anew to Camus's philosophy of the absurd as a voice that with rare and unadorned frankness has expressed the experience of meaninglessness and nonsense which is reaching its final intensification in the technical possibility of an *annihilatio mundi.*

Courage is an ethical concept. Faith as the affirmation of questionable existence as affirmed existence considers itself called to action. It is to accept existence which it knows to be accepted. In many ways, this practical affirmation of questionable existence resembles the humane ethos of the rebel as impressively described in Camus's novel *The Plague.*[330] Action grounded in faith is a protest against everything that is catastrophic that causes the world to become apocalyptic. It is the active proclamation of the meaning whose coming is the *adventus* of God. Faith does not stare anxiously transfixed toward the end of the world, nor does it surrender to apocalyptic pleasure in demise and destruction, but rather affirms both the life God has himself affirmed as well as the world God has affirmed, and does so through active engagement for the sake of both.

The acceptance of existence which one knows to be accepted does not, however, consist only in action, but under certain circumstances also in suffering. In this respect, faith is the courage to suffer. As we have already seen, neither freedom from anxiety nor freedom from suffering is a characteristic feature of the Christian faith. Rather, a specific form of anxiety as well as a specific mode of suffering are part of its essence. According to the apocalyptic understanding, both anxiety and suffering are part of the eschatological tribulations, and as we have already shown, they also determine the attitude of the Christian faith toward existence. It is first of all the suffering from apocalyptic anxiety that faith takes upon itself to endure. It is the suffering under the world's nexus of disaster and calamity, a nexus whose enclosed nature in principle seems sundered and broken through in the fate of Jesus, and yet whose overwhelming power is experienced again and again, tempting and assaulting faith. Finally, it is not only the passive endurance of apocalyptic disaster, but also active co-suffering with the victims of history.

Cosuffering with the victims of an apocalyptically structured world emerges as a consequence of the cross and of the believers' participation in the fate of Jesus. Such participation also includes remembering the suffering and those who suffer. Faith, that is, is participation in the living memory of the crucified one. If the fatal element in Jesus' death consisted in the utter oblivion of the crucified one, then the Easter experience of the disciples consisted in the fact that Jesus was called into their memory, unsummoned, all-powerfully, living. The experience of faith in the resurrection of Jesus consists in no longer being able or permitted to forget the crucified one. This includes the commission and task of transmitting and keeping alive the memory of the crucified one. Precisely as such, however, faith is participation in the memory of the crucified one, i.e., in the memory of the suffering of Christ. Faith is, as J. B. Metz puts it, *memoria passionis.*[331] Hence cosuffering with the crucified one also consists in remembering the suffering of the countless victims of history, remembering which in its own turn can as a subversive act lead to conflict with the perpetrators and thus bring believers themselves into suffering.

The remembrance of suffering takes place equally in relating the passion story of the victims and in active engagement in protest against all that is catastrophic, against all that causes the world affirmed by God to become apocalyptic and worthy of negation. Yet it also takes place in prayer. Prayer is thinking, reflection, and remembrance before God. Cosuffering includes prayer in which those who suffer and the victims of history are recalled in memory before God and are remembered to God in the form of lament, petition, and intercession. This is not an alternative, but rather a corollary to active cosuffering with the victims. Prayer as the remembrance of suffering is simultaneously an expression of the hope of faith that the annihilation of humankind, which has now become possible, does not extinguish the memory of the dead. It assumes a counterposition over against the oblivion prefiguring the nihilistic consequences of the technically possible *annihilatio mundi*, oblivion proleptically allowing the perpetrators to triumph over their victims. Prayer is an expression of hope insofar as, like the Lord's Prayer, it unites the remembrance of suffering[332] with the petition for the coming of the kingdom of God, and issues in the praise of God. This praise is the protest against the absurd.

In the shadow of the threatening end, this petition for the coming of the kingdom of God, along with its hope, itself borders on the absurd. It requires courage. Today, however, we need this courage more than ever.

ABBREVIATIONS

BASOR — *Bulletin of the American Schools of Oriental Research*
BZNW — Beihefte zur Zeitschrift für die neutestamentliche Wissenschaft
EvTh — *Evangelische Theologie*
FG — Festgabe (presentation volume)
FRLANT — Forschungen zur Religion und Literatur des Alten und Neuen Testaments
FS — Festschrift
HTKNT — Herders theologischer Kommentar zum Neuen Testament
KD — *Kerygma und Dogma*
PhRev — *Philosophical Review*
REJ — *Revue des études juives*
RGG — *Die Religion in Geschichte und Gegenwart*
SANT — Studien zum Alten und Neuen Testament
TDNT — *Theological Dictionary of the New Testament*
TRE — *Theologische Realenzyklopädie*
TZ — *Theologische Zeitschrift*
WD — *Wort und Dienst*
WMANT — Wissenschaftliche Monographien zum Alten und Neuen Testament
WUNT — Wissenschaftliche Untersuchungen zum Neuen Testament
ZST — *Zeitschrift für systematische Theologie*
ZTK — *Zeitschrift für Theologie und Kirche*

NOTES

Introduction
THE AGE OF ANXIETY

1. To my knowledge, this designation was first used in reference to our age in the lyrical work *The Age of Anxiety: A Baroque Eclogue*, which W. H. Auden wrote in 1946.

2. Karl Jaspers, *The Future of Mankind*, 255.

3. Karl Jaspers, *Die Atombombe und die Zukunft des Menschen. Politisches Bewusstsein in unserer Zeit*, 399. [This passage was omitted in the Engish translation cited in note 2 above.—Trans.] Cf. also F. Dürrenmatt's story "Der Tunnel," *Die Stadt. Prosa I–IV*, 149ff.: "What should we do," cries the desperate engineer in the train plunging inexorably into the depths of the tunnel. The protagonist, a young man, answers: "Nothing. God has let us fall, and so we plunge toward him."

4. G. Anders, "Über die Bombe und die Wurzeln unserer Apokalypse-Blindheit," in idem, *Die Antiquiertheit des Menschen. Über die Seele im Zeitalter der zweiten industriellen Revolution*, 233–324, here 277.

5. K. Jaspers, *The Future of Mankind*, 322.

6. G. Anders, "Über die Bombe und die Wurzeln unserer Apokalypse-Blindheit," 269.

7. Cf. ibid., 265.

8. Cf. S. Kierkegaard, *The Concept of Anxiety*, 155 (ch. V).

9. G. Anders, "Über die Bombe und die Wurzeln unserer Apokalypse-Blindheit," 279.

10. One need think only of the profound shock experienced by the United States and its feeling of self-worth—"the land of unlimited possibilities"—as a result of the Vietnam War. A lasting economic recession was added, interrupted for only a brief period by a temporary recovery of the American economy and a dramatic increase in the exchange rate of the dollar abroad. The newly awakened feeling of nationalism in the United States is admittedly a different matter altogether.

11. G. Anders, "Über die Bombe und die Wurzeln unserer Apokalypse-Blindheit," 277.

12. Cf. F. Sieburg, *Die Lust am Untergang. Selbstgespräche auf Bundesebene*.

13. See F. van der Meer, *Apocalypse: Visions from the Book of Revelation in Western Art*.

14. The history of the theme of the Apocalypse in painting is well documented in the exhibition catalog *Apokalypse—ein Prinzip Hoffnung. Ausstellung zum 100. Geburtstag von E. Bloch im Wilhelm-Hack-Museum*. See also M. P. Maass, *Das Apokalyptische in der modernen Kunst. Endzeit oder Neuzeit. Versuch einer Deutung*.

15. Cucchi's apocalyptic works are documented in the catalog by A. Ginsberg, *Weisses Totentuch*, published as a guide to the Cucchi exhibition open in Basel until March 4, 1984; see also A. Ginsberg, *White Shroud*.

16. This picture was done in 1979/80 and is now owned by the Kunsthalle Bielefeld.

17. *Malevil* is actually a film version of the novel by R. Merle, *Malevil.*

18. The following selective bibliography can serve as an illustration: A. A. Guha, *Ende. Tagebuch aus dem 3. Weltkrieg;* M. Horx, *Glückliche Reise. Roman zwischen den Zeiten;* Diogenes-Katastrophen-Kollektiv, eds., *Weltuntergangsgeschichten von Edgar Poe bis Arno Schmidt;* C. Berlitz, *Doomsday 1999 A.D.;* O. Friedrich, *End of the World: A History;* the book by the author of *Frankenstein,* M. W. Shelley, *The Last Man;* J. Schell, *The Fate of the Earth.*

19. See, e.g., G. Pausewang, *The Last Children.*

20. M. Ende, *The Neverending Story* (Harmondsworth: Puffin, 1985).

21. *Global 2000: The Report to the President of the U.S.*, 3 vols. (New York: Pergamon Press, 1980).

22. Cf. also R. Kaiser, "Weltende," in *Zumutungen an die Grünen*, 1–5.

23. H. Boehncke, R. Stollmann, and G. Vinnai, eds., *Weltuntergänge.*

24. Ibid., 6.

25. Christa Wolf, *Kassandra.* See also the English translation, *Cassandra: A Novel and Four Essays* (New York: Farrar, Straus, Giroux, 1984). In this context, see also C. Wolf, *Voraussetzungen einer Erzählung: Kassandra. Frankfurter Poetik-Vorlesungen* (Sammlung Luchterhand 456; Darmstadt: Luchterhand, 1983).

26. Ibid., 76f.

27. Ibid., 6.

28. Ibid., 14.

29. U. Horstmann, *Das Untier. Konturen einer Philosophie der Menschenflucht.*

30. Ibid., 17.

31. Ibid., 94.

32. Ibid., 110.

33. See J. Derrida, "Of an Apocalyptic Tone Recently Adopted in Philosophy," *Semeia* 23 (1982) 63–97; also published as "On a Newly Arisen Apocalyptic Tone in Philosophy," in P. Fenves, ed., *Raising the Tone in Philosophy*, 117–71.

34. See the critical view of U. Hornauer, "Abgesang der Postmoderne. Die unvernünftige Rede vom Ende der Aufklärung," *Evangelische Kommentare* 18 (1985) 492–94.

35. O. Spengler, *The Decline of the West* (1926).

36. There are "those who mistakenly take the demise of antiquity to be like that of an ocean liner. The notion of catastrophe is *not* contained in the word demise. If instead of demise one uses the term culmination . . . then the 'pessimistic' aspect is silenced for a while without altering the fundamental meaning of the term" (O. Spengler, *Pessimismus?* Schriftenreihe der Preussischen Jahrbücher, 4, 3f.).

37. As is well known, "Between the Times" was the title of the periodical which from 1923 to 1933 served as the organ for early dialectical theology. The title itself, however, expressed the sentiments not just of theological circles, which is also why Spengler alluded to this name in his assertion that "we live today 'between the ages' " (O. Spengler, *The Hour of Decision, Part One: Germany and World Historical Revolution*, 24).

38. D. Bonhoeffer, *The Cost of Discipleship*, 98.

39. H. Blumenberg, *Schiffbruch mit Zuschauer. Paradigma einer Daseinsmetapher.*

40. Cf. ibid., 58ff.

41. H. M. Enzensberger, *Der Untergang der Titanic. Eine Komödie*, 76f.

42. Christa Wolf, *Kassandra*, 121.

43. Ibid., 41.

44. O. Spengler, *The Hour of Decision*, xiv.

45. F. Lücke, *Versuch einer vollständigen Einleitung in die Offenbarung des Johannes oder Allgemeine Untersuchungen über die apokalyptische Literatur überhaupt und die Apokalypse des Johannes insbesondere.*

46. For a survey of scholarship, see esp. J. M. Schmidt, *Die jüdische Apokalyptik. Die Geschichte ihrer Erforschung von den Anfängen bis zu den Textfunden von Qumran.*

47. Cf. J. Weiss, *Jesus' Proclamation of the Kingdom of God.*

48. Cf. Albert Schweitzer, *The Quest of the Historical Jesus: A Critical Study of Its Progress from Reimarus to Wrede;* this work originally appeared in 1906 with the title *Von Reimarus zu Wrede. Eine Geschichte der Leben-Jesu Forschung.*

49. Cf. the interesting interpretation of Overbeck's work with the aid of the Freudian model of "grief and melancholy" by R. Wehrli, *Alter und Tod des Christentums bei Franz Overbeck,* esp. 216ff., 229f. See also A. Pfeiffer, *Franz Overbecks Kritik des Christentums.*

50. F. Overbeck, *Über die Christlichkeit unserer heutigen Theologie. Streit- und Friedensschrift.*

51. Ibid., 50.

52. F. Overbeck, *Christentum und Kultur. Gedanken und Anmerkungen zur modernen Theologie,* ed. C. A. Bernoulli, 38.

53. Cf. ibid., 51; Overbeck confirms the "interconfessionality of modern theology"; cf. ibid., 277.

54. Cf. F. Overbeck, ibid., 20, 67.

55. Ibid., 66; "Contemporary Christianity has so little room for the whole notion of the return of Christ that it cannot even conceive it historically as a part of primitive Christianity, or at least insists that it is to be viewed as a negligible feature," ibid., 68.

56. "Calm reflection sees plainly that Christianity outfitted itself with a theology only when it wanted to render itself possible in a world which it was actually negating . . . For precisely in the beginnings of theology, i.e., in the oldest Christian Alexandrian theology, it becomes as clear as it possibly can be . . . that Christianity wanted to use its theology to recommend itself to the wise men of the world and to make itself acceptable to them. Viewed in this way, however, theology is nothing more than part of the secularization of Christianity, a luxury it allowed itself which, like every other luxury, is not to be had without a price" (*Über die Christlichkeit unserer heutigen Theologie,* 10).

57. *Christentum und Kultur,* 13.

58. Ibid., 263; cf. also 48.

59. *Über die Christlichkeit unserer heutigen Theologie,* 70.

60. *Christentum und Kultur,* 289.

61. Cf. ibid., 11.

62. Ibid., 291.

63. Ibid., 263f.

64. Karl Barth, *The Epistle to the Romans,* 314 (on Rom. 8:24–25).

65. Ibid., 3. Cf. also Barth's essay "Unsettled Questions for Theology Today," in idem, *Theology and Church,* 55–73.

66. The development and types of eschatology in the twentieth century are discussed by F. Holström, *Das eschatologische Denken der Gegenwart;* W. Ölsner, *Die Entwicklung der Eschatologie von Schleiermacher bis zur Gegenwart;* G. Hoffmann, *Das Problem der letzten Dinge in der neueren evangelischen Theologie;* H. Diem, "Das eschatologische Problem in der gegenwärtigen Theologie," *ThR,* N.S. 11 (1939) 228–47; H. Grass, "Das eschatologische Problem in der Gegenwart," *Dank an P. Althaus,* ed. W. Künneth and W. Joest, 47–78. See also the surveys in W. Kreck, *Die Zukunft des Gekommenen. Grundprobleme der Eschatologie,* 14–76; G. Sauter, *Zukunft und Verheissung. Das Problem der Zukunft in der gegenwärtigen theologischen und philosophischen Diskussion,* 79–145; J. Moltmann, *Theology of Hope,* 37–84.

67. J. Weiss, *Die Predigt Jesu vom Reiche Gottes,* ed. F. Hahn (Göttingen: Vandenhoeck & Ruprecht, 1892; 3rd ed. 1964), 50; this passage not included in the English translation cited in n. 47 above.

68. Cf. K. Koch, *The Rediscovery of Apocalyptic: A Polemical Work on a Neglected Area of Biblical Studies and Its Damaging Effects on Theology and Philosophy*, 57–94.

69. Cf. esp. M. Werner, *Die Weltanschauungsproblem bei K. Barth und A. Schweitzer*, as well as F. Buri, *Die Bedeutung der neutestamentlichen Eschatologie für die neuere protestantische Theologie.*

70. Concerning Barth's problematical reception of Overbeck, see the critical remarks by R. Wehrli, *Alter und Tod des Christentums bei Franz Overbeck*, 44ff.; A. Pfeiffer, *Franz Overbecks Kritik des Christentums*, 79ff.

71. P. Althaus, *Die letzten Dinge*, 77.

72. Ibid. (1st ed. 1922), 95.

73. See esp. the criticism of the conceptions of a supratemporal eschatology in F. Buri, *Die Bedeutung der neutestamentlichen Eschatologie für die neuere protestantische Theologie*, 48ff. Cf. also Albert Schweitzer, *Paul and His Interpreters: A Critical History*, 228: "The term eschatology ought only to be applied when reference is made to the end of the world as expected in the immediate future, and the events, hopes, and fears connected therewith. The use of the word to designate the subjective end of individuals, in connection with which no imminent catastrophe [!] affecting all mankind is in question, can only be misleading, since it creates the false impression—*exempla docent*—that the Pauline eschatology can be paralleled and compared with an eschatology belonging to the mystery-religions. Of eschatology in the late Jewish or early Christian sense there is not a single trace to be found in any Graeco-Oriental doctrine."

74. Among more recent works addressing the history of interpretation of the Apocalypse of John, see G. Maier, *Die Johannesoffenbarung und die Kirche*, WUNT 25; G. Kretschmar, *Die Offenbarung des Johannes. Die Geschichte ihrer Auslegung im 1. Jahrtausend;* On the history of interpretation since 1700, see also the survey in O. Böcher, *Die Johannesapokalypse*, 1–25.

75. As examples see the cassette series by J. Falwell, *Nuclear War and the Second Coming of Jesus Christ*, or by J. Langhammer, *Die Offenbarung Jesu Christi. 12 Vorträge über das letzte Buch der Bibel unter dem Thema "Was bald geschehen wird."*

76. See esp. K. Heim, *The World: Its Creation and Consummation.*

77. Ibid., 113.

78. Ibid.. 124.

79. Ibid., 159.

80. Cf. ibid., 116–21.

81. Cf. ibid., 130f.

82. Cf. ibid., 117: "The whole of reality will be brought back from the polar state into that supra-polar state in which God is. Biblically expressed: 'God will be all in all.' "

83. Similar problems attach to M. Schloemann's attempt to reformulate, in the face of the present ecological crisis, the doctrine of the *consummatio mundi* in the sense of *annihilatio mundi: Wachstumstod und Eschatologie. Die Herausforderung christlicher Theologie durch die Umweltkrise.*

84. One classical attempt is that of G. von Rad, *Old Testament Theology*, 2.306ff.; subsequent German editions contain additional material. On this whole discussion, cf. K. Koch, *The Rediscovery of Apocalyptic*, 36ff., 48ff.

85. G. Sauter, *Zukunft und Verheissung*, 250.

86. Cf. H. Kraft, "Die altchristliche Prophetie und die Entstehung des Montanismus," *TZ* 11 (1955) 149–271.

87. On this whole discussion, cf. K.-H. Schwarte's article on "Apokalyptik/Apopkalypsen V," *TRE* 3.257–75, and R. Konrad's article "Apokalyptik/Apokalypsen VI," *TRE* 3.275–80. Concerning the Reformation and thereafter, see G. Seebass's article "Apokalyptik VII," *TRE* 3.280–89.

88. Cf. G. Podskalski, *Byzantinische Reichseschatologie*, Münchener Univ. schr. R. phil. Fak. 9, 16ff.

89. Hippolytus, *Comm. on Daniel*, IV. 21. 3.

90. Cf. in general H. Grundmann, Ketzergeschichte des Mittelalters.

91. See the recent work of H.-U. Hofmann, *Luther und die Johannes-Apokalypse.*

92. Cf. R. Schwarz, *Die apokalyptische Theologie Thomas Müntzers und der Taboriten;* W. Elliger, *Thomas Müntzer. Leben und Werk;* idem, *Aussenseiter der Reformation: Thomas Müntzer.*

93. Cf. K. Deppermann, *Melchior Hoffman: Social Unrest and Apocalyptic Visions of the Age of Reformation.*

94. Cf. K. Hutten, *Seher, Grübler, Enthusiasten. Sekten und religiöse Sondergemeinschaften der Gegenwart*, 28ff.; M. Schmidt and J. Butscher, "Adventisten," *TRE* 1.454–62.

95. Cited according to K. Hutten, *Seher, Grübler, Enthusiasten*, 33.

96. Ibid., 35f.

97. E. Bloch, *Tübinger Einleitung in die Philosophie, Gesamtausgabe* 13, 183: "an *explosive myth* of liberation (and thus also far removed from the tame series in which Bultmann's neo-bourgeois 'demythologization' stands)."

98. S. N. Bulgakov, "Apokalyptik und Sozialismus. Religiös-philosophische Parallelen (1910)," in idem, *Sozialismus im Christentum*, 53–134, here 64.

99. Ibid.

100. Cf. ibid., 112ff.

101. Cf. ibid., 76.

102. Ibid., 78.

103. E. Bloch, *Geist der Utopie, Gesamtausgabe* 3, new ed., 151.

104. E. Bloch, *The Principle of Hope*, 215; cf. also 157f.

105. E. Käsemann, "The Beginnings of Christian Theology," in idem, *New Testament Questions of Today*, 82–107, here 102.

106. Cf. W. Pannenberg, *Offenbarung als Geschichte.* See also the English translation, *Revelation as History.*

107. Cf. G. Sauter, *Zukunft und Verheissung*, passim.

108. Cf. J. Moltmann, *Theology of Hope*, passim. Concerning the theology of hope, see also the collection *Diskussion über die "Theologie der Hoffnung" von Jürgen Moltmann*, ed. and introd. by W.-D. Marsch. Concerning the renaissance of apocalyptic in systematic theology, see also the survey in K. Koch, *The Rediscovery of Apocalyptic*, 98–111.

109. E. Bloch, *The Principle of Hope*, 3.

110. W. Dantine, *Hoffen—Handeln—Leiden. Christliche Lebensperspektiven*, 21ff., also views hope as the hermeneutical key to the comparison between apocalyptic and Christianity. The alternative between an apocalyptic understanding of existence on the one hand, and Christian faith on the other, prompts Dantine to use the formula "apocalyptic or hope," whereby a series of familiar theological prejudices toward apocalyptic is repeated. Apocalyptic and faith are for Dantine two juxtaposed forms of hope. "In our vocabulary, 'apocalyptic' is to be understood as the current, briefly sketched understanding of a hopeless hope in the ultimate future, while 'hope' is understood in the sense of the Old and New Testaments, in contrast to Jewish apocalyptic [!], as eschatological hope that looks from the certainty of the ultimate fulfillment of the world toward the possibility of a change in history, thus taking future history seriously" (54). The optimistic faith in progress characteristic of the 1960s is clearly speaking here in Dantine's understanding of Christian faith as hope: "Humankind is standing today before yet unimagined possibilities of coming development in future cosmic history" (78).

111. E. Bloch, *The Principle of Hope*, 127; see also 90, 106f.

112. In his discussion with Heidegger, Bloch contests Heidegger's own understanding of F. Hölderlin's verse, "Where there is danger, rescue also grows" (ibid., 111–13).

113. Cf. E. Bloch, *Tübinger Einleitung in die Philosophie, Gesamtausgabe*, 13, 241f.

114. *The Principle of Hope*, 112.
115. Cf. G. Anders, *Die Antiquiertheit des Menschen. Über die Seele im Zeitalter der zweiten industriellen Revolution*, 299ff.
116. U. Horstmann, *Das Untier. Konturen einer Philosophie der Menschenflucht*,110.
117. E. Bloch, *The Principle of Hope*, 3.
118. Ibid.
119. Ibid., 4.
120. Ibid., 12.
121. Cf. ibid., 195ff., 223ff.; *Tübinger Einleitung in die Philosophie*, 210ff.
122. Hope is on its way to the *totum* of history "coupled with the negative, using that variously destructive nothingness. The counter-movement toward nothingness, to the extent this is possible, makes nothingness into an antithesis which itself is then forced into activity; the increasingly negative element becomes thereby the objective criticism of what has become, albeit a criticism which in and of itself, void of the will actually employing it, leads only to destruction" (E. Bloch, *Tübinger Einleitung in die Philosophie*, 259; cf. also 265).
123. *The Principle of Hope*, 7.
124. Ibid., 105; cf. also *Tübinger Einleitung in die Philosophie*, 250ff.
125. M. Heidegger, "Overcoming Metaphysics," in idem, *The End of Philosophy*, 84–110, here 85.
126. Ibid., 87.
127. Ibid., 102.
128. Ibid., 108f.
129. E. Bloch, *Tübinger Einleitung in die Philosophie*, 228.
130. J. Moltmann, *Theology of Hope*, 94.
131. Cf. P. Tillich, *Systematic Theology*, 1.3–68, esp. 59ff.; 2.13–16.
132. Moltmann himself admitted this later and accurately described the situation. Cf. J. Moltmann, " 'Begnadete Angst.' Religiös integrierte Angst und ihre Bewältigung," in *Angst und Gewalt. Ihre Präsenz und ihre Bewältigung in den Religionen*, ed. H. von Stietencron, 137–53, 142f.
133. See the recent work of J. Niewiadomski, *Die Zweideutigkeit von Gott und Welt in J. Moltmanns Theologien.*
134. J. Moltmann, *Theology of Hope*, 338; cf. ibid., 289.
135. J. Moltmann, *The Crucified God: The Cross of Christ as the Foundation and Criticism of Christian Theology*, 5.
136. " 'Begnadete Angst,' " 143.
137. Ibid., 141f.
138. Cf. ibid., 144f. Hope is still kept free of anxiety in Moltmann's exposition concerning the religion of anxiety (*The Crucified God*, 301–3), a religion countered by Christian faith, which is alleged to be free of anxiety. Faith is distinguished from the religion of anxiety as the religion of those "who have not found their freedom in the humanity of God but, for whatever reason, feel anxiety at this God and the freedom that is expected of them" (*The Crucified God*, 301). Although every fear-mongering religion should be decisively opposed, one must emphasize on the other hand that fear of the kind of freedom that opens up a yet uncertain and thus ambiguous future can be quite legitimate.
139. " 'Begnadete Angst,' " 152.
140. Ibid.
141. Ibid., 153.
142. Cf. A. Künzli, *Die Angst als abendälndische Krankheit, dargestellt am Leben und Denken S. Kierkegaards.*
143. Cf. R. Bilz, "Der Subjektzentrismus im Erleben der Angst," *Aspekte der Angst*, ed. H. von Ditfurth, 133–42.

Chapter 1
APOCALYPTIC: PHENOMENOLOGICAL DESCRIPTION

1. So, e.g., *Wahrig Deutsches Wörterbuch* (Gütersloh: Bertelsmann, 1977), 429.
2. K. Koch, *The Rediscovery of Apocalyptic: A Polemical Work on a Neglected Area of Biblical Studies and Its Damaging Effects on Theology and Philosophy*, 18.
3. Ibid., 131.
4. Cf. K. Koch's introduction in idem and J. M. Schmidt, eds., *Apokalyptik*, 18: "The discussion has by no means ended" concerning the various "interpretations of the overall phenomenon 'apocalyptic' " presented thus far; "indeed, scholarship is still learning to walk."
5. F. Lücke, *Versuch einer vollständigen Einleitung in die Offenbarung des Johannes oder Allgemeine Untersuchungen über die apokalyptische Literatur überhaupt und die Apokalypse des Johannes insbesondere*, 23.
6. Ibid., 22.
7. Concerning the current status of scholarship in apocalyptic studies within the parameters of the history of religions, see D. Hellholm, ed., *Apocalypticism in the Mediterranean World and the Near East: Proceedings of the International Colloquium on Apocalypticism. Uppsala, August 12–17, 1979.*
8. The terminological difficulties attaching to the term "apocalyptic" are treated in depth by, e.g., T. Olsson, "The Apocalyptic Activity: The Case of Jamāsp Nāmay," in *Apocalypticism in the Mediterranean World and the Near East*, 21–49, esp. 21–31.
9. J. Carmignac, "Description du phénomène de l'Apocalyptique dans l'Ancien Testament," in *Apocalypticism in the Mediterranean World and the Near East*, 163–70, here 163.
10. "Of course, one must distinguish between 'apocalypse,' which is a literary work, 'apocalyptic,' which is the literary genre serving as the vehicle for such a work, and 'apocalypticism,' which is the systematization of the characteristics of this literary genre. Let us recognize of our own accord that the systematization expressed by the term 'apocalypticism' loses a large part of its interest if it is a matter of a literary style and no longer of a theological tendency" (ibid., 164f.).
11. Ibid., 165.
12. H. Stegemann, "Die Bedeutung der Qumranfunde für die Erforschung der Apokalyptik," in *Apocalypticism in the Mediterranean World and the Near East*, 495–530, here 498.
13. Cf. also L. Hartman, "Survey of the Problem of Apocalyptic Genre," in *Apocalypticism in the Mediterranean World and the Near East*, 329–43.
14. Concerning both this specific point and the results of the International Apocalyptic Colloquium in Uppsala 1979 in general, see K. Rudolph, "Apokalyptik in der Diskussion," in *Apocalypticism in the Mediterranean World and the Near East*, 771–98.
15. Concerning the history of the Greek word *apokalypsis*, see M. Smith, "On the History of APOKALYPTO and APOKALYPSIS," in *Apocalypticism in the Mediterranean World and the Near East*, 9–20.
16. G. von Rad, *Theologie des Alten Testaments*, 2.331, n. 28. In more recent discussion, H. Stegemann also denies the existence of apocalyptic as an independent genre: "The repeated attempts to profile an independent 'genre apocalyptic' should be given up once and for all. They only end up discovering 'genre typical' features common to partial areas of apocalyptic, while then necessarily excluding other apocalypses. At most one can speak of a literary 'genre' only if one does not understand this term in the sense of 'type,' but rather exclusively from the perspective of content" ("Die Bedeutung der Qumranfunde für die Erforschung der Apokalyptik," in *Apocalypticism in the Mediterranean World and the Near East*, 527, n. 107). For Stegemann, however, this primary criterion of

content is the heavenly knowledge disclosed by revelation, knowledge whose content can in its own turn be quite varied.

17. Cf. K. Koch, *The Rediscovery of Apocalyptic*, 28: "Without a distinction between complex and component types there can be no form-critical approach to these writings."

18. P. Vielhauer, in E. Hennecke and W. Schneemelcher, eds., *New Testament Apocrypha*, vol. 2, "Writings Relating to the Apostles; Apocalypses and Related Subjects," 581–607.

19. The most important Jewish apocalypses include Daniel, *As. Mos.*, 4 Ezra, *2 Apoc. Bar.*, *1 Enoch*, as well as *2 Enoch*, *3 Apoc. Bar.*, and the little apocalypses in the *T. 12 Patr.* (*T. Levi* and *T. Jud.*).

20. Cf. also P. Vielhauer, *Geschichte der urchristlichen Literatur*, 485ff.

21. Cf., e.g., K. Koch, *The Rediscovery of Apocalyptic*, 23ff.; idem, *Apokalyptik* (in idem and J. M. Schmidt, eds., Wege der Forschung 365), 12f., who emphasizes that these visions are portrayed esp. in larger discourse cycles. See further J. Lebram, "Apokalyptik/Apokalypsen II. Altes Testament," *TRE* 3.192–202. See further also the special volume of the periodical *Semeia:* J. J. Collins, ed., *Apocalypse: The Morphology of a Genre (Semeia* 14), passim.

22. Cf. K. Müller, "Apokalyptik/Apokalypsen III. Die jüdische Apokalyptik. Anfänge und Merkmale," *TRE* 3.202–51, esp. 223ff. Müller's article also represents a detailed and in part doubtlessly necessary criticism of previous apocalyptic scholarship.

23. Cf. G. von Rad, *Old Testament Theology*, 2.306ff.

24. Cf. German edition, *Theologie des Alten Testaments*, 2.330.

25. Ibid., 2.329.

26. Von Rad accuses wisdom of being insufficiently interested in the phenomenon of history, though he cannot withhold his own respect from wisdom: "In the light of all this, the later wisdom teachers must have been the representatives of a very comprehensive, indeed a practically encyclopedic, theology, at any rate the most comprehensive one which Israel ever achieved" (*Old Testament Theology*, 1.451). "But in the circles of wisdom teaching, interest in the traditions of the saving history had grown weak" (1.449).

27. Cf., e.g., K. Koch, "Vom profetischen zum apokalyptischen Visionsbericht," *Apocalypticism in the Mediterranean World and the Near East*, 413–46.

28. Among recent scholarship, cf. H. H. Rowley, *The Relevance of Apocalyptic;* S. B. Frost, *Old Testament Apocalyptic;* D. S. Russell, *The Method and Message of Jewish Apocalyptic.* The proximity of apocalyptic to the prophecy of Deutero-Isaiah has been defended against von Rad by P. von der Osten-Sacken, *Die Apokalyptik in ihrem Verhältnis zu Prophetie und Weisheit*, P. D. Hanson also claims to have demonstrated a relationship between apocalyptic and Deutero-Isaiah, *The Dawn of Apocalyptic;* idem, "Old Testament Apocalyptic Reexamined," *Interpretation* 25 (1971) 454–79.

29. Cf. J. Lebram, *TRE* 3.195f.; idem, "The Piety of the Jewish Apocalyptists," in *Apocalypticism in the Mediterranean World and the Near East*, 171–210. Here, too, P. Vielhauer's conclusion is classic (*New Testament Apocrypha*, 598): "We would scarcely wish to take away from the strength of von Rad's argument, but the fact that there is no eschatology and imminent expectation in the Wisdom literature corresponding to the presence of Wisdom-motifs in the Apocalypses forms an insurmountable objection to his thesis. The eschatological ideas and the expectation are doubtless primary and so fundamental that the Wisdom elements must be evaluated as colouring, and not as the basis."

30. Cf. W. Harnisch, "Der Prophet als Widerpart und Zeuge der Offenbarung. Erwägungen zur Interdependenz von Form und Sache im IV. Buch Esra," in *Apocalypticism in the Mediterranean World and the Near East*, 461–94.

31. K. Rudolph, "Apokalyptik in der Diskussion," in *Apocalypticism in the Mediterranean World and the Near East*, 783.

32. Cf. K. Koch's introduction to *Apokalyptik*, ed. idem and J. M. Schmidt, 21ff.

33. Scholarship today still considers only a few writings from Qumran to be apoca-

lyptic: the book of giants, the description of the New Jerusalem, and the angelic liturgy. Cf. J. Carmignac, "Qu'est-ce que l'Apocalyptique? Son emploi à Qumrân," *Revue de Qumran* 10 (1979) 3–33; H. Stegemann, "Die Bedeutung der Qumranfunde für die Erforschung der Apokalyptik," *Apocalypticism in the Mediterranean World and the Near East*, passim.

34. K. Koch, *Apokalyptik*, 23.

35. P. Vielhauer, *Geschichte der urchristlichen Literatur*, 493.

36. K. Rudolph, "Apokalyptik in der Diskussion," 776f.

37. E.g., by H. Stegemann, "Die Bedeutung der Qumranfunde für die Erforschung der Apokalyptik," 501f.

38. P. Vielhauer, *New Testament Apocrypha*, 587; cf. also G. von Rad, *Theologie des Alten Testaments*, 329: The "view toward the end of history," i.e., "to an historical consummation with all the attendant manifestations . . . is probably the most characteristic element of apocalyptic."

39. Cf. L. Hartman, "Survey of the Problem of Apocalyptic Genre," *Apocalypticism in the Mediterranean World and the Near East*, 340: "The literary convention of a genre is fluid, it changes and develops, and admits varied and new usages."

40. T. Olsson, "The Apocalyptic Activity," in *Apocalypticism in the Mediterranean World and the Near East*, 22.

41. Ibid., 27f.

42. Cf. C. Colpe, "Vorschläge des Messina-Kongresses von 1966 zur Gnosisforschung," in W. Eltester, ed., *Christentum und Gnosis*, BZNW 37, 129–32.

43. Cf., e.g., the criticism of H.-M. Schenke, "Die Gnosis," in J. Leipoldt and W. Grundmann, eds., *Umwelt des Urchristentums*, 1.371–415, here 375; K. Rudolph, "Randerscheinungen des Judentums und das Problem der Entstehung des Gnostizismus," in idem, ed., *Gnosis und Gnostizismus*, 768–97, here 769ff.

44. Cf. T. Olsson, "The Apocalyptic Activity," 30f.

45. H. Ringgren, "Apokalyptik I. Apokalyptische Literatur, religionsgeschichtlich," *RGG* (3rd ed.) 1.463f., here 463.

46. Cf. G. Lanczkowski, "Apokalyptik/Apokalypsen I, religionsgeschichtlich," *TRE* 3.189–91, here 189f.

47. Cf. J. Ellul, *Apocalypse: The Book of Revelation.*

48. Concerning the following discussion, cf. H. Ringgren, "Apokalyptik I. Apokalyptische Literatur, religionsgeschichtlich," passim; G. Lanczkowski, "Apokalyptik/Apokalypsen I, religionsgeschichtlich," passim (both articles include extensive bibliographies).

49. Cf. the older literature on this subject as well as T. Olsson, "The Apocalyptic Activity," passim; S. S. Hartman, "Datierung der Jungavestischen Apokalyptik," in *Apocalypticism in the Mediterranean World and the Near East*, 61–76; G. Widengren, "Leitende Ideen und Quellen der iranischen Apokalyptik," in ibid., 77–162; A. Hultgård, "Forms and Origins of Iranian Apocalypticism," in ibid., 387–413.

50. Cf. E. Abegg, *Der Messiasglaube in Indien und im Iran.*

51. Cf. in the Koran, esp. the Sūras 81, 82, and 99.

52. Cf. in addition to older scholarship also W. Burkert, "Apokalyptik im frühen Griechentum," in *Apocalypticism in the Mediterranean World and the Near East*, 235–54.

53. Cf. A. Gall, *Basileia tou theou. Eine religionsgeschichtliche Studie zur vorchristlichen Eschatologie*, esp. 48ff.; J. Bergman, "Introductory Remarks on Apocalypticism in Egypt," in *Apocalypticism in the Mediterranean World and the Near East*, 51–60; J. Assmann, "Königsdogma und Heilserwartung. Politische und kultische Chaosbeschreibungen in ägyptischen Texten," in ibid., 345–78.

54. Cf. A. Olrik, *Ragnarök. Die Sagen vom Weltuntergang;* R. Reitzenstein, "Weltuntergangsvorstellungen," *Kyrkohistorisk Areskrift* 25 (1924) 129–212.

55. Cf. A. Métraux, "Migrations historiques des Tupi-Guarani," *Journal de la société*

des américanistes 29 (1927) 1–45; C. Nimuendajú-Unkel, "Die Sagen von der Erschaffung und Vernichtung der Welt als Grundlagen der Religion der Apapocúva-Guarani," *Zeitschrift für Ethnologie* 46 (1914) 284–403.

56. H. Jonas, *Gnosis und spätantiker Geist,* vols. 1 and 2.

57. See M. Krause, "Die literarischen Gattungen der Apokalypsen von Nag Hammadi," in *Apocalypticism in the Mediterranean World and the Near East,* 621–37.

58. Cf. among others G. MacRae, "Apocalyptic Eschatology in Gnosticism," in *Apocalypticism in the Mediterranean World and the Near East,* 317–25.

59. Cf. K. Rudolph, "Randerscheinungen des Judentums und das Problem der Entstehung des Gnostizismus," *Gnosis und Gnostizismus,* 788f.

60. H. Jonas, *Gnosis und spätantiker Geist,* 1.261.

61. W. Schmithals, *The Apocalyptic Movement. Introduction and Interpretation,* 93.

62. Ibid.

63. Ibid., 96.

64. Cf. ibid., 96.

65. G. Kretschmar, "Zur religionsgeschichtlichen Einordnung der Gnosis," *Gnosis und Gnostizismus,* 426–37, here 429.

66. Cf. H. Blumenberg, "Epochenschwelle und Rezeption," *PhRev* 6 (1958) 94–120, here 112f.

67. Cf. G. MacRae, "Apocalyptic Eschatology in Gnosticism," in *Apocalypticism in the Mediterranean World and the Near East,* 323: "Gnosticism may thus be described as the ultimate radicalizing of apocalyptic eschatology."

68. Cf. R. Otto, *The Kingdom of God and the Son of Man,* 15.

69. H. Jonas, *Gnosis und spätantiker Geist,* 1.64.

70. See among others also J. Lebram, "The Piety of the Jewish Apocalyptists," in *Apocalypticism in the Mediterranean World and the Near East,* 207; K. Rudolph, "Randerscheinungen des Judentums und das Problem der Entstehung des Gnostizismus," *Gnosis und Gnostizismus,* 788ff.; idem, *Gnosis: The Nature and History of Gnosticism,* 194ff., 277ff.; R. M. Grant, *Gnosticism and Early Christianity,* 34.

71. This is the implication of G. MacRae's suggestion "that the categories of apocalyptic and Gnosticism should not be too sharply divided" ("Apocalyptic Eschatology in Gnosticism," in *Apocalypticism in the Mediterranean World and the Near East,* 324).

72. Cf. H. G. Kippenberg, "Ein Vergleich jüdischer, christlicher und gnostischer Apokalyptik," in *Apocalypticism in the Mediterranean World and the Near East,* 751–68.

73. K. Koch, "Vom profetischen zum apokalyptischen Visionsbericht," in *Apocalypticism in the Mediterranean World and the Near East,* 430.

74. Cf. P. Vielhauer, in E. Hennecke and W. Schneemelcher, eds., *New Testament Apocrypha,* 2.597; W. Bousset, *Die jüdische Apokalyptik, ihre religionsgeschichtliche Herkunft und ihre Bedeutung für das Neue Testament,* 5ff.

75. Cf. P. Vielhauer, *New Testament Apocrypha,* 2.598; see also O. Plöger, *Theocracy and Eschatology.*

76. Cf., e.g., A. Satake, *Die Gemeindeordnung in der Johannesapokalypse.*

77. So, e.g., O. Plöger, *Theocracy and Eschatology,* passim; P. D. Hanson, *The Dawn of Apocalyptic,* passim; idem, "Old Testament Apocalyptic Reexamined," *Interpretation* 25 (1971), passim.

78. Cf. K. Koch, *Apokalyptik,* 19.

79. So K. Koch, ibid., passim.

80. Cf. T. Olsson, "The Apocalyptic Activity," *Apocalypticism in the Mediterranean World and the Near East,* 44f.

81. Cf. K. Koch, *Apokalyptik,* 10f.

82. Contra E. P. Sanders, "The Genre of Palestinian Jewish Apocalypses," in *Apocalypticism in the Mediterranean World and the Near East,* 447–60.

83. Cf. J. J. Collins, "Jewish Apocalyptic against Its Hellenistic Near Eastern Environment," *BASOR* 220 (1975) 27–36.

84. Cf. G. Theissen, "Wanderradikalismus. Literatursoziologische Aspekte der Überlieferung von Worten Jesu im Urchristentum," idem, *Studien zur Soziologie des Urchristentums*, 79–105.

85. Cf. K. Rudolph, *Gnosis: The Nature and History of Gnosticism*, 208ff.; 291ff.

86. Cf. H. G. Kippenberg, "Ein Vergleich jüdischer, christlicher und gnostischer Apokalyptik," in *Apocalypticism in the Mediterranean World and the Near East*, 763ff.

87. So, e.g., by P. D. Hanson, *Interpretation* 25 (1975) 469: "Prophetic eschatology is transformed into apocalyptic at the point where the task of translating the cosmic vision into the categories of mundane reality is abdicated." Cf. also P. Eicher, "Offenbarungsreligion," in idem, ed., *Gottesvorstellung und Gesellschaftsentwicklung*, 109–26, here 119.

88. Cf. H. G. Kippenberg, "Ein Vergleich jüdischer, christlicher und gnostischer Apokalyptik," 765f.; cf. also K. Rudolph, *Gnosis: The Nature and History of Gnosticism*, 264ff.

89. See P. D. Hanson's warning in *Interpretation* 25 (1971) 455.

90. I. Kant, *Religion within the Limits of Reason Alone* (New York: Harper & Brothers, 1960).

91. I. Kant, *Das Ende aller Dinge (1794)*, in idem, *Werke in zehn Bänden*, ed. W. Weischedel, 9.173–190. See also H. A. Salmony, *Kants Schrift: Das Ende aller Dinge;* H. U. von Balthasar, *Prometheus: Studien zur Geschichte des deutschen Idealismus*, 91ff.; J. Moltmann, *Theology of Hope*, 45ff.

92. I. Kant, *Das Ende aller Dinge*, 179.

93. *Religion within the Limits of Reason Alone*, Book Three.

94. Cf. ibid., 85f. (Book 3, Introduction).

95. Ibid., 129 (Book 3, General Observation).

96. Ibid., 130 (Book 3, General Observation).

97. Ibid., 92 (Book 3, Division 1, Section IV).

98. Cf. ibid., 90ff. (Book 3, Division, Sections III, IV). "We have good reason to say, however, that 'the kingdom of God is come unto us' once the principle of the gradual transition of ecclesiastical faith to the universal religion of reason, and so to a (divine) ethical state on earth, has become general and has also gained somewhere a *public* foothold, even though the actual establishment of this state is still infinitely removed from us" (ibid., 113 [Book 3, Division 1, Section VII]).

99. Cf. ibid., 123 (Book 3, Division 2).

100. Cf. ibid., 125 (Book 3, Division 2).

101. Ibid., 126 (Book 3, Division 2).

102. Ibid., 125 (Book 3, Division 2).

103. *Das Ende aller Dinge*, 181.

104. *Religion within the Limits of Reason Alone*, 126 (Book 3, Division 2).

105. *Das Ende aller Dinge*, 182.

106. Ibid.

107. *Religion within the Limits of Reason Alone*, 125 (Book 3, Division 2).

108. Ibid., 116ff. (Book 3, Division 2).

109. Cf. F. Lücke, *Versuch einer vollständigen Einleitung in die Offenbarung des Johannes, oder Allgemeine Untersuchungen über die apokalyptische Literatur überhaupt und die Apokalypse des Johannes insbesondere* (1st ed. 1832), 27f.

110. Ibid. (2nd ed. 1852), 34.

111. Cf. A. Sabatier, "L'Apocalypse juive et la philosophie de l'histoire," *Revue des études juives* 40 (1900) LXVI–LXXXXVI; German translation: "Die jüdische Apokalyptik und die Geschichtsphilosophie," *Apokalyptik*, ed. K. Koch and J. M. Schmidt, 91–113, here 96.

112. Ibid., 98.

113. Cf. ibid., 110.

114. Ibid., 107.

115. Cf. ibid., 107ff.

116. Sabatier warns emphatically against the fever into which apocalyptic thinking can be fanned: "Unfortunately, we cannot confirm that in all ages the attractiveness of the apocalypses has not caused many people to take leave of their understanding, and caused many others to lose all peace of mind. We find ourselves here on one of those numerous paths which via more or less extended detours ultimately lead to the insane asylum" (ibid., 112).

117. Ibid., 111f.

118. Cf. W. Kamlah, *Christentum und Geschichtlichkeit. Untersuchungen zur Entstehung des Christentums und zu Augustins "Bürgerschaft Gottes"*, 18f.

119. Ibid., 16f.

120. Cf. ibid., 9.

121. Cf. ibid., 34f.

122. Cf. ibid., 42ff.

123. Ibid., 44.

124. Ibid., 24.

125. Karl Löwith, *Meaning in History: The Theological Implications of the Philosophy of History*.

126. Cf. also Löwith's essay "Weltgeschehen und Heilsgeschichte" (1950) in idem, *Sämtliche Schriften*, 2.240–79.

127. *Meaning in History*, 1.

128. Ibid., 6.

129. Ibid., 19. Cf. also 84:

> The living toward a future *eschaton* and back from it to a new beginning is characteristic only for those who live essentially by hope and expectation—for Jews and Christians. To this extent future and Christianity are synonymous. A basic difference between Christianity and secular futurism is, however, that the pilgrim's progress is not an indefinite advance toward an unattainable ideal but a definite choice in the face of an eternal reality and that the hope in the kingdom of God is bound up with the fear of the Lord, while the secular hope for a "better world" looks forward without fear and trembling. They have in common, nonetheless, the eschatological viewpoint and outlook into the future as such. The idea of progress could become the leading principle for the understanding of history only within this primary horizon of the future as established by Jewish and Christian faith, against the "hopeless," because cyclic, world view of classical paganism. All modern striving for improvements and progresses, in the plural, is rooted in that singular Christian progress from which the modern consciousness has emancipated itself,

yet upon which it has nonetheless remained dependent, Löwith suggests, like an escaped slave on its distant master.

130. "The revolution which had been proclaimed within the framework of an eschatological future and with reference to a perfect monastic life was taken over, five centuries later, by a philosophical priesthood, which interpreted the process of secularization in terms of a 'spiritual' realization of the kingdom of God on earth" (ibid., 159).

131. Ibid., 189.

132. Ibid.

133. Ibid., 197. Cf. also Löwith's distinction between religion of progress, the progress of religion, and religious progress (ibid., 112–14).

134. Cf. ibid., viii.

135. Cf. ibid., 143.

136. Ibid., 191.

137. Cf. H. Blumenberg, *The Legitimacy of the Modern Age*, 27ff. [The German original cited by Professor Körtner, *Die Legitimität der Neuzeit* (Frankfurt: Suhrkamp, 1966), did not yet contain the corrections of the second edition, from which the English translation was made. Hence some passages are missing in the translation, others altered or otherwise abbreviated.—Trans.]

138. *The Legitimacy of the Modern Age*, 119.

139. *Die Legitimität der Neuzeit*, 24.

140. Ibid., 35. [Cf. also the altered version in *The Legitimacy of the Modern Age*, 49.]

141. "Thus the formation of the idea of progress and its taking the place of the historical totality that was bounded by Creation and Judgment are two distinct events" (*The Legitimacy of the Modern Age*, 36).

142. Ibid., 39f.; cf. R. Bultmann, *Theology of the New Testament*, 2.38.

143. H. Blumenberg, *The Legitimacy of the Modern Age*, 41.

144. Cf. ibid., 41f.

145. *Die Legitimität der Neuzeit*, 29.

146. *The Legitimacy of the Modern Age*, 42f.

147. *Die Legitimität der Neuzeit*, 30.

148. Cf. *The Legitimacy of the Modern Age*, 45.

149. *Die Legitimität der Neuzeit*, 33f.

150. K. Löwith, *Meaning in History*, 43.

151. Ibid., 44. Cf. also E. Topitsch, "Marxismus und Gnosis," in idem, *Sozialphilosophie zwischen Ideologie und Wissenschaft*, 261–96.

152. Cf. E. Bloch, *The Principle of Hope*, 1293f.

153. E. Bloch, *Atheism in Christianity: The Religion of the Exodus and the Kingdom*, 69.

154. F. Engels, "The Book of Revelation," in *Progress* 2 (1883), 112–16; now in Karl Marx and Frederick Engels, *Collected Works*, vol. 26, *Frederick Engels 1882–89*, 112–17. On the basis of a lecture by Ferdinand Benary Engels heard in the year 1841 (ibid., 115), Engels held the view that the Apocalypse was the only genuine writing in the New Testament, and was composed in the year A.D. 68.

155. Ibid., 113f. Cf. also F. Engels, "On the History of Early Christianity," *Collected Works*, vol. 27, 447–69, esp. 460ff.

156. F. Engels, "Bruno Bauer and Early Christianity" (1882), *Collected Works*, vol. 24, 427–35, here 430.

157. "On the History of Early Christianity," 457.

158. Both citations from "On the History of Early Christianity," 457.

159. Cf. ibid., 460ff.

160. Ibid., 447.

161. Not only is Bloch's language in *Geist der Utopie (The Spirit of Utopia)* in part mystical, his basic understanding of the soul presented there is as well, according to which the soul develops itself in the process of purification in order to reach its heavenly home and the hidden God in us, God as our innermost depths. Concerning the latter point cf., e.g., G. Sauter, *Zukunft und Verheissung. Das Problem der Zukunft in der gegenwärtigen theologischen und philosophischen Diskussion*, 341. Neither should one overlook the home this language also has in expressionism! Cf. A. Jäger, *Reich ohne Gott. Zur Eschatologie Ernst Blochs*, 172f., n. 13.

162. Cf. Bloch's afterword from 1963, *Geist der Utopie, Gesamtausgabe*, 3.347.

163. Among others, G. Scholem has directed attention to the mystical inspiration in Bloch's early piece, though Scholem is reserved toward the continuation and transformation of Bloch's analysis of utopia in *The Principle of Hope:* "The elaborate Marxist montage of his second work stands in poorly concealed contradiction to the mystical inspiration which is basically responsible for Bloch's best insights. Not without a measure of courage, he has managed to draw his insights safely through a veritable jungle of Marxist rhapsodies" (G. Scholem, "Toward an Understanding of the Messianic Idea in Judaism,"

in idem, *The Messianic Idea in Judaism and Other Essays on Jewish Spirituality*, 1–36, here 341, n. 2). See also G. M. Martin, "Erbe der Mystik im Werk von Ernst Bloch," in H. Deuser and P. Steinacker, eds., *Ernst Bloch Vermittlungen zur Theologie*, 114–27.

164. Cf. Bloch, *Geist der Utopie*, 347.

165. Ibid., 304.

166. Ibid., 278.

167. Ibid., 341.

168. Ibid., 336.

169. Ibid., 278.

170. Ibid., 297.

171. Ibid., 287.

172. Ibid., 339.

173. Ibid., 308; cf. also 13.

174. E. Bloch, *Atheism and Christianity*, 101.

175. Ibid., 135.

176. Ibid., 69. For Bloch's view, which draws especially from Albert Schweitzer and J. Weiss (ibid., 51ff.), the following holds true: "His [Jesus'] moral teaching is incomprehensible without its apocalyptic counterpart—even prescinding from the (very late) Revelation of John, which, though not confined to Jesus' doctrine, was continually hinted at in his preaching" (ibid., 125). One should recall at this point Engels's estimation of the Revelation of John!

177. Ibid., 54, 57.

178. Ibid., 105.

179. Ibid., 218.

180. Cf. ibid., 29ff.

181. Cf. ibid., 84ff.

182. Ibid., 163.

183. K. Koch's criticism of Bloch's exegesis is incisive (*The Rediscovery of Apocalyptic*, 121): "Bloch's interpretation is, it is true, accompanied by a fantastic interpretation of the biblical texts which can sometimes distort his undertaking to a ludicrous degree for the critical reader."

184. Cf. E. Käsemann, *Jesus Means Freedom*, 130, 140.

185. A. Jäger, *Reich ohne Gott. Zur Eschatologie Ernst Blochs*, 60.

186. Cf. A. Jäger's critical analysis, ibid., passim.

187. Cf. J. M. Schmidt, *Die jüdische Apokalyptik. Die Geschichte ihrer Erforschung von den Anfängen bis zu den Textfunden von Qumran*, 198, 237, 241f.

188. W. Bousset, *Die Religion des Judentums im neutestamentlichen Zeitalter*, 243f.

189. H. Gunkel, in E. Kautzsch, ed., *Die Apokryphen und Pseudepigraphen des Alten Testaments*, 2.336.

190. J. Metzner, "Der Beitrag der Psychoanalyse zum Verständnis der Apokalyptik," *Wege zum Menschen* 23 (1971) 424–38, here 425. "Only after the apocalyptic account, despite or precisely because of its ambiguity, reveals its linguistic structure and its inner coherency is it legitimate to pose the question concerning the causes prompting apocalyptic thinking" (438).

191. See esp. J. Metzner, *Persönlichkeitszerstörung und Weltuntergang. Das Verhältnis von Wahnbildung und literarischer Imagination.*

192. This was the impulse for K. Jaspers in his study "Der Prophet Ezechiel. Eine pathographische Studie," in *Arbeiten zur Psychiatrie, Neurologie und ihren Grenzgebieten (FS K. Schneider)*, 77–85.

193. Cf. the case studies of A. Wetzel, "Das Weltuntergangserlebnis in der Schizophrenie," *Zeitschrift für die gesamte Neurologie und Psychiatrie* 78 (1922) 403–28.

194. Cf. Schreber's autobiographical piece: D. P. Schreber, *Memoirs of My Nervous Illness*, and S. Freud, *Psychoanalytische Bemerkungen über einen autobiographisch beschriebenen Fall von Paranoia (Dementia Paranoides)*, *Gesammelte Werke*, 8.239–320.

195. J. Metzner, "Der Beitrag der Psychoanalyse zum Verständnis der Apokalyptik," 428.

196. Cf. M. Klein, "Bemerkungen über einige schizoide Mechanismen," in idem, *Das Seelenleben des Kleinkindes*, 101–25, here 124. J. A. Arlow speaks of an "intra-psychic (structural) conflict." Cf. J. A. Arlow and C. Brenner, "Zur Psychopathologie der Psychosen," *Psyche* 23 (1969) 402–18, here 412.

197. Cf. G. Lukács, *History and Class Consciousness: Studies in Marxist Dialectics.*

198. J. Gabel, *False Consciousness: An Essay on Reification*, esp. 288ff.

199. G. Lukács, *History and Class Consciousness*, cited in J. Gabel, *False Consciousness*, 289.

200. J. Gabel, *False Consciousness*, 289–90.

201. Ibid., 102.

202. J. Metzner, "Der Beitrag der Psychoanalyse zum Verständnis der Apokalyptik," 435.

203. Cf. ibid., 428.

204. Cf. I. A. Caruso's introduction to the German translation of Gabel's work, *Ideologie und Schizophrenie. Formen der Entfremdung* (Frankfurt, 1967), 28.

205. See esp. E. Bloch, *The Principle of Hope*, 45–178. On the relationship between utopia and ideology, see 153–65.

206. Ibid., 156.

207. Cf. A. Storch and C. Kulenkampff, "Zum Verständnis des Weltuntergangs bei den Schizophrenen," *Der Nervenarzt* 21 (1950) 102–8.

208. G. M. Martin, *Weltuntergang. Gefahr und Sinn apokalyptischer Visionen*, 58.

209. Cf., e.g., C. Kulenkampff, "Entbergung, Entgrenzung, Überwältigung als Weisen des Standverlustes. Zur Anthropologie der paranoiden Psychosen," *Der Nervenarzt* 26 (1955) 89ff.; now in E. Strauss and J. Zutt, eds., *Die Wahnwelten (Endogene Psychosen)*, 202–17.

210. J. Zutt, "Über Daseinsordnungen. Ihre Bedeutung für die Psychiatrie," *Der Nervenarzt* 24 (1953) 177ff.; now in *Die Wahnwelten (Endogene Psychosen)*, 169–91.

211. C. Kulenkampff, "Zum Problem der abnormen Krise in der Psychiatrie," *Der Nervenarzt* 30 (1959) 62ff.; now in *Die Wahnwelten (Endogene Psychosen)*, 258–87, here 258.

212. Cf. V. E. von Gebsattel, *Prolegomena einer medizinischen Anthropologie.*

213. Cf. C. Kulenkampff, "Zum Problem der abnormen Krise in der Psychiatrie," in *Die Wahnwelten (Endogene Psychosen)*, 258f.

214. Ibid., 282f.

215. Ibid., 283.

216. Cf. ibid., 285.

217. Cf. J. Zutt, "Über Daseinsordnungen. Ihre Bedeutung für die Psychiatrie," passim.

218. C. Kulenkampff, "Entbergung, Entgrenzung, Überwältigung als Weisen des Standverlustes," 204.

219. Ibid., 206.

220. Ibid., 212.

221. Ibid., 211.

222. G. M. Martin, *Weltuntergang. Gefahr und Sinn apokalyptischer Visionen*, 57f.

223. Ibid., 81. Cf. also the contribution of I. Riedel from the perspective of depth psychology, "Apokalyptische Bilder," in P. Dätwyler, ed., *Not-Wendigkeiten. Auf der Suche nach einer neuen Spiritualität*, 51–75.

224. Cf. G. M. Martin, *Weltuntergang. Gefahr und Sinn apokalyptischer Visionen*, 75, 74.

225. E. Drewermann, *Tiefenpsychologie und Exegese*, vol. 2, *Die Wahrheit der Werke und der Worte. Wunder, Vision, Weissagung, Apokalypse, Geschichte, Gleichnis*, 436–591.

226. Ibid., 447ff.

227. Ibid., 452.

228. Ibid., 472. Cf. also 476ff.

229. Ibid., 482.
230. Ibid., 483.
231. Cf. G. M. Martin, *Weltuntergang. Gefahr und Sinn apokalyptischer Visionen*, 58, 81f.
232. G. Scholem, "Toward an Understanding of the Messianic Idea in Judaism," in idem, *The Messianic Idea in Judaism and Other Essays on Jewish Spirituality*, 7.
233. So, e.g., against Bousset's theory, according to which gnosis emerged from a connection between Persian dualism and the spirit of late antiquity: "For me this amounts to chemistry or even alchemy of ideas" (H. Jonas, *Gnosis und spätantiker Geist*, 1.36). For Jonas, on the other hand, it is a matter of "that which is not 'explainable,' but rather only 'understandable' within itself as a total discovery of existence" (ibid., 62).
234. Cf. ibid., 1.13ff.
235. All citations from ibid., 1.58.
236. Ibid., 1.59.
237. Ibid., 1.60.
238. Ibid.
239. Ibid., 1.64.
240. Ibid., 1.60.
241. Ibid., 1.61.
242. Ibid., 1.143.
243. Ibid., 1.110.
244. Ibid., 1.70.
245. E. Schweizer, "Das hellenistische Weltbild als Produkt der Weltangst," in *Mensch und Kosmos. Eine Ringvorlesung der Theologischen Fakultät Zürich*, 39–50; now in E. Schweizer, *Neotestamentica*, 15–27. In connection with this: A. Strobel, *Kerygma und Apokalyptik. Ein religionsgeschichtlicher und theologischer Beitrag zur Christusfrage*, 130. According to Strobel, apocalyptic is "ultimately not only a Jewish way of thinking, but rather one characterizing all of antiquity, an *epochal* way of thinking" (ibid.).
246. E. Schweizer, "Das hellenistische Weltbild als Produkt der Weltangst," 26.
247. Ibid.
248. H. Jonas, *Gnosis und spätantiker Geist*, 1.145.
249. Ibid., 1.68.
250. W. Schmithals, *The Apocalyptic Movement: Introduction and Interpretation*, 106.
251. Cf. ibid., 40.
252. This is also the direction taken by the approach of U. Luck, "Das Weltverständnis in die jüdischen Apokalyptik, dargestellt am äthiopischen Henoch und am 4. Esra," *ZTK* 73 (1976) 282–305. In contrast, H. H. Rowley, who inquires concerning the "enduring message of apocalyptic" (*The Relevance of Apocalyptic*, 150–78), in my opinion takes over too uncritically conceptual models related to salvation history and remains thus behind the questions with which we are here concerned.
253. H. Blumenberg, "Epochenschwelle und Rezeption," *PhRev* 6 (1958) 107.
254. Cf. K. Koch, *The Rediscovery of Apocalyptic*, 114f.
255. Cf. G. Sauter, *Zukunft und Verheissung*, 363ff.

Chapter 2
WORLD ANXIETY

1. O. Spengler, *The Decline of the West*, 1.78–79.
2. Ibid., 1.79; cf. 1.169ff. [The English translation of Spengler's *Decline of the West* renders German *Angst* in this passage as "dread" rather than as "anxiety"; for the sake of consistency regarding the present discussion, I have rendered it as "anxiety" in this context.—Trans.]
3. Cf. ibid., 79; 1.117ff.; 1.165ff.; 1.192ff.; 2.137ff.

4. E. Spranger, *Psychologie des Jugendalters*, 356. Spranger appropriated the concept of world anxiety from Spengler. On the relationship between E. Spranger and O. Spengler, see L. Englert, "Eduard Spranger und Oswald Spengler," in A. M. Koktanek, ed., *Schelling-Studien (FG M. Schröter)*, 33–58, esp. 45f.

5. Cf. W. Schulz, "Das Problem der Angst in der neueren Philosophie," in H. von Ditfurth, ed., *Aspekte der Angst, Starnberger Gespräche*, 13–27.

6. H. Jonas, *Gnosis und spätantiker Geist*, 1.100.

7. Ibid., 1.143.

8. Cf. W. Schulz, "Das Problem der Angst in der neueren Philosophie," 15f.

9. P. Tillich, *The Courage to Be*, 58.

10. Cf. W. Schulz, "Das Problem der Angst in der neueren Philosophie," 16f.

11. M. Scheler, "Tod und Fortleben (1911–1914)," in idem, *Schriften aus dem Nachlass*, ed. Maria Scheler, 1.9–64, here 29. On the dating of this study see 510.

12. Ibid., 29.

13. See esp. Blaise Pascal, *Pensées*, fragment 72 (according to the numbering of Brunschvicg). The following citations are taken from this English translation by W. F. Trotter.

14. Cf. ibid., 23 (fragment 72).

15. Cf. ibid., 24 (fragment 72). To understand this notion of nothingness, one must bear in mind that Pascal's own understanding provides the background according to which there is nothing indivisible in the world, and thus no genuine point. Cf. the annotation by E. Wasmuth, in B. Pascal, *Über die Religion und einige andere Gegenstände [Pensées]* (Berlin: L. Schneider, 1937), 41f.

16. B. Pascal, *Pensées*, 22 (fragment 72).

17. Ibid., 75 (fragment 206).

18. Ibid., 74–75 (fragment 205).

19. Ibid., 234 (fragment 693 [692 in English edition]).

20. Cf. ibid., 23 (fragment 72): "He who regards himself in this light will be afraid of himself, and observing himself sustained in the body given him by nature between those two abysses of the Infinite and Nothing, will tremble at the sight of these marvels." Thus curiosity is transformed by means of terror ultimately into wonderment.

21. F. Schiller, *The Poems and Ballads of Schiller*, 2.200–1.

22. See esp. F.W.J. Schelling, *Of Human Freedom*. On Schelling's later philosophy, see H. Fuhrmanns, *Schellings letzte Philosophie;* W. Schulz, *Die Vollendung des Deutschen Idealismus in der Spätphilosophie Schellings*. On the following discussion, cf. also W. Schulz, "Freiheit und Geschichte in Schellings Philosophie," in F.W.J. Schelling, *Philosophische Untersuchungen über das Wesen der menschlichen Freiheit*, 7–26; idem, "Das Problem der Angst in der neueren Philosophie," 17ff.

23. G.W.F. Hegel, *Hegel's Philosophy of Right*, preface.

24. F.W.J. Schelling, *The Ages of the World*, 230.

25. S. Kierkegaard, "Repetition," *Fear and Trembling/Repetition*, 200.

26. Cf. O. Spengler, *The Decline of the West*, 1.79.

27. Ibid., 1.80.

28. S. Kierkegaard, *The Concept of Anxiety*, 44.

29. Cf. S. Kierkegaard, *The Sickness unto Death*, 146: "The self is a relation which relates itself to its own self, or it is that in the relation [which accounts for it] that the relation relates itself to its own self; the self is not the relation but [consists in the fact] that the relation relates itself to its own self."

30. S. Kierkegaard, *The Concept of Anxiety*, 43: "Man is a synthesis of the psychical and the physical; however, a synthesis is unthinkable if the two are not united in a third. This third is spirit."

31. Ibid., 41.

32. Ibid., 43.

33. Ibid., 44.
34. Ibid.
35. S. Kierkegaard *The Sickness unto Death*, 162.
36. S. Kierkegaard *The Concept of Anxiety*, 42.
37. Ibid.; by the way, English also uses the word "thrill" to refer to anxiety characterized by such pleasure.
38. Cf. Rudolf Otto, *The Idea of the Holy: An Inquiry into the Non-rational Factor in the Idea of the Divine and Its Relation to the Rational*, ch. 4, "Mysterium Tremendum."
39. S. Kierkegaard, *The Concept of Anxiety*, 61.
40. Ibid., 43.
41. Ibid., 42.
42. So, e.g., M. Wandruszka, "Was weiss die Sprache von der Angst?" in W. Bitter, ed., *Angst und Schuld in theologischer und psychotherapeutischer Sicht*, 14–22; F. Riemann, *Grundformen der Angst. Eine tiefenpsychologische Studie*, 19; H. Häfner, "Angst, Furcht," *Historisches Wörterbuch der Philosophie*, 1.310–14, here 310.
43. M. Wandruszka, "Was weiss die Sprache von der Angst?" 16.
44. On the physiological findings relating to anxiety reactions, see among older literature R. May, *The Meaning of Anxiety*. Concerning anxiety from the perspective of biology, see D. von Holst, "Biologie der Angst," in H. von Stietencron, ed., *Angst und Gewalt. Ihre Präsenze und ihre Bewältigung in den Religionen*, 15–26.
45. So, e.g., H. Häfner, "Angst, Furcht," 310. Cf. among others O. Pfister, *Christianity and Fear: A Study in History and in the Psychology and Hygiene of Religion.*
46. Martin Heidegger, *Being and Time*, 230 (German 185).
47. Ibid., 230 (German 186).
48. Ibid., 179 (German 140ff.).
49. Ibid., 180 (German 141).
50. Ibid., 181 (German 142).
51. Ibid., 230 (German 186).
52. Ibid.
53. Ibid., 232 (German 187).
54. Ibid.
55. Ibid., 232 (German 188).
56. Ibid., 229 (German 188).
57. Ibid., 230 (German 185).
58. Ibid., 234 (German 189).
59. Ibid., 235, n. iv (German 190, n. 1).
60. M. Heidegger, "What Is Metaphysics?," in D. F. Krell, ed., *Basic Writings*, 105.
61. Ibid., 104.
62. Cf. S. Kierkegaard, *The Concept of Anxiety*, 61 (IV, 331).
63. M. Heidegger, "What Is Metaphysics?," 103.
64. Ibid., 106.
65. Ibid., 103.
66. Cf. ibid., 105f.
67. P. Tillich, *The Courage to Be*, 36.
68. Ibid., 37.
69. Cf. ibid., 40ff., here 41.
70. O. Haendler, *Angst und Glaube*, 13, 15, and passim.
71. Ibid., 12.
72. Ibid.
73. Ibid., 14.
74. Haendler distinguishes the *forms* of anxiety (the anxiety of flight and of incapacitation) from the various *types* of anxiety (anxiety of catastrophe—anxiety in the face of . . . , anxiety of crisis—anxiety in . . . , anxiety of love—anxiety about . . .) and the various

levels of anxiety (peripheral anxiety, basic anxiety, primal anxiety). Whereas this distinction between anxiety before . . . , anxiety in . . . , and anxiety about . . . recalls that of Heidegger (anxiety before . . . , anxiety about . . .), Haendler's determination of the *content* of anxiety recalls that of Tillich. Whereas Tillich mentions the anxiety associated with fate, guilt, and meaninglessness, according to Haendler the content of anxiety is either associated with fate or guilt. The *elements* of anxiety which Haendler mentions are the sense of being trapped, being pursued by evil powers, and being abandoned by good powers. Cf. O. Haendler, ibid., 21–63.

75. Cf. ibid., 24ff.

76. Such is the case in the example of the young boy locked in a trunk by his classmates (ibid., 24ff.), or of the anxiety of the young boy at the prospect of jumping over a brook because he fears he will get his shoes and socks wet (ibid., 42; here Haendler himself initially puts the term "anxiety" in quotation marks!).

77. Cf. K. Jaspers, *Philosophy*, vol. 2, *Existential Elucidation*, 232.

78. Ibid., 198.

79. Ibid., 232. [The English translation of Jaspers's *Philosophy* renders German *Angst* in this and several other passages as "fear" rather than as "anxiety"; for the sake of consistency regarding the present discussion, I have rendered it as "anxiety" in the present context.—Trans.]

80. Ibid.

81. Ibid., 198.

82. Ibid., 233.

83. J.-P. Sartre, *Being and Nothingness: An Essay on Phenomenological Ontology*, 29. [In this and other passages the English translation of Sartre renders *l'angoisse* as "anguish"; here as in the case of Jaspers I have rendered it as "anxiety" for the sake of consistency regarding the present discussion.—Trans.]

84. Ibid., 30.

85. Cf. ibid., 32.

86. Ibid., 29.

87. Cf. ibid., 35f.

88. Ibid., 39.

89. Cf. W. Schulz, "Die Dialektik von Leib und Seele bei Kierkegaard. Bemerkungen zum 'Begriff Angst,' " in M. Theunissen and W. Greve, eds., *Materialien zur Philosophie S. Kierkegaards*, 347–66, here 353, 362ff. Furthermore, the anxiety addressed by Kierkegaard is dialectical in and of itself, and is not merely the dialectical relationship between two forms of anxiety, namely, world anxiety and self-anxiety, as W. Schulz, ibid., passim, claims to demonstrate.

90. S. Kierkegaard, *The Concept of Anxiety*, 61 (IV, 332).

91. Ibid., 61f. (IV, 332).

92. Cf. ibid., 96ff. (IV, 366ff.), 103ff. (IV, 372ff.).

93. Ibid., 111f. (IV, 379).

94. Cf. ibid., 113ff. (IV, 381ff.).

95. Cf. ibid., 118ff. (IV, 386ff.).

96. Cf. ibid., 155ff. (IV, 422ff.).

97. Cf. ibid., 113 (IV, 382).

98. Consider in this context an expression such as "fear or anxiety" in S. Kierkegaard, *The Sickness unto Death*, 37! In this particular passage Kierkegaard juxtaposes without distinction fear and anxiety over against hope.

99. Cf., e.g., G. Ebeling, "Lebensangst und Glaubensanfechtung. Erwägungen zum Verhältnis von Psychotherapie und Theologie," *ZTK* 70 (1973) 77–100, here 88: "When Kierkegaard conceives the concept" of anxiety (by distinguishing it from fear) "such that he denies that an animal experiences anxiety, then this is obviously forced."

100. M. Wandruszka, "Was weiss die Sprache von der Angst?" 18. Wandruszka also

considers Heidegger's analysis of anxiety to be "extremely revealing" only "as a personal human testimony" (21). Otherwise, however, Heidegger's analysis of existence "has hitherto yielded no other result than endless talk about anxiety and nothing" (19).

101. Concerning Kierkegaard's biography and childhood, cf. among others M. Theunissen and W. Greve, *Materialien zur Philosophie S. Kierkegaards*, 15ff.

102. Cf. S. Kierkegaard, *The Concept of Anxiety*, 43 (IV, 314).

103. Cf. S. Kierkegaard, *Either/Or*, 188, 191f.

104. What Kierkegaard writes about the treatment of the psychologically ill has, in part, unfortunately lost none of its relevance:

> The demonic has been viewed medically-therapeutically. And it goes without saying, with powder and with pills and then with enemas! Now the pharmacist and the physician would get together. The patient would be isolated to prevent others from becoming afraid. In our courageous age, we dare not tell a patient he is about to die, we dare not call the pastor lest he dies from shock, and we dare not tell the patient that a few days ago a man died from the same disease. The patient would be isolated. Sympathy would inquire about his condition. The physician would promise to issue a report as soon as possible, along with a tabulated statistical survey in order to determine the average. And when one has arrived at the average, everything is explained (ibid., 121–22 [IV, 389]).

105. For Kierkegaard, suicide is the result of a misunderstanding of anxiety such that it leads away from faith rather than to it. Cf. *The Concept of Anxiety*, 158f. (IV, 424).

106. All citations from K. Jaspers, *Philosophy*, 2.232.

107. P. Tillich, *The Courage to Be*, 35.

108. Ibid., 66.

109. Cf. Sigmund Freud, *The Standard Edition of the Complete Psychological Works of Sigmund Freud*, vol. 26, *Introductory Lectures on Psycho-Analysis (Part III)*, lecture 25, "Anxiety," 392–411, here 393.

110. S. Freud, *The Standard Edition of the Complete Psychological Works of Sigmund Freud*, vol. 20, "Inhibitions, Symptoms and Anxiety (1926 [1925])," 87–174, here 165.

111. Cf. "On the Grounds for Detaching a Particular Syndrome from Neurasthenia under the Description 'Anxiety Neurosis,' " in *The Standard Edition of the Complete Psychological Works of Sigmund Freud*, vol. 3, 87ff.

112. Cf. "Inhibitions, Symptoms and Anxiety (1926 [1925])."

113. Ibid., 167.

114. Ibid. Cf. also ibid., 165: "By bringing this danger which is not known to the ego into consciousness, the analyst makes neurotic anxiety no different from realistic anxiety, so that it can be dealt with in the same way." Cf. also ibid., 128f.

115. In the lecture on "Anxiety" Freud compares the affect with a hysterical attack. The decisive feature of the affect is the "repetition of some particular significant experience," namely, in the case of anxiety that of the trauma of birth. "A hysterical attack may thus be likened to a freshly constructed individual affect, and a normal affect to the expression of a general hysteria which has become a heritage" (396).

116. Ibid., 395.

117. Ibid., 394.

118. "Inhibitions, Symptoms and Anxiety (1926 [1925])," 165.

119. Ibid., 165; cf. also 134f.

120. Cf. ibid., 132.

121. Cf., e.g., the lecture on "Anxiety," 395; "Inhibitions, Symptoms and Anxiety (1926 [1925])," 165.

122. Concerning criticism of the normal concept of time, see M. Heidegger, *Being and Time*, 274ff., esp. 379ff., 383ff., 429ff. (German 231ff.; esp. 331ff., 334ff., 378ff.). From the theological perspective, see, e.g., G. Sauter, *Zukunft und Verheissung. Das*

Problem der Zukunft in der gegenwärtigen theologischen und philosophischen Diskussion, 15–42.

123. Cf. also Kierkegaard's criticism of the concept of pure temporality, *The Concept of Anxiety*, 85f. (IV, 355f.). Kierkegaard criticizes the concept of pure temporality because it is unable to determine any single moment as being genuinely present, unless by mere arbitrariness. Without such a present moment, however, the past and future cannot be separated from one another, so that for representation this infinite succession of time is "an infinitely contentless present." This means, however, that the concept of time becomes "an illusionary view of an infinite, contentless nothing" which—as with both Kant and Hegel—coincides with space.

124. The concept of time behind the idea of linear time is that of time which is absolute in the physical sense, a concept that A. Einstein, in his special theory of relativity (1905), showed to be untenable. Although modern physics has since given up the concept of absolute time, the understanding of time underlying the contemporary theory of the space-time continuum is nonetheless mathematical. The difference or distance between two events is, viewed physically, spatial-temporal, which for the purely temporal view of events means that one cannot determine in a universally valid fashion which of two events took place earlier than the other. Events that lie in the future for one observer, already belong to the past for a different observer. Concerning these questions, which cannot be discussed here, cf. B. Russell, *The ABC of Relativity*, esp. 71ff. Concerning the spatial character of mathematical and conceptual thinking in the larger sense and its relationship to what has become and to the past, or to death, see G. Simmel, *Lebensanschauung. Vier metaphysische Kapitel*, 108–22, and O. Spengler, *The Decline of the West*, 121ff. Despite M. Theunissen's assumption, Simmel is, as one sees, not the only author of modernity who has recognized this connection. Cf. M. Theunissen, "Die Gegenwart des Todes im Leben," in R. Winau and H. P. Rosemeier, eds., *Tod und Sterben*, 102–24, here 122.

125. M. Heidegger, *Being and Time*, 78ff. (German 52ff.).

126. Ibid., 33 (German 13).

127. Ibid., 26 (German 7).

128. Heidegger expresses the unitary character of the phenomenon through the compound expression "Being-in-the-world." Cf. ibid., 78ff. (German 53ff.).

129. Cf. ibid., 91ff. (German 63ff.).

130. See M. Buber, "Replies to My Critics," in A. Schilpp and M. Friedmann, eds., *The Philosophy of Martin Buber*, 689–744, here 705. The concept of correlation derives in the context of dialogical thinking from F. Rosenzweig, who employs it for the "interrelationship between I and thou." Cf. F. Rosenzweig, *Kleinere Schriften*, 296. Concerning the history of dialogical thinking, see M. Buber "Zur Geschichte des dialogischen Prinzips," *Werke*, vol. 1, *Schriften zur Philosophie*, 291–305. See further H. H. Schrey, *Dialogisches Denken*, Erträge der Forschung 1.

131. M. Buber, "Das Problem des Menschen," *Werke*, 1.307–407, here 404.

132. Ibid., 404f.

133. Ibid., 405. Concerning the concept of the between and criticism of it, see P. Wheelwright, "Buber's Philosophical Anthropology," in *The Philosophy of Martin Buber*, 93f., and G. Marcel, "I and Thou," in *The Philosophy of Martin Buber*, 45; see also M. Buber, "Replies to My Critics," 706f.

134. "Das Problem des Menschen," 405f.

135. Cf. M. Buber, *I and Thou*, 66, "Feelings one 'has': love occurs. Feelings dwell in man, but man dwells in his love. This is not metaphor but actuality: love does not cling to an I, as if you were merely its 'content' or object; it is *between* I and You."

136. "Das Problem des Menschen," 406.

137. G. Marcel, "I and Thou," in *The Philosophy of Martin Buber*, 41–48, here 45.

138. Concerning this problem, cf. M. Buber, *I and Thou*, 57ff., and the critical view of, e.g., H. L. Goldschmidt, *Hermann Cohen und Martin Buber*.

139. Cf. A. Jäger, *Gott. Nochmals Martin Heidegger*, 420, n. 36.
140. M. Heidegger, *Being and Time*, 163f. (German 126).
141. Ibid., 426 (German 374).
142. Cf. ibid., 377 (German 329).
143. Ibid., 426f. (German 374).
144. M. Heidegger, *What Is a Thing?*, 243. Concerning the notion of the between in Heidegger, see A. Jäger, *Gott. Nochmals Martin Heidegger*, 420ff.
145. Cf. E. Jüngel, "Die Welt als Möglichkeit und Wirklichkeit," *EvT* 29 (1969) 417–42, here 419.
146. K. Rahner, *Zur Theologie der Zukunft*, 177.
147. Ibid., 178.
148. Cf. E. Bloch, *The Principle of Hope*, 235ff.
149. Cf. ibid., 195ff.; 223ff.; E. Bloch, *Tübinger Einleitung in die Philosophie*, *Gesamtausgabe* 13, 210ff. See also the criticism of Bloch presented by Jüngel, "Die Welt als Möglichkeit und Wirklichkeit," 423.
150. M. Heidegger, *Being and Time*, 183 (German 143f.).
151. Ibid., 63 (German 38).
152. Cf. K. Rahner, *Zur Theologie der Zukunft*, 149ff., 177ff.
153. E. Jüngel, "Die Welt als Möglichkeit und Wirklichkeit," 436.
154. Cf. A. Jäger, *Gott. 10 Thesen*, 158.
155. Cf. O. Haendler's classification, though it does not speak of three *aspects* of anxiety, but rather categorizes anxiety before, in, and about something as three different *types* of anxiety. See note 74 above.
156. Cf. S. Freud, "Anxiety," in *The Standard Edition of the Complete Psychological Works of Sigmund Freud*, vol. 26, *Introductory Lectures on Psycho-Analysis (Part III)*, lecture 25, 404, 411; also "Inhibitions, Symptoms and Anxiety," *The Standard Edition of the Complete Psychological Works of Sigmund Freud*, vol. 20, 161. "The ego is the actual seat of anxiety" ("Inhibitions, Symptoms and Anxiety," 161).
157. Cf., e.g., Freud, "Inhibitions, Symptoms and Anxiety," 161.
158. W. Schulz, "Die Dialektik von Leib und Seele bei Kierkegaard. Bemerkungen zum 'Begriff Angst,' " 348.
159. To be sure, by anxiety Freud understands a reaction which is not peculiar to human beings, but rather which can be observed among all higher living beings, and thus also among animals whose birth apparently does not take place traumatically. "Therefore there can be anxiety without the prototype of birth," "Inhibitions, Symptoms and Anxiety," 134.
160. Ibid., 137.
161. On this entire complex cf. S. Freud, "Inhibitions, Symptoms and Anxiety," 132ff. (here 140; see also 130). [The translation of Freud's essay renders German *Angst* as fear here instead of as anxiety, as is usually the case; for the sake of consistency in the present discussion I have rendered it as "anxiety."—Trans.]
162. Ibid., 167f.
163. Ibid., 167.
164. Cf. W. Schulz, "Die Dialektik von Leib und Seele bei Kierkegaard. Bemerkungen zum 'Begriff Angst,' " 362; idem, "Das Problem der Angst in der neueren Philosophie," 23f.
165. P. Tillich, *The Courage to Be*, 40.
166. Ibid.
167. Ibid., 40f.
168. Cf. ibid., 41.
169. Cf. K. Jaspers, *Philosophy*, 2.198ff.; 2.232ff.
170. Cf. P. Tillich, *The Courage to Be*, 50f.
171. Ibid., 52.

172. All citations from ibid., 52f.

173. Cf. K. Jaspers, *Philosophy*, 2.198ff; 2.232ff.

174. Cf. ibid., 232.

175. Ibid., 232f.

176. Cf. ibid., 233.

177. "The sensual states of vertigo and trepidation are parables for the notion of absolute consciousness; as all things pass away, that consciousness will touch the source and rise from it" (ibid., 230).

178. Ibid., 232. [Here, too, the English translation of Jaspers's work renders German Angst as "fear," for which I have substituted anxiety.—Trans.]

179. Ibid.

180. J.-P. Sartre, *Being and Nothingness: An Essay on Phenomenological Ontology*, 29.

181. Ibid., 30.

182. Ibid. [The official English translation of this sentence inexplicably omits "not," which is clearly intended in the French original.—Trans.]

183. Ibid., 31.

184. Ibid., 32.

185. Cf. ibid., 32.

186. Ibid., 34.

187. Cf. ibid., 30.

188. Ibid., 34.

189. Cf. W. Schulz, "Die Dialektik von Leib und Seele bei Kierkegaard," 363.

190. Cf. J.-P. Sartre, *Being and Nothingness*, 29.

191. Cf. S. Kierkegaard, *The Concept of Anxiety*, 81ff. (IV, 350ff.).

192. So also W. Schulz, "Die Dialektik von Leib und Seele bei Kierkegaard," 363.

193. Cf. S. Kierkegaard, *The Concept of Anxiety*, 85 (IV, 355).

194. Ibid., 89 (IV, 359).

195. Ibid., 88 (IV, 358).

196. A different view is taken by J. Sløk, *Die Anthropologie Kierkegaards*, 77, for whom it is "clear without further ado" that Kierkegaard is saying the same thing with the concepts body, psyche, and spirit as with the terms time, eternity, and the moment, and "that in a certain sense he can thus arbitrarily substitute terms." However, the fact that Kierkegaard himself already points out that he construes the synthesis of the temporal and the eternal differently than that of the body and psyche (*The Concept of Anxiety*, 85 [IV, 355]) militates against this view. The synthesis between the temporal and eternal initially lacks that third element which in the synthesis between body and psyche is the spirit. This third, the moment, cannot, however, be considered apart from the spirit that posits itself. Rather: "As soon as the spirit is posited, the moment is present" (ibid., 88 [IV, 358]). To this extent the temporal structure of existence is comprehensible only from the perspective of the body-spirit structure.

197. Cf. W. Schulz, "Die Dialektik von Leib und Seele bei Kierkegaard," 352ff.

198. Cf. S. Kierkegaard, *The Concept of Anxiety*, 43 (IV, 315).

199. Cf. ibid., 49 (IV, 319).

200 . Ibid., 43f. (IV, 315).

201. Cf. ibid., 48f. (IV, 319). Sløk's interpretation of the synthesis of body, soul, and spirit (*Die Anthropologie Kierkegaards*, 80), according to which for Kierkegaard a person is "a biological being, characterized by animal functions shared with animals," even though "in addition to this biological determination he is also conscious of himself as soul," accords only in part with Kierkegaard's explication.

202. Cf. S. Kierkegaard, *The Concept of Anxiety*, 49 (IV, 319f.).

203. W. Schulz, "Die Dialektik von Leib und Seele bei Kierkegaard," 362.

204. Ibid., 363f.

205. Cf. ibid., 364. One can ask similarly from the perspective of psychoanalysis how one justifies the demand for a renunciation of one's impulses or drives.

206. M. Wandruszka, "Was weiss die Sprache von der Angst?" 21.

207. W. Jens, in K. Schlechta, ed., *Angst und Hoffnung in unserer Zeit. Darmstädter Gespräch 1963*, 165.

208. A. Jores, in *Angst und Hoffnung in unserer Zeit*, 28.

209. K. Schwarzwäller, *Die Angst—Gegebenheit und Aufgabe, Theologische Studien* 102, 24.

210. J. Moltmann, " 'Begnadete Angst.' Religiös integrierte Angst und ihre Bewältigung," in H. von Stietencron, ed., *Angst und Gewalt. Ihre Präsenz und ihre Bewältigung in den Religionen*, 142.

211. Ibid., 141.

212. E. Bloch, *The Principle of Hope*, 106; cf. M. Heidegger, *Being and Time*, 172f. (German 134).

213. Cf. E. Bloch, *The Principle of Hope*, 74.

214. Ibid., 274.

215. Cf. M. Heidegger, *Being and Time*, 378 (German 329).

216. E. Bloch, *The Principle of Hope*, 75.

217. Ibid., 75.

218. M. Heidegger, *Being and Time*, 386 (German 345); cf. also 175 (German 136).

219. Cf. ibid., 395f., 391 (German 345, 341): "Our temporal Interpretation will restrict itself to the phenomena of fear and anxiety, which we have already analysed in a preparatory manner."

220. E. Bloch, *The Principle of Hope*, 64; cf. also 67, where Bloch refers explicitly to Spinoza: " 'Suum esse conservare,' to preserve one's being, that is and remains however, according to Spinoza's unerring definition, the 'appetitus' of all beings."

221. E. Bloch, *Tübinger Einleitung in die Philosophie*, *Gesamtausgabe*, 13, 210.

222. E. Bloch, *The Principle of Hope*, 65.

223. Ibid., 9.

224. Cf. also E. Bloch, *Avicenna und die Aristotelische Linke.*

225. E. Bloch, *The Principle of Hope*, 207.

226. E. Bloch, *Tübinger Einleitung in die Philosophie*, 223.

227. F.W.J. Schelling, *Philosophische Untersuchungen über das Wesen der menschlichen Freiheit*, 52. See also the English translation *Of Human Freedom.*

228. Ibid., 53.

229. Both citations, ibid., 54.

230. Ibid., 55.

231. Ibid., 56.

232. Ibid., 57.

233. Ibid., 87.

234. Ibid., 74.

235. Ibid., 79.

236. G.W.F. Hegel, *Lectures on the Philosophy of Religion*, 1.276.

237. Ibid.

238. Ibid., 278.

239. Ibid., 279.

240. G.W.F. Hegel, *The Encyclopaedia Logic*, 63. On Hegel's interpretation of the myth of the Fall, cf. 61ff.

241. S. Kierkegaard, *The Concept of Anxiety*, 32 (IV, 304).

242. Ibid., 42 (IV, 313).

243. Ibid., 156 (IV, 422).

244. S. Kierkegaard, *The Sickness unto Death*, 37.

Chapter 3
WORLD ANXIETY AND THE END OF THE WORLD

1. P. Tillich, *The Courage to Be*, 35.
2. P. Tillich, *Systematic Theology*, 1.189.
3. M. Heidegger, *Being and Time*, 276f. (German 233f.).
4. Cf. the interesting remarks by H.-G. Gadamer, "Der Weg in die Kehre (1979)," in idem, *Heidegger's Wege. Studien zum Spätwerk*, 103–16. English translation in idem, *Heidegger's Ways*.
5. Cf. G. Anders, "Über die Bombe und die Wurzeln unserer Apokalypse-Blindheit," in idem, *Die Antiquiertheit des Menschen. Über die Seele im Zeitalter der zweiten industriellen Revolution*, n. 243.
6. Cf. C. Kulenkampff, "Zum Problem der abnormen Krise in der Psychiatrie," *Der Nervenarzt* 30 (1959) 62ff.; now in *Die Wahnwelten (Endogene Psychosen)*, 258–87, here 285.
7. C. Kulenkampff, "Entbergung, Entgrenzung, Überwältigung als Weisen des Standverlustes. Zur Anthropologie der paranoiden Psychosen," *Der Nervenarzt* 26 (1955) 89ff.; now in E. Strauss and J. Zutt, eds., *Die Wahnwelten (Endogene Psychosen)*, 210.
8. M. Heidegger, *An Introduction to Metaphysics*, 151.
9. Ibid., 150.
10. C. Kulenkampff, "Entbergung, Entgrenzung, Überwältigung als Weisen des Standverlustes," 211.
11. G. M. Martin, *Weltuntergang. Gefahr und Sinn apokalyptischer Visionen*, 56.
12. J. A. Arlow and C. Brenner, "Zur Psychopathologie der Psychosen," *Psyche* 23 (1969) 409.
13. Cf. G. M. Martin, *Weltuntergang. Gefahr und Sinn apokalyptischer Visionen*, 57f.
14. On the later distinction between defense and repression, cf. S. Freud, *The Problem of Anxiety*, 144. Freud picks up again the concept of defense, which he gave up for a time, and asserts "that this shall be the general designation for all the techniques of which the ego makes use in the conflicts which potentially lead to neurosis, while repression is the term reserved for one particular method of defense." Cf. also 59f.
15. Ibid., 113f.
16. Ibid., 127.
17. Cf. M. Laubscher, "Krise und Evolution. Eine kulturwissenschaftliche Theorie zum Begriff 'Krisenkult,' " in P. Eicher, ed., *Gottesvorstellung und Gesellschaftsentwicklung*, Forum Religionswissenschaft 1, 131–47. Cf. the criticisms of Laubscher's theses expressed by H. G. Kippenberg, "Krisenkult: Ein ethnozentrisches Konzept?" ibid., 148f.
18. Cf. W. La Barre, "Materials for a History of Studies of Crisis Cults: A Bibliographic Essay," *Current Anthropology* 12 (1971), 3–44, esp. 11.
19. M. Laubscher, "Krise und Evolution," 147.
20. Cf. the extensive bibliography in ibid., 132f., n. 2.
21. Ibid., 146.
22. K. Jaspers, *Philosophy*, vol. 2, *Existential Elucidation*, 277.
23. Ibid.
24. Ibid., 278.
25. Ibid., 158.
26. Ibid., 159.
27. Ibid., 160.
28. Cf. ibid., 338ff.
29. Ibid., 278.
30. Ibid.
31. Ibid., 279.
32. Ibid., 278.

33. S. Freud, *The Problem of Anxiety*, 115.
34. Cf. H. Jonas, *Gnosis und spätantiker Geist*, 1.68.
35. Cf. O. Haendler, *Angst und Glaube*, 30.
36. Ibid., 31.
37. Ibid.
38. Ibid.
39. Ibid., 32.
40. Ibid., 33.
41. Ibid.
42. Ibid., 34ff.
43. Cf., e.g., the reference to the *archē ōdinōn* in the so-called Little Apocalypse of Mark (Mark 13:8; cf. Matt. 24:8).
44. M. Heidegger, *Being and Time*, 235 (German 190f.); cf. 308, 309f. (German 263, 265f.).
45. Ibid., 150 (German 114).
46. Ibid., 150 (German 115).
47. Ibid., 220 (German 175).
48. Ibid., 213 (German 169).
49. Ibid., 234 (German 189).
50. P. Tillich, *The Courage to Be*, 57–63. Concerning this topic, see also the historical work of J. Delumeau, *Angst im Abendland. Die Geschichte kollektiver Ängste im Europa des 14. bis 18. Jahrhunderts* (French original *Le peur en Occident, XIVe–XVIIe siècles).* Delumeau addresses the possibilities and difficulties attaching to a theory of collective anxiety (ibid., 1.25ff.), whereby he tries to transfer to collectives the various psychological theories of anxiety inclusive of their distinction between anxiety and fear.
51. P. Tillich, *The Courage to Be*, 91f.
52. Ibid., 91.
53. Ibid., 92.
54. Ibid., 62.
55. Cf. H. E. Richter in an interview with the *Evangelische Kommentare:* "Umgang mit der Angst. Gespräch mit H. E. Richter," *Evangelische Kommentare* 17 (1984) 141–44, here 144.

Chapter 4
NOTIONS OF THE END OF THE WORLD

1. H. Boehncke, R. Stollmann, and G. Vinnai, eds., *Weltuntergänge*, Kulturen und Ideen, 6.
2. G. M. Martin, *Weltuntergang. Gefahr und Sinn apokalyptischer Visionen*, 38.
3. See the outline by F. M. Wuketits, *Grundzüge der Evolutionstheorie*, passim.
4. Cf. ibid., 44ff. "Paleontology acquired its real significance and its scientific-theoretical foundation understandably only with the establishment of the theory of evolution . . . This is why the significance of fossils for phylogenetics as a whole cannot be overestimated" (45).
5. For example, Cuvier recognized that the mammoth was an extinct type of elephant that was different from contemporary elephants. Admittedly, Leonardo da Vinci already recognized that fossils were not simply jests of nature (*lusus naturae*), but rather the petrified remains of plants and animals. Cf. F. M. Wuketits, *Grundzüge der Evolutionstheorie*, 44f. Findings of mussels and fossils in the interior of the country already played a role among the Stoics, e.g., in Zenon, as an argument for the fixed time limit attaching to the present world condition. Cf. M. Pohlenz, *Die Stoa. Geschichte einer geistigen Bewegung*, 1.77; 2.44.
6. Cf. F. M. Wuketits, *Grundzüge der Evolutionstheorie*, 25. See also H. Hölder,

Geologie und Paläontologie in Texten und ihrer Geschichte, Orbis academicus II/12, 473ff., concerning the theories of catastrophe advanced by Cuvier, F. v. Alberti (1834), Alcide d'Orbigny, A. Oppel, and F. A. Quenstedt.

7. G. M. Martin, *Weltuntergang*, 38.

8. Cf. A. Olrik, *Ragnarök. Die Sagen vom Weltuntergang*, 423ff.

9. Ibid., 437. Cf. also 437ff.

10. J. Moltmann, *Theology of Hope*, 230. Cf. also J. Moltmann, "Exegese und Eschatologie der Geschichte," *EvT* 22 (1962) 31ff., as well as Moltmann's bibliography in the *Theology of Hope*, 230, n. 2.

11. Ibid., 232.

12. We cannot discuss these relationships here. For an introduction, see G. Scherer, *Das Problem des Todes in the Philosophie*, Grundzüge 35, 151ff.

13. In Old High German, the term *Sinvluot* means approximately "the great flood," and not "the flood prompted by sin."

14. On Gen. 6:5ff. as well as concerning the following exposition, cf. C. Westermann, *Genesis 1–11*, 384–458.

15. R. Andrée, *Die Flutsagen ethnographisch betrachtet*, passim, offers 88 texts; J. Frazer, *Folk-Lore in the OT: Studies in Comparative Religion, Legend and Law*, 46ff., offers around 250 texts; J. Riem, *Die Sintflut in Sage und Wissenschaft*, passim, even offers 302 texts. Cf. also M. Winternitz, "Die Flutsagen des Altertums und der Naturvölker," *Mitteilungen der anthropologischen Gesellschaft in Wien* 31 (1901) 305–33.

16. W. von Soden, "Sintflut I. Religionsgeschichtlich," *RGG* (3rd ed.) 6.50f., here 50.

17. C. Westermann, *Genesis 1–11*, 402.

18. Ibid., 398–99.

19. Cf. J. Riem, *Die Sintflut in Sage und Wissenschaft*, 44, 56, 103.

20. C. G. Jung, "After the Catastrophe," *Collected Works*, vol. 10, Bollingen Series 20, 194–217, here 194.

21. Ibid., 214.

22. Ibid., 212.

23. Cf. also Matt. 24:37–39. The Lukan version goes beyond Matt. 24:37ff. by supplementing the recollection of the days of Noah with a reference to the example of Sodom, and augments the flood catastrophe with fire and brimstone. 2 Peter 2:5f. also connects the flood and the downfall of Sodom, a connection already familar to Jewish tradition. Cf. Wisd. 10:4–7; 3 Macc. 2:4f.; *T. Naph.* 3:4f.; Philo, *Vit. Mos.* ii.53–56. See also H. Strack and P. Billerbeck, *Kommentar zum NT aus Talmud und Midrasch*, 1.574.

24. So the title of a 1974 album by Bob Dylan and The Band.

25. M. Kähler, cited by J. Moltmann, *Theology of Hope*, 37.

26. J. W. von Goethe, *Faust I & II*, 36 (lines 1338–41).

27. Cf. E. Abegg, *Der Messiasglaube in Indien und im Iran*, 15.

28. Ibid., 9f. In Vedic literature the names of the Yugas refer to the four possibilities attaching to the throwing of dice, whence derive the names of the world ages.

29. Cf. ibid., 10ff. See also R. Reitzenstein, "Weltuntergangsvorstellungen," *Kyrkohistorisk Areskrift* 25 (1924) 207f.

30. Cf. E. Abegg, *Der Messiasglaube in Indien und im Iran*, 38.

31. A. Olrik, *Ragnarök. Die Sagen vom Weltuntergang*, 458f.

32. M. Eliade, *Cosmos and History: The Myth of the Eternal Return*, 118.

33. Cf. E. Abegg, *Der Messiasglaube in Indien und im Iran*, 23f. The invasions alluded to here commenced with the Saka und Kushana kings and reached their high point with the reign of the Huns. It is disputed whether with respect to religion the invasion of Islam is also being alluded to in addition to Buddhism, that invasion having begun at the end of the first millennium of the common era. In any case, Indian apocalyptic makes extensive use of the device of *vaticinium ex eventu*.

34. Cf. M. Eliade, *Cosmos and History*, 116ff.

35. Cf. M. Pohlenz, *Die Stoa. Geschichte einer geistigen Bewegung*, 1.77. Theophrastus, who in contrast to Zeno asserts that the present world is eternal, does nonetheless have to admit that partial catastrophes have occurred in the past. Cf. ibid., 2.44.

36. Cf. ibid., 1.79f.; 2.45ff.

37. For his own doctrine of the world conflagration and palingenesis, Zeno referred to Hesiod, who had already alluded to this ancient knowledge in myth. Cf. M. Pohlenz, *Die Stoa. Geschichte einer geistigen Bewegung*, 1.79. See also R. Reitzenstein, "Weltuntergangsvorstellungen," 207: "In his overwhelmingly eastern portrayal of the four world ages, Hesiod leads us into the immediate proximity of the notion of the world catastrophe. He did not, however, dare to utter this idea. It is as if pious shyness prevented him from fully conceiving the idea of a destruction of this wonderful cosmos."

38. Cf. F. Nietzsche, *Thus Spake Zarathustra*, 167–70 (part 3, "The Vision and the Enigma," sect. 2). See also K. Löwith, *Nietzsches Philosophie der ewigen Wiederkehr des Gleichen.*

39. So, e.g., Nigidius Figulus and Virgil. Cf. M. Eliade, *Cosmos and History*, 134f.

40. M. Eliade, *Cosmos and History*, 136.

41. U. Horstmann, *Das Untier. Konturen einer Philosophie der Menschenflucht*, 12.

42. Cf. W. Wundt, *Völkerpsychologie*, vol. 6, *Mythos und Religion*, 300f.; E. Abegg, *Der Messiasglaube in Indien und im Iran*, 9.

43. The two derivations do not mutually exclude one another. Contra E. Abegg, *Der Messiasglaube in Indien und im Iran*, 8f.

44. Cf. M. Eliade, *Cosmos and History*, 5.

45. Ibid., 86ff.

46. Ibid., 88.

47. On the apocalyptic of Islam see above, chap. 1, sec. 3. We will discuss the example of the apocalyptic of the Tupi-Guarani (cf. above, chap. 1, sec. 3) again in chap. 5, sec. 5.

48. For an extensive discussion, see A. von Gall, *Basileia tou theou. Eine religionsgeschichtliche Studie zur vorchristlichen Eschatologie*, 83–163; E. Abegg, *Der Messiasglaube in Indien und im Iran*, 203ff., as well as the bibliographical suggestions in chap. 1, n. 30.

49. So, e.g., R. Reitzenstein, "Weltuntergangsvorstellungen," 132.

50. Cf. A. Olrik, *Ragnarök. Die Sagen vom Weltuntergang*, 131f.

51. Cf. R. Reitzenstein, "Weltuntergangsvorstellungen," 203f. Beyond this, Reitzenstein also suspects especially Manichaean influence. Manichaeism might have influenced northern European thinking from Gaul by way of the British Isles as well as from the Balkans through Russia by way of the Baltic Sea. Cf. 194ff.

52. Cf. the extensive exposition in A. Olrik, *Ragnarök. Die Sagen vom Weltuntergang*, 5–132. On the notion of the end of the world within folk legend, see E. Nöth, *Weltanfang und Weltende in der deutschen Volkssage, 23ff.*

53. A. Olrik, *Ragnarök. Die Sagen vom Weltuntergang*, 438. Cf. also, e.g., 80.

54. Cf. ibid., 437; similarly E. Nöth, *Weltanfang und Weltende in der deutschen Volkssage*, 23: "Initially, then, these experiences of fear are the foundation for the construction of myths of the end of the world."

55. Cf. Dan. 8:17f.; 10:8–11, 16ff.; *1 Enoch* 14:13f.; 4 Ezra 10:25ff.; Rev. 1:17 (cf. Ezek. 2:1ff.).

56. On the book of Daniel, see among others K. Koch, T. Niewisch, and J. Tubach, *Das Buch Daniel*, Erträge der Forschung 144.

57. Cf. Dan. 7:15: "As for me, Daniel, my spirit within me was anxious and the visions of my head alarmed me." See further Dan. 4:16.

58. Dan. 7:28: "As for me, Daniel, my thoughts greatly alarmed me, and my color changed."

59. Dan. 8:27: "And I, Daniel, was overcome and lay sick for some days . . . and I was appalled by the vision and did not understand it."

60. Dan. 2:1, 3.

61. Cf. 4 Ezra 5:14. See also *2 Apoc. Bar.* 53:12: "And by reason of my fear I awoke."

62. This does not exclude the possibility that the literary fiction is occasionally dealing with authentic visionary experiences. The phenomenon of anxiety prompted by visions is authentically documented. For example, the painter Albrecht Dürer portrayed a flood vision in some notes concerning his own dream visions from the year 1525. "But when the first waters which came upon the earth had just about come down, they fell with such speed, rage, and storming, and I was so terrified that when I awoke, my whole body was shaking and it was some time before I settled down. But when I got up that morning, I painted it up here, just as I had seen it. May God turn all things to the best" (cited according to I. Riedel, "Apokalyptische Bilder," in P. Dätwyler, ed., *Not-Wendigkeiten. Auf der Suche nach einer neuen Spiritualität,* 53). C. G. Jung reports apocalyptic visions and dreams from the autumn of 1913 in his book *Erinnerungen, Träume, Gedanken.* At one point he says: "The vision lasted about an hour; it confused me and made me sick. I was ashamed of my weakness" (cited according to I. Riedel, ibid., 65).

63. I.e., the fallen angels.

64. The following Jewish apocalypses are cited with occasional alterations according to the translations in *The Old Testament Pseudepigrapha,* 2 vols., ed. James H. Charlesworth (Garden City, N.Y.: Doubleday, 1983), and *The Apocrypha and Pseudepigrapha of the Old Testament,* 2 vols., ed. R. H. Charles (Oxford: Clarendon, 1913). Concerning apocalyptic in Jewish rabbinic thought, see the material in H. Strack and P. Billerbeck, *Kommentar zum NT aus Talmud und Midrasch,* IV/2.799ff.

65. Cf. 4 Ezra 6:36f.: "And on the eighth night my heart was troubled within me again, and I began to speak in the presence of the Most High. For my spirit was greatly aroused, and my soul was in distress."

66. H. Gunkel evaluates 4 Ezra as follows: "This is the most sympathetic book among the apocalypses. The crass, exaggerated fantastic, mythological elements predominating in most of the apocalypses recedes here" (H. Gunkel, in E. Kautzsch, ed., *Die Apokryphen und Pseudepigraphen des Alten Testaments,* 348). We are concerned, however, with acquiring an appropriate understanding of the mythological element in apocalyptic instead of determining where it possibly is eliminated.

67. 4 Ezra 5:1 similarly adduces the anxiety of the inhabitants of the earth as the first among the signs of the end time.

68. Cf. 4 Ezra 7:62ff.; 116ff.

69. Cf. *1 Enoch* 13:3. Anxiety makes the fallen angels speechless (*1 Enoch* 13:5)!

70. Cf. also *1 Enoch* 62:5.

71. J. Lebram, "Apokalyptik/Apokalypsen II. Altes Testament," *TRE* 3.196. "The religious phenomenon of apocalyptic involves a situation in which faith in Yahweh, even in the Palestinian region, takes on the characteristics of a Diaspora-religion" (ibid., 199).

72. M. Buber, cited by J. Moltmann, *The Crucified God: The Cross of Christ as the Foundation and Criticism of Christian Theology, 217.*

73. Cf. 4 Ezra 14:10: "For the age has lost its youth, and the times begin to grow old."

74. Cf. H. Gunkel in *Die Apokryphen und Pseudepigraphen des Alten Testaments,* 337.

75. Cf. 4 Ezra 9:38ff.

76. Cf. O. Kaiser, *Introduction to the Old Testament: A Presentation of Its Results and Problems,* 313–15.

77. Cf. Jer. 25:11f.; 29:10.

78. On Dan. 9:26f., see N. W. Porteous, *Daniel, A Commentary,* OTL.

79. Cf. Dan. 8:12f.; 11:31f.

80. Cf. K. Müller, "Apokalyptik/Apokalypsen III. Die jüdische Apokalyptik. Anfänge und Merkmale," *TRE* 3.220f.
81. Dan. 11:34 speaks of "a little help" granted the afflicted. Cf. N. W. Porteous, *Das Buch Daniel*, ad loc. (141).
82. Cf. *1 Enoch* 92:2.
83. Cf. *1 Enoch* 94ff.
84. Cf. *1 Enoch* 94:6–9; 96:4–8; 97:7–10; 99:11–15.
85. Cf. H. Gunkel in *Die Apokryphen und Pseudepigraphen des Alten Testaments*, 2.352: "The time of the author can be determined precisely on the basis of the eagle vision; he has already experienced the death of Titus (11:35) and is anticipating, even as he writes, that of Domitian (81–96) (12:2, 28)."
86. Cf. H. Gunkel, ibid., 2.404.
87. Cf. also *2 Apoc. Bar.* 48:25ff.
88. Cf. *Sanh.* 97a:41 Bar; *Midr.* Ps. 45 sec. 3 (135a) (H. Strack and P. Billerbeck, *Kommentar zum NT aus Talmud und Midrasch*, IV/2.983).
89. Cf. *1 Enoch* 80:2–8.
90. Cf. Dan. 7—12 as a whole.
91. Cf. F. Lücke, *Versuch einer vollständigen Einleitung in die Offenbarung des Johannes, oder Allgemeine Untersuchungen über die apokalyptische Literatur überhaupt und die Apokalypse des Johannes insbesondere*, 27f.
92. Cf. K. Müller, "Apokalyptik/Apokalypsen III," 232f.
93. Ibid., 2.241.
94. U. Luck makes a similar observation concerning the main problem of apocalyptic: "In my opinion, its main problem is neither history nor the end of history nor any transcending universal history. The 'design' of a history from creation to judgment is the consequence of the understanding of the world which apocalyptic seeks to overcome in its own way" ("Das Weltverständnis in die jüdischen Apokalyptik, dargestellt am äthiopischen Henoch und am 4. Esra," *ZTK* 73 [1976] 286). Cf. also K. Müller, "Apokalyptik/Apokalypsen III," 226, 233.
95. One might think here, e.g., of Dan. 7:25f.
96. K. Müller, "Apokalyptik/Apokalypsen III," 217.
97. The demons are considered to be spirits of the giants which issued from the so-called angel-marriages of the primeval time (cf. Gen. 6:1–4). See *1 Enoch* 15:8ff.
98. Cf. also, however, the qualifying annotation H. Gunkel includes concerning *1 Enoch* 16:1: "What the great course of the world is, is unclear" (*Die Apokryphen und Pseudepigraphen des Alten Testaments*, 2.247).
99. Concerning the rabbinic understanding of the Messiah, his kingdom, and the future world, see the material in H. Strack and P. Billerbeck, *Kommentar zum NT aus Talmud und Midrasch*, IV/2.857ff., 968ff.
100. G. Scholem, "Toward an Understanding of the Messianic Idea in Judaism," idem, *The Messianic Idea in Judaism and Other Essays on Jewish Spirituality*, 1–36, here 7.
101. Ibid.
102. Ibid., 10.
103. Ibid., 11.
104. Cf. also *Midr.* Ps. 44 sec. 2 (135a); *Midr.* Ps. 20 sec. 4 (88a) (H. Strack and P. Billerbeck, *Kommentar zum NT aus Talmud und Midrasch*, IV/2.983).
105. Cf. the thorough discussion, pp. 102f. above.
106. Cf. p. 96f. above.
107. Cf. *2 Apoc. Bar.* 4:2–6.
108. O. Haendler, *Angst und Glaube*, 34ff.; cf. p. 103 above.
109. Cf. Matt. 24:8.
110. Documentation in H. Strack and P. Billerbeck, *Kommentar zum NT aus Talmud und Midrasch*, I.950. Concerning Mark 13:8 par., cf. the substance of 4 Ezra 13:30–32,

though here the reference is to the "bewilderment of mind" which will come over people in the end time rather than to woes. The image of birth pangs is used differently in *1 Enoch* 62:4 (cf. Isa. 13:8; 21:3), though also in 1 Thess. 5:3. Here it is the enemies of God whose pain on the day of affliction is compared with birth pangs. Cf. also *Pesiq. R.* 36(162a) (*Kommentar zum NT aus Talmud und Midrasch*, IV/2.982).

111. Cf. Isa. 65:17; 66:22. In the New Testament see Matt. 5:18; 19:28; Rev. 21!

112. Cf. *2 Apoc. Bar.* 49:3; 51:10.

113. Cf., e.g., *1 Enoch* 51:2; in the New Testament Luke 21:28.

114. Cf. also 4 Ezra 13:57f.

115. See also K. Müller's criticism of such attempts at classification and systematization in "Apokalyptik/Apokalypsen III," 223.

116. *2 Apoc. Bar.* 15:7; 48:50; 14:13; 15:8; 51:14.

117. *2 Apoc. Bar.* 16:1; 83:10–20; 51:16; cf. *2 Apoc. Bar.* 44:9.

118. *2 Apoc. Bar.* 51:14.

119. *2 Apoc. Bar.* 48:50.

120. *2 Apoc. Bar.* 48:50; 51:10.

121. *2 Apoc. Bar.* 15:7f.; cf. *2 Apoc. Bar.* 44:15.

122. *2 Apoc. Bar.* 44:12.

123. Cf. also 4 Ezra 4:2, 27; 6:9, 55; 7:12; 8:1 ("this aeon"); 7:113 ("this age"); 9:19 ("this world"); 7:112 ("this present world"); 6:55 ("this first world").

124. 4 Ezra 7:113; 8:52.

125. 4 Ezra 8:1; cf. 7:47 ("the world to come"); 6:9 ("the age that follows"); 7:13 ("the greater world").

126. Cf. the presentation of W. Bousset, *Die Religion des Judentums im späthellenistischen Zeitalter*, ed. H. Gressmann, 242ff. To the extent the kingdom of the Messiah is not identical with the new aeon, it is variously depicted as an interim kingdom. Cf. *1 Enoch* 91:11–19; 93:1–14; *2 Apoc. Bar.* 29:3; 30:1; 40:3; 74:2. 4 Ezra 7:28ff. anticipates that the Messiah will reign 400 years, while in the New Testament Revelation 20 anticipates a 1,000-year interim kingdom. Talmudic witnesses, which within both the Palestinian as well as the Babylonian tradition give differing estimates, anticipate that the interim kingdom will last between 40 and 7,000 years. Cf. H. Strack and P. Billerbeck, *Kommentar zum NT aus Talmud und Midrasch*, III.824ff.; P. Volz, *Die Eschatologie der jüdischen Gemeinde im neutestamentlichen Zeitalter*, 71–77, 226f.

127. Cf. H. Strack and P. Billerbeck, *Kommentar zum NT aus Talmud und Midrasch*, IV/2.816ff.

128. Cf. ibid., IV/2.844ff. In the New Testament see Matt. 12:32; Mark 10:30; Luke 18:30; 20:34; Eph. 1:21; 2:7; Heb. 6:5.

129. Cf. ibid., IV/2.858ff., 872ff.

130. In various ways the notion of a judgment of catastrophe is associated with the motif of the attack of the nations against Zion and the final battle for the city of God already found in the Old Testament. Occasionally the expectation is that the hostile armies will mutually annihilate one another; so, e.g., *1 Enoch* 56. See already Ezek. 38:21; Hag. 2:22; Zech. 14:13.

131. On this whole complex cf., e.g., *1 Enoch* 99:4, 6–9; 56:5–8; 100:1–4; 91:7ff.; *As. Mos.* 10:3–8; 4 Ezra 7:26ff.; 13; *1 Enoch* 1:3–7.

132. On this whole complex cf. the material in H. Strack and P. Billerbeck, *Kommentar zum NT aus Talmud und Midrasch*, IV/2.880ff.

133. Cf. ibid., IV/2.819f.

134. The various understandings of a resurrection of the dead are completely disparate. In part the resurrection of all dead for the final judgment is anticipated, and in part only a resurrection of the righteous from Israel. Cf. W. Bousset, *Die Religion des Judentums im späthellenistischen Zeitalter*, 269ff.

135. Cf., e.g., 4 Ezra 7:30f. After a 400-year reign the messiah dies. "And the world

shall be turned back to *primeval silence* for seven days, as it was at the first beginnings; so that no one shall be left. And after seven days the world, which is not yet awake, shall be roused, and that which is corruptible shall perish."

136. Cf. *1 Enoch* 80:2ff.; 99:4ff.; 100:1ff.; *Jub.* 23:22ff.; 4 Ezra 4:51–5:13; 6:18ff.; 8:63–9:6; *2 Apoc. Bar.* 25:1–29:2; 48:30–37; 70:2ff.; *Sib. Or.* 2:153ff.; 3:796ff. On the rabbinic traditions cf. H. Strack and P. Billerbeck, *Kommentar zum NT aus Talmud und Midrasch*, IV/2.981ff.

137. Cf. 4 Ezra 14:11ff.; *2 Apoc. Bar.* 53–72.

138. Cf. the apocalypse of ten weeks in *1 Enoch* 93; 91:12–17; *Sib. Or.* 4:47ff.; 4 Ezra 14:11f.

139. Cf. the rabbinic passages in H. Strack and P. Billerbeck, *Kommentar zum NT aus Talmud und Midrasch*, IV/2.989ff.

140. Cf. *As. Mos.* 1:1; 10:1–10, 11f.; 4 Ezra 14:18. Both these writings reckon with a duration of 5,000 years for the first period.

141. Cf. H. Strack and P. Billerbeck, *Kommentar zum NT aus Talmud und Midrasch*, IV/2.996ff.

142. Cf. ibid., IV/2.1001ff.

143. Cf. ibid., IV/2.1011ff.

144. Cf. M. Eliade, *Cosmos and History*, 102ff. Eliade accuses Jewish messianism of "an antihistoric attitude" (111).

145. Cf. R. Bultmann, *The Presence of Eternity: History and Eschatology*. [The expression "dehistoricization of history" (*Entgeschichtlichung der Geschichte*) does not occur in the English version of these lectures. Cf. R. Bultmann, *Geschichte und Eschatologie*, 35.—Trans.]

146. Cf. chap. 5, sec. 5 below.

147. K. Müller, "Apokalyptik/Apokalypsen III," 226.

148. Cf. the documentation in H. Strack and P. Billerbeck, *Kommentar zum NT aus Talmud und Midrasch*, IV/2.1013ff.

149. K. Müller, "Apokalyptik/Apokalypsen III," 228.

150. Ibid., 234.

151. Ibid., 235.

152. On the following discussion, see esp. K. Stock, *Annihilatio mundi. Johann Gerhards Eschatologie der Welt*, Forschungen zur Geschichte und Lehre des Protestantismus, 10th series, vol. XLII, passim. Concerning eschatology during the Reformation period and the modern age see further U. Asendorf, "Eschatologie VII," *TRE* 10.310–34, here esp. 317f.

153. Cf. the documentation in K. Stock, *Annihilatio mundi*, 175, n. 4. One important exception is the eschatology of P. Nicolai. Concerning the understanding of the *annihilatio mundi* of J. A. Quenstedt, see J. Baur, *Die Vernunft zwischen Ontologie und Evangelium. Eine Untersuchung zur Theologie Johann Andreas Quenstedts*, 61, 127–30, 169.

154. Cf. *Confessio Augustana* XVII; *Confessio Helvetica* XI.

155. Cf. D. Korn, *Das Thema des Jüngsten Tages in der deutschen Literatur des 17. Jahrhunderts*, 119ff.

156. Cf. *D. Martin Luthers Werke. Kritische Gesamtausgabe*, vol. 53, 22–184. See also passages such as that in *D. Martin Luthers Werke. Kritische Gesamtausgabe. Die Deutsche Bibel*, II. Band, 2. Hälfte, 1ff.

157. Cf. U. Asendorf, "Eschatologie VII," *TRE* 10.313. On the eschatology of the Reformers, see further T. F. Torrance, "Die Eschatologie der Reformation," *EvT* 14 (1954) 334–58.

158. See, e.g., *Corpus Reformatorum*, vol. 80, 195f. (Calvin's commentary on 2 Thess. 2:1f.).

159. J. Gerhard, *Postilla: Das ist Erklärung der Sontäglichen vnd fürnehmsten Fest-Euangelien/vber das gantze Jahr* (Jena, 1613) 1.27 (cited after D. Korn, *Das Thema des Jüngsten Tages in der deutschen Literatur des 17. Jahrhunderts*, 10).

160. J. Gerhard, *Loci Theologici cum pro adstruenda veritate tum pro destruenda quorumvis contradicentium falsitate per these nervose solide et copiose explicati*, Locus XXIX, "De Novissimimis in genere tractatus IV".

161. Ibid., XXIX, 67–97; cf. K. Stock, *Annihilatio mundi*, 119.

162. J. Gerhard, *Loci Theologici*, XXIX, 7: "prophetae verbis hujus seculi describunt res futuri seculi et a corporalibus beneficiis animos hominum ad spiritualia et coelestia principaliter a Messia expectande evehunt." Cf. also XXIX, 45, 50, 63, 78. See K. Stock, *Annihilatio mundi*, 117ff.

163. Concerning Reformed eschatology see Alexander Schweitzer, *Die Glaubenslehre der evangelisch-reformierten Kirche, dargestellt und aus den Quellen belegt*, vol. 2, 707–47, here esp. 724ff.

164. P. Althaus, *Die letzten Dinge. Lehrbuch der Eschatologie* (5th ed.; Gütersloh: C. Bertelsmann, 1949), 353.

165. Cf. *Confessio Belgica* XXXVII.

166. So, e.g., H. Alting, *Methodus theol. didact.* (1645) (Zurich, 1694) 756: "Mundus peribit non quoad substantiam sed quad accidenta; habebit eas qualitates quae corporibus immortalibus conveniant" (cited after A. Schweitzer, *Die Glaubenslehre der evangelisch-reformierten Kirche*, 727).

167. J. Wolleben, *Theologiae compendium* (2nd ed.; Basel, 1634) 282 (cited after A. Schweitzer, *Die Glaubenslehre der evangelisch-reformierten Kirche*, 727).

168. J. H. Heidegger, *Medulla medullae* (Zurich, 1697) 410 (cited after A. Schweitzer, *Die Glaubenslehre der evangelisch-reformierten Kirche*, 727).

169. J. H. Heidegger, *Medulla medullae*, 409 (cited after A. Schweitzer, *Die Glaubenslehre der evangelisch-reformierten Kirche*, 728).

170. J. Gerhard, *Loci Theologici*, XXIX, 107.

171. Ibid., XXIX, 26. On the concept of the world in Gerhard, see the extensive discussion in K. Stock, *Annihilatio mundi*, 67ff.

172. K. Stock, *Annihilatio mundi*, 87, even considers Gerhard's exegesis of Rom. 8:19ff. to be "an example of dogmatic extortion of biblical texts."

173. Ibid., 33.

174. P. Althaus, *Die letzten Dinge. Lehrbuch der Eschatologie*, 356.

175. Cf. K. Stock, *Annihilatio mundi*, 126ff. On the history of the *annihilatio*-concept, see 6ff.

176. Cf. ibid., 66, 166, 185.

177. Ibid., 123.

178. Cf. J. Gerhard, *Loci Theologici*, XXIX, 11.

179. Cf. ibid., XXIX, 64. See K. Stock, *Annihilatio mundi*, 86.

180. Cf. ibid., 8ff.

181. See p. 33 above.

182. A. Olrik, *Ragnarök. Die Sagen vom Weltuntergang*, 422.

183. "We find, however, that these divisions—which for our own scientific thinking seem clear enough—do not contain distinctions that go very deep" (ibid.).

184. Cf. sec. 3 above.

185. I. Kant, "Die Frage, ob die Erde veralte, physikalisch erwogen" (1754), in *Kant's Werke*, vol. 1, *Vorkritische Schriften I: 1747–1756*, Akademie Ausgabe, 193–213.

186. "I have accordingly dealt with the question of the aging of the earth not definitively, as would the entrepreneurial spirit of a daring natural scientist, but rather analytically, as naturally prompted by the nature of the objection itself" (ibid., 212f.).

187. Ibid., 212.

188. Ibid.

189. Ibid., 213.

190. An arbitrary example would be C. Berlitz, *Doomsday 1999 A.D.*, passim. See also

the thorough work of F. S. Archenhold, *Kometen, Weltuntergangsprophezeiungen und der Halleysche Komet.*

191. Cf. among older works K. Ziegler and S. Oppenheim, *Weltuntergang in Sage und Wissenschaft,* 52ff.

192. I. Kant, "Untersuchung der Frage, ob die Erde in ihrer Umdrehung um die Achse, wodurch sie die Abwechselung des Tages und der Nacht hervorbringt, einige Veränderung seit den ersten Zeiten ihres Ursprungs erlitten habe und woraus man sich ihrer versichern können, welche von der Königl. Akademie der Wissenschaften zu Berlin zum Preise für das jetzt laufende Jahr aufgegeben worden," *Kants Werke,* vol. 1, *Vorkritische Schriften I. 1747–1756,* 183–91.

193. Kant's work did not win, and during his lifetime was hardly made public and was not published a second time. The theory of the slowing of the earth's rotation was renewed in the second half of the nineteenth century by C. E. Delaunay, G. B. Airy, and W. Thomson. See the introduction of the editor of the Kantian treatise, Johannes Raht, in *Kants Werke* I, 539f.

194. K. Ziegler and S. Oppenheim, *Weltuntergang in Sage und Wissenschaft,* 80.

195. Cf. *Global 2000: The Report to the President of the U.S.* (1980), 2.68: "The climate forecasts make no assumptions about technology except that industrial processes will continue to release large amounts of carbon dioxide into the atmosphere, with the possible effect of warming the earth's atmosphere. No other foreseeable technological developments before the year 2000 were considered to have a significant effect on the climate of the planet."

196. Cf. *Global 2000,* 2.51–65.

197. Cf., e.g., *Global 2000,* 2.7–38.

198. See secs. 8 and 9 below.

199. On the following discussion cf. P. Teilhard de Chardin, *The Phenomenon of Man.*

200. See also P. Teilhard de Chardin, *Man's Place in Nature: The Human Zoological Group.*

201. P. Teilhard de Chardin, *The Phenomenon of Man,* 286.

202. Ibid.

203. Ibid., 287.

204. Cf. ibid., 268–72.

205. "Once and once only in the course of its planetary existence has the earth been able to envelop itself with life. Similarly once and once only has life succeeded in crossing the threshold of reflection. For thought as for life there has been just one season. And we must not forget that since the birth of thought man has been the leading shoot of the tree of life. That being so, the hopes for the future of the noosphere (that is to say, of biogenesis, which in the end is the same as cosmogenesis) are concentrated exclusively upon him as such. How then could he come to an end before his time, or stop, or deteriorate, unless the universe committed abortion upon itself . . . *Man is irreplaceable.* Therefore, however improbable it might seem, *he must reach the goal,* not necessarily, doubtless, but infallibly" (ibid., 276).

206. Ibid., 277.

207. Ibid., 276–85.

208. Concerning the "spirit of the earth" cf. ibid., 245ff.

209. Ibid., 287.

210. Ibid., 287–88.

211. On the role of evil in Teilhard's system, cf. ibid., 311–13.

212. "Such an outcome would of course conform most harmoniously with our theory" (ibid., 288).

213. "Though at the same time—since a critical point is being approached—*in extreme tension.* There is nothing in common between this perspective and the old millenary dream of a terrestrial paradise at the end of time" (ibid., 288, n. 2).

214. Ibid., 289.
215. Ibid.
216. Ibid.
217. Ibid.
218. H. v. Ditfurth, *So lasst uns denn ein Apfelbäumchen pflanzen. Es ist soweit*, 15.
219. Cf. ibid., 342ff. See also H. von Ditfurth, *Gedanken zum Leib-Seele-Problem aus naturwissenschaftlicher Sicht;* idem, *The Origins of Life: Evolution as Creation.*
220. H. von Ditfurth, *So lasst uns denn ein Apfelbäumchen pflanzen*, 12.
221. See esp. ibid., 164ff.
222. Cf. ibid., 342ff.
223. Cf. ibid., 357f.
224. Ibid., 358.
225. Ibid., 360.
226. Ibid., 367.
227. Ibid., 366.
228. P. T. d'Holbach, *The System of Nature: Laws of the Moral and Physical World*, 252–53.
229. Ibid., 46.
230. Ibid.
231. E. Drewermann, *Tiefenpsychologie und Exegese*, vol. 2, *Die Wahrheit der Werke und der Worte. Wunder, Vision, Weissagung, Apokalypse, Geschichte, Gleichnis*, 537.
232. Cf. K. Heim, *The World: Its Creation and Consummation*, 89.
233. Cf. H. Fritzsch, *The Creation of Matter: The Universe from Beginning to End*, 166–69.
234. Cf. ibid., 238.
235. Cf. ibid., 238, 251.
236. C. F. von Weizsäcker, *The History of Nature*, 8f.
237. Cf. ibid., 44–59, 52ff.; C. F. von Weizsäcker, *The World View of Physics*, esp. section 6 of the chapter concerning the infinity of the world; idem, *The Unity of Nature*, 138ff.
238. C. F. von Weizsäcker, *The History of Nature*, 53.
239. Ibid., 51.
240. See C. F. von Weizsäcker, *The Relevance of Science: Creation and Cosmogony.*
241. C. Sagan considers the possibility of an oscillating universe and cyclical cosmic deaths to be a given "at the edge of forever." See C. Sagan, *Cosmos*, 245ff.
242. K. Heim, *The World: Its Creation and Consummation*, 98.
243. On K. Heim's eschatology see Introduction, sec. 2 above.
244. K. Heim, *The World: Its Creation and Consummation*, 110.
245. E. Bloch, *The Principle of Hope*, 311.
246. See esp. the posthumous fragments: O. Spengler, *Urfragen. Fragmente aus dem Nachlass*, ed. A. M. Koktanek and M. Schröter. Concerning Spengler's biography, see A. M. Koktanek, *Oswald Spengler in seiner Zeit.*
247. Cf. M. Schröter, *Metaphysik des Untergangs. Eine kulturkritische Studie über Oswald Spengler*, passim, esp. 251.
248. Cf. ibid., 149ff. Schröter calls Spengler's work itself the "last German version of the idea of decline" (13).
249. So also ibid., 252.
250. Cf. K. Löwith, *Meaning in History: The Theological Implications of the Philosophy of History*, 62ff.
251. Ibid., 98ff.
252. See esp. O. Spengler, *Preussentum und Sozialismus;* idem, *Neubau des deutschen Reiches;* idem, *The Hour of Decision, Part One: Germany and World Historical Revolution.*
253. F. Nietzsche, *The Will to Power* (New York: Vintage Books, 1968) 3.
254. Ibid.
255. Ibid.

256. See the longer citation in K. Löwith, *Meaning in History*, 97f.

257. Cf. O. Spengler, *The Hour of Decision*, xi–xiii. "We have entered upon the age of world wars" (24).

258. Ibid., 17f.

259. Cf. C. Breysig, "Der Prophet des Untergangs," *Velhagen und Klasings Monatshefte* 35. Jahrgang (1920/21), Heft 9.

260. So also M. Schröter, *Metaphysik des Untergangs*, 237ff.

261. O. Spengler, *The Hour of Decision*, 21.

262. Ibid.

263. Cf. M. Schröter, *Metaphysik des Untergangs*, 251: "Against his will and contrary to his own expectations, he himself became—in his own work and as its creator—the prophet of the decline which had to occur after the cultural substance had in this way become used up, transparent, and ripe for death."

264. O. Spengler, *Pessimismus?*, 14.

265. Concerning criticism of Spengler see the thorough presentation of the discussion in M. Schröter, "Streit um Spengler. Kritik seiner Kritiker (1922)," *Metaphysik des Untergangs*, 15–158.

266. O. Spengler, *Pessimismus?*, 14.

267. O. Spengler, *The Hour of Decision*, 20.

268. Cf. ibid.

269. Cf. sec. 3 above.

270. In this context, cf., e.g., the criticism of O. Neurath, *Antispengler*.

271. O. Spengler, *The Decline of the West*, 1.17.

272. Ibid., 1.18ff.

273. "The most appropriate designation for this current West-European scheme of history, in which the great Cultures are made to follow orbits round *us* as the presumed centre of all world-happenings, is the *Ptolemaic system* of history" (ibid., 1.18).

274. Ibid.

275. Ibid., 1.50.

276. Ibid., 1.21.

277. Ibid., 1.21–22.

278. Cf. Spengler's synopses, ibid., Table 1, "Contemporary Spiritual Epochs."

279. Ibid., 1.39.

280. "The present is a civilized, emphatically not a cultured time" (ibid., 1.40).

281. Cf. ibid., 1.31ff.

282. Cf. the thorough discussion in M. Schröter, *Metaphysik des Untergangs*, passim.

283. Cf. chap. 2, sec. 1 above.

284. Cf. O. Spengler, *The Decline of the West*, 1.79.

285. M. Schröter, *Metaphysik des Untergangs*, 195.

286. See concluding statements to chap. 2, sec. 1 above.

287. Concerning this problem see also M. Schröter, *Metaphysik des Untergangs*, 213ff.

288. The distinction between longing and direction remains unclear. Cf., e.g., O. Spengler, *The Decline of the West*, 1.122: "Everything living . . . has 'life,' direction, impulse, will, a movement-quality that is most intimately allied to yearning."

289. Ibid., 53ff.

290. Ibid., 79.

291. Ibid., 90.

292. Ibid., 166.

293. Ibid., 166f.

294. Cf. also ibid., 191ff.

295. See chap. 3, sec. 1 above.

296. H. Freyer (1961), cited after H. E. Stier, "Zur geschichtlichen Wesensbestim-

mung Europas," in A. M. Koktanek, ed., *Schelling-Studien (FG M. Schröter)*, 193–210, here 193.

297. E. Spranger in a 1920 review of O. Spengler, *Preussentum und Sozialismus*, cited after L. Englert, "Eduard Spranger und Oswald Spengler," in A. M. Koktanek, ed., *Schelling-Studien (FG M. Schröter)*, 37.

298. Cited after M. Schröter, *Metaphysik des Untergangs*, 26, n. 6. Concerning Spengler's influence see also W. Drascher, "Begegnungen mit Oswald Spengler," in A. M. Koktanek, ed., *Schelling-Studien (FG M. Schröter)*, 9–31.

299. Cf. W. Drascher, "Begegnungen mit Oswald Spengler," 14f., 24f.

300. Cf. W. Drascher, ibid., 15. Among others, L. Wittgenstein also read and admired Spengler's work. See G. Hallet, *A Companion to Wittgenstein's Philosophical Investigations*, 216ff.

301. Cf. W. Drascher, "Begegnungen mit Oswald Spengler," 21.

302. Cf. M. Schröter, *Metaphysik des Untergangs*, 17ff.

303. W. Drascher, "Begegnungen mit Oswald Spengler," 22.

304. Concerning Spengler's friendship with Paul Reusch, see B. Herzog, "Die Freundschaft zwischen Spengler und Paul Reusch," in A. M. Koktanek, ed., *Schelling-Studien (FG M. Schröter)*, 77–97.

305. Cf. M. Schröter, *Metaphysik des Untergangs*, 26ff.

306. W. Elert, *Der Kampf um das Christentum. Geschichte der Beziehungen zwischen dem evangelischen Christentum in Deutschland und dem allgemeinen Denken seit Schleiermacher und Hegel* (Munich: Beck, 1921), 489.

307. P. Althaus, *Die letzten Dinge. Lehrbuch der Eschatologie*, 278.

308. Concerning Althaus's interpretation of, e.g., the First World War as a revelation of God's wrath, see W. Pressel, *Die Kriegspredigt 1914–1918 in der evangelischen Kirche Deutschlands*, 192.

309. Althaus explicitly mentions Spengler in *Die letzten Dinge. Lehrbuch der Eschatologie*, 277.

310. See ibid., 279.

311. Cf. Albert Schweitzer, "The Decay and the Restoration of Civilization (1923)," in *The Philosophy of Civilization*. Without referring to him directly by name, Schweitzer accuses Spengler of withdrawing to the "mild pessimistic supposition that civilization has reached its Indian summer" (39). In contrast, Schweitzer wants for ethical reasons to maintain absolutely "the belief in the possibility of a renewal of civilization." At the same time, he does recognize that both world history and cultural development are currently in a unique crisis.

> Those who regard the decay of civilization as something quite normal and natural console themselves with the thought that it is not civilization, but *a* civilization, which is falling a prey to dissolution; that there will be a new age and a new race in which there will blossom a new civilization. But that is a mistake. The earth no longer has in reserve, as it once did, gifted peoples as yet unused, who can relieve us and take our place in some distant future as leaders of the spiritual life. We already know all those which the earth has to dispose of. There is not one among them which is not already taking such a part in our civilization that its spiritual fate is determined by our own. All of them, the gifted and the ungifted, the distant and the near, have felt the influence of those forces of barbarism which are at work among us. All of them are, like ourselves, diseased, and only as we recover can they recover (39f.).

312. M. Schröter, *Metaphysik des Untergangs*, 257ff. See also 235ff. Because his morphology isolated cultures from one another, Spengler significantly did not share this perspective of a process of world civilization, developed especially by A. Weber, K. Jaspers,

and L. Frobenius; in fact, Spengler explicitly rejected it. Cf. O. Spengler, *The Decline of the West*, 2.37f. See also G. Merlio, "Spengler und die Technik," in P. C. Ludz, ed., *Spengler heute. Sechs Essays mit einem Vorwort von H. Lübbe*, 100–22, here 119f.

313. P. Althaus, *Die letzten Dinge. Lehrbuch der Eschatologie*, 280.

314. Concerning theological criticism of Spengler, cf. M. Schröter, *Metaphysik des Untergangs*, 115ff., especially concerning K. Heim's criticism of Spengler (126ff.).

315. Cf. D. Bonhoeffer, *Letters and Papers from Prison* (New York: Macmillan, 1962) 144 (letter of March 9, 1944).

316. D. Bonhoeffer, *Ethics*, ed. E. Bethge, 41–42. This passage comes from the year 1940.

317. Thus *Ethics*, 44, Bonhoeffer invokes 2 Thess. 2:7 in speaking about the state as the *katechōn*, i.e., the power restraining evil in the end time. This interpretation of the state as the *katechōn* from 2 Thess. 2:6f. derives ultimately from Hippolytus of Rome. Cf. Introduction, sec. 2 above.

318. Cf. G. Anders, *Die atomare Drohung. Radikale Überlegungen*, 176f. In this connection see also G. M. Martin, *Weltuntergang. Gefahr und Sinn apokalyptischer Visionen*, 16f.

319. G. Anders, "Über die Bombe und die Wurzeln unserer Apokalypse-Blindheit," in idem, *Die Antiquiertheit des Menschen. Über die Seele im Zeitalter der zweiten industriellen Revolution*, 345.

320. Ibid., 346.

321. G. Sauter, *Zukunft und Verheissung. Das Problem der Zukunft in der gegenwärtigen theologischen und philosophischen Diskussion*, 365.

322. A. Jäger, *Gott. Nochmals Martin Heidegger*, 439.

323. Ibid., 401.

324. Ibid., 354. Cf. there also in n. 66 Jäger's observations concerning the points of contact between Heidegger and Spengler.

325. A. Baeumler, "Kulturmorphologie und Philosophie," in A. M. Koktanek, ed., *Schelling-Studien (FG M. Schröter)*, 99–124, here 119f.

326. M. Heidegger, "Overcoming Metaphysics," in idem, *The End of Philosophy*, 84–110, here 90.

327. Ibid., 85–86.

328. M. Heidegger, *What Is Called Thinking*, 4.

329. Ibid., 6.

330. Ibid., 4.

331. Heidegger's lectures under the title "What Is Called Thinking" were delivered in the Winter Semester 1951/52 and the Summer Semester 1952 in Freiburg im Breisgau.

332. M. Heidegger, *What Is Called Thinking*, 38.

333. F. Nietzsche, *Thus Spoke Zarathustra* (Part 4), in *The Portable Nietzsche*, 417: "The wilderness [wasteland, desert, *Wüste*] grows: woe unto him that harbors wildernesses."

334. Heidegger's remark "we emphasized that these are words issuing from thought" refers to Nietzsche's expression, not to Spengler's sentence. Contra T. B. Strong, "Oswald Spengler—Ontologie, Kritik und Enttäuschung," in P. C. Ludz, ed., *Spengler heute. Sechs Essays mit einem Vorwort von H. Lübbe*, 74–99, here 79f.

335. M. Heidegger, "Overcoming Metaphysics," 86.

336. Ibid., 89.

337. Ibid., 92.

338. Ibid., 86. Cf. also M. Heidegger, "Der Spruch des Anaximander," idem, *Holzwege*, 296–343, here 343.

339. Cf. M. Heidegger, "The Word of Nietzsche: 'God Is Dead,' " idem, *The Ques-*

tion concerning Technology and Other Essays, 53–112. "And yet Nietzsche never recognized the *essence* of nihilism, just as no metaphysics before him ever did" (109).

340. Ibid., 62.

341. Ibid.

342. M. Heidegger, "Overcoming Metaphysics," 102.

343. Ibid., 101.

344. Ibid., 93.

345. Ibid.

346. Cf. O. Spengler, *The Decline of the West,* 469ff.; 499ff.; idem, *Man and Technics* (London: G. Allen & Unwin, 1932). Concerning Spengler's criticism of technology, see G. Merlio, "Spengler und die Technik," passim.

347. M. Heidegger, "Overcoming Metaphysics," 85. Cf. E. Jünger, *Der Arbeiter. Herrschaft und Gestalt.*

348. "Ernst Jünger's essay on 'total mobilization' appeared in 1930; this essay introduced the basic features of the 1932 book *Der Arbeiter [The Worker].* At that time I discussed these writings in a small circle with my assistant, Brock, and I tried to show how in them an essential understanding of Nietzsche's metaphysics comes to expression insofar as within the horizon of this metaphysics history and the present period of the west are viewed and anticipated. From these writings and even more essentially from their premises we conceptualized what was coming" (M. Heidegger, "Das Rektorat 1933/34. Tatsachen und Gedanken," idem, *Die Selbstbehauptung der Deutschen Universität/Das Rektorat 1933/34,* 21–43, here 24).

349. Concerning the weaknesses of Spengler's interpretation of technology, see also M. Schröter, *Metaphysik des Untergangs,* 235f.

350. See esp. M. Heidegger, "The Question concerning Technology," in idem, *Basic Writings,* 283–317; also published in *The Question concerning Technology and Other Essays,* 3–35 (hereafter cited in this latter edition).

351. M. Heidegger, "Overcoming Metaphysics," 86.

352. Cf. ibid., 104.

353. Cf. ibid., 103ff.

354. On Spengler see M. Schröter, *Metaphysik des Untergangs,* 237ff.

355. Concerning Heidegger's position within the Third Reich, see also his interview in *Der Spiegel* 23 (1976), "Spiegel Interview with Martin Heidegger," *Martin Heidegger and National Socialism: Questions and Answers,* 41–66. Spengler criticized the seizure of power in 1933 and not least of all the person of Adolf Hitler himself. Above all, however, his rejection of socialism separated him from National Socialism, and for just this reason Spengler criticized National Socialism insofar as it was itself socialism (or claimed to be). Cf. in this context H. Lübbe, "Historisch-politische Exaltationen. Spengler wiedergelesen," in P. C. Ludz, ed., *Spengler heute. Sechs Essays mit einem Vorwort von H. Lübbe,* 1–24, here 21ff.; H. Möller, "Oswald Spengler—Geschichte im Dienst der Zeitkritik," *Spengler heute. Sechs Essays mit einem Vorwort von H. Lübbe,* 49–73, here 54ff. " 'Spengler, the antisocialist enemy of the *Volk*'—that was the common denominator encompassing the Spengler-criticism of the National Socialists just after their 'seizure of power' " (H. Lübbe, ibid., 23). From a political perspective Spengler and Heidegger can be described with an expression coined by K. von Klemperer as "progressive Nietzschean conservatives who never found a real political party." Cf. T. B. Strong, "Oswald Spengler—Ontologie, Kritik und Enttäuschung," ibid., 91.

356. Cf. O. Spengler, *The Decline of the West,* 1.36ff.; 2.416ff.; 2.432ff.; 2.452ff.; and passim.

357. M. Heidegger, "Overcoming Metaphysics," 106.

358. Ibid.

359. M. Heidegger, "The Question concerning Technology," 14.

360. Ibid., 15.

361. O. Spengler, *The Decline of the West*, 2.499.

362. Cf. ibid., 2.500.

363. Ibid., 501.

364. Ibid., 502.

365. Ibid., 500.

366. M. Heidegger, "The Age of the World Picture," idem, *The Question concerning Technology and Other Essays*, 115–54, here 116.

367. Cf. M. Heidegger, "The Age of the World Picture," passim, esp. 127ff.

368. Cf. M. Heidegger, "The Question concerning Technology," 22ff.

369. Cf. M. Heidegger, "The Age of the World Picture," 127.

370. In this connection cf. M. Heidegger, "The Age of the World Picture," 122: "Hence the much-cited medieval Schoolman Roger Bacon can never be the forerunner of the modern experimental research scientist; rather he remains merely a successor of Aristotle."

371. Concerning the relevance of Heidegger's criticism of technology on the one hand cf. A. Jäger, *Gott. Nochmals Martin Heidegger*, 402, n. 8; concerning the significance Spengler's criticism of technology holds for the present on the other hand, cf. H. Lübbe's foreword to P. C. Ludz, ed., *Spengler heute. Sechs Essays mit einem Vorwort von H. Lübbe*, IX, as well as G. Merlio, "Spengler und die Technik," ibid., 111.

372. M. Heidegger, "Overcoming Metaphysics," 103.

373. Ibid., 91. Heidegger uses the German term *seinsgeschichtlich*, and occasionally *seynsgeschichtlich*.

374. M. Heidegger, "Der Spruch des Anaximander," 300. In this connection see also A. Jäger, *Gott. Nochmals Martin Heidegger*, 354ff.

375. M. Heidegger, "The Question concerning Technology," 24f.

376. M. Heidegger, "Overcoming Metaphysics," 85.

377. Ibid., 103.

378. M. Heidegger, "The Word of Nietzsche," 108f.

379. Ibid., 110.

380. Ibid., 109f.

381. Ibid., 111.

382. M. Heidegger, "What are poets for?" *Poetry, Language, Thought*, 91–142, here 141.

383. Ibid., 142.

384. "Spiegel Interview with Martin Heidegger," 62.

385. Ibid., 57.

386. Ibid., 66. I consider A. Jäger's thesis (*Gott. Nochmals Martin Heidegger*, 439f.) to be exaggerated according to which Heidegger secretly sees in Hölderlin the Suffering Servant of Deutero-Isaiah, in Nietzsche John the Baptist, and in himself possibly a—new messiah! Against this notion cf. the "Spiegel Interview with Martin Heidegger," 66: "But thinking's greatest affliction is that today, as far as I can see, no thinker yet speaks who is great enough to place thinking, directly and formatively, before its subject matter and therefore on its path." However, a thesis similar to Jäger's is found already in F. H. Heinemann, *Existentialism and the Modern Predicament*, 84–108. Cf. also K. Löwith, *Heidegger. Denker in dürftiger Zeit*, 43.

387. [This verse has been variously translated, even in translations of Heidegger's own work: "Near and / Hard to grasp is the God. / But where danger is, / Deliverance also grows" (as translated in M. Heidegger, "The Question concerning Technology," *Basic Writings*, 310), or "But where danger is, grows / The saving power also" ("The Question concerning Technology," *The Question concerning Technology and Other Essays*, 28). "Near is / And difficult to grasp, the God. / But where danger threatens / That which

saves from it also grows" (as translated in Friedrich Hölderlin, *Poems and Fragments*, 463).—Trans.]

388. M. Heidegger, "The Question concerning Technology," 26.
389. Ibid., 26f.
390. Ibid., 33f.
391. M. Heidegger, "Overcoming Metaphysics," 86.
392. Ibid., 109.
393. M. Heidegger, "The Word of Nietzsche," 111.
394. Ibid., 112 [The English translation renders *Angst* in this passage as "anxious dread," which I have altered to "anxiety."—Trans.]
395. See H. Friedrich, *Kulturkatastrophe. Nachrufe auf das Abendland.*
396. See ibid., 231–302.
397. Cf. ibid., 263.
398. Ibid., 238.
399. Ibid.
400. Cf. ibid., 17.
401. Cf. *Der Tod der Moderne. Eine Diskussion.*
402. H.-J. Heinrichs, cited after U. Hornauer, "Abgesang der Postmoderne. Die unvernünftige Rede vom Ende der Aufklärung," *Evangelische Kommentare* 18 (1985) 492.
403. Kamper, cited according to U. Hornauer, ibid.
404. Baudrillard, cited according to U. Hornauer, ibid.
405. U. Horstmann, *Das Untier. Konturen einer Philosophie der Menschenflucht*, 96.
406. P. Sloterdijk, *Critique of Cynical Reason.*
407. Ibid., 120ff.
408. Ibid., 122.
409. Ibid., 124.
410. Ibid., 126.
411. Cf. ibid., 101ff.
412. Ibid., 124.
413. J. Derrida, "Of an Apocalyptic Tone Recently Adopted in Philosophy," *Semeia* 23 (1982) 63–97, passim; this essay is also published as "On a Newly Arisen Apocalyptic Tone in Philosophy," in P. Fenves, ed., *Raising the Tone in Philosophy*, 117–71.
414. Cf. I. Kant, "On a Newly Arisen Superior Tone in Philosophy," in P. Fenves, ed., *Raising the Tone in Philosophy*, 51–81.
415. J. Derrida, "Of an Apocalyptic Tone Recently Adopted in Philosophy" (cited hereafter according to the Fenves edition), 145.
416. Ibid., 156–57.
417. Ibid., 148.
418. Cf. also Michael Wetzel in his afterword to the German edition of J. Derrida, *Apokalypse. Von einem neuerdings erhobenen apokalyptischen Ton in der Philosophie*, 134.
419. J. Derrida, "Of an Apocalyptic Tone Recently Adopted in Philosophy," 142.
420. Ibid., 158f.
421. Ibid., 161.
422. Michael Wetzel, in J. Derrida, *Apokalypse. Von einem neuerdings erhobenen apokalyptischen Ton in der Philosophie*, 139.
423. J. Derrida, ibid., 167. Cf. also "No Apocalypse, not now (full speed ahead, seven missiles, seven missives)," *Diacritics* 14/2 (1984) 20–31, here 24: "No truth, no apocalypse."
424. Cf. J. Derrida, "No Apocalypse, not now," 20–31.
425. D. L. Meadows et al., *The Limits to Growth: A Report for the Club of Rome's Project on the Predicament of Mankind* (1972), 185f.
426. Other project members included A. A. Anderson, J. M. Anderson, I. Bayar,

W. W. Behrens, F. Hakimzadeh, S. Harbordt, J. A. Machen, D. H. Meadows, P. Milling, N. S. Murthy, R. F. Naill, J. Randers, S. Shantzis, J. A. Seeger, M. Williams, and E.K.O. Zahn.

427. Ibid., 142.

428. Ibid., 181.

429. Ibid., 121.

430. Cf. ibid., 96ff.

431. Ibid., 186.

432. H. von Nussbaum, "Die Zukunft des Untergangs oder Der Untergang der Zukunft—Notate wider die Futurologie des Status quo," in D. L. Meadows et al., *Wachstum bis zur Katastrophe? Pro und Contra zum Weltmodell*, ed. H. E. Richter, 46–71d, here 66.

433. K. Rihaczek, "Advent 2000," in *Wachstum bis zur Katastrophe?* 121–27, here 121f.

434. D. L. Meadows et al., *The Limits to Growth*, 190.

435. From the plethora of publications cf. also P. R. Ehrlich and A. Ehrlich, *Population Resources Environment: Issues in Human Ecology;* J. W. Forrester, *World Dynamics; Umwelt-Report*, ed. H. Schultze; B. Commoner, *The Closing Circle: Nature, Man, and Technology*. See also the critique of civilization in K. Lorenz, *Civilized Man's Eight Deadly Sins*.

436. Cf. G. Picht, "Die Bedingungen des Überlebens," in H. von Nussbaum, ed., *Die Zukunft des Wachstums. Kritische Antworten zum "Bericht des Club of Rome,"* 45–58.

437. H. von Nussbaum, "Die Zukunft des Untergangs oder Der Untergang der Zukunft," 69.

438. Cf. ibid., 66.

439. The Club of Rome itself admits this neglect. Cf. D. L. Meadows et al., *The Limits to Growth*, 121f.; 185f. Concerning the criticism of this method, see among others the discussion *Beyond the Limits*, 72–97.

440. E.g., H. von Nussbaum, "Die Zukunft des Untergangs oder Der Untergang der Zukunft," passim.

441. Guided by the paradigm of real utopia and anticipatory thinking, H. von Nussbaum, e.g., disputes the relevance of the law of entropy for the earth and for humankind: "Neither the world nor society constitutes a closed system . . . As far as the *world* is concerned, i.e., the living space of humankind, this applies at least as long as the dimensions of human access, literally the height and depth of the human biosphere, has not (yet) been definitively established" ("Die Zukunft des Untergangs oder Der Untergang der Zukunft," 56).

442. Cf., e.g., G. Picht, *Mut zur Utopie*, 47ff.; *Zwischen Wachstum und Lebensqualität. Wirtschaftsethische Fragen angesichts der Krisen wirtschaftlichen Wachstums*, ed. by the Sozialwissenschaftliches Institut der EKD; H. Binswanger, W. Geissberger, and T. Ginsburg, eds., *Der NAWU-Report. Wege aus der Wohlstandsfalle;* K. M. Meyer-Abich, ed., *Frieden mit der Natur;* W.-D. Marsch, *Zukunft*, 130ff.

443. See *Global 2000* 2/I, esp. 389ff.

444. Cf. ibid., 2/II.

445. Cf. ibid., 2/III. For a comparison with other world models, see 2/III and 2/IV.

446. Cf., e.g., M. Schloemann, *Wachstumstod und Eschatologie. Die Herausforderung christlicher Theologie durch die Umweltkrise*, 11ff.

447. C. Amery, *Das Ende der Vorsehung. Die gnadenlosen Folgen des Christentums*, 251.

448. D. L. Meadows et al., *The Limits to Growth*, 121.

449. Cf. ibid., 122.

450. Cf. ibid., 89.

451. Cf. ibid., 17ff.

452. Ibid., 195.

453. Cf. ibid., 156ff.
454. Cf. ibid., 175ff.
455. Ibid., 178f.
456. Ibid., 179.
457. Cf. ibid., 180, 195.
458. Cf. G. Picht, "Die Bedingungen des Überlebens," passim.
459. D. L. Meadows et al., *The Limits to Growth*, 195.
460. C. Amery, *Das Ende der Vorsehung*, 22.
461. Cf. C. Amery, ibid., 39ff.; 191ff. See also D. L. Meadows, *Wachstum bis zur Katastrophe?*, 28f.!
462. C. Amery, *Das Ende der Vorsehung*, 21.
463. Ibid., 28.
464. Ibid., 162.
465. Ibid., 158.
466. Ibid., 157.
467. Ibid., 150ff.
468. Ibid., 157.
469. Cf. ibid., 131ff.; 207ff.
470. Ibid., 176.
471. Ibid., 252.
472. H. Gruhl, *Ein Planet wird geplündert. Die Schreckensbilanz unserer Politik.*
473. Cf. ibid., 225ff.: "We have no corresponding event for comparison except perhaps the Copernican revolution. The analogy with this stage, however, is merely formal" (225).
474. Cf. ibid., 313ff.
475. Cf. ibid., 316ff.
476. Cf. ibid., 320ff.
477. Cf. ibid., 330ff.
478. Cf. ibid., 263ff.
479. Cf. in this connection G. L. Ulmen, "Metaphysik des Morgenlandes—Spengler über Russland," in P. C. Ludz, ed., *Spengler heute. Sechs Essays mit einem Vorwort von H. Lübbe*, 123–73.
480. Cf. H. Gruhl, *Ein Planet wird geplündert*, 333f.
481. Finally, Gruhl's preference for Goethe's nature philosophy also recalls Spengler. Cf. H. Gruhl, ibid., 18f. In our century it was Spengler who claimed to have been the first to discover Goethe's philosophy. Cf., e.g., O. Spengler, *The Decline of the West*, 1.25ff.
482. Cf. H. Gruhl, *Ein Planet wird geplündert*, 271ff.
483. Cf. ibid., 25f.
484. Ibid., 26.
485. Ibid., 27.
485. Ibid., 84ff.
487. Cf. ibid., 256ff.
488. Cf. ibid., 345.
489. G. Anders, *Die atomare Drohung. Radikale Überlegungen, XII.* Concerning the resulting weakening of the antinuclear movement, cf. also U. Horstmann, *Das Untier. Konturen einer Philosophie der Menschenflucht*, 68f.
490. Cf. in this context J. Schell, *The Fate of the Earth*, 114f.
491. Cf. ibid., 152ff., esp. 158f.
492. Concerning this term, which has been used in reference to American developments, cf. J. Derrida, "No Apocalypse, not now," in *Apokalypse. Von einem neuerdings erhobenen apokalyptischen Ton in der Philosophie*, 91, n. 1 [not in English-language edition].
493. Karl Jaspers, *The Future of Mankind*, 4.

494. G. Anders, *Die atomare Drohung. Radikale Überlegungen*, 214; cf. also 218.
495. K. Jaspers, *The Future of Mankind*, 4.
496. Ibid.
497. Cf. K. Jaspers, *Die Atombombe und die Zukunft des Menschen*, 405: "Nuclear destruction would be a particular kind of destruction, but would be such that the question concerning just what constitutes Being after that destruction could only be answered with reference to human existence that knows of such Being. This is our own existence. We are reflecting upon Being after such destruction, as if we were yet there, just as we reflect upon the cosmos as it was before all life."
498. Ibid., 410.
499. Cf. K. Jaspers, *The Future of Mankind*, 289f.
500. K. Jaspers, *Die Atombombe und die Zukunft des Menschen*, 410.
501. Cf. ibid., 414ff. [Although this specific section has no equivalent in the English translation of *Die Atombombe und die Zukunft des Menschen*, the translator explains in his foreword why he has rendered the German word *Chiffern* as "symbols" instead of "chiffres." See *The Future of Mankind*, vi.—Trans.]
502. *Die Atombombe und die Zukunft des Menschen*, 402.
503. *The Future of Mankind*, 337.
504. "The threat of total extinction points to thoughts about the meaning of our existence" (ibid., 6).
505. Cf. *Die Atombombe und die Zukunft des Menschen*, 496f.
506. Ibid., 497.
507. Cf. *The Future of Mankind*, 339ff.
508. Ibid., 338. The ground of our existence can—again with a symbol—also be circumscribed as the "hidden deity": "Trust should be accorded the hidden deity" (*Die Atombombe und die Zukunft des Menschen*, 493). On this whole complex cf. K. Jaspers, *Der philosophische Glaube*.
509. K. Jaspers, *The Future of Mankind*, 338.
510. Cf. ibid., 337.
511. Concerning the concept of anxiety in Jaspers, see chap. 2, secs. 2 and 4.
512. K. Jaspers, *The Future of Mankind*, 323.
513. Ibid., 322.
514. Ibid., 327–28.
515. Ibid., 328.
516. Ibid., 329.
517. Cf. K. Jaspers, *Die Atombombe und die Zukunft des Menschen*, 402.
518. K. Jaspers, *The Future of Mankind*, 4.
519. Only such rule, "not simply dictatorship, Marxism, or racial theory," constitutes a danger of equal rank with nuclear weapons. Cf. ibid.
520. Ibid., 287.
521. Ibid., 331.
522. See esp. Albert Schweitzer, "Civilization and Ethics (1923)," in idem, *The Philosophy of Civilization*, 307f.; idem, *Reverence for Life: An Anthology of Selected Writings.*
523. K. Jaspers, *The Future of Mankind*, 332.
524. Ibid.
525. Ibid., 4.
526. K. Jaspers, *Die Atombombe und die Zukunft des Menschen*, 175. See also *The Future of Mankind*, 120ff.
527. K. Jaspers, *The Future of Mankind*, 118.
528. Ibid., 93. A similar view is taken by A. Glucksmann, *La force du vertige.*
529. Cf. K. Jaspers, *Die Atombombe und die Zukunft des Menschen*, 175.
530. K. Jaspers, *The Future of Mankind*, 118.
531. Ibid., 92.

532. Cf. ibid., 121.
533. Ibid., 122.
534. Ibid., 133.
535. Cf. G. Anders, *Die atomare Drohung. Radikale Überlegungen*, 41.
536. J. Schell, *The Fate of the Earth*, 131.
537. Ibid.
538. See G. Anders, *Die atomare Drohung. Radikale Überlegungen*, 41.
539. Ibid., 43.
540. Ibid., 94; cf. also 44. Concerning the criticism of Jaspers, see also 65f.
541. Ibid., 42.
542. Ibid., 41.
543. Cf. ibid., 44, 46.
544. Ibid., IX.
545. G. Anders speaks of the apocalyptic character of end-time expectation in primitive Christianity, and in so doing follows the lead of A. Schweitzer and M. Werner, esp. M. Werner, *The Formation of Christian Dogma*. Cf. G. Anders, *Die atomare Drohung. Radikale Überlegungen*, 215, n. 15; and 217, n. 20.
546. G. Anders, *Die atomare Drohung. Radikale Überlegungen*, 214.
547. Cf. ibid., 214ff.; 217ff. As with Anders, so also does the concept of the end of the world acquire unmetaphorical meaning in the writing of J. Schell, *The Fate of the Earth*, 6–7:

> The annihilation of the belligerent nations would be a catastrophe beyond anything in history, but it would not be the end of the world. The destruction of human civilization, even without the biological destruction of the human species, may perhaps rightly be called the end of the world, since it would be the end of that sum of cultural achievements and human relationships which constitutes what many people mean when they speak of "the world." The biological destruction of mankind would, of course, be the end of the world in a stricter sense. As for the destruction of all life on the planet, it would be not merely a human but a planetary end—the death of the earth.

That the destruction of human civilization, even if the annihilation of humankind itself were not complete, deserves to be called "the end of the world," is a notion that recurs in altered form in J. Derrida. Derrida views the real threat posed by nuclear disaster to be the annihilation of all archives, i.e., of the basis of our civilization ("No apocalypse, not now," *Diacritics* 14/2 [1984] 26):

> Now what allows us perhaps to think the uniqueness of nuclear war, its being-for-the-first-time-and-perhaps-for-the-last-time, its absolute inventiveness, what it prompts us to think even if it remains a decoy, a belief, a phantasmatic projection, is obviously the possibility of an irreversible destruction, leaving no traces, of the juridico-literary archive—that is, total destruction of the basis of literature and criticism. Not necessarily the destruction of humanity, of the human habitat, nor even of other discourses (arts or sciences).

548. G. Anders, *Die atomare Drohung. Radikale Überlegungen*, 96: "we as conscious apocalyptists."
549. Ibid., 179.
550. Ibid., 94.
551. Ibid., 179.
552. Ibid., 93; cf. 61.
553. Cf. ibid., 168f.
554. Ibid., 171.

555. Cf. G. Anders, "Über die Bombe und die Wurzeln unserer Apokalypse-Blindheit," in idem, *Die Antiquiertheit des Menschen. Über die Seele im Zeitalter der zweiten industriellen Revolution*, 243.

556. Cf. ibid., 304; G. Anders, *Die atomare Drohung. Radikale Überlegungen*, 103.

557. G. Anders, "Über die Bombe und die Wurzeln unserer Apokalypse-Blindheit," 239.

558. See sec. 5 above.

559. Cf. G. Anders, "Über die Bombe und die Wurzeln unserer Apokalypse-Blindheit," 299ff. See also 316ff.

560. Ibid., 301.

561. Ibid., 296. J. Schell similarly characterizes nuclear scare tactics as biological and thus also political nihilism. See J. Schell, *The Fate of the Earth*, 218.

562. Cf. G. Anders, "Über die Bombe und die Wurzeln unserer Apokalypse-Blindheit," 294f.; idem, *Die atomare Drohung. Radikale Überlegungen*, 181ff.

563. Cf. Rev. 20:14.

564. G. Anders, *Die atomare Drohung. Radikale Überlegungen*, 95; cf. also 174. Concerning the problem of the second death see also J. Schell, *The Fate of the Earth*, 99ff.

565. Cf. J. Schell, *The Fate of the Earth*, 114ff.

566. Ibid., 147.

567. Cf. G. Anders, *Die atomare Drohung. Radikale Überlegungen*, 55ff.

568. Ibid., 56.

569. Ibid., 68. Cf. also J. Schell, *The Fate of the Earth*, 100: "It is fundamental to the shape and character of the nuclear predicament that its origins lie in scientific knowledge rather than in social circumstances."

570. J. Schell, *The Fate of the Earth*, 188; cf. also 193f.

571. Cf. G. Anders, *Die atomare Drohung. Radikale Überlegungen*, 29ff.

572. J. Schell, *The Fate of the Earth*, 108.

573. G. Anders, *Die atomare Drohung. Radikale Überlegungen*, 176.

574. Ibid., 177.

575. Ibid., 212.

576. Ibid., 204.

577. Ibid., 91.

578. Ibid., 219.

579. Ibid.

580. J. Schell speaks even more pessimistically of a period of grace that now lies behind us and is forever gone: "The period of grace we had in which to ward off the nuclear peril before it became a reality—the time between the moment of the invention of the weapons and the construction of the full-scale machinery for extinction—was squandered" (*The Fate of the Earth*, 183). Insofar as the real nuclear threat consists actually in technical know-how, one must observe that Schell's period of grace was actually only a relative one, or even illusory.

581. Concerning apocalyptic blindness and its roots see the thorough discussion in G. Anders, "Über die Bombe und die Wurzeln unserer Apokalypse-Blindheit," passim, esp. 276ff.; idem, *Die atomare Drohung. Radikale Überlegungen*, 106ff.

582. G. Anders, *Die atomare Drohung. Radikale Überlegungen*, IX.

583. Ibid., 73.

584. Ibid., 185f.

585. Ibid., 64.

586. Cf. ibid., 126ff.

587. J. Schell, *The Fate of the Earth*, 152.

588. Ibid., 182.

589. W. Benjamin, "Zentralpark," idem, *Gesammelte Schriften*, vol. I.1, *Werkausgabe*, eds. R. Tiedemann and H. Schweppenhäuser, 683. Cf. also W. Benjamin, "Einbahnstrasse," idem, *Gesammelte Schriften*, vol. IV.1, 94f.: "Only a reckoning which admits find-

ing in destruction the only *ratio* of the present condition would be able to break out of the enervating gaping at the repetitive monotony of daily life and recognize the phenomenon of decay as the only thing that is really stable, and rescue itself as the only thing that is extraordinary to the point of being virtually miraculous and incomprehensible."

590. In connection with W. Benjamin, see J. Ebach, "Apokalypse. Zum Ursprung einer Stimmung," in F.-M. Marquardt et al., eds., *Einwürfe* 2, 5–61, here 5. But see also the comparable theological ideas in K. Heim, *The World: Its Creation and Consummation*, 110: The possibility does exist "that the world will in fact go on as at present. Then life is not worth living."

591. G. Anders, *Die atomare Drohung. Radikale Überlegungen*, 114.

592. J. Schell, *The Fate of the Earth*, 178.

593. J. Derrida, "Of an Apocalyptic Tone Recently Adopted in Philosophy," 148.

594. Cf. ibid., 147f.

595. G. Anders, *Die atomare Drohung. Radikale Überlegungen*, 51f.

596. Concerning this entanglement, see G. Anders, "Über die Bombe und die Wurzeln unserer Apokalypse-Blindheit," 255f. In this context, Anders has considered the possibility of an expansion of the Hippocratic oath and of a "product strike." Cf. G. Anders, *Die atomare Drohung. Radikale Überlegungen*, 136ff.; "Über die Bombe und die Wurzeln unserer Apokalypse-Blindheit," 307f.

597. Cf. *Die atomare Drohung. Radikale Überlegungen*, 65, 99.

598. Cf. ibid., 61ff.

599. Ibid., 111.

600. Ibid., J. Schell also diagnoses a "sense of helplessness and defeat" (*The Fate of the Earth*, 7).

601. In this connection see esp. G. Anders, "Über die Bombe und die Wurzeln unserer Apokalypse-Blindheit," 267ff.; 271ff.

602. Ibid., 273.

603. Ibid., 274.

604. See "Meditation on the Bomb" in P. Sloterdijk, *Critique of Cynical Reason*, 128ff.

605. Ibid., 130.

606. Ibid.

607. Ibid., 132.

608. This demand is made, e.g., by W. Giegerich. But cf. also I. Riedel, "Apokalyptische Bilder," in P. Dätwyler, ed., *Not-Wendigkeiten. Auf der Suche nach einer neuen Spiritualität*, 68ff.

609. In this connection see Introduction, sec. 1 above. For another attempt at educating our imagination for the sake of sharpening its sensibility for the dimensions of nuclear danger, see also the scenario in J. Schell, *The Fate of the Earth*, 4ff., esp. 47ff.

610. I. Riedel, "Apokalyptische Bilder," 72. Riedel advocates a contemporary spirituality, new, symbolic acts, public activities and rituals which she understands as "public meditation."

611. Cf. by way of association John 9:39–41.

612. See G. Anders, *Die atomare Drohung. Radikale Überlegungen*, 1ff.

613. Ibid., 8.

614. J. Schell, *The Fate of the Earth*, 21.

615. G. Anders, "Über die Bombe und die Wurzeln unserer Apokalypse-Blindheit," 238.

616. Cf. p. 165 above.

617. G. Anders, "Über die Bombe und die Wurzeln unserer Apokalypse-Blindheit," 265.

618. Cf. ibid., 266; G. Anders, *Die atomare Drohung. Radikale Überlegungen*, 127.

619. Cf. G. Anders, *Die atomare Drohung. Radikale Überlegungen*, 97f.

620. Ibid., 98.

621. "Über die Bombe und die Wurzeln unserer Apokalypse-Blindheit," 266.

622. *Die atomare Drohung. Radikale Überlegungen*, 98.
623. Concerning the concept of world anxiety, its semantic scope, and its problematic, see chap. 2, sec. 4 above.
624. See above chap. 3, sec. 1.
625. Concerning the "space of freedom" see chap. 2, sec. 3.
626. G. Anders, *Die atomare Drohung. Radikale Überlegungen*, 205.
627. J. Schell, *The Fate of the Earth*, 172.
628. G. Anders, *Die atomare Drohung. Radikale Überlegungen*, 93.
629. Ibid., 70. Cf. also J. Schell, *The Fate of the Earth*, 173, 174: "With the generation that has never known a world unmenaced by nuclear weapons, a new order of the generations begins." "Formerly, the future was simply given to us; now it must be achieved. We must become the agriculturalists of time."
630. Michael Wetzel in his afterword to the German edition of J. Derrida, *Apokalypse. Von einem neuerdings erhobenen apokalyptischen Ton in der Philosophie*, 138.
631. G. Anders, *Die atomare Drohung. Radikale Überlegungen*, 179.
632. J. Schell, *The Fate of the Earth*, 169.
633. Cf. also P. Sloterdijk, *Critique of Cynical Reason*, 128.
634. H. Kahn, *On Escalation: Metaphors and Scenarios*, 39; cf. U. Horstmann, *Das Untier. Konturen einer Philosophie der Menschenflucht*, 66.
635. So also, correctly, G. M. Martin, *Weltuntergang. Gefahr und Sinn apokalyptischer Visionen*, 126. Horstmann's vacillation between deadly seriousness and biting irony seems to have escaped H. von Ditfurth, *So lasst uns denn ein Apfelbäumchen pflanzen. Es ist soweit*, 323ff., who otherwise subscribes to Horstmann's thesis.
636. Cf. M. Foucault, *The Order of Things* (New York: Pantheon, 1971), cited by U. Horstmann, *Das Untier. Konturen einer Philosophie der Menschenflucht*, 92.
637. Cf. U. Horstmann, ibid., 8.
638. Ibid., 41.
639. Ibid., 55.
640. Ibid., 98.
641. Ibid., 100.
642. See p. 141 above.
643. U. Horstmann, *Das Untier. Konturen einer Philosophie der Menschenflucht*, 110.
644. "Marxism, existentialism, and praxis-oriented attitudes calling themselves peace research and conflict research" are the "final metastases . . . of decaying humanistic doctrine" (ibid., 59). On this whole complex, see ibid., 59ff.
645. Cf. ibid., 106ff.
646. Ibid., 12.
647. Ibid., 100.
648. Cf. ibid., 83.
649. G. M. Martin, *Weltuntergang. Gefahr und Sinn apokalyptischer Visionen*, 127.
650. Cf. K. Jaspers, *The Future of Mankind*, 4f.
651. G. Anders, *Die atomare Drohung. Radikale Überlegungen*, 214.
652. Ibid., 218.
653. Cf. J. Derrida, "Of an Apocalyptic Tone Recently Adopted in Philosophy," 143ff.
654. "No Apocalypse, not now," 23.
655. Ibid.

Chapter 5
THE AMBIGUITY OF APOCALYPTIC

1. See p. 103 above.
2. Regarding the distinction between good and bad utopias among critics of utopian thinking, cf. A. Neusüss, ed., *Utopie. Begriff und Phänomen des Utopischen*, 45ff.

3. Regarding the relationship betwen utopia and ideology, see esp. K. Mannheim, *Ideology and Utopia* (1928/29). See also the outline in A. Neusüss, *Utopie. Begriff und Phänomen des Utopischen*, 14ff. (with a critical posture toward Mannheim, 23ff.).

4. M. Winter, "Don Quijote und Frankenstein. Utopie als Utopiekritik: Zur Genese der negativen Utopie," in W. Vosskamp, ed., *Utopieforschung. Interdisziplinäre Studien zur neuzeitlichen Utopie*, vol. 3, 86–112, subdivides utopian literature into positive, negative, and libertine utopias, distinguished from one another by the notion of the progress of humane behavior: "The goal of positive utopia (e.g., Morus) is the progress of humanity . . . That of negative utopia (Huxley, Orwell), in addition to its own critique of utopia, is the same thing . . . Libertine utopia reverses the humane *telos* of both positive and negative utopias into an anti-humane one" (105). De Sade, for example, outlines this kind of ideal image of evil.

5. Bibliographical information concerning negative utopia can be found in H. U. Seeber and W. Bachem, "Aspekte und Probleme der neueren Utopiediskussion in der Anglistik," in W. Vosskamp, ed., *Utopieforschung. Interdisziplinäre Studien zur neuzeitlichen Utopie*, vol. 1, 143–91, here 154f. Regarding anti-utopias see among others also M. Winter, *Compendium Utopiarum: Typologie und Bibliographie literarischer Utopien*, vol. 1, *Von der Antike bis zur deutschen Frühaufklärung*.

6. Cf. H. Schulte-Herbrüggen, *Utopie und Anti-Utopie: Von der Strukturanalyse zur Strukturtypologie*, 207.

7. Cf. K. H. Bohrer, "Utopie des 'Augenblicks' und Fiktionalität," in idem. *Plötzlichkeit. Zum Augenblick des ästhetischen Scheins*, 180–218, here esp. 185. See also the English translation in idem, *Suddenness: On the Moment of Aesthetic Appearance*.

8. One critical voice against this thesis is R. Levitas, "Sociology and Utopia," *Sociology* 32/1 (1979) 19–33.

9. Cf. K. H. Bohrer, *Der Lauf des Freitags. Die lädierte Utopie und die Dichter. Eine Analyse*.

10. Concerning Bloch's interpretation of apocalyptic, see pp. 15ff., 43ff. above.

11. See, e.g., S.-A. Jørgensen, "Utopisches Potential in der Bibel. Mythos, Eschatologie und Säkularisation," in W. Vosskamp, ed., *Utopieforschung. Interdisziplinäre Studien zur neuzeitlichen Utopie*, vol. 3, 375–401.

12. Ibid., 393.

13. Cf. R. Koselleck, "Die Verzeitlichung der Utopie," in W. Vosskamp, ed., *Utopieforschung. Interdisziplinäre Studien zur neuzeitlichen Utopie*, vol. 3, 1–14.

14. Cf. ibid., 6.

15. L.-S. Mercier, *Memoirs of the Year Two Thousand Five Hundred* (1771; repr. ed., New York: Garland Publishing, 1974).

16. R. Koselleck, "Die Verzeitlichung der Utopie," 6.

17. Concerning the discussion within religious studies of the social locus of apocalyptic, see pp. 33f. above.

18. Cf. J. Moltmann, *The Church in the Power of the Spirit: A Contribution to Messianic Ecclesiology*, 37–50.

19. Cf. ibid., 41ff. Concerning the concept of apocalyptic confessionalism, see 44.

20. Cf. ibid., 44ff.

21. Cf. G. Scholem, "Toward an Understanding of the Messianic Idea in Judaism," idem, *The Messianic Idea in Judaism and Other Essays on Jewish Spirituality*, 1–36, here 24ff.

22. Cf. ibid., 35ff.

23. G. M. Martin, *Weltuntergang. Gefahr und Sinn apokalyptischer Visionen*, 121ff., 133ff., here 135.

24. Cf. A. Neusüss, *Utopie. Begriff und Phänomen des Utopischen*, 34f.

25. M. Winter, "Don Quijote und Frankenstein. Utopie als Utopiekritik: Zur Genese der negativen Utopie," 94.

26. Ibid., 109.

27. See, e.g., J. Falwell, *Nuclear War and the Second Coming of Jesus Christ* [audio cassettes], passim.

28. Regarding the word field of *apokalyptein, apokalypsis* see A. Oepke, "*apokalyptō, apokalypsis,*" *TDNT* 3.563–92; H. Schulte, *Der Begriff der Offenbarung im Neuen Testament.*

29. R. Bultmann, "The Concept of Revelation in the New Testament (1929)," idem, *Existence and Faith*, 67–106, here 68.

30. K. Barth, *Das christliche Verständnis der Offenbarung*, 3.

31. In a reverse fashion, J. Moltmann, *Theology of Hope*, 42ff., criticizes the dogmatic procedure of developing a Christian concept of revelation on the basis of a pre- or extra-Christian understanding of revelation, since such an understanding ends ultimately in the concept of a theophany or epiphany of the deity, a concept that in principle is wholly inappropriate to the biblical God of promise.

32. K. Barth first developed his doctrine of God's self-revelation in an essay on "The Principle of Dogmatics according to Wilhelm Herrmann (1925)," idem, *Theology and Church*, 238–71. Herrmann had presented the thesis that "we can know this God only as he reveals himself to us [German: *uns selbst*] by his work in us" (W. Herrmann, "Gottes Offenbarung an uns [1908]," idem, *Schriften zur Grundlegung der Theologie*, vol. 2, 150–69, here 153; cited by Barth in "The Principle of Dogmatics according to Wilhelm Herrmann," 247), whereby, however, the term "self" [German: *selbst*] referred to human beings as the recipients of revelation. In contrast, Barth takes the term *selbst* to be God's own subjectivity. Concerning the prehistory of the concept of God's self-revelation in the nineteenth century, see also G. Gloege, "Offenbarung VI. Christliche Offenbarung, dogmatisch," *RGG* 4.1609–13, here 1610.

33. See esp. W. Herrmann, "Gottes Offenbarung an uns (1908)."

34. Cf. P. Althaus, "Die Inflation des Begriffs der Offenbarung in der gegenwärtigen Theologie," *ZST* 18 (1944) 134–49.

35. Concerning such formalization of the concept of apocalypse in religious studies, see chap. 1, sec. 2 above.

36. Cf. chap. 1, sec. 3 above.

37. Cf. Dan. 10:14: The angel has come "to make you understand what is to befall your people in the latter days; for the vision is for days yet to come," i.e., the days of the end time.

38. Dan. 2:8, 19, 27, 28, 29, 30, 47; 4:6.

39. E.g., *T. Levi* 2:10; *Sib. Or.* 12:63, and elsewhere. Concerning the term's history, see G. Bornkamm, "*mystērion, myeō,*" *TDNT* 4.802ff.

40. Cf. also Dan. 2:18f., 30.

41. Cf. Dan. 12:4.

42. Cf. chap. 3 above.

43. G. Sauter, *Zukunft und Verheissung. Das Problem der Zukunft in der gegenwärtigen theologischen und philosophischen Diskussion*, 241ff.

44. Ibid., 241.

45. Ibid., 243.

46. W. Pannenberg, "Redemptive Event in History, idem, *Basic Questions in Theology: Collected Essays*, 1.15–80, here 16ff.

47. Ibid., 21.

48. Cf. W. Pannenberg, *Offenbarung als Geschichte*, 91–131. English translation, *Revelation as History*.

49. Cf. G. Sauter, *Zukunft und Verheissung. Das Problem der Zukunft in der gegenwärtigen theologischen und philosophischen Diskussion*, 243, 244, n. 49. Concerning the basic theological issue here, see K. Barth, *Church Dogmatics* I/2, 58: "Revelation is not a predicate of history, but history is a predicate of revelation."

50. Cf. p. 30 above.

51. J. Ellul, *Apocalypse: The Book of Revelation*, 30. Concerning Ellul's methodological consequences for an interpretation of the Revelation of John, see ibid., 11.

52. Ibid., 12.

53. Ibid., 32.

54. Ibid., 17.

55. G. Sauter, *Zukunft und Verheissung. Das Problem der Zukunft in der gegenwärtigen theologischen und philosophischen Diskussion*, 241.

56. J. Ellul, *Apocalypse: The Book of Revelation*, 26.

57. 4 Ezra, like Jewish apocalyptic otherwise, ties the problem of enlightenment to the Law. Thus does 4 Ezra 14:21 explain the condition of darkness: "For your law has been burned."

58. Cf. also Baruch's response to the despairing people: "But I shall go to the Holy of Holies to ask from the Mighty One on behalf of you and Zion so that I may receive in some ways more light, and after that I shall return to you" (*2 Apoc. Bar.* 34).

59. Cf. J. Derrida, "Of an Apocalyptic Tone Recently Adopted in Philosophy," in P. Fenves, ed., *Raising the Tone in Philosophy*, 156.

60. Cf. also J. Ellul, *Apocalypse: The Book of Revelation*, 20, 24.

61. See chap. 3 above.

62. J. Ellul, *Apocalypse: The Book of Revelation*, 27.

63. Ibid.

64. Concerning world negation, see chap. 3, sec. 2.

65. H. Glaser, *Sigmund Freuds Zwanzigstes Jahrhundert. Seelenbilder einer Epoche, Materialien und Analysen*, 170.

66. K. Pinthus, ed., *Menschheitsdämmerung: Dawn of Humanity, A Document of Expressionism*, 61.

67. Cited after H. Glaser, *Sigmund Freuds Zwanzigstes Jahrhundert. Seelenbilder einer Epoche, Materialien und Analysen*, 171.

68. Even if one agrees with J. Ebach, "Apokalypse. Zum Ursprung einer Stimmung," in F.-M. Marquardt et al., eds., *Einwürfe* 2, 25, that the apocalyptic world vision of the American President Reagan constitutes a "usurpation" of the Apocalypse of John, it must still be doubted whether there exists any genuine apocalyptic that is always engaged in political enlightenment in the best sense.

69. J. Ebach, "Apokalypse. Zum Ursprung einer Stimmung," 12.

70. Ibid., 49.

71. Concerning the religio-sociological evaluation of this issue, cf. pp. 33ff. above.

72. H. Nagel, "Anleitungen zumöffentlichen Tod," in H. Boehncke, R. Stollmann, and G. Vinnai, eds., *Weltuntergänge*, 200–21, here 206.

73. In this connection see also H. Boehncke, "Jüngstes Gericht, Verkehrte Welt," in *Weltuntergänge*, 222–35.

74. Cf. also H. Nagel, "Anleitungen zum öffentlichen Tod," 206.

75. See p. 14 above.

76. Concerning collective world anxiety, see chap. 3, sec. 3 above.

77. Cf. pp. 204f. above. Concerning hope in deliverance in various religio-historical variations of apocalyptic, see also A. Olrik, *Ragnarök. Die Sagen vom Weltuntergang*, 458ff.

78. Cf. pp. 15f. above.

79. See esp. E. Bloch, *The Principle of Hope*, 45–336.

80. Cf. ibid., 449ff.

81. Cf. ibid., 925ff.

82. E. Bloch, *Tübinger Einleitung in die Philosophie*, *Gesamtausgabe* 13, 95.

83. Ibid.

84. Ibid., 208.

85. Concerning the phenomenon of hope in Bloch's thinking, see chap. 2, sec. 5 above.
86. E. Bloch, *Tübinger Einleitung in die Philosophie*, 183.
87. E. Bloch, *Atheism in Christianity: The Religion of the Exodus and the Kingdom*, 54, 57.
88. Ibid., 105.
89. Ibid., 218.
90. Cf. pp. 15ff., 17ff., 44–46 above.
91. E. Bloch, *Geist der Utopie, Gesamtausgabe 3*, 151.
92. E. Bloch, *The Principle of Hope*, 215.
93. Concerning the treatment of apocalyptic in utopian studies, cf. pp. 196ff. above.
94. See G. Sauter, *Zukunft und Verheissung. Das Problem der Zukunft in der gegenwärtigen theologischen und philosophischen Diskussion*, 239ff., esp. 242ff.
95. See W. Pannenberg, "Redemptive Event in History," 33ff.
96. Ibid., 18.
97. See D. Rössler, *Gesetz und Geschichte. Untersuchungen zur Theologie der jüdischen Apokalyptik und der pharisäischen Orthodoxie.*
98. See U. Wilckens, "Die Bekehrung des Paulus als religionsgeschichtliches Problem," *ZTK* 56 (1959) 273–93.
99. W. Pannenberg, *Offenbarung als Geschichte*, 97; cf. idem, "Redemptive Event in History," 21. See also the English translation, *Revelation as History.*
100. Cf. W. Pannenberg, "Heilsgeschehen und Geschichte," *KD* 5 (1959) 235.
101. Cf. J. Moltmann, *Theology of Hope*, 76ff.
102. Ibid., 137.
103. Ibid.
104. J. Moltmann, *The Crucified God*, 177.
105. Cf. ibid., 177f.
106. Concerning the catastrophic nature of redemption specifically in Jewish apocalyptic, cf. G. Scholem, "Toward an Understanding of the Messianic Idea in Judaism," idem, *The Messianic Idea in Judaism and Other Essays on Jewish Spirituality*, 7f., 10f., 12ff.; K. Müller, "Apokalyptik/Apokalypsen III. Die jüdische Apokalyptik. Anfänge und Merkmale," *TRE* 3.232ff. See also pp. 126ff. above.
107. Cf. pp. 91ff. above.
108. Dan. 7:25; 12:7.
109. Dan. 12:11f.
110. Concerning this perpetual expectation in the parenetic portion of *1 Enoch*, cf. K. Müller, "Apokalyptik/Apokalypsen III," 221.
111. E. Bloch, *The Principle of Hope*, 1375f.
112. E. Bloch, *Tübinger Einleitung in die Philosophie*, 209.
113. Cf. E. Bloch, *The Principle of Hope*, 1178ff.
114. E. Bloch, *Tübinger Einleitung in die Philosophie*, 98.
115. Ibid., 370f.
116. Ibid., 374.
117. H. Gunkel, in E. Kautzsch, ed., *Die Apokryphen und Pseudepigraphen des Alten Testaments*, 2.337.
118. 4 Ezra 5:49.
119. G. Scholem, "Toward an Understanding of the Messianic Idea in Judaism," 14.
120. Ibid., 15.
121. Concerning the problem of messianic activisim in Judaism, see ibid., 14ff.
122. F. Nietzsche, *The Dawn of Day*, 266 (aphorism 304).
123. Cf. F. Nietzsche, *The Genealogy of Morals.*
124. G. Vinnai, "Die Innenseite der Katastrophenpolitik. Zur Sozialpsychologie der atomaren Bedrohung," in H. Boehncke, R. Stollmann, and G. Vinnai, eds., *Weltuntergänge*, 129–92, here 144: "We are able to yearn for death because it, like orgiastic plea-

sure, is able to provide an end to inner tensions. All of us frequently secretly hope that our world will come to an end; this consciousness can make it clear to us that we ought to bring about the end of a bad world in order to make a better one possible." Such consciousness is to guide this apocalyptic death wish into the proper channels of social change. It is precisely Vinnai's latter remark which contains the entire problematic and ambiguity of messianic activism, since the destruction of the existing world for the sake of a different and better one involves the implicit danger of a complete loss of world. Concerning this issue see sec. 5.

125. J. Ebach, "Apokalypse. Zum Ursprung einer Stimmung," 37.

126. See G. Anders, *Die atomare Drohung. Radikale Überlegungen*, 179.

127. Cf. p. 13 above.

128. Concerning Horstmann, see pp. 190ff. above.

129. U. Horstmann, *Das Untier. Konturen einer Philosophie der Menschenflucht*, 10.

130. Ibid., 109.

131. Ibid., 17.

132. Cf. Horstmann's agreement on this point with the philosophy of Schopenhauer, ibid., 49.

133. Ibid., 89, n. 11.

134. F. Hebbel, "Julia. Ein Trauerspiel in drei Acten [1851]," in idem, *Sämtliche Werke* I/2, 133.

135. A. Glucksmann, *La force du vertige*, 285.

136. Ibid., 284.

137. H. Nagel, "Anleitungen zum öffentlichen Tod," in H. Boehncke, R. Stollmann, and G. Vinnai, eds., *Weltuntergänge*, 220.

138. H. E. Nossack, "Der Untergang," in M. L. Kaschnitz, ed., *Deutsche Erzähler*, II, 572–620, here 580f.

139. Cf. F. Wulf, "Trost," *LTK* (2nd ed.) 10.376–78; W. Hagemann, "Trost," *Handbuch der Pastoraltheologie*, 5.582; H. Tacke, *Glaubenshilfe als Lebenshilfe. Probleme und Chancen heutiger Seelsorge*, 222ff.

140. Cf. also *2 Apoc. Bar.* 81; 82:1.

141. Cf. O. Schmitz and G. Stählin, "*parakaleō, paraklēsis*," *TDNT* 5.773–99.

142. Cf. ibid., 779, 792f.

143. 4 Ezra 9:38–10:59.

144. Cf. 4 Ezra 10:24.

145. 4 Ezra 10:27.

146. Cf. also 4 Ezra 10:40.

147. Cf. also the figure of a *paraklētos*, especially of an interceding angel, in Jewish apocalyptic. For documentation see J. Behm, "*paraklētos*," *TDNT* 5.800–14, here 810.

148. H. Strack and P. Billerbeck, *Kommentar zum NT aus Talmud und Midrasch*, 2.125.

149. Documentation in ibid., 2.125f. Cf. also O. Schmitz and G. Stählin, *TDNT* 5.792f.

150. M. Eliade, *Cosmos and History: The Myth of the Eternal Return*, 118.

151. Ibid., 124.

152. Cf. pp. 143ff. above.

153. Cf. p. 147 above.

154. Concerning Heidegger, cf. pp. 158f. above.

155. *1 Enoch* 91—105.

156. *1 Enoch* 91:1–11, 18f.; 92; 94—105.

157. *1 Enoch* 93; 91:12–17.

158. K. Müller, "Apokalyptik/Apokalypsen III. Die jüdische Apokalyptik. Anfänge und Merkmale," *TRE* 3.221.

159. U. Luck, "Das Weltverständnis in der jüdischen Apokalyptik, dargestellt am äthiopischen Henoch und am 4. Esra," *ZTK* 73 (1976) 289.
160. Ibid., 293.
161. See also 4 Ezra 4:23.
162. See 4 Ezra 14:24ff.
163. 4 Ezra 4:35f.
164. U. Luck, "Das Weltverständnis in der jüdischen Apokalyptik, dargestellt am äthiopischen Henoch und am 4. Esra," 302.
165. K. Müller, "Apokalyptik/Apokalypsen III," 231.
166. Ibid., 232. Cf. also 240f.
167. Cf. pp. 158ff. above.
168. Cf. pp. 169ff. above.
169. Cf. pp. 171ff. above.
170. Cf. pp. 173ff. above.
171. Cf. pp. 175ff. above.
172. Cf. pp. 180, 189ff. above.
173. See pp. 186f. above.
174. G. Anders, *Die atomare Drohung. Radikale Überlegungen*, 98.
175. Cf. *1 Enoch* 38:5.
176. For additional criticism from the theological perspective, see also F. Schleiermacher, *The Christian Faith*, 720–22 (appendix to sec. 163: On Eternal Damnation).
177. F. Nietzsche, *The Genealogy of Morals*, 50 (sec. 16).
178. Ibid., 54 (sec. 16).
179. J. Ebach, "Apokalypse. Zum Ursprung einer Stimmung," 44.
180. Ibid., 45.
181. Cf. pp. 213f. above.
182. F. Kümmel, "Angst als Seinsmodus des Menschen?" in H. v. Stietencron, ed., *Angst und Gewalt. Ihre Praesenz und ihre Bewältigung in den Religionen,"* 27–42.
183. Ibid., 41.
184. Ibid., 42.
185. J. Ebach, "Apokalypse. Zum Ursprung einer Stimmung," 47.
186. J. Moltmann, *Theology of Hope*, 135.
187. J. Moltmann, *The Crucified God*, 19.
188. Cf. also ibid., 19f.
189. Concerning the following discussion, see chap. 3, sec. 2 above.
190. See p. 102 above.
191. R. Bultmann, *Geschichte und Eschatologie*, 35.
192. So, e.g., W. Pannenberg, "Redemptive Event in History," idem, *Basic Questions in Theology: Collected Essays*, 1.20f.
193. Cf. K. Müller's criticism of the theological estimation of apocalyptic universal history presented by Pannenberg, Moltmann, or K. Koch (K. Müller, "Apokalyptik/Apokalypsen III. Die jüdische Apokalyptik. Anfänge und Merkmale," *TRE* 3.243f.).
194. H. Jonas, *Gnosis und spätantiker Geist*, 1.68. Cf. p. 100 above.
195. Cf. K. Müller, "Apokalyptik/Apokalypsen III," 226, 232. On this issue see pp. 133f. above.
196. Cf. U. Luck, "Das Weltverständnis in die jüdischen Apokalyptik, dargestellt am äthiopischen Henoch und am 4. Esra," *ZTK* 73 (1976) 302; K. Müller, "Apokalyptik/Apokalypsen III," 232.
197. G. Sauter, *Zukunft und Verheissung. Das Problem der Zukunft in der gegenwärtigen theologischen und philosophischen Diskussion*, 244.
198. G. Scholem, "Toward an Understanding of the Messianic Idea in Judaism," idem, *The Messianic Idea in Judaism and Other Essays on Jewish Spirituality*, 35.
199. Ibid.

200. Cf. E. Bloch, *Tübinger Einleitung in die Philosophie*, *Gesamtausgabe* 13, 217ff.
201. E. Bloch, *The Principle of Hope*, 1197.
202. Ibid., 1178ff.
203. J. Moltmann, *Im Gespräch mit Ernst Bloch. Eine theologische Wegbegleitung*, 87.
204. G. Anders, "Über die Bombe und die Wurzeln unserer Apokalypse-Blindheit," in idem, *Die Antiquiertheit des Menschen. Über die Seele im Zeitalter der zweiten industriellen Revolution*, 261.
205. On Rev. 18:4 cf. Jer. 51:45, 46, 49; 50:8; Isa. 48:20; 52:11.
206. Cf. Gen. 19.
207. "Christians—this is apparently the meaning of the statement in Rev. 18:4—are to withdraw from the claims of this power [Rome] wherever they can" (A. Lindemann, "Christliche Gemeinden und das Römische Reich im ersten und zweiten Jahrhundert," *Wort und Dienst*, New Series 18 (1985) 105–33, here 122).
208. See C. Nimuendajú-Unkel, "Die Sagen von der Erschaffung und Vernichtung der Welt als Grundlagen der Religion der Apapocúva-Guarani," *Zeitschrift für Ethnologie* 46 (1914) 335f.
209. Concerning the concept of escapism, see chap. 3, sec. 2 above.
210. Cf. G. M. Martin, *Weltuntergang. Gefahr und Sinn apokalyptischer Visionen*, 66.
211. K. Jaspers, *Die Atombombe und die Zukunft des Menschen. Politisches Bewusstsein in unserer Zeit*, 490. [This passage was not included in the English translation of Jaspers's book.—Trans.]
212. Cf. ibid., 490f. A similar evasive maneuver is the notion that some portion of humankind can escape nuclear annihilation by fleeing in spaceships. Cf. J. Schell, *The Fate of the Earth*, 106.
213. J. Schell, *The Fate of the Earth*, 126.
214. P. D. Hanson, "Old Testament Apocalyptic Reexamined," *Interpretation* 25 (1971) 470; cf. also 474f.
215. Ibid., 479.
216. D. Bonhoeffer, *Ethics*, 282.
217. Cf. the criticism of the political conservatism of apocalyptic presented by J. Moltmann, *The Church in the Power of the Spirit*, 38ff.
218. Cf. J. Ebach, "Apokalypse. Zum Ursprung einer Stimmung," 55:

> The history of the student movement and the particular biographical types of the "class of '68" can be described commensurate with this movement of flight. Apocalyptic (i.e., to take this bad pun seriously: the renewed veiling of the contradiction) took place in the form of ever new journeys: Saigon, Havanna, Bejing, Tirana and back again—the long march into academic institutions (distant countries, indeed!), agricultural communes, muesli, KPD/ML/AO/UWE/Zen—the long march inward and, at the same time, into the air with Castañeda's *brujo* and the shamans . . . [Ebach asks further] The development of the peace movement, of the ecumenical conferences, the reception of myth—to mention different and yet interrelated spheres—would be fields of such questions: Who is actually profiting from these journeys? With which "means of transportation" are the return trips taken?

219. P. D. Hanson, "Old Testament Apocalyptic Reexamined," 470.
220. M. Eliade, *Cosmos and History: The Myth of the Eternal Return*, 111.
221. R. Bultmann, *The Presence of Eternity: History and Eschatology*, 30.
222. P. D. Hanson, "Old Testament Apocalyptic Reexamined," 469.
223. Ibid., 477.
224. Cf. J. Gabel, *False Consciousness: An Essay on Reification*, 288ff.
225. K. Mannheim, *Ideology and Utopia*, 86.

226. Concerning the semantic history of the concept of ideology, a concept frequently employed with theoretical imprecision, see the overview in U. Dierse and R. Romberg, "Ideologie," *Historisches Wörterbuch der Philosophie*, vol. 4, 158–85. See also ibid., 170ff. concerning the problematic attaching to Mannheim's own sociological concept of ideology and the criticism of his understanding of ideology presented, e.g., by Tillich, H. Plessner, and representatives of the Frankfurt School.

227. J. Derrida, "Of an Apocalyptic Tone Recently Adopted in Philosophy," in P. Fenves, ed., *Raising the Tone in Philosophy*, 159.

Chapter 6
CHRISTIAN FAITH AND THE APOCALYPTIC WORLD EXPERIENCE

1. Cf. G. Ebeling, "Faith and Unbelief in Conflict about Reality," idem, *Word and Faith*, 374–85.

2. P. Tillich, *Systematic Theology*, 2.99.

3. Cf. also P. Tillich, *Systematic Theology*, 3.394ff., 404.

4. E. Käsemann, *Commentary on Romans*, 221.

5. Concerning the history of scholarship, see K. Koch, *The Rediscovery of Apocalyptic: A Polemical Work on a Neglected Area of Biblical Studies and Its Damaging Effects on Theology and Philosophy*, passim. Cf. also pp. 9ff. above.

6. Cf. A. Strobel, *Kerygma und Apokalyptik. Ein religionsgeschichtlicher und theologischer Beitrag zur Christusfrage*, 135; contra P. Vielhauer, in E. Hennecke and W. Schneemelcher, eds., *New Testament Apocrypha I–II*, vol. 2, "Writings Relating to the Apostles; Apocalypses and Related Subjects," 428ff.

7. See, e.g., 2 Peter 3:3ff.; Heb. 10:35ff.

8. So, e.g., Jude 3ff., 18.

9. E.g., Heb. 12:18ff.; 2 Tim. 4:1.

10. Cf. E. Käsemann, "Sentences of Holy Law in the New Testament," idem, *New Testament Questions of Today*, 66–81; S. Schulz, *Q—Die Spruchquelle der Evangelisten*, 57ff.

11. Concerning the following discussion, cf. the overview in A. Strobel, "Apokalyptik/Apokalypsen IV. Neues Testament," *TRE* 3.251–57, with extensive bibilographical information (255ff.).

12. Concerning this issue, see among others: J. Baumgarten, *Paulus und die Apokalyptik. Die Auslegung apokalyptischer Überlieferungen in den echten Paulusbriefen*, WMANT 44, esp. 55–226; J. Becker, "Erwägungen zur apokalyptischen Tradition in der paulinischen Theologie," *EvT* 30 (1970) 593–609.

13. Cf. 1 Cor. 10:11; 2 Cor. 5:17; Gal. 1:4; see also Gal. 4:4.

14. See Rom. 1:18ff.; 1 Cor. 3:11ff.; 6:2; 1 Thess. 1:9f.

15. 2 Cor. 4:6; 5:17; Rom. 8:17ff.

16. Esp. 1 Cor. 15:20ff.; 1 Thess. 4:13ff.

17. See also the traditional image of the Antichrist and Satan in Rom. 16:20; 2 Cor. 6:14ff.

18. R. Bultmann, *The Presence of Eternity: History and Eschatology*, 41; see also 29, 43.

19. See J. Becker, "Erwägungen zur apokalyptischen Tradition in der paulinischen Theologie," passim.

20. G. Delling, *Zeit und Endzeit. Zwei Vorlesungen zur Theologie des Neuen Testaments*, 57ff. See his analysis of the pertinent passages, 68ff.

21. Ibid., 99.

22. Ibid., 98.

23. E. Käsemann, " 'The Righteousness of God' in Paul," idem, *New Testament Questions of Today*, 168–82, here 181.

24. See U. Luz, *Das Geschichtsverständnis des Paulus*, Concerning Pauline eschatology, see also P. Hoffmann, *Die Toten in Christus. Eine religionsgeschichtliche exegetische Untersuchung zur paulinischen Eschatologie*, esp. 330–41, as well as H. R. Balz, *Heilsvertrauen und Welterfahrung. Strukturen der paulinischen Eschatologie nach Römer 8:18–39*, esp. 124–131.

25. Cf. P. Stuhlmacher, *Gerechtigkeit Gottes bei Paulus.*

26. Cf. A. Grabner-Haider, *Paraklese und Eschatologie bei Paulus. Mensch und Welt im Anspruch der Zukunft Gottes*, See also U. Körtner, "Rechtfertigung und Ethik bei Paulus. Bemerkungen zum Ansatz paulinischer Ethik," *WD*, New Series 16 (1981) 93–109.

27. Cf. E. Käsemann, "On the Subject of Primitive Christian Apocalyptic," idem, *New Testament Questions of Today*, 108–37, here 131f. See also U. Luz, *Das Geschichtsverständnis des Paulus*, 301–58, esp. 332ff.

28. Hence the thesis of U. Wilckens is problematical according to which "the salvation-historical [sic!] outline of Jewish apocalyptic" was determinative also for the Christian theologian Paul, the one difference being that at the decisive juncture Paul eliminated the law from this apocalyptic outline and replaced it with the Christ event. Cf. U. Wilckens, "Die Bekehrung des Paulus als religionsgeschichtliches Problem," *ZTK* 56 (1959) 285f. For a view opposing this linear interpretation of the subject matter, see J. Baumgarten, *Paulus und die Apokalyptik. Die Auslegung apokalyptischer Überlieferungen in den echten Paulusbriefen*, 238.

29. So also G. Delling, *Zeit und Endzeit. Zwei Vorlesungen zur Theologie des Neuen Testaments*, 100.

30. U. Luz, *Das Geschichtsverständnis des Paulus*, 358. J. Baumgarten (*Paulus und die Apokalyptik. Die Auslegung apokalyptischer Überlieferungen in den echten Paulusbriefen*, 239) agrees with Luz's thesis that Paul dealt creatively with the apocalyptic tradition, though he follows J. Becker ("Erwägungen zur apokalyptischen Tradition in der paulinischen Theologie," passim) in objecting to Luz's estimation of Paul as an apocalyptist.

31. Cf. P. Hoffmann, *Die Toten in Christus. Eine religionsgeschichtliche exegetische Untersuchung zur paulinischen Eschatologie*, 340.

32. Cf. U. Luz, *Das Geschichtsverständnis des Paulus*, 356f.

33. J. Baumgarten, *Paulus und die Apokalyptik. Die Auslegung apokalyptischer Überlieferungen in den echten Paulusbriefen*, 239.

34. G. Ebeling, "Der Grund christlicher Theologie," *ZTK* 58 (1961) 227–44, here 234. E. Käsemann cites in agreement Ebeling's dictum here, which was coined in reference to primitive Christian apocalyptic as a whole. E. Käsemann, "On the Subject of Primitive Christian Apocalyptic," 115, n. 9.

35. On Q see also P. Vielhauer, *Geschichte der urchristlichen Literatur*, 311ff.

36. See S. Schulz, *Q—Die Spruchquelle der Evangelisten*, 33ff.

37. Ibid., 65.

38. Concerning the pre- and post-history of Q as well as the genre of sayings source, see J. M. Robinson, "*Logoi sophon.* On the Gattung of Q," in H. Koester and J. M. Robinson, eds., *Trajectories through Early Christianity*, 71–113.

39. Mark 2:10, 28; 8:31, 38; 9:9, 12, 31; 10:33, 45; 14:21, 41, 62.

40. E. Brandenburger, *Markus 13 und die Apokalyptik.*

41. Cf. ibid., 41. Concerning the status of scholarship on this question, see 21ff.

42. Cf. ibid., 69ff.

43. Ibid., 13.

44. Ibid., 114.

45. Cf. D. Lührmann, "Biographie des Gerechten als Evangelium. Vorstellungen zu einem Markus-Kommentar," *WD*, New Series (1977) 25–50.

46. Cf. also A. Vögtle, *Das Neue Testament und die Zukunft des Kosmos*, 67ff.

47. Matt. 21; Luke 24.

48. Luke 17:20ff.

49. Matt. 24:3.

50. Cf. Matt. 13:35; 25:34. Concerning this whole issue, see G. Strecker, *Der Weg der Gerechtigkeit. Untersuchung zur Theologie des Matthäus*, 236ff. R. Walker, *Die Heilsgeschichte im ersten Evangelium*, 114ff.

51. Matt. 10:23; 16:28.

52. Cf. Matt. 24f.

53. See W. Trilling, *Das wahre Israel. Studien zur Theologie des Matthäus-Evangeliums*, 150.

54. Concerning this issue, see G. Bornkamm, "End-Expectation and Church in Matthew," in idem, G. Barth and H. J. Held, *Tradition and Interpretation in Matthew*, 15–51.

55. See esp. Matt. 13.

56. Matt. 13:41. On this whole issue, see W. Trilling, *Das wahre Israel. Studien zur Theologie des Matthäus-Evangeliums*, 143–63.

57. Concerning the interpretation of Luke 17:21 as a reference to the present, cf. W. G. Kümmel, *Promise and Fulfillment: The Eschatological Message of Jesus*, 32f.

58. So the thesis of H. Conzelmann, *The Theology of St. Luke*, 103ff.; E. Grässer, *Das Problem der Parusieverzögerung in den synoptischen Evangelien und in der Apostelgeschichte*, 178ff.; G. Schneider, *Parusiegleichnisse im Lukas-Evangelium*, SBS 74.

59. Cf. W. G. Kümmel, *Introduction to the New Testament*, 100ff.

60. Cf. G. Lohfink, *Die Himmelfahrt Jesu. Untersuchungen zu den Himmelfahrts- und Erhöhungstexten bei Lukas*, 256ff.

61. Concerning Lukan eschatology, see also W. C. Robinson, Jr., *Der Weg des Herrn. Studien zur Geschichte und Eschatologie im Lukas-Evangelium. Ein Gespräch mit Hans Conzelmann*, 45ff.

62. Cf. N. Perrin, *Rediscovering the Teaching of Jesus;* E. Grässer, "Zum Verständnis der Gottesherrschaft," *ZNW* 65 (1974) 3–26; J. Blank, *Jesus von Nazareth. Geschichte und Relevanz.*

63. See Bultmann's own explanation of his position within this discussion of the 1950s in his essay about "Das Verhältnis der urchristlichen Christusbotschaft zum historischen Jesus" (1960), now in R. Bultmann, *Exegetica. Aufsätze zur Erforschung des Neuen Testaments*, ed. E. Dinkler, 445–69. Concerning the following discussion, cf. the bibliography mentioned by Bultmann 445, n. 1.

64. See esp. Albert Schweitzer, *The Mystery of the Kingdom of God: The Secret of Jesus' Messiahship and Passion.*

65. Concerning the history of scholarship, see K. Koch, *The Rediscovery of Apocalyptic: A Polemical Work on a Neglected Area of Biblical Studies and Its Damaging Effects on Theology and Philosophy*, 57ff.

66. See G. M. Martin, *Weltuntergang. Gefahr und Sinn apokalyptischer Visionen*, 86ff. However, cf. also the judgment of R. Bultmann, *The Presence of Eternity: History and Eschatology*, 32: "The preaching of Jesus differs from the apocalypses in so far as he does not give any picture of the coming welfare, except to say that it is life . . . Symbolically, salvation can be described as a great banquet."

67. G. M. Martin, *Weltuntergang. Gefahr und Sinn apokalyptischer Visionen*, 92f.

68. John 5:28f.; 12:45; 6:39f.; 14:2f.

69. Cf. G. Stählin, "Zum Problem der johanneischen Eschatologie," *ZNW* 33 (1934) 225–59; W. G. Kümmel, *Introduction to the New Testament*, 149f. A different view is taken, e.g., by R. Bultmann, *The Gospel of John*, 218f., 261f.; J. Becker, *Auferstehung der Toten im Urchristentum* (Stuttgarter Bibelstudien 82; Stuttgart: Katholisches Bibelwerk, 1976), 117ff.

70. See also J. Blank, *Krisis. Untersuchungen zur johanneischen Christologie und Eschatologie*, 109ff. A different view is taken by L. van Hartingsveld, *Die Eschatologie des Johannesevangeliums. Eine Auseinandersetzung mit Rudolf Bultmann*, who supports the thesis that

the real emphasis of the Gospel of John lies, contrary to Bultmann's interpretation, on future eschatology.

71. Concerning the status of this discussion, see, e.g., W. G. Kümmel, *Introduction to the New Testament*, 154ff.

72. Cf. J. Becker, "Beobachtungen zum Dualismus im Johannesevangelium," *ZNW* 65 (1974) 71–87.

73. Cf. John 1:5; 8:12.

74. Cf. John 3:6, 12, 19–21.

75. Cf. John 15:18–25.

76. L. Schottroff has tried to show that gnosis is the religio-historical background of Johannine dualism; L. Schottroff, *Der Glaubende und die feindliche Welt. Beobachtungen zum gnostischen Dualismus und seine Bedeutung für Paulus und das Johannesevangelium.*

77. O. Böcher, *Der johanneische Dualismus im Zusammenhang des nachbiblischen Judentums*, derives the Johannine dualism in its entirety from Jewish thinking, esp. that of Qumran.

78. See pp. 31ff. above.

79. Cf. O. Böcher, *Der johanneische Dualismus im Zusammenhang des nachbiblischen Judentums*, 120ff.

80. On the following discussion, cf. G. Klein, " 'Das wahre Licht scheint schon,' " *ZTK* 68 (1971) 261–326.

81. See H. R. Balz, *Methodische Probleme der neutestamentlichen Christologie*, 48–128. Cf. further A. Strobel, *Kerygma und Apokalyptik. Ein religionsgeschichtlicher und theologischer Beitrag zur Christusfrage*, 138ff.; idem, "Apokalyptik, Christusoffenbarung und Utopie. Theologisches Zeugnis im Umbruch eines Zeitalters," in G. F. Vicedom, ed., *Das Mandat der Theologie und die Zukunft des Glaubens. Sechs Aspekte zur Gottesfrage*, 104–60, esp. 132ff.

82. E. Käsemann, "The Beginnings of Christian Theology," in idem, *New Testament Questions of Today*, 82–107, here 102. Concerning the debate surrounding this thesis, cf. K. Koch, *The Rediscovery of Apocalyptic: A Polemical Work on a Neglected Area of Biblical Studies and Its Damaging Effects on Theology and Philosophy*, 78ff. A. Strobel, *Kerygma und Apokalyptik*, 132, speaks of apocalyptic as the "well-house" of Christian theology.

83. E. Käsemann, "Zum Thema der urchristlichen Apokalyptik," in idem, *Exegetische Versuche und Besinnungen II* (3rd ed.; Göttingen: Vandenhoeck & Ruprecht, 1970) 111, n. 5. See also the English translation, "On the Subject of Primitive Christian Apocalyptic," idem, *New Testament Questions of Today*, 108–37.

84. Cf. ibid., 112, n. 5.

85. Cf. ibid., 105f., n. 1.

86. E. Käsemann, "Die Anfänge christlicher Theologie," in idem, *Exegetische Versuche und Besinnungen II*, 104. See also the English translation, "The Beginnings of Christian Theology," in idem, *New Testament Questions of Today*, 82–107.

87. E. Käsemann, "Zum Thema der urchristlichen Apokalyptik," 106, n. 1.

88. So W. Schmithals, *The Apocalyptic Movement: Introduction and Interpretation*, 170f., 168; similarly N. Walter, "Zur theologischen Relevanz apokalyptischer Aussagen," in J. Rogge and G. Schille, eds., *Theologische Versuche VI*, 47–72, here 60, 62.

89. N. Walter, "Zur theologischen Relevanz apokalyptischer Aussagen," 59.

90. O. Haendler, *Angst und Glaube*, 159f.

91. Ibid., 160.

92. Ibid.

93. Cf. K. Schwarzwäller, *Die Angst—Gegebenheit und Aufgabe*, 7f.

94. Cf., e.g., O. Haendler, *Angst und Glaube*, 151: "Life anxiety" and "death anxiety" awaken "questions which seek an answer in that which lies 'behind' them."

95. K. Schwarzwäller, *Die Angst—Gegebenheit und Aufgabe*, 10.

96. See D. Bonhoeffer, *Widerstand und Ergebung*, 155f. See also the English transla-

tion incorporating this text, *Letters and Papers from Prison* (4th ed., enlarged; London: SCM, 1971; New York: Macmillan Paperbacks, 1972).

97. D. Bonhoeffer, *Widerstand und Ergebung*, 156.

98. Ibid.

99. Cf. ibid., 170. Similarly also K. Schwarzwäller, Die Angst—Gegebenheit und Aufgabe, 45: "Every statement along the lines of 'you, too, need Jesus, the remedy for anxiety,' is superfluous and absolutely expendable; this kind of pious babbling one must—as always—fear and avoid like sin."

100. See D. Bonhoeffer, *Widerstand und Ergebung*, 159f. Concerning Bonhoeffer's disinclination toward psychology, cf. ibid., 90. This disinclination does admittedly need further explication.

101. O. Pfister, *Christianity and Fear: A Study in History and in the Psychology and Hygiene of Religion.* Starting from 1 John 4:17f., Pfister views freedom from anxiety as the standard for evaluating the individual epochs of church history, though his judgments are admittedly strongly influenced by theological liberalism and in certain instances not at all unproblematical. Cf. the critical views of M. Hartung, *Angst und Schuld in Tiefenpsychologie und Theologie* (Urban Taschenbücher 647; Stuttgart: Kohlhammer, 1979) 56f.

102. K. Schwarzwäller, *Die Angst—Gegebenheit und Aufgabe*, 8.

103. Cf. also R. Affemann, "Die Angst in der Kirche aus der Sicht des Tiefenpsychologen," in R. Bohren and N. Greinacher, eds., *Angst in der Kirche verstehen und überwinden*, 15–43, esp. 29ff.; G. Hasenhüttl, "Theologische Reflexion über die Angst," ibid., 44–57, esp. 50ff.

104. Cf. 1 John 3:21. Concerning *parrēsia*, see further 1 John 2:28; 5:14.

105. On 1 John 4:17f., cf. H. Balz, "Die Johannesbriefe," in idem and W. Schrage, *Die "Katholischen" Briefe*, 194f.; R. Schnackenburg, *The Johannine Epistles*, 222ff.; K. Wengst, *Der erste, zweite und dritte Brief des Johannes*, 191ff. A different view is taken by R. Bultmann, who considers *en tē hēmera tēs kriseōs* in v. 17 to be an interpolation (cf. R. Bultmann, "Die kirchliche Redaktion des ersten Johannesbriefes," in *In memoriam E. Lohmeyer*, 189–201, here 198), and does not associate *kolasis* in v. 18 with the punishment in the last judgment (cf. Matt. 25:46), but rather translates it with "torment." "That would mean that anxiety contains its own chastisement within itself." 1 John allegedly historicized the eschatological concept of *kolasis* to the same extent that John 3:14; 5:24 did the concept of *krisis*. See R. Bultmann, *The Johannine Epistles* in loc. Rom. 8:15 is substantively related to 1 John 4:17b, 18.

106. Concerning John 16:33, see R. Bultmann, *The Gospel of John*, 592f.; R. Schnackenburg, *Das Johannesevangelium*, vol. 3, 187f.

107. So, e.g., Rev. 1:9; 2:9f.; Acts 14:22. Concerning *thlipsis*, see H. Schlier, "*thlibō, thlipsis*," *TDNT* 3.139–48. *Thlipsis* refers quite generally to affliction and is by no means limited to the possible meaning "anxiety," which is not the primary meaning. *Thlipsis* in the sense of anxiety appears in the LXX in Job 15:24; Zeph. 1:15; Isa. 8:22; Gen. 42:21; and elsewhere. Anxiety is an inner affliction (Hebrew *ṣrh*) that emerges in the *anagkē* or *stenochōria*. In the New Testament, too, *thlipseis* refers to afflictions of the most varied sorts, including, as only one among others, anxiety (cf. 2 Cor. 7:5). The afflictions of the church are according to the New Testament view first of all a necessary consequence of the salvation events, then also a means of participation in Christ's sufferings, and finally also a sign of the eschatological situation. The *thlipseis* of the Christian community are the beginning of the eschatological tribulation which in Jewish eschatology is not expected until the future. Some passages, e.g., Rom. 2:9 and 2 Thess. 1:6, speak in the sense of apocalyptic notions of the *thlipsis* of the wicked in the last judgment. Concerning *phobos*, see H. Balz, "*phobeō ktl.* A," *TDNT* 9.189–97; G. Wanke, "*phobeō ktl.* B," *TDNT* 9.197–205; H. Balz, "*phobeō ktl.* C–E," *TDNT* 9.205–19.

108. K. Schwarzwäller, *Die Angst—Gegebenheit und Aufgabe*, 46.

109. Ibid.

110. O. Pfister, *Das Christentum und die Angst. Eine religionspsychologische, historische und religionshygienische Untersuchung*, 18: "Now there is indeed talk of fear here; however, in the New Testament no sharp distinction is made between religious fear and anxiety (*thlipsis*). If even scientific usage employs the two expressions interchangeably, who can then expect from the New Testament a precise distinction between them?" (See also the English translation, *Christianity and Fear.*)

111. Ibid. 1 John 4:17b is not a statement concerning universal experience like that of Seneca: "Love cannot be mixed with fear" (*Epistulae* 47.18). So also K. Wengst, *Der erste, zweite und dritte Brief des Johannes*, 193f. R. Schnackenburg, *The Johannine Epistles*, 224, n. 88, also objects to Pfister's interpretation.

112. O. Pfister, *Das Christentum und die Angst*, 19.

113. Cf. J. Scharfenberg, "Das Problem der Angst im Grenzgebiet von Theologie und Psychologie," *Wege zum Menschen* 20 (1968) 314–24, here 320: "Pfister's book seems to me to be an impressive warning of how the thesis of psychology as an auxiliary discipline does not by itself preclude its being misused as a hermeneutical principle, whereby it is able, with omnipotent hybris, to appropriate for itself the determination of why the interrogation is being carried out in the first place."

114. Cf. O. Pfister, *Das Christentum und die Angst*, 441ff.

115. Ibid., 492.

116. Contra J. Thiele, "Der Ruf in das angstfreie Leben," *Junge Kirche* 44 (1983) 58–60. For Thiele, Christianity's freedom from anxiety becomes an ethical postulate. The "absence of anxiety from within the gospel of peace" (60) is attained only through one's own actions: "Acts of peace, accountable on the basis of faith in the peacemaker Jesus Christ, makes a person free from anxiety" (59).

117. O. Haendler, *Angst und Glaube*, 114. In support, Haendler adduces passages such as Ps. 4:1 and Ps. 71:20.

118. Ibid., 164; cf. also 155f.!

119. Ibid., 158.

120. Cf. ibid., 164.

121. Ibid., 117. "But this God in whom one believes must be the real God, and not the usual impoverished image of God" (ibid.).

122. Ibid., 127.

123. Ibid., 147.

124. Ibid., 118.

125. Ibid., 131; cf. also 152.

126. Ibid., 144.

127. Cf. ibid., 145.

128. J. Scharfenberg, "Das Problem der Angst im Grenzgebiet von Theologie und Psychologie," 315.

129. H. Thielicke, "Theologische Dimensionen der Angst," in W. Bitter, ed., *Angst und Schuld in theologischer und psychotherapeutischer Sicht*, 23–38, here 23.

130. Ibid., 24.

131. Cf. ibid.

132. Cf. ibid., 34f. Thielicke's assertion is virtually misanthropic and unfortunately recalls National Socialist thinking: "The behavior of Bolshevist soldiers has provided astonishing illustrations . . . of the absence of anxiety characteristic of animals" (35).

133. E. Brunner, "Von der Angst (1953)," in idem, *Ein offenes Wort. Vortärge und Aufsätze 1935–1962* (*Werke* II), 287–301, here 297.

134. J. Scharfenberg, "Das Problem der Angst im Grenzgebiet von Theologie und Psychologie," 315.

135. E. Brunner, "Von der Angst," 300.

136. Ibid., 298.

137. Ibid.

138. Ibid., 301.
139. H. U. von Balthasar, *Der Christ und die Angst.*
140. Ibid., 14.
141. See ibid., 16ff.
142. Ibid., 26.
143. Cf. ibid., 33ff.
144. Ibid., 13.
145. Cf. ibid., 33.
146. Ibid., 38.
147. Ibid., 42.
148. Ibid., 32.
149. Ibid., 45.
150. Ibid., 46.
151. Ibid.
152. Ibid., 54.
153. Ibid., 66.
154. Ibid., 48.
155. Cf. ibid., 7ff., 67ff., esp. 84ff.
156. Cf. ibid., 67ff. On Balthasar's critique of Luther, see 54ff.
157. Ibid., 59.
158. Ibid., 90.
159. M. Hartung also assumes a critical position over against Balthasar's theology of anxiety; M. Hartung, *Angst und Schuld in Tiefenpsychologie und Theologie*, 78ff.
160. H. U. von Balthasar, *Der Christ und die Angst*, 13.
161. D. Bonhoeffer, *Widerstand und Ergebung*, 82.
162. Ibid., 87.
163. Cf. ibid., 87f.
164. S. Kierkegaard, *The Sickness unto Death*, 77 (XI 189): "Despair is sin."
165. Attention to this pseudonymity is of central importance for the understanding of Kierkegaard's pseudonymous works. Cf. Kierkegaard's statement that in his pseudonymous writings there is not a single word from himself (VII 546). *The Concept of Anxiety* is an exception to this principle. His manuscripts show that Kierkegaard originally intended to publish the writing under his own name, and decided upon pseudonymity only shortly before actual publication. At the same time, the book's dedication to his teacher Paul Martin Möller remained (*The Concept of Anxiety*, 5 [IV 277]), a dedication that is meaningless as far as the pseudonym is concerned to the extent it is not intended to be Kierkegaard himself. *The Concept of Anxiety* is a writing that very much does contain Kierkegaard's own thoughts, and its observations concerning anxiety doubtless derive from the author's own self-analysis. Cf. E. Hirsch, *Kierkegaard-Studien*, vol. II.3, *Der Denker*, 70ff.; W. Schulz, "Die Dialektik von Leib und Seele bei Kierkegaard. Bemerkungen zum 'Begriff Angst,' " in M. Theunissen and W. Greve, eds., *Materialien zur Philosophie S. Kierkegaards*, 349.
166. S. Kierkegaard, *The Concept of Anxiety*, 16 (IV 288).
167. Ibid., 14 (IV 286).
168. Ibid., 21f. (IV 294).
169. Ibid., 32 (IV 304).
170. Ibid., 20 (IV 292); cf. 22f. (IV 295).
171. Cf. ibid., 15 (IV 287): "The mood of psychology is that of a discovering anxiety, and in its anxiety psychology portrays sin, while again and again it is in anxiety over the portrayal that it itself brings forth."
172. As far as dogmatics is concerned, in the introduction to the *Concept of Anxiety* Kierkegaard praises "Schleiermacher's immortal service to this science. He was left behind long ago when men chose Hegel. Yet Schleiermacher was a thinker in the beautiful

Greek sense, a thinker who spoke only of what he knew. Hegel, on the contrary, despite all his outstanding ability and stupendous learning, reminds us again and again by his performance that he was in the German sense a professor of philosophy on a large scale, because he at any price must explain all things" (ibid., 20 [IV 292]).

173. See H. Fischer, *Subjektivität und Sünde. Kierkegaards Begriff der Sünde mit ständiger Rücksicht auf Schleiermachers Lehre von der Sünde.*

174. Cf. Kierkegaard, *The Concept of Anxiety*, 31f. (IV 304). On Hegel's interpetation of the Genesis account, see p. 90 above.

175. Cf. F. Schleiermacher, *The Christian Faith*, 325–38, where ultimately God is revealed as the originator of sinfulness.

176. Ibid., 302.

177. Ibid., 259.

178. Different than for Schleiermacher, according to Kierkegaard, sexuality, i.e., gender differences and the sexual determination of an individual, is not the presupposition, but rather the consequence of the Fall. Cf. S. Kierkegaard, *The Concept of Anxiety*, 48f. (IV 319f.); 67ff. (IV 337ff.).

179. Cf. ibid., 31f. (IV 304).

180. See p. 89 above.

181. See pp. 90f. above.

182. S. Kierkegaard, *The Concept of Anxiety*, 54 (IV 325).

183. Cf. ibid., 52 (IV 323).

184. Ibid., 56f. (IV 327)

185. Rom. 8:19; cf. S. Kierkegaard, *The Concept of Anxiety*, 57f. (IV 328).

186. S. Kierkegaard, *The Concept of Anxiety*, 60 (IV 331).

187. Ibid., 113 (IV 381).

188. Ibid., 111f. (IV 379f.).

189. Ibid., 114f. (IV 383).

190. H. Fischer, *Subjektivität und Sünde*, 105.

191. S. Kierkegaard, *The Sickness unto Death*, 77 (XI 189); cf. ibid., 81 (XI 193). Admittedly, Kierkegaard also refers to both despair and sin as states (ibid., 21 [XI 135]; 105ff. [XI 215ff.]). When Kierkegaard writes: "Every state of sin is a new sin, or, to express it more precisely, as will be done in this next section, the state of sin is the new sin, is the sin" (ibid., 105 [XI 215]), one should remember that precisely as a position sin is according to Kierkegaard an act (ibid., 99f. [XI 210]). Kierkegaard understands the state of sin as a continued act, something underscored by the fact that Kierkegaard compares the state of sin to the movement of a train (ibid., 106 [XI 216]), and is thus interpreting this state as movement. The state of sin is a continuing one, and this means an internally logical movement. "The reality of despair is not a consequence of the misrelation of the synthesis that relates itself to itself; it derives its reality from the fact that I continually create this misrelation" (H. Fischer, *Subjektivität und Sünde*, 103). Kierkegaard's expositions in the *Sickness unto Death* do differ from those in the *Concept of Anxiety* insofar as the *Concept of Anxiety* describes the act of sin as a leap, while the *Sickness unto Death* emphasizes the continuity of this act. Sin as a state is "a position that on its own develops an increasingly established continuity" (S. Kierkegaard, *The Sickness unto Death*, 106 [XI 216]).

192. S. Kierkegaard, *The Concept of Anxiety*, 53 (IV 324).

193. See ibid., 155ff. (chap. V: "Anxiety as Saving through Faith"; IV 421ff.).

194. Ibid., 52 (IV 323).

195. Ibid., 155 (IV 421).

196. Cf. ibid., 52 (IV 323).

197. Ibid., 155 (IV 421).

198. Ibid., 155 (IV 422).

199. Cf. 158f. (IV 424).

200. Ibid., 161 (IV 426f.).

201. Cf. Kierkegaard's introductory comments in *The Sickness unto Death*, 6 (XI 118): "Once and for all may I point out that in the whole book, as the title indeed declares, despair is interpreted as a sickness, not as a cure."

202. S. Kierkegaard, *The Concept of Anxiety*, 161f. (IV 427).

203. Concerning the basic issue here, see W. Anz, *Kierkegaard und der deutsche Idealismus.*

204. Concerning Hegel's interpretation of Gen. 3, see p. 90 above.

205. Cf. S. Kierkegaard, *The Concept of Anxiety*, 35ff. (IV 307ff.).

206. Ibid., 37 (IV 309).

207. Cf. W. Schulz, "Die Dialektik von Leib und Seele bei Kierkegaard. Bemerkungen zum 'Begriff Angst,' " 350f.

208. W. Anz's critique of Kierkegaard is even more fundamental (*Kierkegaard und der deutsche Idealismus*, 72f.): "Kierkegaard saw with extraordinary clarity that the Idealist experience of the spirit basically contradicts the Christian faith. He failed to see, however, that the dialectic of existence, though incomparably closer to the New Testament, also abbreviates the content of faith in an extremely dangerous fashion."

209. Kierkegaard "would wish that no reader would be so profound as to ask: What if Adam had not sinned?" (*The Concept of Anxiety*, 50 [IV 320]). The question is dismissed as being dumb and unworthy of a serious response.

210. Cf. also A. Paulsen, *Søren Kierkegaard. Deuter unserer Existenz*, 213f. The decisive problem with Kierkegaard's psychological route to the phenomenon of sin resides in the unwanted possibility of the devaluation of the Christian dogmatic concept of sin, and not, as E. Hirsch believes, in the fact that the "human-psychological concept of anxiety . . . , different than the ethical-religious concept of despair, cannot be applied to just any person," and thus Kierkegaard's psychological understanding "at least does not make any easier a primarily religious concept of sin," "at least not for someone who adheres to Kierkegaard's clearly formulated statements." According to Hirsch, all this changes as soon as one proceeds on the assumption "that *for Kierkegaard, behind all anxiety there stands, unexpressed, anxiety before God*" (E. Hirsch, *Kierkegaard-Studien*, II/3.116).

211. Blaise Pascal, *Pensées*, 92 (fragment 262).

212. See Ps. 111:10; Prov. 1:7; 9:10; cf. Job 28:28.

213. See R. Bultmann, *Theology of the New Testament*, 1.320ff. (sec. 35.4). Cf. also H. Balz, *TDNT* 9.213ff.

214. The same holds true for Kierkegaard. Cf. S. Kierkegaard, "To Need God Is a Human Being's Highest Perfection," *Eighteen Upbuilding Discourses*, 297–326, here 323f. (V 103) (this particular essay being one of the *Four Upbuilding Discourses 1844*).

215. Mark 14:34; Matt. 26:28; esp., however, Luke 22:43!

216. Concerning the significance of Jesus' anxiety for a theology of anxiety, cf. S. Kierkegaard, *The Concept of Anxiety*, 155f. (IV 421f.). See also K. Schwarzwäller, *Die Angst—Gegebenheit und Aufgabe*, 51f.

217. Rom. 8:35.

218. Cf. also S. Kierkegaard, *The Concept of Anxiety*, 162 (IV 428): "As soon as psychology has finished with anxiety, it is to be delivered to dogmatics."

219. G. Ebeling, "Lebensangst und Glaubensanfechtung. Erwägungen zum Verhältnis von Psychotherapie und Theologie," *ZTK* 70 (1973) 80, reaches a similar conclusion, though he believes that Kierkegaard's distinction between fear and anxiety ultimately derives exclusively from theological interests.

220. Cf. K. Schwarzwäller, *Die Angst—Gegebenheit und Aufgabe*, 51ff. See further J. Moltmann, *The Crucified God: The Cross of Christ as the Foundation and Criticism of Christian Theology*, 291ff., esp. 301ff.

221. On this formulation, cf. J. Moltmann, " 'Begnadete Angst.' Religiös integrierte

Angst und ihre Bewältigung," in H. von Stietencron, ed., *Angst und Gewalt. Ihre Praesenz und ihre Bewältigung in den Religionen*," 153.

222. Cf. H. U. von Balthasar, *Der Christ und die Angst*, 46.

223. However, see also the use of *phobos* in Jewish apocalyptic literature. Cf. in this context H. Balz, *TDNT* 9.206.

224. Cf. S. Kierkegaard, *The Concept of Anxiety*, 113ff. (IV 381ff.); 102ff. (IV 372ff.).

225. S. Kierkegaard, *Christian Discourses* (1848), 77 (X 78).

226. Cf. Matt. 6:25ff.; Luke 12:22ff.

227. Cf. S. Kierkegaard, *Christian Discourses* (1848) 76f. (X 77).

228. Ibid., 77 (X 78).

229. The dialectic of sublation recalls conceptually the dialectic within the philosophy of Hegel. Our understanding of sublation in connection with apocalyptic, however, differs from that of Hegel in that the sublation in our thesis is not conceived as a synthesis, since we are dealing not with three but rather only with two quantities.

230. Contra N. Walter, "Zur theologischen Relevanz apokalyptischer Aussagen," 59.

231. G. M. Martin, *Weltuntergang. Gefahr und Sinn apokalyptischer Visionen*, 95.

232. Cf. Rom. 10:4.

233. Concerning Christ as the end of history, cf. R. Bultmann, "History of Salvation and History" (1948), in idem, *Existence and Faith*, 268–84, here 281f.; idem, "Prophecy and Fulfillment," in idem, *Essays: Philosophical and Theological*, 182–208, here 190f.; idem, *The Presence of Eternity: History and Eschatology*, 43; and E. Fuchs, "Christus das Ende der Geschichte," *EvT* 8 (1948/49) 447–61, esp. 454ff.

234. See D. Lührmann, *Glaube im frühen Christentum*, esp. 85ff.

235. E. Käsemann, "Zum Thema der urchristlichen Apokalyptik," 119. See also the English translation, "The Beginnings of Christian Theology," in idem, *New Testament Questions of Today*, 82–107.

236. Cf. pp. 76f. above.

237. See E. Brunner, *Eternal Hope* (London: Lutterworth, 1954) 25ff.; A. Rich, *Die Bedeutung der Eschatologie für den christlichen Glauben* (Kirchliche Zeitfragen 31; Zurich: Zwingli Verlag, 1954) 4ff.

238. This distinction between *futurum* and *adventus* is picked up by J. Moltmann, "Kommt Jesus wieder?" *Radius* (1966), Heft 1, 6–13.

239. Cf. E. Bloch, *The Principle of Hope*, 1235f.

240. In addition to the works already mentioned, see W. Pannenberg, *Jesus—God and Man*, 53ff.

241. Cf. the critique of Pannenberg's understanding of prolepsis presented by G. Sauter, *Zukunft und Verheissung. Das Problem der Zukunft in der gegenwärtigen theologischen und philosophischen Diskussion*, 266. Concerning the following discussion, see also Moltmann's criticism, *The Theology of Hope*, 76ff.; idem, *The Crucified God*, 170ff.

242. W. Pannenberg, "Redemptive Event in History," idem, *Basic Questions in Theology: Collected Essays*, 1.21.

243. W. Pannenberg, "The God of Hope," idem, *Basic Questions in Theology: Collected Essays*, vol. 2, 234–49, here 243.

244. Ibid., 246.

245. Ibid., 244.

246. Cf. W. Pannenberg, "Eschatologie und Sinnerfahrung," idem, *Grundfragen systematischer Theologie II* (1980) 66–79, here 71ff.

247. W. Pannenberg, "The God of Hope," 243f.: "For is the future not only of our present but also of every past age?"

248. W. Pannenberg, "Zeit und Ewigkeit in der religiösen Erfahrung Israels und des Christentums," idem, *Grundfragen systematischer Theologie II* (1980) 188–206, here 202.

249. Ibid., 202f.

250. Cf. W. Pannenberg, *Offenbarung als Geschichte*, 91ff. English translation, *Revelation as History*.

251. See K. Barth, *Church Dogmatics* I/2, 58.

252. Concerning the problem of salvation history, see J. Moltmann, *Theology of Hope*, 69ff.; K. G. Steck, *Die Idee der Heilsgeschichte. Hoffmann—Schlatter—Cullmann;* F. Hesse, *Abschied von der Heilsgeschichte*, Concerning von Hoffmann's conception of salvation history, see further E.-H. Wendebourg, "Die heilsgeschichtliche Theologie J. Chr. v. Hoffmanns in ihrem Verhältnis zur romantischen Weltanschauung," *ZTK* 52 (1955) 64–104.

253. G. Sauter uses the term in this sense, *Zukunft und Verheissung, 262ff.*

254. A critical view is also taken by H. D. Betz, "Das Verständnis der Apokalyptik in der Theologie der Pannenberg-Gruppe," *ZTK* 65 (1968) 257–70.

255. J. Moltmann, *Theology of Hope*, 83.

256. Cf. ibid., 154ff. A. Strobel also refers to the Christian understanding of the cross as *eschatologia crucis*, though he classifies this as apocalyptic. Cf. A. Strobel, "Apokalyptik, Christusoffenbarung und Utopie. Theologisches Zeugnis im Umbruch eines Zeitalters," 132ff. Hence today's Christian also must be an apocalyptist. "The tense attitude of the apocalyptist—and for Christians this is primarily that of Jesus himself [!]—becomes a direct challenge and offering to our own age" (A. Strobel, *Kerygma und Apokalyptik. Ein religionsgeschichtlicher und theologischer Beitrag zur Christusfrage*, 131). Thus for Strobel, precisly as *eschatologia crucis* Christian theology must be apocalyptic theology. Cf. *Kerygma und Apokalyptik*, 191ff. Despite certain elements of criticism Strobel directs at Pannenberg's concept, his proximity to Pannenberg's historical theology is unmistakable.

257. J. Moltmann, *Theology of Hope*, 193.

258. J. Moltmann, *The Church in the Power of the Spirit: A Contribution to Messianic Ecclesiology*, 37–50.

259. See also J. Moltmann, *The Crucified God*, 166ff.

260. See H. Weder, "Die Menschwerdung Gottes. Überlegungen zur Auslegungsproblematik des Johannesevangeliums am Beispiel von Joh 6," *ZTK* 82 (1985) 325–60, esp. 333, 334f., 341f.

261. Cf. J. Moltmann, *The Church in the Power of the Spirit*, 47ff.: "Christ as 'the Sign of Hope' is also the Sign of Crisis."

262. Ibid., 49.

263. Ibid., 50.

264. Ibid., 49.

265. J. Moltmann, *The Church in the Power of the Spirit*, 49: "It is wrong to wallow in this dark, gloomy side of Christianity's mission and expansion, let alone to seek to bring on the coming of the end with 'apocalyptic pleasure' over crises and downfalls."

266. Cf. J. Moltmann, *The Crucified God*, 277: "But a trinitarian theology of the cross perceives God in the negative element and therefore the negative element in God, and in this dialectical way is panentheistic." Cf. also ibid., 255f.

267. See Introduction, sec. 2.

268. Albert Schweitzer, "The Decay and the Restoration of Civilization (1923)," in *The Philosophy of Civilization*, 145.

269. Ibid., 143.

270. Ibid., 145.

271. Cf. already Biedermann's criticism of Overbeck. In this context, see E. Vischer's introduction to Overbeck's *Selbstbekenntnisse*, ed. E. Vischer, 55f.

272. M. Kähler, *The So-called Historical Jesus and the Historic Biblical Christ.*

273. J. B. Metz, "Erinnerung des Leidens als Kritik eines teleologisch-technologischen Zukunftsbegriffs," *EvT* 32 (1972) 338–52, here 338.

274. M. Eliade, *Cosmos and History: The Myth of the Eternal Return*, 162.

275. Cf. ibid., 159ff.

276. See S. Kierkegaard, *The Sickness unto Death*, 37ff. (XI 150ff.).

277. Cf. in this context C. Figal, "Die Freiheit der Verzweiflung und die Freiheit im Glauben. Zu Kierkegaards Konzeption des Selbstseins und Selbstwerdens in der 'Krankheit zum Tode,' " *Kierkegaardiana* XIII (1984) 11–23, esp. 21.
278. J. Moltmann, *Theology of Hope*, 20.
279. Ibid., 20f.
280. Ibid., 34.
281. See pp. 91f. above.
282. See pp. 91f. above.
283. P. Tillich, *The Courage to Be*, 1.
284. Ibid., 3.
285. Ibid., 35.
286. Ibid., 163ff.
287. Ibid., 172.
288. Ibid.
289. K. Rahner, "Faith as Courage," idem, *Theological Investigations*, vol. 18, 211–25, here 211.
290. Ibid., 214.
291. Ibid., 214f.
292. Ibid., 215.
293. Ibid., 216.
294. Cf. ibid., 217f.; 220f.
295. Cf. K. Rahner, *Zur Theologie der Zukunft*, 149ff., 177ff.
296. P. Tillich, *The Courage to Be*, 176.
297. Ibid., 177.
298. Ibid., 188.
299. Cf. P. Tillich, *Systematic Theology*, 3.376.
300. Cf. K. Rahner, "Faith as Courage," 222f. See also K. Rahner, "Anonymous Christians," idem, *Theological Investigations*, vol. 6, 390–98; idem, "Atheism and Implicit Christianity," idem, *Theological Investigations*, vol. 9, 145–64.
301. K. Rahner, "Faith as Courage," 213; cf. also 219f.
302. Ibid., 223.
303. Cf. the theory of basic trust developed by E. H. Erikson, *Identity and the Life Cycle*, 57ff.
304. K. Rahner, "Faith as Courage," 224.
305. Ibid., 223.
306. G. Sauter, *Zukunft und Verheissung*, 261.
307. P. Tillich, *Systematic Theology*, 2.100.
308. Cf. ibid., 2.93ff.
309. Ibid., 2.101.
310. Ibid., 3.405.
311. Ibid., 3.399.
312. Ibid., 3.405f.
313. J. Schell, *The Fate of the Earth*, 126.
314. P. Tillich, *Systematic Theology*, 3.422.
315. Cf. esp. the criticism of W. Weischedel, *Der Gott der Philosophen. Grundlegung einer Philosophischen Theologie im Zeitalter des Nihilismus*, vol. 2, 87–111, esp. 97ff.; idem, "Paul Tillich's philosophische Theologie. Ein ehrerbietiger Widerspruch," in *Der Spannungsbogen. Festgabe P. Tillich zum 75. Geburtstag*, 25–47.
316. Cf. Rev. 21:8; 20:6, 14; 2:11.
317. A. Camus, *The Myth of Sisyphus and Other Essays.*
318. Ibid., 8.
319. Ibid., 6.
320. Ibid., 14.

321. Ibid., 15.
322. Ibid., 30.
323. Ibid., 41.
324. Ibid., 40.
325. Ibid., 120.
326. Ibid., 55.
327. Cf. A. Camus, *The Rebel: An Essay on Man in Revolt.*
328. Ibid., 55.
329. Ibid., 31.
330. A. Camus, *The Plague* (New York: Random House, 1948).
331. Cf. J. B. Metz, "Erinnerung," *Handbuch philosophischer Grundbegriffe*, 2.386–96; idem, "Zukunft aus dem Gedächtnis des Leidens. Eine gegenwärtige Gestalt der Verantwortung des Glaubens," *Concilium* 8 (1972) 399–407; idem, "Erinnerung des Leidens als Kritik eines teleologisch-technologischen Zukunftsbegriffs," *EvT* 32 (1972) passim.
332. Matt. 6:13; Luke 11:4b.

BIBLIOGRAPHY

Abegg, E. *Der Messiasglaube in Indien und im Iran.* Berlin and Leipzig: de Gruyter, 1928.

Affemann, R. "Die Angst in der Kirche aus der Sicht des Tiefenpsychologen." In *Angst in der Kirche verstehen und überwinden,* edited by R. Bohren and N. Greinacher, 15–43. Munich: Kaiser; Mainz: Grünewald, 1972.

Althaus, P. *Die letzten Dinge.* Gütersloh: C. Bertelsmann, 1933.

———. "Die Inflation des Begriffs der Offenbarung in der gegenwärtigen Theologie," *Zeitschrift für systematische Theologie* 18 (1944) 134–49.

Amery, C. *Das Ende der Vorsehung. Die gnadenlosen Folgen des Christentums.* Reinbek: Rowohlt, (1972) 1974.

Anders, G. *Die atomare Drohung. Radikale Überlegungen.* 4th ed. of *Endzeit und Zeitenende.* Munich: Beck, 1983.

———. "Über die Bombe und die Wurzeln unserer Apokalypse-Blindheit." In idem, *Die Antiquiertheit des Menschen. Über die Seele im Zeitalter der zweiten industriellen Revolution,* 233–324. Munich: Beck, 1956, 1961; 5th ed. 1980.

Andrée, R. *Die Flutsagen ethnographisch betrachtet.* Braunschweig: F. Vieweg & Sohn, 1891.

Anz, W. *Kierkegaard und der deutsche Idealismus.* Sammlung gemeinverständlicher Vorträge und Schriften aus dem Gebiet der Theologie und Religionsgeschichte 210/211. Tübingen: Mohr (Siebeck), 1956.

Apokalypse—ein Prinzip Hoffnung. Ausstellung zum 100. Geburtstag von E. Bloch im Wilhelm-Hack-Museum. Ludwigshafen (Heidelberg): Braus, 1985.

Archenhold, F. S. *Kometen, Weltuntergangsprophezeiungen und der Halleysche Komet.* Berlin: Verlag der Treptow-Sternwarte, 1910.

Arlow, J. A., and C. Brenner. "Zur Psychopathologie der Psychosen." *Psyche* 23 (1969) 402–18.

Asendorf, U. "Eschatologie VII." *Theologische Realenzyklopädie.* Vol. 10, 310–34.

Assmann, J. "Königsdogma und Heilserwartung. Politische und kultische Chaosbeschreibungen in ägyptischen Texten." In *Apocalypticism in the Mediterranean World and the Near East. Proceedings of the International Colloquium on Apocalypticism, Uppsala, August 12–17, 1979,* edited by D. Hellholm, 345–78. Tübingen: Mohr (Siebeck), 1983.

Auden, W. H. *The Age of Anxiety: A Baroque Eclogue.* New York: Random House, 1947.

Baeumler, A. "Kulturmorphologie und Philosophie." In *Schelling-Studien (FG M. Schröter),* edited by A. M. Koktanek, 99–124. Munich and Vienna: Oldenbourg, 1965.

Balthasar, H. U. von. *Der Christ und die Angst.* Einsiedeln: Johannes Verlag, 1951; 5th ed. 1976.

———. *Prometheus. Studien zur Geschichte des deutschen Idealismus.* Heidelberg: F. H. Kerle, 1947.

Balz, H. "*phobeō ktl.* A and C–E." *Theological Dictionary of the New Testament* 9.189–97, 205–19.

Balz, H., and W. Schrage. *Die "Katholischen" Briefe.* Das Neue Testament Deutsch 10. Göttingen: Vandenhoeck & Ruprecht, 1973.

Balz, H. R. *Heilsvertrauen und Welterfahrung. Strukturen der paulinischen Eschatologie nach Römer 8:18–39. Beiträge zur evangelischen Theologie* 59. Munich: Kaiser, 1971.

———. *Methodische Probleme der neutestamentlichen Christologie.* WMANT 25. Neukirchen-Vluyn: Neukirchener Verlag, 1967.

Barth, K. *Das christliche Verständnis der Offenbarung.* Theologische Existenz heute, New Series 12. Munich: Kaiser, 1948.

———. *The Epistle to the Romans.* London: Oxford University Press, 1933.

———. "The Principle of Dogmatics according to Wilhelm Herrmann (1925)." In idem, *Theology and Church*, 238–71. New York and Evanston: Harper & Row, 1962.

———. *Church Dogmatics.* Vol. I/2. Edinburgh: T. & T. Clark, 1956.

———. "Unsettled Questions for Theology Today." In idem, *Theology and Church*, 55–73.

Baumgarten, J. *Paulus und die Apokalyptik. Die Auslegung apokalyptischer Überlieferungen in den echten Paulusbriefen.* WMANT 44. Neukirchen-Vluyn: Neukirchener Verlag, 1975.

Baur, J. *Die Vernunft zwischen Ontologie und Evangelium. Eine Untersuchung zur Theologie Johann Andreas Quenstedts.* Gütersloh: Gütersloher Verlagshaus G. Mohn, 1962.

Becker, J. "Beobachtungen zum Dualismus im Johannesevangelium." *Zeitschrift für die neutestamentliche Wissenschaft* 65 (1974) 71–87.

———. "Erwägungen zur apokalyptischen Tradition in der paulinischen Theologie." *Evangelische Theologie* 30 (1970) 593–609.

Benjamin, W. *Gesammelte Schriften*, Vol. I.1. *Werkausgabe*, edited by R. Tiedemann and H. Schweppenhäuser. Frankfurt: Suhrkamp, 1980.

Bergman, J. "Introductory Remarks on Apocalypticism in Egypt." In *Apocalypticism in the Mediterranean World and the Near East*, edited by D. Hellholm, 51–60.

Berlitz, C. *Doomsday 1999 A.D.* Garden City, N.Y.: Doubleday, 1981.

Betz, H. D. "Das Verständnis der Apokalyptik in der Theologie der Pannenberg-Gruppe," *Zeitschrift für Theologie und Kirche* 65 (1968) 257–70.

Beyerlin, W., ed. *Religionsgeschichtliches Textbuch zum Alten Testament. Das Alte Testament Deutsch*, Ergänzungsband 1. Göttingen: Vandenhoeck & Ruprecht, 1975.

Bilz, R. "Der Subjektzentrismus im Erleben der Angst." In *Aspekte der Angst*, edited by H. von Ditfurth, 133–42. Starnberger Gespräche. 1964; 3rd ed. Munich: Kindler, 1981.

Binswanger, H., W. Geissberger, and T. Ginsburg, eds. *Der NAWU-Report. Wege aus der Wohlstandsfalle.* Frankfurt: S. Fischer, 1978.

Bitter, W., ed. *Angst und Schuld in theologischer und psychotherapeutischer Sicht.* 4th ed. Stuttgart: Klett, 1967.

Blank, J. *Jesus von Nazareth. Geschichte und Relevanz.* Freiburg, Basel, and Vienna: Herder, 1972.

———. *Krisis. Untersuchungen zur johanneischen Christologie und Eschatologie.* Freiburg: Lambertus, 1964.

Bloch, E. *Atheism in Christianity: The Religion of the Exodus and the Kingdom.* New York: Herder & Herder, 1972.

———. *Avicenna und die Aristotelische Linke.* Edition Suhrkamp 22. Frankfurt: Suhrkamp, 1963.

———. *Geist der Utopie.* 2nd ed. 1923. *Gesamtausgabe* 3. New ed. Frankfurt: Suhrkamp, 1964.

———. *The Principle of Hope.* Cambridge, Mass.: MIT Press, 1986.

———. *Tübinger Einleitung in die Philosophie. Gesamtausgabe* 13. Frankfurt: Suhrkamp, 1970.

Blumenberg, H. "Epochenschwelle und Rezeption," *Philosophical Review* 6 (1958) 94–120.

———. *Die Legitimität der Neuzeit.* Frankfurt: Suhrkamp, 1966.

———. *The Legitimacy of the Modern Age.* Cambridge, Mass.: MIT Press, 1983.

———. *Schiffbruch mit Zuschauer. Paradigma einer Daseinsmetapher.* Suhrkamp Taschenbuch Wissenschaft 289. Frankfurt: Suhrkamp, 1979.

Böcher, O. *Der johanneische Dualismus im Zusammenhang des nachbiblischen Judentums.* Gütersloh: G. Mohn, 1965.

———. *Die Johannesapokalypse.* Erträge der Forschung 41. Darmstadt: Wissenschaftliche Buchgesellschaft, 1975.

Boehncke, H. "Jüngstes Gericht, Verkehrte Welt." In *Weltuntergänge*, edited by H. Boehncke, R. Stollmann, and G. Vinnai, 222–35. Kulturen und Ideen. Reinbek: Rowohlt, 1984.

Boehncke, H., R. Stollmann, and G. Vinnai, eds. *Weltuntergänge.* With contributions by A. Kluge, H. Nagel, and B. Strassmann. Kulturen und Ideen. Reinbek: Rowohlt, 1984.

Bohren, R., and N. Greinacher, eds. *Angst in der Kirche verstehen und überwinden.* Munich: Kaiser; Mainz: Grünewald, 1972.

Bohrer, K. H. *Der Lauf des Freitags. Die lädierte Utopie und die Dichter. Eine Analyse.* Munich: C. Hanser, 1973.

———. "Utopie des 'Augenblicks' und Fiktionalität," in idem, *Plötzlichkeit. Zum Augenblick des ästhetischen Scheins.* Frankfurt: Suhrkamp, 1981, 180–218. English translation in idem, *Suddenness: On the Moment of Aesthetic Appearance.* New York: Columbia University Press, 1994.

Bonhoeffer, D. *Ethics.* Edited by E. Bethge. New York: Macmillan, 1962.

———. *The Cost of Discipleship.* 2nd ed. New York: Macmillan, 1965.

———. *Letters and Papers from Prison.* New York: Macmillan, 1962.

———. *Letters and Papers from Prison.* 4th ed., enlarged. London: SCM, 1971; New York: Macmillan, 1972.

———. *Widerstand und Ergebung.* Edited by E. Bethge. Gütersloh: G. Mohn, 1980.

Bornkamm, G. " *mystērion, myeō.*" *Theological Dictionary of the New Testament.* Vol. 4, 802ff.

———. "End-Expectation and Church in Matthew." In idem, G. Barth, and H. J. Held, *Tradition and Interpretation in Matthew*, 15–51. Philadelphia: Westminster, 1963.

Bousset, W. *Die jüdische Apokalyptik, ihre religionsgeschichtliche Herkunft und ihre Bedeutung für das Neue Testament.* Berlin: Reuther & Reichard, 1903.

———. *Die Religion des Judentums im neutestamentlichen Zeitalter.* 2nd ed. Berlin: Reuther & Reichard, 1906.

———. *Die Religion des Judentums im späthellenistischen Zeitalter.* Edited by H. Gressmann. Handbuch zum Neuen Testament 21. Tübingen: Mohr (Siebeck), 1926.

Brandenburger, E. *Markus 13 und die Apokalyptik.* FRLANT 134. Göttingen: Vandenhoeck & Ruprecht, 1984.

Brunner, E. "Von der Angst (1953)." In idem, *Ein offenes Wort. Vorträge und Aufsätze 1935–1962* (*Werke* II), 287–301. Zurich: Theologischer Verlag, 1981.

Buber, M. "Replies to My Critics." In *The Philosophy of Martin Buber*, edited by P. A. Schilpp and M. Friedman, 689–744. Lasalle, Ill.: Open Court, 1967; London: Cambridge University Press, 1967.

———. "Das Problem des Menschen," *Werke*, 1.307–407.

———. *I and Thou.* New York: Charles Scribner's Sons, 1970.

———. *Werke.* Vol. 1, *Schriften zur Philosophie.* Munich and Heidelberg: Kösel, 1962.

———. "Zur Geschichte des dialogischen Prinzips." In *Werke*, Vol. 1, *Schriften zur Philosophie*, 291–305. Munich and Heidelberg: Kösel, 1962.

Bulgakov, S. N. "Apokalyptik und Sozialismus. Religiös-philosophische Parallelen (1910)." In idem, *Sozialismus im Christentum*, 53–134. Sammlung Vandenhoeck. Göttingen: Vandenhoeck & Ruprecht, 1977.

Bultmann, R. *The Gospel of John*. Philadelphia: Westminster, 1971.

———. "Das Verhältnis der urchristlichen Christusbotschaft zum historischen Jesus." In idem, *Exegetica. Aufsätze zur Erforschung des Neuen Testaments*, 445–69. Edited by E. Dinkler. Tübingen: Mohr (Siebeck), 1967.

———. "The Concept of Revelation in the New Testament (1929)." In idem, *Existence and Faith*, 67–106. New York: Meridian, 1960.

———. *The Johannine Epistles*. Philadelphia: Fortress, 1973.

———. "Die kirchliche Redaktion des ersten Johannesbriefes." In *In memoriam E. Lohmeyer*, 189–201. Stuttgart: Evangelisches Verlagswerk, 1951.

———. *Geschichte und Eschatologie*. 2nd ed. Tübingen: Mohr (Siebeck), 1964.

———. *The Presence of Eternity: History and Eschatology*. New York: Harper & Brothers, 1957.

———. "Heilsgeschehen und Geschichte. Zu Oscar Cullmann, *Christus und die Zeit*." *Theologische Literaturzeitung* 73 (1948) 659–66.

———. *Theology of the New Testament*. 2 vols. New York: Charles Scribner's Sons, 1951–55.

———. "Prophecy and Fulfillment." In idem, *Essays: Philosophical and Theological*, 182–208. London: SCM, 1955.

Buri, F. *Die Bedeutung der neutestamentlichen Eschatologie für die neuere protestantische Theologie*. Zurich: Max Niehans, 1935.

Burkert, W. "Apokalyptik im frühen Griechentum." In *Apocalypticism in the Mediterranean World and the Near East*, edited by D. Hellholm, 235–54.

Camus, A. *The Rebel: An Essay on Man in Revolt*. New York: Knopf, 1956.

———. *The Myth of Sisyphus and Other Essays*. New York: Knopf, 1969.

———. *The Plague*. New York: Random House, 1948.

Carmignac, J. "Description du phénomène de l'Apocalyptique dans l'Ancien Testament." In *Apocalypticism in the Mediterranean World and the Near East*, edited by D. Hellholm, 163–70.

———. "Qu'est-ce que l'Apocalyptique? Son emploi à Qumrân." *Revue de Qumran* 10 (1979) 3–33.

Collins, J. J., ed. *Apocalypse: The Morphology of a Genre. Semeia* 14. Missoula, Montana, 1979.

———. "Jewish Apocalyptic against Its Hellenistic Near Eastern Environment." *BASOR* 220 (1975) 27–36.

Colpe, C. "Vorschläge des Messina-Kongresses von 1966 zur Gnosisforschung." In *Christentum und Gnosis*, edited by W. Eltester, 129–32. BZNW 37. Berlin: Töpelmann, 1969.

Commoner, B. *The Closing Circle: Nature, Man, and Technology*. New York: Knopf, 1971.

Conzelmann, H. *The Theology of St. Luke*. New York: Harper & Brothers, 1960.

Dantine, W. *Hoffen—Handeln—Leiden. Christliche Lebensperspektiven*. Vienna and Göttingen: Vandenhoeck & Ruprecht, 1976.

Delling, G. *Zeit und Endzeit. Zwei Vorlesungen zur Theologie des Neuen Testaments*. Biblische Studien 58. Neukirchen-Vluyn: Neukirchener Verlag, 1970.

Delumeau, J. *Le peur en Occident, XIVe–XVIIe siècles*. Paris: Fayard, *1978*.

Deppermann, K. *Melchior Hoffman: Social Unrest and Apocalyptic Visions of the Age of Reformation*. Edinburgh: T. & T. Clark, 1987.

Derrida, J. "Of an Apocalyptic Tone Recently Adopted in Philosophy." *Semeia* 23 (1982) 63–97. Also published as "On a Newly Arisen Apocalyptic Tone in Philosophy." In P. Fenves, ed., *Raising the Tone in Philosophy*, 117–71. Baltimore and London: Johns Hopkins University Press, 1993.

———. *Apokalypse. Von einem neuerdings erhobenen apokalyptischen Ton in der Philosophie.* Edited by M. Wetzel. Cologne and Vienna: Böhlau, 1985.

Deuser, H., and P. Steinacker, eds. *Ernst Bloch Vermittlungen zur Theologie.* Fundamentaltheologische Studien 6. Munich and Mainz: Kaiser, 1976.

Diem, H. "Das eschatologische Problem in der gegenwärtigen Theologie." *Theologische Rundschau,* New Series 11 (1939) 228–47.

Dierse, U., and R. Romberg. "Ideologie." In *Historisches Wörterbuch der Philosophie.* Vol. 4, 158–85. Darmstadt: Wissenschaftliche Buchgesellschaft, 1976.

Diskussion über die "Theologie der Hoffnung" von Jürgen Moltmann. Edited and introduced by W.-D. Marsch. Munich: Kaiser, 1967.

Ditfurth, H. von. *Aspekte der Angst.* Edited by H. von Ditfurt. Starnberger Gespräche 4, 1964; 3rd ed. Munich: Kindler, 1981.

———. *Gedanken zum Leib-Seele-Problem aus naturwissenschaftlicher Sicht.* Bern, 1979.

———. *So lasst uns denn ein Apfelbäumchen pflanzen. Es ist soweit.* Hamburg and Zurich: Rasch & Röhring Verlag, 1985.

———. *The Origins of Life: Evolution as Creation.* San Francisco: Harper & Row, 1982.

Drascher, W. "Begegnungen mit Oswald Spengler." In *Schelling-Studien (FG M. Schröter),* edited by A. M. Koktanek, 9–31. Munich and Vienna: Oldenbourg, 1965.

Drewermann, E. *Tiefenpsychologie und Exegese.* Vol. 2, *Die Wahrheit der Werke und der Worte. Wunder, Vision, Weissagung, Apokalypse, Geschichte, Gleichnis.* Olten and Freiburg: Walter-Verlag, 1985.

Dürrenmatt, F. "Der Tunnel." In idem, *Die Stadt. Prosa I–IV,* 149ff. Zurich: Die Arche, 1952.

Ebach, J. "Apokalypse. Zum Ursprung einer Stimmung." In *Einwürfe* 2, edited by F.-M. Marquardt et al., 5–61. Munich: Kaiser, 1985.

Ebeling, G. "Faith and Unbelief in Conflict about Reality." In idem, *Word and Faith,* 374–85. Philadelphia: Fortress, 1963.

———. "Der Grund christlicher Theologie," *Zeitschrift für Theologie und Kirche* 58 (1961) 227–44.

———. "Lebensangst und Glaubensanfechtung. Erwägungen zum Verhältnis von Psychotherapie und Theologie." *Zeitschrift für Theologie und Kirche* 70 (1973) 77–100.

Ehrlich, P. R., and A. Ehrlich. *Population Resources Environment: Issues in Human Ecology.* San Francisco: W. H. Freeman, 1970.

Eicher, P. "Offenbarungsreligion." In idem, ed., *Gottesvorstellung und Gesellschaftsentwicklung,* 109–26. Forum Religionswissenschaft 1. Munich: Kösel, 1979.

Eliade, M. *Cosmos and History: The Myth of the Eternal Return.* New York: Harper & Brothers, 1959.

Elliger, W. *Aussenseiter der Reformation: Thomas Müntzer.* Kleine Vandenhoeck-Reihe 1409. Göttingen: Vandenhoeck & Ruprecht, 1975.

———. *Thomas Müntzer. Leben und Werk.* 3rd ed. Göttingen: Vandenhoeck & Ruprecht, 1976.

Ellul, J. *Apocalypse: The Book of Revelation.* New York: Seabury, 1977.

Ende, M. *The Neverending Story.* Harmondsworth: Puffin, 1985.

Engels, F. "Bruno Bauer and Early Christianity" (1882). In idem, *Collected Works.* Vol. 24, 427–35. New York: International Publishers, 1986.

———. "The Book of Revelation." *Progress* 2 (1883) 112–16. Now in Karl Marx and Frederick Engels, *Collected Works.* Vol. 26, 112–17. New York: International Publishers, 1990.

———. "On the History of Early Christianity." *Collected Works.* Vol. 27, 447–69. New York: International Publishers, 1990.

Englert, L. "Eduard Spranger und Oswald Spengler." In *Schelling-Studien (FG M. Schröter,* edited by A. M. Koktanek, 33–58. Munich and Vienna: Oldenbourg, 1965.

Enzensberger, H. M. *Der Untergang der Titanic. Eine Komödie.* Frankfurt: Suhrkamp, 1978.

Erikson, E. H. *Identity and the Life Cycle.* New York and London: W. W. Norton, 1980.

Falwell, J. *Nuclear War and the Second Coming of Jesus Christ* (cassette series). Lynchburg, Va.: Old Time Gospel Hour, 1983.

Fink, E. *Metaphysik und Tod.* Stuttgart: Kohlhammer, 1969.

Fischer, H. *Subjektivität und Sünde. Kierkegaards Begriff der Sünde mit ständiger Rücksicht auf Schleiermachers Lehre von der Sünde.* Itzehoe: H. Dorbandt, 1963.

Forrester, J. W. *World Dynamics.* Cambridge, Mass.: Wright-Allen, 1971.

Frazer, J. *Folk-Lore in the OT: Studies in Comparative Religion, Legend and Law.* 2nd ed. New York: Tudor, 1923.

Freud, S. "Anxiety." In *The Standard Edition of the Complete Psychological Works of Sigmund Freud.* Vol. 26, *Introductory Lectures on Psycho-Analysis (Part III)*, 392–411 (lecture 25). London: Hogarth, 1963.

———. "Inhibitions, Symptoms and Anxiety (1926 [1925])." In *The Standard Edition of the Complete Psychological Works of Sigmund Freud.* Vol. 20, 87–174. London: Hogarth, 1962.

———. "On the Grounds for Detaching a Particular Syndrome from Neurasthenia under the Description 'Anxiety Neurosis.' " In *The Standard Edition of the Complete Psychological Works of Sigmund Freud.* Vol. 3, 87ff. London: Hogarth, 1962.

———. *The Problem of Anxiety.* New York: W. W. Norton and The Psychoanalytic Quarterly Press, 1936.

———. *Psychoanalytische Bemerkungen über einen autobiographisch beschriebenen Fall von Paranoia (Dementia Paranoides). Gesammelte Werke.* Vol. VIII, 239–320. 5th ed. Frankfurt: S. Fischer, 1969.

Friedrich, H. *Kulturkatastrophe. Nachrufe auf das Abendland.* Hamburg: Hoffmann & Campe, 1979.

Friedrich, O. *End of the World: A History.* New York: Fromm International, 1982.

Fritzsch, H. *The Creation of Matter: The Universe from Beginning to End.* New York: Basic Books, 1984.

Frost, S. B. *Old Testament Apocalyptic.* London: Epworth, 1952.

Fuchs, E. "Christus das Ende der Geschichte." *Evangelische Theologie* 8 (1948/49) 447–61.

Fuhrmanns, H. *Schellings letzte Philosophie.* Berlin: Junker & Dünnhaupt, 1940.

Gabel, J. *False Consciousness: An Essay on Reification.* New York: Harper & Row, 1975.

Gadamer, H.-G. "*Der* Weg in die Kehre (1979)," in idem, *Heideggers Wege. Studien zum Spätwerk.* Tübingen: Mohr Siebeck, 1983, 103–16, here 109. English translation in idem, *Heidegger's Ways.* Albany: State University of New York Press, 1994.

Gall, A. *Basileia tou theou. Eine religionsgeschichtliche Studie zur vorchristlichen Eschatologie.* Heidelberg: Winter, 1926.

Gebsattel, V. E. von. *Prolegomena einer medizinischen Anthropologie.* Berlin, Göttingen, and Heidelberg: Springer, 1954.

Gerhard, J. *Loci Theologici cum pro adstruenda veritate tum pro destruenda quorumvis contradicentium falsitate per these nervose solide et copiose explicati.* New edition edited by H. Preuss. 2nd ed. Leipzig: Hinrich, 1885.

Ginsberg, A. *Weisses Totentuch* (published as a guide to the Cucchi exhibition open in Basel until March 4, 1984). Basel, 1984. See also A. Ginsberg, *White Shroud.* New York: Harper & Row, 1986.

Glaser, H. *Sigmund Freuds Zwanzigstes Jahrhundert. Seelenbilder einer Epoche, Materialien und Analysen.* Frankfurt: Fischer, 1979.

Global 2000: The Report to the President of the U.S. 3 vols. New York: Pergamon, 1980.

Gloege, G. "Offenbarung VI. Christliche Offenbarung, dogmatisch." *Die Religion in Geschichte und Gegenwart.* Vol. 4, 1609–13.

Glucksmann, A. *La force du vertige*. Paris: B. Grasset, 1983.
Goethe, J. W. von. *Faust I & II*. Cambridge, Mass.: Suhrkamp/Insel Publishers Boston, 1984.
Goldschmidt, H. L. *Hermann Cohen und Martin Buber*. Geneva: Migdal, 1946.
Grabner-Haider, A. *Paraklese und Eschatologie bei Paulus. Mensch und Welt im Anspruch der Zukunft Gottes*. Neutestamentliche Abhandlungen, New Series 4. Münster: Aschendorff, 1968.
Grässer, E. *Das Problem der Parusieverzögerung in den synoptischen Evangelien und in der Apostelgeschichte*. BZNW 22. 3rd ed. Berlin: Töpelmann, 1977.
———. "Zum Verständnis der Gottesherrschaft." *Zeitschrift für die neutestamentliche Wissenschaft* 65 (1974) 3–26.
Grant, R. M. *Gnosticism and Early Christianity*. 2nd ed. New York: Harper & Row, 1966.
Grass, H. "Das eschatologische Problem in der Gegenwart." In *Dank an P. Althaus*, edited by W. Künneth and W. Joest, 47–78. Gütersloh: Bertelsmann, 1958.
Grimal, P., ed. *Mythen der Völker*. Vol. 3. Frankfurt: Fischer, 1967.
Gruhl, H. *Ein Planet wird geplündert. Die Schreckensbilanz unserer Politik*. Frankfurt: S. Fischer, (1975) 1978; 9th ed. 1981.
Grundmann, H. *Ketzergeschichte des Mittelalters*. Die Kirche in ihrer Geschichte G1. 3rd ed. Göttingen: Vandenhoeck & Ruprecht, 1978.
Guha, A. A. *Ende. Tagebuch aus dem 3. Weltkrieg*. Königstein: Athenäum, 1983.
Häfner, H. "Angst, Furcht." *Historisches Wörterbuch der Philosophie*. Vol. 1, 310–14. Darmstadt: Wissenschaftliche Buchgesellschaft, 1971.
Haendler, O. *Angst und Glaube*. Berlin: Evangelische Verlagsanstalt, 1952.
Hagemann, W. "Trost." In *Handbuch der Pastoraltheologie*. Vol. 5, 582. Freiburg, Basel, and Vienna: Benzinger, 1972.
Hallet, G. *A Companion to Wittgenstein's Philosophical Investigations*. Ithaca: Cornell University Press, 1978.
Hanson, P. D. *The Dawn of Apocalyptic*. Philadelphia: Fortress, 1975.
———. "Old Testament Apocalyptic Reexamined." *Interpretation* 25 (1971) 454–79.
Harnisch, W. "Der Prophet als Widerpart und Zeuge der Offenbarung. Erwägungen zur Interdependenz von Form und Sache im IV. Buch Esra." In *Apocalypticism in the Mediterranean World and the Near East*, edited by D. Hellholm, 461–94.
Hartingsveld, L. van. *Die Eschatologie des Johannesevangeliums. Eine Auseinandersetzung mit Rudolf Bultmann*. Assen: Van Gorcum, 1962.
Hartman, L. "Survey of the Problem of Apocalyptic Genre." In *Apocalypticism in the Mediterranean World and the Near East*, edited by D. Hellholm, 329–43.
Hartman, S. S. "Datierung der Jungavestischen Apokalyptik." In *Apocalypticism in the Mediterranean World and the Near East*, edited by D. Hellholm, 61–76.
Hasenhüttl, G. "Theologische Reflexion über die Angst." In *Angst in der Kirche verstehen und überwinden*, edited by R. Bohren and N. Greinacher, 44–57. Munich: Kaiser; Mainz: Grünewald, 1972.
Hebbel, F. "Julia. Ein Trauerspiel in drei Acten [1851]." In idem, *Sämtliche Werke*. Vol. I/2. Berlin: B. Behr (E. Bock), 1901.
Hegel, G.W.F. *The Encyclopaedia Logic*. Indianapolis and Cambridge: Hackett Publishing Co., 1991.
———. *Hegel's Philosophy of Right*. Great Books 43. 2nd ed. Chicago: Encyclopaedia Britannica, 1990.
———. *Lectures on the Philosophy of Religion*. Vol. 1. London: Routledge & Kegan Paul, 1895; reprint 1962.
Heidegger, M. "The Age of the World Picture." In idem, *The Question Concerning Technology and Other Essays*, 115–54.
———. *Being and Time*. London: SCM, 1962.

———. *An Introduction to Metaphysics*. New Haven, Conn.: Yale University Press, 1959.

———. "The Origin of the Work of Art." In idem, *Poetry, Language, Thought*, 15–87. New York: Harper & Row, 1971.

———. "Overcoming Metaphysics." In idem, *The End of Philosophy*, 84–110. New York: Harper & Row, 1973.

———. "The Question concerning Technology." In idem, *Basic Writings*, 283–317. New York: Harper & Row, 1977. Also published in *The Question concerning Technology and Other Essays*, 3–35. New York: Harper & Row, 1977.

———. "Das Rektorat 1933/34. Tatsachen und Gedanken." In idem, *Die Selbstbehauptung der Deutschen Universität/Das Rektorat 1933/34*, 21–43. Frankfurt: Klostermann, 1983.

———. "Spiegel Interview with Martin Heidegger." In *Martin Heidegger and National Socialism. Questions and Answers*, 41–66. New York: Paragon, 1990.

———. "Der Spruch des Anaximander." In idem, *Holzwege*, 296–343. Frankfurt: Vittorio Klostermann, 1972.

———. *Die Technik und die Kehre*. Opuscula 1. 2nd ed. Pfullingen: Neske, 1962.

———. *What Is Called Thinking*. New York: Harper & Row, 1972, 1986.

———. "What Is Metaphysics?" In idem, *Basic Writings*. Edited by D. F. Krell. New York: Harper & Row, 1977.

———. *What Is a Thing?* Chicago: Henry Regnery, 1967.

———. "What Are Poets For?" In idem, *Poetry, Language, Thought*, 89–142. New York: Harper & Row, 1971.

———. "The Word of Nietzsche: 'God Is Dead.' " In idem, *The Question concerning Technology and Other Essays*, 53–112. New York: Harper & Row, 1977.

Heim, K. *The World: Its Creation and Consummation*. Philadelphia: Muhlenberg, 1962.

Heinemann, F. *Existentialism and the Modern Predicament*. New York: Harper & Brothers, 1953.

Hellholm, D., ed. *Apocalypticism in the Mediterranean World and the Near East: Proceedings of the International Colloquium on Apocalypticism, Uppsala, August 12–17, 1979*. Tübingen: Mohr (Siebeck), 1983.

Herrmann, W. "Gottes Offenbarung an uns [1908]." In idem, *Schriften zur Grundlegung der Theologie*. Vol. 2, 150–69. Theologische Bücherei 36. Munich: Kaiser, 1967.

Herzog, B. "Die Freundschaft zwischen Spengler und Paul Reusch." In *Schelling-Studien (FG M. Schröter)*, edited by A. M. Koktanek, 77–97.

Hesse, F. *Abschied von der Heilsgeschichte*. Theologische Studien 108. Zurich: Theologischer Verlag, 1971.

Hirsch, E. *Kierkegaard-Studien*. Vol. II.3, *Der Denker*. Gütersloh: Bertelsmann, 1933.

Hölder, H. *Geologie und Paläontologie in Texten und ihrer Geschichte*. Orbis academicus II/12. Freiburg and Munich: K. Alber, 1960.

Hölderlin, F. *Poems and Fragments*. Ann Arbor: University of Michigan Press, 1967.

Hoffmann, G. *Das Problem der letzten Dinge in der neueren evangelischen Theologie*. Studien zur Systematischen Theologie 2. Göttingen: Vandenhoeck & Ruprecht, 1929.

Hoffmann, P. *Die Toten in Christus. Eine religionsgeschichtliche exegetische Untersuchung zur paulinischen Eschatologie*. Neutestamentliche Abhandlungen, New Series 2. Münster: Aschendorff, 1966.

Hofmann, H.-U. *Luther und die Johannes-Apokalypse*. Beiträge zur Geschichte der biblischen Exegese 24. Tübingen: Mohr (Siebeck), 1982.

Holbach, P. T. d'. *The System of Nature: Laws of the Moral and Physical World*. Boston: J. P. Mendum, 1853.

Holst, D. von. "Biologie der Angst." In *Angst und Gewalt. Ihre Präsenze und ihre Bewältigung in den Religionen*, edited by H. von Stietencron, 15–26. Düsseldorf: Patmos, 1979.

Holström F. *Das eschatologische Denken der Gegenwart.* Gütersloh: Bertelsmann, 1935.
Hornauer, U. "Abgesang der Postmoderne. Die unvernünftige Rede vom Ende der Aufklärung." *Evangelische Kommentare* 18 (1985) 492–94.
Horstmann, U. *Das Untier. Konturen einer Philosophie der Menschenflucht.* Vienna: Medusa, 1983.
Horx, M. *Glückliche Reise. Roman zwischen den Zeiten.* Berlin: Rotbuch, 1983.
Hultgård, A. "Forms and Origins of Iranian Apocalypticism." In *Apocalypticism in the Mediterranean World and the Near East*, edited by D. Hellholm, 387–413.
Hutten, K. *Seher, Grübler, Enthusiasten. Sekten und religiöse Sondergemeinschaften der Gegenwart.* 5th ed. Stuttgart: Quell-Verlag, 1958.
Jäger, A. *Gott. Nochmals Martin Heidegger.* Tübingen: Mohr, 1978.
———. *Gott. 10 Thesen.* Tübingen: Mohr, 1980.
———. *Reich ohne Gott. Zur Eschatologie Ernst Blochs.* Basler Studien zur historischen und systematischen Theologie 14. Zurich: EVZ-Verlag, 1969.
Jaspers, K. *Der philosophische Glaube.* 7th ed. Munich: Piper, 1981.
———. "Der Prophet Ezechiel. Eine pathographische Studie." In *Arbeiten zur Psychiatrie, Neurologie und ihren Grenzgebieten* (FS Kurt Schneider), 77–85. Heidelberg: Scherer, 1947.
———. *The Future of Mankind.* Chicago: University of Chicago Press, 1961.
———. *Die Atombombe und die Zukunft des Menschen. Politisches Bewusstsein in unserer Zeit.* Munich: Piper, 1958; 7th ed. 1983.
———. *Philosophy.* Vol. 2, *Existential Elucidation.* Chicago and London: University of Chicago Press, 1970.
Jørgensen, S.-A. "Utopisches Potential in der Bibel. Mythos, Eschatologie und Säkularisation." In *Utopieforschung. Interdisziplinäre Studien zur neuzeitlichen Utopie*, Vol. 3, edited by W. Vosskamp, 375–401. Stuttgart: Metzler, 1982.
Jonas, H. *Gnosis und spätantiker Geist.* Vol. 1; FRLANT 51. 3rd ed. Göttingen: Vandenhoeck & Ruprecht, 1964. Vol. 2; FRLANT 63. Göttingen: Vandenhoeck & Ruprecht, 1954.
Jüngel, E. "Die Welt als Möglichkeit und Wirklichkeit." *Evangelische Theologie* 29 (1969) 417–42.
Jünger, E. *Der Arbeiter. Herrschaft und Gestalt.* Hamburg: Hanseatische Verlagsanstalt, 1932.
Jung, C. G. "After the Catastrophe." In idem, *Collected Works.* Vol. 10, 194–217. Bollingen Series 20. New York: Pantheon, 1964.
Kähler, M. *The So-called Historical Jesus and the Historic Biblical Christ.* Philadelphia: Fortress, 1964; 1988.
Käsemann, E. "The Beginnings of Christian Theology." In idem, *New Testament Questions of Today*, 82–107. London: SCM, 1969.
———. *Commentary on Romans.* Grand Rapids: Wm. B. Eerdmans, 1980.
———. *Jesus Means Freedom.* Philadelphia: Fortress, 1969.
———. "On the Subject of Primitive Christian Apocalyptic." In idem, *New Testament Questions of Today*, 108–37. London: SCM, 1969.
———. " 'The Righteousness of God' in Paul." In idem, *New Testament Questions of Today*, 168–82. London: SCM, 1969.
———. "Sentences of Holy Law in the New Testament." In idem, *New Testament Questions of Today*, 66–81. London: SCM, 1969.
Kahn, H. *On Escalation: Metaphors and Scenarios.* New York, Washington, and London: Frederick A. Praeger, 1965.
Kaiser, O. *Introduction to the Old Testament: A Presentation of Its Results and Problems.* Minneapolis: Augsburg Publishing House, 1975.
Kaiser, R. "Weltende." In *Zumutungen an die Grünen*, 1–5. Kursbuch 74, 1983.

Kamlah, W. *Christentum und Geschichtlichkeit. Untersuchungen zur Entstehung des Christentums und zu Augustins "Bürgerschaft Gottes."* 2nd ed. of the work *Christentum und Selbstbehauptung*. Stuttgart: W. Kohlhammer, 1951; 1st ed. 1940.

Kant, I. *Religion within the Limits of Reason Alone*. New York: Harper & Brothers, 1960.

———. *Das Ende aller Dinge (1794)*. In idem, *Werke in zehn Bänden*, edited by W. Weischedel. Vol. 9, 173–90. 3rd ed. Darmstadt: Wissenschaftliche Buchgesellschaft, 1970.

———. "Die Frage, ob die Erde veralte, physikalisch erwogen" (1754). In *Kants Werke*. Vol. 1, *Vorkritische Schriften I: 1747–1756*, 193–213. Akademie Ausgabe. Berlin: Georg Reimar, 1910; reprint Berlin: de Gruyter, 1968.

———. "Untersuchung der Frage, ob die Erde in ihrer Umdrehung um die Achse, wodurch sie die Abwechselung des Tages und der Nacht hervorbringt, einige Veränderung seit den ersten Zeiten ihres Ursprungs erlitten habe und woraus man sich ihrer versichern können, welche von der Königl. Akademie der Wissenschaften zu Berlin zum Preise für das jetzt laufende Jahr aufgegeben worden." In *Kants Werke*. Vol. 1, *Vorkritische Schriften I. 1747–1756*, 183–91. Akademie Ausgabe. Berlin: Georg Reimar, 1910; reprint Berlin: de Gruyter, 1968.

———. "On a Newly Arisen Superior Tone in Philosophy." In *Raising the Tone in Philosophy*, edited by P. Fenves, 51–81. Baltimore and London: Johns Hopkins University Press, 1993.

Kautzsch, E., ed. *Die Apokryphen und Pseudepigraphen des Alten Testaments*. Tübingen: Mohr, 1900. 4th ed. Darmstadt: Wissenschaftliche Buchgesellschaft, 1975.

Kierkegaard, S. "At a Grave." *Three Discourses on Imagined Occasions*. Princeton: Princeton University Press, 1993.

———. *Christian Discourses* (1848). Princeton: Princeton University Press, 1971.

———. *The Concept of Anxiety*. Princeton: Princeton University Press, 1980.

———. *Either/Or*. Princeton: Princeton University Press, 1987.

———. *Fear and Trembling/Repetition*. Princeton: Princeton University Press, 1983.

———. *The Sickness unto Death*. New York: Princeton University Press, 1954.

———. "To Need God Is a Human Being's Highest Perfection." In idem, *Eighteen Upbuilding Discourses*, 297–326. Princeton: Princeton University Press, 1990. This particular essay is one of the *Four Upbuilding Discourses 1844*.

Kippenberg, H. G. "Ein Vergleich jüdischer, christlicher und gnostischer Apokalyptik." In *Apocalypticism in the Mediterranean World and the Near East*, edited by D. Hellholm, 751–68.

Klein, G. " 'Das wahre Licht scheint schon.' " *Zeitschrift für Theologie und Kirche* 68 (1971) 261–326.

Klein, M. "Bemerkungen über einige schizoide Mechanismen." In idem, *Das Seelenleben des Kleinkindes*, 101–25. Reinbek: Rowohlt, 1972.

Koch, K. *The Rediscovery of Apocalyptic: A Polemical Work on a Neglected Area of Biblical Studies and Its Damaging Effects on Theology and Philosophy*. London: SCM, 1972.

———. "Vom profetischen zum apokalyptischen Visionsbericht." In *Apocalypticism in the Mediterranean World and the Near East*, edited by D. Hellholm, 413–46.

Koch, K., T. Niewisch, and J. Tubach. *Das Buch Daniel*. Erträge der Forschung 144. Darmstadt: Wissenschaftliche Buchgesellschaft, 1980.

Koch, K., and J. M. Schmidt, eds. *Apokalyptik*. Wege der Forschung 365. Darmstadt: Wissenschaftliche Buchgesellschaft, 1982.

Körtner, U. "Rechtfertigung und Ethik bei Paulus. Bemerkungen zum Ansatz paulinischer Ethik." *Wort und Dienst*, New Series 16 (1981) 93–109.

Koktanek, A. M. *Oswald Spengler in seiner Zeit*. Munich: Beck, 1968.

Koktanek, A. M., ed. *Schelling-Studien (FG M. Schröter)*. Munich and Vienna: Oldenbourg, 1965.

Konrad, R. "Apokalyptik/Apokalypsen VI." *Theologische Realenzyklopädie*. Vol. 3, 275–80.

Korn, D. *Das Thema des Jüngsten Tages in der deutschen Literatur des 17. Jahrhunderts*. Tübingen: Max Niemeyer, 1957.

Koselleck, R. "Die Verzeitlichung der Utopie." In *Utopieforschung. Interdisziplinäre Studien zur neuzeitlichen Utopie*, edited by W. Vosskamp. Vol. 3, 1–14. Stuttgart: Metzler, 1982.

Kraft, H. "Die altchristliche Prophetie und die Entstehung des Montanismus." *Theologische Zeitschrift* 11 (1955) 149–271.

Krause, M. "Die literarischen Gattungen der Apokalypsen von Nag Hammadi." In *Apocalypticism in the Mediterranean World and the Near East*, edited by D. Hellholm, 621–37.

Kreck, W. *Die Zukunft des Gekommenen. Grundprobleme der Eschatologie*. Munich: C. Kaiser, 1961.

Kretschmar, G. *Die Offenbarung des Johannes. Die Geschichte ihrer Auslegung im 1. Jahrtausend*. Calwer Theologische Monographien, Reihe B, Vol. 9. Stuttgart: Calwer, 1985.

———. "Zur religionsgeschichtlichen Einordnung der Gnosis." In *Gnosis und Gnostizismus*, edited by K. Rudolph, 426–37. Wege der Forschung 262. Darmstadt: Wissenschaftliche Buchgesellschaft, 1975.

Kümmel, F. "Angst als Seinsmodus des Menschen?" In *Angst und Gewalt. Ihre Praesenz und ihre Bewältigung in den Religionen*," edited by H. von Stietencron, 27–42. Düsseldorf: Patmos, 1979.

Kümmel, W. G. *Introduction to the New Testament*. Nashville and New York: Abingdon: 1966.

———. *Promise and Fulfillment: The Eschatological Message of Jesus*. Naperville, Ill.: A. R. Allenson, 1957.

Künzli, A. *Die Angst als abendländische Krankheit, dargestellt am Leben und Denken S. Kierkegaards*. Zurich: Rascher, 1948.

Kulenkampff, C. "Entbergung, Entgrenzung, Überwältigung als Weisen des Standverlustes. Zur Anthropologie der paranoiden Psychosen." *Der Nervenarzt* 26 (1955) 89ff. Now in *Die Wahnwelten (Endogene Psychosen)*, edited by E. Strauss and J. Zutt, 202–17. Frankfurt: Akademische Verlagsgesellschaft, 1963.

———. "Zum Problem der abnormen Krise in der Psychiatrie." *Der Nervenarzt* 30 (1959) 62ff. Now in *Die Wahnwelten (Endogene Psychosen)*, 258–87.

La Barre, W. "Materials for a History of Studies of Crisis Cults: A Bibliographic Essay." *Current Anthropology* 12 (1971) 3–44.

Lampert, W. G., and A. R. Millard. *Atra-hasīs*. Oxford: Clarendon, 1969.

Lanczkowski, G. "Apokalyptik/Apokalypsen I, religionsgeschichtlich," *Theologische Realenzyklopädie*, Vol. 3, 189–91.

Landsberg, P. L. *Die Erfahrung des Todes*. Bibliothek Suhrkamp 371. Frankfurt: Suhrkamp, 1973.

Langhammer, J. *Die Offenbarung Jesu Christi. 12 Vorträge über das letzte Buch der Bibel unter dem Thema "Was bald geschehen wird."* Edited by Kassettendienst der Evangeliums-Mission e.V., Bad Salzuflen, no date.

Laubscher, M. "Krise und Evolution. Eine kulturwissenschaftliche Theorie zum Begriff 'Krisenkult.' " In *Gottesvorstellung und Gesellschaftsentwicklung*, edited by P. Eicher, 131–47. Forum Religionswissenschaft 1. Munich: Kösel, 1979.

Lebram, J. "Apokalyptik/Apokalypsen II. Altes Testament." *Theologische Realenzyklopädie*. Vol. 3, 192–202.

———. "The Piety of the Jewish Apocalyptists." In *Apocalypticism in the Mediterranean World and the Near East*, edited by D. Hellholm, 171–210.

Leipoldt, J. and W. Grundmann, eds. *Umwelt des Urchristentums.* 3rd ed. Berlin: Evangelische Verlagsanstalt, 1973.

Levitas, R. "Sociology and Utopia." *Sociology* 32/1 (1979) 19–33.

Lindemann, A. "Christliche Gemeinden und das Römische Reich im ersten und zweiten Jahrhundert." *Wort und Dienst,* New Series 18 (1985) 105–33.

Löwith, K. *Heidegger. Denker in dürftiger Zeit.* 3rd ed. Göttingen: Vandenhoeck & Ruprecht, 1965.

———. *Meaning in History: The Theological Implications of the Philosophy of History.* Chicago: University of Chicago Press, 1949.

———. *Nietzsches Philosophie der ewigen Wiederkehr des Gleichen.* Stuttgart: Kohlhammer, 1956.

———. "Weltgeschehen und Heilsgeschichte" (1950). In idem, *Sämtliche Schriften.* Vol. 2, 240–79. Stuttgart: Metzler, 1983.

Lohfink, G. *Die Himmelfahrt Jesu. Untersuchungen zu den Himmelfahrts- und Erhöhungstexten bei Lukas.* SANT 26. Munich: Kösel, 1971.

Lorenz, K. *Civilized Man's Eight Deadly Sins.* New York: Harcourt Brace Jovanovich, 1974.

Luck, U. "Das Weltverständnis in die jüdischen Apokalyptik, dargestellt am äthiopischen Henoch und am 4. Esra." *Zeitschrift für Theologie und Kirche* 73 (1976) 282–305.

Ludz, P. C., ed. *Spengler heute. Sechs Essays mit einem Vorwort von H. Lübbe.* Munich: Beck, 1980.

Lücke, F. *Versuch einer vollständigen Einleitung in die Offenbarung des Johannes, oder Allgemeine Untersuchungen über die apokalyptische Literatur überhaupt und die Apokalypse des Johannes insbesondere.* 1st ed. Bonn: E. Weber, 1832; 2nd ed. 1852.

Lührmann, D. "Biographie des Gerechten als Evangelium. Vorstellungen zu einem Markus-Kommentar." *Wort und Dienst,* New Series (1977) 25–50.

———. *Glaube im frühen Christentum.* Gütersloh: G. Mohn, 1976.

Lukács, G. *History and Class Consciousness: Studies in Marxist Dialectics.* Cambridge, Mass.: MIT Press, 1971.

Luz, U. *Das Geschichtsverständnis des Paulus.* Beiträge zur evangelishcen Theologie 49. Munich: Kaiser, 1968.

Maas, M. P. *Das Apokalyptische in der modernen Kunst. Endzeit oder Neuzeit. Versuch einer Deutung.* Munich: Bruckmann, 1965.

MacRae, G. "Apocalyptic Eschatology in Gnosticism." In *Apocalypticism in the Mediterranean World and the Near East,* edited by D. Hellholm, 317–25.

Maier, G. *Die Johannesoffenbarung und die Kirche.* WUNT 25. Tübingen: Mohr, 1981.

Mannheim, K. *Ideology and Utopia* (1928/29). London: Routledge, 1991.

Marcel, G. "I and Thou." In *The Philosophy of Martin Buber,* edited by A. Schilpp and M. Friedmann, 41–48. Lasalle, Ill.: Open Court, 1967; London: Cambridge University Press, 1967.

———. *Searchings.* New York: Newman Press, 1967.

Marsch, W.-D. *Zukunft.* Stuttgart, Kreuz-Verlag, 1969; Gütersloh: G. Mohn, 1979.

Martin, G. M. "Erbe der Mystik im Werk von Ernst Bloch." In *Ernst Bloch Vermittlungen zur Theologie,* edited by H. Deuser and P. Steinacker, 114–27. Fundamentaltheologische Studien 6. Munich and Mainz: Kaiser, 1976.

———. *Weltuntergang. Gefahr und Sinn apokalyptischer Visionen.* Stuttgart: Kreuz Verlag, 1984.

May, R. *The Meaning of Anxiety.* New York, 1950; rev. ed. New York: W. W. Norton, 1977.

Meadows, D. L., et al. *The Limits to Growth: A Report for the Club of Rome's Project on the Predicament of Mankind.* New York: Universe Books, 1972.

———. *Wachstum bis zur Katastrophe? Pro und Contra zum Weltmodell.* Edited by H. E. Richter. Stuttgart: Deutsche Verlagsanstalt, 1974.

Meer, F. van der. *Apocalypse: Visions from the Book of Revelation in Western Art.* London: Thames & Hudson, 1978.

Mercier, L.-S. *Memoirs of the Year Two Thousand Five Hundred.* 1771; reprint ed., New York: Garland Publishing, 1974.

Merle, R. *Malevil.* New York: Simon & Schuster, 1974.

Merlio, G. "Spengler und die Technik." In *Spengler heute. Sechs Essays mit einem Vorwort von H. Lübbe,* edited by P. C. Ludz, 100–22. Munich: Beck, 1980.

Métraux, A. "Migrations historiques des Tupi-Guarani." *Journal de la société des américanistes* 29 (1927) 1–45.

Metz, J. B. "Erinnerung des Leidens als Kritik eines teleologisch-technologischen Zukunftsbegriffs." *Evangelische Theologie* 32 (1972) 338–52.

———. "Erinnerung," *Handbuch philosophischer Grundbegriffe.* Vol. 2, 386–96. Munich: Kösel, 1973.

———. "Zukunft aus dem Gedächtnis des Leidens. Eine gegenwärtige Gestalt der Verantwortung des Glaubens." *Concilium* 8 (1972) 399–407.

Metzner, J. "Der Beitrag der Psychoanalyse zum Verständnis der Apokalyptik." *Wege zum Menschen* 23 (1971) 424–38.

———. *Persönlichkeitszerstörung und Weltuntergang. Das Verhältnis von Wahnbildung und literarischer Imagination.* Tübingen: Max Niemeyer, 1976.

Meyer-Abich, K. M., ed. *Frieden mit der Natur.* Freiburg, Basel, and Vienna: Herder, 1979.

Moltmann, J. " 'Begnadete Angst.' Religiös integrierte Angst und ihre Bewältigung." In *Angst und Gewalt. Ihre Präsenz und ihre Bewältigung in den Religionen,*" edited by H. von Stietencron, 137–53. Düsseldorf: Patmos, 1979.

———. *The Church in the Power of the Spirit: A Contribution to Messianic Ecclesiology.* New York: Harper & Row, 1977.

———. *The Crucified God: The Cross of Christ as the Foundation and Criticism of Christian Theology.* New York: Harper & Row, 1974.

———. "Exegese und Eschatologie der Geschichte." *Evangelische Theologie* 22 (1962) 31ff.

———. *Im Gespräch mit Ernst Bloch. Eine theologische Wegbegleitung.* Kaiser Traktate 18. Munich: Kaiser, 1976.

———. "Kommt Jesus wieder?" *Radius* (1966) Heft 1, 6–13.

———. *Theology of Hope.* New York: Harper & Row, 1967.

Müller, K. "Apokalyptik/Apokalypsen III. Die jüdische Apokalyptik. Anfänge und Merkmale." *Theologische Realenzyklopädie.* Vol. 3, 202–51.

Nagel, H. "Anleitungen zum öffentlichen Tod." In *Weltuntergänge,* edited by H. Boehncke, R. Stollmann, and G. Vinnai, 200–21. Kulturen und Ideen. Reinbek: Rowohlt, 1984.

Neurath, O. *Antispengler.* Munich: G.D.W. Callwey, 1921.

Neusüss, A., ed. *Utopie. Begriff und Phänomen des Utopischen.* Neuwied and Berlin: Luchterhand, 1968.

Nietzsche, F. *The Dawn of Day.* New York: Russell & Russell, 1964.

———. *The Genealogy of Morals.* New York: Russell & Russell, 1964.

———. *Thus Spoke Zarathustra.* New York: Tudor, 1933.

———. *Thus Spoke Zarathustra* (Part 4). In *The Portable Nietzsche.* New York: Viking, 1954.

———. *The Will to Power.* New York: Vintage Books, 1968.

Niewiadomski, J. *Die Zweideutigkeit von Gott und Welt in J. Moltmann's Theologie.* Innsbrucker theologische Studien 9. Innsbruck, Vienna, and Munich: Tyrolia, 1982.

Nimuendajú-Unkel, C. "Die Sagen von der Erschaffung und Vernichtung der Welt als Grundlagen der Religion der Apapocúva-Guarani." *Zeitschrift für Ethnologie* 46 (1914) 284–403.

Nöth, E. *Weltanfang und Weltende in the deutschen Volkssage.* Frankfurter Quellen und Forschungen zur germanischen und romanischen Philologie 2. Frankfurt: M. Diesterweg, 1932; reprint Hildesheim: Gerstenberg, 1973.

Nossack, H. E. "Der Untergang." In *Deutsche Erzähler*, II, edited by M. L. Kaschnitz, 572–620. Frankfurt: Insel, 1971.

Nussbaum, H. von. "Die Zukunft des Untergangs oder Der Untergang der Zukunft—Notate wider die Futurologie des Status quo." In D. L. Meadows et al. *Wachstum bis zur Katastrophe? Pro und Contra zum Weltmodell.* Edited by H. E. Richter, 46–71d. Stuttgart: Deutsche Verlagsanstalt, 1974.

Nussbaum, H. von, ed. *Die Zukunft des Wachstums. Kritische Antworten zum "Bericht des Club of Rome."* Düsseldorf: Bertelsmann Universitätsverlag, 1973.

Ölsner, W. *Die Entwicklung der Eschatologie von Schleiermacher bis zur Gegenwart.* Gütersloh: C. Bertelsmann, 1929.

Oepke, A. "*apokalyptō, apokalypsis.*" *Theological Dictionary of the New Testament.* Vol. 3, 563–92.

Olrik, A. *Ragnarök. Die Sagen vom Weltuntergang.* Berlin and Leipzig: de Gruyter, 1922.

Olsson, T. "The Apocalyptic Activity. The Case of J̌amāsp Nāmay." In *Apocalypticism in the Mediterranean World and the Near East*, edited by D. Hellholm, 21–49.

Osten-Sacken, P. von der. *Die Apokalyptik in ihrem Verhältnis zu Prophetie und Weisheit.* Theologische Existenz heute 157. Munich: Kaiser, 1969.

Otto, R. *The Idea of the Holy: An Inquiry into the Non-rational Factor in the Idea of the Divine and Its Relation to the Rational.* New York: Oxford University Press, 1958.

———. *The Kingdom of God and the Son of Man.* London: Lutterworth, 1938.

Overbeck, F. *Christentum und Kultur. Gedanken und Anmerkungen zur modernen Theologie.* Edited by C. A. Bernoulli. Basel: Schwabe & Co., 1919; reprint of 3rd ed. Darmstadt: Wissenschaftliche Buchgesellschaft, 1973.

———. *Über die Christlichkeit unserer heutigen Theologie. Streit- und Friedensschrift.* Leipzig: E. W. Fritzsch, 1873; 2nd ed. 1903; reprint Darmstadt: Wissenschaftlicher Buchgesellschaft, 1974.

———. *Selbstbekenntnisse.* Edited by E. Vischer. Basel: Benno Schwabe & Co., 1941.

Pannenberg, W. "Eschatologie und Sinnerfahrung." In idem, *Grundfragen systematischer Theologie II*, 66–79. Göttingen: Vandenhoeck & Ruprecht, 1980.

———. "The God of Hope." In idem, *Basic Questions in Theology: Collected Essays.* Vol. 2, 234–49. Philadelphia: Fortress, 1971.

———. *Jesus—God and Man.* Philadelphia: Westminster, 1968.

———. "Heilsgeschehen und Geschichte." *Kerygma und Dogma* 5 (1959) 218–37, 259–88. Now in idem, *Grundfragen systematischer Theologie I*, 22–78. Göttingen: Vandenhoeck & Ruprecht, 1967.

———. *Offenbarung als Geschichte.* Göttingen: Vandenhoeck & Ruprecht, 1961; 5th ed. 1982. English translation, *Revelation as History.* London: Sheed & Ward, 1979.

———. "Redemptive Event in History." In idem, *Basic Questions in Theology: Collected Essays.* Vol. 1, 15–80. Philadelphia: Fortress, 1970.

———. "Zeit und Ewigkeit in der religiösen Erfahrung Israels und des Christentums." In idem, *Grundfragen systematischer Theologie II*, 188–206. Göttingen: Vandenhoeck & Ruprecht, 1980.

Pascal, B. *Pensées.* New York: Random House, Modern Library, 1941.

Paulsen, A. *Søren Kierkegaard. Deuter unserer Existenz.* Hamburg: F. Wittig, 1955.

Pausewang, G. *The Last Children.* New York: Walker, 1990.

Perrin, N. *Rediscovering the Teaching of Jesus.* New York: Harper & Row, 1967.

Pfeiffer, A. *Franz Overbecks Kritik des Christentums.* Studien zur Theologie und Geistesgeschichte des neunzehnten Jahrhunderts 15. Göttingen: Vandenhoeck & Ruprecht, 1975.

Pfister, O. *Das Christentum und die Angst. Eine religionspsychologische, historische und religionshygienische Untersuchung.* Zurich: Artemis, 1944. English translation, *Christianity and Fear: A Study in History and in the Psychology and Hygiene of Religion.* New York: Macmillan, 1948.

Picht, G. "Die Bedingungen des Überlebens." In *Die Zukunft des Wachstums. Kritische Antworten zum "Bericht des Club of Rome,"* edited by H. von Nussbaum, 45–68. Düsseldorf: Bertelsmann Universitätsverlag, 1973.

———. *Mut zur Utopie.* Munich: Piper, 1969.

Pinthus, K., ed. *Menschheitsdämmerung: Dawn of Humanity, A Document of Expressionism.* Columbia, S.C.: Camden House, 1994.

Plöger, O. *Theocracy and Eschatology.* Richmond: John Knox, 1968.

Podskalski, G. *Byzantinische Reichseschatologie.* Münchener Univ. schr. R. phil. Fak. 9. Munich: W. Fink, 1972.

Pohlenz, M. *Die Stoa. Geschichte einer geistigen Bewegung.* Vol. 1. 5th ed. Göttingen: Vandenhoeck & Ruprecht, 1978. Vol. 2 (commentary). 5th ed. Göttingen: Vandenhoeck & Ruprecht, 1980.

Porteous, N. W. *Daniel, A Commentary.* Old Testament Library. Philadelphia: Westminster, 1965.

Pressel, W. *Die Kriegspredigt 1914–1918 in der evangelischen Kirche Deutschlands.* Arbeiten zur Pastoraltheologie 5. Göttingen: Vandenhoeck & Ruprecht, 1967.

Pritchard, B., ed. *Ancient Near Eastern Texts Relating to the Old Testament.* 3rd ed. Princeton: Princeton University Press, 1969.

Rad, G. von. *Old Testament Theology.* 2 vols. New York: Harper & Row, 1962–65.

———. *Theologie des Alten Testaments.* 2 vols. 6th ed. Munich: Kaiser, 1975.

Rahner, K. "Anonymous Christians." In idem, *Theological Investigations.* Vol. 6, 390–98. London: Darton, Longman & Todd; New York: Seabury, 1974.

———. "Atheism and Implicit Christianity." In idem, *Theological Investigations.* Vol. 9, 145–64. London: Darton, Longman & Todd; New York: Seabury, no date (1977?).

———. "Faith as Courage." In idem, *Theological Investigations.* Vol. 18, 211–25. New York: Crossroad, 1983.

———. *Zur Theologie der Zukunft.* Munich: Deutscher Taschenbuch Verlag, 1971. [A collection of essays from Rahner's *Schriften zur Theologie,* Vols. 4–6.]

Reitzenstein, R. "Weltuntergangsvorstellungen." *Kyrkohistorisk Åreskrift* 25 (1924) 129–212.

Richter, H. E. "Umgang mit der Angst. Gespräch mit H. E. Richter." *Evangelische Kommentare* 17 (1984) 141–44.

Riedel, I. "Apokalyptische Bilder." In *Not-Wendigkeiten. Auf der Suche nach einer neuen Spiritualität,* edited by P. Dätwyler, 51–75. Zurich: Arche, 1985.

Riem, J. *Die Sintflut in Sage und Wissenschaft.* 2nd ed. Hamburg: Agentur des rauhen Hauses, 1925.

Riemann, F. *Grundformen der Angst. Eine tiefenpsychologische Studie.* Munich: Reinhardt, 1961/1982.

Rihaczek, K. "Advent 2000," in D. L. Meadows et al., *Wachstum bis zur Katastrophe?,* 121–27.

Ringgren, H. "Apokalyptik I. Apokalyptische Literatur, religionsgeschichtlich." *Die Religion in Geschichte und Gegenwart.* Vol. 1, 463f.

Robinson, J. M. "*Logoi sophon.* On the Gattung of Q." In *Trajectories through Early Christianity,* edited by H. Koester and J. M. Robinson, 71–113. Philadelphia: Fortress, 1971.

Robinson, W. C., Jr. *Der Weg des Herrn. Studien zur Geschichte und Eschatologie im Lukas-Evangelium. Ein Gespräch mit Hans Conzelmann. Theologische Forschung* 36. Hamburg: H. Reich, 1964.

Rössler, D. *Gesetz und Geschichte. Untersuchungen zur Theologie der jüdischen Apokalyptik und der pharisäischen Orthodoxie.* WMANT 3. Neukirchen: Neukirchener Verlag, 1960.
Rosenzweig, F. *Kleinere Schriften.* Berlin: Schocken, 1937.
Rowley, H. H. *The Relevance of Apocalyptic.* London: Lutterworth, 1944; 3rd ed. New York: Association Press, 1964.
Rudolph, K. "Apokalyptik in der Diskussion," In *Apocalypticism in the Mediterranean World and the Near East,* edited by D. Hellholm, 771–98.
———. *Gnosis: The Nature and History of Gnosticism.* San Francisco: Harper & Row, 1984.
———. "Randerscheinungen des Judentums und das Problem der Entstehung des Gnostizismus." In idem, ed., *Gnosis und Gnostizismus,* 768–97. Wege der Forschung 262. Darmstadt: Wissenschaftliche Buchgesellschaft, 1975.
Rudolph, K., ed. *Gnosis und Gnostizismus.* Wege der Forschung 262. Darmstadt: Wissenschaftliche Buchgesellschaft, 1975.
Russell, B. *The ABC of Relativity.* London: G. Allen & Unwin, 1958.
Russell, D. S. *The Method and Message of Jewish Apocalyptic.* Philadelphia: Westminster, 1964.
Sabatier, A. "L'Apocalypse juive et la philosophie de l'histoire." *Revue des études juives* 40 (1900) LXVI–LXXXXVI. German translation: "Die jüdische Apokalyptik und die Geschichtsphilosophie," in *Apokalyptik,* edited by K. Koch and J. M. Schmidt, 91–113. Wege der Forschung 365. Darmstadt: Wissenschaftliche Buchgesellschaft, 1982.
Sagan, C. *Cosmos.* New York: Random House, 1980.
Salmony, H. A. *Kants Schrift: Das Ende aller Dinge.* Zurich: EVZ-Verlag, 1962.
Sanders, E. P. "The Genre of Palestinian Jewish Apocalypses." *Apocalypticism in the Mediterranean World and the Near East,* edited by D. Hellholm, 447–60.
Sartre, J.-P. *Being and Nothingness: An Essay on Phenomenological Ontology.* New York: Philosophical Library, 1956.
Satake, A. *Die Gemeindeordnung in der Johannesapokalypse.* WMANT 21. Neukirchen-Vluyn: Neukirchener Verlag, 1966.
Sauter, G. *Zukunft und Verheissung. Das Problem der Zukunft in der gegenwärtigen theologischen und philosophischen Diskussion.* 2nd ed. Zurich: Zwingli, 1973.
Scharfenberg, J. "Das Problem der Angst im Grenzgebiet von Theologie und Psychologie." *Wege zum Menschen* 20 (1968) 314–24.
Scheler, M. "Tod und Fortleben (1911–1914)." In idem, *Schriften aus dem Nachlass,* edited by Maria Scheler. Vol. 1, 9–64. 2nd ed. Bern: Francke, 1957.
Schell, J. *The Fate of the Earth.* New York: Avon, 1982.
Schelling, F. W. J. *The Ages of the World.* New York: Columbia University Press, 1942.
———. *Of Human Freedom.* Chicago: Open Court, 1936.
———. *Philosophische Untersuchungen über das Wesen der menschlichen Freiheit.* Suhrkamp Taschenbuch Wissenschaft 138. Frankfurt: Suhrkamp, 1975.
Schenke, H.-M. "Die Gnosis." In *Umwelt des Urchristentums,* edited by J. Leipoldt and W. Grundmann. Vol. 1, 371–415. 3rd ed. Berlin: Evangelische Verlagsanstalt, 1973.
Scherer, G. *Das Problem des Todes in the Philosophie.* Grundzüge 35. Darmstadt: Wissenschaftliche Buchgesellschaft, 1979.
Schiller, F. *The Poems and Ballads of Schiller.* 2 vols. Edinburgh and London: William Blackwood & Sons, 1844.
Schilpp, P. A., and M. Friedman, eds. *The Philosophy of Martin Buber.* Lasalle, Ill.: Open Court, 1967; London: Cambridge University Press, 1967.
Schlechta, K., ed. *Angst und Hoffnung in unserer Zeit. Darmstädter Gespräch 1963.* Darmstadt: Neue Darmstädter Verlagsanstalt, 1965.
Schleiermacher, F. *The Christian Faith.* Edinburgh: T. & T. Clark, 1928.

Schlier, H. "*thlibō, thlipsis.*" *Theological Dictionary of the New Testament.* Vol. 3, 139–48.
Schloemann, M. *Wachstumstod und Eschatologie. Die Herausforderung christlicher Theologie durch die Umweltkrise.* Stuttgart: Calwer, 1973.
Schmidt, J. M. *Die jüdische Apokalyptik. Die Geschichte ihrer Erforschung von den Anfängen bis zu den Textfunden von Qumran.* 2nd ed. Neukirchen-Vluyn: Neukirchener Verlag, 1976.
Schmidt, M., and J. Butscher. "Adventisten." *Theologische Realenzyklopädie.* Vol. 1, 454–62.
Schmithals, W. *The Apocalyptic Movement: Introduction and Interpretation.* Nashville: Abingdon, 1975.
Schmitz, O., and G. Stählin. "*parakaleō, paraklēsis.*" *Theological Dictionary of the New Testament.* Vol. 5, 773–99.
Schmökel, H. *Das Gilgamesch-Epos.* 2nd ed. Stuttgart: Kohlhammer, 1971.
Schnackenburg, R. *Das Johannesevangelium.* Vol. 3. HTKNT IV/3. Freiburg, Basel, and Vienna: Herder, 1975.
———. *The Johannine Epistles.* New York: Crossroad, 1992.
Schneider, G. *Parusiegleichnisse im Lukas-Evangelium.* Stuttgarter Bibelstudien 74. Stuttgart: Katholisches Bibelwerk, 1974.
Scholem, G. "Toward an Understanding of the Messianic Idea in Judaism." In idem, *The Messianic Idea in Judaism and Other Essays on Jewish Spirituality,* 1–36. New York: Schocken, 1971.
Schopenhauer, A. *Sämtliche Werke.* Edited by M. Fischreisen-Köhler. 8 vols. Berlin: A. Weichert, no date [1928?].
Schott, S., and W. von Soden. *Das Gilgamesch-Epos.* Stuttgart: Reclam, 1970.
Schottroff, L. *Der Glaubende und die feindliche Welt. Beobachtungen zum gnostischen Dualismus und seine Bedeutung für Paulus und das Johannesevangelium.* WMANT 37. Neukirchen-Vluyn: Neukirchener Verlag, 1970.
Schreber, D. P. *Memoirs of My Nervous Illness.* London: W. Dawson, 1955.
Schrey, H.-H. *Dialogisches Denken.* Erträge der Forschung 1. 2nd ed. Darmstadt: Wissenschaftliche Buchgesellschaft, 1983.
Schröter, M. *Metaphysik des Untergangs. Eine kulturkritische Studie über Oswald Spengler.* Munich: Leibniz, 1949.
———. *Streit um Spengler. Kritik seiner Kritiker.* Munich: Beck, 1922. Now in idem, *Metaphysik des Untergangs,* 15–158.
Schulte, H. *Der Begriff der Offenbarung im Neuen Testament.* Munich: Kaiser, 1949.
Schulte-Herbrüggen, H. *Utopie und Anti-Utopie: Von der Strukturanalyse zur Strukturtypologie.* Bochum: Pöppinghaus, 1960.
Schulz, S. *Q—Die Spruchquelle der Evangelisten.* Zurich: Theologischer Verlag, 1972.
Schulz, W. "Die Dialektik von Leib und Seele bei Kierkegaard. Bemerkungen zum 'Begriff Angst.' " In *Materialien zur Philosophie S. Kierkegaards,* edited by M. Theunissen and W. Greve, 347–66. Suhrkamp Taschenbuch Wissenschaft 241. Frankfurt: Suhrkamp, 1979.
———. "Das Problem der Angst in der neueren Philosophie." In *Aspekte der Angst,* edited by H. von Ditfurth, 13–27. Starnberger Gespräche 4, 1964; 3rd ed.; Munich: Kindler, 1981.
———. "Freiheit und Geschichte in Schellings Philosophie," in F. W. J. Schelling, *Philosophische Untersuchungen über das Wesen der menschlichen Freiheit,* 7–26. Suhrkamp Taschenbuch Wissenschaft 138. Frankfurt: Suhrkamp, 1975.
———. *Die Vollendung des Deutschen Idealismus in der Spätphilosophie Schellings.* 2nd ed. Pfullingen: Neske, 1975.
Schwarte, K.-H. "Apokalyptik/Apopkalypsen V." *Theologische Realenzyklopädie.* Vol. 3, 257–75.
Schwarz, R. *Die apokalyptische Theologie Thomas Müntzers und der Taboriten.* Beiträge zur historischen Theologie 55. Tübingen, Mohr (Siebeck), 1977.

Schwarzwäller, K. *Die Angst—Gegebenheit und Aufgabe. Theologische Studien* 102. Zurich: EVZ-Verlag, 1970.

Schweitzer, Albert. "The Decay and the Restoration of Civilization (1923)." In *The Philosophy of Civilization.* New York: Macmillan, 1949.

———. *The Mystery of the Kingdom of God: The Secret of Jesus' Messiahship and Passion.* London: A. & C. Black, 1925.

———. *Paul and His Interpreters: A Critical History.* London: A. & C. Black, 1912.

———. *The Quest of the Historical Jesus: A Critical Study of Its Progress from Reimarus to Wrede.* New York: Macmillan, 1910; reprint 1968.

———. *Reverence for Life: An Anthology of Selected Writings.* New York: Philosophical Library, 1965.

Schweitzer, Alexander. *Die Glaubenslehre der evangelisch-reformierten Kirche, dargestellt und aus den Quellen belegt.* Vol. 2. Zurich: Orell, Füssli & Comp., 1847.

Schweizer, E. "Das hellenistische Weltbild als Produkt der Weltangst." In *Mensch und Kosmos. Eine Ringvorlesung der Theologischen Fakultät Zürich,* 39–50. Zurich, 1960. Now in E. Schweizer, *Neotestamentica,* 15–27. Zurich and Stuttgart: Zwingli, 1963.

Seebass, G. "Apokalyptik VII." *Theologische Realenzyklopädie.* Vol. 3, 280–89.

Seeber, H. U., and W. Bachem. "Aspekte und Probleme der neueren Utopiediskussion in der Anglistik." In *Utopieforschung. Interdisziplinäre Studien zur neuzeitlichen Utopie,* edited by W. Vosskamp, Vol. 1, 143–91. Stuttgart: Metzler, 1982.

Shelley, M. W. *The Last Man.* London: H. Colburn, 1826. Edited by H. J. Luke. Lincoln: University of Nebraska Press, 1993.

Sieburg, F. *Die Lust am Untergang. Selbstgespräche auf Bundesebene.* Hamburg: Rowohlt, 1954.

Simmel, G. *Lebensanschauung. Vier metaphysische Kapitel.* Munich and Leipzig: Duncker & Humblot, 1918.

Sløk, J. *Die Anthropologie Kierkegaards.* Copenhagen: Rosenkilde & Bagger, 1954.

Sloterdijk, P. *Critique of Cynical Reason.* Theory and History of Literature 40. Minneapolis: University of Minnesota Press, 1987.

Smith, M. "On the History of APOKALYPTŌ and APOKALYPSIS." In *Apocalypticism in the Mediterranean World and the Near East,* edited by D. Hellholm, 9–20.

Soden, W. von. "Sintflut I. Religionsgeschichtlich." *Religion in Geschichte und Gegenwart.* Vol. 6, 50f.

Spengler, O. *The Decline of the West.* New York: Alfred A. Knopf, 1926; reprint 1937.

———. *The Hour of Decision, Part One: Germany and World Historical Revolution.* New York: Knopf, 1934.

———. *Der Mensch und die Technik. Beitrag zu einer Philosophie des Lebens.* Munich: Beck, 1931.

———. *Neubau des deutschen Reiches.* Munich: Beck, 1924.

———. *Pessimismus?* Schriftenreihe der Preussischen Jahrbücher 4. Berlin: G. Stilke, 1921.

———. *Preussentum und Sozialismus.* Munich: Beck, 1920.

———. *Urfragen. Fragmente aus dem Nachlass.* Edited by A. M. Koktanek and M. Schröter. Munich: Beck, 1965.

Spranger, E. *Psychologie des Jugendalters.* 3rd ed. Leipzig: Quelle & Meyer, 1925.

Stählin, G. "Zum Problem der johanneischen Eschatologie." *Zeitschrift für die Neutestamentliche Wissenschaft* 33 (1934) 225–59.

Steck, K. G. *Die Idee der Heilsgeschichte. Hoffmann—Schlatter—Cullmann.* Zurich/Zollikon: Evangelischer Verlag, 1959.

Stegemann, H. "Die Bedeutung der Qumranfunde für die Erforschung der Apokalyptik," In *Apocalypticism in the Mediterranean World and the Near East,* edited by D. Hellholm, 495–530.

Stier, H. E. "Zur geschichtlichen Wesensbestimmung Europas." In *Schelling-Studien*

(FG M. Schröter), edited by A. M. Koktanek, 193–210. Munich and Vienna: Oldenbourg, 1965.

Stietencron, H. von., ed. *Angst und Gewalt. Ihre Praesenz und ihre Bewältigung in den Religionen.* Düsseldorf: Patmos, 1979.

Stock, K. *Annihilatio mundi. Johann Gerhards Eschatologie der Welt.* Forschungen zur Geschichte und Lehre des Protestantismus, 10th series, Vol. XLII. Munich: Kaiser, 1971.

Storch, A., and C. Kulenkampff. "Zum Verständnis des Weltuntergangs bei den Schizophrenen." *Der Nervenarzt* 21 (1950) 102–8.

Strack, H. L., and P. Billerbeck. *Kommentar zum NT aus Talmud und Midrasch.* 4 vols. Munich: Beck, 1922; 8th ed. 1982ff.

Strauss, E., and J. Zutt, eds. *Die Wahnwelten (Endogene Psychosen).* Frankfurt: Akademische Verlagsgesellschaft, 1963.

Strecker, G. *Der Weg der Gerechtigkeit. Untersuchung zur Theologie des Matthäus.* FRLANT 82. Göttingen: Vandenhoeck & Ruprecht, 1962.

Strobel, A. "Apokalyptik/Apokalypsen IV. Neues Testament." *Theologische Realenzyklopädie.* Vol. 3, 251–57.

———. "Apokalyptik, Christusoffenbarung und Utopie. Theologisches Zeugnis im Umbruch eines Zeitalters." In *Das Mandat der Theologie und die Zukunft des Glaubens. Sechs Aspekte zur Gottesfrage*, edited by G. F. Vicedom, 104–60. Munich: Claudius-Verlag, 1971.

———. *Kerygma und Apokalyptik. Ein religionsgeschichtlicher und theologischer Beitrag zur Christusfrage.* Göttingen: Vandenhoeck & Ruprecht, 1967.

Strong, T. B. "Oswald Spengler—Ontologie, Kritik und Enttäuschung." In *Spengler heute. Sechs Essays mit einem Vorwort von H. Lübbe*, edited by P. C. Ludz, 74–99.

Stuhlmacher, P. *Gerechtigkeit Gottes bei Paulus.* FRLANT 87. 2nd ed. Göttingen: Vandenhoeck & Ruprecht, 1966.

Tacke, H. *Glaubenshilfe als Lebenshilfe. Probleme und Chancen heutiger Seelsorge.* 2nd ed. Neukirchen-Vluyn: Neukirchener Verlag, 1979.

Teilhard de Chardin, P. *Man's Place in Nature: The Human Zoological Group.* London: Collins, 1966.

———. *The Phenomenon of Man.* 2nd ed. New York: Harper & Row, 1965.

Theissen, G. "Wanderradikalismus. Literatursoziologische Aspekte der Überlieferung von Worten Jesu im Urchristentum." In idem, *Studien zur Soziologie des Urchristentums*, 79–105. Wissenschaftliche Untersuchungen zum Neuen Testament 19. 2nd ed. Tübingen: Mohr (Siebeck), 1983.

Theunissen, M. *Der Andere. Studien zur Sozialontologie der Gegenwart.* Berlin: de Gruyter, 1965.

———. "Die Gegenwart des Todes im Leben." In *Tod und Sterben*, edited by R. Winau and H. P. Rosemeier, 102–24. Berlin and New York: de Gruyter, 1984.

Theunissen, M., and W. Greve, eds. *Materialien zur Philosophie S. Kierkegaards.* Suhrkamp Taschenbuch Wissenschaft 241. Frankfurt: Suhrkamp, 1979.

Thiele, J. "Der Ruf in das angstfreie Leben." *Junge Kirche* 44 (1983) 58–60.

Thielicke, H. "Theologische Dimensionen der Angst." In *Angst und Schuld in theologischer und psychotherapeutischer Sicht*, edited by W. Bitter, 23–38. 4th ed. Stuttgart: Klett, 1967.

Tillich, P. *The Courage to Be.* New Haven: Yale University Press, 1952.

———. *Systematic Theology.* 3 vols. in 1. Chicago: University of Chicago Press, 1967.

———. *Der Tod der Moderne. Eine Diskussion.* Tübingen: Konkursbuchverlag, 1983.

Topitsch, E. "Marxismus und Gnosis." In idem, *Sozialphilosophie zwischen Ideologie und Wissenschaft*, 261–96. Soziologische Texte 10. 2nd ed. Neuwied and Berlin: H. Luchterhand, 1966.

Torrance, T. F. "Die Eschatologie der Reformation." *Evangelische Theologie* 14 (1954) 334–58.

Trilling, W. *Das wahre Israel. Studien zur Theologie des Matthäus-Evangeliums.* Studien zum Alten und Neuen Testament 10. 3rd ed. Munich: Kösel, 1964.

Ulmen, G. L. "Metaphysik des Morgenlandes—Spengler über Russland." In *Spengler heute. Sechs Essays mit einem Vorwort von H. Lübbe,* edited by P. C. Ludz, 123–73.

Umwelt-Report. Edited by H. Schultze. Frankfurt: Umschau-Verlag, 1972.

Vielhauer, P. Introduction to "Writings Relating to the Apostles; Apocalypses and Related Subjects." In *New Testament Apocrypha,* edited by E. Hennecke and W. Schneemelcher. Philadelphia: Westminster, 1963–65; rev. ed. 1991. Vol. 2, 581–607.

———. *Geschichte der urchristlichen Literatur.* Berlin and New York: de Gruyter, 1975; reprint 1978.

Vinnai, G. "Die Innenseite der Katastrophenpolitik. Zur Sozialpsychologie der atomaren Bedrohung." In *Weltuntergänge,* edited by H. Boehncke, R. Stollmann, and G. Vinnai, 129–92. Kulturen und Ideen. Reinbek: Rowohlt, 1984.

Vögtle, A. *Das Neue Testament und die Zukunft des Kosmos.* Kommentare und Beiträge zum Alten und Neuen Testament. Düsseldorf: Patmos, 1970.

Volz, P. *Die Eschatologie der jüdischen Gemeinde im neutestamentlichen Zeitalter.* Tübingen: Mohr (Siebeck), 1934.

Vosskamp, W., ed. *Utopieforschung. Interdisziplinäre Studien zur neuzeitlichen Utopie.* 3 vols. Stuttgart: Metzler, 1982.

Walker, R. *Die Heilsgeschichte im ersten Evangelium.* FRLANT 91. Göttingen: Vandenhoeck & Ruprecht, 1967.

Walter, N. "Zur theologischen Relevanz apokalyptischer Aussagen." In *Theologische Versuche VI,* edited by J. Rogge and G. Schille, 47–72. Berlin: Evangelische Verlagsanstalt, 1975.

Wandruszka, M. "Was weiss die Sprache von der Angst?" In *Angst und Schuld in theologischer und psychotherapeutischer Sicht,* edited by W. Bitter, 14–22. 4th ed. Stuttgart: Klett, 1967.

Wanke, G. "*phobeō ktl.* B." *Theological Dictionary of the New Testament.* Vol. 9, 197–205.

Weder, H. "Die Menschwerdung Gottes. Überlegungen zur Auslegungsproblematik des Johannesevangeliums am Beispiel von Joh 6." *Zeitschrift für Theologie und Kirche* 82 (1985) 325–60.

Wehrli, R. *Alter und Tod des Christentums bei Franz Overbeck.* Zurich: Theologischer Verlag, 1977.

Weischedel, W. *Der Gott der Philosophen. Grundlegung einer Philosophischen Theologie im Zeitalter des Nihilismus.* Vol. 2. Munich: Nymphenburger, 1979.

———. "Paul Tillichs philosophische Theologie. Ein ehrerbietiger Widerspruch." In *Der Spannungsbogen. Festgabe P. Tillich zum 75. Geburtstag,* 25–47. Stuttgart: Evangelischer Verlagswerk, 1961.

Weiss, J. *Jesus' Proclamation of the Kingdom of God.* Philadelphia: Fortress, 1971.

Weizsäcker, C. F. von. *The History of Nature.* Chicago: University of Chicago Press, 1949.

———. *The Relevance of Science. Creation and Cosmogony.* London: Collins, 1964.

———. *The Unity of Nature.* New York: Farrar, Straus & Giroux, 1980.

———. *The World View of Physics.* Chicago: University of Chicago Press, 1952.

Weltuntergangsgeschichten von Edgar Poe bis Arno Schmidt. Edited by Diogenes-Katastrophen-Kollektiv. Zurich: Diogenes-Verlag, 1975, 1981.

Wendebourg, E.-W. "Die heilsgeschichtliche Theologie J. Chr. v. Hoffmanns in ihrem Verhältnis zur romantischen Weltanschauung." *Zeitschrift für Theologie und Kirche* 52 (1955) 64–104.

Wengst, K. *Der erste, zweite und dritte Brief des Johannes.* Ökumenischer Taschenbuchkommentar zum Neuen Testament. Gütersloh: G. Mohn, 1978.

Werner, M. *Die Weltanschauungsproblem bei K. Barth und A. Schweitzer*. Munich: Beck, 1924.

———. *The Formation of Christian Dogma*. London: Adam & Charles Black, 1957.

Westermann, C. *Genesis 1–11*. Minneapolis: Fortress, 1984.

Wetzel, A. "Das Weltuntergangserlebnis in der Schizophrenie." *Zeitschrift für die gesamte Neurologie und Psychiatrie* 78 (1922) 403–28.

Widengren, G. "Leitende Ideen und Quellen der iranischen Apokalyptik." In *Apocalypticism in the Mediterranean World and the Near East*, edited by D. Hellholm, 77–162.

Wilckens, U. "Die Bekehrung des Paulus als religionsgeschichtliches Problem." *Zeitschrift für Theologie und Kirche* 56 (1959) 273–93.

Winter, M. "Don Quijote und Frankenstein. Utopie als Utopiekritik: Zur Genese der negativen Utopie." In *Utopieforschung. Interdisziplinäre Studien zur neuzeitlichen Utopie*, edited by W. Vosskamp. Vol. 3, 86–112. Stuttgart: Metzler, 1982.

———. *Compendium Utopiarum: Typologie und Bibliographie literarischer Utopien*. Vol. 1, *Von der Antike bis zur deutschen Frühaufklärung*. Stuttgart: Metzler, 1978.

Winternitz, M. "Die Flutsagen des Altertums und der Naturvölker." *Mitteilungen der anthropologischen Gesellschaft in Wien* 31 (1901) 305–33.

Wiplinger, F. *Der personal verstandene Tod*. Munich and Freiburg: K. Alber, 1970.

Wolf, C. *Kassandra*. Darmstadt: Luchterhand, 1983; 8th ed., 1984. English translation, *Cassandra: A Novel and Four Essays*. New York: Farrar, Straus & Giroux, 1984.

———. *Voraussetzungen einer Erzählung: Kassandra. Frankfurter Poetik-Vorlesungen*. Sammlung Luchterhand 456. Darmstadt: Luchterhand, 1983.

Wuketits, F. M. *Grundzüge der Evolutionstheorie*. Grundzüge 42. Darmstadt: Wissenschaftliche Buchgesellschaft, 1982.

Wulf, F. "Trost," *Lexikon für Theologie und Kirche*. 2nd ed. Vol. 10, 376–78.

Wundt, W. *Völkerpsychologie*. Vol. 6, *Mythos und Religion*. 3rd ed. Leipzig: W. Engelmann, 1922; 1951.

Ziegler, K., and S. Oppenheim. *Weltuntergang in Sage und Wissenschaft*. Aus Natur und Geisteswelt 720. Leipzig: B. G. Teubner, 1921.

Zimmerli, W. *Man and His Hope in the Old Testament*. Naperville, Ill.: A. R. Allenson, [1971?].

Zutt, J. "Über Daseinsordnungen. Ihre Bedeutung für die Psychiatrie." *Der Nervenarzt* 24 (1953) 177ff. Now in *Die Wahnwelten (Endogene Psychosen)*, edited by E. Strauss and J. Zutt, 169–91.

Zwischen Wachstum und Lebensqualität. Wirtschaftsethische Fragen angesichts der Krisen wirtschaftlichen Wachstums. Edited by the Sozialwissenschaftliches Institut der EKD. Munich: Kaiser, 1980.